P9-ELH-965

Praise for

# A New World Begins

"A fresh and fair-minded account of the revolution overflowing with vivid narrative detail and clear exposition."      —*Wall Street Journal*

"When it comes to showing how events can scramble the prospects of even the most determined plotters, Popkin has no equal, and readers will find in his pages a deeply satisfying account of the inevitable messiness of rapid change."      —*New York Review of Books*

"Popkin's expertise on revolutionary-era France is keenly demonstrated here—from prerevolutionary thought through the history of the country up to Louis XVI and his Hapsburg wife, Marie-Antoinette, and beyond, to the years of upheaval and the reign of Napoleon Bonaparte."
      —*Booklist*

"Sweeping in coverage, *A New World Begins* offers a fresh and richly detailed account of French revolutionary politics. Jeremy Popkin is an outstanding scholar of the French and Haitian Revolutions, and his deep layers of expertise shine through the pages of this book. This thought-provoking account will push readers to reflect deeply on the contradictions and complexities of modern democracy."
      —Suzanne Desan, professor of history, University of
      Wisconsin-Madison and author of *The Family
      on Trial in Revolutionary France*

"This is a book that has been needed for a long time: a lucid, engaging, authoritative, accurate, and up-to-date history of the French Revolution. Jeremy Popkin is one of the great living experts on the subject, and he has drawn on a half-century of study to produce this first-rate work. Particularly impressive is the way he integrates the history of the Haitian Revolution into that of the French Revolution. A New World Begins will appeal to experts, students, and general readers alike."

—David A. Bell, professor of history, Princeton University
and author of Men on Horseback: Charisma
and Power in the Age of Revolutions

"Jeremy Popkin is one of the most eminent scholars working on the French Revolution, and his A New World Begins provides us with the best, fullest and most up-to-date history of the Revolutionary decade from 1789 through to the advent of Napoleon. Writing with an insight that distils a lifetime's study, Popkin is particularly alert to the range of experience of those who lived through the Revolutionary years. There is heart and compassion here as well as wit and intelligence: Popkin does not flinch from recounting the Revolution's more sombre legacies, but can still elicit in his readers a bitter-sweet sense of excitement about a moment in western history when, indeed, a new epoch in the history of humanity seemed to be blossoming."

—Colin Jones, author of The Great Nation: France
from Louis XV to Napoleon 1715–99

"Based on nearly half a century of research and teaching, Jeremy Popkin's new study of the French Revolution brilliantly brings alive the complex goals and emotions of the men and women and people of color struggling to create a new world. It is especially effective in exploring what that struggle meant, both for the generation of Revolutionaries and for our own day. A New World Begins is an outstanding synthesis that is sure to stand as basic reading on the subject for many years to come."

—Timothy Tackett, professor emeritus of history,
UC Irvine and author of Becoming a Revolutionary and
The Coming of the Terror in the French Revolution

# A NEW
# WORLD
# BEGINS

ALSO BY JEREMY D. POPKIN

A History of Modern France

From Herodotus to H-Net: The Story of
    Historiography

A Concise History of the Haitian Revolution

You Are All Free: The Haitian Revolution and the
    Abolition of Slavery

Facing Racial Revolution: Eyewitness Accounts of the
    Haitian Insurrection

A Short History of the French Revolution

Revolutionary News: The Press in France,
    1789–1799

THE HISTORY OF THE
FRENCH REVOLUTION

# A NEW WORLD BEGINS

## JEREMY D. POPKIN

BASIC BOOKS
New York

Copyright © 2019 by Jeremy D. Popkin

Cover design by Chin-Yee Lai
Cover images: *The Taking of the Bastille*, 14 July 1789 (oil on canvas), French School (18th century) / Chateau de Versailles, France / Bridgeman Images; © MaxyM / Shutterstock.com
Cover copyright © 2021 Hachette Book Group, Inc.

Hachette Book Group supports the right to free expression and the value of copyright. The purpose of copyright is to encourage writers and artists to produce the creative works that enrich our culture.

The scanning, uploading, and distribution of this book without permission is a theft of the author's intellectual property. If you would like permission to use material from the book (other than for review purposes), please contact permissions@hbgusa.com. Thank you for your support of the author's rights.

Basic Books
Hachette Book Group
1290 Avenue of the Americas, New York, NY 10104
www.basicbooks.com

Printed in the United States of America

Originally published in hardcover and ebook by Basic Books in December 2019
First Trade Paperback Edition: October 2021

Published by Basic Books, an imprint of Perseus Books, LLC, a subsidiary of Hachette Book Group, Inc. The Basic Books name and logo is a trademark of the Hachette Book Group.

The Hachette Speakers Bureau provides a wide range of authors for speaking events. To find out more, go to www.hachettespeakersbureau.com or call (866) 376-6591.

The publisher is not responsible for websites (or their content) that are not owned by the publisher.

Print book interior design by Amy Quinn.

Library of Congress Cataloging-in-Publication Data

Names: Popkin, Jeremy D., 1948- author.
Title: A new world begins : the history of the French Revolution / Jeremy D. Popkin.
Other titles: History of the French Revolution
Description: First edition. | New York : Basic Books, [2019] | Includes bibliographical references and index.
Identifiers: LCCN 2019019101| ISBN 9780465096664 (hardcover) | ISBN 9780465096671 (ebook)
Subjects: LCSH: France--History--Revolution, 1789-1799.
Classification: LCC DC148 .P665 2019 | DDC 944.04--dc23
LC record available at https://lccn.loc.gov/2019019101
ISBNs: 978-0-4650-9666-4 (hardcover), 978-0-4650-9667-1 (ebook), 978-1-5416-2017-9 (paperback)

LSC-C

Printing 2, 2022

To my parents, Richard H. Popkin (1923–2005) and Juliet Popkin (1924–2015), who inspired me with a love of learning, and my grandmother Zelda Popkin (1898–1983), who made me want to be a writer.

The force of things has perhaps led us to do things that we did not foresee.

Louis-Antoine de Saint-Just, 1794

# Contents

Contents

# Preface

# WHY A NEW HISTORY OF THE FRENCH REVOLUTION?

A T THE END OF 1793, A PRINTER IN THE AMERICAN FRONTIER SETTLEMENT of Lexington, Kentucky, as far away from the French Revolution as any point in the Western world, published *The Kentucky Almanac, for the Year of the Lord 1794*. Along with a calendar and weather forecasts for the coming year, the almanac's main feature was a poem, "The American Prayer for France." Addressing the deity as the "Protector of the Rights of Man," the anonymous poet implored him to "make thy chosen race rejoice, / and grant that KINGS may reign no more." His message was clear: the outcome of the French Revolution mattered, not just to France's "heroes brave, her rulers just," but to all those around the world who believed that human beings were endowed with individual rights and that arbitrary rulers should be overthrown. At the same time, however, the poet's words showed how hard it was to interpret the upheaval that had started in France in 1789 from a distance. Even as the Kentucky author implored God's protection for the Revolution, the revolutionaries were suppressing religious worship in France, and as he praised the justice of their actions, their Revolutionary Tribunal was straining the definition of justice to its limits.[1]

Today, more than two hundred years since the dramatic events that began in 1789, the story of the French Revolution is still relevant to all who believe in liberty and democracy. Whenever movements for freedom take place anywhere in the world, their supporters claim to be following the example of the Parisians who stormed the Bastille on July 14, 1789. Whoever reads the words of the Declaration of the Rights of Man and Citizen, published in August 1789, immediately recognizes the basic principles of individual liberty, legal equality, and representative government that define modern democracies. When we think of the French Revolution, however, we also remember the violent conflicts that divided those who participated in it and the executions carried out with the guillotine. Likewise, we remember the rise to power of the charismatic general whose dictatorship ended the movement. As I sit in my study in Lexington today, making sense of the French Revolution is as much of a challenge as it was for the anonymous author of the *Kentucky Almanac*.

When I began my own career as a scholar and teacher in the 1970s, the memory of the worldwide student protest movements on university campuses in the 1960s was still fresh. Those movements had inspired interest in the French Revolution, which seemed to stand alongside the Russian Revolution of 1917 as one of the great examples of a successful overthrow of an oppressive society. Ironically, the understanding of the French Revolution in those years of upheaval seemed largely fixed: virtually all historians agreed that it had resulted from the frustrations of a rising "bourgeois" class determined to challenge a "feudal" old order that stood in the way of political and economic progress.

By the time I participated, along with researchers from all over the globe, in commemorations of the bicentennial of the French Revolution in 1989, the situation had changed drastically. The communist regimes in Eastern Europe were now tottering, and the fact that the French Revolution had inspired the Soviets was a reason to ask whether France's upheaval had foreshadowed totalitarian excesses more than social

2

progress. The polemical essays of a dynamic French historian, François Furet, challenged the orthodoxy that had dominated study of the Revolution; among other things, he appealed to scholars in the English-speaking world to turn to the subject with fresh eyes.

The decades since 1989 have brought even more questions about the French Revolution to the fore. In 1789, the French proclaimed that "all men are born and remain free and equal in rights"—but what about women? At the start of the American Revolution, John Adams's wife, Abigail, famously urged him in a letter to "remember the ladies, and be more generous and favorable to them than your ancestors."[2] In revolutionary France, the issues about women's rights and relations between the sexes that still preoccupy us today were openly debated in the press, in political clubs, and even in the nation's legislature. Mary Wollstonecraft, recognized as the pioneer of modern feminism, wrote her trailblazing *Vindication of the Rights of Women* in revolutionary Paris, but a French reviewer commented that women there had already shown they could do more than even Wollstonecraft imagined.[3] Some of the women of the period—the playwright and pamphleteer Olympe de Gouges, the novelist and salon hostess Madame de Staël, the backroom politician Madame Roland, and the unhappy queen, Marie-Antoinette—became prominent public figures and left ample records of their thoughts. Others took part in mass uprisings or exerted influence through their daily grumbling about bread prices. Under the new laws on marriage and divorce, some women welcomed the possibility of changes in family life; others played a key role in frustrating male revolutionaries' efforts to do away with the Catholic Church. A history of the French Revolution that does not "remember the ladies" is incomplete.

In today's world, the issues of race and slavery during the French Revolution also command attention they did not receive in the past. On the map, the scattered islands of France's overseas empire in 1789 looked insignificant compared to the holdings of the British, the Spanish, and the Portuguese, but their importance was out of all proportion to their size. In 1787, the colonies provided 37 percent of the goods imported into France and took 22 percent of its exports. One French colony alone—Saint-Domingue, today's Haiti—provided half the world's supply of sugar and coffee. These profits came from the labor of enslaved black men and women. In 1789, the 800,000 slaves in the French sugar islands in the Caribbean and the Indian Ocean outnumbered the 670,000 in the thirteen newly independent American states; indeed, the number of Africans being transported to the French colonies reached its all-time peak just as the French revolutionaries were proclaiming that "men are born and remain free and equal in rights." The French colonies and their slaves were far away from Europe, but they preoccupied the minds of thinkers in France. The abbé Guillaume Raynal's *History of the Two Indies*, a multivolume work with passages condemning colonialism and slavery, was a bestseller in the prerevolutionary years. In 1788, Marie-Antoinette authorized the gift of a gilded watch for "Jean-Pierre, Madame de Boisnormand's mulatto," a playmate of her son.[4] The question of how to reconcile the principles of freedom with the economic importance of the colonies tormented revolutionary leaders throughout the 1790s. After much controversy, they voted to abolish slavery and to grant full rights to people of all races, but only after they were faced with history's largest slave uprising, the beginning of a "Haitian Revolution" that ended in 1804 with the creation of the first independent black nation in the Americas. A history of the French Revolution that gives this previously neglected topic the attention it deserves changes our understanding of the movement's meaning.

The events of the first decades of our century, which have led to widespread questioning of traditional political institutions, also send us back to the French Revolution. Revolutionary-era protests against economic globalization and the consequences of free trade often sound eerily similar to the demands of present-day movements. Because they argued that government needed to represent the will of the people, the French revolutionaries were the forerunners both of modern political democracy and of modern anti-elitist populism, and the events of the 1790s in France vividly demonstrate the conflicts that can arise between the two. As the world attempts to cope with a resurgence of militant nationalism, the ways in which the French Revolution turned the word "nation" into an explosive force demand new attention. The Revolution's violent debates about the proper place of religion in society, and the powerful resistance to its efforts to impose secular values, also foreshadow conflicts of our own time. Like people today, participants in the

French Revolution felt they were experiencing a transformation of the communications media; the proliferation of newspapers and pamphlets, for example, made it seem as though time itself had speeded up, and difficulties in distinguishing between political truth and false rumors were a constant of the period. Finally, in an era in which "disruption" has become a political program, the history of the French Revolution's experiment in deliberately demolishing an existing order has never been more relevant. Our own experience of disruption also lends new relevance to the revolutionaries' efforts, in the five years between the end of the Reign of Terror and the rise of Napoleon, to stabilize their society without undoing the movement's positive achievements.

The French Revolution unfolded at a moment when public taste favored melodramatic plays and novels featuring stark confrontations between good and evil. Histories of the Revolution often repeat this pattern, even if their authors disagree about which figures and movements should be cast as heroes and which as villains. My own personal itinerary as a scholar of the Revolution has inclined me to strive for a balanced view of the men and women of the revolutionary era. My first research projects on French revolutionary history were devoted to writers and journalists who opposed the movement. Although I never embraced their conservative philosophies, I was challenged by learning that intelligent and articulate people had argued so strenuously against the ideals of liberty and equality that I accepted as self-evident. As I broadened my studies on the journalism of the revolutionary period, I had to engage with the writers who favored the movement, or who even thought it had not gone far enough, and grapple with the paradox that the loudest proponents of democracy during the Revolution, such as Jean-Paul Marat and the pseudonymous Père Duchêne, were also vociferous advocates of overt violence.

Midway through my scholarly career, I found myself exploring the dramatic events that led the French revolutionaries to their historic declaration, in 1794, that slavery was an unacceptable violation of human rights, and that the black populations of their colonies should be full French citizens. I discovered that although in one obvious sense the Revolution was a drama in black and white, it was not a simple confrontation between heroes and villains. Abolitionist reformers in France understood the injustice of slavery and racial prejudice, and yet many of them were so convinced that blacks were not yet ready for freedom that they hesitated to draw what now seem the obvious conclusions from their own principles. The blacks in the French colonies who revolted against oppression did not always see the French revolutionaries as allies. Toussaint Louverture, the main figure in the movement that eventually led France's largest and most valuable overseas colony to independence, initially told the French that he was fighting for "another liberty," not the form of freedom the revolutionaries were prepared to offer.

Hardly any of the hundreds of figures readers will meet in these pages can be portrayed in simple terms. Louis XVI and Marie-Antoinette could not comprehend the revolutionary principles of liberty and equality, but they had a sincere devotion to what they saw as their duty to defend the nation's long-established institutions. Prominent revolutionary leaders, from Mirabeau to Robespierre, advocated admirable principles, but they also approved measures with a high human cost in the name of the Revolution. Ordinary men and women were capable of both acts of courage, such as the storming of the Bastille, and acts of inhuman cruelty, including the September massacres of 1792. Certainly all of the participants could have agreed on at least one thing: the truth of the words of a young revolutionary legislator, Louis-Antoine de Saint-Just, when he remarked that "the force of things has perhaps led us to do things that we did not foresee."[5]

The continuing relevance of the French Revolution does not mean that the events of 1789 are simple or that they can offer clear answers to the questions of our own day. Our new perspectives on the role of women in the Revolution, on the importance of the revolutionaries' debates about race and slavery, and on the ways in which revolutionary politics prefigured the current dilemmas of democracy may give us a new view of the movement, but the Revolution's message and its outcome remain ambiguous. Liberty and equality turned out to mean very different things to different people at the time, as they have ever since. One of the most relevant lessons of the Revolution, first driven home by the conservative critic Edmund Burke, and most forcefully articulated by the great nineteenth-century political theorist Alexis de Tocqueville, is that actions inevitably have unintended consequences. An equally important lesson of the Revolution, however, is that it is sometimes necessary to fight for liberty and equality, despite the risks that conflict entails. The respect for individual rights inherent in the Revolution's own principles does require us to recognize the humanity of those who opposed it, and it requires us as well to consider the views of those who paid a price for objecting that the movement did not always fulfill its own promises. Despite its shortcomings, however, the French Revolution remains a vital part of the heritage of democracy.

# 1

# TWO FRENCH LIVES IN
# THE OLD REGIME

O N January 21, 1793, Louis XVI, king of France and Navarre, heir
to fourteen centuries of French monarchy, mounted the steps of
the scaffold in Paris and met his death under the guillotine. His death
became the symbol of the victorious revolutionary movement that had
begun with the storming of the Bastille and the passage of the Declaration of the Rights of Man and Citizen in 1789. Among those who
watched the king's carriage on its way to his execution were thousands
of the commoners of Paris: the artisans, workers, and shopkeepers whose
fervent embrace of the promises of liberty and equality had enabled that
movement to topple France's old order. A few years later, a glazier (or
glassfitter) named Jacques-Louis Ménétra would become one of the few
ordinary people to write an account of his own life before and during
the Revolution.

The experiences Ménétra recalled in his memoirs put him on
one side of the gulf between the two worlds—the world of hierarchy
and privilege, in which Louis XVI was raised, and the world of ordinary people—that collided so violently during the French Revolution.

Ménétra's experiences growing up had prepared him, if not to make a revolution, at least to understand the possibilities of a world in which individuals could make important choices about their own lives and expect to be treated as equals. Louis XVI, in contrast, had been taught from childhood that the existence of society depended on people accepting the ranks assigned to them by birth. Louis XVI did not always enjoy the strictly programmed life he had been given; at times, he may have dreamed of living a freer existence, one more like Ménétra's. Certainly his wife, Queen Marie-Antoinette, had imagined such an existence: she had an artificial village, the "Hameau," constructed on the grounds of Versailles, so that she and her companions could play at being peasants. Neither the king nor the queen, however, could imagine a society in which individuals were free to change the situation into which they had been born. What brought them to their deaths in 1793 was their inability to accept the values that had come to seem natural and just to their former subjects.

Louis-Auguste, the future Louis XVI, born in 1754, was the living symbol of the hereditary privileges and social inequalities the revolutionaries were determined to overturn. From the time of his birth, his life was shaped by his ancestry. Raised in the palace of Versailles, which his famous great-great-great-grandfather, Louis XIV, had built to showcase the grandeur of the French monarchy, he learned about the intricacies of status from an early age. He had an older brother, the duc de Bourgogne, and little Louis-Auguste would have been constantly reminded that it was this older sibling who would someday be the king, and that, as his subject, it would be his duty to obey him. Even as a small child, Louis learned to play his part in court rituals, dressed in elaborate costumes that emphasized his status. As was customary in aristocratic households, he saw little of his parents. They left childrearing chores to a staff overseen by the royal governess, who preferred his older brother, the presumed heir to the throne, and his younger brothers, the comte de Provence and the comte d'Artois, both livelier and more engaging children.

In the hothouse environment of Versailles in which the future Louis XVI was raised, the adults he encountered were either titled nobles, acutely conscious of the minute gradations of status among themselves, or servants whose obsequiousness served to emphasize their masters' and mistresses' sense of importance. Centuries earlier, dukes and barons had been warriors who ruled over their own local fiefdoms. Over the centuries, Louis XVI's ancestors had deprived the nobles of their political independence, but the members of their caste whom the young prince encountered in Versailles remained influential as courtiers and as holders of well-paid positions in the royal administration and the Catholic Church. The courtiers of Versailles were part of a network whose members were scattered throughout the kingdom, bound together by their special legal and social status. To bind its most faithful servants more fully to them, monarchs such as Henri IV and Louis XIV rewarded judges and high officials with titles of nobility, even if they came originally from commoner families. This practice created a division between the *noblesse d'épée*, the "nobles of the sword" whose ancestors had been warriors, and the *noblesse de robe*, who had gained their status through service to the state.

Noble status was highly valued in French society because it brought with it important privileges. Nobles were exempt from many of the most onerous taxes, for example, particularly the *taille*, the basic tax levied on peasants. The most prestigious positions in the government as well as in the Church were reserved for them, as were a specified number of seats in the royal academies and almost all officer posts in the army and navy. Nobles had the right to wear swords at their side in public and to emphasize their status by adding the name of their estate to their family names with the noble "particle" *de*. They had special seating privileges in their local churches and at public ceremonies and the exclusive right to put weather vanes on their chateaux or manor houses in the countryside. Only nobles had the right to hunt game in the countryside: they could trample over peasants' fields as they chased after stags and hares. When nobles were condemned to death, they had the privilege of having their heads cut off. This was considered a more dignified method of execution than hanging, which was reserved for commoners.

To make it clear that they were motivated by honor rather than monetary considerations, nobles were not supposed to engage in the grubby business of commerce or in any kind of manual labor. Various mechanisms allowed wealthy commoner families to obtain noble status, a process that usually took several generations, but once they became *anoblis*, they abandoned the occupations that had made their fortunes. In theory, nobles were expected to live on the incomes they derived from their landed estates, although in practice they found ways to share in the profits of France's expanding commerce and manufacturing during the eighteenth century by investing in enterprises ranging from factories to slaving voyages. A small group of very wealthy aristocrats surrounded the king at Versailles, squabbling over the most desirable court positions and royal rewards. At the other extreme were impoverished noble families who owned little but their titles and a few acres of land, and who frequently resented the favors lavished on the well-connected court nobility. Still, nobles were, on average, richer than even the most prosperous members of the bourgeoisie. Commoners watched their expenses carefully, knowing they could lose their social status if they failed to pay their bills. Nobles had no such worries: their standing was secure, and as a class, they were notoriously careless about running up debts.

In the first years of his life, young Louis would have looked forward to a life as an unusually privileged member of the nobility, but he would not have expected to ever occupy a position of real power. When he was seven years old, however, his older brother died, leaving him second in line to the throne, after his father, the Dauphin. Even royal status could not confer immunity to the many diseases for which eighteenth-century medicine had no remedies.

To prepare him for the responsibilities he now stood to inherit, Louis received an intensive education from a variety of tutors. Religion was an important part of his upbringing, partly in reaction against his grandfather, the ruling king Louis XV, who notoriously flouted the rules of Catholic morality. The king's official mistress during Louis XVI's early years, Madame de Pompadour, exercised highly public influence at court, while a succession of younger women were brought in to satisfy the king's insatiable sexual appetite. Louis's parents made sure their son was raised in an atmosphere of piety and strict moral rules. Only on rare occasions were the royal children allowed some informal fun. One of those occasions, as the glassfitter Ménétra remembered years later, was when he and some other artisans were hired to repair windows at Versailles. In the evenings, "we climbed up on the tables and pretended to fence," Ménétra recalled. "The royal children were brought in to watch our antics."[1]

The future king grew up to be a shy young man who never became comfortable speaking in public. His reluctance to engage in conversation led those who met him to underestimate his intellectual abilities, which were nevertheless considerable. Louis took a special interest in geography; a skillfully drawn map of the area around Versailles demonstrates how well he had mastered the subject. Yet Louis XVI had almost no experience of the world represented in his maps. Except for ceremonial visits to Paris and the royal family's annual stays at other palaces near the capital, he saw nothing of his future kingdom. Even after he became ruler, he made only two brief trips to the provinces, one for his coronation in the cathedral city of Reims in 1775 and another for the inauguration of new harbor facilities in the Norman port city of Cherbourg in 1786, and he never traveled abroad. The tutors who prepared young Louis XVI for the duties he would someday assume did not spend much time teaching him about the population spread across the territories he studied in his maps. In his own notes to his son, dictated nearly a century earlier, Louis XIV had observed that "every profession contributes, in its own way, to the support of the monarchy," but he had accorded just one sentence to peasants and one to artisans.[2] Louis XVI learned little more about the wealthier and more educated commoners—lawyers, doctors, merchants and manufacturers, lower-level government officials— who might, on Sundays, put on their best clothes and visit Versailles to gawk at the splendor of the palace and its elegant courtiers. No matter how successful such men became, they remained, like peasants and artisans, part of the "Third Estate," the catch-all category for all royal subjects except titled nobles and members of the clergy.

Young Louis learned Latin, as did all educated young men in eighteenth-century France, and several modern languages. From his parents, the stern and gloomy Dauphin and the devout Maria-Josepha, he acquired an early interest in history. His father was especially fond of the British historian David Hume's *History of Charles I*, the story of the seventeenth-century monarch who had been executed by his subjects in 1649. The image of a king brought to the scaffold by his own subjects was engraved in the future Louis XVI's mind; he would later recommend the book to his wife, Marie-Antoinette. When Hume was received at Versailles in 1763, the nine-year-old Louis delivered a little formal speech to welcome him. The lengthy summary of the principles of French royal absolutism that Louis copied out for his *gouverneur*, the duc de la Vauguyon, during his early teenage years shows that he knew the major accomplishments of his royal ancestors and the lessons he was supposed to have learned from the many crises France had experienced through the centuries.

In most ways, the future Louis XVI's childhood could not have been more different from that of his future subject Jacques Ménétra, whose horseplay had once entertained him at Versailles. Ménétra was born in 1738 in Paris. His father was a glazier, and Ménétra's birth probably took place in the cramped apartment in the center of the city where the family lived. Like the future king, the future glasscutter saw little of his parents during his infancy: as was customary among Paris artisans, he was placed with a wetnurse so that his mother could return as quickly as possible to helping her husband run the family business. Ménétra was still boarding with the wetnurse's family when his mother died giving birth to her next child: commoners' families were even more familiar than the king's with the ravages caused by eighteenth-century medicine's helplessness in the face of disease. According to his memoirs, Ménétra's wetnurse tried to supplement the meager payments she received for caring for him by teaching him "the profession of begging." Stopping by to check up on him, his grandmother was appalled to see that the son of a respectable artisan was in danger of slipping into a life of poverty. She took him home with her and raised him until he was eleven.[3]

Whereas the future Louis XVI's childhood and education were strictly regulated, Ménétra's early years were chaotic. He had a sweet voice and was briefly a choirboy at the family's neighborhood church, where he would have received an education that might have led to a career in the clergy, but he could not adjust to the school's discipline and soon returned to his grandmother's home. He did learn to read and write—by the middle of the eighteenth century, most boys in Paris got at least some schooling, although their sisters often did not—but in his memoirs he was more eager to recall how he became "one of the leading mischief-makers in my neighborhood."[4] From an early age, Ménétra was also immersed in the adult world of work. Just as Louis XVI was prepared for the family profession of kingship, from an early age Ménétra was trained to follow in his glassfitting ancestors' footsteps.

Whereas young Louis XVI had only the most limited exposure to the realities of other people's lives, Ménétra came into contact with all levels of French society. The glazier's trade took Ménétra into the homes of the wealthy, and he spent a good deal of time working in churches, whose structures incorporated more glass than other buildings of the time. Exposure to religion made the future king a dutiful Catholic, but Ménétra's work gave him a behind-the-scenes perspective on the Church that had the opposite effect. Working in the abbey of Saint-Denis, where the kings of France were traditionally buried, he learned that the monks themselves didn't know which saints' bones were in the reliquaries they displayed to earnest pilgrims, and he lost his faith in the sanctity of the Catholic Mass when he witnessed a priest giving out unconsecrated hosts to his parishioners. "So I never wanted to be with these hypocrites and have never liked their company," Ménétra concluded.[5]

From his history lessons, Louis XVI learned to think of himself as a link in a chain of kings that extended back for over a millennium; Ménétra remembered episodes that affected the common people of Paris but that would never have found a place in the future ruler's schoolbooks. In his memoirs, Ménétra described a popular riot that broke out in May 1750, when he was twelve, sparked by a rumor "that they were taking young boys and bleeding them and that they were lost forever and that their blood was used to bathe a princess suffering from a disease that could only be cured with human blood."[6] The story was false, but the willingness of the Parisians to believe it showed that the common people harbored a deep distrust of the elites who governed them.

An angry crowd that included Ménétra's father responded to the rumor by attacking a police station and burning a suspected informer alive. Although the riot was put down and three ringleaders were executed, it taught Ménétra that commoners could wield power when they acted together. In 1757, just before he set out from Paris on the *tour de France* that would complete his training as a glassfitter, he witnessed a very different kind of historical event, one meant to demonstrate the power of the monarchy: the torture and execution of Louis Damiens, a domestic servant who had stabbed Louis XV with a penknife. Damiens was drawn and quartered, his arms and legs torn from his body by straining draft horses in a prolonged procedure meant to inflict as much excruciating pain as possible.

By the time he witnessed the gruesome execution of Damiens, Ménétra was eighteen and nearing the end of the apprenticeship that prepared him for his adult responsibilities. Louis XVI's transition from childhood to adulthood came more abruptly: his father died in 1765, making his eleven-year-old son, the Dauphin, the direct heir to the throne. Even though Louis's grandfather, Louis XV, was still a vigorous man in his mid-fifties, the boy now knew that he might find himself obliged at any moment to take on the responsibilities of kingship. It was at this time that the royal governor, the duc de la Vauguyon, decided to have the young Louis write out a two-hundred-page summary of the main features of the French monarchy, an exercise that was meant to prepare him for his future obligations.

When Louis XVI's mother died in 1767, it fell to his grandfather to take the place of his parents. In some ways, young Louis may have appreciated the change: his father had forbidden him to go hunting, so Louis XV, a passionate hunter himself, introduced his grandson to the sport. It became one of the future king's great passions and the main theme of the daily journal he began to keep in 1766, when he was twelve. The practice of keeping private diaries to record the events of individual lives was just beginning to spread in France at the time. Although some of Louis's contemporaries used their journals to record their private thoughts and develop a sense of themselves as distinct individuals, the dry and unemotional entries the future king put down give little clue to his personality. Instead, they faithfully record the thousands of stags, boars, and birds he shot in the royal forests that surrounded Versailles. Hunting was a privilege reserved for France's nobility that set its members apart from the common people. Louis's obsession with the sport put him on one side of the great divide that separated the privileged from the Third Estate, to which Ménétra belonged.

It was probably during his teenage years that Louis developed another hobby that, curiously, gave him something in common with Ménétra. The future king enjoyed working with his hands. A master craftsman named Gamain was engaged to teach him the skill of lockmaking, just as Ménétra learned his glasscutting skills from older artisans. Gamain claimed that, "in teaching his trade to Louis XVI, [he] treated him with a tone of authority," although one imagines that his pupil was spared the beatings that were a normal part of an apprentice's training. Eventually, a workshop was set up for Louis in a room in Versailles, where he frequently escaped to get away from palace routine. At the court, his interest in the mechanical arts was regarded as a bizarre eccentricity rather than as something that might bring him closer to his ordinary subjects.[7]

Surrounded by courtiers who hoped to advance their own careers by winning his favor, Louis was taught by his religious confessor to "never let people read your mind," an injunction that strengthened his natural inclination to avoid conversation. Louis's position as heir to the throne after his father's death made it essential for him to be married as quickly as possible, so that he could carry out his most important royal duty: the production of a male heir who would assure the continuation of the Bourbon dynasty. That the king's marriage would be arranged for him was a given, as was the fact that he could only be paired with a princess from another royal dynasty. Louis XVI's grandfather and father had both been married to women from relatively minor ruling houses that were not in a position to demand much from the French in return for the honor of such an alliance. The arrangement that brought the fifteen-year-old Austrian Habsburg princess Marie-Antoinette to Versailles in 1770 to be united with the sixteen-year-old Louis was an entirely different matter.

Along with the Bourbons, the Habsburgs were the most illustrious and powerful of Europe's dynasties. For centuries, the two families had been each other's archenemies. The royal history young Louis had been made to memorize was a long saga of wars against Marie-Antoinette's ancestors, and the aristocratic generals who commanded the king's troops had also been raised on stories of victories over the "Kaiserlichs." It was a shock to them and to the whole continent in 1756 when Louis XV and his closest advisers engineered a "diplomatic revolution" that made Austria, rather than Prussia, France's main ally. Indeed, Austria and Prussia were bitter rivals, and the ambitious ruler of the latter, Frederick the Great, had plunged Europe into an era of conflict in 1740 when he had seized the valuable province of Silesia from his Habsburg neighbor.

The marriage of Louis and Marie-Antoinette was meant to consolidate the alliance between the Bourbon and Habsburg dynasties. Whether the two teenagers were compatible with each other was irrelevant to the diplomats who negotiated the arrangement. Nor were they concerned about how the deep unpopularity of the Austrian alliance in France might affect the royal couple. The marriage was the last major victory of the minister Étienne-François de Choiseul, a fervent partisan of the pact who was ousted from power and exiled to his country estate shortly after its conclusion. Young and inexperienced in politics as she was, Marie-Antoinette understood that Choiseul's disgrace left her without an ally in French court circles. She would quickly acquire a reputation for self-interested intrigue because of her efforts to win court favors for Choiseul's supporters and bring him back to prominence.

Louis XVI's bride was young and pretty, and Louis XV and his court became infatuated with her. "Nothing was spoken of except her charms, her liveliness and the cleverness of her responses," her lady-in-waiting Madame Campan wrote in her memoirs. Her new husband was less intrigued. His governor, the duc de la Vauguyon, had warned him to be on his guard against any attempt to influence him in favor of Austrian interests. The spectacular fireworks display in honor of their marriage in Paris turned into a disaster when a panic in the crowd set off a stampede in which over a hundred spectators were trampled and suffocated. The young royal couple did not witness the event—much to Marie-Antoinette's annoyance, Louis XV did not allow them to visit Paris for the first time until three years after their marriage—but the fact that their union began with a calamity was a bad omen. Ménétra never forgot the event. By 1770, he had completed his tour of France, returned to Paris, and married; he and his wife lost sight of each other in the crowd at the "night of celebration" that "changed into a night of mourning," and he spent anxious hours before they were reunited.[8]

The young royal couple turned out to be woefully ignorant about how to accomplish their most important duty, the production of an heir. It took seven frustrating years before Marie-Antoinette's brother, the Austrian emperor Joseph II, discovered that Louis "stays there for perhaps two minutes without moving, withdraws without ever discharging, and bids good night," and explained to the "two incompetents" what they needed to do in order to consummate their marriage. By that time, Louis's inability to get his wife pregnant had become the talk of Versailles and Paris, sorely undermining his reputation. Florimond-Claude, comte de Mercy d'Argenteau, the Austrian ambassador to France, served as Marie-Antoinette's "minder," lecturing her regularly on her duties and reporting the smallest details of her life to her mother, the Habsburg empress Maria Theresa. He found "the coldness of the heir to the throne, a young husband of twenty, with regard to a pretty woman . . . inconceivable," and wondered if he suffered from some kind of physical deformity. Despite her best efforts, Marie-Antoinette could not divert Louis from his two passions, hunting and what Mercy described as "his extraordinary taste for everything that has to do with building, like masonry, carpentry and other things of that sort." On one occasion, the two teenagers squabbled in front of their courtiers until Marie-Antoinette's complaints about Louis's behavior reduced him to tears.[9]

Distant as he may have seemed, Louis XVI was not entirely closed off from the world outside of Versailles. One of the first purchases he made when Louis XV gave him a personal allowance was a set of the volumes of the *Encyclopédie*, a reference work notorious for its expression of the critical spirit of the Enlightenment. He may have appreciated its detailed explanation of the various mechanical trades that interested him so much, but he could hardly have failed to notice its controversial articles on politics and religion. Not satisfied with the censored news in the official *Gazette de France*, he subscribed to the *Gazette de Leyde*, an uncensored newspaper published outside the kingdom.[10] Nevertheless, when the celebrated author Voltaire, the symbol of the Enlightenment, made a triumphal visit to Paris in 1778 after years of exile in Switzerland, Louis firmly vetoed any suggestion that he be received at court, lest it appear that the monarchy approved his critiques of aristocracy and revealed religion.

The unhappy Marie-Antoinette, bored with the formality of a court routine that forced her to spend most of her time with older women—such as her husband's unmarried aunts—developed her own social life. Once she was finally allowed to visit Paris, she often made evening outings to attend plays and masked balls, leaving Louis, who always wanted to be in bed by eleven o'clock, behind in Versailles. These expeditions inspired malicious gossip, as did the attention paid to her by various courtiers, including the king's younger brother the comte d'Artois, and her close relations with two young friends, the princesse de Lamballe and the comtesse de Polignac. Even when she stayed at Versailles, her conduct caused scandal. Especially after Louis XV died, her passion for high-stakes gambling set tongues wagging and discouraged proper society women from frequenting the court.

Jacques Ménétra shared the young Marie-Antoinette's penchant for amusement and adventures. By the time the young glassfitter set off on his tour of France, the traditional culmination of a skilled artisan's training, he had already mastered the art of lovemaking that posed such a challenge for his future monarch. After learning the basics from a chambermaid in one of his clients' homes, Ménétra became a regular customer of the prostitutes of Paris. "These interludes were so pleasant that every day I tried to make new conquests," he wrote in his memoirs, although "in the end my reward was what you might well imagine and that made me a little wiser." Whatever lessons he learned from his first bout of venereal disease, it hardly slowed him down. His memoirs mention fifty-two sexual relationships prior to his marriage at twenty-seven, a typical age for ordinary Frenchmen of the time, and an additional thirteen extramarital affairs afterward.[11]

The king may have been at the pinnacle of a society based on privileges, but his subjects had their own spheres of freedom, as Ménétra's busy sex life proved. The glassfitter's adventures reflected a sense of masculine entitlement shared by Louis XVI's notorious grandfather. Ménétra left several of his partners pregnant—one confronted him and, he claimed, tried to stab him—and a number of the encounters he described crossed the boundary between seduction and rape. Marie-Jeanne "Manon" Phlipon, a young woman who grew up in an artisan's household and who became famous as Madame Roland, an important figure in revolutionary politics, left one of the rare testimonies of the impact that casual sexual assaults like Ménétra's could have on their targets. Aggressively molested on several occasions by one of her father's apprentices, she was troubled by the memory for years. "Every time I tried to reflect about it, disturbing thoughts made the meditation difficult for me," she recalled.[12]

The seven years Ménétra spent traveling around France gave him an acquaintance with the kingdom far more extensive than what Louis XVI learned from studying his beloved maps. In the course of his wanderings, Ménétra crossed the wheat-growing plains of France's breadbasket around Paris; followed the slow-moving Loire River through cities such as Orléans, Tours, and Angers; sailed around the long Brittany peninsula on a privateering ship at the start of the Seven Years' War; and stopped in the slave-trading port cities of Nantes, La Rochelle, and Bordeaux. In the Atlantic ports, he might have met blacks from the French colonies, some enslaved and some who were members of the "intermediate race" of free people of color produced by unions between white men and black women. These educated colonials would have been brought to France to serve their masters and to learn artisanal skills like his own, and like Ménétra, some of them would later join the revolutionary movement. From Bordeaux, Ménétra traveled through the southern provinces of Gascony and Languedoc to the Mediterranean coast and its main port of Marseilles, trekked up the valley of the Rhône to the silk-manufacturing center of Lyon, and then continued north through the Burgundian capital of Dijon and back to the capital. In general,

Ménétra followed the well-maintained high roads that were one of the great achievements of Louis XV's reign. Much admired by visitors from the rest of Europe, these roads knit the kingdom together so that by the last decades of the century, the trip from Paris to Lyon took only three and a half days by coach. (Today's high-speed trains do it in two hours.)

As he tramped along, Ménétra passed by hundreds of villages, the homes of the rural peasantry who made up the vast majority of France's population. They rarely figure in his memoirs. Able to read and write, equipped with a set of specialized skills and contemptuous of religion, Ménétra had little in common with country folk. Peasants were not potential customers for a glazier: their cottages seldom had glass windows. Ménétra and his companions thought nothing of stealing a peasant's sheep to roast for their dinner; the owner of one farm set her dog on him, telling him that the animal was "doing his duty."[13] He was pleasantly surprised when another peasant offered him a meal, let him sleep overnight in his barn, and even gave him a little money to help him on his way.

Ménétra's travels taught him little about the realities of peasant life. Neither he nor the villagers themselves would have had any idea that the country's rural population had been growing rapidly since the last great climate crisis, the fearful winter of 1709–1710. He might have noticed how the main crops growing in the fields he passed changed from region to region—wheat in the Beauce near Paris; buckwheat and rye in poorer areas, including Brittany and the Sologne south of the Loire; wine grapes outside of Bordeaux; olive trees in the Mediterranean climate of Provence—but he did not care about the ways in which the lives of the peasants who worked those fields differed depending on what they raised, how much land they owned or rented, and what their relations were with their local *seigneur*, or lord. He certainly did not know that the introduction of new crops, such as American corn and potatoes, and of new farming practices were raising overall productivity and thus making an increase in population possible.

To Ménétra, the titled aristocrats, clergy, and wealthy bourgeois who held legal rights over the land were potential clients; to peasants, they were powerful presences who could grant or withhold leases, demand dues and payments that took a considerable portion of the crops, and control the local courts that administered justice in the countryside. Unable to appreciate this tangled web of relationships between seigneurs and peasants that would play such an important role in setting off the French Revolution, Ménétra was also oblivious to the ways in which peasants organized themselves in order to look after their community affairs and defend their interests. Even if few of them could read or write, peasants had a strong sense of their rights. Village councils, usually dominated by the heads of the wealthiest households, bargained with the local seigneur, or, more often, with his estate manager, about communal needs; with the priest about the upkeep of the church; and with the tax collectors about the community's annual bill, which council members then had to collect from the inhabitants. The local priest, itinerant peddlars, and visits to nearby towns meant that peasants were not completely ignorant of the wider world.

Louis XVI understood that the peasantry made up the majority of his subjects and that their welfare mattered to him, because the taxes they paid were an essential part of the monarchy's revenue. Distant as his life was from theirs, king and peasants shared the Catholic faith that Ménétra rejected. Within the little worlds of their villages, better-off peasant families also shared the royal Bourbons' obsessive concern about making good marriages for their children. A good marriage for the king meant one that promised to keep the kingdom intact and even enlarge it; a good match in a village kept a family farm from being divided and ensured that the new couple would inherit their parents' position in their community. Peasant families kept a close watch on their children to make sure they would be marriageable: in a village, no young man would have been able to compile a list of sexual conquests like Ménétra's. The schoolmaster Pierre Delahaye, who kept a diary, noted the noisy charivari rituals villagers held to punish marriages with "outsiders" from other communities, and how unmarried women who became pregnant had to leave the town to hide their shame.

The world that really interested Ménétra was that of the towns where he stopped on his tour of France, often for months at a time, and looked for work. In the towns he visited, Ménétra met a far more varied range of people than Louis XVI encountered at Versailles, or than peasants saw in their villages. As a member of a journeymen's organization, or *compagnonnage*, he could count on a friendly welcome in every town he entered, where he would be lodged in a local inn run by the compagnonnage's *mère*, or "mother," and put on the list of glassfitters available for hire. Long before 1789, the journeymen's compagnonnages were practitioners of what would become the revolutionary ideal of fraternity. Members were supposed to treat each other as comrades, care for each other in case of illness or accidents, and stand up for each other in conflicts with employers, with local authorities, and above all, with members of rival compagnonnages. Neither the artisans' compagnonnages nor the Masonic lodges, which attracted nobles and wealthy commoners, promoted subversive ideas, but members of both learned to govern themselves according to rules they had voluntarily sworn to obey. As a result, they began to think of themselves as parts of national and—in the case of the Masons—international networks that transcended local concerns.

The clients for glaziers' services included local nobles who wanted the windows and mirrors in their chateaux repaired; members of the clergy, whose churches' ancient stained glass needed new lead joints; prosperous local merchants and lawyers, whose elegant townhouses lined the streets of provincial cities; and municipal officials, who often wanted to imitate Paris by putting up glass lanterns to light their streets. In southern France, Ménétra encountered members of France's Protestant minority and liked them better "than those fanatics who gave me a headache with their priests and their superstitions." He attended some of the Protestants' clandestine religious services and became convinced of the injustice of the laws that restricted their religious freedom. Initially, he was less sympathetic to the Jews he met in the Rhône valley town of Carpentras, one of the few places where they were legally allowed to live. Yet after seeing how badly the Jews were treated by the Catholic clergy, he reflected that "they are our brothers and . . . they are equal to us in the eyes of the Eternal."[14]

Quick to make friends and always ready to join in drinking bouts, Ménétra lived up to his nickname, *Parisien le bienvenu*, the "welcome

Parisian," wherever he went. If we are to believe his memoirs, local women were among those who welcomed him most eagerly. The length of his stay in each location generally depended on how long it took before he decided he needed to move on, in order to avoid a permanent commitment to his latest girlfriend. The surprising number of widows he claimed to have bedded indicates that he paid special attention to women whose artisan husbands had left them the ownership of a functioning enterprise. Writing nearly forty years later, he regretted having turned down the most attractive of them, a woman in the southern town of Nîmes, because of religious differences. Such women needed a man with glassfitting skills to keep their businesses running; in return, they offered Ménétra the possibility of establishing himself as a master artisan with his own shop and an experienced partner to keep the books. Although he regarded most women as "prey," Ménétra understood that these widows wielded real economic power.

According to the official doctrine of absolutism taught to the young Louis XVI, kings in France ruled, and subjects, especially those of lowly status, such as artisans, obeyed. Ménétra, although he was hardly a revolutionary before 1789, knew that reality was different. As a group, artisans had considerable power. If they objected to the pay and working conditions they were offered in a town, they could boycott its local guild masters, who would find themselves without qualified workers. When they became upset with the terms offered by the masters' representative in Nantes, Ménétra and his comrades threw him out a window. In Angers, he claimed to have taken part in a battle between rival compagnonnages that involved over a thousand participants and resulted in a number of deaths; the local authorities stood by helplessly, outnumbered by the artisans and afraid to confront them. In Bordeaux, Ménétra represented several thousand artisans who objected to being drafted into the militia in negotiations that brought him face to face with the officials charged with strengthening the country's defenses in the Seven Years' War. He showed no fear in presenting their case to the royally appointed administrator of the province; the haughty head magistrate of the local royal court, or *parlement*; and even the duc de Richelieu, the royal governor and a member of the family of the famous Cardinal Richelieu, the seventeenth-century architect of the absolutist monarchy.

Clashes between compagnons were just one of the many forms of collective violence punctuating French life throughout the eighteenth century. Such events showed that members of the lower classes had ways of asserting their interests. In years of bad harvests, villagers used force to prevent middlemen from buying up grain to ship it to distant markets, and townspeople rioted to force local officials to set a maximum price on bread. Smugglers' gangs could often rally local support when they confronted the armed guards of the tax-collecting *ferme générale*, or general farm, the octopus-like enterprise that worked, among other things, to enforce the unpopular state monopoly that drove up the price of tobacco.

Subjected to much harsher discipline than artisans and peasants in France, the slaves in France's plantation colonies nevertheless had strategies of resistance of their own. A few were able to obtain their freedom: in the French colony of Saint-Domingue in the 1770s, the future black leader Toussaint Louverture even briefly owned a small plantation and a handful of slaves of his own.[15] Other enslaved blacks became *maroons*, running away from abusive owners and overseers and sometimes negotiating for improved conditions before they would return. Whites who depended on their black servants to prepare their food and care for their children lived in fear of the poisons Africans supposedly knew how to prepare. In 1758, shortly after the gruesome execution of Damiens in Paris, the authorities in Saint-Domingue staged a similar public execution, burning an accused sorcerer named Macandal at the stake. The memory of his martyrdom would help spur a slave uprising during the Revolution.

In 1764, after seven years of provincial life, Ménétra finally returned to Paris, where he would spend the rest of his days. Compared to the other French cities he had visited during his tour of France, the capital was in a class by itself. The second-largest city in Europe, with a population that grew from around 450,000 in 1715 to 600,000 by 1789, it was surpassed only by London in the European world. Concentrating within its walls the wealthiest elites in the kingdom, it was the main market for every kind of luxury product, from the fancy furniture turned out by the skilled artisans of the Faubourg Saint-Antoine around the Bastille to the elaborate dresses Marie-Antoinette and her court entourage ordered from her favorite designer, Rose Bertin. The sheer mass of the city's population made it a voracious consumer of grain, meat, wine, firewood, and all the other basic necessities of life. Contemplating the capital's appetite, one observer wrote that "one would have trouble imagining that there are sources capable of meeting the needs of this vast pit."[16]

The Paris of the mid-eighteenth century was very different from the city tourists see today. The broad tree-lined boulevards of modern Paris would not be built until the 1850s and 1860s, and the Eiffel Tower would not give the city its universally recognized symbol until 1889. The center of the city was a maze of narrow streets lined with four- and five-story buildings whose inhabitants routinely emptied their chamberpots out their windows, letting the next rain wash the contents into the Seine River. The streets were constantly crowded with pedestrians dodging horse-drawn carriages, and vendors offering everything from water to dentistry: the Pont-Neuf bridge was well known as the place to go to have an aching tooth pulled.

The growth of the city meant that it was constantly changing. New public monuments, such as the church of Sainte-Geneviève, begun in 1758 and still unfinished when the Revolution transformed it into the Pantheon, altered the appearance of the city and kept hundreds of artisans like Ménétra employed. Whereas peasant villagers all followed the same daily routines, Parisians constantly encountered people from other social classes and professions whose lives were very different from their own. Louis-Sébastien Mercier, whose twelve-volume *Tableau de Paris* was a best seller in the 1780s, thought city life was bound to make people ask why some should be rich and others poor, why some rode in carriages while others went on foot, and why the population had to endure so many inconveniences when the possibilities of improvement seemed so obvious.[17]

Paris was also the center of France's and Europe's cultural and intellectual life. The royal academies of science, literature, and art attracted the most accomplished men in their fields. Women were allocated a handful of places in the art academy but excluded from most of the others. Actresses, however, were as important, if not more important, than their male colleagues in the troupes of the capital's theaters and its opera. With its thirty-six licensed publishers and numerous bookstores, Paris was the center of the French book trade, even if controversial works were often printed abroad to avoid censorship. The authorities generally looked the other way when such works were smuggled into the capital: courtiers and government officials were often among their most enthusiastic readers, and many wrote provocative works themselves. The city's hundreds of coffeehouses and reading rooms, where customers could pay for the privilege of scanning the latest periodicals, were the basis for the growing phenomenon of *opinion publique* (public opinion) a term that entered the French language around 1750 to describe the imagined consensus of educated individuals on matters of general concern.

As well as attracting the country's elites, Paris was also home to France's largest concentration of the poor. In the minds of the authorities and the upper classes, the urban working classes—such as Ménétra and his wife—were not that different from the truly destitute and the worlds of crime and prostitution. Charitable institutions and public workhouses, or *hôpitaux*, which took in beggars as well as orphans old enough to work, the chronically ill or disabled, and the elderly who could not care for themselves, attracted even the poor from the surrounding countryside. The desperately poor often engaged in petty theft, and women easily fell into prostitution, especially in the capital, where the sex trade ran the gamut from elegant courtesans, who sometimes had formal contracts with their lovers, to the less fortunate who sold sex for a few coins on the streets. By modern standards, however, violent crime, particularly murder, was relatively rare. Lower-class urban neighborhoods were tightknit communities in which everyone knew everyone else's business and helped enforce social norms. Though wives were often treated with casual brutality, this was kept within certain limits by social pressure from other women, who would intervene collectively to scold abusive husbands. The urban poor were theoretically expected to attend church, but it was much harder for city parish priests, or *curés*, to supervise their flocks than it was for their counterparts in the countryside. More effective in maintaining order, as Ménétra's memoirs indicate, were the police, whose agents kept a close eye on public gathering places, such as the cabarets, where working men went to drink.

Ménétra had no trouble making himself at home once he returned from his travels. He might have joined the family business, but relations with his irascible father were so poor that he preferred to strike out on his own. After a brief continuation of his womanizing, drinking, and brawling, a friend introduced him to "a nice good girl who had a little property," and the two soon reached an agreement. As was common for couples from the popular classes, the bride brought with her savings that allowed her husband to purchase a workshop that would become the family business. Since he was over twenty-five, Ménétra did not need his father's permission to marry. Because marriage was a religious sacrament, however, Ménétra had to get a certificate of confession from a Catholic priest, no easy matter in view of the life he had led. He found an obliging clergyman who gave him what he needed in exchange for "a few bottles and three livres," but the transaction did nothing to improve his opinion of the Church.[18]

The match was no happier than the one between Louis XVI and Marie-Antoinette. "Getting ahead was her main passion and mine was to enjoy myself it was impossible to reconcile the two," Ménétra wrote in his unpunctuated prose. Although the law made him the unquestioned head of the household, as was customary in lower-class families, reality was more complicated. Ménétra's wife handled the family finances, paying for supplies and collecting from clients; she also invested the family savings without consulting her husband. Ménétra, for his part, never hesitated to give "the old marriage contract a few healthy stabs all in secret" when the opportunity presented itself.[19] Some of his liaisons were with prostitutes, but others involved women who, to judge by his descriptions, possessed the same independence of spirit that made it difficult for him to live with his wife.

Just as in the days when he was on his tour of France, Ménétra continued to socialize with members of all levels of society. For a while, he even forged a friendship with the most celebrated French writer of the day, Jean-Jacques Rousseau, who had been allowed to return to the French capital by 1770, after being forced into exile for his controversial works in 1762. Ménétra met Rousseau when he was hired to do some repair work for the author's landlord. Rousseau, himself the son of an artisan, enjoyed the tales Ménétra told about his adventures, and for a time the two met regularly. They went for walks or drank and played checkers in a café, an egalitarian setting where anyone who paid the price of a beverage could enter. Ménétra got a taste of Rousseau's own difficult marriage and listened as the writer poured out the story of his unhappy life. Ménétra clearly enjoyed the friendship, but he knew he was not Rousseau's equal. "Both of us had the same clothes but not the same knowledge," he wrote. Another of his close friends was Henri Sanson, the official executioner of the city of Paris, who would conduct the guillotining of Louis XVI in 1793. "His profession aside he was a gentle friendly kindly man," Ménétra recalled.[20]

Had Louis XVI had better fortune managing the affairs of the country, Ménétra might have lived out his days in obscurity, enjoying his friendships, his love affairs, and his work. Nothing in his memoirs suggests a man who felt oppressed by the institutions of prerevolutionary France. He was arrested occasionally and even once briefly imprisoned, owing to the frequent scrapes and quarrels he got himself into, but he took these misadventures in stride rather than cultivating a sense of injustice. Nevertheless, Ménétra's story shows that, long before the Revolution, even members of France's lower classes had come to value individual freedom and to regard themselves as the equals of their social betters. Ménétra never hesitated to stand up for himself, and he also knew how to work with others to defend their common interests. It is unlikely that he ever read his friend Rousseau's famous political tract, The Social Contract, or his best-selling novel Emile, whose hero was brought up to be a self-supporting artisan, but in many ways, Ménétra exemplified the ideal of the autonomous individual that Rousseau's works promoted. When the Revolution broke out, men like Ménétra— and some of the independent-minded women whom he encountered— would recognize themselves in its language of liberty and equality.

In contrast, Louis XVI's personal life after his ascension to the throne in 1774 did little to prepare him for the crisis he would face in 1789. Only twenty years of age when smallpox suddenly claimed his grandfather's life, the new king was overwhelmed by the responsibilities that immediately descended on him; unlike Ménétra, he had no opportunity for an apprenticeship to help him grow into his adult role. Pressured from all sides by ambitious courtiers, he called on an older political figure, Jean-Frédéric Phélypeaux, comte de Maurepas, to act as his mentor, but even with Maurepas's help, he found it difficult to steer a steady policy course. Few of his ministers held office for more than a short period, and there was little coordination between them. Louis acquired an unfortunate reputation for appointing men who would try to push through significant reforms and then dismissing them as soon as their actions incited opposition.

For the first three years of his reign, Louis XVI's marriage with Marie-Antoinette remained under great strain because of his inability to make her pregnant. Finally, on December 19, 1778, the queen gave birth to a child. It was under circumstances that reminded the royal couple of how heavily their specially privileged positions weighed on every aspect of their lives. Time-honored ritual dictated that a royal child's birth had to be a public event, so that there could be no doubt about the infant's parentage. "The rule of letting everyone in . . . was observed in such an exaggerated way," Madame Campan remembered, that "the flood of spectators . . . almost made the queen perish." Told that her baby was a girl rather than the longed-for male heir, Marie-Antoinette fainted, leading to a moment of panic when it was feared that she had died.[21] The experience was so traumatic that precedent was broken and attendance limited at her subsequent deliveries.

The birth of a son in 1781 finally secured the future of the Bourbon dynasty, but the royal couple still clashed. The queen had always resented the strictness of French court etiquette, which was much more formal than Habsburg court etiquette in Vienna. Louis XVI indulged her, giving her the Petit Trianon palace in the Versailles gardens as a private retreat, and allowing her to build the imitation peasant village, where she and her friends played at being milkmaids. He seems

CORONATION OF LOUIS XVI: This engraving celebrating Louis XVI's official coronation ceremony emphasized the divine origin of his authority and gave no hint of the challenges to the church and the monarchy that led to the French Revolution. *Source: Bibliothèque nationale de France.*

to have looked the other way when she made the dashing young Swedish nobleman Axel von Fersen her lover; evidence suggests that Fersen fathered the last two children she bore.[22] Like Ménétra and his wife, however, Louis and Marie-Antoinette argued regularly over money. Marie-Antoinette gambled heavily in the years before the birth of her first child, counting on the king to cover her debts, and she lobbied for extravagant favors for the families of her favorites, especially the countess Jules de Polignac. The sums she paid to her dressmaker, Rose Bertin, inspired nasty criticism at court, as did the designs she favored, which were often made from imported cotton fabrics rather than the heavy silks produced by the weavers of Lyon, whom the court was traditionally expected to support with its patronage. Marie-Antoinette's unconventional taste in dress was featured in the portraits she commissioned from her favorite artist, Elisabeth Vigée-Lebrun, another strong-minded and independent woman.

Just as Ménétra settled down as he reached his late twenties, Louis XVI eventually seemed to become accustomed to his routine as king. Mercy d'Argenteau noted that, in spite of the many hours he spent each day hunting, he took his duties seriously, spending three or four hours every morning meeting with his ministers and minimizing the time he spent on formal ceremonies, such as the king's daily *lever*, the elaborate ritual he had inherited from Louis XIV, in which courtiers had the privilege of handing him the various articles of his clothing. He might be impatient with court routine, but he did not question the necessity of maintaining it. So, too, the king expected that the monarchy he embodied and the country he ruled would continue to function as they had under his predecessors. That something might happen to shake the foundations of the palace of Versailles, and put power in the hands of men like the glassfitter who had once amused him when he was a child, never crossed his mind. Nor did it occur to Ménétra. And yet changes were afoot in France that would overturn the worlds of both the king and his subjects.

# 2

# THE MONARCHY,
# THE PHILOSOPHES,
# AND THE PUBLIC

L OUIS WAS YOUNG AND INEXPERIENCED WHEN HIS GRANDFATHER'S DEATH
made him king on May 10, 1774, but the monarchy he had inherited
had a long history behind it. During the carefully programmed tutoring
he received to prepare him for his duties, Louis XVI was imbued with
the glories of that history and with the principles of royal absolutism
as they had been articulated by important seventeenth-century figures.
These included the minister Richelieu and Louis XIV's court preacher,
Bishop Bossuet, whose *Politics Drawn from the Very Words of Holy
Scripture* provided a comprehensive justification of France's monarchy.
In the long summary of French history and absolutist principles that the
future king copied out as a young teenager, he wrote that the French
kings "have received from God himself the greatest and most absolute
power over other men that has ever been entrusted to one man: the
power to make laws for improvement, administration to control them,
judicial authority to punish and compensate." In 1766, just after the

death of Louis XVI's father had made the young boy the heir to the throne, his grandfather Louis XV had resoundingly restated the principles of French royal authority, reminding his subjects that "I alone exercise the power of making laws, independently and undividedly." At his desk, the young boy dutifully echoed those words: "A defining characteristic of the French monarchy is that all power resides with the king alone, and that no body or person can make itself independent of his authority."[1]

Young Louis knew that, according to the theorists of absolutism, his power was not arbitrary: he could not simply follow his caprices, as French political writers imagined that the "despots" of non-European kingdoms and empires did. The French king was bound to follow the dictates of the reason with which God had imbued human beings, and to respect his subjects' rights, which Louis listed in his lessons as "life, honor, liberty, and the property of the goods that each individual possesses."[2] This list was not so far removed from the "life, liberty, and the pursuit of happiness" that the American revolutionary Thomas Jefferson would speak of in the Declaration of Independence, and to the rights that the French revolutionary legislators would define in 1789; the similarities were a reminder that French absolutism and American and French revolutionary liberalism shared roots in the philosophical tradition of natural law. The most significant difference between the future king's notion of rights and that of the revolutionaries was young Louis's reference to *honneur* (honor), a promise to maintain the elaborate differences in rank and status on which France's hierarchical society was based. Respect for honor meant rejection of equality, which would have put nobles and commoners on the same footing.

In theory, French absolutism was a strikingly simple system of government in which the ruler was free to take whatever measures the welfare of the state demanded. In practice, the French government was a bewilderingly complicated assortment of poorly coordinated institutions that no one, not even the king, fully understood. In the late 1750s, Louis XV assigned the royal historiographer Jacques-Nicolas Moreau the task of compiling the legal documents that would establish, once and for all, the basic outlines of the French "constitution," the fundamental laws governing the kingdom. Moreau's researches took him all over the country in pursuit of moldy medieval charters and scattered copies of obscure royal edicts, but he never succeeded in completing his mission. In 1789, the revolutionaries would decide that the effort to rediscover the true principles of the French constitution was impossible; instead, they would set out to give the country a completely new set of fundamental institutions.

Louis XVI was no revolutionary: he could never accept the idea of simply dismissing the legacy of the French past, of which the monarchy itself was the most important part. French historians trumpeted the fact that the country's line of kings went back further than that of any other European country. They traced its origins to Clovis, who in 486 proclaimed himself king of the Franks, the Germanic tribe that ruled what had been the Roman province of Gaul. In the early Middle Ages, the kingship had been wrested away from the Merovingian descendants of Clovis by a second dynasty, the Carolingians, whose most illustrious member was Charlemagne. At its height, Charlemagne's empire took in most of the kingdom Louis XVI would inherit in 1774 as well as much of Germany and northern Italy. The territories east of the Rhine River and south of the Alps were soon separated from the French crown, and the Carolingian dynasty lost its position to the rival family of Hugues Capet, who was proclaimed king in 987. From that point on, every French monarch claimed blood descent from a royal Capetian ancestor.

The Salic Law, a medieval invention supposedly based on Roman precedents, made France one of several European monarchies that barred women from occupying the throne or passing it to their descendants: French kingship could only be inherited through the male line. Yet women had often exercised decisive influence in France: in his history lessons, Louis XVI would have learned about the two Italian Medici princesses, Catherine and Marie, powerful queen mothers who had served as regents in the sixteenth and seventeenth centuries after the deaths of their husbands, and Anne of Austria, who had preserved the throne for her five-year-old son, Louis XIV, when his father died in 1643. For French legal theorists, however, the Salic Law made France the European kingdom where male authority was most firmly established and created a precedent for excluding women from political life. In his summary of his lessons, the future Louis XVI repeated the warnings he had received that "women involve themselves in everything in France" and that "they are behind all the intrigues," even if a few of them "have merit above their sex."[3]

Over the centuries, the kings of France had gone from being feudal overlords dependent on their vassals' uncertain loyalty to exercising an extensive array of powers. Above all, they were the source of the kingdom's laws, which each monarch, at his coronation ceremony, swore to maintain and defend. Royal decrees covered every aspect of their subjects' lives, from the rights of property and inheritance to the definition of crimes and the punishments for them. The king appointed judges to the royal tribunals and served as the ultimate court of appeal from their decisions. In 1539, François I issued the Edict of Villers-Cotterets, making the king's French the language of law throughout his realm. Although much of the population continued to speak regional dialects, or languages such as Breton, Basque, or Flemish that were unrelated to French, this royal decision ensured that there were at least some people in every part of the country who understood French, thus contributing to the development of a sense of common nationhood.

Although the king was the supreme judge throughout his realm, the monarchy's laws were far from uniform. The differences in laws in the provinces reflected the long process through which the kingdom had been built up. The growth of France had been an unplanned process, and the boundaries of the kingdom had shrunk and expanded many times over the centuries. The core of the kingdom was the Île de France, the "island of France" surrounding Paris, which was established as the capital in the early Middle Ages. The rich farmland of northern France provided the crops to feed its population, and the city's location on the Seine facilitated the arrival of bulky necessities such as firewood. Vulnerable to invaders crossing the flat plains to its north and east, as Habsburg armies did many times after 1500, Paris's location forced the French kings to be continually prepared for war.

After the breakup of the overly extended empire of Charlemagne in the ninth century, the French kingdom grew through conquests to the south. Among other things, these territories had preserved the heritage of Roman law, whereas the northern parts of the kingdom lived under customary laws rooted in the traditions of the Germanic tribes, including the Franks, who had settled in those regions. The bloody Albigensian crusades of the twelfth and thirteenth centuries brought the provinces of Languedoc and Provence under royal control, extending the kingdom to the Mediterranean. These wars against heretics who dissented from orthodox Catholic teachings emphasized the role of the French kings as defenders of the Church. By 1375, the papacy confirmed that the rulers of France, and they alone, could claim the title of "most Christian" kings. As a sign of their sacred status, they were thought to possess the ability to cure the painful disease of scrofula, the "king's evil," by touching sufferers, a ceremony Louis XVI dutifully performed at his coronation in 1775.

Louis XVI's history lessons would have taught him about the Hundred Years' War, the desperate struggle against the English kings who claimed the province of Aquitaine in southwestern France and key port cities on the North Sea coast. Throughout the conflict, which raged in the fourteenth and fifteenth centuries, the very survival of the kingdom was in doubt, until Joan of Arc, the "Maid of Orléans," dramatically galvanized the French war effort. The king would also have learned about his ancestors' rivalry with the dukes of Burgundy, which Louis XI had ended through his annexation of that eastern province in 1477, and about the marriages of Charles VIII and Louis XII to the duchess Anne of Brittany, which added the western peninsula jutting out into the Atlantic to the kingdom in 1532.

The Protestant Reformation in the sixteenth century interrupted the expansion of France and posed an even more serious threat to its unity than earlier conflicts. Under the banner of religion, both Protestant and Catholic noblemen formed armed factions that fought each other and intrigued to bring the monarchy under their control. Although they were hardly glorious moments in royal history, the young boy would have been taught the story of the Saint Bartholomew's Day massacre of 1572, in which Catholics in Paris murdered several thousand Protestants, and the grim tale of how King Henri III's complicity in the assassination of the Catholic duc de Guise in 1588 led to the king's own murder a few months later. Louis XVI's tutors would have made sure he knew how Henri IV, a distant relative of the Valois branch of the royal family, of which Henri III had been the last male member, had founded the Bourbon dynasty. He would have learned how Henry IV had declared that Paris was "worth a Mass," and how he had abandoned his Protestant faith in order to claim the throne and bring peace to a country that for four decades had been ravaged by violent religious warfare. Remembered fondly for his outgoing personality and his promise to his subjects that there would be "a chicken in every pot" under his rule, Henri IV also launched France's first successful colonial venture overseas, the planting of settlements in Québec.

Young Louis probably shuddered when he first heard how a Catholic religious fanatic had stabbed Henri IV to death in the streets of Paris in 1610. Louis XIII came to the throne as a child, as would his own successor, Louis XIV, and Louis XVI's grandfather Louis XV: immature as he was when he found himself king at the age of twenty, Louis XVI was actually older than his three predecessors had been at the beginning of their reigns. Louis XIII had leaned heavily on the wily minister Richelieu, who built on Henri IV's achievements, increasing the power of the monarchy by imposing a greatly increased tax burden on the population and adding islands in the Caribbean to France's empire. In pursuit of gains in Europe, Richelieu plunged France into the Thirty Years' War in Central Europe. The outcome of that great struggle was still uncertain when he and the king he had loyally served died in quick succession in 1642 and 1643. The throne then passed to the five-year-old Louis XIV, with Richelieu's hand-picked successor, the Italian cardinal Mazarin, as chief minister.

No doubt the young Louis XVI was also taught to shudder at the mention of the Fronde, an almost incomprehensibly complicated tangle of rebellions that had nearly brought down the monarchy in 1648, when his celebrated predecessor, Louis XIV, had been a mere child. Mazarin and Anne of Austria had outmaneuvered the Fronde rebels, and Louis XIV reacted to the trauma of that event by concentrating all his effort on making sure that no such revolt could occur again. To do so, he centralized authority more tightly in his own hands than any of his predecessors had done. No single minister would be allowed to make himself indispensable, as Richelieu and Mazarin had. The "Sun

King" employed able collaborators, such as Jean-Baptiste Colbert, who imposed regulations on the kingdom's economy, seeking to bolster the king's revenues. Colbert also built up a system of administrative record-keeping that would continue to function until the Revolution. The king, however, kept all important decisions to himself and incited rivalries among his ministers, making sure they could not form a united front to influence him. The palace Louis XIV built for himself at Versailles, twelve miles outside of Paris, was an integral part of his program to strengthen royal authority. The imposing building and its elaborate gardens radiated an image of the king's power; they were also safely outside of the turbulent city of Paris, whose population had resisted Henri IV during the wars of religion and forced the young Louis XIV and his mother to flee during the Fronde. Louis XVI never knew his mighty ancestor, but he lived all but the last tumultuous years of his life in the house Louis XIV had built.

Determined to resume the pursuit of new territory in Europe that had been interrupted for nearly a century, Louis XIV pushed France's boundaries farther north, into Flanders, and east, gaining the Habsburg enclave of Franche-Comté and securing the German-speaking province of Alsace along the Rhine; he also added islands in the Indian Ocean and trading posts in Africa and South Asia to France's colonial empire. Although Louis XVI's history lessons emphasized the greatness of his ancestor, he would also have heard about how Louis XIV had struggled to overcome the Europe-wide coalition of enemies his ambitions generated. The need to overcome the staggering debts run up in those wars set the stage for the wild speculative schemes of the Scottish financier John Law that created the "Mississippi bubble" during the regency that followed the Sun King's death, and for their spectacular failure in 1720. The collapse of Law's system of foreign trade and financing left French rulers and their subjects with a lasting distrust of banks, stock companies, and paper money and an abiding fear of royal bankruptcy.

Chosen by Louis XV, Louis XVI's tutors would certainly have emphasized the successes of that monarch's reign. Known optimistically as the *Bien Aimé*, the "Well-Beloved," Louis XV had let his cautious chief minister, André-Hercule de Fleury, keep France out of major wars for several decades, a period of peace that put the country on a sounder financial footing. France entered the first major conflict of his reign, the War of the Austrian Succession, in 1743, and it ended on favorable terms in 1748. The years of Louis XVI's childhood, however, were darkened by the disastrous Seven Years' War, in which France lost its overseas colonies in Canada and India and suffered humiliating defeats on European battlefields. Even so, like most of his ancestors, Louis XV left the kingdom larger than it had been when he inherited it. In 1766, France completed the absorption of the province of Lorraine in the northeast, and in 1768 it took over the island of Corsica off the Mediterranean coast. The occupation of Corsica meant that when a local woman there gave birth to a son named Napoleone Buonaparte in 1769, her child was a French subject.

The kingdom Louis XVI inherited from his long line of ancestors was the largest in Europe. Over the course of the eighteenth century, French royal officials had become increasingly interested in calculating the number of its inhabitants, although they still lacked the resources to carry out a national census. Modern historians estimate that the population was probably about twenty-six million to twenty-eight million at the time of the Revolution in 1789, up from around twenty million at the beginning of the eighteenth century. By 1789, close to a million more people lived in the French overseas colonies, most of them enslaved blacks. France was more populous than all the dozens of small German states combined, and it had well over twice as many people as its chief competitor, England. Even though Louis XVI never knew how many subjects he had, he knew they were the source of his kingdom's wealth and power. More people meant more taxpayers, and therefore greater royal revenue. It meant more potential recruits for the royal army in times of war. More enslaved blacks in the colonies meant more valuable tropical crops, such as sugar and coffee, lucrative exports that French merchants sold to the rest of Europe.

The extent of France's territories and the size of its population challenged the capacity of the royal government to administer them effectively. In an age in which galloping couriers could still take over a week to reach the most distant corners of the kingdom, and in which sailing ships took more than four months to go from the port cities of Bordeaux or Marseille to the Île de France or the Île Bourbon in the Indian Ocean, it was a constant struggle to enforce laws, collect revenue, and maintain order. And yet, as the thousands of registers of handwritten documents in the French National Archives attest, the eighteenth-century monarchy was surprisingly successful in meeting this challenge. The subjects of the king of France expected the royal government to settle their local quarrels and protect their lives and property. In 1764 and 1765, for example, when marauding wolves killed several dozen peasants in a remote central region, the local authorities appealed to Versailles, which dispatched a royal huntsman to pursue "the beast of Gévaudan." When the French Revolution broke out in 1789, the kingdom's inhabitants did not demand a government that would leave them alone; instead, they wanted a government that would be even more involved in their lives.

The creation of a government apparatus that could actually control such a large territory and its population was the greatest collective achievement of the Bourbon kings. The pursuit of this achievement started with Henri IV and his chief minister, Maximilien de Béthune, duc de Sully, and was carried forward by Richelieu, Mazarin, and Louis XIV. Louis XIV appointed *intendants*, officials whose authority came directly from the king, to carry out his orders and govern the thirty-odd provinces of his realm. Unlike the great nobles who had led factions during the wars of religion or staged revolts during the Fronde, and the royal governors entrusted with military powers in the provinces, the intendants, usually from lesser noble backgrounds, had no independent power bases of their own, and they were regularly rotated from place to place to prevent them from becoming too entrenched in any one locality. They were the first avatars of a professional civil service, recruited to serve the state. At the time, no other European government had such a bureaucracy, and the intendancy system was widely admired by other monarchs. Louis XIV's intendants had to contend with powerful local nobles, independent-minded judges, municipal officials, and high-ranking clergy, all of whom often had strong networks of support and powerful protectors at the royal court. Louis XIV had never intended to sweep away all these other local power brokers when he created his intendants; indeed, his system depended as much on encouraging them to compete for his favor as it did on the bureaucracy he was starting to create. But the intendant system gave him dependable representatives to protect his interests in the interminable conflicts that made up local political life in the provinces.

By the time Louis XVI came to the throne in 1774, the network of intendants stationed in provincial capitals and their *subdélegués,* or representatives, in smaller cities had become a familiar feature of French life. Their duties included maintaining law and order; seeing that roads and bridges were kept up; appointing and supervising local mayors and other officials; approving the budgets of communities, from the smallest villages to large provincial governments; and implementing new laws and edicts from Versailles. Intendants also cooperated with the Church to arrange for the maintenance or replacement of its buildings. They were the government's eyes and ears throughout the country, sending regular reports on the situation in their region. When crop failures, natural disasters, or epidemics struck, the intendants stepped in to organize a response. The more energetic intendants actively promoted economic activity; they also encouraged townspeople to come together to build civic institutions, such as the theaters that were the pride of French provincial cities, and sponsored the creation of provincial newspapers that would provide an outlet for local authors and advertisers. Accustomed to a much more decentralized system, in which local landowners dominated rural government, the observer Arthur Young, an English agricultural expert conducting a survey of French agriculture, worried about the "enormous power" of these officials, who, he said, were "constantly acting, and from which no man was free."[4]

Through the network of intendants, the French monarchy seemed to have equipped itself with a modern mechanism for governing its population. But the young Louis XVI would have learned that this *bureaucratie*—the word itself entered the French language in 1759, when he was five years old—had to coexist with other institutions that frequently complicated its functioning. Some of France's most important provinces, such as the sprawling territory of Languedoc in the southwest, and the western peninsula of Brittany, had provincial estates. These were bodies composed of representatives of the local nobility, the upper clergy, and the more important towns, which claimed the right to share the administration of their region with the intendant. The provincial estates traced their history back to the days before their regions had been fully integrated into the kingdom, and they zealously defended the historical privileges their regions had enjoyed when they became part of France. When Brittany joined the kingdom in 1532, for example, its population had been promised that they would not be subject to the *gabelle*, the unpopular royal tax on salt collected in the rest of France. From the start of the seventeenth century, royal officials tried to weaken or even abolish provincial estates; in many provinces, these assemblies had ceased to meet for a century or more. Where provincial estates continued to function, however, intendants had to negotiate with them about tax collection and other issues.

Even more important to the functioning of the French government than the provincial estates were the sovereign courts, of which the most significant were the thirteen *parlements* that met in Paris and the main provincial capitals. Tracing their origins to the thirteenth century—the Parlement of Paris had been established in 1278—these courts heard appeals from lower courts throughout the realm. More importantly, they insisted that it was their duty to verify that royal laws and edicts did not violate the fundamental rights of the king's subjects, which each French monarch solemnly swore to uphold when he was crowned. The parlements asserted the right to send the king *remontrances* (remonstrances) containing their criticisms and objections to new laws, and the right to delay registering laws until their complaints had been dealt with. In the last analysis, the parlements recognized that the king had the power to compel them to accept laws they objected to, but only after he had gone through a complicated ritual, which went by the curious name of a *lit de justice*, or "bed of justice." This procedure required the king to come personally to the court, or, in the case of provincial parlements, to send his representative to order the judges to comply. Staging a *lit de justice* was a time-consuming business, sure to stir up agitation, and royal ministers tried to avoid it.

The ability of the parlements to resist royal demands was anchored in a deep conviction, shared by the king and his subjects alike, that the legitimacy of absolute monarchy depended on its observance of the laws. The parlements also enjoyed considerable independence, because the king could not simply appoint judges who would go along with his wishes. From the late 1500s, the French monarchy had developed the practice of selling seats on the courts, as well as many other offices, and allowing their purchasers to bequeath them to their heirs. Such positions were known as venal offices, and the practice became more widespread and entrenched in France than anywhere else in Europe. Selling venal offices raised revenue and reduced royal expenses, since officeholders received only minimal salaries, which they supplemented by charging litigants fees for hearing their cases. To make the purchase of judgeships more attractive, the monarchy granted their holders hereditary titles of nobility. Initially, the descendants of the warrior nobles of earlier centuries looked down on these newly created *nobles de robe*, whose titles referred to the judicial robes they wore in court. But as the internal administration of the kingdom became more extensive, and the notion of a state governed by laws became fundamental to the monarchy, the parlementary judges gained status.

By the time Louis XVI became king, the judges of the parlements had constituted themselves as the most prestigious members of the French nobility, with the exception of the so-called princes of the blood, who could claim direct royal ancestry. The court in Paris was the most important, but the twelve other parlements located in the provinces were often even more outspoken than their colleagues in the capital. The strong-willed Louis XIV had succeeded in forbidding the parlements from issuing remonstrances until after they had registered his decrees, thus preventing them from slowing down the enforcement of new laws. When Louis XIV died in 1715, however, leaving the throne to his five-year-old great-grandson, Louis XV, the judges exploited the weakness of the monarchy to recover their right to delay new laws while they argued about their provisions.

The parlements found a defender in the baron de Montesquieu, a magistrate in the Bordeaux Parlement and the most influential political thinker of eighteenth-century France. In his *Spirit of the Laws*, his critical discussion of political institutions, Montesquieu made a powerful argument for the value of a division of powers as a way of preventing rulers from acting as tyrants. Montesquieu was a great admirer of Britain's constitutional monarchy, in which Parliament limited the power of the king, and his ideas strongly influenced the American colonists when they drafted their own revolutionary constitution. In France, Montesquieu argued, the law courts, with their judges who could not be ousted from the positions they had purchased or inherited, served as a brake on the power of the king. Even though they were not elected, the judges made the parlements into what Montesquieu called "intermediary bodies" between the monarch and his subjects.

Montesquieu was more than just a defender of the aristocratic parlements: he was one of a growing number of writers who raised questions about the basic features of French society. In the same years when young Louis XVI was diligently copying down the rules of absolutism, these *philosophes*, as they styled themselves, were collaborating on a project that was meant, as its main editor, Denis Diderot, said, to cause "a revolution in the minds of men." He promised that it would "not be to the advantage of tyrants, oppressors, fanatics and bigots."[5] The success of their project, the *Encyclopédie*, was so great that Louis XVI himself, as we have seen, used some of his own money to purchase a copy. Its editors, Diderot and the mathematician Jean Rond d'Alembert, were representatives of a generation whose thinkers would not accept religious or political dogmas without examining their foundations. They would devote themselves to making the world a better place, even if that meant reforming or abolishing traditional institutions.

D'Alembert and Diderot conceived of their project not just as a collection of information, but as a chance to apply the principles of reason and empirical observation to every subject, from manufacturing processes to religious doctrines. Encyclopedias were one of the new media in which information and ideas were being made accessible to an ever-growing public in the eighteenth century. The long and torturous history of the work's publication, which extended over more than twenty years, from 1751 to 1772, when the last volume of illustrations came out, demonstrated the delicate balance between the advocates for change and their opponents in mid-eighteenth-century France.

Government officials at times intervened to favor the publication of the *Encyclopédie* and at other times put obstacles in its way. In the end, they let it proceed, but without acknowledging its legality. From its inception to its completion, the *Encyclopédie* was also the subject of intense debates carried on in the full range of media of the day. Discussed in Paris salons, denounced and defended in pamphlets, periodicals, and manuscript newsletters, praised and ridiculed on the stage, the project demonstrated both the growing power of public opinion and the depth of the divisions in France about issues such as religion and politics. In the end, however, response to the work was so enthusiastic that its spread could not be halted. By 1789, cheap small-format editions of the work meant that nearly anyone in France who had the capacity to read had access to it.

The ideas propagated in the more controversial articles of the *Encyclopédie* were those of the European Enlightenment. In his "Preliminary Discourse," d'Alembert gave full credit to a series of thinkers who had, in his view, shown the power of human reason to escape from religious dogma and other sources of error, emphasizing in particular the seventeenth-century philosophers and scientists Francis Bacon, René Descartes, Isaac Newton, and John Locke. More radical figures who had explicitly challenged the bases of religion, particularly the Dutch Jew Benedict Spinoza, were not mentioned in the "Preliminary Discourse," but many contributors to the *Encyclopédie* were familiar with his ideas and the simplifications of them that had circulated clandestinely throughout Europe for half a century, such as the sulfurous *Treatise of the Three Impostors*, in which Moses, Jesus, and Muhammad were depicted as charlatans who had deliberately set out to dupe their followers.

By the time the *Encyclopédie* was launched, the ideas it would popularize had already been articulated by a number of important French authors. The most famous was Voltaire, the illegitimate son of a nobleman, who had overcome his lack of social status through his writings. His greatest talent was his ability to present serious ideas in witty words;

posterity remembers him above all as a master of irony and satire. For Voltaire himself, the great cause of his life was the campaign against revealed religion and especially against religious intolerance. Voltaire insisted that he believed in the existence of God, but his abstract and impersonal deity was a clockmaker who created the universe and then left it to run itself. "When His Highness sends a ship to Egypt, does he worry about whether the mice in it are comfortable?" a character in Voltaire's novel *Candide* asks, expressing the author's conviction that humans had no choice but to "cultivate our garden" without divine guidance.[6] Voltaire was less radical politically than he was in religion; indeed, he put more faith in the possibility of converting rulers to rational ideas than of educating the common people. Voltaire contributed numerous articles to the *Encyclopédie*, although he also criticized its editors for being too cautious. He used his own *Dictionnaire philosophique* to make more radical statements on many issues.

Voltaire's name was often conjoined with that of Montesquieu, whose masterwork, *The Spirit of the Laws*, appeared just as the *Encyclopédie* was getting under way. In it, Montesquieu suggested that there was no single pattern of legislation, or "constitution," appropriate for all societies, and that institutions necessarily differed in accordance with national customs, climate, and other variables. He gave a favorable portrayal of the British monarchy, praising its division of powers between the king and Parliament as a protection of liberty. Montesquieu's comments on France were more critical. In the absence of a true equivalent to the British Parliament, France seemed to him to be dependent on its aristocracy's sense of honor, which kept it from submitting slavishly to arbitrary rule, and on "intermediate bodies," such as the parlementary courts—Montesquieu was himself a member of the Bordeaux Parlement—which imposed a certain restraint on the king. Whether these restraints would always be sufficient to prevent France from degenerating from monarchy into despotism—the kind of government Montesquieu identified with non-European states such as Turkey and China—remained an open question for him. Contributors to the *Encyclopédie* drew liberally on *The Spirit of the Laws* for inspiration, sometimes simply copying whole passages from Montesquieu's work.

The relationship of the third member of the French Enlightenment's trinity of celebrities, Jean-Jacques Rousseau, to the *Encyclopédie* was quite different from that of Voltaire or Montesquieu. At the moment when the project was being organized in the late 1740s, Rousseau was a close friend of Diderot's. Diderot enlisted Rousseau to write most of the *Encyclopédie*'s articles on music, and it was while he was on his way to visit Diderot, during his friend's imprisonment in 1749, that Rousseau suddenly had the inspiration for the argument about the morally corrupting effect of civilization that made his *Discourse on the Arts and Sciences*, published in 1750, a sensation. To Diderot, Rousseau's argument was a *jeu d'esprit*, a paradox that could hardly be taken seriously by someone who had committed himself to the *Encyclopédie*, which celebrated the advance of science and technology. To Rousseau, however, the critique of civilization that he put forward in his prizewinning essay grew into an all-consuming passion. He tried to structure not just his thought but his life around the ideas he had advanced in this work.

By the time the *Encyclopédie* had reached its midpoint, Rousseau had turned into one of its most vehement critics, precipitating a personal rupture with d'Alembert and Diderot. The split widened because of Rousseau's religious views. Like Voltaire and Montesquieu, he rejected organized religion, but he could not accept the idea of an abstract deity indifferent to human fate. "I have suffered too much in this life not to look forward to another," he wrote in a letter to Voltaire, who had questioned the idea of a beneficent God.[7] His rationalist opponents denounced him for opening the door to a return of religious faith and intolerance. Meanwhile, conservative critics of the *Encyclopédie* continued to lump him together with his former associates as a dangerous enemy of established orthodoxy.

The subversive originality of the *Encyclopédie* was to present the ideas of its seventeenth-century predecessors and of the great minds of eighteenth-century French letters as if they were simply common sense, so obviously true that they could be put forth without fear of contradiction. The fundamental premise underlying the entire content of the *Encyclopédie* was that human reason, a characteristic shared by everyone, was sufficient to explain the world and improve people's lives. A diagram of the "tree of knowledge" classified all branches of knowledge as outgrowths of three basic mental faculties: memory, reason, and imagination. In the diagram, "knowledge of God" was lumped together with "knowledge of good and evil spirits," "divination," and "black magic," suggesting that there was little difference between religion and superstition. The category of "ethics," a subbranch of "knowledge of man," sufficed, according to the chart, to provide "knowledge of good and evil" and to demonstrate "the necessity of being virtuous."[8]

To outwit the royal and ecclesiastical censors, whose approval was needed if the *Encyclopédie* was to be published in Paris and sold without interference, Diderot developed a devious strategy. Entries on obviously sensitive subjects, such as "Christianity," were carefully phrased to avoid arousing objections. Cross-references in "Christianity" led readers to other articles that were less orthodox, however. The entry on "Miracles," for example, summarized Spinoza's argument that God could not cause something contrary to the laws of nature to happen. The essay on "Toleration," also cross-referenced under Christianity, cast doubt on the ability of human beings to ever arrive at complete certainty about anything, including religious truth, and suggested that, in view of the intolerant nature of Christianity, no one could blame "a prince in Asia or the New World who hanged the first missionary that we sent to convert him," rather than letting him cause conflicts among his people.

In his article on "Political Authority," Diderot undercut the bases of royal absolutism by insisting that "no man has received from nature the right to command others." Another collaborator, Paul-Henri Thiry, baron d'Holbach, insisted that legitimate government required that the nation should have freely chosen representatives to defend its interests. In addition to the "Nation" entry, his article on "Representatives" used words such as "citizens" and "national assembly" that would become central in the revolutionary era. His insistence that representation should be limited to "those individuals who are citizens by virtue of their possessions and whose status and enlightenment enables them to know the interests of the nation and the needs of the people" showed, however, that even the most radical philosophes were not prepared to embrace political democracy.[9] D'Holbach's distrust of the poor—the majority of the population—would be shared by many revolutionary legislators.

Although d'Holbach drew a sharp distinction between property-owners and the poor, he wanted to break down the barriers between nobles, clergy, and commoners: anyone who owned significant property, especially land, should be able to vote and serve as a representative. Another contributor was François Quesnay, who had invented the slogan *laissez faire, laissez passer* to sum up his teaching that individuals should be allowed to do whatever they wanted with their economic resources. His articles on "Farmers" and "Grains" expressed the ideas of the distinctive French school of economic thinking known as *physiocratie* (physiocracy, or "government of nature," from its Greek roots) that he had helped found, which favored unrestricted trade. Quesnay's contributions urged government policies that would favor "big farms to be highly developed by rich farmers," whom he counted on to adopt productive new methods. Like d'Holbach, Quesnay had little respect for the poor. "It is . . . a great drawback to accustom the people to buying wheat at a price that is too low," he wrote. "They do not work as hard, they live on inexpensive bread, and they become lazy and arrogant." As was often the case in the *Encyclopédie*, however, its contributors vigorously disagreed with each other on this matter. "Who would believe that, in our days, anyone would have dared to put forward this maxim . . . that such men should not live comfortably, in order to make them hard-working and obedient?" demanded the chevalier Louis de Jaucourt in his article "People."[10]

Along with political and economic liberty, contributors to the *Encyclopédie* raised important questions about equality. Jaucourt, a workhorse who wrote more articles than any other contributor, stated that "natural equality is that which is found among all men solely by the constitution of their nature. This *equality* is the principle and foundation of liberty." Where equality was compromised, "the princes, the courtiers, the principal ministers, those who control the finances, possess all the riches of the nation," he continued, "while the rest of the citizens have only the necessities of life, and the great majority of people groan in poverty."

Lest anyone think he was calling for a social upheaval, however, Jaucourt hastened to add: "I am only speaking here of the *natural equality* of men. I know too well the necessity of different ranks, grades, honors, distinctions, prerogatives, subordinations that must prevail in all governments." Nevertheless, he had laid out a critique of inequality that would be heard again many times after 1789. In his article on "Woman," Jaucourt even broached the thought that "it would be difficult to demonstrate that the authority of the husband comes from nature, because this principle is contrary to the natural equality of humanity."[11]

The subject of women brought out a diversity of opinion among the philosophes. "Women, due to the fragility of their sex and their natural delicacy, are excluded from many functions and incapable of certain activities," the editorial team's main legal expert, Boucher d'Argis, pronounced, while another contributor deplored women's skill at dissimulation and penchant for flirtation, and urged them to find happiness in "the duties of wife and mother." Diderot's article on "Enjoyment" was an encomium to sexual pleasure, which he argued "imperiously solicits both sexes as soon as they have been granted their share of strength and beauty." He accepted the idea, however, that "the propagation of beings is the greatest object of nature," thereby making heterosexual intercourse the only acceptable expression of this instinct, and motherhood a female obligation.[12]

The contributors to the *Encyclopédie* were as divided about racial equality and slavery as they were about the status of women. Jaucourt's article on the slave trade was quite outspoken: "This buying of Negroes, to reduce them to slavery, is one business that violates religion, morality, natural laws, and the rights of human nature," he wrote. "Let the European colonies be destroyed rather than make so many unfortunate people." Samuel Formey's article on the "Negro," however, questioned whether whites and blacks were members of the same species, and talked about the "ugliness" of the latter. An anonymous article on "Commerce in Negroes" justified the slave trade and warned potential purchasers of enslaved Africans that "their hard nature requires that one not treat them with too much indulgence."[13]

The issue of equality, in a more abstract sense, was also central in the widely remarked upon article on "Political Economy," written by

Jean-Jacques Rousseau. Many of the key ideas in Rousseau's more extended political treatise, *The Social Contract*, were already laid out in this article, in particular his doctrine of the "general will," the perception of what best served the purposes of a community. The general will, expressed in the form of the law, he said, overrode all the particular special interests of individuals and social subgroups. "The first and most important maxim of legitimate or popular government, that is to say, of government whose object is the good of the people, is, therefore, as I have said, to follow in everything the general will," Rousseau wrote. Because all members of a state must ultimately prefer its interest to their own private concerns, they might find themselves in the position of having the state "enforcing their consent over their own refusal," but they would still be free. To be legitimate, the state must treat all citizens equally. Such a state could only thrive if its citizens were imbued with virtue, the willingness to put the general interest ahead of their own selfish desires. The abstract equality of citizens required as much genuine social equality as possible: "It is therefore one of the most important concerns of government to prevent the extreme inequality of fortunes," Rousseau wrote.[14]

Concerned about the freethinking tendencies of many of the Encyclopédistes, conservative officials and devout Catholics were not taken in by Diderot's rhetorical precautions. But d'Alembert and Diderot also found important allies in the highest circles of government. Guillaume-Chrétien de Lamoignon de Malesherbes, the head of the royal censorship office, worked tirelessly behind the scenes to keep the project alive and protect its participants, and Madame de Pompadour, whose adulterous relationship with Louis XV embroiled her in conflict with the Church, also offered discreet support. The connections that d'Alembert and Diderot had forged in the capital's various salons, where both of them made regular appearances, helped create a network of influential sympathizers. The debates about the *Encyclopédie*, carried on not only in aristocratic salons but in the increasingly numerous cafés and *cabinets de lecture*, or reading rooms, in French cities, gave substance to the invisible but very real phenomenon of public opinion, which was becoming increasingly important as a force in shaping culture.

As important as the *Encyclopédie* and other printed publications were in influencing public views, the climate of opinion was also molded by other media, especially the theater. That plays could have a political impact was clear from the runaway success of a historical drama, *The Siege of Calais*, that turned an episode of the Hundred Years' War into an anti-English statement. The play, written by Pierre-Laurent de Belloy and first performed in 1765, resonated powerfully because of the humiliating Seven Years' War. "The performances of *The Siege of Calais* were an event, and seemed to cause a revolution. . . . [T]hey revealed to the French the secret of their love for the state," wrote one eighteenth-century commentator. Besides editing the *Encyclopédie*, Diderot was also a playwright, and he was a firm believer in the power of the stage to transform its audience. His "bourgeois dramas" featured characters whose lives and speech resembled those of their audience in place of the poetry-spouting kings and queens of French classical drama. "Natural situations!" Diderot promised his spectators, swearing to put on the stage "the man of letters, the philosophe, the merchant, the judge, the lawyer, the politician, the citizen, the financier, the great lord, [and] the intendant," and to make drama out of ordinary family relations.[15]

It was the subject of the theater that provoked the final break between Rousseau and the other philosophes. He was scandalized by an article by the project's coeditor d'Alembert about Rousseau's birthplace, Geneva, which suggested that the city's life would be improved if it had a theater like the ones in Paris. In *A Letter to M. D'Alembert on Spectacles*, Rousseau held up as models the simplicity of Swiss peasants and the ancient Greek republic of Sparta, where all the citizens had been completely devoted to the public good rather than to their own private interests and pleasures. Moreover, in Sparta the differing roles of men and women had been rigorously upheld, a distinction that broke down in the theater, where both sexes mingled. A free people, Rousseau contended, would replace the theater with public festivals in which all could participate, an idea the revolutionaries would make central to their project. Rousseau's polemic was a scathing critique both of the *Encyclopédie* and of the society from which it had emerged. During the Revolution, devotees of Rousseau, such as Maximilien Robespierre, would echo his denunciation of rationalist intellectuals and commercial society and his glorification of the simple life of the poor.

Another philosophe, Gabriel Bonnot de Mably, took Rousseau's idealization of republican governments even further. Mably's vision of a good society was one in which everyone put the public interest ahead of private concerns. "Let every citizen devote himself to the defense of his country, let him spend some time every day practicing with his weapons, and let the entire city acquire the discipline of an armed camp," Mably wrote in his popular *Entretiens de Phocion*, published in 1763. "Not only will this policy provide you with invincible soldiers, but it will give a new force to the civic virtues as well."[16]

Rousseau's fear of the influence of the theater on society was not unfounded. Theater performances brought people together, promoting social interchange and discussion. On stage, actresses were the equals of their male colleagues, and indeed, the most popular women performers were often paid more than the male leads. Theater audiences were also socially mixed. Nobles and wealthy bourgeois reserved box seats, but members of Jacques Ménétra's world could pay for the right to stand or sit on benches in the *parterre*, the part of the auditorium directly in front of the stage. During Louis XV's reign, theater mania spread throughout the kingdom, and local citizens helped fund the construction of playhouses. In colonial cities, special seating sections were created for free people of color and even enslaved blacks. Regardless of their social status, spectators assumed the right to express their opinions about the performances they were watching, booing lustily or interrupting to demand the repetition of passages they particularly appreciated. Theater audiences served as a living embodiment of the abstract notion of public opinion.

In addition to the theaters, the authorities kept an eye on other places where common people gathered, and took note of what they were saying. In an age before public opinion polling, police surveillance was a way of assessing the popular mood and anticipating trouble before it started. In Paris especially, a network of paid agents filed regular reports on any "bad remarks" they heard in the streets, marketplaces, and popular drinking places where workers congregated. The police knew that public spaces, such as the Tuileries Gardens near the Louvre and the

Luxembourg Gardens on the Left Bank of the Seine, were regular meeting places for people who wanted to exchange gossip about the latest political developments. At streetcorners and on the city's bridges, performers sang improvised ballads about recent events; sometimes they offered passersby illustrated broadsheets that combined news reports, illustrations, and lyrics so that purchasers could make their own music. Just outside the toll barriers, where food and wine destined for the city were assessed for taxes, entrepreneurs set up cabarets selling untaxed wine at bargain prices. The crowds flocking to the most famous of these, Ramponeau's, came from a wide spectrum of society; here, aristocrats could be found slumming in the exotic world of ordinary people, both members of the bourgeoisie and the lower classes. A popular drinking song honored "the illustrious Ramponeau, appreciated by all of Paris, / who offers fresh wine and girls who aren't difficult."[17] The bawdy "culture of laughter" that emanated from Ramponeau's also characterized the informal "boulevard theaters" on the newly constructed avenues in the growing city. One of the familiar characters from boulevard-theater skits, the foul-mouthed "Père Duchêne," would inspire the most successful popular newspaper of the French revolutionary years.

Although the controversies about radical ideas were heated, they did not have as much immediate impact during the years of Louis XVI's adolescence as the confrontations between the king's ministers and the parlements. Throughout these years, judges became increasingly confrontational in their attitudes toward the monarchy. In particular, they put themselves forward as defenders of a purist sect within the French Catholic Church known as the Jansenists. They also styled themselves as the protectors of the taxpayers against efforts by the king's ministers to increase government revenues. Although the judges' remonstrances, their main weapon in these conflicts, were supposed to be secret communications to the king, the parlements became increasingly brazen about publishing their denunciations of arbitrary royal power. As a result, more and more of the population was able to read these texts, in which the judges warned that government actions were threatening the kingdom's basic laws and the rights of subjects.

The Jansenist controversy was a long-running battle that dated back to the seventeenth century, when some French Catholics became attracted to the austere teachings of a Belgian theologian, Cornelius Jansen, who criticized the papacy for endorsing religious doctrines that allowed too much scope for moral laxity. Both Louis XIV and the papacy saw the Jansenists as dangerous. Their doctrine of predestination undermined the authority of priests to guide their parishioners' behavior, since, according to the Jansenists, how people conducted themselves had no bearing on their chances of salvation. From the king's point of view, the Jansenists encouraged people to think for themselves about religious questions, a practice that might lead to undesirable political consequences.

Throughout much of the eighteenth century, the church hierarchy's attempt to compel the country's Jansenists to renounce their convictions was the most divisive issue in French life. The quarrel became intertwined with the issue of the rights of the parlements to challenge royal power, as judges repeatedly put themselves forward as defenders of the Jansenists. Sympathetic lawyers argued that the king's Catholic subjects had the right to appeal to the royal courts against anti-Jansenist clergy and against the interference of a "foreign" power—the papacy—in France. In contrast to developments in Britain's North American colonies, where religious freedom came to be identified with the separation of church and state, in France religious freedom came to be defined as a value to be defended through the state, if necessary against the Church itself.

The passions aroused by the Jansenist quarrel reached a peak in the last quarter-century of Louis XV's reign starting in 1749, when the archbishop of Paris ordered priests to refuse the Catholic sacraments to anyone who would not renounce the sect's principles. In 1761, a bankruptcy case involving the business affairs of the Jesuit order handed the Jansenists a new weapon. The legal proceedings brought to light a copy of the "constitution," or rules, of the Jesuits, the Jansenists' bitter enemies. This Jesuit document had been kept secret by the Vatican since the founding of the order. The revelation that Jesuit priests had to swear an oath of unconditional obedience to the pope allowed their opponents to portray them as potential subversives, whose first loyalty was not to the king and the laws of France, but to the Church. A reluctant Louis XV found himself unable to defend the Jesuits without seeming to undermine the very principles of absolutism that justified his authority. In 1764, he signed a decree banning the Jesuits from France.

Just as they put themselves forward as defenders of the religious freedom of the king's subjects, the parlements under Louis XV increasingly cast themselves as opponents of arbitrary taxation and excessive government borrowing. The extraordinary costs of the Seven Years' War in the late 1750s and early 1760s, which forced the government to scramble to raise new revenue, triggered a number of confrontations with the courts. In 1760, the Parlement of Rouen in Normandy urged Louis XV to "assist . . . the peoples who are succumbing under the unbearable weight of taxes; it is their tears that we are presenting to you."[18] The rhetoric the parlementary judges used in this case resembled the kind of argumentation that was being honed in Britain's North American colonies during the same years. The magistrates insisted that French citizens possessed rights they were entitled to defend and were not simply subjects who had to bend to the will of their monarch. Parlementary remonstrances began to use the word *nation* to describe the collectivity of the citizens, and to insist that the *nation* had rights, including the right to be heard on the subject of taxes.

To be sure, none of the parlements called for elections or any other mechanism by which the population at large could actually express its wishes. Instead, the judges insisted that they were the nation's representatives; during the 1750s, the judges of the various courts had begun to claim that they were just geographically separated parts of a single body that constituted a sort of national assembly. The fact that they were also wealthy and privileged and had an important personal stake in preventing tax increases made royal ministers regard them with skepticism. One memorandum denounced them as a selfish elite, men who were trying to protect their own fortunes by setting themselves up as "a national tribunal which holds the balance between the king and the nation." Nevertheless, the judges' proclamations, regularly printed and widely circulated despite royal prohibitions, familiarized the public with the claim that taxation should imply consent and representation. Louis XVI was acutely aware of the danger of the parlements' claims, which were being voiced more strongly than ever during the years of his child-hood. "They are courts of justice created by our kings," he wrote in his lesson book, emphasizing their subordination to royal power. "They are not in any way representatives of the nation."[19]

When Louis was in his late teens, and in the midst of adjusting to his marriage with Marie-Antoinette, the lessons he had been taught about the dangerous pretensions of the parlements suddenly took on stark rel-evance. Louis XV, at the end of his patience with the judges' defiance, launched an assault on the parlements so drastic that contemporaries called it a "revolution." The courts had refused to register the royal tax edicts needed to produce revenue to pay off debts from the Seven Years' War. A bitter quarrel with the Parlement of Brittany reached the point where the Paris Parlement put the king's commissioner, the duc d'Ai-guillon, on trial for violating the province's rights. Louis XV and his advisers remembered that the English revolution that had cost Charles I his head had begun with the impeachment and trial of one of Charles's ministers by Parliament; d'Aiguillon himself warned the king that if he was found guilty, the parlement would have set a precedent allow-ing it to condemn "all those who have acted under orders, ministers, commandants, intendants, commissioners."[20] The king caused outrage among the judges by invoking his absolute powers to end d'Aiguillon's trial and declare him innocent.

When the Paris judges denounced the king's intervention, the gov-ernment struck back with an "edict of discipline" ordering them to end their protests. As they had on several earlier occasions, the parlemen-taires responded by going on strike and refusing to perform their judicial functions. The chancellor René Maupeou, the royal minister who super-vised the judicial system, undertook to break this resistance. His plan, often called the "Maupeou coup," was simple. On the night of January 20–21, 1771, armed soldiers knocked on the doors of the judges of the Paris Parlement and offered them a choice: either promise in writing to obey the king's orders, or face exile to remote provincial towns and the confiscation of their valuable judicial offices. In their place, if they chose not to comply, new judges would be appointed. The new judges would have to pledge to accept royal policies; they would also have to agree not to insist on their right to issue remonstrances, or to obstruct ministerial actions.

To supporters of the parlements, Maupeou's coup threatened the very basis of French liberty. If the king's ministers could simply replace long-established institutions, such as the parlements, with ones designed to go along with whatever policies the government wanted to carry out, they charged, there would be no check on arbitrary royal power. "There is nothing sacred in the State that one could not overturn by this means," one pamphleteer wrote. Unable to prevent the arrest of the judges, the parlements' defenders flooded the country with tracts denouncing Maupeou. These pamphlets introduced new terms into the French political vocabulary that were destined to play an important role in the French Revolution: they baptized the pro-parlementary movement as "the party of patriotism" and said its proponents were determined to combat "political despotism." Lawyers and court clerks, who were dependent on the goodwill of the judges, supported the exiled parlementaires by refusing to take part in proceedings in the new courts. No lawyers appeared at the first session of Maupeou's replacement parlement. When a dog was heard barking, according to a widely repeated anecdote, "someone cried out, 'there's a lawyer willing to plead.'"[21]

Maupeou's assault on the parlements was accompanied by a forceful effort to deal with the government's finances. A new finance minister, the abbé Terray, carried out a partial repudiation of the royal debt and reimposed traditional restrictions on the grain trade that had been lifted during the 1760s. In earlier years, Louis XV had shown a reluctance to push through controversial policies. In this case, however, with his spine stiffened by the last and most controversial of his mistresses, Madame du Barry—whose ascension, accomplished in spite of her commoner origins and the widespread rumor that she had been a professional prostitute, deeply offended many traditional courtiers—the king remained steadfast in supporting his ministers.

By early 1774, three years after the start of Maupeou's coup, resistance was beginning to weaken. Most lawyers finally agreed to appear in the new courts, and some of the former parlementary judges finally yielded their seats or even accepted appointments to the new courts. Maupeou had shown that, in the face of determined action, the parlements were not able to sustain the role of "intermediary bodies" limiting the king's powers that their defenders had claimed for them. Terray's measures had gotten the government through the worst of the financial crisis, and d'Aiguillon, appointed as foreign minister, had given the coup an international dimension, by supporting the Swedish king, Gustav III, when he took similar measures to limit the powers of his country's parliament in 1772. Those who feared the consequences of unrestrained absolutism realized that it would take institutions more powerful than the parlements, and with a more direct connection to the population, to balance the power of the monarchy.

Had Louis XV lived a few years longer, his ministers might have succeeded in giving the French monarchy powers that would have enabled it to deal with the crises that would lead to the Revolution of 1789. A stronger, more authoritarian royal government might have reacted more effectively to the renewed fiscal problems that developed in the 1780s, and efforts to realize the ideals of liberty and equality would have faced more determined opposition. In May 1774, however, Louis XV fell ill with smallpox, and it quickly became clear that he would not survive. Madame du Barry was hastily sent off to a convent so that the king could reconcile himself with the Church and receive the sacraments. The future of the controversial program he had embarked upon in 1770 was left to his heir, the twenty-year-old Louis XVI. The tutors appointed by the old king had done all they could to imbue their pupil with the conviction that he needed to radiate authority. Now they would see how he applied those lessons.

# 3

# THE MONARCHY ADRIFT

## 1774–1787

THE DEATH OF LOUIS XV ON MAY 10, 1774, WHICH PROPELLED HIS twenty-year-old grandson to the throne, came as a shock, but one the French monarchy's institutions were prepared to absorb. Since the death of Louis XVI's father in 1765, everyone had known that, barring his own death, the youth would be the next king. His precocious marriage to Marie-Antoinette may have been unhappy and, as of 1774, still unfruitful in terms of producing an heir, but it had settled a major question about the future of the dynasty and promised continuity in France's foreign policy. The old king's liaison with the disreputable Madame du Barry, and his backing of the Maupeou coup against the parlements, had so discredited Louis XV in Paris that the court decided to hold his burial at night and almost in secret. His unpopularity, however, did not extend to the monarchy as an institution. "Every day gives new hope by the prospect of an imminent improvement. The new monarch's sense of economy, his disdain for luxury and appearances, seem to guarantee it," wrote a journalist who had led the opposition to Maupeou.[1]

Louis XVI certainly wanted to make some changes. Gossip about royal mistresses would no longer swirl around the court, and the elderly comte de Maurepas persuaded the young king to dismiss Louis XV's controversial team of hardline ministers and recall the parlements. At the ceremony for the reinstallation of the Paris Parlement, the judges were sternly instructed not to resort to the obstructionist tactics they had used against Louis XV. Undaunted, they soon showed that they still saw themselves as entitled to resist the king and his ministers. Warned that the restoration of the parlements might weaken his authority, Louis XVI supposedly replied, "It may be considered politically unwise, but it seems to me that it is the general will, and I wish to be loved."[2]

Whereas the reinstatement of the parlements was a return to tradition, Louis XVI's appointment of Anne Robert Jacques Turgot as his finance minister represented a break with the past. It raised the hopes of those who looked to the new king to implement the enlightened ideas of the Encyclopédistes and especially of the Physiocrats, the economic theorists whose advocacy of deregulation had already inspired several previous efforts at reform under Louis XV. As intendant in the province of the Limousin in the 1760s, Turgot had vigorously promoted policies to modernize agricultural methods and had shown his willingness to do away with institutions such as the *corvée*, the system under which peasants were required to work for several days a year on repairing roads and other projects, a practice the Physiocrats condemned as an inefficient interference with personal liberty. In an article on charitable foundations that he contributed to the *Encyclopédie*, Turgot had argued that institutions rooted in the past could be abolished if they failed to meet the needs of the present or limited the rights of individuals. He thus advanced the notion that all aspects of French life were open to reform. Elevated to the ministry, Turgot took aim at the system of laws that limited the free sale of grain within the kingdom. Meant to ensure that speculation did not lead to sharp rises in the price of bread in years of bad harvests, these rules restricted the movement of grain from one region to another and allowed local authorities to control its price.

Physiocratic theorists argued that regulations on the sale of grain were an unjust restriction on individual property rights. Such regulations discouraged landowners from investing in improvements to agriculture, because they could not be sure they would be allowed to reap the profits from increased production. Consumers—a group that included both urban populations and much of the peasantry, since few farmers grew the grain for their own bread—were unconvinced. As one Physiocrat, Quesnay, had openly said in his articles for the *Encyclopédie*, the abolition of regulations was meant to push prices up and force the poor to work harder to earn their bread, hardly a recipe for gaining popular support. A growing economy, however, would, in his view, and Turgot's, benefit the monarchy by enlarging its revenue base without the necessity of raising taxes.

Like earlier efforts to end grain-trade restrictions in the 1760s, Turgot's reforms were poorly timed. The 1774 harvest was less successful than usual, especially in northern France, the region most dependent on the grain crop, and the result was the broadest wave of social unrest the kingdom had experienced in many decades. For nearly a month in the spring of 1775, as grain prices rose and supplies ran low, a wave of riots known as the *guerre des farines*, the "flour war," broke out across the region. In the towns, crowds stormed bakeries and demanded that bread prices be lowered. In the countryside, peasants blocked merchants' efforts to ship grain out of their districts; they also confronted wealthy landowners, who were suspected of holding crops off the market to wait for higher prices. The disturbances affected the royal residence of Versailles and the capital, where a major outbreak took place on May 3, 1775. One journalist mentioned rumors that "the rebels want to seize the Bastille" only to dismiss the threat as "physically impossible."[3] Women were often prominent in these disturbances: making sure their families could afford bread for their daily needs was always one of their major concerns. At Brie-Comte-Robert, Madelaine Pochet, described in police reports as "the woman with the red scarf on her head," insulted local farmers and demanded that they sell their reserves at a price approved by the crowd.[4] The government reacted strongly, mobilizing twenty-five thousand troops around Paris and insisting on the need to protect the rights of property-owners, although Turgot also opened "charitable workshops" to enable the unemployed to earn what they needed to support themselves.

The flour war was brought under control after a few weeks, but the outbreaks showed how powerful a popular protest could become and how quickly it could spread. The uprisings sparked the first major political debate of Louis XVI's reign and brought to the surface issues that would be central in the French Revolution fifteen years later. Whereas Turgot, like neoliberal economists today, argued that ending regulation would bring long-term benefits for the kingdom as a whole by encouraging more efficient farming methods and increased production, the recently restored parlementary law courts seized the opportunity to pose as protectors of the population by criticizing his measures. Eager to prove that objections like those of the parlements were not just the expression of special interests, the distinguished magistrate Malesherbes, who had defended the *Encyclopédie* in the 1750s and was now the spokesman for the government's fiscal court, the Cour des Aides, inserted a radical twist into the familiar argument about the need for intermediate bodies to check the ministers' arbitrary actions. He called for the revival of the Estates General, an elected assembly that had met at intervals during the medieval and Renaissance eras but that France's absolutist kings had ceased to convene after 1615. Malesherbes insisted that "in France, the nation has always been profoundly conscious of its rights and of its freedom," showing that memories of France's distant past could have potentially revolutionary implications in the present. His complaint that the principles protecting French freedom "have never been duly drawn up" in the form of a constitutional document also looked forward to the demands that would be made at the start of the Revolution.[5]

While the parlements and Malesherbes revived history-based arguments against reforms, Turgot's ambitious rival, the banker Jacques Necker, attacked from a different direction. Launching the career that would keep him at the center of French politics until the Revolution, Necker published an *Essay on the Commerce in Grains* that denounced Turgot's measures as ill-timed and impractical. It was the first time an aspirant for ministerial office tried to win power by appealing openly to public opinion and offering a contrasting program. Outraged, Turgot and his friends blamed Necker for inciting the grain riots. An anonymous journalist raised a question that would be debated even more vehemently during the French Revolution: Should the right of property take precedence over the needs of the poor? "To refuse to one's fellow man the nourishment he needs, if he cannot pay the price one wants for it, is an action as highhanded as that of a robber in the forest, who uses his pistol to demand that a traveler give up his purse or his life," he wrote.[6]

Once the flour war had been quelled, Turgot, still confident of Louis XVI's backing, pushed ahead with other reforms. In April 1776, he persuaded the king to issue a package of six edicts, all of them reflecting his conviction that individuals should be freed as much as possible to pursue their economic interests and that special privileges should be done away with. As he had tried to do in the Limousin when he was an intendant, Turgot proposed to abolish the *corvée* system of forced labor that provided for the upkeep of roads and public works. In its place, he wanted to impose a tax paid by all landowners regardless of their social status, a measure that inspired fierce resistance from nobles, who objected to being treated the same as commoners. Equally controversial was Turgot's proposal to abolish the guilds to which skilled artisans like Jacques Ménétra belonged and open all trades to anyone who wanted to practice them. Throughout France, aggressive entrepreneurs were already finding ways around guild restrictions by shifting production to rural areas where those rules did not apply. They were also sometimes illegally hiring journeymen and even women workers.

Turgot's edict legalized these practices and did away with regulations on manufacturing procedures that had been justified as a way to protect consumers from shoddy goods. In Turgot's mind, the elimination of guild privileges would benefit not only business owners but also "that class of men, who, owning nothing except their ability to work, have more than others the need and the right to use to their full extent the only resources they have to make a living."[7]

Turgot's edicts, like his earlier effort to deregulate the grain trade, ran into vehement opposition. Guild masters and skilled artisans complained that they were being deprived of rights they had spent years to earn and that consumers would suffer because of a decline in the quality of workmanship. Turgot's reforms also threatened government finances: payments for guild licenses and other privileges were a significant source of royal and municipal revenue. The monarchy had often encouraged corporate groups such as guilds to borrow in their own name in order to pay their taxes, since these groups could often secure loans at better rates than the king himself. In the Paris Parlement, a young magistrate, Jean Jacques Duval d'Eprémesnil, began to make a name for himself with his vehement opposition to the radical doctrines that he detected behind all of Turgot's actions. Duval d'Eprémesnil would play a major role in the crisis leading to the Revolution in 1789. At almost the same moment when, on the other side of the Atlantic, Thomas Jefferson was drafting the American Declaration of Independence's ringing words about liberty and equality, Duval d'Eprémesnil drew up remonstrances warning that "any system tending under the guise of humanity and benevolence to establish an equality of duties between men, and to destroy these distinctions, necessary in a well-ordered monarchy, would soon lead to disorder." Unrestricted liberty, he concluded, "would soon be transformed into license, opening the door to every abuse."[8]

Louis XVI initially seemed committed to backing Turgot, staging a *lit de justice* in early May 1776 to compel the Paris Parlement to accept the six edicts. Had he remained steadfast, he might have been remembered as a forceful reforming monarch. Within a few weeks, however, the young king changed his mind, saddling himself instead with an enduring reputation as a waverer who could not stick to a consistent policy. Louis's change of heart reflected several factors. Turgot had insisted that his reforms needed to be accompanied by reductions in wasteful government spending, which had brought him into conflict with Marie-Antoinette and other influential court figures. In line with the thinking of the Physiocrats, Turgot had also envisaged a system of local and regional assemblies, chosen by taxpayers without regard for social status, that would cooperate with the intendants in levying taxes and supervising expenditures. His ideas were openly discussed in publications such as the *Gazette de Leyde*, which Louis XVI read regularly. In the *Gazette*, the king would have seen an editorial comment that "it would not be one of the least remarkable singularities of our century that France should return to the nation the right of taxing itself . . . while England works to take it away from its American subjects." One of Turgot's close collaborators, Pierre Samuel Dupont de Nemours, prepared a "Memorandum on Municipal Assemblies" outlining a plan that would have done away with traditional provincial institutions such as estates and parlements. When Louis XVI read the document, he concluded that his minister wanted to "establish a new form of government in France, and to denigrate the old institutions, which the author considers as the products of centuries of ignorance and barbary."[9] Louis had certainly not been brought up to stage such a sweeping revolution in his kingdom.

Ironically, however, one of the biggest reasons for Turgot's downfall was his resistance to French involvement in another revolution, the one in Britain's North American colonies that had begun in 1775, almost at the same moment as France's flour war. Some of the French saw aiding the Americans as an opportunity to strike back at the rival power that had inflicted a stinging defeat on their country in the Seven Years' War. Others, like the young Gilbert du Motier, the marquis de Lafayette, were inspired by the ideals of freedom articulated in the rebels' manifestos, such as Thomas Paine's Common Sense. At court, Louis XVI's foreign minister, Charles Vergennes, a normally cautious diplomat, and the navy minister, Antoine de Sartine, urged the king to approve clandestine aid to the Americans, despite the dangerous precedent of supporting a popular revolt against a monarchy. Turgot, acutely aware of the debt burden left behind by the Seven Years' War, strongly opposed involvement in another costly conflict. Even though he had little of the warrior about him, Louis XVI could not resist the appeal of humbling the British and reestablishing France as Europe's dominant power.

On May 12, 1776, Turgot was abruptly dismissed from office, and his ambitious reform plans were largely scrapped. Louis XVI would not go down in history as an enlightened despot, wielding royal powers to impose radical changes. The fall of Turgot did not result in a complete return to the previous status quo, however. By appointing Turgot's critic, Necker, to oversee the monarchy's finances, Louis XVI opted for a man whose policies were more pragmatic than his rival's but whose ascent also represented an innovation. Originally a Genevan banker, Necker was a commoner, a foreigner, and, most shockingly, a Protestant.

Whereas Turgot had dreamed of remaking fundamental features of France's economy and social structure, Necker thought he could master the kingdom's financial problems by reducing waste in government spending and abolishing unnecessary offices. He hoped to avoid open confrontations with the parlements and unpopular tax increases. His immediate problem, however, was to finance the French involvement in the American war. News of the major American victory over the British at the Battle of Saratoga, which reached France at the end of 1777, persuaded Louis XVI to accept Vergennes's recommendation that France move from covert support to open alliance with the Americans and war with the British. Although the conflict was fought overseas and involved relatively small numbers of French troops, it required a huge investment in the French navy. Trees all over France were felled to provide the timber to build the ships of the line that were the eighteenth century's costliest weapons. Throngs of sailors were recruited from the country's coastal regions, and money had to be found to pay for the supplies they needed on their months-long voyages across the Atlantic. Necker proved indispensable in lining up loans that made the war possible, at the price of adding staggering sums to the monarchy's already formidable debt.

The French effort paid off when Admiral François Joseph Paul de Grasse's ships successfully blockaded General George Cornwallis's forces at Yorktown, allowing George Washington to force the British to surrender. The defeat drove the British to accept American independence, but the French hopes for an outcome that would have decisively shifted the worldwide balance of imperial power were disappointed when a British naval victory in the Caribbean in April 1782 scuttled a planned attack on the major sugar island of Jamaica. The Treaty of Paris, signed on January 20, 1783—ironically, almost exactly ten years to the day before the execution of Louis XVI in 1793—was a humiliation for the British, but it gave the French few tangible gains.

France's support for the American rebels had important domestic repercussions. In the Caribbean colony of Saint-Domingue, free men of color were recruited to serve in an attack on the city of Savannah,

Georgia. The assault failed, but service in the army gave its participants military experience and the conviction that they deserved the same rights as whites. French soldiers and officers who served in North America did not necessarily return to Europe as convinced advocates of revolution and republicanism—many of them were put off by the rough manners of the Americans and the undisciplined nature of their military effort—but printed reports and American propagandists inspired a wave of enthusiasm for the supposed virtues of the simple American farmers who had defeated the haughty British. Foremost among the propagandists was the elderly Benjamin Franklin, who arrived in Paris in 1776 as the official spokesman for the movement. Franklin shrewdly concealed the sophistication he had acquired over his many years as a public figure in America and Britain. Sporting a fur hat unlike anything seen before at Versailles, he played the role of a rustic sage with great success. Women swooned over him, and future revolutionaries, such as Count Mirabeau, listened eagerly to his political ideas. The image of America as a land of "new men" living in harmony with nature was the main theme of the best-selling *Letters of an American Farmer*, written by the French-born Hector St. John de Crèvecoeur. Crèvecoeur was not entirely uncritical of America—he devoted part of one chapter to denouncing the evils of slavery—but he presented the country as a radical alternative to the aristocratic and inegalitarian societies of the Old Continent.

Other publications spread American political ideas as well. During his years in France, Franklin oversaw translations of key revolutionary documents, including the Declaration of Independence and the republican constitutions adopted by the various American states. Some influential French figures were deeply impressed by these experiments in republican liberty. The idea of defining the fundamental features of a political system in a written constitution and limiting governmental powers through a declaration of rights had an undoubted influence on the French Revolution. Other French thinkers, however, such as Turgot and the republican theorist Mably, were more critical. Turgot blamed the Americans for reproducing too many of the irrational features of the British monarchy, such as bicameral legislatures, in their new governments, and Mably warned that the unrestricted freedom of speech promised in the country's constitution might allow opponents of freedom to undermine it. These critiques foreshadowed ways in which the French Revolution would diverge from the American one.

By the time the American war ended, Necker's time in office was also over. Even though they were modest compared to Turgot's projects, his own reform efforts provoked strong opposition. Convinced, like Turgot, that the monarchy would benefit from the introduction of some form of representation, Necker had tried to create elected assemblies in two French provinces, leading his ministerial rival, Vergennes, to complain to Louis XVI that "English and Genevan principles are filtering in to our administration."[10] Necker's efforts to eliminate unnecessary government positions and put the collection of taxes under government control, at the expense of the private financiers who had traditionally profited from the process, made other enemies. Most controversially, Necker decided in early 1781 to take the unprecedented step of publishing a summary of the monarchy's annual revenues and expenses. His *Compte rendu au roi* (Account to the king) became a runaway best seller: for the first time, royal subjects were offered a comprehensive overview of the sources of the king's income and how it was spent. The goal of Necker's initiative was to convince the public that the French government was creditworthy: his figures purported to show that its regular income exceeded "ordinary" expenses by a healthy margin. Critics were quick to point out, however, that Necker had not included the cost of the ongoing war, and the payments that would be needed to pay back the loans he had taken out to finance it. Conservatives were appalled at the idea of provoking a public discussion about the secrets of the government.

Sensing that his support was fading, Necker forced Louis XVI to make a decision: either give him firm support by officially appointing him to the royal council, in spite of his Protestantism, or else let him go. The king accepted Necker's resignation, thereby adding to his reputation for abandoning reform-minded ministers when they found themselves in difficulty. After the flurry of discussion set off by Necker's *Compte rendu*, the issue of royal finances ceased to be a major topic for a few years. The heavy debts Necker had incurred to pay for the war still had to be repaid, but temporary wartime taxes were still in effect, giving the government breathing space. Public attention shifted to other matters, such as the pioneering balloon ascensions of daring aeronauts like Jean-François Pilâtre de Rozier, who made the first manned flight, reaching an altitude of three thousand feet, on November 21, 1783. "It was a moment which can never be repeated, the most astounding achievement the science of physics has yet given to the world," the popular author Louis-Sébastien Mercier wrote, and the ascent, witnessed by the king himself, seemed to position France as Europe's leader in science as well as politics.[11]

The king found a new finance minister he trusted in the person of Charles-Alexandre Calonne, who promised that the monarchy's expenses could be met through energetic promotion of economic growth, without the controversial reforms his predecessors had tried to introduce. The first three years of his time in office saw a rapid increase in stock-market speculation, sometimes directly encouraged by the government in the hopes that new companies would spur spending and investment. Calonne also hoped to expand French foreign commerce. An edict issued in August 1784 allowed French colonists to trade directly with merchants from other countries, especially the newly independent United States. This breach of the traditional *exclusif*, the system that reserved colonial trade for metropolitan French merchants, was unpopular in port cities such as Bordeaux and Le Havre, but it had strong support from Caribbean plantation owners. Their happiness about the trade reform was not enough to offset their outrage when Calonne's colleague Charles de Castries, the navy minister, issued an edict in December 1784 meant to curb the worst excesses of the slavery system in the islands. "This edict violates the sacred rights of property, and puts a dagger in the hands of the slaves, by giving control over their discipline and their regime to someone other than their masters," one colonist wrote of the limits imposed on the punishments owners could inflict.[12]

In 1786, Calonne took an even more sweeping step in the direction of opening up the French economy by negotiating a free trade treaty with the British. Well aware that British manufacturers, especially the makers of textiles, were introducing new mechanized production methods that allowed them to sell their products more cheaply than their

French rivals, Calonne hoped the pressure of competition would drive his own countrymen to modernize and become more efficient. In the meantime, he calculated that increased exports of French agricultural products, such as wine, would offset the impact on manufactured goods. Just as the Castries edict outraged slaveowners, the Eden Treaty, named for the British diplomat who negotiated it, set off a furious backlash from French manufacturers, who feared being overwhelmed by British competition, as well as from workers, who worried about losing their jobs. Jean-Marie Roland, Madame Roland's husband and a future revolutionary politician, wrote that "we have just concluded a commercial treaty with the English which may well enrich our great-grandchildren but has deprived 500,000 workers of bread and ruined 10,000 commercial houses."[13] In Lyon, France's largest manufacturing city, silkworkers fearing competition from cheap English-made fabrics staged the largest urban rebellion in decades in August 1786, forcing the government to send in troops to restore order.

As his ministers adopted policies that angered key sectors of public opinion, Louis XVI's ability to back them was undermined by a scandal that severely damaged the reputation of the queen. On August 15, 1785, a great nobleman, Cardinal Rohan, was publicly arrested in the palace of Versailles, accused by the king in person of having falsely claimed that Marie-Antoinette had asked him to buy a fabulously expensive diamond necklace on her behalf. Rohan had fallen for an elaborate scheme concocted by an adventuress by the name of Madame de la Motte and her husband. Madame de la Motte had pretended to be a confidante of the queen and assured the cardinal that arranging the purchase of the necklace would win him her favor. Rohan obtained the necklace, showing the jewelers letters forged by the conspirators promising that the queen would pay for it, and turned the jewels over to La Motte to be given to the queen. Instead, La Motte and her accomplices broke up the necklace and sold the diamonds separately, netting a handsome profit.

The scheme was exposed when the jewelers, impatient for payment, presented the forged letter with Marie-Antoinette's signature to Versailles. Marie-Antoinette, well aware of how her reputation for extravagance had undercut her popularity, was appalled and demanded harsh punishment for the cardinal. Louis XVI obliged her by arranging for a public arrest in front of the rest of the court. The revelations that ensued exposed the cardinal's involvement with a cast of dubious characters, including one Count Alessandro di Cagliostro, an Italian con man who claimed to be over a thousand years old. The spectacle of a great nobleman and church dignitary consorting with such company did nothing to improve the reputation of the French aristocracy. But Rohan also had powerful supporters, including leading members of the Paris Parlement, where his case was heard. His advocates insisted that he had been the innocent dupe of the La Mottes, a defense that implied that it was reasonable for him to have believed that the queen's love of luxury might have led her to turn to him to obtain the necklace. Louis XVI was left looking powerless, as if he could not control his wife's behavior, a devastating blow for a ruler who was supposed to be the "father of the people."

After twelve years on the throne, the still young Louis XVI—he was only thirty-two in 1786—found himself beleaguered from all sides. He was tied to a wife who had become a symbol both of female excesses and of the unpopular Austrian alliance; his own apparent weakness as a husband had undermined his authority, perhaps irreparably; and his ministers' policies had alienated influential parts of the population. Then, in August 1786, after three years spent reassuring the king that the monarchy's finances were under control, the finance minister, Calonne, suddenly informed his master that unless something drastic was done, he would face another disaster: the threat of government bankruptcy. Firmly convinced that it was up to him to decide how to respond to this crisis, Louis XVI was about to discover that his subjects were no longer willing to let him set his country's course.

# 4

# "EVERYTHING MUST CHANGE": THE ASSEMBLY OF NOTABLES AND THE CRISIS OF 1787–1788

I T CANNOT HAVE BEEN EASY FOR LOUIS XVI'S FINANCE MINISTER, CALONNE, to inform the king that the French monarchy was on the verge of financial collapse. Calonne had made his name as an unswerving defender of absolutist principles: according to rumor, he had helped draft the bellicose "flagellation speech" in which Louis XV had denounced the parlements in 1766. He had fought his way to office in 1783 by promising that he could resolve the monarchy's financial problems without imposing drastic reforms. As he realized in the summer of 1786 that his policies had increased the royal deficit without producing the economic growth he had counted on—and that opposition to him was mounting—Calonne reacted by upping the stakes. Something had to be done: a special tax imposed during the American war was due to expire in 1787, depriving the government of vitally needed revenue just as the cost of servicing the loans taken out to pay for the war reached its peak. With half of the king's annual revenue pledged to pay interest on the debt, the financial situation had become unsustainable. Lenders, increasingly nervous about the possibility of a royal bankruptcy, were demanding ever higher rates of interest. A drastic change of course was imperative.

In a lengthy memorandum for the king, Calonne announced that "the only way to bring real order into the finances is to revitalize the entire state by reforming all that is defective in its constitution." The plan he suggested was mostly borrowed from proposals originally put forward by his predecessors, Turgot and Necker. Calonne called for the abolition of the special tax privileges that had set the nobility and the Church apart from the rest of the population. As the Physiocratic economic reformers had long advocated, a myriad of special taxes would be replaced by a single tax on landed property, which would be levied on owners regardless of their social status. Critics immediately realized that Calonne's proposed land tax promised the crown a stream of income that would grow automatically as the economy expanded without allowing the parlements to object as they traditionally did when ministers proposed new taxes. To deflect charges that he was trying to make the government more powerful, Calonne offered taxpaying landowners a voice in decision-making: they would be allowed to elect provincial assemblies, which would have the power to review expenditures and offer advice on policies. In contrast to the traditional estates that existed in some provinces, the provincial assemblies would represent all property-owners and would not have reserved seats for nobles and high clergy. Turgot's former adviser André Morellet excitedly called the plan "an announcement of liberty and equality."[1]

A career spent in royal service battling the aristocratic parlements, for whom social equality was anathema, and for whom liberty meant opposing royal authority, convinced Calonne that it would be impossible to promulgate his radical program in the form of ordinary laws. Instead, he proposed to revive a long-forgotten institution, last resorted to in 1626, by convoking an "Assembly of Notables" made up of deputies handpicked by the government. His hope was that endorsement of his program by a group of prominent figures, including representatives of the parlements themselves, would stifle opposition.

Calonne's first challenge was to win over the king. Louis XVI was not a backward-looking conservative: since coming to the throne in 1774, he had approved a number of reforms, including the abolition of serfdom on the royal estates and the end of torture in judicial proceedings. Cautious by nature, however, he had no ambition to play the part of an enlightened despot, unlike his Habsburg brother-in-law, the Austrian emperor Joseph II, who had created an uproar throughout his lands in the early 1780s by curtailing the powers of the Catholic Church, granting toleration to Protestants and Jews, and trying to impose a single scheme of rational administration on disparate territories scattered from Belgium to Hungary.

Throughout the second half of 1786, Calonne worked to overcome the king's fears that "the proposed plan is too broad and involves changes that are too great." Anticipating the language that would be used by the revolutionaries who would soon succeed him, Calonne urged Louis to recognize that "one cannot do great things if one is stopped by fear of difficulties." The financial crisis was an opportunity for the king to "immortalize" himself by freeing the monarchy once and for all from its chronic lack of revenue.[2] And so Louis XVI, who had already reluctantly let himself be persuaded to embark on one history-altering adventure when he approved French intervention on behalf of the American colonists, allowed Calonne to set in motion the series of events that would lead to the complete overthrow of his monarchy.

Although the summoning of an Assembly of Notables had respectable precedent in French law, the sudden decision to revive such a long-forgotten institution jolted the public almost as much as the content of Calonne's reform proposals. Such an event "could hardly take place under an absolute monarch and despotic ministers, except in a disastrous crisis to which they do not know any remedy," one chronicler wrote.[3] Although the same journalist warned that the Notables would find themselves acting like toy "Chinese pagodas," the eighteenth-century version of bobblehead figures, by doing nothing but nodding their approval of Calonne's proposals, ambitious courtiers, church prelates, and magistrates scrambled for places in the upcoming assembly.

While the convocation of the Notables alarmed some and spurred the ambitions of others, it also encouraged utopian hopes that went far beyond the solution of France's financial problems. At the beginning of January 1787, as Calonne was assembling the Notables, a man with ambitions of another kind, Jacques-Pierre Brissot, convened a very different kind of group: a club of reform-minded intellectuals. Born in 1754, the same year as Louis XVI, Brissot, the son of an innkeeper from the cathedral town of Chartres, was typical of a younger generation who dreamed of following in the footsteps of the philosophes who had compiled the *Encyclopédie*. Whereas Diderot, d'Alembert, and their colleagues in the 1740s and 1750s had taken on an entrenched conservative establishment, Brissot's generation came on the scene at a time when the principles of the Enlightenment had become conventional wisdom among France's educated classes. Middle-aged disciples of the philosophes monopolized positions in the prestigious Académie française and the editorships of France's major periodicals, but none of them seemed to have many fresh ideas. Those younger still, including Brissot, imagined themselves capable of great things, but had to struggle to find places for themselves.

At the same time, despite decades of criticism by the philosophes, French institutions remained largely unchanged. An absolute monarch still ruled from Versailles, a hereditary aristocracy still monopolized prestigious positions, and the Catholic Church still imposed its rules on a population increasingly detached from its teachings. Brissot took up the causes the earlier philosophes had espoused, attacking religious dogma, entrenched privileged groups, and oppressive laws. Like Voltaire, he visited England, where he wrote for a French-language newspaper and tried unsuccessfully to found a cosmopolitan society to bring together progressive thinkers from many countries. When he returned to France in 1784, he was accused of writing scandalous pamphlets and became, like so many other French writers before him, an unwilling guest in the Bastille. Released from prison, he found an outlet for his literary talents and a source of badly needed income by helping to compose publications designed to either promote or denigrate the new joint-stock companies encouraged by Calonne's policies.

The American Revolution inspired Brissot: its success demonstrated that real changes in the world could happen. In 1787, Brissot and his friend Étienne Clavière, a Genevan banker, collaborated on a short book defending the new American republic against its critics. Clavière had been exiled from Switzerland for his participation in an unsuccessful revolutionary movement there in 1782. Brissot also followed the Dutch Patriot movement, which used republican rhetoric about patriotism to challenge the country's ruler, the stadholder, in the mid-1780s. Through his British connections, Brissot kept up with the first stages of the movement for the abolition of the slave trade. Interested in everything and known for his ability to write quickly and fluently, Brissot built up a circle of acquaintances that ranged from fellow underemployed writers with advanced ideas to great nobles. Through his wife, Félicité, who had once been a governess to the children of the duc d'Orléans, the king's cousin, Brissot gained entrée to the circle of the richest man in the kingdom.

For Brissot and his friends, the convocation of the Assembly of Notables suddenly opened the prospect of hitherto undreamed-of reforms in France. Brissot hastened to invite like-minded friends to take advantage of the opportunity by joining his "Gallo-American Society" to work "for the good of all men." He and his friends held no positions of power, but they knew how to get ideas into circulation, a talent that would become increasingly valuable in the years ahead. Among the proposals the ever-inventive Brissot and his colleagues batted around were a campaign to promote the planting of potatoes in France, in order to increase the food supply and relieve the misery of the poor; the possibility of expanding Calonne's free trade treaty with Britain to include other nations, as a way of ensuring world peace; and "the destruction of Negro slavery."[4]

Brissot and his friends were only a few of the many figures who saw the summoning of the Assembly of Notables as a sign that truly radical changes in French government and society were suddenly possible. Many of them, including Brissot himself, would go on to play major roles in the French Revolution. Some of the future revolutionaries, such as the marquis de Lafayette and the marquis de Condorcet, were political insiders. Lafayette, who came from a wealthy court family and had married into an even wealthier clan, had become a celebrity because of his engagement in the American war of independence. Condorcet, from a more modest noble family, was a brilliant mathematician, a former collaborator of the reforming minister Turgot, and a member of the major royal academies. He was an active pamphleteer who had, among other things, put forward a proposal for the gradual abolition of slavery as early as 1781. Other figures galvanized into activism in 1787 were still known only locally. Henri Grégoire, for example, the local priest of the small Lorraine town of Emberménil, had argued for reform of the Church; he attracted attention in 1787 with an essay advocating civil equality for the Jews, an unusual position for a Catholic priest. Some of the younger future revolutionaries, such as the law student Jean-Marie Goujon, were just beginning to translate their youthful emotions into political ideas. Goujon's family had sent him on a long voyage to one of France's Indian Ocean colonies, where he had witnessed "the whites' antisocial contempt for the blacks," as his friend and biographer Pierre-François Tissot later recalled. There, he absorbed his "first lessons of humanity" when he was a mere seventeen.[5]

The most visible of these future revolutionaries could claim to be both an insider and an outsider. Honoré Gabriel Riquetti, comte de Mirabeau, came from a distinguished noble family. His father, the Victor Riquetti de Mirabeau, had been converted to Physiocratic economic doctrines and had written one of the mid-eighteenth century's most widely read works on economics, *L'ami des hommes* (The friend of man), published in 1760. Despite his reputation for philanthropic concern for the betterment of humanity, the elder Mirabeau was in constant conflict with his son from childhood on. So badly disfigured by a childhood case of smallpox that he was often called "the ugliest man in France," Count Mirabeau became notorious for his outrageous behavior. Despite his scarred face, the future revolutionary proved irresistible to women; he spent money on a prodigious scale, threatening to deplete the family fortune. He courted and won a wealthy local heiress, but the match did not settle him down. When his father punished him by obtaining a *lettre de cachet*, a royal order calling for his detention in a provincial town, he got himself condemned to death for running off to the Netherlands with a married woman. The sentence was not carried out, but, after being extradited back to France, Mirabeau found himself imprisoned more strictly, again at his father's request.

Mirabeau used his time in prison to write several scandalous pornographic works, but he also developed a talent as a political polemicist. Upon his release, he issued a lengthy denunciation of the arbitrary justice to which he had been subjected. "Oh my blind compatriots! It would be no more difficult to erase your name than mine from the list of citizens," he warned.[6] He called for a government in which laws were made by elected representatives who would protect individual liberty. Mirabeau's emergence as a public figure did not temper his private behavior. He continued to run up debts and plunge into new love affairs, even as he brought a widely publicized lawsuit against his own wife. Pleading his own case, Mirabeau revealed the extraordinary oratorical talent that would make him the dominant figure of the early French Revolution.

The controversies of the mid-1780s provided Mirabeau opportunities to build his reputation. Benjamin Franklin encouraged him to step into a debate aroused by French participation in the American Revolution. There had been a proposal to create a special status for veterans of the war by making them and their descendants members of an exclusive "Society of the Cincinnati," an idea Franklin opposed. Mirabeau used the American dispute as an opportunity to make a scathing criticism of hereditary privileges in general. The spectacle of a titled nobleman denouncing the ancestors of the *noblesse d'épée* as "thirty thousand ironclad oppressors," and the forefathers of the *noblesse de robe* as "calculating vampires who have . . . sucked the blood of twenty million French," added to his notoriety.[7] Mirabeau joined Brissot in selling his writing talents to investors who wanted to promote stock market schemes. To stop the flow of Mirabeau's pamphlets, Calonne sent him off to the Prussian capital of Berlin in 1786, where he composed a denunciation of anti-Jewish prejudice, adding to his reputation as a defender of liberty and equality. The announcement of the Assembly of Notables brought him rushing back to Paris: he saw that Calonne would need public spokesmen, and he hoped to be appointed as the assembly's official secretary. When he was passed over in favor of the less controversial economist Dupont de Nemours, however, he prepared to throw his weight against Calonne and his program. The ability of men like

Mirabeau and Brissot to influence public opinion would soon make them a real force.

The Notables selected by Calonne and the king were neither utopian dreamers like Brissot nor "class traitors" like Mirabeau. They included seven "princes of the blood" who stood in the line of royal succession, fourteen archbishops and bishops, and an impressive contingent of "dukes and peers," including "marshals of France" representing the military aristocracy; marquis, including the young Lafayette, the hero of the American war; and a lowly baron. The royal administration was represented by a selection of councilors of state and intendants, outnumbered nearly three to one by judges from the various parlements. Twenty-five mayors, nearly all of them nobles, were to speak for the interests of France's cities. Urban artisans like Jacques Ménétra and peasants were entirely excluded, as were the parish priests who made up the majority of the clergy. All the Notables were, it went without saying, male; whatever influence women exercised on their deliberations was indirect, through the ability of wives, mistresses, and fashionable salon hostesses to put ideas in their heads.

Nevertheless, the Notables were not entirely isolated from the currents of change affecting French society. The ambitious archbishop of Toulouse, Étienne Charles de Loménie de Brienne, was so imbued with Enlightenment ideas that Louis XVI had refused to appoint him as archbishop of Paris in 1781. "An archbishop," Louis said, "should at least believe in God."[8] Lafayette brought with him the spirit of republican liberty he had witnessed during his time in America. Many of the Notables had experience in public administration, and they were well aware of the difficulties facing the monarchy. Many of them also bore scars from the bitter political fights between the crown and the parlements during the last decade of Louis XV's reign, and in particular, Chancellor Maupeou's attempt to replace those refractory courts with a more pliable judiciary. Although Calonne had been one of Maupeou's henchmen, he did not systematically exclude opponents of the Maupeou coup from the Assembly of Notables. He also appointed several prominent "Neckerists" loyal to his bitter rival.

Calonne had originally hoped to move quickly, but his schedule was thrown off when the foreign minister, Vergennes, died on February 13, 1787. Louis XVI had trusted Vergennes deeply and lamented his passing, saying, "I have lost the only friend I could count on, the only minister who never deceived me."[9] Although temperamentally more conservative than Calonne, Vergennes had recognized that the monarchy's financial ills were depriving it of resources to play the role of a great power abroad and had therefore given his support to Calonne's project. On February 22, the Notables finally convened for their opening session. Unaccustomed to public speaking, Louis XVI read only a few words, not enough to impress the Notables with his determination. It was left to Calonne, a far more polished orator, to lay out his program and try to convince his audience that it represented the king's views.

Calonne's sweeping proposals threatened the special interests of the privileged groups from which the Notables were drawn, but they also raised serious questions that concerned all the king's subjects. Showering the Notables with figures, Calonne argued that the new land tax would raise more revenue without affecting the poorer subjects. The Notables pointed out, however, that Calonne himself talked of a royal budget deficit of more than a hundred million livres a year, and the new tax, according to his own estimates, would produce only about a third of that sum in increased revenue. They objected to the unlimited revenue the new taxes would bring in as well as to the details of how they were supposed to be collected. Most importantly, however, the Notables asserted that they lacked the authority to approve new taxes. "It would require the Estates General to give an adequate consent to a tax of this nature," one of them insisted, reviving the demand first voiced twelve years earlier by the reforming minister Malesherbes after the Maupeou coup.[10]

Other parts of Calonne's program also aroused opposition among the Notables. The provincial assemblies he intended to create, in which half the seats would be reserved for representatives of the Third Estate, while the other half would be filled by the clergy and the nobility, struck many of the Notables as a threat to the kingdom's traditional social hierarchy. "At every turn the Plebeian finds himself the equal of the Minister of the Altar, of the Noble or of the Magistrate," the duc d'Harcourt complained.[11] In a foretaste of the bitter personal rivalries that would poison revolutionary politics, Calonne also found himself fighting a proxy duel with Necker. By insisting that the budget had been in balance when Necker was in office, the "Neckerists" put the blame for the financial crisis entirely on Calonne's shoulders and insinuated that he could not be trusted to resolve it.

Frustrated by the Notables' unexpectedly stubborn opposition, Calonne was also weakened by an attack from a coterie of pamphleteers led by Mirabeau. Their collectively written *Denunciation of Speculation* exposed Calonne's use of government funds to buy off speculators who had threatened the launch of the new India Company a few years earlier. But Mirabeau, Brissot, and their collaborators raised more fundamental issues that would loom increasingly large as the crisis facing the monarchy deepened. France's problems could only worsen, they warned, "as long as we have no constitution," a set of rules that would make it impossible for someone as untrustworthy as Calonne to exercise power. To have a constitution, they wrote, would mean replacing the uneven patchwork of existing laws with national institutions "guided by a single spirit . . . according to uniform principles," and a society in which citizens would be "classified from now on according to the useful contributions they make to society."[12] The pamphlet's language suggested a revolutionary remaking of the country that would eliminate such basic features of French life as the differences between provinces and the existence of privileged classes.

Now far behind the timetable he had anticipated, Calonne decided to take yet another risky gamble. Initially, his proposals and the Assembly of Notables' proceedings were supposed to be secret. On March 30, 1787, however, Calonne abruptly brought the whole of the French population into the debate by having the royal printer in Versailles publish his proposals, together with a cover letter denouncing the selfish motives of his opponents. Free copies of Calonne's cover letter, or "Avertissement," were distributed in the streets, and parish priests were directed to read it aloud to their congregations. Within two weeks, according to one chronicler, "people arriving in Paris said they had seen it distributed in the marketplaces of the smallest towns." Some readers responded positively: Jérôme Pétion, a future revolutionary mayor of Paris, for example, wrote to his friend Brissot that "there are excellent views in Calonne's projects, views very favorable to the people." The Notables, however, reacted with outrage. The minister, they claimed, was trying to incite the mass of the population against them. Lafayette, despite his enthusiasm for the American Revolution, had to agree that "even in Boston this appeal would have been regarded as an act of sedition."[13] Calonne's opponents convinced the king that if there was to be any hope of getting the Notables to approve significant reforms, the minister had to go. A week after the publication of the "Avertissement," he found himself out of office.

Calonne's dismissal did nothing to resolve the financial problems that had led to the Assembly of Notables being held in the first place. For a few weeks, Louis XVI, showing unaccustomed energy, tried hard to persuade the Notables to accept a modified version of Calonne's plan. But even the king's personal meetings with leading members of the Notables proved fruitless. Estimates of the deficit escalated steadily, making the public and the stock market increasingly nervous. Unwilling to give in to pressure from many of the Notables to summon Necker, the king finally agreed to turn the management of royal finances over to Brienne, Calonne's main critic among the Notables. The king hoped that Brienne could win their endorsement of at least some significant measures.

Initially, Brienne pushed for modified versions of Calonne's proposals: for example, he amended the land tax so that it would be collected in cash rather than in agricultural produce, and he put a limit on the amount of revenue it would produce, thinking this would quell opposition to the idea. The assembly's secretary, Dupont de Nemours, optimistically concluded that Brienne had conceded the principle that there could be no taxation without the consent of the governed, and that, as a result, France would now be "a *republic*, where there remains a magistrate, decorated with the title and honors of royalty, but perpetually obliged to assemble his people and to ask them to provide for his needs." Brienne quickly learned, as many others would discover during the Revolution, that accepting a government position drastically altered his standing with his former allies. The Notables remained steadfast in their opposition to any increase in taxes or alteration of privileges. They cloaked their objections in language about defending the public good and protecting liberties, making it difficult to denounce them as selfish defenders of special interests. The assembly was willing to endorse the creation of provincial assemblies and to approve a new loan to enable the government to pay its most pressing bills, but they wanted to see the royal power to collect and spend revenue severely restricted, an idea that one journalist likened to treating the king like a "prodigal son" who needed to be taught not to "repeat the same mistakes."[14]

Within a few weeks, Brienne and the king concluded that there was no point in prolonging the Notables' sessions and sent them home. The assembly's failure demoralized the king; according to the Austrian ambassador, he lost interest in his official duties, spending his time hunting, eating, and drinking to the point where he sometimes "lost his reason." The Notables were as frustrated as the king and his minister: in one of the last meetings of the bureau to which he had been assigned, Lafayette startled its chairman, the king's younger brother the comte d'Artois, by openly calling for the convocation of the Estates General. Calonne's gamble that radical reforms could be brought about through a voluntary consensus among the kingdom's elites had failed, and his attempt had badly undermined the credibility of existing institutions. As the great nineteenth-century French political thinker Alexis de Tocqueville would remark, Calonne had demonstrated that "the most perilous moment for a bad government is when it seeks to mend its ways."[15]

Left to proceed with little input from the king, Brienne began to implement the changes in local and provincial government that the Notables did approve, supported significant reforms in the military, and moved ahead with a proposal to grant limited civil rights to the kingdom's Protestant minority, a major shift in policy that appealed to enlightened opinion but alarmed many of the Catholic clergy. Had he succeeded, Brienne might have been remembered as a great reforming minister. The financial problems facing the government did not permit him the time he would have needed, however, and in the public debate about the underlying issues that the proposed reforms had opened up, it became clear that many groups would no longer accept radical changes without a real voice in shaping them.

During his first year in power, Brienne tried all the timeworn tactics for dealing with the parlements that had developed during the reign of Louis XV. The older magistrates who had taken part in the noisy struggles of the Maupeou era were familiar with this playbook. Younger members, such as the talented orator Duval d'Eprémesnil and the ambitious radical Adrien Duport, put forward a heady, if confused, brew that combined traditional arguments with new ideas. On the traditional side, they spoke of how the parlements functioned as a check on royal power; more radically, they praised representative government and cited the examples of England and the United States. Beleaguered defenders of the ministry complained that the young hotheads in the Paris Parlement had become addicted to demagogic opposition for its own sake. "The more dangerous and violent [an opinion] is, the more it exposes them to the opprobrium of the Court, the more glorious it becomes to profess it," a critic wrote.[16]

After approving an emergency loan to keep the government afloat in May 1787, the Paris Parlement accepted several of Brienne's reforms that did not involve new taxes. When proposed stamp and land taxes were presented for registration at the beginning of July, however, the magistrates balked. Adopting the tactics of the Notables earlier in the year, they called on the king to present them with a comprehensive account of royal revenue and expenditures and a detailed list of the cuts in expenditures that he would make. The king's representative, his younger brother the comte d'Artois, indignantly rejected these demands as violations of the king's right to govern without interference. On July 16, the parlement issued another remonstrance, this time asserting its "wish to see the nation assembled before any new taxes. Only it, knowing the true state of the finances, can do away with great abuses and offer great resources."[17] The judges thus endorsed the call for the convocation of the Estates General that Lafayette had made at the end of the Assembly of Notables.

In a formal ceremony at Versailles on August 6, the king compelled the parlement to register the tax decrees, but as soon as they returned to their Parisian chambers, the magistrates voided them. Days later, they further challenged the king by voting to indict Calonne for financial malfeasance, and rejecting any tax that treated nobles and commoners in the same way. The ministry struck back with a countermeasure that had frequently been employed under Louis XV, exiling the magistrates to the provincial town of Troyes. As was equally traditional, law clerks and others whose jobs depended on the presence of the judges staged noisy public demonstrations in the capital. Meanwhile, the exiled magistrates issued proclamations inciting judges in the lower courts to refuse to recognize the tax edicts. Brienne tried to avoid a brutal confrontation with the parlements by suggesting a compromise: he would renounce the new stamp and land taxes and instead continue collecting the wartime taxes imposed years earlier, which were due to expire. In his view, this measure would not require the judges to approve any new taxes. He would bring the deficit down by implementing rigorous cuts in government expenditures, and in the meantime, he would take out new loans that would be easier to repay once the government's credit had improved. And, once he had demonstrated that his program of financial recovery was succeeding, he would satisfy the public clamor by calling a meeting of the Estates General in five years' time. Despite the inflammatory rhetoric of their public declarations, the parlement judges were rapidly tiring of their forced vacation in Troyes. Assured that the parlement would ratify his measures, Brienne allowed the magistrates to return to Paris.

The government's eagerness to resolve the standoff with the parlement was intensified by a humiliating foreign crisis that reached its peak in September 1787, when Prussia sent troops to occupy the Netherlands, one of France's traditional allies. Their aim was to quash the "Patriot" movement against the country's ruler, the stadholder, that had been developing there for several years. In Versailles, the ministry recognized that it simply did not have the money to oppose the Prussians. The Dutch Patriot movement prefigured the revolution about to break out in France. Calling for a government elected by all citizens, Patriot propagandists were the first to use the word "democracy" in its modern sense.

In 1785, they circulated a proposed declaration of rights whose language anticipated that of the French declaration of 1789. The Prussian intervention made many of the Dutch Patriots flee to France, where they denounced the French court for abandoning them. Lafayette, who saw the Dutch movement as an echo of the American struggle for independence, called the French failure to support the Patriots "a blot which it will be difficult to wash out."[18] Even conservative French diplomats and military officers blamed the government for letting itself get into a situation where it could not stand up to foreign rivals and protect the national interest.

Brienne and his colleague Chrétien-François Lamoignon, marquis de Basville, the minister of justice, prepared carefully for a formal ceremony at the Paris Parlement on November 19, 1787. The judges had been promised that they would be allowed to speak freely and take a vote on the ministry's proposals. After more than eight hours of debate, they were finally ready to vote when Louis XVI suddenly intervened, announcing: "I order that my edict be registered." This was the formula traditionally employed at a *lit de justice* ceremony. A wave of shock ran through the hall at this reversion to the procedures of absolute monarchy. The king's cousin the duc d'Orléans, the person closest to the line of succession after the king's sons and brothers, declared the king's action illegal, and Louis XVI replied with words that his ancestor Louis XIV would have endorsed: "It is legal because I will it."

In the short run, the king's will prevailed. The duc d'Orléans's protest earned him a *lettre de cachet* exiling him to one of his country estates, and several magistrates who had supported him were arrested and imprisoned. Investors eagerly subscribed to the first of Brienne's planned loans, which offered favorable terms. The government turned its attention to installing the newly approved provincial assemblies, which Brienne hoped might become a mechanism for implementing features of the land tax the parlements had rejected, particularly the extension of tax collection to the property of the privileged orders. Among other things, this reform brought changes to peasant villages. Accustomed to managing many of their local affairs through various traditional arrangements with their seigneurs, or overlords, villagers now discovered that they were supposed to adopt a uniform system of municipal government.

In the tiny village of Silly-en-Multien, the diary-keeping schoolteacher Pierre Delahaye noted the details of the unfamiliar voting procedure. There, as in many rural communities, the reform caused a substantial shift in the local balance of power. Wealthy peasants dominated the new elected village councils at the expense both of the seigneur and of their poorer neighbors.

While the government pushed forward with its reform efforts, the loose network of radicals that had begun to coalesce around Brissot, Mirabeau, and their friends also continued to develop. In February 1788, Brissot founded the Société des amis des noirs (Society of the Friends of the Blacks). Inspired by the abolitionist movement in England, the Friends of the Blacks quickly attracted a list of members that read like a "Who's Who" of future revolutionaries. They included Mirabeau, Lafayette, Condorcet, Clavière, and the abbé Emmanuel Sieyès. Open to nobles and commoners alike and even to women, who played a large role in the British antislavery movement, the society was the first example of the kind of institution that would play a large role after 1789: the revolutionary political club. Brissot recognized that the cause of abolition offered a way to put the issue of liberty on the agenda without openly challenging the government. Clavière met with Brienne in March 1788 and reported back to the club that the minister had said "it pained him to see that the slave trade and the slavery of the Negroes were continuing, [and] that it would be desirable to find a way to abolish them," although he warned that any reform would have to also be "in the interest of the planters and the treasury."[19] Brissot, Mirabeau, and a growing number of other pamphleteers also continued to develop their talents at using the press to stir up public discussion. Mirabeau obtained permission to put out a journal that became a vehicle for abolitionist propaganda. He also published documents such as the proposed declaration of rights drawn up by Dutch Patriot republicans in 1785.

Despite the initial success of the measures forced through the parlement in November, Brienne knew he still faced a volatile situation. He had hoped that an edict granting civil toleration to France's Protestant minority, presented to the parlement on November 19 along with his controversial financial measures, would help him in the battle for public opinion. It did in fact split the parlementary firebrands:

Duval d'Eprémesnil opposed it, siding with conservative Catholics, while Adrien Duport supported it. The leading spokesman for the French Protestant community, the pastor Jean-Paul Rabaut Saint-Étienne, was disappointed that public Protestant worship would still not be permitted; he became one of the pamphleteers demanding an expanded version of political liberty. Meanwhile, the Catholic bishop of Dol, spokesman for the provincial estates of Brittany, warned the king that granting rights to the Protestant minority would "violate his Coronation Oath, and that such a measure would infallibly be a source of civil dissensions, and commotions in his kingdom."[20] The debates about the measure were a foretaste of the violent controversies about religion that would take place during the Revolution.

In the early spring of 1788, Brienne and Lamoignon decided to broaden their efforts with a set of reforms to France's judicial system even more sweeping than Maupeou's coup in 1771. They wanted to create a new central *Cour plenière*, a plenary court, to replace the various parlements in registering royal edicts. The parlements themselves would be restricted to hearing appeals from judgments rendered in lower-level courts, whose jurisdictions would be augmented. Brienne and Lamoignon hoped that the expanded responsibilities granted to lower courts at the expense of the parlements would win them the support of provincial judges and enable them to weather the storm they knew would break out when their plan was announced. To broaden the appeal of their reform, Brienne and Lamoignon also decreed that litigants would no longer have to pay judges to hear their cases; moreover, judicial procedures would be simplified.

Forewarned of what was coming, the members of the Paris Parlement prepared to resist. On April 29, 1788, the judges issued a decree denouncing any efforts to change the procedures for the collection of taxes, and on May 3 they went even further, setting down in writing what they proclaimed to be the fundamental constitutional principles of the kingdom. Their declaration acknowledged that "France is a monarchy," but asserted that the king was required to govern "according to the laws." Those laws included, they claimed, "the right of the Nation to freely consent to taxes through regularly convoked and regularly organized meetings of the Estates General." Other fundamental laws that they claimed the king could not alter included the permanence of judicial appointments and guarantees against arbitrary arrest and imprisonment.[21] Rather than speaking of royal subjects, the declaration used the term "citizens." The privileged judges of the parlement thus became the first to insist that freedom depended on the recognition of fundamental constitutional laws that stood above the power of the king and to demand a true representative assembly to speak for the nation.

With its defiant declaration, the Paris Parlement raised the political stakes beyond anything that had occurred in any of its previous clashes with the monarchy over the course of the eighteenth century. The judges and their supporters prepared themselves for the government's inevitable reaction. Cheered on by an unruly crowd of supporters, the magistrates waited while royal troops, the Gardes françaises, surrounded their building, and then, between 1:00 and 2:00 a.m. on May 6, 1788, finally entered their chamber to arrest Duval d'Eprémesnil and one of his allies. After a lengthy standoff, the two magistrates finally gave themselves up. With his sense of theater, Duval d'Eprémesnil announced, "I am the victim who is being sacrificed on the altar; my crime is to have defended public liberty against the innumerable attacks made on it." His words resonated in the heart of the young legal apprentice Goujon, who wrote to his parents, "Sensible people say nothing, but lament in their hearts all these changes that attack the essence of our constitution and our liberty." Goujon, whose evolution over the next few years would make him the very model of a perfect revolutionary, was only one of many who were stirred by the judges' resistance. The lawyer Charles Lacretelle, later to become one of the Revolution's first historians, never forgot "the impression made on me by the sight of those magistrates who came to offer themselves and perhaps to sacrifice themselves to save freedom, which seemed at that time to have no other shelter than their togas."[22]

# 5

# A NATION AROUSED

### *June 1788–May 1789*

A S DRAMATIC AS THE RESISTANCE OF THE PARIS JUDGES MAY HAVE BEEN, it was the reactions of the rest of the population to the court reform plan that were more indicative of events to come. The most drastic response was not long in coming. On June 7, 1788, in the mountain-ringed city of Grenoble, the capital of the southeastern province of Dauphiné and home of the regional parlement, wrote one historian, "the alarm bells sounded from all sides, the town's gates were closed and nailed shut." Soldiers "opened fire on the people and charged them with bayonets and sabers. . . . The people tore up parts of the streets and armed themselves with the stones. They climbed up on the roofs and used tiles and paving stones to drive the troops away."[1]

Grenoble's "Day of the Tiles" was the first outbreak of revolutionary political violence in France—the first moment when the population rose up and overwhelmed the authorities. The royal commander's report left no doubt about the gravity of the situation. "The people . . . [were] out of control. . . . The countryside joined in, peasants came from all over, armed with axes, pitchforks and guns," he wrote. His own residence and office had been overrun and looted, and he decided he had no choice but to release the parlementary judges he had been ordered to arrest. He then allowed them to reoccupy their palace.[2]

The Day of the Tiles and the protests against the Brienne-Lamoignon court reform in other parts of the country showed a much greater determination to contest royal authority than the pamphlet campaigns and lawyers' strikes that had greeted the Maupeou coup in 1771. Even more worrisome for the king and his ministers, however, was the chain of events that unfolded in Dauphiné in the weeks and months following the uprising in Grenoble. As the central government tried to carry through its program, resistance in that province prepared the way for a genuine revolution in France's political institutions, one whose principles found an echo in many other parts of the country.

Brienne and Lamoignon had expected fierce resistance to their reform from regional capitals such as Grenoble that were the seats of parlements, but they had assumed they would find support from the population at large, to whom they promised speedier and less expensive judicial procedures. Events in Dauphiné quickly demonstrated that parlementary rhetoric against "ministerial despotism," the liberal ideas of the Enlightenment, the example of the American Revolution, and government ministers' own criticisms of the deficiencies of the monarchy were not so much trickling as pouring down to people of all classes. In particular, the Day of the Tiles showed that the lower classes, the overwhelming majority of the population, could be mobilized in a political cause even if it was not directly linked to the price of bread and other immediate concerns. Brienne and Lamoignon had not imagined that peasants might take up their pitchforks to support privileged judges and educated lawyers.

Just as they had not anticipated that peasants might intervene in a constitutional dispute, the ministers had not imagined that commoners might displace members of the privileged classes as leaders of a political movement. That happened for the first time in Dauphiné, where even local nobles accepted the program articulated by the local judge Jean-Joseph Mounier, a typical successful member of France's Third Estate.

The son of a cloth merchant, Mounier was just twenty-nine years old at the time of the Day of the Tiles. Like so many lawyers, he admired the British government, with its balance of powers and its structure that promoted cooperation between aristocrats and the better-off members of the rest of the population. Mounier's special gift, in the summer of 1788, was his ability to see how to turn the anger at absolutism that had boiled over in Grenoble into an organized movement to transform France into a constitutional monarchy.

Just a week after the Day of the Tiles, Mounier helped convene a meeting of local officials in Grenoble that set in motion a genuine local revolution. The meeting's participants condensed political ideas that had been germinating for several decades into a manifesto announcing that "taxes can only be legally imposed with the consent of the population, united in a national assembly of freely elected representatives." To make this abstract principle a reality, they called for an assembly of representatives from the whole province of Dauphiné. This proposal openly defied the royal government, which had not authorized any such initiative. Mounier and his allies foreshadowed the passions of the Revolution when they described their opponents as "traitors to the country" and claimed for themselves the label of "patriots."[3]

The provincial assembly Mounier and his supporters advocated met a month later in the small mountain town of Vizille, outside of Grenoble, now the home of the national museum dedicated to the French Revolution. Mounier had worked carefully to get representatives of the two privileged orders, the clergy and the nobility, to cooperate with spokesmen for the Third Estate like himself and his even younger colleague Antoine Barnave, another future revolutionary leader. The Vizille assembly adopted resolutions proclaiming that "the law should be the expression of the general will," words that evoked Rousseau's *Social Contract* and that would find their way into the Declaration of the Rights of Man and Citizen a year later.[4] The most influential aspect of the assembly's resolutions was their proposal to reconstitute Dauphiné's provincial estates. The Vizille delegates proposed that the three estates of the province—clergy, nobles, and commoners—continue to elect deputies separately, but they called for the "doubling" of the Third Estate's allotment: the latter would have twice as many deputies as the other orders, so that the assembly as a whole would be evenly divided between the privileged groups and the commoners. Instead of meeting as three separate bodies, all the members of the estates would form one assembly and vote "by head," so that majority rule would prevail.

The plan for the Dauphiné estates was an ingenious attempt to lay out a path by which France could make the transition from an absolute monarchy to a constitutional system without setting off a dangerous social upheaval. The proposal for the "doubling of the Third" in the provincial estates was meant to satisfy demands for a greater public role for the more educated and wealthier members of the bourgeoisie, even though the clergy and the nobility would still have an influence out of proportion to their numbers. The plan assumed that the issues uniting members of all three estates, particularly their opposition to arbitrary royal power, would outweigh the matters on which they might disagree. While the Vizille resolutions stressed the historic rights of the province, the delegates had no intention of breaking up the kingdom. In response to letters from like-minded reformers in the southwestern province of Béarn who were also trying to revive their local estates, the Dauphinois insisted that "we should see our fatherland in the whole of France."[5]

The resistance to the court reform plan was not limited to Dauphiné. Assembled to vote on their annual "free gift" to the government, representatives of the Catholic clergy denounced the proposed changes in the "ancient constitution" and blamed "the errors of that rash philosophy which seems to have been trying for so long to give new laws to the world." In Brittany, the province's nobles organized a network that flooded the province with pamphlets against the reforms. From the far-off Caribbean colony of Saint-Domingue, where the government had cracked down on the island's equivalent of the parlement by abolishing the Conseil supérieur (Superior Council) of the main port city, Cap Français, in 1787, denunciations of "ministerial despotism" swelled the chorus of complaints. The polemics inspired by the crisis had a profound impact on those who read the published tracts. When Madame Roland, the brilliant daughter of a Paris artisan, now married to an older man devoted to the cause of reform, declaimed one tract aloud, she found herself "sounding much like one possessed," she wrote, adding, "There is stuff to fill the chest of a stentor and to bring down the ceilings."[6]

Brienne had hoped that the elements of "philosophy" incorporated in the reforms would win support, and that they would drive the king to ally with members of the Third Estate. "Since the nobility and the clergy abandon the king, who is their natural protector," he told one confidant, "he must throw himself into the arms of the commons and use them to crush the other two." Even many of those who sympathized with the spirit of Brienne's measures still opposed the use of the king's absolute power to force them through, however. As one lawyer wrote, "there are now three parties in the realm and in Paris: Royalists, Parlementaires, and Nationals." And "the last two [were] making common cause," even though the "Nationals" had no real love for the judges.[7]

Looming over the debate about the court-reform plan was the ongoing government financial crisis. As the failure of the Assembly of Notables and the resistance of the parlements had shown, no one wanted to take responsibility for helping the government raise taxes. The only solution, as both Brienne and his opponents recognized, was to get the consent of a genuinely representative assembly, one whose authority to make laws and impose taxes could not be contested. Within the framework of the French monarchy, this meant summoning the Estates General, and inviting all of the king's subjects, or at least the men among them, to express their "grievances" and to elect representatives who would debate governmental policy. When Brienne insisted that the king approve the convening of the Estates, Louis XVI exclaimed, "What, Archbishop, you must think we are lost! . . . They might overturn the state and the monarchy."[8]

Despite the king's fears, on July 5, 1788, Brienne announced the drastic step of immediately calling the Estates General. A proclamation issued the next day had the king announce, "It is in the midst of the Estates that I wish, in order to assure forever the liberty and happiness of my people, to consummate the great work I have begun of regenerating the kingdom." Since the last meeting of the Estates General had been in 1614–1615, there was no institutional memory of how deputies should be chosen and what procedures they should follow. Brienne suspended political censorship, inviting anyone who wished to voice an opinion on these questions to do so, a move that unleashed a torrent of new pamphlets. He may well have hoped to delay the actual meeting of the body for as long as he could, and even to demonstrate that consensus on these issues could not be achieved; an observer at the time complained that "he raised endless questions designed to divide the people, to persuade us that holding the Estates had become almost impossible."[9] In the meantime, he also continued to try to cope with the financial crisis through new loans, hoping to buy time and perhaps make the summoning of the Estates General unnecessary.

Unfortunately for Brienne, the monarchy's credit was no longer sufficient to give him the time he hoped for. By the beginning of August 1788, the royal treasury was virtually empty, and no bankers were willing to lend the government more money. On August 16, Brienne announced that the government would have to pay its obligations by printing paper treasury notes that would be redeemed at some future date. The measure was, in effect, a declaration of bankruptcy. "The alarm was universal," the journalist Jacques Mallet du Pan wrote. "The public funds dropped sharply; many people gave up their carriages and some of their domestics. . . . The financial distress was at its peak; only four hundred thousand livres in the royal treasury."[10] There was no choice except to call in the one man who always seemed able to get bankers to lend: Jacques Necker, the finance minister Louis XVI had dismissed seven years earlier.

On his way to Paris the day after the announcement, one traveler "heard the cries of happiness of the inhabitants in all the small towns and villages" as the news of Necker's appointment spread.[11] Through his connections with the world of finance, Necker obtained the short-term loans Brienne had been unable to arrange. The justice minister Lamoignon was dismissed shortly afterward and Necker reinstated the parlements, leaving it up to the Estates General to decide whether to make reforms to the court system. Initially, Necker wanted to convene that assembly as quickly as possible, but it soon became apparent that the effort would take time: there were too many difficult questions about how the elections should be organized to make a date earlier than May possible. In places where movements like the one in Dauphiné to restore or reinvigorate provincial estates had blocked the Notables' plans to create provincial assemblies, Necker gave in to local demands, further eroding the authority of the royal government.

In addition to dealing with financial and political issues, Necker also had to confront the most serious social and economic crisis France had experienced since the last years of Louis XIV's reign—one even worse than 1775, the year of the flour war. The decade of the 1780s had been a hard one for the French population. After many years of increases, prices for crops began to fall around the start of the decade, just as landlords had started a widespread push to raise rents on leases that had been set years earlier on favorable terms for tenants. Landowners were in a strong bargaining position because of the continued growth of the population, which left more poor peasants competing for the chance to rent land; population growth also caused the subdivision of peasant landholdings, leaving many of them too small to support a family. These trends were exacerbated by a cycle of bad weather. In a country whose economy was so dependent on agriculture, the aftereffects of a string of bad years could not be easily overcome. As their income shrank, the peasant farmers who made up the overwhelming majority of the population cut back on their spending, hurting commerce and manufacturing even before Calonne's 1786 free trade treaty with Britain flooded the country with cheap imported goods.

The year 1787 saw a successful harvest, allowing landowners to refill granaries that had been depleted. They also took advantage of the opportunity to export their crops, permission to do so being one of the reforms Calonne had proposed and that Brienne had implemented in June 1787. From the spring onward, unfortunately, 1788 was a disaster for much of the countryside. During the planting season, drought conditions prevailed. Summer brought devastating storms that ruined crops in wide areas. The worst of these, a pelting hailstorm that flattened wheat fields across northern France, struck on July 13, 1788. That was in the midst of the ongoing crisis over the court reforms, just a week after Brienne's announcement of elections for the Estates General. The archbishop of Paris wrote that farmers' losses "are so great, and their situation so deplorable that it has not been possible to overstate them."[12] One did not need to be an economic expert to foresee the consequences that would follow over the next twelve months. Grain would be in short supply, especially in northern France, where both the heavily populated rural areas and the insatiably hungry capital had to be fed. Bread prices would inevitably rise, provoking protests and outbreaks of violence against grain merchants and bakers. As consumers were forced to use most of their income for food, demand for other goods would fall, which would raise unemployment and force businesses into bankruptcy.

The local authorities who were normally expected to maintain order and ensure adequate supplies were in disarray. On August 17, 1788, the intendant of the province of Champagne in northeastern France wrote to Brienne describing the critical situation in the textile-manufacturing center of Troyes: "The journeymen and workers are beginning to grumble, and they are even putting up placards in which they threaten to burn down the merchants who refuse to buy." But the intendant hesitated to act until he received instructions from the government, whose attention was completely absorbed by the financial crisis. In the meantime, tension in Troyes became so acute that the local officials "believed it necessary to establish day and night patrols in order to overawe the evil-minded."[13] By the time the intendant's letter reached Versailles, Brienne, the minister to whom it had been addressed, was gone, leaving local officials with little clue about what they were supposed to do.

It was in these troubled circumstances that the preparations for the Estates General were carried out. Brienne's lifting of censorship restrictions in early July unleashed a cacophony of opinions about how the Estates should be structured and what powers they ought to have. As soon as the judges of the Paris Parlement were allowed to resume their functions, they weighed in with a pronouncement meant to settle the debate. On September 25, 1788, the parlement decreed that the upcoming assembly should follow the "forms of 1614," the procedures followed at the Estates' last meeting. This meant that the three orders—the clergy, the nobility, and the Third Estate—would each have approximately the same number of deputies, and that each group would meet and vote separately. Unanimous support from all three would be needed to pass any laws or approve new taxes.

The judges provided no explanation of their ruling; most likely, they wanted to prevent the king and the ministers from setting their own rules for the assembly. But their intervention backfired badly. Everyone realized that the parlement's decree would give the two privileged orders an ironclad veto against any significant reforms. Hopes for an increased political voice for the Third Estate would be crushed, even though the clergy and nobility seemed prepared to concede that they would pay the same taxes as commoners. As Mallet du Pan wrote, "the public debate has been transformed. Now the king, despotism, the constitution, have become secondary: it is a war between the Third Estate and the two other orders." Madame Roland told a friend that the parlement had left the country with the choice of "vegetating sadly under the rod of one despot, or suffering under the iron yoke of several assembled despots."[14] Reluctant to clash openly with the parlement, Necker and the king decided to reconvene the Assembly of Notables and ask their advice on the procedures to be followed in the Estates General.

Alarmed by the spread of disorder and the radical ideas circulating in the country, the Second Assembly of Notables, which met from November 6 to December 12, 1788, took a far more conservative position on the questions presented to it than its predecessor. Liberal nobles such as Lafayette and the duc d'Orléans were outnumbered by a majority that firmly backed the Paris Parlement. Even as the Notables resisted demands for change, however, members of the Third Estate were becoming more vocal in demanding it. In assemblies in cities and even in some villages, resolutions were passed urging the "doubling of the Third" and equality of taxation. Members of social groups that had previously been content to leave politics to traditional elites now demanded to be heard. In the small town of Limoges, the 72 members who signed a resolution included 22 merchants, 16 lawyers and local officials, 27 representatives of the artisanal trades, and 4 peasants. In the larger southern city of Nîmes, 1,100 people participated in a public meeting.[15]

The province of Brittany, which, like Dauphiné, had maintained its traditional estates, became a battleground that showed how violent the conflict between the privileged groups and their opponents could become. The province had a large population of poor nobles who felt especially threatened by the increasingly wealthy merchants and lawyers of its towns, many of them beneficiaries of the growth of slave trading and overseas commerce. The Breton Estates were due to hold their annual meeting in December 1788. In early October, the municipal council of the provincial capital, Rennes, spoke out strongly for reforms in favor of the Third Estate similar to those that had been adopted in Dauphiné. The movement quickly spread to the other cities of the province; meanwhile, the nobles struck back with a resolution of their own opposing any changes to the provincial constitution. As the two camps hurled pamphlets at each other, local authorities also had to contend with a string of bread riots that affected most of the towns in the region.

Forced to choose between the intransigent Notables and an increasingly powerful movement of public opinion, Necker and the king tried to find a compromise. On December 27, they issued a decision. The Third Estate got its key demand: it would be allowed to elect some 600 deputies, twice as many as the other two orders. Necker also insisted that the Third Estate be allowed to elect deputies who were members of the clergy or the nobility. This provision opened the way for some liberal nobles and clergy to win seats they would otherwise have been denied by the members of their own order. Knowing that these decisions would anger members of the privileged orders, Necker optimistically assured them that "it will never enter the minds of the Third Estate to seek to diminish the prerogatives . . . of the first two orders."[16] Dodging the most controversial question, the royal announcement said nothing about whether the Estates General would meet as a single assembly with vote by head, or as three separate chambers, in which case the doubling of the Third would not enable them to outvote the other orders.

Diminishing the prerogatives of the privileged orders was precisely the aim of the most effective propagandist for the Third Estate, the abbé Emmanuel Sieyès. Like many sons of modest commoner families, Sieyès had studied for the priesthood more because it offered a secure career than out of any sense of religious vocation. For a decade prior to the Revolution, Sieyès was a canon and church administrator for the diocese of Chartres, home of France's most famous medieval cathedral. In his free time, he devoted himself to studying political theory. Like so many of those who would become revolutionaries, he was frustrated to see less intelligent men promoted ahead of him because they had noble status. By 1788, he was ready to join the chorus of critics denouncing aristocratic privilege.

Sieyès's polemical tract *What Is the Third Estate?* put the case against the privileged classes more strongly than any other prerevolutionary pamphlet. "The plan of this work is very simple," Sieyès announced. "We have three questions to ask: 1st. What is the Third Estate? Everything. 2nd. What has it been in the political order up to now? Nothing. 3rd. What does it demand? To become something." Members of the Third Estate performed all the useful work necessary for society to function, he said: they raised the crops, manufactured the necessities of life, and, like Sieyès himself in his church post, did the work for which nobles and church dignitaries claimed credit. The Third Estate, Sieyès wrote, "has . . . within itself all that is necessary to constitute a complete nation." He emphasized the numerical disparity between the 25 million members of the Third Estate and "about 200,000 nobles or priests." Despite their impressive titles, the nobility were nothing more than parasites living off the sweat of the commoners. "If the privileged order were abolished," Sieyès wrote, "the nation would be not something less but something more." The nation, he explained, was "a body of associates living under a *common* law and represented by the same *legislature*." If the privileged orders did not accept these common laws, they thereby excluded themselves from membership in the nation.[17]

Pursuing the logic of his argument that the Third Estate constituted the true nation, Sieyès also insisted that it had the power to disregard all existing institutions. "If we lack a constitution we must make one; the nation alone has that right," he announced. He did offer the holders of privileges a pathway to citizenship: if they were willing to give up all claims to special status and live under the same laws as everyone else, they could, as individuals, become members of the national community. As property-owners, the majority of them would still be better off than most of the population. But Sieyès insisted that any truly national legislature had to consist of only one chamber in which all votes would be counted equally. In contrast to more moderate Third Estate spokesmen, such as Jean-Joseph Mounier, Sieyès meant to defeat the nobility, not to reach a compromise with them. On the subject of the clergy, the group to which he himself belonged, Sieyès was less vehement. He included working parish clergy as part of the Third Estate, although he opposed giving the Church any special political representation.

Sieyès was one of a number of activists who belonged to the "Society of Thirty," a loose network of radical reformers who came together in an attempt to make sure the elections to the Estates General would favor their ideas. The society's membership was a mixture of two main groups: on the one hand, liberal nobles and clergy who were prepared to sacrifice the prerogatives of their order for what they saw as the greater good, and on the other, Third Estate figures eager to seize the opportunity to create a new society in which their talents would give them leading roles. Many members of the Society of Thirty also belonged to Brissot's antislavery group, the Friends of the Blacks, and had developed their ideas about liberty and equality in its debates.

Although the propagandists of the Society of Thirty all shared certain objectives, they differed on the details. What they shared was a hostility to hereditary privilege, as well as a conviction that royal power needed to be put under constitutional control through the establishment of a representative legislature. Sieyès saw little role for the king, who would simply be the head of the government that would be established by the "constituent" or constitution-making assembly he hoped to see convened. Other patriot pamphleteers were willing to concede to the king a greater role, provided he committed himself to a new role as a constitutional monarch and allied himself with the Third Estate. Mirabeau, well aware of how the nobility and the Church had often opposed royal initiatives, promised that if he was elected to the Estates General, he would be "a zealous monarchist" who would work to "restore royal authority" at the expense of ministers and privileged groups. Only a few isolated individuals rejected the whole idea of remaking the French constitution. In his private journal, the marquis de Bombelles, a well-connected courtier, complained that "many of our friends are becoming crazy; anyone who raises his voice in favor of the old forms is dismissed out of hand."[18]

The issues that would divide the country became increasingly clear as the assemblies that were to choose deputies for the Estates General began to convene in early 1789. Brittany remained a flash point. In January, when the Breton Estates met, fighting broke out in the streets of Rennes as domestic servants of the local nobles attacked bourgeois law students. Accounts written by Third Estate supporters denounced "the odious conspiracy of the nobility, this abominable race," and complained that "the Third Estate is nothing, gets nothing, is left with exclusions, humiliations and tax burdens."[19] Third Estate groups from Nantes and other cities in the region hurried to the capital to support their colleagues, and the province nearly descended into civil war. In the end, the Breton nobles never did elect deputies to the Estates General, and the province's Third Estate delegation was one of the most radical, bringing its experience of polarizing conflict to Versailles.

In most parts of France, the election process proceeded more smoothly. The rules laid down by the government allowed almost every adult male to take part in an assembly, but the regulations also underlined the distinctions in status that were fueling the debates about equality all over the country. Nobles holding fiefs—properties with seigneurial rights—could participate personally in their baillage assembly, although *anoblis*, individuals who had not inherited their status, found themselves assigned to the Third Estate. Whereas the rules for the nobility favored the group's more privileged members, those for the order of the clergy had the reverse effect. All parish clergy—the priests, almost all originally commoners, who actually conducted services in churches—had the right to vote personally in the assemblies. They heavily outnumbered the bishops and other members of the church hierarchy, who were usually nobles. Government officials deliberately favored the lower clergy because, as one intendant put it, they were in a position to give "the most accurate picture of the needs and the misery of the people." They also correctly assumed that the often underpaid parish priests would be more willing than their wealthy superiors to give up the Church's tax immunity.[20] Monks and nuns, who often came from noble families, were familiar targets of Enlightenment criticism and were thus limited to one representative per community.

Electoral procedures were more complex for the Third Estate than for either of the privileged orders. One reason was that the ranks of the Third Estate were far more numerous. In the countryside, assemblies were held in every parish. Although all male residents could attend, the need to draw up written *cahiers de doléances*, or statements of grievances, meant that the assemblies were usually dominated by the most literate. The parish assemblies compiled cahiers and chose delegates for a district assembly, which then sent delegates to the baillage assemblies. There, so-called general cahiers were drafted, and then deputies to the Estates General were finally chosen. In towns and cities, guild organizations held their own assemblies, which sometimes witnessed fights between guild masters and journeymen. A general assembly then chose the town's representatives to the baillage assembly. Although almost all male members of the Third Estate had a chance to participate at some level, the multilayered nature of the process acted as a filter that favored the election of the most articulate and educated, especially members of the legal profession. Those finally chosen for the Estates General included no artisans and only one peasant, even though the peasantry made up the overwhelming majority of the population.

The thousands of cahiers drafted by the electoral assemblies constituted an extraordinary survey of public opinion, that phenomenon that had come to loom so large in the eighteenth century's political thinking. There was a clear difference between the parish-level cahiers compiled in village and guild assemblies, which often highlighted concrete local issues, and the more general cahiers from the baillages, which sometimes turned into veritable treatises on political theory. The literate lawyers and others who gained influence as the electoral process moved from its initial stages to the baillage general assemblies unquestionably changed the tone of the Third Estate cahiers, but they did not simply ignore the concerns of the poor and less educated. A statistical analysis of the cahiers carried out in the late twentieth century convincingly showed that the lower-level cahiers reflected genuine peasant concerns, especially their hostility to the numerous seigneurial privileges that affected their daily lives. The clumsily written cahier of the parish of Longnes in the western province of Maine asked for the elimination of taxes on salt and foodstuffs, the ending of noble tax exemptions, and a ban on abuses benefiting the nobles, such as expensive road projects. The Longnes cahier also included requests for closer regulation of millers and harsher punishments for horse thieves. In the northern French village of Silly-le-Multien, the schoolteacher Pierre Delahaye noted with pleasure that the peasants had not hesitated to denounce the damage their local seigneur, the mighty prince de Conti, caused to their crops during his hunts.[21]

The general cahiers from the Third Estate added political and constitutional issues that were rarely mentioned at the village level: demands for elected provincial estates and regular meetings of the Estates General, legal protections for individual freedoms, the abolition of the *lettres de cachet* that Mirabeau had denounced, and the end of various forms of noble privileges. On constitutional matters, the cahiers of the nobility were often in tune with those of the Third Estate: four of the six most frequent demands in both sets of cahiers were the same, including the issues of taxation in general, the creation or revival of provincial estates, regular meetings of the Estates General, and a veto on taxation for that body. Both groups denounced censorship and infringements on individual liberty (such as the *lettres de cachet*).[22] The clergy, too, joined in this critique of the principles and practices of royal absolutism: as Louis XVI had feared, the summoning of the Estates General revealed a generalized demand for representative government.

Where the Third Estate and the nobility differed most sharply was on the issue of noble privileges: both peasants and urban bourgeois elites were hostile to them, whereas nobles, although generally willing to accept equal taxation, defended their other privileges as "property" that deserved to be protected by law. Unlike the liberal nobles of Dauphiné, who had agreed that all their province's deputies should be chosen in a single assembly of all three orders, those in the rest of the kingdom were generally unwilling to endorse voting by head in the upcoming Estates General, which they saw as a dangerous threat to their position. The intransigence of the nobility reflected the strong influence of the group's more conservative provincial members. Issues such as the reservation of military officer posts for their sons and hunting rights mattered more to them than they did to the wealthy grandees at Versailles.

The clergy cahiers differed from those of the other two orders in a number of ways. The cahier of the clergy in the diocese of Digne, in Provence, wanted any issues involving religion that came up in the Estates General to be referred to a general council of the Church. The priests of Digne also wanted stricter policing of drinking establishments, "whose frequentation," they noted, "is so pernicious to religion." They wanted bans on gambling and on fairs on religious holidays, which often turned into raucous popular festivals. Rather than the freedom of the press sought by the other orders, the priests of Digne wanted an end to "the circulation of works against religion and good morals"; they also sought a promise that Protestant rights would still be limited. At the same time, however, their cahier called for social equality within the Church, where "benefices, dignities and ecclesiastical appointments should be acquired solely on merit." Relatively few cahiers from any of the orders made any mention of slavery, but several cahiers from the clergy used explicitly religious arguments to denounce it. "In the eyes of religion the difference in skin colors cannot create any distinction among its children," the clergy of Melun wrote.[23]

In addition to drafting cahiers, the assemblies had to choose deputies. The noble deputies came from the upper ranks of the aristocracy, starting at the top with the duc d'Orléans, a cousin of the king. They included a number of prominent liberals, such as Lafayette and the duc de la Rochefoucauld-Liancourt, who had been members of the Friends of the Blacks and the Society of Thirty. Reform-minded nobles, however, were outnumbered by conservatives, who intended to defend their hereditary privileges. More than four-fifths of the noble deputies had been military officers at some point in their lives and had therefore absorbed a respect for hierarchy and a concern with honor that set them apart from their colleagues from the other orders.[24] The electoral regulations guaranteed that the deputies representing the clergy would be less aristocratic. Given the chance to outvote their hierarchical superiors in the election process, ordinary curés took advantage of their superiority in numbers; three-quarters of the clergy's deputies came from their ranks. The parish priests included the largest group of deputies from genuinely humble social backgrounds, including several sons of artisans and peasants.

Among the 600 deputies from the Third Estate, the dominant groups were those with legal training: 218 of them had held positions as judges or magistrates, and an additional 181 identified themselves as lawyers. By definition, members of these two groups were educated and had a considerable investment in the idea of the law itself as the main instrument for structuring society. Sharing their educational background were several dozen doctors, professors, and men of letters. A few of these had distinguished themselves as pamphleteers during the previous years, but on the whole, men of letters were poorly represented in the assembly; Brissot, for instance, failed to win a seat. The same was true of manufacturers and merchants, cutting against the long-held tendency to regard the French Revolution as a "bourgeois" revolution made in the interests of promoting a capitalist economy based on the free market. Only about 100 of the Third Estate's deputies came from such professions. Most of the Third Estate deputies were economically well off and certainly richer than the peasants, artisans, and laborers who made up the overwhelming majority of the unprivileged population, and quite a few of them had made it to the borderline of noble status and had close relations with members of the aristocracy. They were men who had succeeded under the rules of the existing society, but many were also frustrated that their status meant that "all roads to advancement [were] barred," as Antoine Barnave, one of the leaders of the Dauphiné delegation, lamented in his journal.[25]

The art of political campaigning was new to France in 1789, and it was considered unseemly for individuals to put themselves forward too brazenly. No one violated that precept more flagrantly than Mirabeau. Sure that his talents and his booming voice would make him a major figure, he was prepared to go to any lengths to make sure he would have a seat in the Estates General. He tried to secure a nomination from several different provinces and even negotiated with the wealthy colonists of Saint-Domingue, a possibility that fell through when he learned that he would have to own a plantation with at least fifty slaves in order to represent them. Frustrated by his efforts to win a seat among the nobles, Mirabeau finally turned to the Third Estate of his native Provence, boasting of his rejection by his own order and convincing the electors that, in spite of his aristocratic title, he would be "the man of public liberty, the man of the constitution."[26] He was triumphantly elected to represent the city of Aix.

Mirabeau was not the only one to pour his efforts into the pursuit of a deputy's seat. In the northern French town of Arras, a young lawyer, Maximilien Robespierre, put himself forward as a spokesman for the common people. In doing so, he defied the local municipal officials, who had expected to be elected easily. To outmaneuver them, Robespierre and his allies had to prevail in four different local meetings, starting with the committee of the local lawyers and culminating with the municipal electoral assembly. By contrast, the marquis de Ferrières, who would represent his order in the district of Saumur, claimed that he was chosen "without having sought it, or foreseen it," even though "several richer and more important persons worked hard to get themselves elected." This was not because the contests among the privileged orders were less heated than those among the Third Estate: the nationally known mathematician and writer Condorcet complained that he was blocked by the nobility of Mantes because of opposition from "the aristocrats, the parlement judges, the plantation owners, zealous Catholics and half of the slave-traders."[27]

As the elections proceeded, social unrest continued to rock the country. In late April, violence exploded in the working-class *faubourg* of Saint-Antoine in Paris when a rumor spread that a wealthy elector, the wallpaper manufacturer Jean-Baptiste Reveillon, had said that workers' wages were too high. A large crowd attacked his house in the Saint-Antoine, on the eastern side of the city. "They carried away everything they found, burned the papers, the wallpaper designs and even banknotes, devastated the gardens, cut down the trees," the noble deputy Ferrières wrote to his wife. Elsewhere in the city, crowds "stopped everyone passing by, asked if they were from the Third Estate, and insulted or mistreated those who were nobles."[28] At least sixty rioters were killed; rumors at the time put the death toll much higher. Such outbreaks of violence were a warning that the deputies making their way to Versailles for the meeting of the Estates General would be under pressure not just to approve constitutional reforms, but to convince the mass of the population that something would be done to meet its immediate needs.

The anger that fueled the Reveillon riot was given political expression in a number of pamphlets whose authors claimed to speak for a "fourth estate" made up of those too poor to have had a voice in the electoral assemblies. One radical pamphlet claimed to be a "petition from 150,000 workers and artisans of Paris." It complained that "one can hardly identify, among the 400 electors, four or five who, knowing our needs, our situation, and our sufferings, can take an informed interest in them." This populist current found a particularly eloquent spokesman in the fictitious person of the Père Duchêne, a rough-hewn man of the people who was destined to play a major role in French life for the next ten years. This "gruff, ill-mannered, warm-hearted stove setter" had been invented as a character in a popular play, but now he was co-opted for a wider audience. Given a voice by pamphleteers, he was ready to denounce "the atrocious and criminal abuses that have enslaved and eaten away at us for so many centuries!" Duchêne was styled as a former sailor whose every other word was *foutre* (fuck) or *bougre* (bugger), and the idea of speaking directly to his social betters did not scare him. "If the king is there," he proclaimed, "I'll explain myself with even more assurance." He demanded that the powerful elites respect "the poor man who works tirelessly to feed them, and whom they have the barbarous vanity to treat with disdain," and he laid out a program for the Estates General that included an end to the luxury of the upper clergy, a reformed tax system that would hit the rich "without pity," and laws that would "punish the selfish monopolists, the insatiable hoarders who stuff themselves with wealth at the expense of the indigent multitude." Addressing the deputies, he cried out, "Let wheat be cheaper, and let the worker live. . . . Do something for the subsistence of the poor. . . . That is your first obligation."[29]

The figure of the Père Duchêne, given voice in this case by an obscure writer named Antoine-François Lemaire, would be used by numerous journalists in the years to come to show that the common people were no longer asking for pity but instead had very real demands. In this case, he called for a repeal of Calonne's free trade treaty with Britain and for the institution of a single method of capital punishment for all, regardless of their social standing. Such pleas would be a constant challenge to the wealthier and more educated elites who dominated the Estates General elections. Other pamphlets were similarly challenging. One, titled *Remonstrances, Complaints and Grievances of French Women*, challenged the claim of the Estates General to represent "the whole nation, when half and more of the Nation will not have seats there." The author called for French women to form their own Estates General to put forward their demands.[30]

Over the course of the elections, millions of people had the unprecedented experience of taking part in open debates about the most fundamental aspects of their society. Even after the electoral assemblies finished their work, those who had participated in them remained mobilized. In many towns, committees of electors continued to meet, expecting to receive regular reports from the deputies they had chosen, and ready to remind them of the commitments they had made to push for specific reforms. Hopes were high, but so were fears. Would the king be willing to accept real limits on his power? Nobles worried about the future of their privileges, and clergy feared a backlash against the Church fueled by Enlightenment ideas. Most importantly, however, members of the Third Estate feared that the privileged orders would find a way to stop the movement for equality and ignore their pressing needs, despite the momentum they had gained in the months leading up to the opening of the Estates General. The propertied classes feared the anger of the common people, as expressed in outbreaks like the Reveillon riot and the other disturbances sweeping the country. To satisfy so many contradictory expectations and calm so many conflicting fears would be a monumental challenge.

# 6

# REVOLUTION IN A TENNIS COURT: FROM THE ESTATES GENERAL TO THE NATIONAL ASSEMBLY

*May–July 1789*

On May 4, 1789, the deputies to the Estates General solemnly marched to the church of Saint Louis in Versailles to attend a service marking the opening of the assembly. "If you had seen the king, you would have said, 'How good he is! How joyful he is!'" wrote Jean-François Gaultier de Biauzat, a Third Estate member.[1] Just six weeks later, on June 20, he and the other deputies from that body found themselves locked out of their meeting hall by the king's officials. They responded by taking a dramatic oath not to let any opposition, even that of the king, prevent them from creating a new constitution based on the principles of liberty and equality for France. By the beginning of July, the deputies had carried out a true revolution, claiming power for themselves in the name of the nation they represented. The king's only chance to stop their movement was a resort to force, and the storming of the Bastille on July 14 would demonstrate that he no longer had the means to uphold the absolutist system he had been born to maintain.

Although the financial crisis had forced the king into summoning the Estates against his will, the pageantry surrounding its opening aimed to emphasize not only the authority of the monarchy but also that of the other institutions to which it was so closely tied, the Church and the nobility. The royal master of ceremonies notified the upper clergy that they were to appear in their most splendid ecclesiastical robes. Nobles were to wear cloaks with gold trim and "hats with white plumes in the style of Henri IV"; one noble deputy spent 1,300 livres on his costume. The Third Estate deputies, however, were forbidden to show off and told to purchase somber black cloaks. "The distinction in dress could give the idea that there will be others, either in the method of receiving the cahiers or in the counting of votes," a disgruntled Third Estate deputy wrote.[2]

The commoners defied instructions to group themselves according to their home provinces and instead mingled with their new colleagues from other parts of the kingdom, a gesture that emphasized their claim to speak for a united French people. The huge crowd that lined the streets of Versailles to watch the elaborate parade used the occasion to make a statement of its own. The spectators reserved their most enthusiastic cheers for the simply dressed deputies, who truly "represented the nation," as the Protestant pastor Rabaut Saint-Étienne, a Third Estate deputy, put it. There was an especially warm welcome for "père Gérard," the one peasant deputy, a Breton farmer who wore his crudely tailored Sunday clothes. Among the deputies, Necker's daughter, the brilliant young Madame de Staël, distinguished one man in particular: Mirabeau, whose "great head of hair stood out." It helped him make the impression of "a power such as one imagined in a tribune of the people," she wrote.[3]

The formal opening session, held on May 5, 1789, put the political and social hierarchy of the monarchy on full display. As the deputies took their seats in one of the grand halls of the palace, the Salle des Menus Plaisirs, Louis XVI looked down on them from his throne, with Marie-Antoinette seated to his left. Below the monarchs, on either side of a table reserved for the principal ministers, the deputies of the two privileged orders sat facing each other. At the far end of the hall, opposite the king, were the benches reserved for the representatives of the Third Estate. Around three sides of the hall, galleries allowed as many as two thousand spectators to watch the proceedings. The staging of the session impressed the deputies, but the content did not. The king made only brief remarks. Necker, the finance minister, delivered the main speech, taking three hours to read an explanation of the government's dire financial situation. The marquis de Ferrières, writing to his wife, said the oration was "much beneath what one had the right to expect from a man with such a great reputation." He was careful not to say so to Madame de Staël, however, who was already poised to use her salon to exercise political influence. Necker wanted to avoid falling into the trap that had led to Calonne's failure at the Assembly of Notables, that of seeming to withhold vital information from the deputies. Where he saw an opportunity, Necker tried to demonstrate his and the king's sympathy for good causes. Toward the end of his speech, he denounced the suffering inflicted on the victims of the slave trade, whom "we stuff into the hold of a vessel in order to proceed under full sail to deliver them to the chains that await them," and expressed the hope that France and Britain could work together to end this "barbarous trade."[4] What Necker's speech completely lacked, however, was a plan of action for the deputies to debate, either on the slave trade or any other subject. Above all, he did not address the most pressing issue facing the deputies: whether to meet and vote by head or by order.

On the morning of May 6, when they arrived at the meeting hall, the Third Estate deputies immediately found themselves confronting a momentous decision. The clergy and the nobles were directed to separate rooms to begin verifying their credentials. If the Third Estate agreed to do likewise, it would be acquiescing to the idea that the Estates General consisted of three distinct chambers. Mirabeau immediately made his first decisive intervention: he convinced his colleagues that the only way to compel the clergy and nobility to accept voting by head in a single assembly was for the Third Estate to refuse to take any action in the absence of the deputies from the other orders.

This strategy was not without risks. As the stalemate continued, rumors spread that the king might declare the Estates General a failure and impose his own decrees to deal with the financial crisis. Few Third Estate deputies were genuinely eager for an outright confrontation with the clergy and the nobility, and many responded positively to efforts to negotiate some kind of compromise. The Third Estate delegation from Brittany, the province where hostilities between commoners and nobles had been most violent, led the opposition to such proposals. From the start of the meeting, the Breton deputies held regular meetings to agree on a common position in the debates. Their "Breton Club" soon attracted members from other provinces, particularly those where there had been conflicts during the elections, and began to take on the appearance of an organized faction.

As the stalemate dragged on, the six hundred Third Estate deputies, most of whom had known only a few other colleagues from their local district when they arrived, began to learn each other's strengths and weaknesses. By May 19, when the Third Estate agreed to name representatives to meet with the other orders to seek a solution to the impasse, Adrien Duquesnoy was able to characterize almost all of them: "Rabaut de Saint-Étienne, ambitious, a writer of books, but they say he is moderate and wise . . . Le Chapelier, a very violent madman, an extremist Breton . . . Barnave, gilder of words without great ideas, fairly dangerous." Mirabeau stood out: "This man is a ferocious beast, an *enragé*," wrote Duquesnoy. "He speaks in convulsions, his face is contorted, he spits out his words in a fury." Throughout the month of May, a clear majority of the Third Estate deputies continued to support the moderates. Not all the deputies from the privileged orders were bent on confrontation. At the beginning of June, Ferrières told his wife, "It doesn't really matter to me, in the last analysis, whether we vote in common or separately." Among the clergy, many of the parish priests rebelled against the hard line preached by their aristocratic superiors. Meanwhile, some Third Estate deputies were already talking openly about a unilateral move to break the deadlock. Despite his own personal doubts, as early as May 15 Duquesnoy had written, "I have no doubt that, before the end of the month, the Third will have decided to declare that it alone is the nation."[5]

From the moment the Estates General opened, some deputies turned to the media to rouse public support. Mirabeau was at the forefront of this effort; conveniently enough, his mistress of the moment, Madame Lejay, owned a printing shop in Paris, and she was eager to help him launch a newspaper that promised to help pay for his exorbitant spending. Mirabeau's sometime collaborator Brissot, the activist behind the Friends of the Blacks, saw newspapers as essential if the country was going to make reforms. With newspapers, said Brissot, "one can teach the same truth at the same moment to millions of men; through the press, they can discuss it without tumult, decide calmly and give their opinion." When the government banned the two publicists' initiatives, Mirabeau insisted that he had the right to publish what he called *Lettres à mes commettants* (Letters to my constituents). Many other deputies also sent regular reports back to their home communities, where some of them were printed and sold: Mirabeau's innovation was to publish his letters in Paris and offer them to the public there as well as to his voters in Provence. More or less faithful versions of motions made in the sessions of the three orders were quickly rushed into print in Paris, and by the end of May, Gaultier de Biauzat was complaining that journalists were less concerned with accuracy than with filling their pages.[6]

These early newspapers were overwhelmingly supportive of the Third Estate. Étienne Le Hodey de Saultchevreuil, one of the first independent journalists, denounced the nobles' "wall of pride that tries to halt the torrent of the general opinion." He warned against a maneuver by the clerical deputies to lure the Third Estate into accepting the separate existence of its order: "It's a sneaky trick, characteristic of the clergy. For more than eight hundred years, it has always behaved the same way." Such editorial comments made journalists active participants in shaping public reactions, and the population responded eagerly to their efforts. The English traveler Arthur Young, who found himself in Paris in June 1789, observed the intense public interest in the proceedings and in anything published about them. "The business going forward at present in the pamphlet shops of Paris is incredible," he wrote in early June. "Every hour produces something new. Thirteen came out today, sixteen yesterday, and ninety-two last week."[7]

For those most engaged with the ongoing political struggle, reading printed accounts was not enough. They were impelled to express themselves directly. In the Palais-Royal, the main gathering place in Paris for newshounds, Young saw "expectant crowds . . . at the doors and windows" of coffeehouses, "listening *à gorge déployé* [with their mouths agape] to certain orators, who from chairs or tables harangue each his little audience." He added, "The eagerness with which they are heard, and the thunder of applause they receive for every sentiment of more than common hardiness or violence against the present government, cannot easily be imagined." Those who could manage it—such as the young Parisian lawyer Camille Desmoulins, whose schoolmate Maximilien Robespierre was among the deputies—took public coaches to Versailles and crowded into the public gallery to listen to the Third Estate deputies. Young joined them. "The room is too large," he grumbled. "None but stentorian lungs, or the finest clearest voices can be heard; however the very size of the apartment, which admits 2000 people, gave a dignity to the scene." On the day he attended, he heard an all-star lineup that included an hour-long improvised oration by Mirabeau, delivered with "warmth, animation, and eloquence," as well as speeches by Sieyès, Mounier, Rabaut Saint-Étienne, and Barnave. Young was, however, alarmed that "the spectators in the galleries are allowed to interfere in the debates by clapping their hands, and other noisy expressions of approbation." Such manifestations of public opinion, he feared, could "overrule the debate and influence the deliberations."[8] What Young feared was just what many supporters of the Third Estate hoped for: that by bringing behavior familiar from public theaters into politics, ordinary people could influence the course of events.

Young's visit to the Estates General happened to fall on a crucial day, June 15, 1789, as the Third Estate deputies were on the brink of moving from their parliamentary sit-down strike to a genuine revolution. Representatives of the privileged orders were prepared to yield their special tax privileges, but the majority of both the clergy and the nobility adamantly refused to give way on the question of their separate existence. In both of their chambers, however, a minority was prepared to accept union with the Third Estate, which gave Third Estate leaders hope that if they kept up the pressure long enough, they would eventually prevail. The conservative opposition counted on support from the royal court, where the king's younger brother the comte d'Artois and the queen actively opposed any concessions and worked to undermine the position of Necker, who, for his part, still hoped to find a compromise that would lead to a British-style constitution. The royal family was distracted, however, by a domestic tragedy: on June 4, their oldest son died, making it difficult for the king to give public affairs his full attention.

By the second week of June, even moderates had become convinced that radical steps were necessary to end the deadlock with the privileged orders. At a meeting of the club formed by the Breton deputies, Sieyès offered a plan: the Third Estate would announce a roll call of all the deputies from the three orders and declare that, once this procedure was completed, the resulting assembly would be the sole representative of the nation. The Third Estate, Sieyès's motion proclaimed, "cannot wait any longer for the deputies of the privileged classes without making itself guilty in the eyes of a nation which had an undoubted right to demand from it a better use of its time."[9] The sense of urgency reflected in Sieyès's motion was heightened by the reports the deputies received daily about disorder in the provinces, where riots over bread prices continued. Peasants' nerves were on edge because of rumors about "brigands" supposedly plotting to sabotage the crops in the fields before they could be harvested.

Sieyès's motion had revolutionary implications. The Third Estate deputies were now claiming the power to take action without the consent of the representatives of the other two orders or the approval of the king. If their move succeeded, it would overturn the absolute monarchy and the centuries-old French social hierarchy. For the moment, however, the deputies were simply six hundred men who were, as they very well knew, going well beyond what the electoral assemblies that chose them had authorized. The noble deputies were not impressed: the marquis de Ferrières described the motion as "an insolent act." The first sign that the Third Estate might nevertheless prevail came on June 13. The names of the Third Estate deputies from the province of Poitou had just been read off when three parish priests from that province who were deputies to the clergy entered the hall. "We come . . . led by the banner of reason, guided by love of the public good and the cry of our conscience, to place ourselves with our fellow citizens and our brothers," the curé Jacques Jallet announced. The *Journal des Etats Généraux* helped readers share the emotions of the moment, telling them how "the room echoed with applause; everyone crowded around the curés; tears of joy flowed, they were embraced."[10]

The debate that Arthur Young heard two days later marked a new stage in the unfolding of the parliamentary revolution Sieyès had launched: the issue was the name the deputies would give themselves now that they were no longer merely the representatives of one estate but instead of the whole population. The assembly rejected the cautious Mounier's wordy proposal that they call themselves the "legitimate assembly of the representatives of the larger part of the nation, acting in the absence of the smaller part." When Mirabeau suggested "representatives of the French people," there were objections that the word "people" would confer too much influence on the lower classes, whom even he admitted were "not yet ready to understand the system of its rights and the holy theory of liberty." The deputies finally settled on two simple words: "National Assembly."[11] The meaning was clear: the deputies asserted that they were the sole representatives of the entire French community, leaving no room for particular groups such as the nobility or the clergy or even the king. To underline this claim, the Assembly declared on June 17 that it was "one and indivisible."

What the Assembly meant to do with the powers it claimed became clear on June 17, the day on which, as Sieyès put it, the Assembly definitively "cut the cable" binding it to existing institutions. The deputies, their ranks now strengthened by a number of other clergy who had followed the example of the three priests from Poitou, struck at the heart of royal authority by declaring that existing taxes, which had "not been consented to by the nation, are all illegal." Recognizing that the government needed revenue, the Assembly hastened to add that the old taxes would continue to be collected until they could be replaced by a new system, but it left no doubt that it meant to strip Louis XVI of the power to raise money on his own authority. Furthermore, the deputies "put the creditors of the state under the protection of the honor and loyalty of the French nation," objecting in advance to any move by the king to declare bankruptcy and thus free himself from the Assembly's authority.[12]

An absolute monarch could not let such a direct challenge go unanswered, but the king was slow in responding. In the meantime, his own cousin, the duc d'Orléans, tried to persuade the noble deputies to join the Third Estate. Although only eighty-eight of them supported him, they included some of the most prominent members of their order. On June 19, a majority of the clergy voted to join the National Assembly. When the members of the National Assembly convened on the morning of June 20, however, they found the doors of the Salle des Menus Plaisirs closed. The king had ordered preparations for a "royal session" at which he would announce his intentions. Fearing that the king might be about to dismiss the Estates General or even put them under arrest, the deputies searched for a room large enough to hold them. Eventually they found the king's indoor tennis court, the *jeu de paume*. There, their president, Sylvain Bailly, led them in swearing the "Oath of the Tennis Court," a promise that they would not allow themselves to be dispersed until they had given France a constitution. Defiantly, they announced that "the National Assembly exists wherever its members come together": even if the king succeeded in forcing them to quit Versailles, they would still assert their right to reunite in some other location and continue their work. A delegation of wealthy plantation-owners claiming to represent the colony of Saint-Domingue, who had been seeking admission to the Assembly, seized the opportunity to identify themselves with the patriotic cause by offering to swear the oath along with the deputies; in the heat of the moment, their offer was accepted. The question of whether their inclusion meant putting the institution of slavery under the protection of the nation, and thereby creating a major contradiction that would haunt the Assembly's efforts to guarantee the ideal of liberty, was not brought up.

Inside the royal palace, the king, his ministers, and members of the royal family frantically tried to craft a response to what the king's younger brother, the comte d'Artois, called the "illegality of the deliberation of June 17 and the defiance of the session at the tennis court."

Necker and the ministers closest to him urged the king to avoid a confrontation. If the king took a hard line, warned the foreign minister, the comte de Montmorin, "the Third may not dissolve itself, and then the troubles will reach their peak"; this crisis, moreover, would occur at a time when the government had no resources to combat the rebellious group.[13] But making an alliance with commoners was psychologically impossible for the monarchs, who had spent their entire lives among their fellow aristocrats. All of Louis XVI's education and experience militated against such a gamble, and Marie-Antoinette, who had been included in meetings of the royal council since late 1788, was even more opposed to concessions. Necker, dismayed by the king's intransigence, offered his resignation; he did not accompany the monarch when the royal session was held on June 23.

At the royal session, the king promised some substantial reforms. He assured the deputies that all taxes would henceforth require the "consent of the representatives of the nation," and he implied that there would be regular meetings of the Estates General, although he did not specify how often they would take place. Throughout the kingdom, there would be provincial estates, structured more or less on the model proposed in Dauphiné in 1788. The Estates General was invited to reform the system of *lettres de cachet* and to "investigate and make known to His Majesty the most suitable means of reconciling liberty of the press with the respect due to religion, morals, and the honor of citizens."

Yet even as he offered reforms that went beyond anything he had conceded before, the king also made it clear that he would not accept either the political revolution or the social revolution implied by the National Assembly's declarations. He "declared void the resolutions made by the deputies of the Third Estate on the 17th of this month, and all subsequent ones," and he emphatically asserted that the "distinction of the three orders of the State" remained "inherent in the constitution of his kingdom." He decreed that the deputies of the three orders would deliberate in common "upon matters of general welfare," but insisted that they meet and vote separately on any issues that concerned the privileges of the nobility or the clergy. Recognizing the strength that the new National Assembly drew from the publicity of its proceedings, he prohibited the admission of spectators to the meetings. He reasserted his exclusive command of the military, and he ended with an unmistakable threat, telling the deputies that, "if, by a calamity remote from my mind, you abandon me in so worthy an undertaking, alone I will effect the happiness of my people, alone I will consider myself their true representative."[14]

As many deputies recognized, Louis XVI was resorting to the procedures of a *lit de justice* to override opposition. Once his words had been read, he left the hall, and the royal master of ceremonies, the marquis de Dreux-Brézé, ordered the deputies to disperse. The nobles and the upper clergy obeyed, but the other deputies remained in their seats. Sieyès and the Assembly president, Bailly, addressed their colleagues, trying to convince them that, as Sieyès put it, "you are today what you were yesterday," but it took Mirabeau, with his flair for dramatic improvisation, to find words to restore his colleagues' courage. Speaking directly to Dreux-Brézé, he thundered, "I tell you that if you have orders to make us leave here, you should ask for orders to employ force, because we will only be driven from our places by bayonets."[15] Emboldened by Mirabeau's oratory, the deputies reaffirmed their stand and declared the members of the Assembly immune to arrest.

By the time the king ordered troops to clear the hall, the Assembly had ended its session on its own terms and the news of its actions was spreading throughout Versailles and Paris. "The ferment in Paris is beyond conception," Arthur Young wrote. "The language that was talked, by all ranks of people, was nothing less than a revolution in the government, and the establishment of a free constitution." In Versailles, a crowd surrounded the palace, demanding Necker's reinstatement. Having failed to overawe the deputies, the king was forced to give way. "The royal session only served to make the Third triumph," the noble deputy Ferrières wrote. On the 24th, the majority of the deputies from the clergy joined the Assembly's ranks. When the crowd outside spotted the archbishop of Paris, who was still refusing to do so, stones were thrown at his coach, breaking the windows. Ferrières reported rumors that forty thousand Parisians were coming to attack the recalcitrant nobles; discipline among the Gardes françaises, the military garrison of the capital, was said to be disintegrating.[16] A day later, with the duc d'Orléans at their head, some fifty noble deputies defected from their order and joined the Assembly.

A few court figures still tried to convince the king to stand firm, but by the 26th, he had decided that, at least for the moment, further resistance was impossible. On June 27, the National Assembly was debating yet another act of defiance of royal authority—the admission of deputies representing the French colony of Saint-Domingue, whom the king had explicity excluded from the Estates General—when word of a new development arrived: the monarch had instructed the remaining holdouts among the clergy and the nobility to enter the Assembly even if the mandates from their electors explicitly forbade them to accept vote by head in a single chamber. The question of whether France's overseas slave colonies formed an integral part of the nation was postponed, and the president, Bailly, called on the deputies to "abandon themselves to the joy that a so ardently desired reunion . . . must produce in the heart of all the French." In Paris, Arthur Young, concluding that "the whole business now seems over, and the revolution complete," packed his bags to resume his tour of the countryside.[17]

In fact, as Young and the rest of the world would soon discover, the Revolution was just beginning. Many of the nobles deeply resented the order to join the National Assembly and obeyed it only when the comte d'Artois warned them that the king's life might be in danger if they continued to resist. Still, they did so with "tears in their eyes and rage and despair in their hearts," according to one deputy. Many noble deputies insisted that they had to return home to obtain permission from their electors to ignore their mandates not to agree to a common assembly. The Assembly responded on July 7 by declaring such mandates void and announcing that it would continue its work despite the absence of the noble deputies. And, with the great question of vote by head settled, the National Assembly started on the work of fulfilling its promise to give France a free constitution. On July 3 and 4, the deputies returned to the question they had been debating on June 27, when the arrival of the nobles had interrupted them: Would France's overseas slave colonies be fully included in the nation? The deputies, a number of whom either owned property in the colonies or represented cities dependent on colonial trade, recognized that they were confronting one of the issues that had sparked the American Revolution. "If the British Parliament had admitted colonial deputies, America would still be English," the marquis de Sillery said. The deputy Dominique-Joseph Garat agreed that representatives of the slaveowning colonists should be seated in the Assembly, although he would have liked them to promise "that they will never oppose any effort that the assembly may make to find ways to end this crime as soon as possible."[18] On July 4, in the first recorded roll-call vote in the Assembly, a motion to seat six deputies from Saint-Domingue, was approved. France thus became the first European country to make its overseas territories integral parts of the nation. It was at the price, however, of creating an obvious contradiction between the principles of liberty and equality, on the one hand, and the reality of slavery, on the other.

From the colonial issue and slavery, the deputies turned to laying the bases of the constitution. On July 6, a thirty-man committee was appointed to propose the basic outlines of a new constitution, and on July 9, the Dauphinois deputy Mounier laid out the main issues that would have to be decided. As he had in his native province, the moderate Mounier hoped to incorporate some elements of existing institutions into the new order, even as he recognized there would also have to be fundamental changes. "We will never abandon our rights, but we will know not to exaggerate them," he proclaimed. "We will not forget that the French are not a new people, just emerging from the heart of the woods to form an association, but a great society of 24 million people . . . for whom the principles of the true monarchy will always be sacred."[19]

Just before they listened to Mounier's careful weighing of the issues involved in designing a constitution, the deputies had a sharp reminder that their ability to carry out that project was still not assured. For more than a week, reports had been streaming in that military units were on the march, heading toward Paris from their frontier garrisons. The deputies were particularly anxious because the regiments being assembled were primarily composed of foreign troops, and it was feared that they did not share the enthusiasm for the revolutionary movement that the soldiers of the Gardes françaises in Paris had demonstrated.

Mirabeau put the deputies' concerns into sharp words, as he had so many times before: "As troops advance from all directions, as camps form all around us, as the capital is surrounded, we ask ourselves with astonishment: does the king doubt the loyalty of his peoples?" The deputies were not the only ones fearful about the buildup of troops. A published *Letter of the Ladies of Paris to the Officers of the Camp* asked them, "Would you pierce a pretty breast, caressed by the innocent hands of a little citizen? Would you make our beloved children, our husbands, our brothers, fall at our feet?"[20]

Mirabeau's speech was in response to a statement by the king justifying the summoning of troops to the area: it was out of concern, the king said, about the continuing popular disturbances, and the increasing unreliability of the main force charged with maintaining order in Paris, the Gardes françaises. "There is a spirit of insubordination and independence among the troops that is indeed difficult to control," the deputy Duquesnoy wrote on June 30.[21] Two soldiers from the Gardes françaises had been arrested for disobedience; on June 29, a crowd had freed them and brought them back in triumph to the Palais-Royal. This alliance between the unruly population in Paris and the mutinous soldiers was a sign, from the government's point of view, that it risked losing all control of the capital.

Behind the scenes, conservative courtiers pressed Louis XVI to take decisive action. The Assembly's determined resistance to the king on June 23 had caught him and his more conservative advisers unprepared, but by the beginning of July, a plan was ready. The baron de Breteuil, one of the royal ministers, agreed to take Necker's place, and the baron de Batz, a financial speculator, put together a scheme to issue paper money and raise an emergency loan to provide the necessary funds. On July 4, Breteuil's confidant the marquis de Bombelles wrote in his private journal, "We have the hope of seeing the royal authority reestablish itself for the greater good of this country, for which no other government except pure monarchy is appropriate."[22]

The crucial question was whether the army would obey orders in the face of popular resistance. The royal military commander, Victor-François, duc de Broglie, warned that "if there is an uprising, it will not be possible for us to defend all of Paris." Nor was it clear what Louis XVI planned to do if the National Assembly stood firm and he lost control of the capital. One idea was for the royal family to move to the fortress of Metz in Alsace, close to the border where he might hope to obtain foreign support. Broglie was not persuaded. "Yes, we can go to Metz, but what will we do once we get there?" he asked, doubtful that it would be possible to bring the country back under control if the king abandoned Paris. In spite of Broglie's hesitation, however, on the night of July 11, the plan was set in motion. Necker was abruptly dismissed and ordered to leave the kingdom without passing through Paris or communicating with anyone, and the commanders of the troops stationed in the capital were told to be ready to deal with any protests there. Gaston de Lévis, a noble deputy with ties to the king's brother, the comte de Provence, passed a warning to his wife in Paris: "Don't go out at all tomorrow, there will surely be a dreadful commotion, one can't know how things will go."[23] France would now find out which was more powerful: the ringing words of the National Assembly's resolutions of the previous month, or the bayonets of the king's soldiers.

# 7

# A PEOPLE'S REVOLUTION

*July–August 1789*

O N JUNE 17, 1789, WHEN THE THIRD ESTATE DEPUTIES IN VERSAILLES PRO-claimed themselves the National Assembly, they set a revolution in motion. Despite the radical nature of their actions, however, they had hoped that their movement would succeed without violence. When the king commanded the deputies from the privileged orders to join the Assembly on June 27, those hopes seemed to have been fulfilled. Two threats menaced their hopes for a peaceful outcome to their actions. One was the possibility that the king would resort to military force to dismiss them and restore the absolutist regime; the other was that popular unrest, spurred by the high price of bread combined with fears for liberty, would boil over into uncontrollable violence that would threaten the very foundations of society.

On the night of July 11, both of the deputies' fears were realized. In Versailles, Louis XVI dismissed his chief minister. At the same time, even before the news of Necker's dismissal had arrived, the population in Paris turned to violence, attacking and burning several of the toll gates, or *barrières*, that surrounded the city, where taxes were levied on the food and drink the common people bought every day. Like the king, the people of Paris were ready for a showdown. Using the force of their numbers, they would either make the government take action to meet their demands or else resort to violence to repress them. By the evening of July 14, just three days later, the movement that had begun when the deputies of the Third Estate named themselves the National Assembly was transformed from a revolution of words into a revolution of deeds, and from a movement led by a small elite into a movement of the common people.

Revolutionaries though they were, and focused as they were on the danger from the king and his troops, the deputies were also deeply concerned about the danger of the kind of popular violence the assaults on the Paris toll gates exemplified. As property-owners themselves in a society where the majority of the population lived in poverty, they knew this fear was warranted: the people might undermine the stability of the "common laws" that Sieyès had called the very basis of the nation. Even before the crisis that exploded on July 11, the deputies were aware of the potential contradiction between their desire for a social order based on laws and the popular demand for immediate actions to improve their lives. The letters many of them received from their home districts, telling them of violent disturbances sparked by bread prices and unemployment, were a constant reminder that the population faced problems that were more immediate than the making of a new national constitution. Mirabeau warned that "it is too easy to get [the people] to abandon the constitution for bread."[1]

The contradiction between respect for the law and demands for action had already surfaced in the first important speech given by the deputy Bertrand Barère, a future member of the Committee of Public Safety, which would govern France during the most radical phase of the Revolution. The speech was on June 19, just two days after the proclamation of the National Assembly. On the one hand, Barère acknowledged, the high price of bread was reducing the people to eat "food that is unfit for consumption, unhealthy and insufficient"; on the other hand, the emergency bans on the circulation of grain, meant to keep supplies from being shipped out of areas in need, violated the legal "rights of citizens and landowners" to do as they pleased with their property. Convinced, as a good disciple of the economic theorists of the eighteenth century, that the fertile soil of France must be producing enough food for its population, Barère concluded that the food shortage could only be the result of "the disastrous projects of enemies of the people, enemies of humanity," who needed to be "discovered, intimidated and punished."[2] Speeches like Barère's contributed to fears of conspiracies that helped incite direct popular action.

The reaction to Necker's sudden ouster and the riots at the toll barriers brought together two powerful currents of popular unrest: fear of a royal coup d'état against the National Assembly, and the demand for immediate relief from hunger. By midday on July 12, the news had spread throughout Paris. A crowd gathered at the Palais-Royal, whose arcades, cafés, and shops made it a forum for public opinion. As the news of Necker's dismissal and the violence at the toll barriers flooded in, public opinion turned into public action. In the central garden, groups gathered around impromptu orators. The young lawyer Camille Desmoulins, who had spent the previous few weeks feverishly rushing between Paris and Versailles to keep up with events, climbed up on a table to make himself better heard. He cried, "Citizens, you know that the Nation wanted Necker to be kept in office; he's been chased out! Could anyone insult you with more insolence? After this, there's no telling how far they will go." He ended his oration with a ringing call: "To arms! To arms!"[3]

Around noon, a crowd of several thousand headed into the streets around the Palais-Royal. To show their unity, the demonstrators plucked leaves from the trees in the garden of the Palais-Royal and put them on their hats. The marchers' first action was to demand that the theaters in the neighborhood cancel performances. As the crowd passed the door of another of Paris's attractions, Philippe Curtius's wax museum, where lifelike figures of leading public figures were exhibited, demonstrators stopped to take its busts of Necker and the duc d'Orléans. The latter was seen by some as a possible replacement for his stubborn cousin Louis XVI. The two men's effigies announced a political program: a government headed by men supported by the people.

By 5:00 p.m., the agitated crowd had reached the Place Louis XV, the great square at the western end of the Tuileries Gardens now known as the Place de la Concorde. The gardens themselves were filled with Parisians, many of them members of the city's more prosperous classes: unlike the Palais-Royal, with its prostitutes, the Tuileries was considered safe ground for families and women concerned about their reputation. On this day, however, soldiers and cavalrymen from the regiments recently brought to Paris on the king's orders were assembled at the square. They were ordered to stand their ground as the angry crowd jeered and threw rocks at them. Among those who passed by during this standoff was Thomas Jefferson, the American ambassador to France. Having helped start one revolution, he now became an eyewitness to the beginning of another.

After several hours, the troop commander, the baron de Besenval, tried to stop the disorder by ordering his cavalrymen to force the crowd back into the Tuileries. It was a disastrous mistake: the troops' action gave substance to the rumors that the army was about to be turned loose on the Parisians, even those from the middle classes. The cavalrymen who penetrated into the Tuileries were driven back when the crowd pelted them with heavy stones taken from a nearby construction site. Besenval reported to his superior, the duc de Broglie, that—as Broglie had feared even before the crisis erupted—it would be impossible to restore order in Paris by military force. Besenval then withdrew his soldiers: they would play no role in the events of the next two days. As the real threat from the army diminished, however, the population's fear of an attack worsened. From every part of the city, rumor reported imaginary columns in uniform, ready to massacre civilians.

With the forces of order paralyzed, disturbances continued to spread in Paris during the night of the 12th; by morning, forty of the fifty-four customs barriers around the city had been destroyed. Inside the city, improvised groups organized to maintain order. In the neighborhood around the Palais-Royal, the pamphleteer Brissot helped organize volunteers to guard the royal treasury and the stock exchange.[4] Abandoned by the government and the army, an uneasy coalition of royal officials (led by Jacques de Flesselles, the *prévot de marchands*, a position equivalent to the mayor of Paris) and members of the assembly of electors (chosen the previous April to select deputies to the Estates General) tried to keep control of the city. At dawn, they ordered the churches in the city to sound the *tocsin*, a monotonous tolling of the steeple bells that served as a warning for emergencies. The purpose was to summon members of the electoral assembly to a meeting at the Hôtel de Ville, the seat of the city government, but the sound of the bells brought the entire population out in the streets. Early in the morning, rioters stormed and pillaged the convent of Saint-Lazare. The large quantities of flour and wine they found—stocks that the monks had accumulated so they could carry out their mission of providing charity to the poor—gave substance to accusations that privileged groups were hoarding food in order to drive up prices.

Expecting a military attack at any minute, the crowd demanded weapons. Throughout the day of the 13th, huge throngs gathered at the Hôtel de Ville and even forced their way into the building in search of guns and powder. They confiscated some obsolete museum pieces, including halberds and crossbows, from a royal warehouse, but these were hardly adequate to stand up to a modern army. In the afternoon, a crowd converged on the Invalides, the complex built by France's most celebrated king, Louis XIV, to house retired veterans, but its commander succeeded in keeping them away from its stocks of arms. (The complex now contains the tomb of Napoleon Bonaparte, the man who would later end the Revolution.) At the Hôtel de Ville, Flesselles repeatedly sent groups on what proved to be fruitless searches for arms in other parts of the city. Rumors spread that he was deliberately deceiving the people, trying to buy time until the army intervened.

While Flesselles was trying to cope with the crowd outside the Hôtel de Ville, an emergency committee of members of the electoral assembly was rapidly taking over his powers. Throughout the day, "news of disasters kept arriving with great rapidity," the assembly's official minutes noted.[5] Acting on their own, groups in different parts of the capital arrested and sometimes hanged suspects they branded as troublemakers. The Place de Grève, the large square in front of the Hôtel de Ville, became cluttered with coaches and wagons seized by vigilantes, who insisted that they belonged to conspirators trying to smuggle arms and valuables out of the city.

Many of the electors and city officials surely remembered that just a few years earlier, in 1780, rioting crowds in the British capital, London, had burned and looted much of the city during the so-called Gordon riots, causing immense property damage. How were they to defend the cause of liberty without unleashing the forces of anarchy? The emergency committee decided to form a "bourgeois guard" composed of respectable citizens to replace the royal troops, whom the population no longer trusted, and the spontaneous groups that were springing up in the streets. As the radical Breton deputy Jean Le Chapelier put it in supporting the decision, "it is the people who should protect the people."[6] So that the guardsmen could be identified, they were told to pin a red and blue cockade, a piece of ribbon in the colors of the coat of arms of the city of Paris, to their hats or jackets. This cockade quickly replaced the green leaves the crowd had adopted the previous day as the symbol of the patriotic movement. Although the formation of the National Guard was less dramatic than the following day's assault on the Bastille, it was equally significant. The revolutionary movement now had an armed force of its own, one that thousands of citizens would join in the years to come. Control of the National Guard would be crucial in the power struggles that determined the course of the Revolution.

As dawn broke on Tuesday, the 14th of July, women in Paris went out to perform the daily chore of buying bread for their families at local bakeries. They returned home irate: the price of the loaves that were the basis of the ordinary Parisian's diet had spiked to the highest point in decades. No wonder one of the first chroniclers of the day's events reported that "women made their husbands go out and urged them on, telling them, 'Get going, coward, get going; it's for the king and the country.'"[7] Early in the morning, a crowd larger than any of those on the previous days surrounded the Invalides on Paris's Left Bank. This time, they were determined to seize the thousands of muskets its commander had refused to distribute the day before. The crowd might have been dispersed by Besenval's five thousand regular soldiers, who remained camped a few hundred yards away on the Champ de Mars, but they did not stir. Their officers feared that the men would not fire on the people, and that they might even join them.

Eventually members of the crowd pushed their way into the Invalides. The veteran soldiers refused to fire on the intruders; the crush in the building's basement, where arms were stockpiled, was so bad that people were trampled and nearly suffocated. The watchmaker Jean-Baptiste Humbert, one of those who would soon distinguish himself in the fighting at the Bastille, found that the only way he could get out of the building was to "force a way through the unarmed crowd . . . by threatening to bayonet them in the gut."[8] The guns they seized were passed out freely, with no attempt to restrict them to the respectable bourgeois citizens who were supposed to form the new civic guard. The arsenal contained no cartridges or gunpowder, however. If the Parisians were going to be prepared to mount an effective defense against a possible attack by the army, they needed to get their hands on the barrels of powder stored in the Bastille.

Located in the Faubourg Saint-Antoine, a working-class neighborhood on the eastern side of the city, the Bastille, with its crenellated towers, was a genuine relic of the Middle Ages and a powerful symbol of royal authority. In 1782, when he published a lurid account of his captivity in the Bastille, the dissident writer Simon-Henri-Nicolas Linguet illustrated his story with a striking engraving: it showed a lightning bolt toppling the Bastille's towers while grateful subjects knelt before a statue of Louis XVI in front of the fortress. The message was clear, and also prophetic: if the French were to be free, the Bastille had to be destroyed. Now the moment had come to translate Linguet's image into action.

The Bastille's commander, the marquis Bernard-René Jourdan Delaunay, was aware of the dangers surrounding him and had been preparing for more than a week. Residents of the neighborhood had been able to watch as the gunports in the fortress's towers were enlarged to give its cannon a clearer field of fire, and cartloads of heavy paving stones were carried up to the top of the fortifications so they could be thrown down on assailants. As a crowd began to gather around the Bastille in mid-morning on July 14, Delaunay initially seemed ready to negotiate. He met with several delegates from the municipal committee at the Hôtel de Ville, and even invited some of them to share his breakfast. Delaunay promised that he had no intention of opening fire, but he drew the line at allowing members of the newly formed civic guard to join his troops inside the fortress's walls, and he refused to open its gates to the angry crowd outside.

The crowd swarming around the Bastille came from a very different social universe than the prosperous, educated electors who were trying to maintain a minimum of order at the Hôtel de Ville. Opponents of the Revolution denounced them as a "rabble" drawn from the lowest orders of the city's population, but in fact the majority of them were established residents of the Saint-Antoine neighborhood with regular occupations. In June 1790, 954 individuals—953 men and 1 woman, the laundress Marie Charpentier—were officially recognized as "conquerors of the Bastille." Of the 661 whose professions were listed, the majority were skilled craftsmen—men like the glazier Jacques Ménétra, self-confident and experienced at carrying out collective actions to assert their interests. Alongside the residents of the faubourg on July 14 fought soldiers from the Gardes françaises and deserters from some of the other regiments brought to the city. Perhaps a sixth of the "conquerors" came from the middle class or bourgeoisie, such as the brewery owner Antoine-Joseph Santerre, who would go on to become a major figure in Parisian revolutionary politics. The oldest of the "conquerors" was a man of seventy-two, the youngest a boy of eight.

At around 1:30 in the afternoon, a loud explosion from the Bastille announced the catastrophe the whole city had dreaded for the past three days: the troops in the fortress had opened fire on the crowd. In the confusion at the scene, no one could say who fired the first shot. Members of the crowd had succeeded in forcing their way past the Bastille's outer gate and had lowered a drawbridge that gave access to the inner courtyard. There, they faced the heavily defended entry to the central fortifications and were easy targets for the soldiers posted above them. The sequence of events convinced the attackers that Delaunay had deliberately lured them into the courtyard so they could be mown down by fire from the towers. As cries of "treason!" filled the air, the fighting became more intense. Without artillery, however, the assailants could not blast their way past the main door of the fortress, and the parapets of the towers protected the soldiers from rifle fire. Only one of the soldiers would be killed during the fighting.

Back at the Hôtel de Ville, the municipal committee was at a loss for ideas. Two electors were dispatched to Versailles to alert the deputies of the National Assembly and beg it to take measures to "spare the city of Paris the horrors of civil war." The committee knew, however, that any assistance from that quarter would come too late to affect the course of events. While the committee members dithered, Pierre-Augustin Hulin stepped into action. Hulin, one of the orators who had launched the popular movement at the Palais-Royal on July 12, found two companies of soldiers from the Gardes françaises assembled in front of the Hôtel de Ville and began haranguing them. "Don't you hear the cannon . . . with which the criminal Delaunay is assassinating our fathers, our wives, our children?" he demanded. "Will you let them be slaughtered?"[9]

With Hulin in the lead, the soldiers headed for the Bastille, bringing with them two small cannon taken from the Invalides earlier in the day. They reached the fortress around 3:30 p.m., about two hours after the start of the fighting. There, they joined another group of soldiers, led by an army lieutenant named Élie, and brought their cannon into position for a systematic assault on the Bastille's fortified gate. Inside the fortress, Delaunay realized he could not hold out very long. For a moment, he threatened to detonate the 250 barrels of gunpowder stored in the fortress rather than surrender. Such a gigantic explosion would have destroyed not only the Bastille but the neighborhood around it. His own soldiers stopped him from acting on this impulse and refused to go on firing. When the crowd rejected any terms other than unconditional surrender, Delaunay and his soldiers yielded and lowered a small drawbridge next to the main gate. "The people then showed an unheard-of resolution," one eyewitness reported. "They threw themselves into the moat of the Bastille, used the shoulders of the stronger ones as ladders, climbed on each other's backs. A dozen of the most vigorous, armed with axes, broke the gate . . . two thousand people rushed in, and soon a white flag announced that the Bastille was ours."[10]

The victorious crowd swept through the building, grabbing the weapons the defenders had abandoned and tossing archival documents out the windows. The attackers had expected to find numerous prisoners

*REVEIL DU TIERS ETAT.*

*Ma foimte, il étoit tems que je me réveillasse, car l'opression de mes fers me donnoie le cochemar un peu trop fort.*

AWAKENING OF THE THIRD ESTATE: Figures representing the nobility and the clergy recoil in alarm as a commoner from the Third Estate breaks his chains and prepares to take up arms. In the background, a crowd carries the heads of the Bastille's commander, the marquis Delaunay, and Jacques de Flesselles, who led the city government. Easily understood images like this conveyed the meaning of the events of 1789 even to those who could not read. *Source: Library of Congress.*

and were surprised to find only seven, most of them victims of mental illness being held at their families' request. They were set free and triumphantly paraded through the streets, although at least one of the deranged men had to be incarcerated in another institution the following day. It took several days before the victors convinced themselves that there were no other inmates hidden in secret cells.

The passions stirred up during the fighting doomed the Bastille's commander and several of his officers. Convinced that Delaunay had deliberately lured the attackers into the Bastille's outer courtyard in order to massacre them, the crowd dragged him and the other captured officers through the streets back to the Hôtel de Ville. Hulin, who had led the Gardes françaises soldiers who intervened, tried to protect Delaunay so that he could be turned over to the municipal authorities, but as they reached the building, he was overwhelmed. Struggling to protect himself, Delaunay kicked one of the men surrounding him, an unemployed cook named Desnot, in what Desnot delicately called "the parts." As the cook cried out in pain, other members of the crowd stabbed Delaunay with their bayonets. After Delaunay had fallen, the attackers gave Desnot the honor of decapitating him and putting his head on a pike, crying out that "the Nation demands his head to show to the public."[11]

The unfortunate Delaunay soon had company. Inside the Hôtel de Ville, the hundreds of ordinary citizens who had invaded the building demanded punishment for Flesselles, whom they accused of sending them on futile chases for gunpowder in order to buy time for troops who might come to the rescue of the Bastille's defenders. Flesselles consented to go to the Palais-Royal for an impromptu trial, but he never made it. At the Place de Grève in front of the Hôtel de Ville, a young man put a bullet through his head. Flesselles's head was also mounted on a pike, and the crowd paraded their two bloody trophies through the streets. The killings of Delaunay and Flesselles and the spectacle of heads on pikes were mentioned in almost every one of the dozens of accounts of the day's events: no one could ignore the violence woven into the Revolution from its start.

While some members of the crowd were wreaking vengeance on Delaunay and Flesselles, others were turning the day's events into a story of the triumph of liberty. The playwright Louis-Abel Beffroy de Reigny rushed to the scene to take down testimony from Hulin and several members of the Gardes françaises. He then composed a pamphlet with a long title: "Accurate Summary of the Taking of the Bastille, written in the presence of the main participants who played a role in the expedition, which was read that very day at the Hôtel de Ville." At the site of the fortress, Pierre-François Palloy, a wealthy building contractor who had joined his workers in the assault, immediately began organizing its demolition. In the following days, he led tours of the cells; eventually he had stones from its walls carved into miniature models of the Bastille, which he dubbed "relics of freedom." He sent them to provincial cities, where they were received with great ceremony and put on display, so that all French citizens could feel they had taken part in the epic struggle for freedom.[12]

As darkness fell, the clouds that had covered the sky for most of the long summer day of July 14 turned to heavy rain. Exhausted after seventy-two hours of anxiety and agitation, many Parisians were no doubt relieved by the respite. The thunderbolt of revolutionary action that Linguet had predicted in 1782 had struck the Bastille. Only "legislators and enlightened spirits" had understood the profound significance of the creation of the National Assembly a month earlier, wrote Bailly, who now took Flesselles's place as mayor of Paris, but "the Bastille, taken and razed, spoke to the whole world."[13]

What the violence that swept Paris on July 13 and 14 portended was at first far from clear to the deputies of the National Assembly in Versailles. On the morning of the 13th, as the tocsin sounded throughout Paris, the deputies were trying to grapple with the consequences of Necker's dismissal, and with the appointment of a ministry bent on restoring the king's power that had been announced the previous day. The Assembly declared itself in permanent emergency session, but Mounier opened the discussion on the 13th by urging his colleagues to continue their work on the constitution. Any chance that the Assembly could stay focused on that subject disappeared when a deputy who had been in Paris arrived and reported that the city was "in a terrifying fermentation." As further dispatches came in, the anxiety of the deputies mounted. Several nobles who had previously been reluctant to embrace their new role in the combined assembly rose to exclaim that it was time to put aside all divisions and "unite to save the country." The Assembly sent a delegation to meet with the king and urge him to withdraw the troops he had sent into the capital. Louis's response was anything but reassuring. He stood by "the measures that the disorders in Paris have forced me to take" and insisted he was "the sole judge of what is necessary."[14]

The day of July 14 was even more nerve-racking. The deputies tried again to focus on constitution-making. They managed to appoint an eight-man committee to draft a declaration of rights, and the abbé

Grégoire, the parish priest from Lorraine who was already emerging as one of the most forceful advocates of radical change, strove to assure his colleagues that "it will be in vain if rivers of blood flow, the Revolution will still succeed." As evening fell, however, the vicomte de Noailles hurried in and told the deputies about the citywide insurrection, the seizure of arms at the Invalides, the capture of the Bastille, and the death of Delaunay. "This news produced the saddest impression on the Assembly. All discussion ceased," wrote one journalist.[15] The Assembly sent a delegation to beg the king to recall the troops whose presence had incited the Parisians to resistance, but the king, not yet willing to yield, gave them an equivocal answer.

Anxious deputies remained in their meeting hall all night, in case emergency action was needed. All morning on July 15, the deputies waited for further reports from Paris and for a sign of the king's intentions. Meanwhile, the king, who had entered a single word, "Rien" (Nothing), in his private journal under the date of July 14, indicating that he had not gone hunting, absorbed the significance of the fact that his soldiers "would not fight against their fellow citizens," as the duc de Broglie put it. Finally, Louis XVI decided to address the National Assembly personally. Accompanied by his brothers, the counts of Provence and Artois, he announced that he had ordered the withdrawal of the troops from Paris. For the first time, he referred to the body by the title it had given itself, "National Assembly," instead of calling it the Estates General, and he asked the deputies to send a delegation to Paris to calm the fears of the population.[16]

The deputies were overwhelmed as they heard the king promise to work with them to end the crisis without mass bloodshed. The marquis de Ferrières tore open an already sealed letter to his wife to add to it, telling her how a crowd "drunk with joy" had surrounded the king and his two brothers as they returned to the palace after the king's speech and then cheered as the royal family appeared on the balcony. The delegation of deputies sent to Paris were welcomed with wild celebrations. In his memoirs, Bailly remembered "acclamations and expressions of joy . . . tears, cries of 'Long live the Nation! Long live the king! Long live the deputies!' They were given red, blue and white cockades; people surrounded them and embraced them."[17] The addition of a white stripe to the red and blue cockades improvised on the previous day was a gesture of reconciliation between the monarch and the people: white was the symbolic color of the Bourbon dynasty, which was now combined with the colors of Paris. The cockades, manufactured in silk for the well-to-do and cheaper woolen versions for the poor, became the first of a flood of symbolic objects, such as pottery decorated with patriotic motifs, that advertised their purchasers' support for the revolutionary cause.

The tumultuous welcome they received in Paris on the 15th convinced the deputies that, rather than threatening the social order, the city's population supported their efforts to remake the country. Their confidence in the people's support stiffened the deputies' resolve to compel the king to dismiss the Breteuil ministry and recall Necker. "The prayers of the people are orders," the marquis de Lally-Tollendal, a liberal noble, said during debates on the 16th. At a meeting of the royal council that morning, Louis XVI conceded not only that there was no further possibility of using military force to restore his authority, but that he could not resist the demand for Necker's return, even though it meant accepting the principle that government policies would now be set by the Assembly rather than by the monarch. The comte d'Artois and several court figures closely tied to Marie-Antoinette, including her favorite, the duchess of Polignac, hurriedly packed their bags and fled the country. They were the first of what would become a stream of counterrevolutionary émigrés seeking refuge abroad.

If he was to retain any power at all, Louis XVI had to convince the deputies and the population of the capital that he was prepared to accept his new status as a constitutional monarch with limited powers. With grave forebodings, the king prepared on July 17 to venture into the middle of the city that had driven out his soldiers just three days before. Escorted by a delegation of Assembly members and a huge crowd, he was greeted at the gates of the city by the newly installed mayor, Bailly, who announced that "the people has reconquered its king." As the procession crossed the city to the Hôtel de Ville, the Austrian ambassador, Mercy d'Argenteau, noted that there were few cries of "Long live the king!" but many shouts of "Long live the Nation!" At the Hôtel de Ville, Bailly handed the king a tricolor cockade, and the king stuck it on his hat. Awkward as always when he had to speak in public, Louis XVI managed to assure the crowd that "you can always count on my love," and he was cheered when he appeared on the balcony of the Hôtel de Ville with his cockade. The Portuguese ambassador could hardly believe that he had seen "a king of France in a rustic carriage, surrounded by bayonets and the muskets of an immense crowd of people, and finally obliged to wear on his hat the cockade of liberty." More enthusiastically, Thomas Jefferson called it "an apology such as no sovereign had ever made, or any people ever received."[18]

At ten o'clock that night, Louis XVI finally reached the palace of Versailles, where Marie-Antoinette had been anxiously waiting for him, concerned for his safety. We do not know his innermost thoughts about the extraordinary events the country had just witnessed: seven days that had begun with his attempt to reassert his authority by dismissing Necker, and had ended with the emotional scene of reconciliation at the Hôtel de Ville. As he had been taught in childhood, the king kept his secrets to himself.

The deputies were more voluble. As they realized that the troops that had been menacing them were being sent away, and that the conciliatory minister Necker was being recalled, they hastened to frame the story of the crisis in reassuring and even inspiring terms for their correspondents. A Third Estate deputy, Jean-Antoine Huguet, put it this way:

> It is unique, in the annals of the universe, to see a people, in just five days, arm itself in the greatest order, use force to procure the necessary arms, take and destroy a fortress, the bulwark of despotism; to see, on the fifth day of the Revolution, the ruler whom these hostile actions seemed to threaten, come put on, in the midst of this people in revolt, the cockade that they had taken to obtain liberty for themselves; to see this same ruler receive from this same people the most touching signs of love and fidelity. It was reserved for the French nation to give this example to the universe.[19]

Like most of the deputies, Huguet chose to emphasize the magnitude of the threat the people had faced, the courage with which it had responded, and the reconciliation between king and people with which the crisis had ended. In Paris and Versailles, few dared to describe the events in any other terms. From the safety of the Dutch city of Leiden, the editor of the continent's most respected newspaper used more critical language. In the *Gazette de Leyde*, the crowd in Paris was described as "a vile populace, which, in giving itself over to pillage and to the most awful excess, spread terror and panic everywhere" until it was successfully contained by the armed bourgeoisie. The storming of the Bastille merited only a half-sentence in this report and was overshadowed by the killings of Delaunay and Flesselles. Nevertheless, the paper could not help applauding the final triumph of the National Assembly and the end of the last resistance from the privileged orders. "It is thus that good comes out of the most extreme evils," the account concluded.[20]

Whether they regarded it as a triumph of freedom or a breakdown of order, everyone who experienced the crisis recognized that they had just lived through an exceptional event. Europe's most powerful monarch had been forced to bow to the people and to the authority of an elected assembly. The representatives of the French nobility and the established Catholic Church had abandoned their claims to political privilege and agreed to join in the making of a new society based on the principles of equality and individual liberty. The American Revolution had been carried out by a "new" people on the fringes of the Western world, far from the center of European civilization. With the storming of the Bastille, a revolution was now unfolding at that civilization's very heart. Its consequences would affect not only the twenty-eight million people of France and its colonies, but the entire world.

# 8

# FROM THE "GREAT FEAR" TO THE DECLARATION OF RIGHTS

## *August 1789*

THE TRICOLOR COCKADE, MADE BY PUTTING THE WHITE COLOR OF THE Bourbon monarchy between the red and blue of Paris's emblem in concentric circles, became the symbol of the revolutionary movement. This symbol enshrined the capital's centrality to the Revolution's victory. The French Revolution would not have succeeded, however, if it had been limited to Paris. The response of the rest of the country to the electrifying news of the capture of the Bastille not only consolidated the Parisians' triumph but also accelerated the revolutionary movement, driving the National Assembly to take steps that launched France into a new world that few could have anticipated when the Estates General first met.

Unrest reached extraordinary levels in many parts of the country even before the crisis set off by Louis XVI's dismissal of Necker and the riots at the Paris toll barriers on July 11, 1789. The number of outbreaks of collective violence, usually fewer than ten per month in calmer times, had soared to over a hundred in March and April. After falling off slightly in May and June as the public anxiously awaited action from the Estates General, the number of incidents reached its all-time peak of over a thousand incidents in July; on July 27 alone, the most troubled single day of the entire revolutionary period, there were 145 such episodes.[1] The reports streaming in to royal officials and to the deputies of the National Assembly aroused fears that the very basis of social order was disintegrating.

Governmental authority had already eroded badly even before the dismissal of Necker. The transformation of city government that accompanied the storming of the Bastille, with the ousting of royally appointed local officials, the installation of municipal councils supported by the mass of the population, and the formation of citizen militias to maintain order, was imitated throughout the country. In Brittany's capital of Rennes, news of the disorder in Paris on July 13, the day before the storming of the Bastille, set off a local revolution on July 15. Within four days, four thousand men had been enrolled in the local "national army." "Commanded by simple townsmen, it carries out its duties as regularly as if it were under the orders of the most experienced officers," a local pamphleteer boasted. Recognizing the force of the popular movement, he added, nobles had publicly renounced their privileges and agreed to accept the status of ordinary citizens. Meanwhile, in the larger Breton city of Nantes, rumors that foreign troops were being sent to the region provoked a massive mobilization: thirty thousand men were reported to have taken up arms to protect the city.[2]

The details of the local revolutions in France's cities differed from place to place, depending on how strongly old governing elites resisted sharing their power and how militant outsiders were in challenging them. In the city of Troyes in Champagne, for example, the local magistrates, confronted on July 20 with a crowd they estimated at seven thousand to eight thousand people demanding reduced prices for bread, formed an emergency committee composed almost exclusively of judges and military officers who already held government positions. Over the course of the next two months, popular pressure, culminating in a veritable insurrection on August 28, forced them to yield power to a General

Committee elected by the citizens and dominated by merchants, shop-keepers, and artisans, who had previously been excluded from power. In Strasbourg, the capital of Alsace, the municipal revolution took a violent form. The English agricultural expert Arthur Young watched as a crowd invaded the local town hall and threw "a shower of casements, sashes, shutters, chairs, tables, sophas, books, [and] papers" from the building's windows while troops stood nearby, refusing to intervene.[3]

As Young continued to make his way across the countryside, de-termined to complete the survey of French agriculture he had begun several years earlier, he witnessed the dramatic upsurge of popular ac-tivism that was transforming the peasantry. While townspeople turned against the traditional elites who had governed municipal affairs, the population of the countryside rose up against the seigneurs, the privi-leged landlords who had always dominated rural life. "The whole coun-try is in the greatest agitation," Young noted on July 26. "At one of the little towns I passed, I was questioned for not having a cockade of the Third Estate. They said it was ordained by the Third, and if I was not a Seigneur, I ought to obey." On July 27, the day on which the num-ber of violent outbreaks around the country reached its peak, Young added that "many chateaux have been burnt, others plundered, the sei-gneurs hunted down like wild beasts." One of the noblemen he talked to summed up the situation for him: "He considers all rank, and all the rights annexed to rank, as destroyed in fact in France."[4]

This wave of violence was part of what historians have come to call the "Great Fear," a series of panics that raged across the countryside as peasants heard rumors that brigands in the pay of aristocrats hostile to the Revolution were coming to cut down or burn the crops in the field, threatening to worsen the famine from which the country was al-ready suffering. The rumors started near Paris and other major cities in the days following the storming of the Bastille and eventually reached most of the country. Local officials in the towns helped spread these re-ports. In Mamers, in the Loire region, the authorities had heard that in "neighboring provinces" there were "vagabonds, men without stable jobs who, in order to trouble public security and tranquility, threaten public warehouses, tax collections, and maybe even the property of private individuals." The rioting near Grenoble escalated when the peasants heard rumors that "the king had given permission to burn the nobles' chateaux, but only for three days." In reality, there were no brigands. The truth was that the frightening rumors drove peasants in one small region to band together, and that their own assemblies became the basis for distorted reports in other nearby regions, thus spreading a wave of fear. When the rumors reached the schoolteacher Delahaye's village, he wrote that "the tocsin was sounded twice and the curé ran through the village to gather the men and boys, all armed, a few with guns, the others with pitchforks, pikes, axes, whatever each one could find." Led by the curé, they set off to warn the neighboring villages while the rest of the population brought their valuables to the church for safekeeping.[5]

Although peasants had at best a hazy idea of what had happened since the Estates General had opened in early May, they expected at least a reduction in the various feudal dues they owed to their seigneurs. When no changes in their situation were announced after several months, it was natural for them to assume that the nobility was blocking reforms. The jolt provided by news of the violence in Paris, in whatever garbled form it arrived, galvanized the peasants to take direct action by marching on the manor houses of the local noble landowners. In the western region of Bas-Maine, an estate manager found himself confronted by "an infinite number of individuals . . . armed with guns, pitchforks, pikes and other weapons," who demanded money and "the papers and titles of the seigneurie." Overwhelmed, and "seeing himself menaced on all sides and his life itself in danger," he "begged to be allowed to go to the garden to relieve himself"; permitted to do so, he used the opportunity to flee, leaving the crowd to destroy the legal documents they seized.[6]

Few noble landowners were actually killed during the Great Fear, and the number of noble chateaux actually burned was also relatively modest. But the impact of the wave of peasant uprisings was considerable. The destruction of seigneurs' legal documents left many of them without any proof of the basis for their claims to dues and privileges. The assaults on nobles' homes also had a psychological impact,

demonstrating that the traditional customs of deference to
that had sustained the hierarchical social order no longer h
numbered and acutely conscious that the king and his intendants no
longer had the power to intervene on their behalf, aristocrats recognized
the truth of what Sieyès had said in his pamphlet: a privileged minority
of two hundred thousand could not stand alone against twenty-six million commoners.

As they contemplated the reports of revolts streaming in from the countryside, the deputies were also traumatized by a shocking episode of violence in Paris itself. On July 21, a week after the fall of the Bastille, angry
peasants seized a senior royal official, Joseph Foulon de Doué, who had
taken refuge in a village outside the city. Foulon was accused of having
engaged in speculation that had raised the price of grain. Brought to
Paris, he was being held at the Hôtel de Ville on July 22 when a crowd
gathered and demanded his immediate punishment. The new city leaders installed a week earlier, the mayor Bailly and the National Guard
commander Lafayette, were unable to protect him. Foulon was dragged
out of the city hall, hanged from a nearby lamppost, and then decapitated; his heart was cut out and put on the end of a pike. His son-in-law
Louis Bénigne François Bertier de Sauvigny, the intendant of Paris, was
also lynched by the crowd; before his death, he was confronted with the
severed head of his father-in-law and ordered to "kiss papa."

The witnesses to these killings included the future radical Gracchus Babeuf, who would be executed in 1797 for plotting to establish a
communist regime in France. Babeuf recorded his mixed feelings in a
letter to his wife: "I was both satisfied and unhappy; I said all right and
too bad. I understand that the people want to execute justice, I approve
this justice when it is satisfied with the annihilation of the guilty, but
couldn't it now not be cruel?" The problem, he decided, was that an
unjust society had set a bad example: "The masters, instead of making us more civilized, have made us barbaric, because they themselves
are." Whereas Babeuf had some hesitations about the killing of opponents of the Revolution, Madame Roland wrote to a friend that further

executions were needed to deter its enemies. "If this letter doesn't reach you," she added, "may the cowards who read it blush at learning that it is from a woman, and may they tremble in thinking that she might create a hundred enthusiasts who would make millions of others."[7]

Madame Roland's vehemence was not unusual. An anonymous pamphlet, typical of the cruel and mocking humor that would become characteristic of the Revolution, depicted Hell happily welcoming Foulon, Bertier, and the two earlier victims Delaunay and Flesselles: "What a superb acquisition for [the Devil] in just eight days!"[8] Whereas most National Assembly members had been willing to excuse the killings of Delaunay and Flesselles, which had been committed during the excitement following the storming of the Bastille, the murders of Foulon and Bertier seemed less justifiable. The Dauphiné deputy Barnave, a major Third Estate leader, justified the killings, saying, "This blood that was shed, was it then so pure?" These words would haunt him and the revolutionary movement in general for years afterward. In a few terse words, Barnave had suggested that the stakes in the Revolution justified actions that violated ordinary norms of justice and that there were certain categories of people who might, simply by virtue of their identity, deserve punishment without trial.

Despite Barnave's attempt to justify them, most of the deputies were shocked at the violent killings in Paris and dismayed at the seemingly universal disorder in the provinces. The country had been badly shaken by recent events, and the chaos underlined the urgency of restoring order. They could not look to the king or his ministers for leadership: the royal government remained leaderless until Necker, who had gone home to Switzerland, arrived back in Versailles on July 30. It immediately became clear that Necker could not depend on the support of the Assembly: at Mirabeau's urging, the deputies voted down his proposal to declare an amnesty for those who had helped oust him during the crisis of mid-July. With Necker paralyzed, the initiative fell to the more determined deputies, particularly the members of the "Breton committee." Convinced that the only way to calm the unrest in the countryside was to take decisive action in favor of the peasantry, they crafted a plan for a dramatic gesture: the nobility would renounce their seigneurial rights.

On August 4, the Assembly convened for a special evening session. The vicomte de Noailles, a descendant of one of the kingdom's most distinguished noble families, rose to move that all of his group's tax privileges should be abolished and that peasants should be allowed to buy out the dues they owed to their seigneurs. He was immediately upstaged by the duc d'Aiguillon, who offered a more detailed and specific proposal. "In this century of enlightenment," he told the Assembly, it was time to "establish as promptly as possible that equality of rights that should exist among all men, and which alone can assure their liberty."[9] Like Noailles, d'Aiguillon intended to assure that the nobles were properly compensated for the rights they would lose; he was careful to specify that existing payments should continue until arrangements for reimbursing them were made. Nevertheless, what struck the other deputies was d'Aiguillon's broad reference to equality and liberty and his willingness to abandon the most fundamental privileges that had defined the noble order.

What followed Noailles's and d'Aiguillon's speeches exceeded anything the radical deputies had anticipated when they had planned the session. Once prominent spokesmen for the nobility had offered up their privileges, representatives of other groups competed to make similar sacrifices. Swept along by a rising tide of exaltation, deputies shouted out propositions that were endorsed so rapidly that no one was sure afterward what they had agreed to. The session continued until two o'clock in the morning of August 5. "Never, without a doubt, has any people offered such a spectacle," wrote the Third Estate deputy Duquesnoy. "Everyone offered up, gave, laid at the feet of the nation. I'm a baron from Languedoc, I abandon my privileges;—I'm a member of the estates of Artois, I also offer my loyalty;—I'm a magistrate, I vote to make justice free of charge;—I have two clerical benefices, I vote against allowing anyone to have more than one. No more privileges for the towns; Paris, Bordeaux, Marseille give them up. Great and memorable night! We cried, we embraced. What a nation! What glory, what honor to be French!"[10]

It took a week for a committee to reduce the multiple propositions offered on the night of August 4 to a coherent form. The final version of the decrees began with a sweeping pronouncement that was bound to resonate with the country's restless peasantry: "The National Assembly abolishes the feudal regime entirely." In reality, the deputies, many of whom possessed feudal rights, did not entirely mean what they said: although they abolished rights associated with personal serfdom without indemnity, they made most seigneurial dues "redeemable." This meant the peasants would have to compensate their landlords for the loss of payments they had been entitled to collect. It would soon become clear that, by trying to satisfy peasants without damaging the financial interests of landowners, the Assembly had created a conflict that would prove impossible to resolve peacefully.

Whereas the provisions of the August 4 decrees on the redemption of seigneurial rights reflected a reluctance to threaten the wealth of the landowning classes, other parts of the legislation were more radical. The abolition of tax privileges and the promise that "collection shall be made from all citizens and on all property, in the same manner and in the same form," the basic issue raised by Calonne's proposals to the Assembly of Notables at the beginning of 1787, now seemed simply a matter of course. The nobility's monopoly on hunting was done away with, and the seigneurial courts that had given landlords so much authority over their vassals abolished. The Church lost the tithes that had provided its income and the Assembly committed itself to "providing in some other manner for the expenses of divine worship" and the welfare services the clergy provided, a promise that would propel the deputies into a sweeping reform of the country's largest institution that would have momentous consequences.[11]

The declaration that "venality of judicial and municipal offices is suppressed" implied the end of the parlements and of city governments made up of men who had purchased their positions. "Since a national constitution and public liberty are more advantageous to the provinces than the privileges which some of them enjoy," the Assembly decreed, it would put an end to all special provincial, municipal, and corporate rights and create laws "common to all Frenchmen." Provinces that had enjoyed special tax privileges or the right to trade with foreign countries without paying customs taxes lost those rights. The royal court did not escape unscathed. The August 4 decrees promised a review of the "pensions, favors, and stipends" handed out by the king. One institution clearly inimical to the new notions of liberty and equality that did survive was slavery. Under existing French law, the slaves in the colonies were a form of property, legally purchased and paid for, and none of the slaveowning deputies in the Assembly came forward to propose to give it up. The duc de la Rochefoucauld-Liancourt's proposal that the Assembly at least promise "to take up this matter before it ends its sessions" was ignored.[12]

Even as they did away with almost all the other fundamental institutions that had defined French society for so many centuries, however, the deputies still hoped to make the king their ally rather than their enemy: as the emotion-laden session of August 4 drew to its close, they declared Louis XVI "the Restorer of French Liberty." In the face of the disorder in the country, they still felt the need for some kind of central authority. A few of them, especially Mirabeau, privately thought the sweeping measures offered an opportunity to strengthen the monarchy, since the decrees virtually eliminated the independent power of the nobility, the parlements, the Church, and the provinces, all traditionally obstacles to royal authority. But the deputies also arrogated to themselves two customary royal privileges: "In memory of the impressive and momentous deliberations just held for the welfare of France," they ordered the striking of a commemorative medal, and they decreed that a special Te Deum ceremony, normally reserved for military victories and the births of royal heirs, be celebrated in every church in France.

The deputies hoped that their measures would bring an end to the wave of popular disorder in the country. Their rhetoric about abolishing the "feudal regime" spread the idea that France was truly undergoing a complete transformation. The entire complex of institutions that had existed up to 1789 was now stigmatized as the ancien régime, the "old regime," with the implication that every aspect of the past had been unjust and irrational and now deserved to be replaced. The outlines of the new society were still vague, but the term ancien régime itself was a powerful weapon that could be wielded against individuals, institutions, and even patterns of behavior. Whatever the new order would look like, it would be a society that had been "regenerated," another term that was suddenly on everyone's lips. Carrying religious implications of purification, and biological overtones suggesting rebirth, the idea of regeneration, like that of the old regime, had a dynamic power of its own. Together, the two terms suggested an almost limitless project of transformation that would change not only society but also the very nature of the individuals who composed it.

Whether or not they saw themselves as regenerated, the French peasants, whom the decrees of August 4 had originally been intended to pacify, were certainly ready to bury the old regime and exercise their new rights. "The great news just arrived from Paris, of the utter abolition of tithes, feudal rights, game, warren, pigeons etc., has been received with the greatest joy by the mass of the people," Arthur Young noted on August 12. Later in the month, he observed that "one would think that every rusty gun in Provence is at work, killing all sorts of birds": country folk were taking advantage of their new right to hunt. "In the declarations, conditions and compensations are talked of," Young added, "but an unruly ungovernable multitude seize the benefit of the abolition, and laugh at the obligations or recompense."[13] Seigneurial rights were not the only targets of the disorder, however. In Alsace, which had elected a violent anti-Semite, François Hell, as one of its deputies, peasants turned on the local Jewish population, accusing them of overcharging for the loans they provided. These riots were a warning of the passions that would be aroused by proposals to grant rights to France's Jewish minority.

On August 10, while it was still trying to agree on the list of privileges and institutions that had been abolished on the night of August 4, the National Assembly moved to quell disorder by passing a law making the National Guard, the citizen militia improvised in Paris and other cities during the crisis in mid-July, an official military force separate from the royal army. Guardsmen were to take an oath "to be faithful to the nation, the King, and the law," a formula that put the community of citizens above the monarch.[14] Admission to the ranks of the new force was supposed to be limited to respectable property-owning citizens. "Our bourgeoisie is putting itself more and more on a military footing," one observer wrote, going on to describe in loving detail the elegant and costly uniforms prescribed for those who joined its ranks.[15] The guardsmen were intended to form a bulwark both against the king and the aristocracy and against the restless mass of the population that threatened to drive the Revolution beyond the limits to which the deputies hoped to confine it.

The August 4 session was the third major milestone of the Revolution. The first had been the session of June 17, when the deputies had named themselves the National Assembly and asserted their right to make the country's laws; the second had been the *journée*, or revolutionary "day," of July 14, when the population of Paris had stormed the Bastille and symbolically destroyed the authority of the king. In these three events, what decades of rational discussion of the need for reform had not accomplished was carried out in a surge of emotion. The changes affected not only members of the privileged orders but the entire population. Babeuf, for example, who had made his living drawing up the documents that itemized seigneurs' rights, realized that "the profession of feudal rights specialists is over."[16] Hoping that the enthusiasm inspired by their actions, along with a combination of repressive measures and the promise of a successful new harvest, would bring the widespread disorder in the country under control, the National Assembly turned its attention to what the deputies considered to be their most important task: drafting the national constitution they had sworn to create.

The most enduring accomplishment of the National Assembly's constitutional labors was the Declaration of the Rights of Man and Citizen, which was hammered out in a series of impassioned debates that stretched from the beginning of July to the end of August 1789. In these debates, the deputies struggled to translate the notions of liberty and equality that had been at the heart of political and philosophical disputes all through the eighteenth century into a single coherent statement. Most of the deputies initially thought that creating a declaration of rights would be a straightforward matter. The notion that all men were equally endowed with natural rights was basic to the thought of the Enlightenment, and it had been memorably expressed by Thomas Jefferson in the American Declaration of Independence. The debates about politics on both sides of the Atlantic had produced a broad consensus in favor of freedom of speech and expression, religious toleration, the protection of property, and the need for safeguards against arbitrary arrest and imprisonment. That some form of representative government was the best way to protect these rights was also widely accepted.

By the fall of 1788, leaders of the patriot movement were busy drafting philosophically grounded declarations of rights based on the assumption that "all men are free and equal," as Mirabeau put it in his own proposal. Such a declaration, Sieyès argued, would "imbue the generality of citizens with the principles essential to any human association that is legitimate, that is, *free*." Condorcet agreed that citizens needed to "be aware of their rights." He was also concerned, however, that men might have "errors or false ideas about the nature and extent of their rights." One of his concerns was to ensure that property-owners would be allowed "to make any use of their property that is not contrary to the rights of others." As befitted a onetime collaborator of Turgot, Condorcet saw government restrictions on the grain trade, village rules about farming, and artisan guilds as infringements on individual economic liberty, meaning that his definition of rights was bound to encounter opposition from the popular classes. On the other hand, he stressed the right of all citizens to an equal voice in the political process through participation in elections, a point that did not figure in the American bills of rights that influenced some of the French discussions.[17]

Another former collaborator of Turgot, the economist Dupont de Nemours, shared Condorcet's concern about guaranteeing the freedom of economic enterprise, but the list of rights he wrote into his district's cahier stood out because of its explicit insistence that "everyone in the state of childhood, disability, old age, illness, has the right to free assistance from others," a call for welfare entitlements that went far beyond anything the American revolutionaries had considered. Dupont de Nemours also identified education as a basic right, on the grounds that citizens could not participate fully in civic life if they did not know how to read or write. The most "American" of the participants in the French discussions was Lafayette, who was in close touch with Thomas Jefferson. The distinctively Jeffersonian phrase "pursuit of happiness" appeared in an unpublished draft declaration that Lafayette shared with the American ambassador in June 1789.[18]

Even as some French revolutionaries were expanding the range of issues that might be incorporated into a bill of rights beyond what the Americans had included, others were questioning the wisdom of discussing "superfluous issues of abstract metaphysics," as the deputy Jacques François Laurent de Visme put it. A former colonial official, Pierre Victor Malouet, pointed out that in Saint-Domingue twenty-four thousand white landowners were outnumbered by five hundred thousand black slaves. "It is therefore not permitted to a citizen to excite those five hundred thousand men and to call them to examine and exercise their rights as free men," he insisted.[19] Some Catholics also looked askance at the mania for declaring rights. Many clergy, battered for decades by the philosophes' assaults, feared the consequences that freedom of speech and freedom of worship would have for the Church.

On July 9, 1789, the National Assembly's constitutional committee, headed by Mounier, recommended that the constitution begin with a declaration of rights, but that the drafting of the declaration be postponed until the rest of the constitution had been completed. To give out a list of "arbitrary and philosophical ideas" before working out the other details of the constitution would open the door to demands that the Assembly might not want to adopt.[20] Mounier's report cleared the way for a legislative debate about a declaration of rights, and on July 11, Lafayette, prepared by his private meetings with Jefferson, became the first deputy to put forward an actual proposal in the Assembly. The crisis provoked by Necker's dismissal later that day, however, sidetracked consideration of the matter for several weeks.

During this interval, proposals published by two of the most prominent deputies, Sieyès and Mounier, clarified the issues at stake in defining rights. The abbé Sieyès's proposal was prefaced with a comprehensive treatise on the nature of society. This was in keeping with his argument that a meaningful declaration could not simply present a series of propositions as "articles of faith," but needed to back them up with "reasoning and evidence." His declaration distinguished between what he called "natural and civil rights," those possessed by all members of society, on the one hand, and "political rights," or the right to participate in making and carrying out the laws, on the other. Inventing terms that would play an important role in the subsequent course of the Revolution, he called the first category of rights "passive rights" and the second "active rights." The latter, he argued, could only be given to those who had a real stake in society through their ownership of property. Those who should have only passive rights, in his view, included children, foreigners, and those too poor to pay any taxes. To this list he added women, "at least in the present state of things," a qualification that suggested that their exclusion was not necessarily a fixed principle; he was one of the few male writers who even mentioned the question in 1789.[21]

Sieyès's didactic proposal helped the majority of the deputies recognize what they did not want to see in such a document. They reacted more favorably to the short declarative sentences in the draft offered by Mounier, much of which would, with minor modifications, be incorporated in the final declaration. Mounier's proposal, like Sieyès's, was radical in its affirmations of equality. It declared that "nature has made men free and equal in rights" and said "the law should be the expression of the general will." Its author's caution was reflected, however, in its suggestion that government should not only protect citizens' rights but also "prescribe duties." Mounier's draft included among the rights of man the "honor" that nobles prized, and it insisted that religious freedom should be allowed only insofar as it did "not trouble the public cult" of the Catholic Church.[22]

At the beginning of August, a four-day debate about the declaration revealed deep fissures in the Assembly. Conservatives wanted no declaration at all. The bishop of Auxerre argued that a declaration of rights might be appropriate in a society like that of the Americans, where all citizens owned property and were already equal, but that it was unsuited to France. Malouet foresaw that, in practice, laws would often have to restrict supposedly natural rights. "Why promise men the full extent of their rights when they are only allowed to exercise them within just limits?" he asked. If there was to be a declaration of rights in the constitution, many deputies insisted, it should be accompanied by a declaration of duties. Even the abbé Grégoire, one of the clergymen who was most enthusiastic about the Revolution, supported the idea. "In an insurrectionary moment when the people . . . recovers rights that had been invaded and is reborn to liberty, it can easily go to extremes," he warned. "Show it not only the circle within which it can move, but also the limit that it cannot violate."[23]

In the eyes of the majority of the deputies, however, the proposal to balance the declaration of rights with a declaration of duties contradicted the assertion that men, by their nature, possess natural rights, and that the laws they agree to obey are based on their own consent, not on obedience to religious maxims or blind respect for authority. During the daytime session on August 4, 1789, just prior to the evening session in which the deputies would do away with legal privileges, and following a debate so animated that at times "the speakers could not make themselves heard," a roll-call vote took place. The final tally was 570 against a declaration of duties and 433 in favor of one.[24] The debate itself, meant as a means of unifying the French nation, thus underlined the divisions that would increasingly beset the Revolution as it proceeded.


After the night of August 4, a committee headed by Mirabeau was appointed to assemble a single proposal for a declaration of rights that could be voted on. The committee's proposal, presented on August 17, 1789, met with almost universal condemnation. Mirabeau himself confounded the Assembly, first by proposing to postpone any further discussion of the declaration until after the completion of the rest of the constitution, and then by arguing for the right to bear arms, an idea that had not been mentioned in any of the numerous proposed declarations circulated since the start of the year, and that would not be included in the final declaration. Discouraged and frustrated, the deputies decided to scrap the Mirabeau committee's proposal. Instead they turned to a discussion of a much shorter and less controversial proposal that had been drawn up by the Sixth Bureau, one of the groups into which the Assembly had been divided to facilitate debate. "The draft lacked energy," the deputy Gaultier de Biauzat later remarked. "But this was a much less dangerous defect than the errors that we had seen in many other projects."[25]

On the next day, the legislators began going through the proposal article by article and immediately decided that its language was too flat and uninspired. They wanted a statement that would, as the deputy Duquesnoy put it, speak "to all eras and to all peoples."[26] Suddenly, an eloquent paragraph that Mirabeau had proposed as a preamble in the committee draft took on a new appeal. "The Representatives of the French People," it said, "having constituted themselves as a National Assembly, concluding that ignorance, forgetting, or disregard for the rights of man are the only causes of public misfortunes and the corruption of governments, have resolved to set out, in a solemn declaration, the natural, inalienable, and sacred rights of man." The sonorous words clearly announced the purpose of the document. To satisfy the more religious deputies, the Assembly added a phrase stating that they were acting "in the presence and under the auspices of the Supreme Being." The Assembly then moved on to the basic articles defining individual rights and the role of government in protecting them.

Like Mirabeau's preamble, the propositions adopted were clearly and forcefully worded: "Article 1: Men are born and remain free and equal in rights. Social distinctions can only be justified if they are useful to the community. Article 2: The purpose of any political association is to protect the natural and imprescriptible rights of man. These rights are liberty, property, security, and resistance to oppression. Article 3: The basis of all sovereignty resides essentially in the nation. No group, no individual can exercise any authority that does not expressly derive from it." Article 4 defined liberty as the right to do anything that did not harm others, and Article 5 specified the circumstances under which individual liberty might be restricted by law. In a few sentences, the declaration outlined a theory of government as an agreement among free and equal citizens, defined the rights that the constitution was to protect, and asserted that only a representative government could claim legitimate authority.

A particularly heated debate broke out over the wording of what became the declaration's sixth article, which dealt with the crucial question of how Article 3 would be carried out. Article 3 promised that only the nation could exercise the sovereign power to make laws. Charles Maurice de Talleyrand, an aristocratic bishop destined for future notoriety as Napoleon's foreign minister, proposed a paragraph that wove together the promise of representative government and the question of equal access to government positions. His opening sentence, "The law is the expression of the general will," echoed Rousseau's controversial *Social Contract*, although the concept of "general will" was so widespread in eighteenth-century French political thought that Louis XVI himself had used it in the summary of absolutist principles he copied out as a young teenager. The article then stated that "all citizens have the right to participate personally or through their representatives" in the making of laws. By declaring themselves the National Assembly, the deputies had already asserted their right to act on behalf of the voters who had chosen them, but Article 6 held out the theoretical possibility of a direct democracy in which citizens would participate personally in the lawmaking process. The article would also be cited by colonial slaveowners, who used it to insist that no changes could be made to their rights without their consent.

Talleyrand's Article 6 continued by declaring that the law "must be the same for all, whether it protects or punishes," thereby barring any return to the special laws and privileges that had characterized the old regime. The last sentence of the article was the most contentious. It promised that, since all citizens were now legally equal, they would all be "equally eligible for all honors, appointments, and public positions, according to their capacities, and without regard to any distinction other than that of their virtues and their talents." The sticking point for many deputies was the phrase "according to their capacities," put forward by Mounier. Did it simply mean that no one should be eligible for a public office unless he had the ability to perform its functions, or was it a way of reintroducing a form of aristocracy by requiring a certain background or level of wealth for some appointments? "No motion suffered so many amendments, no session was ever so stormy," one chronicler commented.[27] After much sound and fury, the article was approved with Mounier's amendment, but the violence of the debate showed how easy it would be to rouse fears about a return of special privileges that would violate the ideal of equality.

There was much less controversy about the next three articles of the declaration, which laid down guidelines concerning arrests, judicial procedures, and punishments. A main goal was to rule out arbitrary practices such as the *lettres de cachet* that Mirabeau had famously denounced before the Revolution. Suspects could only be indicted or arrested if they had violated a law that existed at the time of the supposed offense. They were to be presumed innocent until found guilty, and punishments were limited to what was "clearly and obviously necessary." The deputies also declared, however, that "any citizen summoned or seized according to the law must obey immediately": they did not intend to undermine respect for law and order.

If there was consensus about judicial rights, there was none with regard to the next two articles, which dealt with religious freedom and freedom of expression. The draft declaration from the Sixth Bureau strongly endorsed the necessity of religion and of a "public cult" or state-supported church. Its grudging concession to the idea of religious liberty provided only that "any citizen who does not disturb the established cult should not be restricted." Advocates of religious freedom vehemently opposed this wording. The comte de Castellane proposed replacing the Sixth Bureau's article with a single sentence: "No one should be harassed for his religious opinions, or restricted in the practice of his religion." Mirabeau denounced the notion of toleration itself as "tyrannical . . . since the existence of an authority with the power to tolerate violates the liberty of thought, since what it tolerates, it might also not tolerate." "It would be hard to imagine the cries, the murmurs, the intrigues, the declamations that this project excited," the deputy Duquesnoy wrote in his journal.[28]

The debate continued more vehemently than ever during a long session on the following day. One deputy, the marquis de Clermont-Lodève, insisted that "without religion, it is useless to make laws, rules[;] one simply has to commit one's life to chance." In the longest speech of the debate about the declaration, the Protestant spokesman Rabaut Saint-Étienne replied that there could be no distinction between the rights of the majority and those of religious minorities. "Your principles are that liberty is a common good, and that all citizens have an equal right to it," he said. "Liberty must then belong equally and in the same manner to all the French." Going beyond the issue of his own group, he made the first appeal in the Assembly for rights to be granted to the Jews, "this people torn out of Asia, always wandering, always proscribed, always persecuted for almost eighteen centuries." Rabaut's views failed to carry the day: his colleagues instead adopted what Duquesnoy called a "detestable" and "absurd" article stating that "no one should be disturbed because of his opinions, even about religion [*même religieuses*], provided that their practice does not disturb the public order established by the law." The word for "even" (*même*) seemed to suggest that religious ideas did not really deserve the same protection as others. Although Duquesnoy regretted the article's timidity, he admitted that one reason the majority had voted for it was that "the tolerators made their demands with a heat and an activity that was a little intolerant."[29] As his comment suggested, the eagerness of some revolutionaries to establish complete religious freedom risked convincing the Catholic Church and its supporters that the Revolution was a campaign against them.

Deputies concerned about the limits on religious freedom in Article 10 were somewhat mollified by the wording of Article 11, which established freedom of the press but made it "subject to responsibility for abuse of this freedom in cases determined by law." An intervention by the young lawyer from Arras, Maximilien Robespierre, made it into the parliamentary record: "You should not hesitate to emphatically declare the freedom of the press. Free men are never permitted to pronounce their rights in an ambiguous manner." His colleagues would soon learn to recognize Robespierre's uncompromising devotion to his principles. Many Catholics did not see freedom of the press in such a positive light. "How much has religion suffered from the attacks that licentious writings have made on it!" the bishop of Amiens exclaimed.[30] On this point, however, the conservative members of the clergy found themselves isolated, and the article passed easily.

Having defined the individual freedoms that citizens were to be guaranteed in the constitution, the deputies now turned to a series of articles justifying certain constraints on them. Article 12 declared that "the protection of the rights of man and citizen requires a public force." Article 13 drew the logical consequence that taxes were necessary to pay for that protection and for other government functions, so long as the burden was "shared equally among the citizens, according to their means." When one deputy proposed wording that cast taxes in a negative light, by calling them "a portion taken away from private property," Mirabeau replied that taxes were "the price you pay to possess your properties."[31] Article 14 gave the citizens "the right to ascertain, by themselves or through their representatives . . . the necessity of the general tax, to freely consent to it, to know how it is used, and to decide on its rate," thus asserting the principle that there should be no taxation without representation. Article 15, which said that "society has the right to require every public official to account for his administration," provided a legal basis for citizens to hold members of the government accountable if they violated the laws.

After nearly a week of sessions devoted to the declaration, the deputies were eager to finish the job. Their working document included an article on the separation of powers, a reflection of the ideas of Montesquieu and the American constitution-makers. The Assembly adopted the proposed wording as Article 16: "Any society in which the protection of rights is not assured, or the separation of power is not determined, has no constitution." This statement barred any return to the principles of absolutism that Louis XV had so memorably enunciated in the "flagellation session" at the Paris Parlement in 1766.

At this point, many of the deputies were ready to turn to other aspects of the constitution. Some of them, however, still wanted to insert other articles into the declaration. Only one of them succeeded: the parlementary magistrate Adrien Duport, who proposed declaring that property was "an inviolable and sacred right." Article 17's defense of property led many critics, particularly the nineteenth-century socialist Karl Marx and his followers, to criticize the Declaration of Rights for elevating economic rights over other aspects of liberty. Duport's article, however, also made property the only right of which individuals could be deprived: it included a provision for eminent domain, the appropriation of private property for "public necessity," with appropriate compensation. At the time, the Assembly's decision to cut off discussion of the declaration on August 26 was not meant to preclude the addition of other articles. On August 27, the deputies voted to "recognize that the Declaration of the Rights of Man and Citizen is not finished," with a promise that they would consider adding to it when the rest of the constitution was completed.[32]

Although the deputies thought they would revisit the Declaration of the Rights of Man and Citizen later on, the preamble and seventeen articles they had approved immediately took on a life of their own. Quickly translated into other languages and distributed throughout Europe and North America, the document became the authoritative statement of the principles of the French Revolution. By the time the Assembly finally completed the rest of the constitution in August 1791, the thought of changing it had already become inconceivable. According to the deputy Jacques-Guillaume Thouret, "this declaration has acquired . . . a sacred and religious character. It has become the creed of all the French, it is published in every format, it is posted on the walls in all public

DECLARATION OF RIGHTS: In this allegorical engraving, the National Assembly's Declaration of the Rights of Man and Citizen separates the sunlit world of liberty from the dark realm of feudal rights and privileges. *Source: Bibliothèque nationale de France.*

places and even in the homes of peasants; it has been used to teach children to read."[33]

Once uttered, the words of the Declaration of the Rights of Man and Citizen changed the world. Although the course of the Revolution would lead legislators to replace the original declaration with not just one but two modified versions, a more radical one in 1793 and a more conservative one in 1795, the basic principles articulated in 1789 endured. All three declarations taught Frenchmen to regard themselves not as subjects obligated to obey a superior authority, but as rights-bearing citizens equal to one another and entitled to a voice in making the laws under which they lived. Once this idea had been broadcast as an official pronouncement in the name of the nation, rather than simply philosophical speculation, it proved impossible to eradicate entirely from the minds of people around the world. Both for the French and for the inhabitants of other countries, it became a definitive statement of natural rights. The declaration's seventeen articles explicitly contradicted the basic premises underlying absolute monarchy and the hierarchy of social privileges that had characterized the old regime. Even those who rejected constitutional government and individual freedom, such as the conservative monarchs of nineteenth-century Europe and the totalitarian dictators of the twentieth century, would have to come to terms with it, publicly refuting its premises rather than simply ignoring them.

At the same time, the Declaration of Rights forced its own supporters to confront new questions. That the document's wording would encourage claims the deputies had not considered became clear even before its drafting was completed. On August 26, 1789, the Jews of Paris became the first group to cite the language of the declaration to seek rights for themselves. Addressing the deputies, the petitioners asserted that "in returning man to his original dignity . . . you have not meant to make any distinction between one man and another; this title belongs to us as to all other members of society; the rights that derive from it thus belong equally to us." Representatives of the free men of color in the French colonies made similar arguments, and the doctrine of natural rights clearly threatened the basis of slavery. The issue of women's rights was never mentioned in the debates, given the all-male body of legislators, but women were among the spectators in the galleries at Versailles, and some of them no doubt thought that they, too, deserved equal rights. Satirical pamphlets inspired by the declaration raised questions about sexual freedom: one, claiming to speak in the name of the prostitutes of the Palais-Royal, argued for their right "to do anything they want with their bodies," and therefore to practice their trade openly; another cited "the success of the Rights of Man" to defend homosexual acts.[34]

The issue of how inclusive the declaration's definitions of "man" and of "rights" were was only one of the questions the document raised. The deputies had been concerned to maintain a balance between the affirmation of individual liberty and the need for order. But would the citizens whose freedom they had promised to protect be ready to acknowledge laws passed by their representatives as expressions of their own will that needed to be obeyed? Or would they cite their right of "resistance to oppression" to justify opposition to laws they did not like? In a society with such a yawning gulf between rich and poor, would the mass of the population accept the document's emphasis on property rights, or would the poor insist on the "right of subsistence" that had already been spoken of during the flour war in 1775, but that was not mentioned in the declaration? Even as it fixed the principles of the new order that would replace the old regime, the Declaration of Rights opened new issues for debate.

# 9

# CONSTITUTION-MAKING
# AND CONFLICT

*September–December 1789*

THE DECLARATION OF THE RIGHTS OF MAN AND CITIZEN WOULD COME to be regarded as the most important statement of the French Revolution's principles. Nevertheless, the debate over its provisions divided and exhausted the deputies, leaving them eager to move on to the substance of the new constitution. Within a few months, they defined the major features of a new system of government that would, they hoped, effectively protect the individual liberty now guaranteed to all citizens and give them a real voice in making the laws under which they would live. At the same time, they began tackling other urgent questions, from how to solve the financial crisis to how France's territorial divisions might be reshaped. Their answers to these questions had profound effects on every individual and community in the country.

At every step, the revolutionary legislators were forced to take the reactions of the population into account. The public's hopes had been raised by the extraordinary events of the previous few months, but its fears had also been ignited. Now able to follow events more closely than ever through the political press, the public was also able to intervene through new local governments and participation in the National Guard. Peasants rejoiced at the prospect of the abolition of feudal dues, but they worried that landlords might find ways to protect their interests. Members of the bourgeoisie celebrated the end of noble privileges, but they wondered whether aristocrats would accept the end of their special status peacefully. Changes in the status of the Church were profoundly unsettling for the clergy and for much of the population. The urban and rural poor demanded bread, and citizens of all classes were troubled by the disorder that continued to disrupt daily life.

While expressing satisfaction that the National Assembly was moving from abstract theoretical questions to practical ones, the deputy Duquesnoy noted that his colleagues were splitting into opposing groups. "The room is divided in such a way that, in one part, one finds men who sometimes, without a doubt, have exaggerated opinions but, in general, have a high idea of liberty and equality. . . . [T]he other part is occupied by men whose less idealistic ideas and less firm opinions give them a character of weakness, of caution, very regrettable in present circumstances," he wrote.[1] The deputies who supported the Revolution sat on the left side of the meeting hall, while their opponents occupied the seats on the right; the terms "left" and "right" soon became the recognized labels for progressives and conservatives that continue to be used around the world.

As the differences among the deputies became clearer, like-minded legislators began to form clubs in which they could come together outside the Assembly to plot strategy with their allies. Many of the "patriot" radicals had participated in the club formed by the Breton deputies earlier in the year. Once the Assembly moved to Paris in mid-October 1789, the group rented a meeting room conveniently close to the legislature's new hall. Officially, the group called itself Les amis de la constitution (The Friends of the Constitution), but they became better known simply as the "Jacobins," because the Jacobin religious order had leased the space to them. Membership was at first limited to deputies, but within a few months it was opened also to ordinary citizens, provided they could afford the relatively steep dues. Meanwhile, the patriots' rivals created their own organizations. The more moderate among them, identified as *monarchiens*, defenders of the monarchy, saw themselves as working to replace absolutism with a British-style constitutional monarchy. They therefore supported the Revolution's early stages. A more conservative group of deputies was known as the *noirs*, or "blacks," because many of them had originally been representatives of the clergy and wore black robes. The noirs openly opposed the basic principles of the Revolution and hoped for its collapse.

The debate about whether the king should have the power to veto laws passed by the assembly of the people's representatives became the first focus of the disagreements among these factions. The monarchiens, led by the Dauphiné lawyer Joseph Mounier and several liberal nobles, accepted the idea that the king needed to share power with a legislature representing the will of the people. But, in their view, the king needed to have real authority to maintain public order and to oppose ill-considered laws. Still chairman of the Assembly's constitutional committee, Mounier used his position on August 28, 1789, a day after the conclusion of the debates on the Declaration of Rights, to put forward a proposal that gave the king the right to veto laws he opposed.

The debate over the king's veto went to the heart of the question of what was meant by Article 3 of the Declaration of Rights, which said that "the basis of all sovereignty resides essentially in the nation." If the elected deputies of the National Assembly truly represented the nation, the "patriots" asked, by what right could a single individual, even the king, reject their decisions? The issue was particularly explosive, because the king had not yet accepted either the August 4 decrees or the Declaration of Rights itself. "The nobles and the clergy want to make use of the veto to have all of our reforms rejected," one nervous deputy wrote. In response to the monarchiens' proposal, Parisian radicals at the Palais-Royal proclaimed themselves a "patriotic assembly" and warned conservative deputies that "fifteen thousand men [were] ready to set their chateaux and their houses alight" if they persisted in their efforts.[2] On August 30, a crowd even tried to march to Versailles to pressure the Assembly. Lafayette, the commander of the Paris National

Guard, dispersed the demonstrators, but the incident reminded the legislators that a restless population was watching closely and could easily turn on them.

The debate about the royal veto clarified the distinction between the constitution and ordinary laws. If the king had the power to veto the constitutional laws that set limits on his power, the Revolution would indeed be undone. Even Mounier agreed that "the king has no consent to give to the constitution; it is anterior to the monarchy." But the monarchiens considered the king's power to veto ordinary laws as a necessary safeguard against an elected assembly that might pass hasty measures under the pressure of an excitable populace. Sieyès, however, insisted that any kind of veto would be "a *lettre de cachet* launched against the national will, against the entire nation."[3] In the middle stood a number of deputies who proposed what they called a "suspensive" veto, giving the king the right to delay laws, but only for a certain period of time. Advocates of this compromise argued that it would allow the people to make the final decision. If they then reelected deputies committed to overriding a royal veto, it would be clear what they wanted.

Before they finally resolved the veto issue, the deputies took up another major question: Should the future national legislature consist of just one chamber, or, like the British Parliament and the United States Congress, of two houses that would both have to approve proposals before they became laws? Concerned that a one-house legislature would be too vulnerable to public opinion, the monarchiens wanted a "senate," whose members would be named for life, to balance an elected lower chamber. To their opponents, this amounted to the restoration of a privileged aristocracy that could stand in the way of the will of the people. Tempers flared to the point where "an f-word came out of the mouth" of one speaker, setting off a "universal tumult" that brought debate to a halt.[4] The resort to swearwords in the midst of a debate about a major constitutional issue undermined the notion that the deputies were being guided only by reason as they struggled to draft the constitution. Even so, the monarchiens' proposal was defeated. Altogether, 849 of the 1,060 deputies voted for the creation of a one-house legislature. Those who helped to pass the measure included a number of noirs, who

hoped to discredit the Revolution by encouraging its m⌣
tendencies.

On September 11, at the end of a debate that dragged on until 4:⌣
a.m., the Assembly gave the king a suspensive veto. He would have the
power to make three successive legislative assemblies pass a law before it
could go into effect over his opposition. No one was satisfied with this
outcome: radicals objected that the king could obstruct the will of the
people, even if only for a certain number of years, whereas conservatives
claimed that a suspensive veto was not enough to maintain a genuine
balance of powers between the monarch and the legislature.

The debates about the royal veto and the creation of a bicameral
legislature inflamed public opinion, especially in Paris. The high bread
prices that had provoked agitation throughout the year continued to
weigh on the population as they waited anxiously for the results of the
new harvest. Moreover, the many artisans in the capital who depended
on aristocratic customers suffered as their clients stopped spending or
even fled the country. The king's refusal to declare his acceptance of the
August 4 decrees and the Declaration of Rights left a cloud of uncertainty hanging over the direction of the Revolution. The government's
financial crisis continued to worsen: the breakdown of order meant that
taxes were no longer coming in, driving the Assembly to appeal to citizens to make voluntary contributions to keep the government solvent.
Delegations of women offering their jewelry, students donating their
silver shoebuckles, clergy sacrificing treasures from their churches, and
Jews hoping that their contributions would help win them rights visited the Assembly to make "patriotic gifts," but they were not enough
to cover the government's needs. Mirabeau felt compelled to denounce
proposals to resolve the financial crisis by declaring bankruptcy, which
some legislators had come to see as a way of making the rich pay while
sparing the rest of the population. "Will you be the first to show the
world the spectacle of a people assembled in order to betray the public
trust?" he demanded.[5]

In Mirabeau's own mind, his success in talking the National Assembly into taking the unpopular decision to approve more borrowing showed what could be achieved if only a strong leader was given

the necessary authority. Mirabeau's evident ambition was to persuade Louis XVI to embrace the Revolution and to appoint a chief minister—himself, of course—who, unlike the cautious Necker, could dominate the legislature. In this endeavor he encountered obstacles from all sides. The king deeply distrusted the rebellious nobleman who had done so much to undermine royal authority in June and July. Mirabeau's fellow deputies were equally suspicious of a man who, after leading the defiance of the king at the royal session of June 23, had later defended an absolute royal veto. Mirabeau enthusiastically embraced media-driven politicking by creating a newspaper, the *Courrier de Provence*, which was very successful. This, and his demonstrated ability to rouse crowds, deepened the fear of his less talented colleagues that he might gain power at their expense. Behind the scenes, Mirabeau was trying to establish direct contact with the king and queen to offer them advice on how to bolster royal power within the framework established by the Revolution. Had they known this, the other deputies would have been even more reluctant to trust him. When popular violence broke out in Paris on October 5, 1789, leading to an armed march on Versailles, many suspected that the ambitious deputy must have somehow had a hand in provoking it.

Although Mirabeau and the Assembly's radicals profited from the "October Days," it was the women of Paris who played the major role in the second of the Revolution's journées. In addition to their anxiety about the price of bread, the women who began gathering outside of Paris's city hall early on the morning of October 5 were agitated by the latest news from Versailles. For the first time since the July crisis, the king had summoned a unit of foreign soldiers, the Flanders regiment, reviving fears that he planned military action against the Revolution. On the evening of October 1, officers of the king's bodyguard gave a banquet to welcome the newcomers. The royal family briefly appeared to greet the participating officers, who responded with cheers of "Long live the king!" The reports about the banquet that circulated in Paris depicted it as a veritable counterrevolutionary orgy: regaled with food and drink by the court, the military officers had supposedly adorned themselves with white and black ribbons, symbols of the Bourbon and Habsburg dynasties, and trampled on revolutionary tricolor cockades.

By 8:00 a.m. on October 5, a crowd of angry women began to form in front of the Hôtel de Ville, the site of the Paris city government. Prominent among them were the *dames de la Halle*, the tough and determined marketwomen from the city's wholesale food market, a group that traditionally expressed the sentiments of the city's working population on public occasions. The women called on the city fathers to authorize a march of the National Guard to Versailles to demand punishment of the aristocratic officers who had insulted the national colors; they also wanted immediate action to increase the city's food supply. Recognizing Stanislas Maillard, a National Guard captain who had helped storm the Bastille in July, they called on him to lead their protest, telling him that "the men were not strong enough to be revenged on their enemies and that they (the women) would do better," as Maillard recalled the following year.[6]

By the time Lafayette, the National Guard commander, arrived at 11:00 a.m., some women had already set out for Versailles. They recruited others they found in the streets to join them and armed themselves with "broomsticks, lances, pitchforks, swords, pistols, and muskets." Maillard, who tried to persuade them to leave their weapons behind, estimated their number at seven thousand to eight thousand. The mood of the armed male National Guards at the city hall was also turning mutinous. Not only did they make it clear to Lafayette that they would not fire on "women begging for bread," but many of them wanted to join the march. Until the middle of the afternoon, Lafayette remained at the Hôtel de Ville, trying to calm the crowd. But by this point, in spite of a cold rain, thousands of Parisians were heading for Versailles, carrying whatever weapons they could find and dragging along some of the National Guard's cannons. A "prisoner of his own troops," as an American observer put it, Lafayette finally decided that he had no choice but to join the throng himself.[7]

As the crowd began to arrive in Versailles in midafternoon, some of the king's advisers urged him to take flight, but the opportunity passed before the monarch could make up his mind to act. The demonstrators flooded into the National Assembly's meeting room, disrupting its proceedings. "Soon the hall was filled with drunken women, who danced, climbed up the president's desk, [and] embraced him," the scandalized Duquesnoy wrote in his journal. Madeleine Glain, a forty-two-year-old housewife, demanded the deputies' attention and told them that the women "were asking that they not be lacking bread." A delegation of women were admitted to present their demands for bread to the king himself. "His Majesty answered them that he was suffering at least as much as they were, to see them lacking it," said the lacemaker Marie-Rose Barré, according to a summary of her testimony the next year; he promised to see that grain shipments to Paris were protected.[8] The king met with Mounier, the presiding officer of the Assembly, and finally agreed to accept the August 4 decrees and the Declaration of the Rights of Man and Citizen. By the time Lafayette reached Versailles, the king's concessions seemed to have calmed the situation. The main problem appeared to be finding food for the hungry marchers, many of whom had not eaten all day, and places for them to sleep.

As dawn broke on October 6, marchers who had spent the night in Versailles began to force their way into the palace. When the royal bodyguards tried to drive them out, violence exploded. Two bodyguards were killed and decapitated, and Marie-Antoinette, fearing for her life, fled from her private bedroom in her nightgown. Lafayette persuaded the National Guardsmen to protect the royal family, and he had the bodyguards affirm their loyalty to the nation by putting on tricolor cockades. But he made it clear to the king that the only way to prevent further bloodshed was for the king to agree that he and his family would immediately move to the capital. The crowd cheered the king when he appeared on the palace balcony to make the announcement, but no one knew how they would react to the queen, whom many Parisians regarded as the Revolution's main opponent. It took considerable courage for her to show herself on the balcony. When she did, she was accompanied by Lafayette, who risked his own popularity by bowing and kissing her hand. The crowd's anger subsided enough to bring the crisis to an end, but the queen was deeply shaken. "No one would ever believe what has happened in the last twenty-four hours," she told her Austrian confidant Mercy d'Argenteau when she was finally able to write to him.[9]

By midday, the royal family had completed its hasty preparations, and the huge mass of protesters, National Guardsmen, and courtiers began a slow march to Paris. As they trudged along, the crowd called out that they were "bringing back the baker, the baker's wife, and the baker's boy," a reference to the king, the queen, and the little heir to the throne, whose presence in the capital would supposedly guarantee the supply of bread. They also carried the severed heads of the two royal bodyguards they had killed that morning, a grim warning of the fate that awaited those who opposed the Revolution. Popular engravings of the October Days throughout the country highlighted the extraordinary role women had played in the event. Several showed the victorious Paris marketwomen suggestively straddling the barrels of National Guard cannon. Some depictions singled out a striking-looking young woman named Théroigne de Méricourt, whose flamboyant red riding jacket stuck in witnesses' minds. De Méricourt, originally from Belgium, was one of a number of foreigners who had been so inspired by the outbreak of the Revolution that they had moved to Versailles to follow the National Assembly debates in person. As the Revolution progressed, she would become one of the leading activists calling for women to take a direct role in politics, but she would also become a leading target for misogynist attacks.

The idea that women's actions had forced a decisive reversal of the relations between the king and the people underlined the degree to which the Revolution was putting fundamental aspects of French society into question. The initiative women had taken during the October Days was so disturbing that many men preferred to believe that a good part of the crowd had been men disguised in women's clothing. Men who could not bring themselves to accept that women could intervene so forcefully in politics would have been even more upset if they had read two manifestos published soon after the October Days. One of them declared that men, "with their systems of equality and liberty, with their declarations of rights, . . . leave us in a state of inferiority, truly, of slavery." In addition to demanding political representation, both these pamphlets called for equal marriage rights between husbands and wives; one even wanted a reform of the French language, so that "the masculine gender will no longer be regarded, even in grammar, as the more noble." The journalist

Brissot, who applauded the political results of the October Days, stayed true to his Rousseauist principles about the distinct roles of the sexes, a view shared by many male revolutionaries. Brissot insisted that once the Assembly relocated itself to Paris, women should be banned from its public galleries. "They can only create a spirit of frivolity there, cause distractions and throw the discussions into disorder," he opined. "We are still too childish to debate in front of women."[10]

The effect of the women's march on the October Days was to force both the king and the National Assembly itself, which moved to Paris along with the monarch, to recognize the power of the people of the capital. The royal family was now installed in the Tuileries Palace in the center of the city, a building that would be destroyed in another Paris uprising, the revolt of the Commune in 1871. After moving to the city, the Assembly began holding its sessions in the nearby Salle de Manège, the royal riding hall. The king and the deputies were now dependent on the municipal government of Paris to guarantee their safety. This meant relying on Lafayette and on the city's Assembly of Representatives, even though Lafayette could barely control his National Guard, and the Assembly of Representatives faced pressure from activists like the rabble-rousing lawyer Georges Danton, who supported a kind of direct democracy at the local level.

Some of the more conservative deputies found the thought of being so closely surrounded by the easily aroused Parisians threatening. Mounier, labeled "Monsieur Veto" in the press, because of his stand during the debate about the king's powers, retreated to his native province of Dauphiné. He thus became the first of many politicians who, after initially supporting the revolutionary movement, found themselves stigmatized as counterrevolutionaries when they decided it had turned too radical. Others saw opportunities in the new situation, however. Madame de Staël, the daughter of the minister Necker, was one of these. Exercising a more traditional form of female influence on politics than the women who had marched on Versailles, she brought men from different groups into her salon for conversations. These included men from the Third Estate, "distinguished by their intelligence and their talents," as well as "gentlemen more proud of their merit than of the privileges of their group." As she liked to recall later, as a result of her hospitality, "the greatest questions that the social order ever gave rise to were treated by the minds most capable of discussing and understanding them." The king and queen were less assured about their safety and the course of the Revolution than Madame de Staël and her friends. Outwardly, Louis XVI tried to give the impression that he now accepted his position as a constitutional monarch; secretly, he sent a "solemn protestation" to his Bourbon relative, the king of Spain, denouncing "all the acts contrary to royal authority that have been extracted from me since last July 15."[11]

At first, Lafayette appeared to be the major winner from the October Days crisis: he had succeeded in limiting the violence at Versailles while prodding the royal family into moving to Paris. But Lafayette's initial efforts to stop the march to Versailles on October 5, and his intervention to protect the royal family on October 6, made the more radical patriots distrustful of him. In any event, he lacked the temperament to seek power for himself. Mirabeau had no such scruples, but rumors that he had worked to inspire the October Days hurt his already dubious reputation. On November 7, Mirabeau's rivals in the Assembly blocked his ambitions by passing a decree that prohibited sitting deputies from serving as royal ministers: France's constitutional monarchy would not imitate the British system, in which royally appointed ministers managed Parliament while also directing the government. Ostensibly, the National Assembly's decision was justified as a way to protect the separation of powers required by Article 16 of the Declaration of Rights, but everyone understood that it was aimed at Mirabeau. "An eloquent genius directs you and subjugates you," the deputy Jean Denis Lanjuinais told his colleagues. "What would he not do if he were minister?"[12]

With Lafayette unwilling and Mirabeau unable to take control of the revolutionary movement, new personalities took leading positions in the Assembly and the clubs. Among the patriotic members of the Jacobin Club, a "triumvirate" of young deputies, Antoine Barnave, Adrien Duport, and Alexandre Lameth, emerged as leaders. Barnave, originally a close collaborator of Mounier's in the Dauphiné provincial movement barely a year earlier, was a talented speaker who did not hesitate to measure himself against Mirabeau in the Assembly debates. Duport, a young magistrate from the Parlement of Paris, had turned against that institution and played an important role in the Society of Thirty. Lameth, less active as a speaker, was a skillful behind-the-scenes politician. Devoted to making the Revolution work, the "triumvirs" had little patience for what they saw as the doctrinaire democratic positions that Robespierre and a handful of other radicals defended. The Jacobin leaders also had to deal with opposition from the right. Despite the defection of their recognized leader, Mounier, the monarchiens still had a number of effective speakers, such as Malouet. On the far right, the abbé Maury, a Catholic priest with experience as a preacher, was a powerful presence at the podium.

As it turned out, the October Days would be the last major upsurge of popular violence in the capital until the summer of 1791; after months of nearly continuous turmoil, the deputies could now resume their work on the constitution under calmer circumstances. Although the Assembly no longer had to fear direct popular pressure after its move to Paris, the deputies now found themselves closely scrutinized and pressured by new media called into existence by the Revolution: the political press and the politicized theater. The first revolutionary newspapers largely confined themselves to reporting what the deputies did, condensing hours of confused debate to brief summaries; even so, it was soon evident that their editors, by the choices they made about which speeches to emphasize, and the language in which they described events, were actively shaping their readers' reactions. The deputies themselves quickly recognized the indispensability of these printed news bulletins, which spared them the effort of composing their own summaries of the debates for their friends and supporters back home.

The storming of the Bastille transformed the revolutionary press. Throughout the summer and fall of 1789, dozens of new periodicals tried to satisfy the public's insatiable appetite for political news and polemics. The weekly *Révolutions de Paris*'s breathless description of the taking of the fortress, featured in its first issue on July 19, showed how journalism could make readers feel they were in the heart of revolutionary action: "The fury was at its height, no one cared about death or danger . . . Numerous women helped us with all their strength. Even children, after each salvo from the fort, ran here and there to pick up the cannonballs. . . . We pressed ahead, we reached the staircase, we seized the prisoners, we penetrated everywhere. . . . This glorious day should astonish our enemies, and promise us the triumph of justice and liberty."[13] The journal's epigraph—"Those above us look powerful only because we are on our knees. Stand up!"—captured the essence of the extraordinary events it recounted.

Not only did the new papers plunge readers into the rush of events as they happened, but they were also far more outspoken than their old-regime predecessors. Typical was Brissot's *Patriote français*, whose motto was "A free newspaper is a sentinel always on watch for the people." Intent not only on reporting the news but also on telling readers what to think about it, Brissot did not hesitate to lecture deputies who, in his view, did not properly understand the principles of democracy. He also used his paper to continue the campaign against slavery that he had launched in February 1788, when he had founded the Society of the Friends of the Blacks. In his view, the liberty for which the French were fighting needed to be universal.

No other journalist had as much impact as Jean-Paul Marat, an older man previously known primarily for his attacks on established medical and scientific authorities. His *Ami du peuple* (Friend of the people) quickly attracted attention for its vehement denunciations of deputies and officials whom Marat accused of trying to subvert the Revolution. He also became known for his criticism of the people, whom he chastised for their failure to "demand without let-up the punishment of public enemies." Marat outdid all other journalists in his zeal to expose hidden opponents of the Revolution and denounce their indifference to the sufferings of the common people. Other revolutionaries worried that his unceasing vilification of all but a handful of the movement's leaders, and his open celebration of violence—the privileged orders would never have given up their rights "without the bloody scenes that followed the storming of the Bastille," he wrote in his first issue—would make stability impossible. Within a few weeks of the launch of Marat's newspaper, the newly installed municipal government tried to shut him down for criticizing one of its officials. It was only the first of many brushes with the authorities that let him pose as a persecuted martyr. Other "patriot" journalists were reluctant to condemn him, fearing that to do so would open the door to an imposition of limits on their own activities. "I regard him as a good citizen who goes too far out of an excess of zeal," the woman journalist Louise de Kéralio wrote to Brissot.[14] Marat's provocations changed the boundaries of revolutionary discourse and made him a genuine force in political life.

By the time another celebrated pamphleteer, Camille Desmoulins, began his own weekly newspaper, the *Révolutions de France et de Brabant*, in late November 1789, so many other periodicals had already started up that he complained he could hardly find a title that wasn't already taken. Whereas Marat was consistently pessimistic about the prospects for the Revolution's success, Desmoulins started with a hopeful attitude. The reference to the Belgian province of Brabant in his title reflected optimism that the revolt against Austrian rule that had recently broken out there was a sign that the principles of the French movement were spreading beyond the country's own borders. Desmoulins promised to treat the news with a sense of humor; it was the only characteristic he shared with the creators of the *Actes des Apôtres* (Acts of the Apostles), a sharply satirical counterrevolutionary title whose denunciations of the Revolution were as violent as Marat's polemics. Its contributors included several well-known poets and wits as well as the revolutionary leader Mirabeau's own brother.

Between the extremes of the pro-revolutionary left and the anti-revolutionary right, other newspapers promised an impartial account of the news. The most important of them, started in November 1789 by the publisher Panckoucke, became the Revolution's generally acknowledged newspaper of record. Twice the size and price of other newspapers, Panckoucke's *Moniteur* had the space to give a full transcript of the Assembly's debates, rather than just a summary. Reading rooms and cafés made newspapers accessible even to those who could not afford private subscriptions. A German visitor to Paris, Johann Heinrich Campe, observed how workers in Paris would find "one of their comrades, who possesses the rare advantage of being able to read," and have him read the latest news out loud to them.[15] In the provinces, village priests and local officials performed the same function, sometimes translating papers into the local dialect. By the early fall, revolutionary politicians were acutely aware that their every move was being watched and criticized by an audience spread throughout the country and even beyond.

The collapse of censorship made the stage another powerful venue for the spread of political ideas. Marie-Joseph Chénier, who had been struggling for several years to get his play about the massacre of the Protestants on Saint Bartholomew's Day in 1572 staged, achieved his ambition in November 1789. The play, *Charles IX*, recounted the story of a French king lured into committing a crime by a foreign-born queen, and a Catholic prelate preaching murder in the name of religion. Answering critics who warned that it might cause a public disturbance, Chénier replied, "If it is dangerous to make fanaticism and tyranny detestable; if it is dangerous to make virtue, laws, liberty, tolerance admirable, let me boast that there are few works as dangerous as 'Charles IX.'"[16] Another frustrated playwright who was suddenly able to gain a hearing was Olympe de Gouges, whose abolitionist drama *Mirza and Zamore*, in which a black slave escapes punishment after killing a white man, provoked a riot at the end of 1789. The play launched de Gouges as a one-woman media phenomenon: for the next four years, she bombarded Parisians with theater pieces, pamphlets, wallposters, and public speeches. Like journalists, actors willing to take a political stand became celebrities overnight: when his older colleagues at the Comédie française declined to take leading roles in Chénier's and Gouges's plays, the young François-Joseph Talma stepped in and quickly became the era's most famous performer. His adoption of Roman togas in place of elaborate eighteenth-century costumes for plays set in antiquity helped promote the cult of classical republicanism. It also helped him forge a friendship with another ambitious young man, the military officer Napoleon Bonaparte, that would pay off handsomely after the Revolution.

Watched closely by journalists after their move to Paris and acutely aware of the passions that could be aroused in the theaters, the king and the deputies continued their confrontation over the country's future. The October Days gave the deputies more leverage over the king, who now promised to accept the fundamental decisions they had taken in August, but the women's march reminded them that an angry crowd could still intervene decisively in the political process. When a Paris baker accused of holding bread off the market was lynched outside his shop on October 20, 1789, in a riot in which women again played a major role—one of them tied the noose around the victim's neck—the Assembly reacted by passing a law authorizing the imposition of martial law to stop riots. The deputy Robespierre, already identified as the leading spokesman for the interests of the common people, objected strenuously to a measure that aimed to "push back the people" instead of addressing their complaints about high food prices. The more conservative Duquesnoy, in contrast, longed for a "violent blow to reestablish order," adding, "A clearcut explosion is needed, some people who form themselves into a mob need to perish."[17]

From Robespierre's point of view, things became even worse on the following day, when the Assembly decided to limit the right to vote in elections to men who paid taxes equivalent to the value of three days of an ordinary laborer's wages. A higher qualification was set for members of the electoral colleges, who would choose legislators, and an even higher one, the so-called *marc d'argent*, for future deputies themselves. Following an argument advanced by Sieyès, this rule created a distinction between "active" citizens, who would have the right to vote and hold office, and "passive" ones, who would be subject to the law but could not participate directly in making or enforcing it. Rising again in defense of the poor, Robespierre charged that the measure "could easily erect an aristocracy of the rich on the ruins of the feudal aristocracy." For him, the exclusion of poorer citizens from the right to vote violated the basic principle of equality enshrined in the Declaration of Rights. A year and a half later, in March 1791, he was still demanding to know how "the law can be termed an expression of the general will when the greater number of those for whom it is made can have had no hand in its making."[18] Robespierre's position has become basic to modern definitions of democracy, whereas open advocacy of property qualifications for voting has disappeared; in practice, however, Sieyès's distinction between "active" and "passive" citizens often seems to more accurately describe how modern-day societies function.

By the standards of the time, the voting law was actually fairly inclusive: somewhat more than half of the adult male population, including much of the peasantry, qualified to vote, although the number eligible to be chosen as deputies was only around seventy-two thousand. Because the urban poor were less likely than peasants to pay the required amount of direct taxes, the proportion of passive citizens in cities was higher than in the countryside. In the Faubourg Saint-Antoine, the heart of revolutionary Paris, only 12 to 14 percent of the residents qualified for voting rights. Under the law, those who could not vote were also not eligible to serve in the National Guard, the citizen militia that was now tasked with keeping public order. In the capital, especially, the division the law created between the wealthier, active citizens and the rest of the population was a constant provocation to the ordinary men and women who had stormed the Bastille in July and forced the king to accept the Revolution and move to Paris in October. The journalist Marat's populist denunciations of a system that favored "the capitalists, the bankers, the speculators . . . the merchants, the retailers, those who live on their investments, more concerned with their fortunes than with liberty," while denying a political voice to "the little people, the only decent part of the capital," had an obvious appeal.[19]

Even as the majority of the deputies to the National Assembly voted for a system they thought would defend the rights of property-owners, another of their decisions changed the ownership of much of the land in the kingdom and set in motion a sequence of events that would create a divisive conflict about religion. On November 2, 1789, at the conclusion of an emotional debate that had lasted nearly a month, the deputies voted by a narrow margin—510 to 345—to put the property of the Catholic Church "at the disposal of the Nation." By abolishing the tithes and payments to clergy for performing religious rituals as part of the August 4 decrees, the National Assembly had committed itself to funding the Church. To do so, the deputies needed to find a source of revenue, making the Church's property an obvious target. Talleyrand, a prorevolutionary bishop, had formally proposed the measure on October 10. Born into an aristocratic family but barred from traditional careers, including the military, because of a club foot, Talleyrand was one of many members of the clergy suspected of having gone into the Church despite having no real commitment to religious concerns. According to his optimistic calculations, selling off the Church's assets would not only provide enough revenue to raise the income of most parish priests, but also enable the government to pay off its existing debt.

The effects of the expropriation and sale of the church lands, begun the following April, were felt in every corner of France. "What a change this single decree and the consequences that it is necessarily going to have are going to make in . . . the arrangements of all kinds that have existed in France for many centuries," Adrien-Joseph Colson, a lawyer employed to manage one nobleman's estate, wrote to his client.[20] The Church owned more than 10 percent of all French real estate, including rural land leased out to farmers and many choice urban properties. The income from its holdings supported schools, hospitals, orphanages, and other institutions as well as churches, convents, and monasteries. The government would now have to decide which of these establishments it would still support, thus involving itself in the internal affairs of an institution that held deep meaning for much of the population.

Most of the French clergy had initially welcomed the Revolution; a former court preacher, Claude Fauchet, had delivered the eulogy for the revolutionaries who had been killed in the storming of the Bastille. There was little sympathy, even among the clergy itself, for enabling aristocratic bishops and abbots to maintain lavish lifestyles. Many deputies held up the holy poverty of the first Christians as an example worthy of the clergy's imitation, and underpaid parish curés were willing to let the government reform an institution they saw as having lost touch with its true mission. Adrien Lamourette, one of these "patriot" priests, urged his colleagues to accept the expropriation of ecclesiastical property with "gratitude and joy, as a blessing from Providence to regenerate the Church."[21]

It was clear, however, that many deputies, imbued with the Enlightenment's critical attitude toward the Catholic Church, saw the restructuring of the institution as a chance to reduce its influence and autonomy. "Whether the assembly has acted . . . entirely through patriotism or from a great desire of lowering the clergy I will not pretend to say," an English observer wrote. Opponents such as the abbé Maury, one of the most articulate members of the noirs, denounced the nationalization of the church lands as a sign of a "crisis of delirious impiety." Its origins, he said, could be found in the pages of that monument of hostility to religion, the Encyclopédie.[22]

The deputies were also acutely aware that this measure could be seen as a threat to property rights. The property of the Church, the deputies in favor of expropriation asserted, was made up of donations given to ensure the performance of religious and charitable services; it had not been given to any specific individuals, and if alternative sources of funding were provided for these purposes, it could legitimately be taken over by the state. Opponents of the measure warned that overriding the Church's claims to property it had owned for many centuries would open the door to assertions that "all the members of a nation and all the goods they possess in its territory belong to the nation."[23]

The practical obstacles to converting the church lands into a source of revenue for the state were also daunting. Talleyrand noted that if all church properties were put up for sale at once, the market would be flooded and the government would not get full value for them. He proposed the issuance of certificates backed by the value of the church lands that the state would use to pay its expenses. Individuals could then exchange these assignats for church lands when they found property they wanted to purchase. In this way, the government would get the financial benefit of the operation immediately, without having to wait until the entire stock of church property was sold off. Since they could be converted into something tangible—real estate—the assignats were initially seen as something different from paper money, a form of currency distrusted in France ever since the spectacular failure of John Law's financial schemes at the start of Louis XV's reign.

In view of the desperate financial situation facing the French government, the lure of the scheme to sell the church lands was strong. Tax collections had virtually collapsed, and once the deputies ruled out a state bankruptcy, money had to be found somewhere. Many "patriot" members of the clergy accepted the notion that the Church needed to make sacrifices for the public good; they were also pleased with the promise of a relatively substantial income for the curés who actually served in churches. Ostensibly, the question of church property did not touch on the nature of Catholic belief or change familiar rituals. Nevertheless, it was clear to everyone that the Church would now be firmly subordinated to the state. "Religion was annihilated, its ministers reduced to the deplorable condition of agents appointed by brigands," the conservative bishop of Tréguier in Brittany complained. Mirabeau and other supporters of the measure had foreseen that purchasers of church lands, or *biens nationaux* (national properties), as they came to be known, would be turned into loyalists to the Revolution; they had not anticipated that the purchasers would also be condemned as enemies of religion and sometimes threatened with excommunication. The expropriation thus created a dynamic of polarization that soon pushed the National Assembly into an even broader restructuring of the Church.

Just one day after the vote to make the church lands state property, the deputies, at Sieyès's urging, decided to completely remake the map of France, replacing historical geographic entities with new units. The provinces were to be replaced by new *départements* (departments). Once the plan was implemented, in 1790, the 130-odd Catholic dioceses were also to be redrawn so that their boundaries would coincide with those of the departments. The jurisdictions of the law courts were changed to fit with the new geographic subdivisions of the kingdom as well. Of the many measures taken by the National Assembly, few have been as successful and long-lasting as the creation of the departments, which are still the fundamental subdivisions of France today.

To the revolutionary reformers, the map of the kingdom, to which Louis XVI had devoted such attention in his youth, exemplified the irrational nature of the institutions inherited from the past. The overlapping boundaries of provinces, court districts, and dioceses had been established haphazardly over the centuries. The provinces varied tremendously in size, population, and wealth. Most importantly, in Sieyès's mind, was the fact that they were a psychological obstacle to the creation of a unified nation of equal citizens. His plan was to "melt the various peoples of France into a single people, and the various provinces into a single Empire." He warned, "If we miss this occasion, it will not return again, and the provinces will guard eternally their esprit de corps, their privileges, their pretensions, their jealousies."[24]

Sieyès's original plan called for creating eighty square units of equal size, each one subdivided into nine smaller subunits for local administration. The straight lines of Sieyès's map ignored geographic realities, such as the location of rivers and mountains, as well as the pattern of transportation routes and market regions. The plan that was ultimately adopted tried to avoid separating towns from the rural areas that supplied them with food. Although the legislators wanted to abolish the distinct identities of the historical provinces, they accepted a proposal by Mirabeau to draw the new map in such a way that most departments were carved out of single provinces, avoiding arrangements that would have thrown together populations that sometimes had a long history of mutual hostility; some smaller provinces survived almost intact under new names.

Named after natural features such as rivers—for example, there are departments named after the "Lower Loire" and the "Upper Loire"—or mountains, such as the "Puy-de-Dôme," the departments were not supposed to inspire the kind of psychological identification inhabitants felt toward their historical provinces. Many people accepted the idea that local interests needed to be subordinated to those of the nation. A Lyon newspaper editor, for example, commented at the end of 1789 that his paper had "ceased to be the journal of Lyon, to become . . . almost exclusively the journal of the National Assembly." But there were others who were unhappy about this loss. A group of Norman nobles protested that "all the French have been rudely cut off from their customary affections by the preaching of a vague and restless false patriotism and a general system of equality and uniformity."[25] In fact, provincial identities were not so easily uprooted. They would experience a revival in the nineteenth century, which witnessed a surge of interest in regional history, folklore, and dialects, and the French today still identify themselves as Alsatians or Provençaux more often than as residents of a particular department.

The decision to replace traditional political, legal, and religious units with the new departments set off an intense competition among provincial towns bidding to be chosen as the administrative centers of

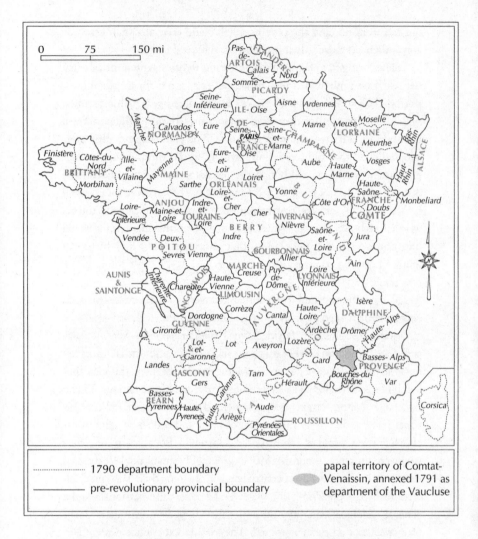

**0    75    150 mi**

| | | |
|---|---|---|
| Finistère | | |

**FLANDERS**
Pas-de-Calais
**ARTOIS**
Somme
Nord
**PICARDY**
Seine-Inférieure
**ILE-** Oise
Aisne
Ardennes
Calvados
Eure
**DE-**
**NORMANDY**
Seine-et-
**PARIS**
Seine-et-Marne
Marne
Meuse
Moselle
**LORRAINE**
Meurthe
Orne
Eure-et-Loir
**FRANCE**
Oise
**CHAMPAGNE**
Vosges
Finistère
Côtes-du-Nord
Ille-et-Vilaine
Mayenne
**MAINE**
Sarthe
**ORLEANAIS**
Loiret
Loire-et-Cher
Aube
Haute-Marne
**BRITTANY**
Morbihan
Haute-Saône
**FRANCHE-**
Doubs
Monbeliard
**COMTE**
Loire-Inférieure
**ANJOU**
Maine-et-Loire
**TOURAINE**
Indre-et-Loire
Cher
**BERRY**
Yonne
Côte d'Or
**BURGUNDY**
Vendée
Deux-Sèvres
**POITOU**
Vienne
Indre
Nièvre
**NIVERNAIS**
Saône-et-Loire
Jura
**BOURBONNAIS**
Allier
Ain
**AUNIS**
**&**
**SAINTONGE**
Charente-Inférieure
**ANGOUMOIS**
Charente
**MARCHE**
Creuse
Haute-Vienne
**LIMOUSIN**
Puy-de-Dôme
Loire
**LYONNAIS**
Rhône-Inférieure
Isère
**DAUPHINE**
Dordogne
**GUYENNE**
Gironde
Corrèze
Cantal
**AUVERGNE**
Haute-Loire
Ardèche
Drôme
Hautes-Alps
Lot-et-Garonne
Lot
Aveyron
Lozère
Gard
Basses-Alps
**PROVENCE**
Landes
**GASCONY**
Gers
Tarn
**LANGUEDOC**
Hérault
Bouches-du-Rhône
Var
Basses-**BEARN**
Pyrenees
Haute-Pyrenees
Haute-Garonne
Ariège
Aude
**ROUSSILLON**
Pyrénées-Orientales
Corsica

**Legend:**
........ 1790 department boundary
——— pre-revolutionary provincial boundary

papal territory of Comtat-Venaissin, annexed 1791 as department of the Vaucluse

THE TRANSFORMATION OF THE MAP OF FRANCE: This map details the replacement of France's historical provincial loyalties and relocated institutions such as courts and bishoprics with departments. The redrawing of the map has proved to be one of the most lasting accomplishments of the Revolution. *Credit: Richard Gilbreath.*

the new units, or at least of one of their subdivisions. The new arrangements were a demotion for some of the cities that had housed provincial parlements or intendancies under the old regime, but the redrawing of the map gave many places that had not housed major institutions before 1789 a new importance. In each department, an elected "directory" was to take over most of the functions previously exercised by royal officials. Within the departments, towns and villages would also elect their own local leaders. The National Assembly assumed that with a common spirit of patriotism, these local governments would carry out the laws decreed by the legislators; the top-down bureaucratic system of the old regime was swept away, leaving the king and the ministers dependent on the voluntary cooperation of local officials over whom they had no control.

As 1789 drew to a close, the Assembly took up another fundamental question: Could members of religious minorities exercise the full rights of citizens, including the right to hold public office? The Declaration of Rights had promised these groups freedom of worship, but Catholicism remained the only state-backed religion. The deputy Brunet de Latuque pointed out that several Protestants had been elected to the Assembly and concluded that there was no basis for excluding them from other positions. Other deputies then raised the issue of rights for practitioners of two professions, public executioners and actors, that were generally denigrated in French society at the time. The conservative abbé Maury defended these prejudices: men who put others to death, or who publicly pretended to be something they were not, did not deserve the same respect as other citizens. The monarchien Stanislas de Clermont-Tonnerre countered that "the executioner only obeys the law"; as for actors, since everyone attended the theater, "we should either forbid plays altogether or remove the dishonor associated with acting."[26]

Having agreed that Protestants, executioners, and actors should have the same rights as other French citizens, the Assembly then turned to one last group whose status had not been settled: France's forty thousand Jews. Maury and Clermont-Tonnerre again took opposing sides.

The abbé insisted that Jews were members of a foreign nation with its own laws and had "never undertaken anything other than commerce based on money." He was prepared to tolerate them as resident aliens, but not to admit them as French citizens. Clermont-Tonnerre agreed that no minority group should be allowed to have its own laws and courts, as Jews had under the old regime, but if they were willing to give up those rights and accept French laws, they deserved citizenship rights. If they continued to keep up some distinctive practices, such as opposing intermarriage and refusing to eat certain foods, that was their business. "Is there a law that obliges me to marry your daughter?" he asked. Deviating from the logic of its rulings on other minority groups, the Assembly decided to postpone any decision on Jews' rights. "Unhappy Jews, remain forever strangers to the nation whose justice you invoke!" a radical newspaper wrote.[27] At the beginning of 1790, the wealthy and assimilated Sephardic Jews of Bordeaux and Bayonne succeeded in obtaining citizenship, but the decision was not extended to the poorer and more numerous Ashkenazi community in Alsace until the Assembly's next-to-last day of business in September 1791.

In an address to the French people summing up the remarkable year 1789, Talleyrand reminded them of how their lives had changed. "Raised to the rank of citizens, eligible for all jobs, informed critics of the administration when you are not part of it, knowing that everything is done by you and for you; equals before the law, free to act, to speak, to write; owing no obedience to men, only to the common will, what an improvement in your condition!"[28] The new national constitution was still far from finished, he admitted, and the details of many of the Assembly's decisions still needed to be fleshed out. Nevertheless, the historic nature of the year's events was indeed obvious to everyone. Even peasants in remote villages and humble urban artisans had done things they had never dreamed of before. They had drawn up *cahiers de doléances* and participated in elections. In many cases, they had risen up against their seigneurs and municipal authorities. The expropriation of church properties and the redrawing of the boundaries of provinces portended further transformations.

For Parisians, the revolutionary year 1789 had been especially intense, punctuated by the journées of July 14 and October 5–6, which had taught them that they could, by their own actions, make history. The citizens of the capital had come to expect to hear the cries of newspaper vendors in their streets, and to join the animated discussions about public events taking place in their cafés and public squares. Whether they experienced these changes as traumas, as Louis XVI and Marie-Antoinette unquestionably did, or welcomed them, like many of the country's ordinary people, everyone understood that life in France would never be the same.

# 10

# A NEW WORLD DIVIDED

*January 1790–June 1791*

F OR MANY PARTICIPANTS, THE CELEBRATION OF THE FIRST ANNIVERSARY OF the storming of the Bastille, the event that had opened the path of the Revolution, was as memorable as the journée itself. Held on the Champ de Mars, the large open space on Paris's Left Bank that is now the site of the Eiffel Tower, on July 14, 1790, the celebration, known as the Festival of Federation, drew a crowd of over three hundred thousand. Whereas the "victors of the Bastille" had been drawn mostly from the neighborhood immediately around the fortress, the participants and spectators at the festival came from all over the country. To symbolize the unity of the new national community proclaimed by the Revolution, members of the patriotic militia, the National Guard, marched to Paris from every one of the newly established departments to join soldiers from the regular army, the deputies, and the king himself in swearing a public oath of loyalty to the nation and the new constitution.

Preparations for the huge oval of grandstands and for the field to be used for the festival were still not completed in the days prior to the event, and a call went out for volunteers to wield spades and fill carts with debris to clear the ground for the "altar of the fatherland" and other structures needed for the ceremony. The king himself visited the construction site, and "the most distinguished society ladies gave themselves over to this patriotic work with a graciousness that redoubled the enthusiasm," the Jacobin deputy Alexandre Lameth remembered. "It would be impossible for those who didn't see these extraordinary days to imagine what they were like . . . the truest happiness, the most original remarks, patriotic songs, lively exchanges, the free opening up of hearts, the quick sharing of hopes, the anticipation of the beautiful future that was being prepared for France . . . formed something that had never existed on earth before this great moment of political regeneration."[1] As the volunteers toiled, they sang a catchy ditty, "Ça ira, ça ira" (Things will go fine), that became an anthem of the Revolution. Numerous verses could be fitted to the song's simple refrain, and singers often joined hands in a circle dance, the carmagnole, as they sang. In 1790, the song reflected popular optimism that "in spite of the mutineers everything shall succeed"; later versions became more explicit in calling for punishment for aristocrats and other opponents of the movement.

On the morning of the event at the altar erected in the center of the grounds, the deputy and bishop Talleyrand led two hundred priests in celebrating Mass to bless the country. Like the Church, Louis XVI made a show of accepting the new order by swearing a solemn oath of loyalty to the constitution. "I heard him pronounce it and fifty thousand people heard it as I did," Ferrières wrote.[2] But the high point of the ceremony came when Lafayette, in his uniform as commander of the National Guard, strode to the center of the massive arena and led the assembled guardsmen in taking the oath. If the king symbolized the old regime that had originally given him his authority, Lafayette was the embodiment of the revolutionary movement for liberty and equality that he had joined in America and that had now come to France.

Attending the ceremony was a life-changing experience for the young Jean-Marie Goujon. Inspired by the Revolution, Goujon had abandoned a promising law career and cut his hair short in "the most natural, the simplest, the healthiest [style]," in order to proclaim his political sympathies. At the festival, he later wrote to his mother, he "saw five hundred thousand men assembled, their arms raised to the Supreme Being, offering him free souls worthy of virtue. I saw it, I joined them, my flaming heart sought in nature a more beautiful title than that of French citizen, and I felt glorious because it was given to me. . . . I will live free or die."[3] His words were more prophetic than Goujon knew: five years after dedicating himself heart and soul to the Revolution, he would literally give his life for the movement.

The enthusiasm with which the Parisians helped complete the preparations, the enormous turnout, and the willingness of the crowd to endure the rain that poured down for most of the day showed that the Festival of the Federation had tapped into a widely shared wish for the success of the Revolution. But the feelings generated by the festival could not dissipate the tensions that continued to grow as proponents of the radical measures taken to promote liberty and equality in 1789 sought to put them into practice, and as those who feared the Revolution's consequences stiffened their opposition. Rather than remaining united, French men and women found themselves making choices that increasingly divided them into hostile camps. On June 20, 1791, less than a year after he swore to uphold the new constitution on July 14, 1790, Louis XVI would dash the hopes of people like Goujon when he tried to flee Paris and force a reversal of the Revolution.

Even the events that had led up to the festival reflected the tensions running through the country. The national festival was a carefully choreographed elaboration of celebrations that had begun on a local level in the previous winter in southwestern France, where peasants were eager to see the promise of "the abolition of feudalism" carried out. A veritable wave of disturbances had affected at least three hundred parishes spread across eight of the newly created departments. Groups of armed men would go to a neighboring village and urge the inhabitants to join them in attacking symbols of noble privilege, such as the weather vanes on the local seigneurs' houses and the coats of arms of aristocratic families on church walls or pews. These gatherings frequently culminated in the erection of a "liberty tree," similar to the maypoles raised during annual spring festivals. Liberty trees were decorated with symbols of the Revolution: tricolor ribbons, panels painted with revolutionary slogans, and sometimes representations of the gallows as a threat against opponents of the Revolution. Boisterous locally organized federations, frequently accompanied by drinking and the random discharge of gunfire, were joyous occasions, but they also showed how strong popular fear of a reaction against the Revolution remained and how easily it might spill over into violence.

In the spring of 1790, the federation movement spread from the countryside to the towns, reaching almost every part of the country. Gatherings of National Guards from entire regions came together to swear loyalty to the nation and the constitution. The small town of Tain, considering that "such confederations can only accelerate the regeneration of the kingdom," voted to provide funds to send all three hundred of its National Guardsmen to Lyon for a regional event at the end of May. The Lyon ceremony, which stretched over three days and included concerts and a fireworks show, attracted fifty thousand guardsmen and fifty thousand civilians. The Lyonnais paid a local sculptor to create a seventy-six-foot-high artificial mountain topped with a female statue of Liberty "in the Egyptian style," and had souvenir medals struck to commemorate the occasion. The city's official address promised support for the National Assembly's decrees and menacingly declared "the rebels who oppose[d] them despicable and traitors to the country."[4]

The militant tone of such declarations and the insistence of regular army soldiers that they be allowed to participate in the federations along with the "patriots" of the National Guard alarmed the government. Most denunciations of the aristocracy might be dismissed as empty rhetoric, but soldiers who directed such epithets at their noble officers threatened to plunge the army into "the most turbulent anarchy," as the army minister warned the National Assembly on June 4. The grand assembly in Paris on July 14 was designed to channel and control the patriotic enthusiasm that had started the confederation movement. Only uniformed soldiers and National Guardsmen were allowed to participate actively, and initiatives from below, such as that of Madame Mouret, who proposed a parallel "confederation of French women," were discouraged. These efforts to set strict boundaries to the festival angered radicals like the journalist Marat. Always suspicious of the motives of men in power, he vociferously denounced the "criminal oath" that would bind the soldiers and National Guardsmen to blindly obeying an assembly that had denied voting rights to the poor; he warned the populace against the "lures of this festivity, where your implacable enemies will promise you fraternal friendship."[5]

Both the authorities' fears and Marat's anger grew out of the many conflicts unleashed by the revolutionary reforms of the previous year. The successful harvest in the fall of 1789 did reduce one source of unrest: riots over bread prices remained relatively rare until 1792. Local elections in January and February of 1790 were also largely peaceful. Turnout was high, especially in rural areas, and the results seemed to indicate that members of all three former orders were willing to accept the new system. Peasant voters frequently chose local nobles or village priests as mayors, and their willingness to accept these responsibilities showed that members of the former privileged orders were ready to give the new regime a chance. The king gave the same impression on February 4, 1790, when he made a surprise appearance at the National Assembly. Addressing the deputies in person for the first time since the October Days, he promised to uphold the new constitution, raising hopes of a peaceful transition to a new regime.

At the same time as the local elections were being held, however, the wave of peasant unrest that started the federation movement was setting off alarm bells. Reporting to the National Assembly about these troubles on February 9, 1790, the abbé Grégoire attributed them to "fear that the decrees of August 4 would not be implemented, to the false interpretation of these decrees," and called for the deputies to quickly make it clear which feudal rights would be abolished outright and which ones peasants would have to buy out.[6] The Assembly answered that question in mid-March, when the veteran feudal lawyer Philippe-Antoine Merlin de Douai presented the results of months of debate in the committee charged with implementing the decrees passed the previous August. In almost impenetrable language full of archaic words such as *gavenne, poursoin, sauvement,* and *avourie*—regional terms for dues paid to a lord in exchange for the theoretical protection he owed his vassals—the proposal separated the hundreds of privileges that seigneurs had accumulated over the centuries into those that were considered outright violations of individual natural rights and those that could be classified as legitimate properties of their holders. The Assembly had recognized the former in its declaration, and they had been abolished without compensation; peasants would have to buy out the latter.

The committee's proposal heavily favored the former seigneurs. The rates at which they were to be paid for the extinction of the dues they had traditionally collected were high, and the procedures established made it difficult for peasants to actually liberate themselves from their obligations. If there was a dispute about the legitimacy of a particular claim, it was up to the former vassal to prove that it was not justified. Peasants were further disappointed by the committee's treatment of the tithe. Now that the clergy were to be paid by the state out of tax revenues, cultivators who leased land had expected their burdens to be reduced. Instead, the deputies decided that tithes should be considered part of the legitimate rent due to the owners of property. Most of the benefits from the abolition of the tithe wound up in the pockets of former seigneurs and of bourgeois landowners rather than going to those who worked the land.

As news of the details of the Assembly's plan filtered out to the countryside, peasants reacted angrily. "The people . . . not only refuse to pay or recognize these rights, but threaten the owners and the notaries who try to collect them," a local official in the department of Nièvre complained.[7] Rural populations were especially frustrated to learn that they were expected to continue paying dues even on former church properties that now belonged to the nation: the revolutionary government still wanted the revenue from these holdings until they were sold off. Now that they were officially free and equal citizens, peasants saw no reason why they should be subject to the same obligations that had marked their inferior status before 1789. Although the letter of the law was largely on their side, former seigneurs were no happier with the legislation. They quickly realized that they had little chance of collecting the compensation they were promised, and they complained that they were not allowed to free themselves from traditional restrictions on the use of their property, such as the requirement to let villagers glean leftover grain in the fields after the harvest.

The National Assembly's increasingly radical decrees on religious matters were just as controversial as its decisions on feudal rights. On February 13, 1790, the deputies voted to abolish the religious orders of monks and nuns, with the exception of congregations that provided necessary services, such as nursing and education. Enlightenment critics had long had the orders in their sights; unlike the parish clergy, who supposedly instilled moral virtues in their flocks, cloistered religious did not, in the philosophes' view, perform any useful functions at all. The very idea of lifetime vows of celibacy struck Barnave as "incompatible with the rights of man" and with the prescriptions of nature itself. The revolutionaries were convinced that nuns, especially, were unwilling victims of families eager to avoid the cost of dowries for their daughters. Caricaturists churned out pictures of smiling young women throwing off their habits and joining hands with liberated male monks, and Olympe de Gouges wrote a melodramatic play about a young novice saved from a life of celibacy by her gallant lover. Protests such as that of the Carmelite nuns of Paris, who denied indignantly that they were "victims slowly consumed by regrets," failed to move the deputies. After all, the deputies expected, as the economist Dupont de Nemours said, that taking over the property of the convents and monasteries would be "an excellent operation from the financial point of view." Initially, about half the male members of religious orders—and an even higher proportion of women religious—tried to take advantage of provisions in the Assembly's decree that would have allowed them to continue living in voluntary religious communities. As the pressures on them mounted, however, increasing numbers melted into the general population. A conservative Catholic complained that "women who had vowed to espouse Jesus, monks who had voluntarily sacrificed themselves to chastity . . . prostituted their hearts with adulterous oaths" by leaving their orders and marrying.[8]

The abolition of the religious orders made it urgent for the Assembly to find new ways to carry out the charitable works for which the Church had been responsible. In a report to the National Assembly that he delivered at the end of May 1790, the duc de la Rochefoucauld-Liancourt, a liberal noble known for his philanthropic concerns, laid down the basic principles for a secularized welfare state administered by the government. Instead of accepting the existence of poverty as an inevitable aspect of society, he argued, the goal should be to eliminate it entirely. "Society owes all its members subsistence or work," he announced. While he and his colleagues expressed no sympathy for able-bodied individuals who refused employment, they envisioned a comprehensive system that would "aid the indigent, the weak and the infirm of all ages, in all social situations, and in every part of the kingdom." This would include creating jobs for those who could not find them on their own. The Church had used the "humiliating word 'alms'" to describe aid to the poor, Rochefoucauld-Liancourt stated. The new terms of "assistance and obligation should ennoble both the nation that gives and the unfortunate person who receives." Poor citizens were "an integral part of the nation," another deputy, Jacques-Guillaume Thouret, insisted, and their needs therefore ought to be covered by "the revenue of the nation."[9]

Implementing the lofty goal of protecting all citizens through a comprehensive safety net of welfare measures, the Assembly recognized, would be a massive challenge. The deputies promised the newly created departmental administrations the funds they would need to set up workshops for the unemployed, maintain hospitals, and care for the aged, orphans, and the insane, but the money they appropriated was far short of the need. The actual effects of these idealistic reforms fell very unequally on men and women. Although the ongoing crisis in the country's largest industry, textile manufacturing, put more female spinners and lacemakers than male weavers out of work, little was done to provide women with employment; moreover, the committee's calculations of what constituted a living wage paid no attention to the fact that women's pay was invariably much less than men's. Legislators praised the "precious citizennesses" who served as wetnurses for abandoned children, but their reforms disrupted the sources of funding that were supposed to pay for this care. To make sure hospitals remained staffed, the decree abolishing the religious orders actually required that the nursing sisters who worked in them continue performing their functions, but under the administration of male doctors.

This takeover of welfare functions by the state caused less controversy in the Assembly and among the public than issues concerning the Church. Two months after the decree abolishing religious orders, the Assembly carried through on its decision to expropriate all church property. Forced to resign themselves to this loss, the Church's supporters in the Assembly rallied behind a proposition put forward on April 12, 1790, by Christophe Antoine Gerle, one of the first members of the clergy to join the National Assembly as a deputy in June 1789. The proposition declared Catholicism the "dominant" religion in France, and the ensuing debate showed once again how the subject of religion drove speakers on both sides to take extreme positions. A clerical deputy demanded that his colleagues bear witness that if the motion was defeated, he did not deserve to be cursed by God, since he had done his utmost to oppose it. Mirabeau countered with a reminder of France's past history of religious intolerance, pointing out that "from this tribune from which I am speaking to you, one can see the window from which the hand of a French monarch . . . fired the arquebus that signaled the Saint Bartholomew's Day massacre."[10] The final vote was 495 to 400 against Gerle's motion.

The deputies who had voted against declaring Catholicism the state religion justified their position by arguing that "the word 'dominant'" implied "a superiority contrary to the principles of equality, which are the basis of our constitution."[11] They denied any hostility toward Catholicism and pointed out that the Catholic Church would continue to be the only one receiving public financial support. Nevertheless, many Catholics concluded that the Revolution was turning against their most cherished beliefs. Particularly in regions where there was a significant Protestant minority, Catholics saw the rejection of Gerle's motion as a renewal of the religious conflicts of the sixteenth century. "Calvinism has taken charge of the committees," one pamphleteer insisted. "It is drawing up speeches, it is seizing control of the forces of the National Guard, and it is furiously propagating . . . the sentiments of hate, intolerance, and vengeance which animated Calvin, its founder." Passions boiled over in several southern cities where the Revolution had allowed prosperous Protestant merchants and manufacturers to gain control of local governments and National Guard units. The worst outbreak was in the city of Nîmes, a major center of textile production, where peasants from the countryside joined Catholic artisans in attacking the Protestants. Three days of violence in mid-June claimed some three hundred lives, a larger number of casualties than in any other episode of the Revolution up to that time. The National Assembly's official report took the side of the Protestants, blaming the bloodshed on "a party that was formed to oppose the constitution, at the time of your [the National Assembly's] . . . first decrees on the property of the clergy."[12]

The troubles in Nîmes seemed like a revival of religious violence from the past, but the revolutionaries' own actions were rapidly creating a new conflict within the Catholic Church. The Assembly's decision to take over the entirety of the Church's property made it imperative for the legislators to agree on new arrangements to govern the country's largest institution. Known as the Civil Constitution of the Clergy, the law, hammered out in debates extending from late May to early July 1790, radically restructured the French Church. An American-style separation of church and state was hardly conceivable in France, where members of a single denomination made up the overwhelming majority of the population. Government and religion there had been deeply intertwined since the establishment of the kingdom more than a millennium earlier. Just as they had been unwilling to concede the king any voice in determining what powers he would have under the new constitution, on the grounds that to do so would be to undermine the sovereignty of the nation, the deputies were also unwilling to negotiate with the Church about the reforms they had in mind. They were even less disposed to allow the pope, a foreigner, to weigh in on issues that, as far as they were concerned, were strictly national concerns.

Many advocates of government-dictated reform had been inspired by the arguments of the Jansenists, a party within the Church that had regularly turned to the king and to the parlements for protection from hostile bishops and even the papacy. "Your decrees will not carry any attack on this holy religion: they will only return it to its primitive purity, and you will truly be the Christians of the Gospel," one advocate of reform told his colleagues in the Assembly. Deputies imbued with the rationalist ideas of the Enlightenment were happy to see the institution literally cut down to size as the Assembly suppressed many parishes as well as fifty-two bishoprics, redrawing the boundaries of dioceses so that they matched those of the newly created departments. For Catholics who regarded bishops as divinely consecrated continuators of the work of the original apostles, this was much more than a "mechanical and purely temporal operation," as one apologist called it. The same theologian endorsed the Civil Constitution's provisions for bishops to be elected by the departmental electoral assemblies (which were also to choose deputies), and for priests to be named by the lower-level district assemblies. The plan simply "exchanged an arbitrary government for a communal one, so conformable to the church's true spirit," he wrote.[13] Opponents objected that the electoral assemblies selecting Catholic clergymen might include Protestants, nonbelievers, and even Jews.

Although the Assembly insisted on its authority to enact the Civil Constitution of the Clergy, it now had to face the question of whether the clergy and the population would accept these sweeping changes. At first, the signs seemed favorable. Many parish clergy were willing to support reforms that elevated their status and their income at the expense of monks and priests who had little contact with the laity. A long tradition of loyalty to the French government and a genuine enthusiasm for the Revolution's project of national regeneration worked in favor of acceptance. This enthusiasm had been shown by the willingness of many members of the clergy to participate publicly in the federation festivals held while the debate about the Civil Constitution was under way. The French Church's "Gallican" tradition of independence from the papacy, embodied in the concordat signed in 1516 between the monarchy and the Vatican, limited the pope's power to intervene in its affairs. The current pope, Pius VI, not wanting to provoke the revolutionaries into annexing the papal territory of Avignon in southern France, said nothing about the Civil Constitution during the legislative debates. In view of the pope's silence, Louis XVI approved the measure on July 22, 1790. A dutiful Catholic, he accepted the argument that the new rules for the Church did not affect the substance of religious belief. He was deeply pained a few days later, however, to receive a letter from the pope warning that the law might "lead the entire nation into error, the kingdom into schism, and perhaps be the cause of a cruel civil war."[14] The king now found himself caught between his loyalty to the Church and his public duty as head of the French government.

The first half of 1790 was also marked by controversies involving France's relations with its colonies and with other countries and with a major extension of the campaign against the nobility. After the night of August 4, defenders of the colonial system warned plantation owners that the French were "drunk with liberty" and might take steps to undermine slavery. The fact that so many leaders of the revolutionary movement were members of Brissot's Society of the Friends of the Blacks made such fears plausible. In late August 1789, slaves on two plantations in Martinique "refused to work, saying loudly that they were free," according to the colony's governor, who forwarded to France anonymous letters purporting to come from black conspirators. When news of the fall of the Bastille reached Saint-Domingue, blacks were reported to have interpreted it to mean that "the white slaves had killed their masters and that now they are free."[15]

The news of the uprising in Paris inspired not only the slaves in Saint-Domingue but also the white colonists. The latter staged a colonial version of the municipal revolutions that had swept metropolitan France, setting up local assemblies in the different parts of the colony and forcing the royal intendant to flee. By this time, plantation owners living in Paris had created the Club Massiac, a group dedicated to lobbying for their interests. Free men of color in Paris formed their own movement to protest their exclusion from representation. Since the wealthier free men of color were often slaveowners in their own right, they initially thought they might be able to persuade the members of the Club Massiac to work with them; Vincent Ogé and Julien Raimond, wealthy men of mixed race from Saint-Domingue, addressed the club in early September, only to be told that its members were determined to limit the organization to whites.

After this rebuff, the free men of color sought allies among the white revolutionaries. Although few members of the Friends of the Blacks had ever visited the colonies, and they had said nothing about the situation of free men of color in their numerous pamphlets, they were happy to embrace their campaign. Defending the rights of men like Raimond, who had three white grandparents, spoke and wrote French fluently, and was wealthy enough to meet the new constitution's criteria of active citizenship, was simpler than challenging slavery itself; indeed, many whites in

France could not understand why those in the colonies did not see how advantageous it would be for them to ally with the free people of color to form a single bloc of property-owners opposed to the more numerous slaves. The white colonists, who claimed that any concession to people of mixed race would lead inexorably to the overthrow of slavery, were stigmatized as "aristocrats of the skin." It took an all-out effort for them to defeat a proposal advanced in late November 1789 to grant the free people of color in Saint-Domingue two representatives in the National Assembly. Despite this success, colonists and merchants remained on their guard. Mirabeau, the Assembly's most effective orator, was known to be corresponding with the British abolitionist leader Thomas Clarkson, and he had told his speechwriting team to work on a proposal to abolish the slave trade. "We live in perpetual fear of the effects of a metaphysics that extends to everything with a truly dangerous exaggeration," a proslavery trader in the French port city of La Rochelle wrote.[16]

News of the white revolts against the colonial administration reached France at the end of February 1790. "Letters from Martinique and Saint-Domingue report that these colonies have declared their independence from the metropole," one newspaper told its readers.[17] The reports created a frenzy in trading centers like Bordeaux, where supporters of slavery organized a deputation to Paris. The city's merchants claimed to accept the principles of the Declaration of Rights, a local chronicler noted, "but cannot conceive that the Africans, like others, are born and remain free and equal in rights."[18] Such pressures drove Mirabeau to tone down his long-anticipated speech to the Jacobin Club on March 2. To the colonists' great relief, he stopped short of urging immediate measures against the slave trade, calling instead for negotiations with the British on the issue. In the National Assembly, another patriot firebrand, Barnave, in his capacity as chair of a hastily created committee on colonial affairs, concentrated his efforts on conciliating the white colonists. They were promised that the Assembly would not pass any measures concerning "the status of persons"—a circumlocution referring to slaves and people of color—without the prior approval of the colonists themselves.

Barnave brought forward decrees on March 8 and 28, 1790, endorsing the assemblies that had sprung up in the colonies. The abbé

Grégoire, a strong supporter of the cause of the free men of color, demanded assurances that members of that group who met the property qualification for voting would be allowed to participate in colonial elections. Barnave privately reassured him, but the absence of any mention of the issue in the decrees allowed the white colonists to exclude their rivals. This ambiguity set the stage for further troubles. Fearing that the French legislators might change their minds, an all-white colonial assembly meeting in the city of Saint-Marc drafted its own constitution for Saint-Domingue, asserting its power to make its own laws without approval from the French legislature. Recognizing the determination of the whites in the colony to exclude them from power, free men of color on both sides of the ocean began organizing to demand the rights they thought the decrees of March 1790 were meant to give them.

The colonies, vital to the French economy, were also part of the kingdom's global competition with other imperial powers. The issue of who would decide when the country's interests required resort to war suddenly flared up in mid-May 1790, when Spain came into conflict with Britain over rights in the Nootka Sound in the northern Pacific. Spain had been allied to France through a "family compact" since Louis XVI's ancestor Louis XIV had succeeded in installing a Bourbon relative as king there in 1713. When Louis XVI prepared to back Spain if the dispute over this remote territory led to conflict, the patriot deputies in the Assembly objected. Declaring war was a privilege of the nation, not the monarch, they insisted. "It is in a minister's interest to declare war," Barnave warned, "because then one is forced to let him manage the immense subsidies that are required, because then his authority is increased without limit." In contrast, an elected assembly representing the people would be naturally inclined to peace. "Each of us has properties, friends, family, children, a whole set of personal interests that might be compromised by war," the Jacobin leader concluded.[19]

Fifty thousand Parisians crowded the streets around the meeting hall on May 22, following the debates through handwritten bulletins passed out the windows. Inside, the Jacobin triumvirate of Barnave, Duport, and Lameth were battling Mirabeau, who once again was defending royal powers while secretly trying to persuade the king and queen to commit themselves to the basic principles of the Revolution. Mirabeau, who wanted the king and the Assembly to share the authority to declare war, "was incredible yesterday," one noble deputy, Gaston de Lévis, wrote to his wife. "He pulverized the aristocrats, brought down the kings, elevated the peoples, vexed the extremists and won the admiration of all." In the end, it was decided that the king could propose a declaration of war, but that only the Assembly could officially make the decision. The Jacobins regarded the outcome as a victory: they confidently assumed that France would never again engage in a war of conquest or send soldiers into battle merely to gain glory for its ruler. They brushed aside warnings like those of the conservative marquis d'Estourmel, who prophetically foresaw two dangers: either France's rivals would "profit from our enthusiasm for philosophical reveries" by seizing territories and commercial advantages for themselves, or France, deciding that its democratic principles required it to intervene when other powers committed aggressions, would "be at war with every nation that we consider unjust, or which will not accept our system."[20]

What d'Estourmel saw as a danger—the possibility that France would commit itself to bringing its revolutionary principles to the rest of the world—inspired others, who hoped that the ideals of liberty, equality, and democracy would soon spread beyond the country's borders. Already in late 1789, the journalist Camille Desmoulins and other French revolutionaries had welcomed the start of a revolt against Austrian rule in the Belgian provinces just north of the French border. Although the Belgian rebels were deeply divided between traditionalists, who opposed the rationalist reform program that the Habsburg emperor, Joseph II, wanted to impose from above, and democrats, who sought a reduction in the privileges of the local nobility and the Catholic Church, Desmoulins assumed that the movement would follow in the footsteps of the French one. The Belgian movement overthrew Austrian rule in December, but by the following March, the traditionalist party, led by Hendrik Van der Noot, had driven out the rival supporters of the democrat, Jean-François Vonck. Vonck's followers took refuge in France and lobbied for intervention against the aristocrats in their own country.

Vonckist exiles from Belgium were just some of a growing number of foreigners inspired by the spectacle of the French Revolution. Others included the Dutch Patriots who had been forced to flee their country after the defeat of their movement in 1787; the Polish Jew Zalkind Hourwitz, who had competed against Grégoire in an essay contest about Jewish emancipation in 1787; a German journalist, Konrad Oelsner, who joined the Jacobin Club in 1790, and who translated Sieyès's writings into his native language; and the Spanish colonial military officer Francisco Miranda, who would later help start an independence movement in his native Venezuela. The American poet Joel Barlow had arrived in 1788 to promote a land-speculation scheme, the Scioto Company, that attracted the attention of Brissot and other revolutionaries. The English-woman Helen Maria Williams, who settled in Paris in 1790, welcomed a stream of visitors over the years, including the pioneering feminist Mary Wollstonecraft and Thomas Paine, whom the French revolutionaries regarded as a hero, because of his role in promoting American independence. Through their personal contacts, their correspondence, and their publications, the members of this foreign colony in France helped spread revolutionary ideas abroad and encouraged the French revolutionaries to believe that they had support in other countries.

Pro-revolutionary foreigners obtained public recognition when a group of them, dressed in exotic costumes, appeared at the National Assembly on June 19, 1790, asking to participate in the upcoming Festival of Federation. The delegation included "Arabs, Americans, Chaldeans, Indians," and representatives from over a dozen European countries. Their spokesman, a Prussian baron named Anacharsis Cloots who called himself "the orator of the human race," introduced them as "free men whose countries are in irons, whose fatherlands will be free someday thanks to the influence of your unshakable courage and your philosophical laws."[21] The Assembly welcomed them but stopped short of promising any concrete support to revolutionary movements in other countries; nevertheless, the incident underlined the conviction of the French revolutionaries that their principles were universal and encouraged the activists hoping to transform their homelands. Many of them believed that France would support them.

On the same day that it welcomed Cloots's delegation, the Assembly voted to abolish the institution of hereditary nobility and outlaw titles such as count, baron, and marquis. Their use, asserted one liberal noble, Charles de Lameth, Alexandre's brother, "offends the equality that forms the basis of our constitution; they come from the feudal regime that you have destroyed." Lafayette and other prominent nobles supported him; only the abbé Maury, the counterrevolutionary priest of commoner origins, tried to head off the decision. Maury protested that social distinctions were an essential aspect of French life, and that "if there is no more nobility, there is no more monarchy." The marquis de Ferrières tried to downplay the significance of the measure, telling his wife that, after the abolition of feudal rights the previous August, "the nobility was already gone for all practical purposes." In any event, he continued, the decree was "absurd, since one cannot keep a son from descending from his father." Even as he promised to try to persuade the other nobles from their province to submit to the new law, however, he hedged his bets by instructing his wife to "save our family titles . . . and put them in a safe place."[22]

The Assembly's measure drove an increasing number of members of the former privileged class to take the step of emigrating from France. The phenomenon of noble emigration had begun during the summer of 1789: immediately after the storming of the Bastille, courtiers associated with the unsuccessful effort to replace Necker, including the comte d'Artois, the younger of Louis XVI's two brothers, had sought refuge abroad. In the face of the peasant uprisings that followed the fall of the Bastille, many other nobles also decided to cross the nearest border. Some revolutionaries initially claimed that "it is a good thing for the nation to see its bad citizens flee," but before long, the émigrés began to be seen as a threat to the Revolution.[23]

By September 1789, the comte d'Artois had taken up residence in Turin, the capital of his father-in-law's kingdom of Savoy on France's southeastern border. There, he gathered other exiles around him. Assisted by the former minister Calonne, who had fled after his dismissal in 1787, and who hoped to win back royal favor by helping to restore the monarchy, Artois wrote to other European rulers, claiming that Louis XVI was not acting freely in appearing to accept the Revolution. He urged military action to rescue the French monarchy. Emigration thus took on the appearance of a deliberately counterrevolutionary act intended to thwart the will of the French people. By mid-1790, a number of military officers and aristocratic members of the upper clergy had also joined the emigration. The prince de Condé, another high-ranking member of the royal family, had emigrated to the German city of Coblentz. He began organizing émigré officers into an army, while émigré clergy stirred up opposition to the National Assembly's church reforms. The emigration movement embarrassed Louis XVI, who was acting as though he accepted the Revolution while privately hoping that the movement's internal conflicts would hasten its collapse. He appealed to Artois and Condé to return to the country, but they ignored his instructions, which led others to suspect that he secretly approved of their actions. Inside the country, disgruntled nobles took the lead in organizing a counterrevolutionary federation of their own in a town called Jalès in the southern department of the Gard near the city of Nîmes, where religious violence had broken out earlier in the year. Reports about this "camp of Jalès" heightened patriots' fears of counterrevolutionary plots.

The French military was one of the institutions most affected by the growing distrust between commoners and former nobles. Officers' ranks in the prerevolutionary army and navy had been almost exclusively limited to aristocrats; the ordinary soldiers and sailors they commanded could never expect to rise to higher positions. The promise of "careers open to talents" proclaimed in the August 4 decrees and the Declaration of Rights appealed to the commoners in the military but offended their superiors, who saw a gentleman's profession being thrown open to less educated and sophisticated competitors. The morale of the army was also undermined by the creation of the National Guard, whose members' claims to be the truest patriots often offended soldiers from the professional line infantry. That the National Guards were often better paid than the regulars added to the soldiers' grievances. The growing number of noble officers who abandoned their posts to join Condé's émigré army fueled distrust of those who remained. Justifying the resistance that soldiers often showed to their superiors, the *Révolutions de Paris* asked, "Don't nobles, privilege-holders, occupy all the places of officers? Should one think that they are loyal to the Revolution?"[24]

The seriousness of the tensions between soldiers and officers became evident on August 31, 1790, when a mutiny broke out among troops in the garrison of Nancy, a major military stronghold near the border with Austrian territory. For months, soldiers in Nancy had complained that they were not receiving their full pay; moreover, they said, men who protested were being unjustly punished. The soldiers found support among the local authorities, but reports of the soldiers' insubordination led the National Assembly in Paris to order an aristocratic general, François Claude Amour, marquis de Bouillé, to assemble a force of loyal units and quash the disturbances. As his expedition of five thousand men approached the city, soldiers from the Châteauvieux regiment prepared to defend themselves and handed out weapons from the Nancy arsenal to their civilian supporters. Bouillé's forces suffered some three hundred casualties; the losses on the rebels' side were probably even higher. The courts-martial that followed resulted in twenty-three executions and the sentencing of several dozen soldiers to long terms in the galleys. The majority of the National Assembly saw the loss of life and the severe repression as the price that had to be paid to restore discipline in the army, and the king and queen warmly congratulated Bouillé. Democratic radicals such as Robespierre and the journalist Marat, however, deplored the harsh line taken against the soldiers.

Less bloody than the conflict in Nancy but equally disquieting was the naval mutiny that broke out in France's Atlantic fleet in the port city of Brest in Brittany in September. Loyal to their traditions, the members of the aristocratic naval officer corps angered their crews by resisting the replacement of the white flag of the Bourbon dynasty with the new tricolor of the nation. In addition, the officers rejected proposals to open their ranks to merchant captains, who, in their view, had made their careers pursuing profit rather than being "uniquely concerned with glory," as one veteran captain put it.[25] Sailors protested the maintenance of the severe disciplinary regulations handed down from the old regime and resisted orders to sail for the Caribbean, an unpopular assignment that could easily keep them away from home for more than a year. The Brest city government, distrustful of the aristocratic naval officers, took the side of the men and encouraged their movement. The mutineers were further fired up by the arrival from Saint-Domingue of the warship *Léopard*, whose crew had sided with the Colonial Assembly when the royal governor had opposed its demand for autonomy from France. Convinced that the white colonists were patriots whose rights were being trampled on, the *Leopard*'s sailors ejected their captain and took eighty-five members of the Colonial Assembly on board, bringing them to France so they could carry their protest to the National Assembly. While the colonial deputies went on to Paris, the *Léopard*'s sailors encouraged the other sailors in the fleet to resist their officers. The local Jacobin Club promised them that the unpopular disciplinary regulations would be revoked, and the National Assembly decided it had no alternative but to give in to their demands. Like the revolt in Nancy, the mutiny at Brest revealed the deep distrust between officers and the lower-ranking men and raised serious questions about the revolutionary government's control of the military.

The National Assembly's reaction to the naval mutiny provided the German visitor Gerhard-Anton Halem, one of the many foreigners drawn to Paris to see the extraordinary spectacle created by the Revolution, with an opportunity to see how the new French political system worked. By the time he arrived in early October 1790, Halem, a great theater fan, already knew that the National Assembly was the best show in town. Admission to the spectators' galleries was free, but he had to get to the Manège, the former riding school converted into a meeting hall for the deputies after the October Days in 1789, by 6:30 a.m. to be sure of obtaining a good seat. On October 20, the patriots seized on the navy crisis to demand that the king dismiss his ministers, whom they accused of deliberately remaining inactive in order to let anarchy overwhelm the Revolution. Halem was particularly impressed by Barnave, who, as he put it, "combined energy and precision with ease and elegance in his speeches." But he also praised the eloquence of the conservative deputy Jacques Cazalès, who defended the king's right to choose his own ministers. Halem, who came from a German

principality where, as in all of the rest of Europe at the time, public political debate was unknown, was struck not only by the performance of
the deputies but also by the active role of the spectators. Those looking
on regularly interrupted the speakers with applause and murmurs. He
also remarked on the presence of journalists, who by now had a loge
reserved for them behind the president's desk. From that vantage point,
they recorded not only what the deputies said but how the galleries
reacted.[26]

After eight hours of debate, the Assembly defeated an attack on
the ministers by the deputies on the right. But Halem soon learned
that this was hardly the final word on the matter. He could see that the
population of the city took an active interest in politics: he visited the
Palais-Royal, the center of public discussion, and listened to an orator
denouncing the distinction between active and passive citizens as a violation of the principle of equality, because it kept the lower classes from
influencing decisions. He overheard a "well-dressed man who read long
passages from the *Ami du peuple*, full of invectives against the ministers, to an attentive crowd," and he observed the impact of the evening
papers, which published summaries of the day's parliamentary debates
within a few hours of the end of the Assembly's sessions. Exhausted
though he must have been, at 6:00 p.m. Halem joined a thousand other
people who were prepared to listen to more oratory at the meeting of
the Jacobins. As he looked at the dusty volumes of theology that lined
the walls of the meeting room, Halem reflected that their authors would
have "trembled with horror" if they could have heard the revolutionary
politicians' speeches. Listening to the reading of letters from provincial Jacobin clubs that opened the session, he realized that the club was
building up a nationwide network. After hearing the stars of the revolutionary left, including Mirabeau, Barnave, the Lameth brothers, and
Robespierre, Halem went home assured that the club session had given
the left-wing deputies, who had temporarily been outvoted earlier in the
day, "a new enthusiasm" to return to the fight.[27]

In 1790, the Jacobin Club was still limited to fairly wealthy and respectable members. Would-be admittees needed to be recommended
by existing participants and pay dues equal to several days' wages for
an ordinary worker. Not everyone shared Halem's impression that this

requirement kept the club's debates sensible. Invited to address the Jacobins on the subject of British policy toward the Revolution, another foreign visitor, William Miles, acknowledged that the members had listened to him with interest, but he was still unnerved by their "wild and dangerous effervescence"; he feared that the Jacobins "may soon provoke a spirit that will deluge the country in blood."[28] Even if they had doubts about the Jacobins, the two foreign visitors both saw that moderates were having a hard time competing with them. A more elitist group founded at the beginning of 1790, the Club de 1789, had never attracted a popular following. This club brought together celebrities from the first few months of the Revolution, such as Sieyès, Lafayette, Mirabeau, and Condorcet, who were concerned about the growing radicalism of the Revolution. By the fall of 1790 its members had returned to the Jacobins in the hope of recovering some influence there. Meetings of an openly royalist club, the Amis de la constitution monarchique (Friends of the Monarchical Constitution), were harassed by supporters of the Revolution, who denounced its attempts to win support among the members of the lower class by giving out bread at below-market prices and stirring up agitation against shops that sold imported British goods.

Realizing that "we are now in the season of clubs," as the Paris bookseller Nicolas Ruault, himself a Jacobin member, put it, both Halem and Miles visited another, much less exclusive gathering, the Cercle des amis de la vérité (Circle of the Friends of Truth), whose weekly public sessions, held in the circus arena at the Palais-Royal, drew crowds of four thousand or more. Whereas the Jacobins focused on the political issues confronting the National Assembly, members of the Cercle kept alive the utopian spirit that had inspired Brissot's Gallo-American Society in 1787. They dreamed of remaking the universe and creating a new religion of humanity. The Cercle's founders were Nicolas Bonneville, a religious mystic with democratic beliefs, and the radical priest Claude Fauchet, who preached a gospel that combined elements of Christianity with lofty ideas about universal human fraternity. Halem recognized some of Fauchet's ideas as coming from the Masonic movement. The French Revolution, Fauchet proclaimed, was the opening of new era: "The moment approaches when the veil of mystery can be safely lifted, when the statue of humanity will be brought to life by the Prometheuses who have kept the celestial flame alive." A Paris journalist was bemused by "this mixture of apocalyptic phrases, Oriental expressions, Jewish parables, political terms and words of love, bound together in poetic fashion," but he admitted that it "marvelously astounded the audience."[29]

Later renamed the Cercle social (Social Circle), the club eventually absorbed the members of the antislavery Society of the Friends of the Blacks and opened itself to new ideas about the public role of women. In March 1791, the Dutch-born Etta Palm d'Aelders, one of the militants working to change the relations between the sexes, congratulated the group for having been "the first to have admitted us to patriotic sessions." She used its platform to call for the creation of a nationwide network of women's clubs that would defend the Revolution by keeping its enemies under surveillance; in addition, it would take over tasks formerly performed by religious establishments, such as the regulation of wetnurses, the provision of schooling for young children, and the distribution of aid to the poor.[30]

Foreign visitors also found their way to the most radical of the Paris clubs, the Cordeliers. From its origins in 1789 as the district assembly in a neighborhood peopled by journalists, printshop workers, and actors from the nearby Théâtre français (now known as the Odéon and still a feature of the Paris landscape), this group developed a reputation as "the terror of the aristocracy and the refuge for oppressed political activists in the capital," as one radical newsman put it. The first president of the Cordeliers was Georges Danton, a lawyer whose oratorical skills were often compared to those of Mirabeau, although Danton's radical democratic principles struck even many Jacobins as "absolutely impossible in a big city like Paris." The journalists Marat and Desmoulins were also active members, and when Marat ran afoul of the municipal authorities in 1790, the Cordeliers helped him evade the police. "About three hundred persons of both sexes filled the place," one visitor to the club reported. "Their dress was so unkempt and so filthy that one could have taken them for a gathering of beggars. The Declaration of the Rights of Man was stuck on the wall, crowned by crossed daggers. Plaster busts of Brutus and William Tell were placed on each side, as if to expressly guard the Declaration."[31] The club's symbol was an all-seeing eye, a sign of the surveillance its members intended to exercise on the people's behalf.

A network of "fraternal societies" spread the Cordeliers' influence. These had originally been founded to explain the principles of the Revolution to uneducated members of the lower classes, whom the Jacobins firmly excluded from their sessions. Political factions of all sorts tried to reach the common people through cheap pamphlets and newspapers attributed to the fictional Père Duchêne and similar characters. The early months of 1791 were the high tide of pamphlets attributed to "Mère Duchêne," whose vigorous voice was a match for that of her voluble husband. Among the most industrious journalists churning out this populist literature was Jacques-René Hébert, the son of a provincial bourgeois family. Hébert had ruined his prospects in a messy sex scandal and eked out a living before the Revolution on the fringes of the Paris theater world. He was not the most inventive of the Père Duchêne journalists, but he developed political instincts that his competitors lacked. Before long, his newspaper made him a genuine force as the voice of the ordinary people.

The "season of clubs" was not limited to Paris. By the end of 1790, every French town of any size had at least one political group; some sixty cities had clubs for women. Club mania even reached the colonies, where local patriots in Cap Français, the largest city in Saint-Domingue, gathered to denounce royal officials; after their meetings, they "exited inflamed with a divine fire," according to one newspaper account.[32] Provincial Jacobin clubs attracted local officials, journalists, members of the professions, and military officers; as in Paris, they required membership fees, which discouraged artisans and workers from joining. Besides keeping their members abreast of political developments in the capital, provincial clubs took it on themselves to keep the local authorities—both those who had won municipal elections at the beginning of 1790 and the departmental officials chosen later that year—under close surveillance; they denounced any signs of "aristocratism" to the Paris club.

The spread of the Jacobin movement reflected a strong current of support for the Revolution in most of the country in spite of the many controversies its reforms were generating. Protests were as likely to come from groups that wanted to push the movement even further as from conservative opponents. Those in the former camp included the peasants, particularly those who refused to pay compensation for abolished feudal rights; the radical democrats of the Cordeliers Club; and some of the white population of the colonies, who proclaimed themselves "patriots" even as they demanded greater autonomy and protections for slavery. Unable to establish a public club movement to counterbalance the Jacobins, opponents of the Revolution relied on informal networks of former nobles, clergy, and their supporters. Counterrevolutionaries proved as adept at using the press as their opponents, however. The earliest monarchist periodicals had specialized in satire and leveled personal attacks against leading revolutionaries; indeed, the counterrevolutionary forces were more likely in these years than the supporters of the Revolution to single out specific politicians and incite violence against them. By 1790, royalists could count on daily papers that followed the National Assembly's debates as closely as their pro-revolutionary rivals, even though one of their editors complained that doing so was a "truly sad, truly humiliating task." It involved nothing but recording "assaults, arson, murders, ravages, imprisonments, atrocious acts of vengeance," he wrote.[33]

For all the vehemence of their language, the counterrevolutionary journals lacked a coherent philosophical perspective to match the ideas that the revolutionaries had inherited from the philosophes. The most cogent critique of the Revolution in its early phases came not from a French polemicist, but from the British politician and publicist Edmund Burke, who published his *Reflections on the Revolution in France* in November 1790. Burke had followed events in France closely for many years. He knew the weaknesses of the old monarchy, but he was convinced that its institutions should have been reformed rather than being completely overthrown. "You began ill, because you began by despising everything that belonged to you," he told the French. Above all, he criticized the revolutionaries for trying to create an entirely new system based on abstract philosophical principles defined by reason. In Burke's view, human reason was too fallible to serve as a guide in politics, and society was too complex to be remade overnight. "We are afraid to put men to live and trade each on his own private stock of reason, because we suspect that the stock in each man is small," he wrote. "The nature of man is intricate; the objects of society are of the greatest possible complexity."[34]

The theory of natural rights, in Burke's view, was bound to lead to destructive anarchy. "Their abstract perfection is their practical defect," he insisted. The real purpose of government was to satisfy human wants or needs, and "among these wants is to be reckoned the want . . . of a sufficient restraint upon their passions," which required an authority that could stand up to public opinion rather than following its dictates. The exercise of such authority was made tolerable, according to Burke, by time-honored rituals and beliefs—such as the sacredness of monarchy—even if they were in the category of "pleasing illusions." His indignation rose to a peak in a celebrated passage about the assault on Marie-Antoinette during the October Days of 1789: "I had thought ten thousand swords must have leaped from their scabbards to avenge even a look that threatened her with insult," he wrote. "But the age of chivalry is gone. That of sophisters, economists, and calculators has succeeded; and the glory of Europe is extinguished forever."[35] Convinced that the principles of the Revolution contradicted the realities of social life, Burke predicted that the French would end up executing their king; that their new paper currency, the assignat, would become worthless; and that they would succumb to a military dictatorship, prophecies that would all eventually be fulfilled.

Burke's real audience was in Britain: he wanted above all to counter the enthusiasm of many reformers there who saw revolutionary France as a model to be imitated. His lasting achievement was to found a tradition of conservative political philosophy that has lasted down to our own day. At the time, however, most reactions to Burke's *Reflections* were negative. The work was considered scandalous, not only because of its denunciations of reason and democracy, but because it seemed to represent a repudiation of Burke's own principles. "Burke had been warmly loved by the most liberal and enlightened friends of freedom," the British libertarian theorist William Godwin wrote, "and they were proportionably inflamed and disgusted by the fury of his assault, upon what they deemed to be its sacred cause." Godwin was attempting to explain why his wife, the pioneering feminist Mary Wollstonecraft, had rushed into print to refute him. Burke had defended the American Revolution and denounced corruption in the British political system; in the years before the French Revolution, he had fought a lonely campaign against abuses in the administration of Britain's establishments in India. "One can hardly imagine how Mr. Burke could have dishonored his own judgment by the production of such a work," Brissot opined in his newspaper.[36]

A much greater concern for French supporters in the last months of 1790 and the first part of 1791 than Burke's polemic was a new phase of the conflict over the reform of the Church that further widened the distrust between supporters and opponents of the Revolution. The National Assembly had assumed that priests would accept the Civil Constitution peacefully, but on October 30, more than 120 clerical deputies signed a document protesting its provisions about the election of bishops and the redrawing of dioceses. This stand by church leaders encouraged local parish priests to resist the implementation of the reform, which in turn provoked local authorities in anticlerical regions to take stronger measures to enforce it. "No one could doubt any longer that most bishops have formed a seditious league in order to light up the torch of fanaticism everywhere and attempt a counter-revolution by this means," the administrators of the Bouches-du-Rhône department asserted.[37]

The patriot majority in the National Assembly saw its entire work in jeopardy as a result of the resistance to the Civil Constitution. Among other things, religious protests threatened to disrupt the sale of church properties, on which they had pinned their hopes of climbing out of the financial abyss that had precipitated the Revolution. On November 26, 1790, one of the deputies, Jean Georges Charles Voidel, read out a long catalog of incidents in which members of the clergy had opposed legislation affecting the Church. He warned the recalcitrant members of the clergy that "now all the citizens of the empire must bow their heads before the majesty of the laws," and exhorted them to "pacify the people, irritated by your resistance, by a prompt submission." At his urging, the overwhelming majority of the deputies voted to require all priests

*Moyen de faire prêter serment aux Evêques et Curés aristocrates, en présence des Municipalités suivant le décret de l'Assemblée Nationale.*

THE CLERGY OATH: This engraving, issued in 1791, captures the divisions stirred up by the controversy over the clergy oath. Several men dressed in the clothes of respectable provincial bourgeois are using ropes and pulleys to make a priest raise his hands, while young altarboys and some older women look on in dismay. Two uniformed National Guardsmen, holding their muskets, watch the proceedings with satisfaction, and two pretty young women smile at the soldiers. Two older gentlemen, who appear to be *ci-devant* (former) nobles, seem disgruntled. The prominent role of the women in this picture corresponded to reality: observers noted that female congregants often took the lead in opposing the oath. *Source: Bibliothèque nationale de France.*

and bishops who wanted to remain in their posts and continue drawing their salaries to swear a public oath of obedience to the new national constitution and the new laws governing the Church. When some deputies representing the clergy tried to square the Civil Constitution with their consciences by stating that they would obey its provisions except with regard to "spiritual questions," the Assembly insisted that all oaths had to be "pure and simple," without any qualifying language.[38]

Legally speaking, only the curés and vicars who actually led church services had to decide whether to take the oath, but their flocks often

had a crucial influence on the choices they made. The public ceremonies in which priests either accepted or rejected the law were often explosive occasions, as an engraving titled "A New Method to Make Curés
Take the Oath" illustrated.

Nationwide, slightly more than half of the fifty thousand parish
clergy initially swore the oath; they were called *jureurs* (jurors, a term
related to *jurer*, "to swear"), or "constitutional clergy." The percentage,
however, varied widely from region to region. Oathtakers were a clear
majority in most of the departments of the Paris basin and in the southeast, between the Rhône River and the Alpine frontier, and in parts of
the southwest, where one conservative Catholic observed sourly, "Half
the diocese will take it because self-interest, vile self-interest, is the great
mover."[39] "Refractory clergy," or *non-jureurs* (non-jurors)—those who refused to accept the new arrangements—dominated in western France,
in the country's mountainous south-central region, and in peripheral departments in the north, east, and southwest. The close division between
supporters and opponents intensified the conflict. If a clear overall majority of the clergy had accepted the Civil Constitution, there might
have been less pressure to force recalcitrants into line; if its opponents
had had a convincing edge, the Assembly might have had to modify
its policy. As it was, neither side was willing to concede victory to the
other. The heavily aristocratic upper clergy, who lost far more from the
reform than the ordinary pastors did, were overwhelmingly hostile to
the Civil Constitution. Because of these divisions, the question of who
would ordain new priests and bishops became even more crucial.

The rhetoric on both sides of the oath controversy was heated. For
the opponents of the reform, Catholicism itself was in jeopardy, and
the basic rights of its followers were being suppressed. Women were as
divided as men about the issue. In Paris, according to Adrien Colson,
"the marketwomen punished the Gray Sisters and the nuns of Mira-
miones the way one treats children," by publicly whipping them on
their bare buttocks. "The crime of the Sisters was to have taught their
pupils a catechism of hatred, contempt, and revolt against the clergy
who have sworn the oath . . . and that of the nuns was to have insulted and mistreated their new curé." Political opponents of the Revolution seized on the opportunity to turn Catholics against the whole

movement. Gaston de Lévis, who had always known the king's brother, the comte de Provence, as a devotee of Enlightenment ideas, remarked ironically that the prince had suddenly become an expert on church law: "He knows every passage from the church councils, he bores me to tears with evangelical citations. . . . [T]here isn't a refractory priest who knows more about the Civil Constitution and its defects." But Lévis also understood that the sale of church lands had created many supporters for the Civil Constitution. "Every acre sold makes a convert and a man who wouldn't be moved by liberty or intrigue will fight like a hero to save his acre," he wrote. Backers of the Civil Constitution accused their opponents of "preaching, from the pulpit of peace and truth, lies and the principles of fanaticism"; they demanded that "the guilty be given over to the vengeance of the laws."[40] Surprised by the number of priests who refused to take the oath, local authorities had to scramble to find replacements, and violence often broke out when congregations refused to allow these "intruders" to take possession of their churches.

Local authorities were drawn into the oath controversy, either attempting to enforce the law in the face of resistance or, if they themselves were sympathetic to non-juring priests, trying to avoid having to take action against them. When Talleyrand and Jean-Baptiste-Joseph Gobel, the only two bishops in the National Assembly who had agreed to swear the oath, took the initiative of consecrating new bishops according to the procedures established in the Civil Constitution, Pope Pius VI broke the cautious silence he had maintained on the subject. His condemnation of the Civil Constitution and his threat to suspend priests who swore the oath deepened the conflict in France and drove some clergy to retract the oaths they had sworn.

No one anguished more over the conflict caused by the Civil Constitution than Louis XVI. Although he reluctantly endorsed both the Civil Constitution and the clerical oath, his dislike for the Assembly's religious policy led him to consider proposals secretly presented to him in the fall of 1790 to organize his escape from Paris. Marie-Antoinette was equally determined to see her husband and the royal family freed from their humiliating and dangerous situation, even if it meant calling on other European powers, particularly her Habsburg brother Leopold II, for help. Leopold had inherited the throne when their brother Joseph II had died at the beginning of 1790. From the French royal family's perspective, the situation in Paris was becoming increasingly critical in the early months of 1791. When the king's two elderly aunts tried to leave the country in February, local authorities arrested them en route. It took a forceful intervention by Mirabeau to get them freed and allow them to continue their journey. On February 28, a rumor that the king was in danger inspired several hundred royalists to rush to the Tuileries to defend him, provoking a backlash from patriots, who demanded closer surveillance of the palace. The king's opposition to the Civil Constitution provoked another confrontation on April 18, a day after Louis XVI had shown his opposition to the religious oath by taking communion from a non-juring priest. When the royal family attempted to travel to the palace of Saint-Cloud, outside of Paris, a crowd blocked their carriage for several hours; the National Guards responsible for their security joined the demonstration, saying that "the friend of our enemies cannot be our friend." "Now you can see we are not free," Marie-Antoinette told the soldiers as she reentered the palace.[41]

On April 11, the departmental administration of Paris tried to find a compromise on the religious issue by announcing that it would let non-juring priests rent church buildings that were not being used for the officially sanctioned services of their "constitutional" colleagues and hold services. On the following Sunday, a hostile crowd gathered outside the "aristocratic Sanhedrin," where one such gathering had been announced, and prevented Mass being celebrated. The incident alarmed even some of the National Assembly's strongest supporters of the Civil Constitution. Talleyrand, who had sworn the oath and defied the pope by consecrating new constitutional bishops, reminded the deputies of the promise of religious freedom enshrined in the Declaration of Rights, but more radical deputies were unwilling to support any compromise on the issue. "If you allow this exception," the deputy Jean Denis Lanjuinais said, "the oath law that has cost us so many troubles, so many perplexities, so many millions and above all so much anxiety . . . will have been useless."[42]

By the spring of 1791, as local authorities became increasingly em-broiled in the quarrels caused by the Civil Constitution and the oath, the deputies of the National Assembly were approaching the point of exhaustion. For nearly two years, they had been meeting daily, both to hammer out the new constitution and to deal with the innumerable immediate problems confronting the government. Overwork, combined with the flamboyant private life he persisted in pursuing, was blamed for the premature death of the great orator Mirabeau on April 2. Mirabeau's efforts to create a strong monarchy that would defend individual liberty and social equality had undermined his influence with the more radical Jacobins, but the force of his personality had made him the one fig-ure who could still rein in their most dangerous impulses without being accused of siding with the counterrevolution. Despite his best efforts, however, Mirabeau had been unable to convince the king and queen to sincerely embrace the new constitution. Without their support, his vision of a democratic monarchy could not be realized.

As news of Mirabeau's illness spread, the street in front of his house was covered with straw to keep the noise of carriage wheels from disturb-ing him. Nevertheless, the dying man "heard the whole people talk of his illness as an event that threatened the Revolution," a journalist wrote. To honor Mirabeau, the National Assembly decided to convert the huge domed church of Saint Genevieve, which Louis XV had ordered con-structed on the hill dominating Paris's Latin Quarter, into the Pantheon, a secular monument to the memory of "great men" who had served the nation. Previously, only French kings and queens, laid to rest in elab-orate tombs in the basilica of Saint-Denis north of Paris, had received such public honors. With the Pantheon, which remains one of France's national monuments, the Revolution created its own way of conferring immortality on its heroes. In the village of Meudon, where he had settled and joined the local Jacobin Club, Jean-Marie Goujon gave a eulogy of Mirabeau. It was "so beautiful and full of the warmest patriotism" that the municipality had it published, launching him on a political career. A good head taller than the average Frenchman of the day, with "a majes-tic appearance and a decisive attitude," according to his intimate friend Pierre-François Tissot, Goujon was beginning to discover that he had the qualities to actively promote the revolutionary spirit.[43]

With the death of their sparring partner Mirabeau, the Jacobin triumvirs, Barnave, Duport, and Alexandre Lameth, and their allies took over
his policy of attempting to rein in the growing radicalism of the Revolution and prevent the total destruction of royal power. Throughout
the spring, they promoted a series of measures aimed at keeping poorer
members of society, the passive citizens, out of politics. Confrontations
with urban artisans and workers increased after the Assembly took up
the issue of the urban guilds and workers' organizations, the institutions
that had played such a large role in the prerevolutionary life of Jacques
Ménétra and other artisans. Economic reformers had long condemned
the guilds as obstacles to free enterprise, and Turgot had tried to eliminate them in 1776. On August 4, 1789, however, the deputies had not
dared to do away with the organizations that had traditionally kept urban workers under control. Throughout 1790, the status of the guilds
remained unsettled. Many journeymen, kept under the thumb of their
masters, now claimed the right to set up their own shops, and business
entrepreneurs, who had already found ways around guild privileges before 1789, were emboldened to openly ignore them. When it passed a
new occupational tax law that explicitly permitted any citizen to practice any profession, the National Assembly realized that it had to make
a decision. On March 2, 1791, the deputies abolished the guilds. "These
dispositions should be regarded as one of the greatest benefits that the
legislature has yet extended to the nation," one newspaper proclaimed.
"The guilds [enjoyed] exclusive privileges that deprived the vast majority
of citizens of one of the foremost rights of man, that of working. . . . All
men will have the means to make use of their skills; they will not need
considerable sums to establish themselves."[44]

The guilds had been legally recognized corporate bodies that included both employers and workers. Their abolition raised the question
of the status of other workers' organizations, such as the compagnonnage to which Ménétra had belonged. In the minds of the deputies,
these entities—through which workers tried to impose standardized
rates of pay on employers, sometimes by means of strikes—were even
more dangerous than the guilds. Three months after the guilds had
been outlawed, the deputy Isaac René Guy Le Chapelier, originally
one of the Third Estate firebrands from Brittany, brought forward an

extraordinarily harsh law against them. "Citizens who practice a partic-ular profession must not be allowed to assemble for their supposed com-mon interests," he asserted. "There are no more group interests within the state, there are only the private interests of individuals and the gen-eral interest." Even mutual-aid societies that helped unemployed or sick members of a given trade violated that principle, Le Chapelier insisted, and were contrary to the public interest. "It is up to the nation . . . to provide work for those who need it for their existence and aid for the infirm."[45]

The Le Chapelier law is often cited as proof that the legislators of the National Assembly were bent on furthering the interests of the bourgeois class, from which so many of them came. When he intro-duced his law, Le Chapelier defended himself against such accusations by calling for salaries that would be high enough so that workers would be able to escape "that absolute dependency that comes from being de-prived of basic necessities"; he also claimed that collective groups sim-ilar to modern trade unions violated the individual freedom of workers as well as employers. In fact, the Assembly had already applied the prin-ciples in Le Chapelier's law to a number of middle-class occupations. The Paris bar association had been dissolved, its members were forbid-den from using the label *avocat* (lawyer), and the same law that broke up the guilds made it legal for anyone to offer medical services, without any requirement for training or licensing. Looking back with a shudder after the end of the Revolution, a leading nineteenth-century lawyer wrote that "this was one of the first abuses of freedom, that the right was left to anyone, without scrutiny, nor any apprenticeship, to prac-tice the liberal professions, especially the profession where confidence should best be proven before handing over the honor of families, the fate of the widow and the orphan."[46] In practice, middle-class profes-sionals did fare better than manual workers in the individualistic soci-ety created by the Revolution, but not all members of the bourgeoisie were enthusiastic about the changes imposed by the movement.

Even though the Le Chapelier law against associations affected bourgeois professional groups as well as manual workers, there is no doubt that he and his allies—including the Jacobin triumvirs in the Assembly and Bailly and Lafayette, the two officials most involved in maintaining order in the streets of Paris—were primarily concerned with the behavior of the lower classes. Lafayette's National Guards, even those who came from relatively poor backgrounds themselves, encountered increasing hostility in the streets as they tried to enforce the crackdown on workers' groups and break up crowds hostile to non-juring priests. A month before he introduced the law with which his name would remain associated, Le Chapelier had also been the spokesman for another piece of restrictive legislation. This law, passed on May 10, 1791, proposed banning collective petitions, and on that occasion, he had allowed himself a truly violent outburst against the passive citizens. According to their defenders, they would be prevented from expressing their views by the prohibition. But, according to Le Chapelier, "the men who are separated from society by their restlessness, their laziness, their refusal to practice any useful occupation" did not deserve rights, since they were "a burden on society rather than serving it." His message to the poor was clear: "Do something useful with your limbs, find work, cultivate this fertile soil, and you will receive the title of citizen." Robespierre and his closest ally in the Assembly, Jérôme Pétion, answered Le Chapelier powerfully. Pétion asked, "How can there be men, other than slaves, who are not legally allowed to protest against laws that oppress them?" The Assembly's support for the ban, however, showed that fear and hostility toward the lower classes was widely shared.[47]

The word for "slaves" (*esclaves*) may have come to Pétion's mind because the consideration of the ban on petitions interrupted the Assembly's most tumultuous debate on the colonies, another piece of business still unaddressed as it neared the end of its work on the constitution. When the eighty-five deputies from the Saint-Domingue assembly who had come to France with the mutineers of the *Léopard* reached Paris, they were severely dressed down by the National Assembly, which reminded them in no uncertain terms that they had no right to make laws for themselves. Even as he scolded the colonists, however, Barnave, the head of the colonial committee, renewed his promise from March 1790 that they could decide on the rights of both slaves and free people of color. For the colonists, this was the crucial issue, and they treated the

Assembly's statement as a major victory. Within the Jacobin movement, however, it marked the beginning of the downfall of the triumvirs, Barnave and his allies Duport and Lameth. Brissot lambasted Barnave for leaving the fate of the slaves to their masters. "A patriot wants liberty for all men. He wants it without exception, without modification," Brissot proclaimed.[48] Just as the triumvirs had outflanked the monarchiens in the early months of the Revolution, by accusing them of compromising the movement's basic principles of liberty and equality, Brissot now put the spotlight on the limits of Barnave's commitment to those ideals.

The determination of Brissot and his supporters to challenge the colonial racial order increased at the end of 1790, when disturbing news from Saint-Domingue reached France. Vincent Ogé, a free man of color and an officer in the Paris National Guard, had gone to the colony to insist on the extension of political rights to members of his group, which he claimed was the clear intention of the National Assembly's decree of March 8, 1790. "He made it clear that he did not make any demands concerning slavery," Brissot's *Patriote français* reported.[49] When the white colonists rejected his demands, he raised a rebellion among the free men of color in the northern part of the colony. Ogé's movement was quickly put down, but it profoundly shook the white plantation owners. After a hasty trial, Ogé was broken on the wheel, the most painful of France's forms of capital punishment, and a number of his followers were hanged.

Reports about Ogé's rebellion intensified debates about race in metropolitan France. Supporters of the white colonists resorted to overtly racist arguments, claiming that blacks were a separate species intermediate between humans and apes. In response, the spokesman for the free people of color, Julien Raimond, became the first writer to assert that racial prejudices were social constructions with no roots in reality. When the news of Ogé's execution reached France, Brissot wrote, "In Saint-Domingue, it is the heads of the defenders of liberty that fall on the scaffolds."[50] A few days later, news of more violence in that colony arrived: soldiers sent from France and sailors from the French fleet had joined white colonists in Port-au-Prince in murdering Colonel Thomas-Antoine Mauduit, the military commander who had dispersed the Colonial Assembly the previous year. The National Assembly concluded that the only way to restore order in the colonies was to decide once and for all how they would be integrated into the new order.

For more than a week, from May 7 to 15, the deputies clashed over whether a nation devoted to freedom and equality could tolerate slavery and racial discrimination in its colonies. "The question concerns both Europe and America," a leading proslavery newspaper wrote. "The assembly's decision could be a decree of life or death, or slavery or freedom for millions of men, and the signal of the prosperity or the downfall of commerce." It was clear from the outset that the majority was not prepared to decree the immediate abolition of slavery, because of the economic repercussions such a drastic step would cause. Nevertheless, some colonists, such as the deputy Élie Médéric Louis Moreau de Saint-Méry, insisted that, in order to reassure plantation owners, the promise of white supremacy incorporated into the Assembly's previous decrees needed to be written into the constitution. When other deputies hesitated to preclude the possibility of abolishing slavery at some later date, by protecting it in the constitution, Moreau de Saint-Méry challenged them directly: he moved to decree that "no law on the status of slaves in the American colonies, no change in the status of men of color be made except in response to a precise and spontaneous request from the colonial assemblies."[51]

Moreau de Saint-Méry's motion set off one of those firestorms that had regularly marked the Assembly's contentious debates. The idea that the word "slavery" (esclavage) might appear in a constitution that proclaimed that "men are born and remain free and equal in rights" outraged many of the deputies. Paraphrasing a line from the Encyclopédie's article on the slave trade, Robespierre exclaimed, "Let the colonies perish rather than abandon a principle!" These became the words for which he was best known until the height of the Reign of Terror two years later. Nevertheless, the most that he and the other radical deputies could achieve was to get esclaves changed to the euphemistic expression non libres (unfree persons).

The debate then shifted to the issue of free people of color. Over the vehement objections of the pro-colonial deputies, Julien Raimond was allowed to address the Assembly. It was the first time a man of African descent was allowed to speak in the debates of a Western legislature.

Raimond argued that men like himself, who owned property and slaves, met all the requirements for active citizenship laid down in the constitution, and indeed, that they were essential to keeping the slaves in the colonies in subordination. Defenders of the colonists replied that allowing anyone descended from slaves to achieve equality with whites would fatally undermine the racial distinctions on which plantation society depended.

Raimond's appeal for rights for all members of his group was rejected, and the pro-colonial side appeared to have won the debate. Then, however, the Alsatian deputy Jean-François Rewbell offered an amendment that he claimed would assure white supremacy while making a small concession to the free people of color. Rewbell's proposition granted citizenship rights to free men of color whose parents had been free and legally married. Only a small minority of the free colored population in the colonies met these requirements, but the colonial deputies in the Assembly objected that Rewbell's seemingly minor amendment contradicted the promise just made: that no changes to the status of nonwhites would be allowed unless they were initiated in the colonies themselves. When the majority of the deputies nevertheless endorsed the Rewbell amendment, Moreau de Saint-Méry and his colleagues announced that they were resigning their seats.

This angry debate had forced the deputies to confront the contradiction between their idealistic principles and the unpleasant reality of slavery. Perhaps it was still in the deputies' minds the next day, when they overwhelmingly endorsed a motion by Robespierre that barred any of them from holding seats in the new legislature that would be elected once the constitution was completed. This "self-denying ordinance," meant to demonstrate that personal ambition to remain in power had played no role in the design of the constitution, would be "a great example of love of equality, of pure devotion to the good of the country," Robespierre told his colleagues.[52] Few of them dared to oppose his motion and appear to be expressing their personal ambition; many were no doubt also happy to make sure their opponents were excluded from the next assembly, and others were simply worn out by the all-consuming task they had imposed on themselves two years earlier. The end of their labors appeared to be in sight, even though the feeling of unity that had been generated for the Festival of Federation the previous July had become a distant memory.

As the deputies struggled to complete the constitution, they were hit by an unexpected blast of criticism questioning whether they were truly accomplishing the goals of the prerevolutionary philosophes. The abbé Guillaume Raynal, whose *History of the Two Indies*, first published in 1770, had sparked Enlightenment debates about colonialism and slavery, publicly denounced the Revolution as a "false interpretation of our principles." In France, he claimed, he saw only "religious conflicts, civil debates, the consternation of some, the tyranny and presumption of others, a government enslaved to popular tyranny . . . soldiers without discipline, leaders without authority, ministers without resources," and, above all, "a king, the first friend of his people . . . outraged, threatened, stripped of all authority." Power now rested with "clubs where ignorant and uneducated men dare to pronounce on all political questions."[53] In Marseille, Raynal's home, members of the Jacobin Club responded by carrying Raynal's bust from their meeting room to the local insane asylum; in Sevrès, the young Jacobin Goujon followed up his successful oration in honor of Mirabeau by writing an address to the National Assembly denouncing the abbé. Raynal's diatribe reflected a growing disillusionment with the results of the Revolution even among devotees of the Enlightenment. Meanwhile, even as Raynal unleashed his denunciation, Louis XVI and Marie-Antoinette were plotting an initiative that threatened to scuttle the movement altogether.

# 11

# A RUNAWAY KING AND A
# CONSTITUTIONAL CRISIS

*June–September 1791*

Few politically informed Parisians could have been entirely surprised on the morning of June 20, 1791, when they woke to the news that the king and the entire royal family had disappeared from the palace of the Tuileries. Talk of a royal escape had been a constant feature of life in the capital since the storming of the Bastille two years earlier. More surprising was the outcome of the king's flight. Many had expected that such a move would provoke civil war within the country, foreign war against Europe's other monarchies, and the end of kingship in France. All of these things would ultimately come to pass within little more than a year, but in the summer of 1791, the royal escape attempt did not result in a major domestic or international conflict or the king's removal from the throne. The decisions the National Assembly took in June and July to resolve the crisis caused by the king's flight allowed implementation of the new constitution, but they ended up adding to the unresolved tensions that would soon undermine the effort to transform France into a constitutional monarchy.

Desperate to protect the king and the traditional authority of the throne, courtiers had tried to convince Louis XVI to flee to some location at a safe distance from Paris in July 1789. They tried again at the time of the October Days later that year. Worried about the safety of his family and genuinely reluctant to set off a civil war among his subjects, the king would not commit himself to any of their plans. An unlucky conspirator, the marquis de Favras, was hanged in February 1790 for his participation in a plot to kidnap the king and move him out of Paris. The crisis caused by the Civil Constitution of the Clergy convinced Louis that he had to try to escape from the capital, but he now had to choose between rival plans. As part of his effort to convert the king to his vision of a genuinely popular monarchy, Mirabeau urged Louis XVI to flee to a safe location inside the kingdom, where he could negotiate with the National Assembly without involving foreign powers in French affairs. The queen and the baron de Breteuil, the leader of a network of émigré supporters of the monarchy, put forward a rival plan in which the king would escape to a fortress near the Belgian border, where Austrian troops could intervene on his behalf if necessary. Louis XVI finally accepted this option. Months of secret negotiations secured a promise from Marie-Antoinette's brother Leopold to provide the necessary funds and forces if the escape plan succeeded. "To lull the faction parties to sleep concerning his true intentions," as a key conspirator put it, Louis personally addressed the National Assembly on April 19 to renew his promise to accept the new constitution, and he sent a public statement to other European courts with the same message.[1]

The escape attempt on June 20 required lengthy preparations. From the time of the October Days, Louis XVI had insisted that he would not abandon his family to secure his own safety; he and the queen decided that, in any flight attempt, they and their children would have to travel together. Axel von Fersen, the Swedish nobleman who had become the queen's lover before the Revolution, handled the practical details of getting the royal party out of Paris. He had a large carriage, or *berline*, constructed with room for the king, the queen, the two children, their governess, and Louis XVI's sister Elisabeth. The royal family would have to slip out of Paris unescorted, but royalist military officers with small detachments of loyal men would be stationed at key points along the route, ready to protect the passengers once they were in the countryside. The presence of these troops could alert the population that something unusual was happening, but the conspirators assumed that country folk would be sympathetic to the king. The soldiers were told that they would be guarding a "treasure"; they may have assumed that this meant money for the pay of troops at the frontier. General Bouillé, who had put down the army mutiny in Nancy the previous August, would be waiting near Montmédy with a strong contingent of soldiers, ready to back up the king's authority with force.

Even after cavalrymen along the route had arrived at their stations, the date of the escape had to be postponed several times. As the cavalrymen lingered in the countryside, local peasants took notice and became increasingly alarmed by their presence. Nevertheless, the first stages of the plan went off successfully. In the afternoon of June 20, the king said goodbye to his brother, the comte de Provence, who left to make his own way to Belgium, disguised as an English merchant. After their customary nighttime rituals, the royal family retired to their bedrooms. Then, one by one, they made their way out of the darkened palace through an unguarded door and joined Fersen in a Paris horse cab. In the dark, the queen nearly stumbled into Lafayette, the National Guard commander, who had unexpectedly visited the palace. He had tied the king up in conversation for quite a while earlier in the evening, delaying the escape, but he did not recognize the queen.

Fersen drove the royal family to a nearby street where their carriage awaited; he then set off on his own secret journey to the frontier. Louis XVI promised him that "whatever may happen to me, I shall never forget all that you are doing for me," but he forbade his wife's lover from traveling with them. Three loyal bodyguards escorted the fugitives; they had been given yellow uniforms, an unfortunate decision because yellow, a color associated with the émigré prince de Condé, attracted hostile attention along their route. At 2:30 a.m., the group was finally ready to begin their journey, several hours later than originally planned but still well before sunrise. As their large and conspicuous carriage jolted along the main road to the east, Louis XVI was in a good mood, telling his family that "once I'm back in the saddle, I'll be very different from what you've seen up to now." He imagined how he would welcome back the émigrés and reestablish the Church.[2]

Relieved to be away from Paris and its hostile crowds, the king incautiously got out of the carriage at relays while the horses were changed and even engaged in conversation with bystanders. Rumors of possible sightings of the king spread along the route. Louis XVI had assumed that, outside of Paris, he would find loyal supporters, but in fact local officials and National Guardsmen, already alarmed by the unexplained presence of soldiers along the roads, went on heightened alert. At 6:30 p.m., the royal family reached the posthouse where the first detachment of loyal cavalrymen was supposed to be waiting for them. To their consternation, there was no sign of the troops or their commander, the young Claude Antoine Gabriel Choiseul. When the carriage hadn't appeared at the scheduled time, Choiseul had decided that something must have gone wrong with the plan and decided to leave before his presence aroused too many suspicions. He sent a confusing message to the other units waiting farther along the route; it did not occur to him to leave anyone behind who could let the travelers know what he had done.

With no other choice, the royal party continued down the highway. When they reached the town of Sainte-Menehould, the local postmaster, Jean-Baptiste Drouet, thought he recognized the king when he peered into the berline after hitching up fresh horses to it. Drouet communicated his suspicions to town officials, who sent him and a companion to chase after the carriage. At 11:00 p.m., the king and his family reached Varennes, the last town where they were to change horses before reaching the planned rendezvous with Bouillé and his troops. Precious minutes were lost because of a mix-up about where the travelers' fresh horses were waiting for them. Meanwhile, Drouet arrived. He improvised a barricade to block the bridge out of town and alerted Jean-Baptiste Sauce, the town *procureur*, or manager. Sauce inspected the passengers' documents and found no reason to arrest them, but Drouet made such a fuss that it was finally decided to keep them in the town until morning. As the fugitives were settling down unhappily for the night, a local resident who had once visited Versailles was brought to the town inn. Recognizing the monarch, he could not keep himself from kneeling in homage. His identity given away by a loyal subject, Louis XVI replied wearily, "Yes, I am indeed your king."[3]

The townspeople were initially swayed when the king appealed for their aid, telling them how he and his family had been "forced to live in the capital in the midst of daggers and bayonets." But the town's church bell sounded the tocsin, bringing several thousand National Guardsmen and ordinary peasants to Varennes to prepare defenses against any effort to attack the town. The town council, made up of humble residents, reached a decision: they would not obey the king's orders. Although they assured him of their love, they told him "that his residence was in Paris, and that even those living in the provinces eagerly and anxiously called him to return there." As dawn approached, two couriers sent in pursuit of the king by the National Assembly two days earlier reached Varennes, carrying a decree requiring all local officials to compel him to return to the capital. "There is no longer a king in France," Louis XVI sadly concluded.[4]

Realizing that their gamble had failed, the exhausted royal family reluctantly returned to their ill-fated carriage. Bouillé reached a hill overlooking Varennes with four hundred cavalry shortly after their departure, but with thousands of armed men now surrounding the carriage, he decided that liberating the royal family was not possible. Any illusions Louis XVI still cherished about the population's sympathy for his cause were severely tested by the hostile receptions he received at most of the towns along the route back to Paris. Local officials, Madame de Tourzel recalled, "had only one thought in mind: to glory in their own triumph and to humiliate the royal family."[5] A nobleman who cried out "Vive le roi!" as the carriage passed by was killed by local peasants. The return journey proceeded much more slowly than the attempted escape had, since the berline now had to move at the pace of the guards marching alongside it. The heat was sweltering, and the cloud of dust stirred up by the thousands of marchers made breathing difficult.

Halfway back to Paris, the royal party was met by three National Assembly deputies who had been appointed to accompany them.

Reflecting the Assembly's effort to unite in the face of the crisis caused by the king's flight, the delegation consisted of a devoted royalist, Charles Latour-Maubourg; a leader of the mainstream Jacobin faction, Barnave; and a democratic radical and close ally of Robespierre, Pétion. Hoping that direct exposure to the king and queen might soften their hostility, Latour-Maubourg let his two colleagues ride inside. So cramped that Pétion had to hold the royal princess on his lap, they listened to a long harangue by the king's sister, Madame Elisabeth, who emphasized above all the measures the revolutionaries had taken against the Church. "This speech made such an impression on Barnave that from that moment on, he changed his conduct and his ideas," Madame de Tourzel claimed.[6]

In reality, Barnave and his closest associates had already begun to distance themselves from the more radical Jacobins. Indeed, they had tried to establish secret contact with the king. Barnave and Marie-Antoinette clearly reached some kind of understanding during the hours they spent in the carriage; after their return to Paris, Barnave would follow in the footsteps of Mirabeau and establish a secret correspondence with her. In these letters, he attempted to forge an alliance between the king and the Assembly and negotiate a revision of the constitution to restore some royal powers. Even as the king and queen began to realize that there might still be a chance of saving a portion of his authority, they still had to face the hostility of the Paris populace. At several points as they neared the city, crowds surged toward the carriage, threatening to kill the three royal bodyguards who had assisted in the escape attempt. Lafayette, the National Guard commander, gave orders for guards and spectators to maintain a strict silence and to keep their hats on their heads, rather than removing them in the traditional gesture of respect for authority. Five days after they had left, the royal family found themselves back in the Tuileries.

More surprising than the king's desperate flight to Varennes was the reaction of the National Assembly and the population to the crisis. The king's valet had been the first to realize the royal family had left the palace, and within an hour of the discovery, the news had spread throughout the capital. Large, angry crowds gathered around the Tuileries and the Hôtel de Ville, the seat of the city government. Lafayette and Bailly, the mayor of Paris, who were responsible for the king's security, fell under suspicion because they had failed to stop the plot. When the deputies accepted Bailly's assertion that "the king and some of his family were carried off last night by enemies of the public welfare," revolutionary patriots extended their suspicions to the National Assembly as a whole. The story that the king had been abducted, "as if he had been given a sleeping potion and hauled away without his knowledge," as a skeptical journalist put it, fell apart within hours, when it was discovered that he had left behind a lengthy denunciation of the Revolution. In this document, Louis XVI declared all the actions he had taken during his "captivity" invalid because they had been performed under duress. He claimed that for two years, he had been powerless as he watched "the destruction of the monarchy, the subversion of all authority, the violation of properties, the endangerment of personal security, crime left unpunished and the establishment of a complete anarchy."[7]

Even moderate deputies were outraged by the king's violation of the repeated oaths he had sworn to accept the new constitution and his apparent willingness to risk the outbreak of a civil war. The Assembly quickly asserted its authority to issue decrees and orders to the ministers without his approval. It dispatched couriers to alert local officials throughout France and banned anyone from leaving the country. The Assembly's actions gave France its first taste of what would come to be called "revolutionary government," the invocation of emergency powers justified by an overwhelming crisis. In the streets, ordinary people took their own revenge on their unfaithful monarch. "All the signs, where 'Perfumer to the king,' or 'to the Queen,' or 'Royal lottery,' &c. was written up, are knocked down, and perhaps in a short time their names will not even be mentioned," an Englishwoman wrote. Madame Roland, who had scrupulously confined herself to "the kind of influence that seemed proper for my sex," decided that circumstances required her to take a public role and signed up as a member of a political club that admitted women.[8]

For the first time since the Revolution began, serious voices now put forward the idea that France could do without a king at all. Thomas

Paine, who had helped establish one republic in America, now sought to help found another. He hoped that the French would see "the absurdity of monarchical governments; here will be a whole nation disturbed by the folly of one man." On June 21, while the royal carriage was still rolling toward Varennes, the radical Cordeliers Club issued a proclamation calling "royalty, especially hereditary royalty . . . incompatible with liberty." The club urged the National Assembly to "immediately declare that France is no longer a monarchy, that she is a Republic." Radical journals, such as Jean-Louis Carra's *Annales politiques*, the favorite newspaper of provincial Jacobin clubs, denounced the king in the strongest terms: "This morning, Louis XVI deserted the throne, the capital, the empire, and, by this cowardly defection, intended to come back, with foreign executioners, to rule over twenty-five million corpses." There was considerable popular support in Paris for these ideas. On June 24, two days after news of the king's capture had reached the capital, some thirty thousand people marched to present a Cordeliers petition to the National Assembly. For devoted royalists, the king's flight sent a different kind of message. On June 23, just before he learned that the king had been stopped at Varennes, the outspoken editor of the *Gazette de Paris* gave free rein to his excitement. "He found a way to break his chains, this unfortunate king. . . . In whatever place where he has sought asylum, he will have found real Frenchmen. What inexpressible joy they must feel in crying, 'The king! The king!'"[9]

The leaders of the National Assembly and the city government were determined to save their constitutional project from both republicans and royalists. When Cordeliers representatives tried to read their proclamation to the more mainstream Jacobin Club on June 22, a speaker reminded the members that "you are the Friends of the Constitution and . . . the monarchy is part of the constitution." The club voted unanimously not to listen to the petitioners. As the many Assembly deputies who belonged to the Jacobins realized, their own legitimacy depended on the still-uncompleted constitution, and the monarchy was an essential element of the elaborate structure they had been drawing up. Preoccupied for months before the king's flight with the problem of containing popular unrest, the Assembly was not eager to restart the revolutionary process. The law passed on May 10 banning collective petitions, and the Le Chapelier law against workers' organizations, showed their mood. The mayor and the National Guard commander would not tolerate the behavior of radical individuals, such as the wagondriver who was arrested for "having dared to say that M. Bailly and M. Delafayette must be hanged."[10]

Outside of Paris, the king's flight and arrest set off a variety of reactions. In border regions, and especially in the northeast, where Louis had hoped to take refuge, there was fear of a foreign invasion. Local authorities sometimes arrested nobles, refractory priests, and others suspected of harboring royalist sympathies, a foretaste of the increasingly harsh measures that would characterize the Revolution in the coming years. In rural Brittany, a National Guard unit tried to track down a refractory priest who had come out of hiding when he learned the news of the royal family's attempted getaway. He "cried out in the village of Génezé, with a face radiant with joy, 'Good news, my friends, the king has fled, it's good news for us.'" A petition from the Jacobin club in the city of Montpellier, on the Mediterranean coast, urged the establishment of a republic, showing that it was not only Parisians who were willing to consider this radical option. Some of the deputies in Paris were convinced by the letters they received from their home regions urging them to do away with the monarchy. One constituent wrote that the nation was "ready to set an example of a people that knows how to manage without a king."[11] Once it became clear that the National Assembly intended to preserve the monarchy, these debates faded away. Nevertheless, the possibility of a republican government had been established in the minds of at least a part of the population.

Unwilling to consider an alternative to the monarchy or even to the existing monarch, the leaders of the National Assembly handled the king gingerly after he returned. The suspension of his powers until the circumstances of the flight could be clarified was too much for the royalist deputies in the Assembly, who refused to take any part in the proceedings. Disregarding their protests and those of the radicals, the Assembly's leaders decided that the king would be treated as "the first victim of a conspiracy formed by the enemies of France," as a centrist journalist put it, rather than as a suspect.[12] Louis was allowed to make a statement about his motives without being subjected to interrogation; while he did not pretend to have been kidnapped, he promised not to continue opposing the constitution and said he now recognized that the population supported it. General Bouillé, who had fled to safety in Belgium, provided cover for the royal family by announcing, falsely, that he had initiated the plot.

Arguments in favor of maintaining the monarchy combined appeals to political theory with practical considerations. No less an authority than Montesquieu, the most widely quoted political thinker during the early years of the Revolution, had insisted that republican government was possible only in small states; the new United States had not existed long enough to show the French that he was wrong. The *Gazette universelle*, a newspaper that supported the moderates in the Assembly, editorialized, "It is not for Louis XVI that the monarchy has been established. . . . It is to prevent a perpetual clash of private ambitions striving for the highest post; it is to assure the separation of powers, without which there is neither liberty nor constitution; it is to maintain the indivisibility of the empire, without which we are at the mercy of any ambitious neighbor." More candidly, Lafayette told a British friend that the Assembly's leaders thought it was in their interests "to keep a monarch who is weak, in truth, and who has not been sincere with us," but who could be pressured into accepting the nearly completed constitution. Fear of foreign governments' reactions was a genuine concern: the leaders of the Assembly wrote to Emperor Leopold II, hoping to convince him to endorse the French constitution rather than expressing hostility toward it. The latter could easily drive the French population to demand "a complete overturning of everything" and a war against all other monarchies.[13]

On July 12, 1791, the committee appointed by the National Assembly to propose a response to the crisis issued its report. Since the constitution had promised that the king would be inviolable and could not be punished for his actions, the committee members concluded that he should be reinstated, provided that he was willing to swear to obey the constitution once it was completed. The radical minority in the National Assembly was incredulous. "How could you ever restore the nation's confidence in Louis XVI?" Grégoire asked. "If he promises to be loyal to the constitution, who would dare vouch for him?" Speaking for the majority, Barnave, still remembered as one of the patriot firebrands of 1789, hammered home the argument that removing the king would threaten the basis of society. "Are we going to conclude the Revolution, are we going to start it all over again?" he asked. "Is there any other aristocracy left to destroy except that of property? . . . It is time to conclude the Revolution. . . . It needs to stop now that the nation is free and that all the French are equals."[14] On July 15, the Assembly approved the committee's recommendation.

The National Assembly's decision to restore the king to the throne set off a showdown with the newly emboldened democratic radicals, led by the Cordeliers Club. The Cordeliers immediately sought support from other groups, including the Society of the Friends of Truth and the Jacobins. A petition drawn up by the journalist Brissot after a joint meeting of the clubs on the evening after the Assembly vote asserted that "it would be as contradictory to the majesty of the outraged nation as to its interests to continue to entrust the reins of the empire to a man who has lied, betrayed, and fled."[15] Robespierre, respected by the radicals because of his unswerving devotion to the popular cause in the National Assembly, urged them not to circulate the petition. He was trying to head off a confrontation that he feared would be used to justify a crackdown on the democratic movement; his advice, however, went unheeded. The Cordeliers and the more cautious Jacobins spent several hours arguing about exactly what the petition should say: Should it call for the king to be removed "by constitutional means," or should it leave open the possibility of calling for a popular insurrection?

The day of July 16 was filled with political intrigue. The deputies who had followed Barnave's lead in pushing for the reinstatement of the king set out to disrupt and defeat the radical movement. Warned by Barnave's close collaborator Alexandre Lameth, several prominent Cordeliers, including Danton and Desmoulins, dropped out of sight, but others called for a mass meeting at the Champ de Mars, where the "altar of the fatherland" from the great Festival of the Federation in July 1790

still stood. While the Cordeliers were trying to mobilize their supporters, Barnave's allies quit the Jacobin Club and founded a new group, the
Feuillants, so called because it met in a former monastery by that name.
Of the some three hundred Assembly deputies who had been Jacobin
members, only six, led by Robespierre, remained. Initially, the majority
of the provincial societies affiliated with the Jacobins backed the Feuillants, whose meeting place was next door to the Manège, giving it the
appearance of being an annex of the legislature.

Meanwhile, the Cordeliers' supporters gathered at the altar of the fatherland to draft yet another petition. They were careful not to directly
challenge the authority of the Assembly by calling for a republic, but
they asked that the question of the king's fate be referred to the "primary
assemblies" that would soon be gathering everywhere in the country to
choose deputies for the new legislature. As they dispersed for the night,
they announced that citizens would be invited to come to the Champ
de Mars on the next day to sign the new petition, which would then
be delivered to the Assembly. People began to gather at the Champ de
Mars on the morning of July 17. The meeting was disrupted when two
men were pulled from under the platform at the altar, where they had
been drilling a hole, probably in the hope of looking up the skirts of
women coming to sign the petition. With the city crackling with political tension, however, members of the crowd imagined that they might
have been planning to disrupt the rally or even plant explosives. The
two men were hustled to the nearest police station and then killed.

News of this incident provided the pretext that hardliners in the
Assembly and the city government had been waiting for to suppress the
radical movement. The Assembly rushed through a resolution calling
on the mayor to disperse the crowd at the Champ de Mars. Lafayette
and Bailly assembled their forces and marched across the city, carrying with them a red flag to announce the imposition of martial law.
Many of the National Guardsmen, frustrated by months of trying to
contain an unruly population, were more than ready to use force. As
the troops reached the Champ de Mars, a shot rang out, causing panic
in the crowd and among the guards, who immediately charged toward
the "altar of the fatherland." They did not give the warning that was

supposed to precede the use of force, and at least sixty members of the crowd were killed. The shock caused by the massacre was enormous. For the first time, the National Guard, the citizen militia created by the revolutionary movement itself, had become "f—ing villains and rogues who had the baseness to fire on the people," as a cabdriver arrested on the following day said.[16]

The Cordelier journalists were temporarily silenced, although the chronicler Nicolas Ruault told his brother that "their opinion has nevertheless become stronger; it's the usual effect of persecution."[17] Plans to stage a mass trial of those arrested were shelved, as it was clear that eyewitness testimony would not back up claims that the crowd had started the fighting. Two months later, when the National Assembly was winding up its meetings, it approved a general amnesty for political crimes. Many who had sided with the Cordeliers never forgot the massacre, however. Two years later, when Mayor Bailly was caught up in the Reign of Terror and sentenced to death, the guillotine was transported to the Champ de Mars so that he could be executed on the site of what his enemies regarded as his greatest crime.

With the issue of the king's fate settled and the radical opposition temporarily silenced, the National Assembly undertook a final push to finish work on the constitution. The efforts of the Feuillant leaders Barnave and Duport were complicated by the continuing reluctance of the king and queen to sincerely embrace the constitution. Barnave tried to persuade the royal couple that Louis's powers under the new arrangements would still be eminently respectable. His veto power would be more effective than the rights he had previously possessed to override the parlements; he would still choose all the important government officials; and his "civil list," the money he could spend at his own discretion, would be greater than that of any other European ruler. "What more does it take to be king?" Barnave asked. Although Marie-Antoinette sent her brother Leopold II a letter, essentially dictated by Barnave, asking him to promise to respect Louis's acceptance of the constitution, she continued to regard it as a "tissue of impractical absurdities." In secret notes she told the Austrian government that she and the king were just pretending to go along with the Feuillants, "in order to better double-cross them later."[18]

Although Leopold remained reluctant to get drawn into French affairs, the failure of the flight to Varennes put pressure on him and other European rulers to make some gesture on behalf of their fellow monarch. Up to this point, the major European powers had been content to treat the turmoil in France as an internal French matter; some of them were secretly pleased to see the continent's major power sidelined while they pursued their own agendas. For the three eastern powers, Austria, Prussia, and Russia, developments in Poland were more pressing than the situation in France. On May 3, 1791, "patriot" reformers, acting together with King Stanislas, staged a parliamentary revolution, trimming the powers of the aristocracy and granting political rights to wealthier urban residents, although not the peasantry. The *Gazette de Leyde* contrasted the Polish revolution, which "has not cost a drop of blood," with the upheaval in France, but Poland's neighbors, who were not prepared to tolerate a movement that threatened their influence, began planning military intervention that would result in a partition of the country in 1792.[19]

Emperor Leopold and the king of Prussia met in the Saxon town of Pillnitz on August 17, 1791, and issued a joint declaration calling "the present position of His Majesty the King of France . . . a matter of common concern to all the sovereigns of Europe," thus designating the French Revolution as an international issue. They avoided making any firm commitment to defeat it, however. In fact, they made it clear that they did not intend to act unless all the other European powers agreed, a condition unlikely to be met. As the loyal Fersen, now in exile in Brussels, told the queen, for many European powers "it is useful that disorder and anarchy continue and the kingdom is thereby weakened, without them seeming to contribute to it and without it having cost them a thing." The king's brothers, now together in Coblentz after the comte de Provence's successful escape from France, had the Pillnitz declaration published and circulated in France along with their own cover letter, in which they optimistically insisted that the European monarchs were now ready to intervene in France. They adjured Louis XVI not to abandon "the fundamental maxims of the monarchy" and outraged him by trying to appoint a new royal governor for the colony of Saint-Domingue without his approval.[20] The royal brothers' actions raised fears about an invasion of France and undercut the credibility of the king's assurances of support for the constitution.

Meanwhile, Barnave, Duport, and the other leaders of the newly formed Feuillants worked to revise the constitution in ways that they claimed would give further protection to property rights and strengthen the executive branch of the government. They proposed raising the property requirement for voting to a level that would have completely excluded peasants and urban artisans. Barnave insisted that "for most men, tranquility is more important than liberty," which allowed the radicals to portray him as a hypocrite. They claimed that he had abandoned the core values of the Revolution that he had done so much to launch in the summer of 1789. Robespierre, who had taken on the mission of salvaging the Jacobin Club after the split with the Feuillants, was at his most devastating in denouncing them for their efforts to create a new aristocracy: "What good does it do for me as a citizen if there are no more nobles," he demanded to know, "if I see that privileged class succeeded by another to whom I am forced to give my vote so that it can discuss my most cherished interests?" Popular militants demanded that poorer citizens be allowed to participate in the elections for the new assembly that was about to be chosen. "Workers are urged to rise up on the pretext that, since all men have been declared equal by the law as well as by nature, one should not let wealth create differences among them," the chronicler Adrien Colson reported.[21]

The Feuillant leaders' efforts to revise the constitution were deeply unpopular, and this allowed Robespierre to regain the loyalty of many of the Jacobins who had initially shifted their loyalty to the new club. He emphasized his unswerving commitment to the constitution and his lack of personal ambition at a moment when Barnave and Duport appeared to be trying to find some way to make it possible for them to be appointed as ministers, despite the provisions of the self-denying ordinance passed the previous May. Robespierre gained the nickname of "the Incorruptible," and became known as a politician who was ready to put the public interest ahead of his own career. In the provinces, patriotic militants like Goujon stood by the Jacobin network and worked to win over the population. Goujon browbeat the local priest into letting him use the church to give lectures to the local villagers every Sunday. He did not aim to destroy religion—"he admired above all the morality of Jesus, in which he found all the principles necessary for the happiness and the peace of families and society," his friend Tissot wrote—but he thought priests distorted the true teachings of Christianity. Through his lectures, he enacted the revolutionaries' dream of "regenerating" the population by explaining the Declaration of Rights and announcing that "the poor and virtuous farmer, bent over the soil that he works with his hands . . . is a thousand times greater . . . than the haughty rich men who think that they have been raised above other men." Tissot later remembered seeing tears in the peasants' eyes as Goujon depicted for them "the happiness that true liberty promises."[22]

On September 13, 1791, the king announced that he would accept the constitution as it stood, without further revisions. By this time, the elections for the new Legislative Assembly that would replace the National Assembly were well under way. Although many of the new deputies shared the views of the Feuillants, it was clear that the Jacobins would also have powerful spokesmen in the new body, including well-known figures such as Brissot and Condorcet and new ones like Pierre Vergniaud, who represented Bordeaux. However, there would be no more deputies elected to represent the privileged orders of the old regime, who had made up half of the original membership of the National Assembly. In the last days before they handed over power to their successors, the deputies of the National Assembly reversed the decisions they had made earlier on several controversial issues. After long hesitations, they voted to annex the papal enclave of Avignon in southern France, setting a precedent that threatened to cause conflicts with the country's neighbors. Barnave roused himself to defend the white colonists of Saint-Domingue, who had vowed to "bury themselves under its ruins, rather than to allow the promulgation of the decree of May 15," which had granted rights to free men of color born to free and legally married parents. As the deputies listened to Barnave's reminder that "this regime is oppressive, but it provides a living in France for several million men," they were unaware that thousands of enslaved blacks in the country's richest colony had just risen up against that oppression; news of the rebellion that began on the night of August 22, 1791, would not reach Paris for another month. After a debate as angry as the original clash on the issue in May, Barnave won a last political triumph by getting the National Assembly to repeal the decree of May 15. The deputies would leave the issue of rights for free men of color to the discretion of the white colonists.[23]

Although it refused to maintain its earlier stand on behalf of the rights of free people of color, the Assembly then overturned the restrictions it had continued to impose on the Ashkenazi Jews of Alsace. A decree adopted on September 28 offered them citizenship rights on the same basis as all the other inhabitants of the country, although, unlike members of other minority groups, they were required to take a civic oath. As part of this oath, they had to explicitly renounce the special privileges and legal exemptions that organized Jewish communities had previously held; these had allowed them to follow their own laws on matters such as marriage and divorce and to settle legal disputes among themselves in Jewish courts. Whereas the status of the Jews occasioned considerable debate, another minority saw its status transformed without any discussion. As part of a general revision of the country's criminal code, the deputies voted to eliminate penalties for "those phony offenses, created by superstition, feudalism, the tax system, and despotism."[24] Among those "phony offenses" were homosexual acts: France thus became the first country to completely decriminalize them.


On September 30, 1791, the deputies of the National Assembly gathered for the last time in the Salle de Manège, the improvised meeting hall created for them when they had come to Paris from Versailles. There was no equivalent to the elaborate ceremony that had opened the Estates General more than two years earlier. Some of the leading personalities who had decisively shaped the Assembly's extraordinary history were missing. Mirabeau, whose thundering oratory had rallied the deputies to defy the king at the royal session of June 23, 1789, was dead; Mounier, so influential in the early debates, had resigned after the October Days and returned to his native Dauphiné. On their last day of work, as usual, the deputies had a crowded agenda. It included a report on the financial situation, mention of troubles in the provinces, and last-minute amendments to various decrees. Their president thanked the staff who had assisted them in their work and reminded them of the etiquette to be observed when the king came to officially declare their session over.

It was left to Emmanuel Pastoret, a newly elected deputy to the Legislative Assembly that was about to replace the National Assembly, to deliver the only substantial assessment of what the legislators had accomplished during the twenty-nine months of their labors. "Liberty had fled beyond the seas, or hidden itself in the mountains," he told them:

> You put it back on its throne among us. Despotism had erased all the pages of the book of nature; you put back into it this immortal declaration, the Decalogue of free men. . . . You created a political representation that . . . made the law the general expression of the will of the French. . . . You broke all the links of the feudal chain under which [the people] was oppressed. Pride had separated men; you worked to reunite them. Equality had been so distorted that it was regarded as a privilege to defend the country. All citizens have become soldiers. . . . You made the service of the altar more venerable. . . . You freed commerce, agriculture, industry, thought. Not satisfied with having created the most beautiful constitution in the universe, you gave yourself over to such immense labor on the laws that those who may someday try to imitate you will perhaps say . . . what Alexander said of Philip: he left me nothing to conquer.[25]

Few of the deputies who listened to Pastoret could have entirely accepted this rosy vision of their accomplishments. There were official celebrations of the completion of the constitution—the king paid for the illumination of the Tuileries Gardens and the Champs-Élysées on September 25, and the city put on an even larger display a week later. But even as the deputies took part in these events, they were well aware that the country was still beset by conflicts. Many nobles signed a protest against the constitution, and the pace of emigrations picked up. On the left, dissatisfaction with the constitution was equally strong. The *Révolutions de Paris* told its readers how street demonstrators had surrounded Robespierre and his close ally Pétion and placed crowns of oak leaves on their heads, honoring them for their dogged opposition to the document's antidemocratic features. As for the rest of the deputies, the journal wrote, "They are gone, these faithless representatives, covered with gold and curses." The militant and self-proclaimed atheist Sylvain Maréchal told the departing deputies that they had accomplished nothing: "I still see, as before, two distinct castes, the rich and the poor . . . in spite of the Declaration of Rights."[26]

As she saw the constitution going into effect without any mention of rights for women, the always outspoken Olympe de Gouges was inspired to rewrite the document's most celebrated section in the form of a "Declaration of the Rights of Woman," beginning with the assertion that "woman is born free and lives equal to man in her rights." Her creative appropriation of the National Assembly's own language gave her document special force. She insisted that "male and female citizens, being equal in the eyes of the law, must be equally admitted to all honors, positions and public employment," and she defended the right of women to speak in public with a striking formulation: "Woman has the right to mount the scaffold; she must equally have the right to mount the rostrum." She concluded her manifesto with a call for a completely egalitarian marriage contract.[27] In the uproar of 1791, de Gouges's publication attracted little attention, but with the rise of modern women's movements, it has come to be recognized as a milestone of feminist thought.

As they prepared to disperse, many of the deputies had come to regret the sweeping changes brought about by the decrees they had voted for on the night of August 4, 1789; others were convinced that not enough had been done to fulfill those promises to establish equality and extinguish the remnants of feudalism. Still, most of the deputies were proud of the Declaration of the Rights of Man and Citizen, which they had left untouched in August 1791 during their debates about revising the constitution, even though they were acutely conscious of the bitter disputes that had divided them about the meaning of its principles.

Ferrières assured his wife that "the king and the queen seem to be entirely for the constitution," but it required considerable optimism to believe in their sincerity.[28] Whether deputies had supported or opposed the Civil Constitution of the Clergy, they could hardly have agreed with Pastoret's claim that their legislation had settled the religious questions facing the country. They knew how divided the military had become as a result of the changes wrought by the Revolution. Another of their last acts in September 1791 had been an effort to reconcile the principles of economic freedom Pastoret celebrated with the realities of life in the peasant communities, whose unrest continued to trouble them. Whatever their true feelings about the Assembly's accomplishments, however, the departing deputies knew they had made immense changes in their country's life. For better or for worse, they had truly inaugurated a new era of history, for their own country and for the world that surrounded it.

# 12

# A SECOND REVOLUTION

*October 1791–August 1792*

O N OCTOBER 1, 1791, THE DAY AFTER THE FINAL SESSION OF THE NA-
tional Assembly, the 745 members of the first legislature to be
elected under the new constitution took their predecessors' places
in the Manège, the riding hall that had been converted into a parliamentary meeting place two years earlier. Whereas half of the legislators
in the National Assembly had originally been elected as representatives of the old regime's privileged orders, the clergy and the nobility,
the overwhelming majority of the new legislature's members had been
part of the Third Estate before the Revolution. Under the rules passed
in 1789, they had to be wealthy enough to pay the equivalent of a *marc
d'argent* in taxes, which distanced them from the urban populace of
Paris and from the peasantry who made up the vast majority of the
French population. Thanks to Robespierre's "self-denying ordinance,"
none of the new deputies had been members of the previous assembly.
The new deputies were supporters of the Revolution: two-thirds of them
had held local office since the start of the movement. Like the members
of the National Assembly, they came from all over the country, and

few knew many of their new colleagues before they found themselves charged with making the new constitution function.

With diehard members of the nobility having emigrated and clergy who opposed the Civil Constitution ineligible to run, there were no outspoken defenders of the old regime to take the place of the deputies of the National Assembly, such as the abbé Maury, who had regularly denounced the revolutionary experiment. But only a handful of the new legislators, such as Antoine Christophe Merlin de Thionville, Claude Basire, and François Chabot, were associated with the radical Cordeliers Club in Paris, which had called for the replacement of the monarchy by a democratic republic after the king's flight. Just fifty-two of the new deputies joined the Jacobin Club, which, true to its official name, Friends of the Constitution, hesitated to openly criticize the new constitution that had just gone into effect. Traveling through the countryside on her way to Lyon, Madame Roland wrote to Robespierre, with whom she was still friendly, that the population "raised their hackles at the word of republic, and a king seems to them essential to their existence." Her letter strengthened his conviction that the supporters of the Revolution should vigilantly defend the document's provisions and put the onus for violating them on the king. In mid-October 1791, when the firebrand journalist Camille Desmoulins predicted that the new constitution would not last long, because of the glaring contradiction between its "divine preface," the Declaration of the Rights of Man and Citizen, and its other provisions, many Jacobins attacked him for undermining the new institutions.[1]

The Feuillants, the group of moderates who had broken away from the Jacobins at the time of the massacre of the Champ de Mars in July 1791, initially had more sympathizers among the new deputies. The popularity of the Feuillants reflected a widespread hope that the king would cooperate and help to make the new constitutional monarchy work. Behind the scenes, the former Feuillant leader Barnave kept up his correspondence with Marie-Antoinette, urging her to press the king to make more convincing gestures to show his acceptance of the new regime. Events had turned the giddy princess whose escapades had scandalized Versailles into a calculating political strategist. The queen largely replaced the king in trying to save the monarchy, both from the revolutionaries and from "the follies of the princes and emigrants" whose efforts to promote a foreign invasion of the kingdom put the royal couple's lives in danger. Marie-Antoinette remained opposed to any genuine cooperation with the Revolution. In one letter to Fersen, she wrote, "There is nothing to be done with this current Assembly, it is a collection of criminals, fools and idiots."[2] Nevertheless, she was convinced that the only chance of defeating the movement was to let its own internal contradictions destroy it.

As it became clear that Louis XVI was not prepared to make genuine compromises with them, the Feuillant club lost its appeal to the deputies. The Jacobins, in contrast, continued to extend their network of provincial affiliates, and the debates at their meetings in Paris, extensively publicized in the press, mobilized public support for their ideas. Robespierre, who had done so much to preserve the Jacobin network after the split with the Feuillants, remained an important presence in the Paris club, even though he was now out of office. The most dominant representative of the movement, however, was the journalist and newly elected deputy Brissot. He found support from a group of deputies from the department of the Gironde, the area around Bordeaux. They included Pierre Vergniaud, a dazzling orator, and his colleagues Élie Guadet and Armand Gensonné. Hostile journalists soon began to speak of "Girondins" or "Brissotins" as an organized faction, although the group had no formal organization or clear program. Attracted by the brilliant and witty Madame Roland, Brissot and many of his allies met regularly at the apartment she and her much older husband occupied. Unlike Olympe de Gouges or Etta Palm d'Aelders, Madame Roland did not speak out on issues of women's rights, but she was eager to promote the success of the Revolution and energetically encouraged the men in her circle to stand up for its principles.

There was a certain amount of justification for Brissot's conviction that he deserved to lead the revolutionary movement. His role in founding the Society of the Friends of the Blacks showed a genuine commitment to the ideal of freedom for all men, even when it meant challenging strong vested interests, and in 1789 he had been among the strongest advocates for freedom of the press and the notions of natural rights and national sovereignty. When his sometime associate Mirabeau had embarked on his perilous effort to combine support for the Revolution with advocacy for a strong monarchy, Brissot had retained his deep suspicion of royal power. He had also been quick to turn against the early Jacobin leaders, such as Barnave and Duport, when they began retreating from what he regarded as the essential principles of liberty and equality. Until his election to the Legislative Assembly, Brissot had generally been an ally of Robespierre, although his prerevolutionary experiences, which had included extensive foreign travel and contact with influential political figures, convinced him that he had a more sophisticated knowledge of the world than the earnest provincial lawyer from Arras. Comfortable holding forth in assemblies dominated by middle-class participants or among small groups of friends, such as those who gathered in the Rolands' apartment, Brissot lacked Danton's ability to bond easily with the common people of Paris, and his newspaper lacked the populist appeal of the publications attributed to the Père Duchêne or Marat's *Ami du peuple.* In the long run, Brissot's inability to hold the trust of the Jacobin radicals or win over the popular movement would prove fatal to him and his network of allies. But for nearly a year, no one had a greater influence on the direction of the Revolution.

As Brissot and the Jacobins squared off against the more conservative Feuillants, a new word entered the revolutionary vocabulary: *sans-culottes,* literally, "without breeches." At first, the epithet was used dismissively by conservatives to stigmatize men from the lower classes who wore long workingmen's trousers rather than the knee breeches and stockings required in respectable society. Soon, however, left-wing journalists turned the term into a label for true supporters of the people's cause, particularly those from the lower classes. The most famous answer to the question, "What is a sans-culotte?" defined him as "a being who always goes on foot, who has no millions . . . and who lives simply on the fourth or fifth story with his wife and children, if he has any. He is useful, because he knows how to plow a field, to work a forge, a saw, a file, to cover a roof, make shoes and give the last drop of his blood for the Republic."[3]

Je fuis le véritable père Duchefne, foutre.

## LA CONFESSION
### DU
# PERE DUCHESNE
## A L'ABBÉ MAURI,

ET CELLE DE L'ABBÉ MAURI
AU PERE DUCHESNE,

SA CONVERSION A LA CONSTITUTION, SON
ACCEPTATION D'UN VICARIAT DE
VILLAGE, SON DÉPART AVEC DES LETTRES
DE RECOMMANDATION DU PERE DU-
CHESNE.

L'ABBÉ MAURY, homme très-charitable
pour le falut de fon prochain, ayant appris que
le pere Duchefne étoit dangéreufement malade,

---

Je suis le véritable Père Duchêne ci devant
rue du vieux colombier n°. 30 actuellement
rue du Four St. Germain n°. 17.

## PRÉDICTION
### DU
# PÈRE DUCHÊNE
Des grands événemens qui arriveront bien-
tôt. Tableau alarmant de la situation de
la France. L'aveuglement des Parisiens,
seul auteur de tous les maux. Grandes fêtes
de Condé et du cardinal Collier, lors de
la fuite du roi. Massacres en Bretagne,
Promesse du Père Duchêne à l'abbé Maury d'un bout de corde patriotique.

LA France aujourd'hui est une mer bat-
tue par des vens contraires, c'est une voi-

---

THE VOICE OF THE PEOPLE: Two examples of newspapers attributed to the Père Duchêne, written in simple language the common people could understand. On the left, an issue from 1790 shows the Père Duchêne wearing a respectable coat. In the image on the right, from 1791, he wears rough workingman's clothes. The two pistols in his belt, the hatchet brandished over his head, and the musket in easy reach leave no doubt about his revolutionary militancy. *Source: Newberry Library.*

In practice, many of those who came to call themselves sans-culottes were wealthier and more educated than this stereotype suggested. To be a sans-culotte was as much a matter of political behavior as of social class. Many of the leaders of the Paris sans-culotte movement were small businessmen like the veteran glassfitter Jacques Ménétra, whose election to numerous positions of responsibility in his Paris section showed the extent of his local connections. Others, like the brewery owner Antoine-Joseph Santerre or the Polish nobleman Claude François Lazowski, won acceptance through their leadership during revolutionary journées. The sans-culotte was the virtuous opposite of the *aristocrate*, but was also increasingly opposed to the wealthier and more educated stratum of the Third Estate. Radical militants began using the term "sans-culottes" to rally opposition not just to the former nobles, but to all those who refused to identify themselves with the common people.

Although the popularity of the term projected the urban lower classes into the center of political debate, the attitudes of the peasantry would prove equally important in shaping the outcome of the Revolution. Among the many last-minute enactments of the outgoing National Assembly was a rural code that was meant to institutionalize the sweeping changes in laws affecting the lives of villagers, who made up the overwhelming majority of the French population. Legislators in Paris had a mental image of simple country folk whom they could mold into a new "regenerated" citizenry, but they recognized that they could not change the harsh economic realities of rural life. As the editors of the Feuille villageoise, an inexpensive weekly newspaper aimed at a rural audience, wrote, "being unable to bring wealth to the villages, we will at least try to give them truth and instruction."[4] The attitude of many deputies toward the rural population was reflected in the paper, which openly told its readers that they lacked the basic knowledge to understand political debates unless they were presented in the simplest terms.

Peasants may not have followed the intricacies of politics as closely as the Paris sans-culottes, but they had a keen sense of their own interests. The country population was not the uniform mass that the deputies often imagined. Rural communities in the crowded wheat-growing regions of northern France were deeply divided by tensions between their minority of wealthy farm entrepreneurs and their majority of nearly landless laborers, whereas villages where property was more equally distributed were more harmonious. Prosperous villages with extensive holdings of common land and forests did not have the same interests as poor settlements with few shared resources. Reactions to the Revolution in rural regions where the peasants were deeply religious were very different from reactions in areas where devotion to the Church was more tenuous, and experiences were different as well depending on whether a community's residents spoke French or not as their everyday language.

Although many peasants may not have understood the details of the extraordinary events that began in Versailles and Paris in 1789, they quickly realized that their place in society had radically changed. One ex-seigneur complained that "the former vassals believe themselves to be more powerful than kings."[5] After the night of August 4, landlords and their representatives no longer ran the local courts; nor could they compel the population to use their mill or their winepress. Local legal disputes, formerly settled in seigneurial courts, were now handled by locally elected justices of the peace. In their improvised courtrooms, litigants were allowed to present their arguments orally, instead of having to pay lawyers and clerks to write them down, and the justices tried to settle as many quarrels as possible through informal mediation. Cheaper and simpler than the courts of the old regime, the new system showed peasants that the Revolution did have some real benefits.

Although most peasants could not read, there were at least a handful of newspaper subscribers in even the smallest communities, and they shared the latest reports with their neighbors. The revolutionary assemblies bombarded humble village mayors with laws and decrees that they were expected to enforce, and public festivals, such as the federations of 1790, linked the population to national events. The formation of National Guard units, which took place even in rural villages, put arms in the hands of the peasantry and gave them the power to defend their interests. In the department of the Haute-Saône alone, thirty villages with populations of under six hundred had their own guard units.[6] In the early years of the Revolution, rural National Guards served primarily as a local police force and as a symbolic presence at patriotic ceremonies; membership was not particularly onerous. When the National Assembly called on the guardsmen to help pressure local priests to take the oath supporting the Civil Constitution, however, some of them found themselves uncomfortably at odds with their fellow villagers.

From 1789 on, the middle-class lawyers who dominated the revolutionary assemblies consistently promoted the idea that property-owners should be able to do whatever they wanted with their land and the crops it produced. This individualistic ideal was rooted in the economic theories of the eighteenth-century Physiocrats and articulated in numerous articles in the *Encyclopédie*, but few peasants were prepared to embrace it, despite lectures from the editors of the *Feuille villageoise*, who scolded them, with exasperation, that "you want the big producers, the land-owners, to hire you and raise your wages, and you don't want them to have the right to sell the fruits of their fields." The rural code enacted by the National Assembly on September 28, 1791, contained bold language promising that landowners were "free to vary at their will the cultivation and management of their lands, to manage their harvests as they wish, and to dispose of all the products of their property within the kingdom and outside of it." From the peasants' point of view, this meant that landowners, often outsiders to the village, could disregard long-established practices that protected the poorer members of the community, such as requirements that all village livestock be allowed to graze on the fields once the grain had been cut. Recognizing that their effort to implement free-enterprise principles in the countryside was likely to encounter resistance, the authors of the rural code added that landowners' freedoms were limited to those that could be exercised "without harming the rights of others, and while conforming with the law," a qualification that protected gleaning and pasturing rights.[7] Many of these traditional limitations on land use persisted long into the nine-teenth century.

Many peasants had hoped that the changes wrought by the Rev-olution would give them the chance to acquire land of their own or expand their holdings. The sale of the church lands, and later of prop-erties confiscated from nobles who fled the country, might have offered them such opportunities, but in fact only a relatively small fraction of these holdings initially wound up in peasant hands. Revolutionary administrators, under pressure to bring in as much money as possible, considered it most advantageous to sell these national lands as large parcels rather than subdividing them to make them affordable for poorer peasants. As a result, the majority of them were purchased by wealthy urban residents rather than villagers. The nobleman Gaston de Lévis noted that the "capitalists" who "bought large areas" then of-ten "sold them in small units to poorer city-dwellers and peasants," so over the years, an increasing amount of land did wind up in the hands of the peasantry.[8] In 1791, however, it was easy for peasants to conclude that they were not yet receiving the benefits the Revolution had prom-ised them.

Faced with a restive urban population in Paris and a peasantry unconvinced that the Revolution favored its interests, the newly elected Legislative Assembly also quickly found itself dealing with a crisis in France's most valuable overseas colony. A massive insurrection among the enslaved blacks in the North Province of Saint-Domingue began on the night of August 22, 1791, and quickly swept through the wealthiest sugargrowing district of the island. The rebels set fire to the highly flammable sugarcane fields, creating columns of smoke that could be seen for miles, and attacked their masters' houses, killing a number of plantation owners and managers. The white colonists, convinced that black slaves could never have organized such an effective revolt on their own,

Vorstellung der auf der Französchen Colonie St: Domingo von denen schwartzen Sclaven eingebildete Französchen democralische Freyheit, welche selbige durch unerhörte Brausamkeit zu erwerben gedachten. Sie ruinirten viele hundert Coffe und Zucker-Plantagen und verbranten die Mühlen, sie melzelden auch ohne Unterschied alle Weise die in ihre Hände fielen, dabeß ihnen ein weises Kind zur Fahne diente, schändelen Frauen und schlepten sie in elende Gefangenschaft, 1791. allein ihr Vorhaben wurde zu nichte.

UPRISING IN SAINT-DOMINGUE: The revolt in the French Caribbean colony of Saint-Domingue (today's Haiti) was the largest challenge to slavery in history. Its outbreak forced the French revolutionaries to confront the contradiction between their principles of liberty and equality and the reality of the oppressive plantation system. This fanciful illustration of the uprising was produced in Germany, hinting at how the German population may have viewed events in France. *Source: Bibliothèque nationale de France.*

blamed metropolitan *philanthropes* (lovers of humankind) like Brissot for putting explosive ideas about liberty into their heads. Distrustful of the legislators in France, the leaders of Saint-Domingue's Colonial Assembly appealed to the neighboring British and Spanish colonies for help before they communicated with their own government. This convinced Brissot and his supporters that the colonists preferred a foreign occupation of their island over the arrival of French troops to put down the rebellion, because the latter might bring revolutionary ideas with them.

Some of the participants in the black uprising may indeed have heard echoes of French revolutionary debates, which the colonists had freely discussed among themselves. But the insurgents drew more motivation from a widespread rumor that the French king wanted to improve their lot by granting them three days a week to work for pay and earn money that they could use to purchase their own freedom. The black population also found the revolutionary campaign against the Church hard to understand. Some of the colony's Catholic priests maintained contacts with the insurrection's leaders and served as intermediaries, attempting to limit the violence of the revolt. Paradoxically, the Saint-Domingue slave uprising thus began as a movement more sympathetic to the values of throne and altar than to the abstract principles of liberty and equality that had been proclaimed in 1789 but not applied to the colonies. Metropolitan revolutionary ideas had more of an impact on Saint-Domingue's free people of color, who began their own insurrection in parts of the island's West and South provinces almost simultaneously with the slave revolt in the north. Determined to claim the rights promised to them in the May 15 decree, they did not call for the freeing of the slaves, since many of them were themselves plantation owners, but they did supplement their own forces by arming some of the blacks.

Because of the time it took for ships to cross the Atlantic, news of the uprisings in Saint-Domingue only reached Paris at the end of October 1791. The reports put the revolutionary advocates of liberty and equality in an awkward position. Olympe de Gouges, whose play *Mirza and Zamore*, first performed at the end of 1789, had brought the abolitionist cause to the stage, now denounced the violence of the black insurgents: "Men are not born to be in chains, and you prove that they are necessary." Brissot and the Friends of the Blacks had always insisted that they were advocating only a gradual and peaceful phase-out of slavery, not an upheaval that would endanger the lives of the whites and the national economy. They denied that their criticisms of slavery could have set off the revolt. Just as the colonists immediately suspected a Jacobin conspiracy behind the slave insurrection, the white reformers jumped to the conclusion that the movement must have been inspired by royalists. That idea that seemed plausible, because the uprising had begun at almost the same time as the arrival in Saint-Domingue of the news of the king's attempted escape from Paris.[9]

The government dispatched six thousand troops to Saint-Domingue, the beginning of a military deployment that would continue throughout the revolutionary decade. Barnave assured Marie-Antoinette that the news would make "all the commerce and all the manufactures of France pronounce in favor of the government and against the troublemakers." As the months went by without a resolution of the crisis, Brissot and his allies blocked additional military forces until the white colonists agreed to grant rights to the free people of color. While the legislators in Paris fought verbal battles over the issue, whites and people of color in the colony's administrative capital, Port-au-Prince, clashed on November 21, 1791. Half of the city's buildings burned in the fracas. The troubles in Saint-Domingue sent sugar and coffee prices soaring in France, leading to riots at food shops. At the Jacobin Club, speakers proposed that members show their patriotism by renouncing both products until their prices came down, but few Parisians were prepared to go without the luxuries that had become the symbol of civilized urban life. Called on to put down the disturbances, the commander of a Paris National Guard unit recognized that his men would not obey him, because "they were part of the people more than they were National Guards."[10]

In addition to the disputes about colonial policy, the Legislative Assembly soon found itself divided by struggles about the émigrés and the Church that brought the king into direct confrontation with the majority of the deputies. For the more radical deputies, such as the

Girondin leader Vergniaud, there was no doubt that "clemency . . . has merely emboldened the enemies of liberty and the Constitution," and that "the time has now come to clamp down on their criminal audacity."[11] A decree passed on November 9, 1791, took aim at the royal princes who were lobbying foreign governments to intervene in France. The decree ordered them to return to the kingdom by the beginning of 1792 or else face execution if they ever reentered French territory. Louis XVI could hardly endorse such a draconian measure against his own brothers, and he promptly exercised his constitutional right to veto the law. A second law, passed on November 29, 1791, tried to put a stop to disruptive agitation by refractory priests. It offered those who were willing to tone down their hostility to the new government the option of taking a civic oath that did not involve an explicit acceptance of the Civil Constitution of the Clergy in its entirety. Again the king used his veto, convincing the revolutionaries that he was determined to protect their worst enemies.

Fearing that the survival of the Revolution and the country was at stake, the patriot leaders embarked on a high-stakes gamble: led by Brissot, they began to campaign for a declaration of war against the foreign powers that were providing refuge to the émigrés. In the spring of 1790, when the question of the king's right to declare war had been debated, the supporters of the Revolution had argued that a free people would never embark on a war of aggression. Now, in a series of vehement speeches at the Jacobin Club, Brissot, citing examples from antiquity and the recent American war of independence, proclaimed that "a people which has conquered its freedom, after twelve centuries of slavery, needs a war to consolidate it, to test itself, to show that it is worthy of freedom." Adopting the exalted language common at the Society of the Friends of Truth, where Brissot and his supporters often appeared, he announced that "such a war is a sacred war, a war ordained from on high, and like the heavens, it will purify our souls." A war for liberty would also be a war for equality: "By mixing men and ranks, elevating the plebeian, bringing down the proud patrician, war alone can make all equal and regenerate souls."[12]

If the king sought to betray the country by committing treason, Brissot argued, so much the better: "We need great betrayals: they will save us, for powerful doses of poison still exist in France, and it will take strong explosions to expel them." The American revolutionaries, he recalled, had emerged strengthened despite the treachery of Benedict Arnold. If the French launched a "crusade for universal freedom," Brissot promised, they could be sure of support from the populations of other countries. "All the nations secretly invite it," he said. "It will topple all the foreign Bastilles."[13] He was not worried about the disorganization in the French army caused by the emigration of aristocratic officers. Fighting for a noble cause, he insisted, French soldiers would surely be invincible. Brissot's close ally, the banker Étienne Clavière, claimed that war would restore the value of the Revolution's depreciating paper currency, the assignats, which he alleged was being deliberately undermined by foreign governments. For her own reasons, the influential Madame de Staël joined in the campaign for war: her lover, the handsome comte de Narbonne, had just been appointed war minister and hoped to distinguish himself by conducting a limited offensive against Trier, a small German state where a number of émigrés had taken up residence.

The Feuillants and moderates in the Legislative Assembly had grave doubts about such an adventure, but they feared appearing to defend the émigrés and the diehard opponents of the Revolution. Barnave emphasized to Marie-Antoinette the importance for the king of taking a firm position against the Austrian government's protection of the émigrés in the German principalities close to the French frontier. In a secret letter to her longtime confidant Mercy d'Argenteau, the queen gave an assessment of the situation that was very different from Brissot's unbounded confidence in French success. "I don't need to go on at length to show how absurd this policy is: without an army, without discipline, without money, we are the ones who are going to attack." Nevertheless, Marie-Antoinette explained, Louis XVI was going to support the demand for war. "The king is not free, he has to follow the general will, and for our personal safety here, he has to do what he is told."[14]

Paradoxically, the most forceful critic of Brissot's war policy was not a moderate or a royalist but rather the most consistent defender of radical democracy among the revolutionaries, Robespierre. In speeches at the Jacobin Club, he challenged Brissot's assurance that the French would find broad support if they invaded foreign countries. "The most extravagant idea that can arise in the head of a politician is to believe that it is enough for a people to enter a foreign territory with military force to get them to adopt our laws and our constitution. No one likes armed missionaries," he warned. In his view, before the French tried to bring the principles of liberty and equality to others, they needed to win their struggle against their enemies at home. He also feared that war would provide the king and his ministers with an opportunity to subvert the constitution. Robespierre's sober assessment of the risks of trying to export democratic ideas through armed intervention was prophetic, but initially, its main effect was to isolate him from the mainstream of the French revolutionary movement. Madame Roland made an unsuccessful last attempt to keep him from turning against his former allies; after a private meeting, she wrote to him, "I saw, with pain, that you are persuaded that any intelligent person who thinks differently from you about the war is not a good citizen." Robespierre's position also put him at odds with the patriotic volunteers who were eagerly joining the army. "How enthusiastically we would go into combat!" one of them wrote. "In fighting for the cause of our country we would at the same time be fighting for that of all peoples."[15]

The Austrian government attempted to avoid an open conflict by urging local German rulers to curb the émigrés' activities, but Vienna promised to fight back if the French took military action. As rhetoric in Paris became increasingly heated, the Austrians and their longtime rivals, the Prussians, made a secret agreement to act together in case of war. By this time, Louis XVI and Marie-Antoinette had decided to take the risk of helping Brissot achieve his goal. Fersen, who had succeeded in returning to Paris for a secret meeting with the queen in mid-February, reported to the Swedish king that the royal couple had decided that "there is no way of restoring their authority except through force and foreign assistance": in other words, the king would help plunge the country into war in the hope that his own armies would be defeated and that foreign troops would rescue him.[16] The king's decision was signaled by his appointment, on March 15, 1792, of a "Jacobin" ministry dominated by close allies of Brissot. Although Brissot himself, as a member of the legislature, was barred from holding a ministerial position, he was considered the real power behind the ministry. Clavière, the new finance minister, had been a close associate of Brissot's even before the Revolution, and the interior minister, Roland, was the husband of the woman at the center of the "Brissotin" network. Foreign policy was put in the hands of Charles-François Dumouriez, an older military officer who had long argued for an aggressive policy toward Austria.

As part of this awkward agreement between the outspoken revolutionary patriots and the monarch, Brissot achieved one of his most cherished objectives. On April 4, the king approved a law granting full civil and political rights to the free population of color in the French colonies. It also provided for the dispatch of a civil commission to Saint-Domingue with powers to replace the white colonists' local assemblies with new bodies in which they would share power with their mixed-race rivals. For the first time in history, a European government declared that nonwhites could be full citizens in its empire. The law of April 4 said nothing about ending slavery, however, and the civil commission it established was to be accompanied by a new contingent of six thousand troops, to help defeat the uprising that had begun the previous August. By overturning the National Assembly's concession of granting extensive autonomy to the colonies, the law put them under the direct control of the metropole. Opposition in the Legislative Assembly blocked the appointment of the mixed-race spokesman Julien Raimond to the commission, but on the other side of the Atlantic, members of Raimond's mixed-race group had already obtained major concessions even before news of the April 4 law reached Saint-Domingue. Convinced that the white colonists' rigid opposition to any change in the system of racial hierarchy was making it impossible to defeat the slave rebellion, the colony's governor and other officials who had already been sent from France forged an alliance with the leader of the free colored movement, Pierre Pinchinat, and the mixed-race Conseil de paix et d'union (Council of Peace and Union) that he had created as an alternative to the all-white Colonial Assembly.

Brissot's victory on the colonial front was quickly overshadowed by the consequences of his and Dumouriez's war policy. Dumouriez, who had been born close to France's northern border with Belgium, had strongly supported the revolt there against Austrian rule in 1789–1790.

He argued that the troops the Austrians had stationed in the area after their defeat of the Belgian uprising were a menace to French security, and he shared Brissot's confidence that "these provinces are permeated by the spirit of liberty" and would eagerly welcome French troops if war broke out. On April 20, 1792, Louis XVI gave Dumouriez the green light for his policy by going to the Assembly and calling for a declaration of war. A moderate deputy, Louis Becquey, found himself echoing the arguments that the radical Robespierre had made in his debate with Brissot: "We shall appear as aggressors; we shall be portrayed as a disorderly country which upsets the peace of Europe in defiance of treaties and our own laws."[17] Despite this opposition, Brissot's heady rhetoric and Dumouriez's brash confidence carried the day: only six deputies voted against the declaration.

Enthusiasm for the war was not limited to politicians: the ranks of the army were filled by patriotic volunteers. When news of the declaration of war reached the Alsatian city of Strasbourg, a fortified city on the Rhine that was bound to play a major part in the struggle, the local mayor called on a young military officer with musical talents, Claude Joseph Rouget de Lisle, to compose a patriotic song to mark the occasion. In one night, Rouget de Lisle jotted down six stanzas, beginning with the words, "Allons enfants de la patrie! Le jour de gloire est arrivé" (Arise, children of the fatherland! The day of glory has arrived). Meant to rouse nationalist fervor, the lyrics called upon citizens to "form your battalions" and "let an impure blood water our fields." The words were fitted to a stirring melody and titled "War Song for the Army of the Rhine." Within two months, as soldiers circulated around the country, the new song had reached the other end of France. It was performed at a patriotic ceremony in Marseille on June 22, 1792, and a local newspaper provided the first printed version the next day, allowing the local volunteers to take copies with them as they headed north.

The declaration of war transformed the nature of the French Revolution. To be sure, none of those who launched it knew they were starting a conflict that would draw in all the powers of Europe, or that this conflict would continue, in one form or another, for more than twenty years. Brissot and Dumouriez, who anticipated popular uprisings that would overthrow the other governments of Europe, underestimated the determination of their adversaries and the resources they would be able to mobilize. So did Louis XVI and Marie-Antoinette, who assumed that the shaky revolutionary regime would quickly collapse. As Robespierre had warned, the faith of the revolutionary warhawks that other peoples would eagerly welcome the French proved unfounded. Brissot's expectation that war would push the Revolution in a more radical direction, however, was confirmed. The need to recruit soldiers from among the ranks of the passive citizens, that is, the poor, and to call on the entire population to make sacrifices for the war effort, made it ever more difficult to defend their exclusion from political participation. It even created openings for women to demand recognition for their contributions by volunteering to take up arms. Two young women in particular, the Fernig sisters, so impressed the general defending Valenciennes that he promised to "put them in the line of fire at the first opportunity," according to one news report. Only in April 1793 were women officially barred from combat.[18]

These expressions of women's patriotism did not result in an expansion of their rights. The Legislative Assembly did make a major change in policy with respect to the nagging question of compensation for feudal dues, however. This was an issue that mattered intensely to millions of peasants whose sons would now be called on to serve in the military. A law enacted on June 18, 1792, reversed earlier legislation that had favored former seigneurs: landowners who wanted to make peasants pay them compensation for abolished feudal dues would now be the ones who would have to come up with documentary evidence to justify their claims. The Assembly's action shored up peasant support for the revolutionary government at a time when the war crisis was forcing the government to make ever more exacting demands on the population.

As the war pushed the Revolution in a more democratic direction, it also made political conflicts more explosive. When the Brissot ministry ordered the release of the soldiers imprisoned after the army mutiny in Nancy in 1790, they were hailed as heroes who had exposed the tyranny of their aristocratic officers, a risky message to spread as the troops were preparing for battle. An elaborate procession welcomed them to Paris. Moderates responded by organizing a "Festival of the Law" to honor a small-town mayor who had been killed by a crowd demanding bread. The *Révolutions de Paris* complained that the festival's organizers "had set their hearts on humiliating and subduing the people" by "supposing that it needed to be constantly recalled to order."[19] All sides increasingly saw their opponents not just as misguided but as traitors to the country who needed to be physically eliminated, even if this meant severely limiting the freedoms that the Revolution had promised to protect.

Ironically, however, it would not be Brissot and his Girondin allies who would emerge to lead the movement toward greater democracy and radicalism, but Robespierre and the more extreme revolutionaries. The Incorruptible's paranoid fear that the military effort would allow for a restoration of royal authority was soon shown to be wrong. Robespierre's concern that war would create opportunities for ambitious and charismatic military leaders to attempt to seize power was more prophetic, however. The man who ultimately proved the point was not one of the aristocratic generals who led the French forces in 1792, but an obscure artillery lieutenant whose name was completely unknown outside of the remote island of Corsica when the war began. In 1792, the ambitious military man most in view was not Lieutenant Napoleone Buonaparte, who was still debating whether to commit himself to the French Revolution or to a movement for the independence of his native island, but the minister Dumouriez.

In accordance with Dumouriez's plan, French troops quickly crossed the Belgian frontier, but it immediately became clear that their expectations for a glorious crusade on behalf of liberty were far removed from the realities of warfare. "It is not with addresses, petitions, festivals and songs that one holds off experienced, disciplined troops skilled in tactics," a veteran officer later explained to the politicians in Paris.[20] When poorly prepared French soldiers were ambushed by Austrian defenders near Tournai and took heavy losses, the survivors turned on their own commander, General Théodore Dillon, hanging him from a lantern and burning his body. In the Legislative Assembly, the deputies responded to military setbacks by demanding stronger measures against the customary suspects, refractory priests and émigrés. Brissot and his legislative allies stepped up their attacks on what they called the "Austrian committee," the secret council through which, they claimed, Marie-Antoinette was conspiring to sabotage the war effort. The king vetoed the harsh new laws against counterrevolutionaries, further fueling the distrust surrounding the court. Had the Austrians and their Prussian allies been more prepared for the war, they might have quickly taken advantage of the disarray caused by the initial French military setbacks and the political chaos in Paris, but their generals, sure of success, took their time preparing their campaign.

In Paris, disagreements about the conduct of the war divided the Jacobins. "Robespierre and Brissot, the two chiefs of the different parties, each have their partisans, and so war is declared, as unfortunate in the club as on the frontier. It puts us on the edge of the abyss," Rosalie Jullien, a keen observer of politics, lamented to her husband. The military defeats made open conflict between the new Jacobin ministers and the king inevitable. On June 10, 1792, the interior minister, Roland, published an open letter to Louis XVI, drafted in large part by his wife, demanding that he take immediate measures against priests and others who were causing unrest. The king, Roland insisted, needed to understand the emotional force of the new passion for the country that the Revolution had created. "The fatherland is not just a word embellished by imagination; it is something tangible for which one has made sacrifices," he wrote. If the king did not prove his loyalty, this intense devotion to the nation would force local officials in the departments to take "violent measures, and the angry people will add to them through its excesses."[21] No French minister had ever dared address a ruler in such a tone, and the king reacted swiftly by dismissing Roland and the other Jacobin ministers, who had only just been appointed in March. As the Jacobins voiced their outrage, Lafayette, who had long seen himself as the one man who could maintain the balance between the court and the revolutionary radicals, became increasingly alarmed. From his position at the frontier, where he was now commanding one of the French armies, he sent a strongly worded denunciation of the Jacobins. To those who remembered how Roman generals had used their soldiers to destroy the republic, the man who had been a national hero in 1789 now began to appear as a menace to the Revolution.

If Louis XVI and Lafayette were unwilling to accept the dictates of the pro-revolutionary militants, the revolutionaries were equally unwilling to back down in the face of the king's resistance. On June 20, 1792, a week after the ministers' dismissal, a massive crowd of twenty thousand to twenty-five thousand men and women, many of them National Guardsmen carrying weapons, forced its way into the meeting hall of the Legislative Assembly and then invaded the neighboring Tuileries Palace, where they surrounded the king and kept him backed up against a window for several hours. Louis XVI faced this ordeal with unexpected courage. He allowed protesters to put a red "liberty cap," a symbol of sans-culotte militantism, on his head, and he drank a toast to the nation, but he refused the crowd's demands to withdraw his vetoes and recall the Jacobin ministers. He insisted that he was exercising his legitimate constitutional powers. Even more overt anger was directed at the queen, but she was not physically assaulted either. Toward evening, the pro-revolutionary mayor of Paris, Pétion, belatedly appeared at the palace. Determined not to provoke a confrontation with the sans-culottes that might end in bloodshed, like the massacre of the Champ de Mars a year earlier, he had accepted the demonstration organizers' promise that they would not resort to violence. The king reproached him bitterly for allowing the invasion of the palace. Marie-Antoinette, who had made it her business to win the sympathy of the National Guard officer assigned to the palace so that she could pump him for information about public opinion, was also furious. The officer had failed to protect them. "She glared fiercely at me and spoke in a tone that betrayed all her anger," he later recalled.[22]

The protest had been organized by Jacobin militants and activists in the Paris *sections*, the new subdivisions of the city, each of which had its own assembly and National Guard unit. It was the first such political intervention by the ordinary people of Paris since the October Days in 1789. Unlike the October Days, however, the journée of June 20 did not break the political deadlock that threatened to paralyze the government. Louis XVI's firm and dignified behavior in the face of the demonstrators spurred a reaction in his favor, especially in the provinces. Over seven thousand Parisians signed a petition denouncing Mayor Pétion for his failure to take active measures to stop the demonstration, and the conservative administrators of the department suspended him from office. Lafayette left his army at the frontier to come to Paris and denounce the militant movement. Radical journalists accused him of threatening a "civil war by means of which he hopes to impose a tyrannical protectorate." "If, instead of talking, Lafayette had acted," a National Guard officer who sympathized with him later wrote, "it would have been the end of all the Jacobins in the world."[23]

In the Legislative Assembly, a constitutional clergyman, Adrien Lamourette, tried to heal the inflamed political divisions. On July 7, he called on the deputies to set aside their differences and embrace one another. As men who had barely spoken to each other for months shared emotional hugs, Louis XVI hurried over from his palace to renew his oath of support for the constitution. The deputies' enthusiastic participation in "the kiss of Lamourette" revealed the emotional appeal of national unity, but the moment of reconciliation was fleeting. Both moderates and radicals had become convinced that true harmony could only be achieved by eliminating their opponents. Only two days after Lamourette's intervention, Brissot unleashed a renewed attack on the king. Demanding that the deputies declare "the country in danger," he insisted that France faced a crisis because "its forces have been paralyzed": "And who has paralyzed them?" he asked. "One man: he whom the constitution has made their leader."[24]

Brissot demanded a special committee to decide whether the king's actions amounted to a violation of his solemn oath to uphold the constitution. He also called for the elimination of the distinction between "property-owners and non-property-owners" that kept the latter from having the status of active citizens. Outside of the Assembly, "the firmest patriots and the republicans of Paris" began to organize a movement to force the king from the throne. These organizers included the Jacobin leaders, their militant allies in the Paris sections—where efforts to exclude the poor had already broken down—and the radical journalists. They aimed to "carry out a second revolution[,] whose necessity they recognized," as one of them later put it. By the first week of July, Paris newspapers such as the *Trompette du Père Duchêne* were outlining the radicals' program, calling for a popular uprising to force the Legislative Assembly to suspend the king's powers, the installation of a provisional government to replace the royally chosen ministers, and elections for a national convention to determine the future of the monarchy and draft a new constitution.[25]

The anniversary of the storming of the Bastille provided the Paris radicals an opportunity. As in 1790 and 1791, a great gathering of *fédérés*, patriotic volunteers from all over the country, was scheduled in the capital for a celebration. The armed participants would then be sent to the frontiers to strengthen the army. While they were in Paris, however, the Paris radicals decided that the fédérés, who had been selected for their revolutionary enthusiasm, could provide the muscle to overcome Louis XVI's resistance. Among the provincial militia groups, the fédérés from Brest and Marseille had especially radical reputations. As soon as the men from Marseille landed from the riverboat that brought them down the Seine, they provoked a street fight with some well-dressed Parisians who had insulted them. "The poorer people of Paris took the side of the Marseillais," the chronicler Ruault wrote.[26] The men from Marseille not only brought a new militancy to the streets of Paris: they also brought the first printed copies of the new patriotic song that Rouget de Lisle had composed in April. The stirring melody and the bellicose words of this "song of the Marseillais" became indissolubly identified with the group that brought it to Paris. "La Marseillaise," now France's national anthem, remains the one melody from the revolutionary era that is immediately recognizable around the world.

The Legislative Assembly was reluctant to endorse the radicals' demands or the strong-arm tactics of the fédérés, but even the moderate deputies recognized the danger of the situation. The country was bracing for a foreign invasion, and the head of the government and his ministers were suspected of collusion with the enemy. On July 22, a week after the celebration in honor of Bastille Day, while the out-of-town fédérés were still in the city, the Assembly finally accepted Brissot's recommendation to declare the "country in danger." Its decree ordered all local governments to take any measures they thought necessary to respond to the crisis, without waiting for instructions from the king or his ministers. Rendered virtually powerless by this decree, the ministers the king had appointed to replace the sacked Brissotins resigned, creating a vacuum in the executive branch and demonstrating that the constitutional monarchy had ceased to function. Nevertheless, the Assembly's moderates were still reluctant to support firm measures. They defeated a motion to censure Lafayette, for example, even after he announced he would use his troops to oppose any threats against the king.

As the constitutional system inaugurated just a year earlier broke down, both sides prepared for a violent struggle. Inside the Tuileries Palace, the members of the royal family feared for their lives. Although the king and queen distrusted many of the National Guardsmen assigned to protect them, they felt they could count on the loyalty of the units of professional Swiss soldiers who shared that duty. Armed with artillery, the defenders could at least hope to inflict heavy casualties if the palace was attacked. Perhaps this would enable the royal couple to hold out long enough for a rapid advance of the Austrian and Prussian armies to rescue them. By late July, the forces of the two foreign monarchies were finally ready to cross the French frontier. To the frustration of the French émigrés whose presence in Germany had done so much to trigger the war, the Austrians and Prussians refused to give them a leading role in the invasion, fearing that their presence would inflame resistance. Instead, the allied powers insisted that they were intervening only to uphold Louis XVI's legitimate authority. On July 28, 1792, the commander of the allied army, the duke of Brunswick, issued a manifesto warning that the population of Paris would be severely punished if the royal family was harmed.

The threats in Brunswick's manifesto convinced supporters of the Revolution that there was no more time to spare in dealing with the king. Men like Fournier l'Américain, a former Saint-Domingue colonist who had helped lead the assault on the Bastille and the October Days march in 1789, had concluded that "the French legislators only showed real energy when the people rose up and forced them to act."[27] On August 3, 1792, the assembly of the Mauconseil section of Paris issued a manifesto demanding that the Legislative Assembly remove Louis XVI from the throne. If the legislators did not do so, the people of Paris would use force to oust the monarch. Behind the scenes, a secret committee of militants from the Cordeliers Club and the sans-culotte movement prepared to launch the National Guard battalions of the Paris sections against the Tuileries. The militants calculated that if their movement succeeded, radical politicians would have no choice except to satisfy their demand for the elimination of the opponents of the Revolution.

Brissot and the Girondin deputies thought the threat of an insurrection would intimidate Louis XVI into reappointing the ministers he had dismissed in June and letting them direct the war effort, but they were hesitant about completely overturning the constitution. The consequences of an armed popular uprising were unpredictable. They worried that the army might not accept the outcome of a violent uprising in Paris, and that Lafayette might find support among his troops to intervene against it. Brissot himself feared that the country was not ready for a radical shift from monarchy to republic. In his memoirs, which he wrote after his own defeat and arrest a year later, he recalled that he "knew very well that this single word [republic] would have offended many people, and perhaps caused the failure of the revolution that was coming."[28] Earlier, the Girondin newspapers had joined in agitating for the deposition of the king, but now they began to transmit confusing signals, suggesting that a direct confrontation should be postponed. After the decisive clash, the Girondins' apparent last-minute doubts about the wisdom of overthrowing the monarchy by force would be used to discredit them.

Unlike the spontaneous and disorganized uprising that had led to the capture of the Bastille, the insurrection of August 10, 1792, was carefully plotted. Under cover of night, the activists summoned their troops and took control of the Commune, the government of Paris based in the Hôtel de Ville. They dismissed its elected assembly and replaced it with their own loyalists from the sections. For the next month and a half, this revolutionary Commune would compete with, and sometimes overshadow, the national government. Pétion, the mayor who had failed to prevent the mass demonstration on June 20, was put under house arrest, and the commander of the National Guard, suspected of being loyal to Lafayette, was summoned to the Hôtel de Ville and murdered. The brewer Santerre, a leading figure in the popular radical movement from the time of the storming of the Bastille, took his place, and the

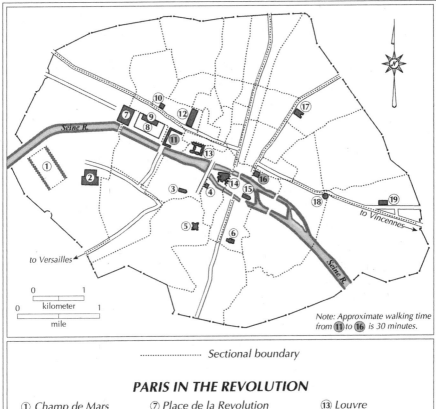

## PARIS IN THE REVOLUTION

1. Champ de Mars
2. Invalides
3. Abbaye Prison
4. Cordelier Club
5. Luxembourg Palace
6. Pantheon
7. Place de la Revolution
8. Tuileries Gardens
9. National Assembly (Manège)
10. Jacobin Club
11. Tuileries Palace
12. Palais Royal
13. Louvre
14. Conciergerie Prison
15. Notre Dame
16. Hôtel de Ville
17. Temple
18. Bastille
19. Reveillon's Factory

.................. Sectional boundary

*Note: Approximate walking time from (11) to (16) is 30 minutes.*

REVOLUTIONARY PARIS: The densely populated city of Paris played a unique role in the revolutionary drama. The Bastille, the meeting halls of the revolutionary assemblies and clubs, the royal palace of the Tuileries, the seat of the city government at the Hôtel de Ville, and the working-class faubourgs, where insurrections often started, were all within close walking distance of each other. *Credit: Richard Gilbreath.*

281

tocsin was sounded to summon the guard units, especially those from the militant sans-culotte strongholds of the Faubourg Saint-Antoine and the Faubourg Saint-Marcel. Inside the Tuileries Palace, the king's defenders listened as church bells and drums sounded from all directions. By 6:00 a.m. on August 10, the section battalions were marching toward the Tuileries, armed with the long pikes that had become the favored weapons of the armed people. Inside the palace, Louis XVI and Marie-Antoinette prepared themselves for what might be their last moments. As the king reviewed his troops, Marie-Antoinette tore a pistol from an officer's belt and handed it to her husband, telling him, "Now is the time to show who you are." But some of the National Guards who were supposed to defend the Tuileries now revealed their true sentiments, shouting, "Down with the traitor!" Then they abandoned their posts.[29]

Had Louis followed his wife's prompting and allowed himself to be cut down at the head of his defenders on the steps of the palace, the result would have been fatal for the king, but it might have restored some luster to the monarchy. Instead, he turned to the former Jacobin National Assembly deputy Pierre-Louis Roederer for advice. Roederer, now a municipal official, persuaded him that the only way to save himself and his family was to abandon the palace and take refuge in the meeting hall of the Legislative Assembly. This response saved the royal family from a possible violent death, but it also made them prisoners. At the same time, it left the Legislative Assembly with the awkward question of what to do with them. To avoid violating the constitutional provision that forbade the king from being present during deliberations of the Assembly, the royal family was sequestered in the space normally reserved for the journalists who kept a record of the deputies' speeches. There they stayed until late in the night while the legislators discussed their fate.

Louis XVI's decision to abandon the Tuileries had disastrous consequences for his most loyal defenders, the Swiss Guards. By 9:30 a.m., the aggressive fédérés from Marseille had forced their way into the interior courtyard of the Tuileries. When they managed to grab two of the defenders and disarm them, the Swiss soldiers' comrades responded with a volley. Firing into the densely packed crowd, the Swiss Guards' guns claimed hundreds of victims; the final death toll of well over a thousand would make the journée of August 10 by far the bloodiest day of the Revolution in Paris. "The women ran through the streets crying and lamenting, because each of them feared a cruel loss," Rosalie Jullien reported. Outraged that the Swiss had killed patriotic citizens even after the royal family was out of danger, radical activists were convinced that they had been victims of "a crime unheard of until this epoch that the court planned against the nation," as the *Révolutions de Paris* wrote.[30] Hearing the gunfire from his refuge in the Assembly hall, Louis XVI attempted to end the bloodshed by instructing the Swiss to cease fire, but it was impossible to deliver his order in the midst of the fighting.

The Swiss soldiers' resistance infuriated the attackers, and once the attackers were able to overwhelm their opponents with their superiority in numbers, the result was gruesome. As Ruault recorded, "the people . . . went through all the apartments and massacred all the Swiss they found. The corridors, the offices, the attack, all the secret passageways and even the cupboards were searched; all the unfortunates discovered in these corners and byways were massacred; others were thrown alive from the windows, despite begging vainly for their lives, and run through with pikes on the garden terrace and the pavement of the courtyard."[31] Crowd members destroyed the furnishings of the palace. As they ransacked cabinets and drawers, they also found hundreds of letters and documents offering evidence of the court's opposition to revolutionary policies.

The violence at the Tuileries and the idea that the king's troops had deliberately opened fire on the people made any effort to stand up to the demands of the radicals impossible. Bloodshed was not confined to the palace: crowds lynched a royalist journalist and the moderate ex-deputy Clermont-Tonnerre, as well as a number of individuals accused of looting. The printing shops of royalist and moderate newspapers were attacked, and numerous ex-nobles, royal officials, and refractory priests were imprisoned. The offices of the white colonial slaveholders' Club Massiac were raided and its papers seized. Sans-culotte militants not only went after living supporters of the monarchy but also its symbols, such as the equestrian statue of Louis XIV in the Place des Victoires and the statue of Henri IV on the Île de la Cité. Napoleon Bonaparte, who witnessed the attack on the palace from the window of a nearby building, mingled with the crowd afterward. "The anger was extreme everywhere one went," he later recalled. "Hatred was in their hearts and could be seen on their faces, even though they were not at all from the lower classes."[32] The experience left him with a lasting distaste for popular violence.

With the radical Commune moving rapidly to seize power in the city, the Legislative Assembly had to act quickly to retain any influence at all. The Girondin deputy Gensonné put forward a motion to suspend the king from his functions, which would repeat what had happened after his attempted flight in June 1791. The deputies called for the election of a National Convention that, like the National Assembly of 1789, would have full authority to express the will of the people. The arguments that Sieyès, Barnave, and so many other politicians had made to justify excluding the poor from participation in politics were tossed aside; the legislators now decreed that any man over twenty-one years of age who was gainfully employed and who was not a household servant would be allowed to participate in the elections. At a time when many of the American states still had wealth qualifications for voting, revolutionary France became the first country in the world to embrace universal manhood suffrage.

On August 11, the Assembly passed a series of additional emergency measures. The royal family would be held as prisoners, and a special guardian was appointed for the Dauphin, the child heir to the throne, to remove him from the influence of his parents. Royal ministers were replaced with a new Executive Council that included Roland and Clavière, members of the Brissotin team named the previous March. But the council also included several new faces, of whom the most important was Georges Danton, who was now closely associated with the revolutionary Commune. Although he had held only a modest position as second assistant to the Commune's chief prosecutor when the August 10 insurrection broke out, Danton quickly filled the vacuum of leadership created by the uprising. For a crucial six weeks, until the newly elected Convention met on September 20, 1792, he was the one figure capable of dominating both the insurrectionary forces and the legislature. The former, he remarked, had been unleashed by what he described as "this so indispensable supplement to the revolution of July 14."[33] The latter, at this point, was struggling to keep the country together in the face of a crisis that made even the earlier revolutionary journées seem tame. Physically imposing, and, like Mirabeau, scarred by a childhood bout of smallpox, Danton stood out among the Revolution's great orators. He had a genius for improvisation: very few of his speeches were written out in advance and he rarely bothered to have them circulated in printed form. His appointment as minister of justice was meant to give the emergency Executive Council appointed to run the government credibility with the militant movement that had just overthrown the monarchy.

Danton and his colleagues had their hands full trying to satisfy the revolutionary activists in Paris while keeping some control over the rest of the country and dealing with the enemy invasion. In the capital, the victorious radicals demanded swift punishment for the political suspects they blamed for the "conspiracy" that had resulted in the deaths of so many patriots on August 10. The Legislative Assembly at first tried to defend the principle that all defendants should be judged according to normal procedures, but on August 17 it bowed to demands from Robespierre and others and agreed to establish a special Revolutionary Tribunal to handle their cases. Its judges and jurors were chosen for their patriotic convictions, and their verdicts could not be appealed. This first Revolutionary Tribunal operated only for three months, but it set a precedent for the creation of special political courts that would be revived on a much larger scale in 1793 and 1794. The first defendants convicted by the court and executed in accordance with its decisions included court officials, the commander of the Swiss Guards, and the royalist journalist Barnabé Farmian Durozoi, the first of many writers to find that the constitution's guarantee of press freedom was no protection in the heated revolutionary atmosphere.

The Revolutionary Tribunal's trials attracted large crowds of cheering spectators who often insulted the defendants as they were taken to be executed. The editor of the tribunal's official bulletin defended their behavior, calling it an expression of "the passion of a free people, satisfied to see itself delivered of an enemy." The executions, conducted by Jacques Ménétra's old friend Henri Sanson, were carried out using the guillotine, the mechanical beheading machine destined to become the Revolution's most enduring symbol. Developed in response to a motion made in 1789 by the National Assembly deputy Joseph-Ignace Guillotin, the guillotine was intended to give victims a swift and painless death, in contrast to the protracted and painful methods of capital punishment used under the old regime. "In less than two minutes, everything was over," Adrien Colson recorded after witnessing a double execution.[34] The guillotine's introduction also represented a victory for equality: all those condemned, regardless of their social status or their crime, would now be put to death in the same way. The guillotine was first used on common criminals in April 1792; the executions ordered by the Revolutionary Tribunal linked it indelibly with revolutionary politics.

The outgoing deputies of the Legislative Assembly and the provisional ministers named after August 10 hardly had time to think about the consequences of their adoption of the guillotine as an instrument of political vengeance. They were more concerned with defining the principles that the new constitution would embody, although it would be created not by them, but by the National Convention they had summoned. More emphatically than ever, the revolutionaries promised to create a society based on the principles of liberty and equality. The elimination of the distinction between active and passive citizens marked a major extension of the idea of equality, even if Danton felt obligated to insist that they were not aiming for "the impossible equality of goods, but an equality of rights and of welfare." The Constitution of 1791 had been based on the premise that liberty and equality were compatible with a monarchical form of government, but the events of August 10 and the ongoing war now ruled out any such compromise. A proclamation drafted by Danton and issued on August 25, 1792, told the population that "the French people and the kings confront each other, already the terrible struggle begins, and in this combat . . . there is no choice but victory or death."[35] As in July 1789, when the storming of the Bastille had set off "municipal revolutions" across the country that put power in the hands of the movement's supporters, news of the August 10 uprising in Paris led to considerable turmoil in local governments. Radicals in the departments, including Goujon in the Seine-et-Oise, began to oust their moderate opponents.

As the new power-holders in Paris set a radical course, the greatest threat was from Lafayette, who had already strongly condemned attacks on the constitutional monarchy in June. When the Legislative Assembly sent three deputies to his headquarters to make sure of his loyalty, the man who had been the first to propose a declaration of rights in 1789 showed how alienated he had become from the radical direction of the Revolution: he had them arrested. But Lafayette had lost sway over his men. "The news of the ouster of the king . . . spread joy and happiness among our volunteers," one soldier observed. "'No more king! No more king! that is their cry.'" When Lafayette tried to make his men swear to defend the monarchist constitution of 1791, they refused.[36]

Recognizing that his effort to oppose the overthrow of the monarchy had put him in danger, Lafayette abandoned his troops and gave himself up to the Austrians, who promptly imprisoned him. In Paris, a newspaper announced that Philippe Curtius, the proprietor of the wax museum, "having recognized his misjudgment of the traitor Lafayette who was for a long time one of the main attractions of his display, . . . had cut off the head of this untrustworthy hero." The general, to be sure, continued to see himself as a supporter of "the people, whose cause is dear to my heart, and whose name is now profaned by brigands."[37] But he and most of the other "men of 1789" who had led the Revolution in its early stages were now totally discredited.

As elections for deputies to the Convention began in late August, the news from the military front turned increasingly dire. The Austro-Prussian forces were advancing rapidly. First the key fortress town of Longwy and then the even more strategic city of Verdun, the last major obstacle on the road to Paris, surrendered to the Prussians on August 29 without a struggle. The news of the loss of Verdun caused panic in the capital. Danton exhorted the citizens to redouble their efforts, calling on all able-bodied men to volunteer for the army and demanding searches of the homes of potential political suspects. "The tocsin we are sounding is not an alarm signal," he told the deputies on

September 2, 1792. "It is the call to charge against the country's enemies. To defeat them, gentlemen, we need to dare, to dare again, and
France will be saved!"[38] The nineteenth-century statue of Danton summoning the French to repel the invaders that stands today on Paris's
busy boulevard Saint-Germain captures something of the great tribune's
revolutionary energy.

For the most committed activists, however, words alone, even the soaring
rhetoric of a Danton, were not enough when the survival of the Revolution was at stake. As Danton was addressing the Legislative Assembly,
militants from the Commune and the sections were taking over the prisons in the city, which were crowded with hundreds of suspects who had
been arrested in the wake of the August 10 uprising. Claiming that the
prisoners planned to take advantage of the departure of volunteers for
the front to stage an uprising as the enemy army approached, they set up
improvised "people's courts." Terrified captives—former nobles, refractory
priests, relatives of émigrés, and ordinary people who had been swept up
in the hunt for counterrevolutionaries—were brought out of their cells,
given summary hearings, and, in most cases, thrust out the prison doors
into the courtyards of the prisons or the streets in front of them, where
they were immediately hacked to death. Among the prominent victims
was the princess de Lamballe, who had been an intimate friend of Marie-
Antoinette's. Her body was torn apart in the street. Unable to get at
the queen and the royal family, who were closely guarded in the Temple
prison, some of those in the crowd waved her head under their window
to send what one journalist called "a message worth heeding."[39]

François Jourgniac Saint-Méard, an army officer and contributor to
royalist newspapers, recorded the prisoners' experience in *My Agony of
Thirty-Eight Hours*, the most widely distributed contemporary account
of the September massacres, which continued over the next three days.
Saint-Méard had been arrested ten days before the start of the killing and was being held in the abbey of Saint-Germain, one of several
confiscated religious buildings that had been turned into prisons. On
the afternoon of September 2, killers arrived at the abbey and began
taking victims down to the courtyard. From the window in his cell,

Saint-Méard could hear what happened to those who were convicted. "It is completely impossible to express the horror of the profound and somber silence that prevailed during these executions," he wrote. "It was interrupted only by the cries of those who were sacrificed, and by the saber blows aimed at their heads. As soon as they were laid out on the ground, murmurs arose, intensified by cries of 'long live the nation' that were a thousand times more terrifying to us than the terrible silence."[40]

Saint-Méard was among the lucky prisoners who survived their ordeal. A friendly guard let him watch the interrogations of other prisoners, so he could see what tactics offered the best chance of winning

THE SEPTEMBER MASSACRES: Revolutionary militants' violent reaction to the threat of foreign invasion permanently stained the movement's reputation. The deputies elected to the National Convention realized that they had no choice but to adopt whatever measures were necessary to ensure the Revolution's survival. Although revolutionary leaders were eager to put the outbreak of violence behind them, images of the killings were included with the widely distributed weekly *Révolutions de Paris. Credit: © Musée Carnavalet / Roger-Viollet.*

an acquittal. At 1:00 a.m. on September 4, Saint-Méard found himself facing the improvised popular court. "Two men in bloodstained shirts, sabers in their hands, guarded the door," he recalled. His hearing was interrupted while the judges quickly sentenced a priest to death. Returning to Saint-Méard's case, they decided for acquittal. Three militants—a mason, an apprentice wigmaker, and one of the fédérés who had participated in the August 10 uprising, a typical sample of the militants involved in the massacres—accompanied him home to ensure his safety. When he tried to offer them a gift of money, they indignantly refused, insisting that they and the other participants in the killings were acting purely out of patriotic motives.

The Legislative Assembly and the delegates from the sections who made up the assembly of the Commune were informed of the massacres soon after they began on September 2. Both bodies sent representatives to the prisons to try to talk the killing squads into stopping their activities, but with no success. "We are doing our duty. Go back to yours," one militant told them. Since the prisoners' killers were drawn from the militia units of the sections, which constituted the only police force in the city, the authorities had no way to officially stop their activities. The vehement speech calling for "daring" that Danton, the minister of justice, had given on the morning of September 2 helped to create an atmosphere in which extreme measures seemed justified. Danton himself remained conspicuously silent throughout the three days of killings. Among the other leading radicals, the journalist Marat, who, like Danton, was about to enter the Convention as a deputy, openly associated himself with a justification of the killings by signing a letter issued by the Commune's surveillance committee on September 3. The people, the committee claimed, had decided that the executions were "acts of justice that seemed indispensable to them in order to deter, through the use of terror, these legions of traitors . . . at a moment when it was about to march out to meet the enemy. . . . We will not leave behind us brigands who will slaughter our children and our women."[41]

Among the many consequences of the September massacres was the creation of an unbridgeable gap of distrust among the revolutionary radicals who had collaborated during the summer of 1792 in order to remove the king from the throne. It was not the massacres themselves that completed the rupture between Brissot and the Girondins, on the one hand, and Robespierre and the more radical Jacobins, on the other: neither group had a hand in organizing the killings, but neither rushed to condemn them once they started. On September 3, Brissot's close ally Roland, the minister of the interior, complained that the Parisian militants were disrupting his efforts to maintain order, but he referred to the previous day's massacre as an event "that we should perhaps leave behind a veil." He added, "I know that the people, terrible in its vengeance, still is exercising a kind of justice." The only action he demanded from the Legislative Assembly was a declaration that it had been powerless to stop the killings.[42]

Within a few hours, however, Roland and Brissot were almost swept up in the bloodshed themselves. Commune officials issued arrest warrants for them that could have resulted in their being sent to one of the prisons where inmates were being killed. At the Commune assembly, Robespierre called Brissot and other leading members of the Legislative Assembly "perfidious intriguers working with the armed enemy powers against French liberty." Madame Roland had no doubt that the arrest warrants had been inspired by their political rivals. "We are under the knife of Robespierre and Marat," she wrote to a friend. "Danton is, behind the scenes, the leader of this gang."[43] No evidence has ever shown that Robespierre, Marat, or Danton were responsible for the arrest warrants, but they had certainly come to doubt the loyalty of Brissot and his allies as a result of their wavering behavior in the last days before the August 10 uprising. The Brissotins, however, were convinced that their rivals in the revolutionary movement had tried to take advantage of the massacres to have their leaders killed. There was now little possibility of the two groups working together.

The prison massacres shocked contemporaries at the time and must necessarily trouble all those who think that the contribution the French Revolution made to modern ideas of liberty and equality puts the movement in a different category from those of the Nazis, the communists, and the instigators of recent genocides. The September massacres stand out from most other episodes of violence in the Revolution both for the large number of victims and for their one-sided nature. The casualties during the fighting on August 10 may have equaled those in the massacres, but August 10 was a battle between two armed groups in which both sides thought they were defending their lives, whereas the victims of the *septembriseurs* had no chance to resist. The massacres are also particularly troubling because of the way in which they were integrated into the revolutionary narrative, even by figures who were in principle opposed to arbitrary violence. The killers were never identified or punished, and most of the revolutionary leaders agreed that it was best to cover the episode with a "veil of silence" rather than disrupt efforts to ward off the foreign invasion. The idealistic Jean-Marie Goujon said nothing about the similar massacre in his town of Versailles.

Newspapers close to the Girondins, who had nearly become victims of the movement, were quiet about the episode until several months later, when they realized the propaganda advantage of challenging the radicals. One journalist demanded to know "how many killers must be assembled, in order that a murder committed by them ceases to be a crime and becomes an act of the people's justice." Some publications close to the radicals openly justified the massacres. The people "took the extreme measure, but the only appropriate one, of forestalling the horrors that were being prepared against it, and of showing itself merciless toward those who would not have shown it any mercy," the *Révolutions de Paris* wrote. The journal's editor even blamed the municipal authorities for not disposing of the victims' bodies more discreetly, although he also sent subscribers no less than six graphic engravings of the killings, images that have kept the memory of the massacres alive ever since.[44]

Although the news of the surrender of Verdun precipitated them, the massacres were not just an expression of panic or popular brutality. The fact that the popular courts set up in the prisons spared inmates who were being held for common-law crimes or failure to pay their debts showed the participants' political purpose. Like the insurrection of August 10, the prison killings were organized by militants from the sans-culotte movement, men who had come to distrust not only all those who had belonged to the privileged classes under the old regime but also the more educated and privileged members of the Third Estate. Faced with the possibility that enemy armies might reach Paris, sans-culotte activists meant to show the political leaders, who were struggling to fill the vacuum created by the fall of the monarchy, what could happen to them if they showed any sign of weakness. Although the number of those directly involved in the killings was relatively small—one contemporary estimated it at no more than 150—the reaction of the crowds that gathered outside the prisons suggests that they had broad support. Even women demanded punishment for those accused of opposing the Revolution. On September 2, as the executions were starting, a delegation of women urged the Legislative Assembly to protect inmates who were being held for not having paid fees to wetnurses, but to "destroy all the others."[45]

However crude their understanding of politics may have been, a considerable part of the population had come to believe that the basic achievements of the Revolution were in mortal danger, and that even the most drastic measures were justified to defend them. The lesson was not lost on the deputies elected to the new National Convention, who were about to take on the challenge of defending the embattled Revolution. Six months later, with the memory of the September massacres vivid in his mind, Danton would support the reestablishment of the Revolutionary Tribunal that had first been created in August 1792 by crying out, "Let us be terrifying, in order to spare the people from having to be so."[46] The September massacres thus opened the way to the more systematic and controlled but equally troubling excesses of the Reign of Terror.

# 13

# A REPUBLIC BORN IN CRISIS

*August 1792–May 1793*

WITH FOREIGN ARMIES INVADING THE COUNTRY AND SANS-CULOTTE militants defying the established authorities in the capital, no one could have any assurance that the Revolution would survive. Prominent figures who had helped promote the movement in its early stages—including Talleyrand, who had proposed the expropriation of church property, and Madame de Staël, whose salon had been a meeting place for the revolutionary elite—found themselves forced to emigrate, but they were greeted with hostility by the diehard royalists who had fled earlier. As electoral assemblies were convoked to choose deputies to the National Convention, the outgoing Legislative Assembly continued to meet in Paris. It was symbolically appropriate that, on the last day of its session, September 20, 1792, the Legislative Assembly turned its attention from war and factional politics to the passage of two laws applying the Revolution's individualistic principles to citizens' private lives. One of them established a secular, state-run system for the registration of identity, the *état civil*; the other legalized divorce. Despite the crisis surrounding them, the deputies were under pressure to deal with these issues because their restructuring of the Church had ended that institution's jurisdiction over personal status and marriage without putting anything in its place.

Although there was little debate about the law on the *état civil*, everyone recognized its importance. By establishing procedures for municipal officials to register births, marriages, and deaths, it marked a watershed in the shift from a society in which religion pervaded every aspect of life to one in which the individual's relationship with the state became primary. Having proof of being born in France was crucial to determining who qualified for citizenship. By linking children to their parents, birth certificates established parents' obligations to support their offspring and heirs' rights to inherit property. In later life, they were crucial in determining who was liable for military service, eligible for state-provided benefits, old enough to marry, or qualified to hold political office. Marriage licenses authorized the establishment of new families and defined spouses' claims to shared property, whereas death certificates ensured an orderly disposition of that property. Under the old regime, Catholic priests had kept the documents that established the legal identity of royal subjects. The 1787 law granting civil status to non-Catholics had created awkward alternative procedures for Protestants and Jews, but, as one deputy said in the September 1792 debate, if all citizens were now to be completely equal, "there cannot be different ways to recognize births, marriages and deaths."[1]

The transfer of these functions from the church to the state was more than just a matter of relocating record books from the parish church to the local mayor's office. As the deputies understood, registration of major life events was a ritual that identified individuals with the institution that guaranteed their identity. Simple in principle, the implementation of the law encountered many difficulties in practice, especially in the countryside. Refractory priests who rejected the reorganization of the Church did their best to continue the old practices. "They baptize, marry and bury, keep registers of everything and tell the ignorant people that they don't need to go to public officials," local administrators in one region complained.[2] In non-French-speaking areas, local officials often did not know French well enough to complete the forms properly, and many members of the country's Jewish minority did not have family names as the law required. Nevertheless, the state-run *état civil* eventually became a permanent legacy of the Revolution.

Finalized on the same day as the *état civil*, the divorce law defined marriage as a purely civil arrangement rather than a religious sacrament. The Catholic Church had prohibited divorce and established complicated and costly procedures for the granting of annulments and legal separations; the 1792 divorce law excluded religious considerations, ending church control over a fundamental social institution. The law also recognized that women, even if they did not enjoy political rights, deserved to have significant rights within the family. "Is it not time to give some recognition in our government, in our legislation, to the reason and the spirit of women which, in many regards, are not inferior to the spirit and reason of men?" one deputy, Mathurin-Louis-Étienne Sédillez, asked in proposing that an all-woman jury decide whether a husband bringing suit against his wife should be allowed to divorce her.[3]

Sédillez's proposition was rejected, but the Assembly did endorse the argument of another deputy, Louis Robin, who pointed out that the right to divorce was a necessary consequence of the individual liberty proclaimed in 1789. "Individual freedom can never be renounced in an indissoluble way by any contract," he asserted. The rules for divorce were strikingly egalitarian and designed to avoid court cases like Mirabeau's scandalous clash with his wife in the prerevolutionary years. Couples seeking to end their marriage had to meet with a "family council" consisting of three relatives from each side, who would try to help them work out a settlement. Unless the couple agreed otherwise, the mother would retain custody of all children under the age of seven; the father was normally to keep sons older than that. Both parents were to share the cost of child support. The only special restriction imposed on women was that they could not remarry for a year after the granting of a divorce, so that the paternity of any child born in that period would be clear; men only had to wait six months. Women clearly saw the law as an opportunity to free themselves from abusive husbands: they filed more than two-thirds of the divorce suits brought during the revolutionary period.

Always a model of revolutionary zeal, Jean-Marie Goujon, now an official of the department of the Seine-et-Oise, adopted the new rules about civic ceremonies in both his public and private life. As a magistrate, he took it upon himself to perform the first "civic baptism" in Versailles. As he did so, he proclaimed that imposing a religious ritual on a newborn would be "a violation of the freedom of a future citizen"; he bestowed on the child the first name "Republican" and exhorted the parents to make sure their child "learns from you to babble the names of fatherland and liberty . . . and when he hears the tale of crimes of our kings, may hatred of tyrants rise in his heart along with the first notions of humanity and justice." Around the same time, Goujon proposed marriage to a young woman. Before he committed himself, however, he told his intended that the *patrie* would always have to come first for him. He asked whether, if they married, "you would raise my courage, or would you try to turn me away from my duty?" She wrote back to assure him that "distracting you from your duty of making yourself useful to your fellow citizens is what I would never do," and the match went ahead.[4]

While the outgoing legislators finished their work, the voters weighed in on their replacements. The electorate now included almost all men over the age of twenty-one, although domestic servants and the unemployed, who were considered to lack the economic independence that even radical Jacobins regarded as necessary for full citizenship, were still excluded. Women, to be sure, were still denied voting rights: the arguments that Olympe de Gouges had advanced in her "Declaration of the Rights of Woman" in 1791 had made few converts. The majority of the male population did not make use of its right to vote, however. Participation was about 20 percent, below what it had been in the elections to the Legislative Assembly in 1791. Out of fear or reluctance to endorse the Revolution's radical turn, many conservatives and moderates stayed home. In Arras, Robespierre's hometown, a local lawyer complained that the Incorruptible's supporters arrived at the electoral assembly "with heavy sticks in their hands . . . crying out against the royal family, the clergy and the nobility." They proceeded to intimidate anyone who dared to disagree with them.[5]

These circumstances favored the election of men prepared to take decisive measures to protect the achievements made since 1789.

"To help organize a republican government, establish order and calm in all of France, but above all to drive out the foreigners and silence the aristocracy, that was my mandate," wrote René Levasseur, a young deputy from Le Mans in western France.[6] Levasseur was a newcomer to national politics, but 283 of the 749 *conventionnels* were veterans of one or the other of the two previous revolutionary assemblies and had a personal stake in defending what those bodies had done. Some prominent figures, including Robespierre, Sieyès, and Grégoire, returned to the national legislature after a year's absence. To symbolize the Revolution's universal aspirations, the Convention approved the election of two foreigners. One was Thomas Paine, famous for his role in the American Revolution, as well as for his reply to the British conservative Edmund Burke when he attacked the French movement. The other was Anacharsis Cloots, the self-proclaimed "orator of the human race." Their colleagues included the leading members of the left-wing movement in the Legislative Assembly. Brissot and his Girondin allies were strongly represented, even though they found themselves excluded from the symbolically important Paris delegation and had to settle for seats representing provincial departments.

The militant Jacobins, known as the Montagnards, or "the men of the mountain," because they regularly sat on the highest benches in the Assembly's hall, dominated the elections in Paris itself. Robespierre was the first choice of the Parisian electors, followed by Danton and a number of other radicals, including the journalists Desmoulins and Marat, known as the "Friend of the People," from the title of his newspaper *Ami du peuple*. Surprisingly, the last deputy chosen in Paris was the former duc d'Orléans, the king's cousin, who had renamed himself "Philippe-Egalité" and affiliated himself with the Jacobins. The election of Marat, whom even many radical Jacobins disliked because of his open defense of violence, meant that the most extreme version of revolutionary ideology now had a spokesman in the national legislature. While public attention focused on deputies who already had a reputation, half of the *conventionnels* were newcomers, known only in their own regions, and many of them were reluctant to take sides in the quarrels that already separated the Girondins from their more radical opponents. Neither the Montagnards nor the Girondins were able to obtain a dependable majority in the Convention as a whole: for the first eight months of its existence, the two hostile factions fought to win votes from the unaffiliated deputies, who displayed their independence by sitting between the Montagnards and the Girondins. The independents were called *le Plaine* or *le Marais* (the Plain or the Marsh) because their seats were lower in the hall, on benches arranged on the floor.

The hostility between the Girondins and the Montagnards colored every debate in the Convention until the Montagnards succeeded in eliminating their opponents. The differences in social background between the two groups were not significant: both came overwhelmingly from the urban bourgeoisie, and primarily from the legal profession. Both professed their republicanism, and neither had any desire to bring back the distinction between richer, active citizens and the rest of the population. Members of both groups also vowed to protect the rights of property and to oppose anything that smacked of an "agrarian law," a redistribution of wealth to benefit the poor. The Montagnard leader Robespierre had opposed the declaration of war, but now that the conflict was under way, all members of both factions insisted that it had to be prosecuted vigorously. Both groups supported the harsh measures the Legislative Assembly had passed against émigrés and refractory clergy. As the Convention began its sessions in September 1792, the most obvious distinction between the two groups grew out of their reactions to the popular violence that had accompanied the uprising of August 10 and boiled over in the September massacres. In the Montagnards' view, the Girondins had betrayed the revolutionary cause when they had, at the last minute, tried to head off the popular insurrection against the king. As the Girondins saw it, the Montagnards' acceptance of the killings in September, and especially the effort to have Brissot and Roland arrested, proved their willingness to use violence to achieve their ends.

Initially, the Girondins were more successful than the Montagnards in the competition to control the Convention. Throughout the last months of 1792, their candidates regularly won the contests for the body's presidency, and they could count on the support of most of the provincial Jacobin clubs and the Paris newspapers. Reinforced by radicals from the Cordeliers, however, the Montagnards dominated the influential Paris Jacobin Club, whose well-attended public sessions allowed them to influence public opinion in the capital. Brissot and his allies, who had driven Barnave and his supporters out of the Jacobins in early 1791, now suffered the same fate: in early October, when he was challenged to defend himself or give up his membership, Brissot did not even bother to appear. The most influential anti-Girondin publications, Marat's *Ami du peuple* and Jacques-René Hébert's *Père Duchêne*, spoke a populist language that often went beyond what the majority of the Montagnards endorsed. The two papers' editors had independent followings among the Paris population and even beyond: the provincial Jacobin newspaper in Dijon featured articles attributed to a "nephew of Père Duchêne" that tried to imitate Hébert's distinctive style.

Brissot remained the Girondins' most visible spokesman. His devoted friend Madame Roland helped him keep the loyalty of old collaborators and recruit new ones. Fully aware of the prejudice against women in politics, Madame Roland avoided intervening overtly in the discussions among the men whom she and her husband, once again installed as minister of the interior, hosted in their apartment, but she was widely suspected of drafting many of the proclamations issued in her husband's name. Comparing his activities as minister to Roland's, Danton snidely commented, "Everyone knows that Roland was not alone in his office. I was alone in mine."[7] In time, Madame Roland fell in love with François Buzot, one of the younger Girondins, and her Rousseauist commitment to emotional honesty made her feel obliged to tell her husband about her feelings, injecting a painful personal drama into the group's political struggles. It was testimony to the two Rolands' commitment to their convictions that they continued to work together until the moment of the Girondins' defeat.

The ties binding the most prominent Montagnards to each other were much looser, and indeed, the Girondins' constant attacks on the new triumvirate of Robespierre, Danton, and Marat created the impression of a closer relationship between the three of them than actually existed. Robespierre had made his mark in the National Assembly with his unyielding defense of democratic principles. From 1789 to 1791, he had often been an isolated voice; after August 10, his principles became official policy. In the early years of the Revolution, Robespierre had been friends with Brissot and had sometimes visited Madame Roland's gatherings, but the debate about the war broke those connections. When not attending the Convention or the meetings of the Jacobin Club, Robespierre spent much of his time with the family of his landlord, a prosperous carpenter named Maurice Duplay. Duplay had connections with sans-culotte activists in Paris and helped Robespierre build contacts with them. The Duplays were devoted to him, and their older daughter, Eléonore, was a favorite of his, although there is no evidence that their friendship ever became more than platonic. Always fastidious about his appearance, Robespierre continued to dress in the formal clothes of the old regime. He always had his hair carefully powdered before he appeared at the Convention, where he read his major speeches from prepared manuscripts.

In personality and appearance, Robespierre cut a strong contrast with Danton, the Cordeliers Club firebrand who had become a national figure for his role as leader of the provisional government after August 10. Madame Roland found Danton's manners too crude for her salon; he was more comfortable with the militant activists of the Paris clubs and sections. Whereas Robespierre was untouched by suspicions that he might have used his political position for his own benefit, there was widespread speculation about how Danton, a not particularly successful lawyer, had managed to pay off the debts he had acquired at the start of his career; in 1791, he had also purchased several properties in his hometown. When he joined the Convention, his explanation of how he had spent the funds of the justice ministry, which he had headed after August 10, were unconvincing, and rumors of corruption continued to follow him throughout the rest of his career. Whereas Robespierre kept his emotions under tight control, Danton was unrestrained, both in his oratory and in his private acts. In early 1793, following a mission that had taken him away from the city, he returned to Paris to discover that his first wife had died in childbirth; she had already been buried, but he insisted on having her coffin dug up so that he could embrace her one last time. For more than a year after the start of the Convention, the two men generally supported the same policies, but Danton, in spite of his public image as a revolutionary hothead, was more open to compromise than Robespierre. In the hope of avoiding a complete breakdown in the assembly, he cultivated contacts with leading members of the Plain, the Convention's uncommitted middle group, and even with some of the Girondins.

Compromise was not the style of Marat, the third member of the supposed Montagnard triumvirate. The Friend of the People had made himself a force to be reckoned with through his vociferous denunciations of almost every important figure in revolutionary politics. Positioning himself as an uncompromising defender of the interests of the common people, Marat constantly exhorted his readers to assume the worst about the intentions of anyone in authority. Long before the Revolution, in his tract *The Chains of Slavery*, he had concluded that only the constant threat of popular insurrection could deter rulers from violating the rights of their subjects. The first three years of the Revolution did nothing to change his views. Like Danton, he had joined the Cordeliers Club and encouraged the most radical militants in the Paris sections. Greeted with hostility by the overwhelming majority of the deputies in the Convention when he was elected in September 1792, Marat proved unexpectedly effective at defending himself and provoking his opponents into making clumsy efforts to silence him. Robespierre had little desire to be associated with him; the two men were never close and hardly ever spoke. Nevertheless, the Incorruptible was one of the few politicians Marat approved of, and he rendered Robespierre and the Montagnards valuable services in keeping their Girondin opponents off balance.

Just a year earlier, when the Legislative Assembly had convened, there had been hopes that the disruptions caused by the Revolution were coming to an end. By the opening session of the National Convention, the mood had changed. The deputies knew they were taking up their duties in the midst of a terrifying crisis. Their very first act, meant to win the confidence of a population made mistrustful of all leaders by the chaos of the preceding three years, was to adopt a motion made by the radical Jacobin deputy Georges Couthon, a future member of the all-powerful Committee of Public Safety. Couthon, who had become a leading Jacobin despite his paralyzed legs—his wheelchair is one of the prized exhibits in Paris's history museum, the Musée Carnavalet—proposed that the new plan of government they would draft be submitted to the citizenry for approval. This was a major concession to the democratic principle that the laws should truly express the will of the citizens. Next, Danton called on his colleagues to "reject all exaggeration" by promising to protect "every form of property, territorial, individual, and industrial." Several weeks earlier, he had privately promised representatives of the colonial plantation owners that this promise would even cover the enslaved blacks on their plantations. At the same time, however, he sketched out a vast and ambitious program for the new legislature: "We have to look again at everything, recreate everything . . . the Declaration of Rights itself is not without faults, and it deserves to be reviewed by a truly free people."[8]

Despite having begun by proclaiming that it would respect limits to its own authority, the Convention immediately showed that it would interpret its mandate very broadly. Jean-Marie Collot d'Herbois, who, like Couthon, was a future member of the Committee of Public Safety, moved that the monarchy be abolished. Only a handful of electoral assemblies had endorsed such a radical step, and some deputies hesitated to take such a bold move without discussion or time for the public to express itself. Henri Grégoire, one of the priests who had sat in the National Assembly and now a constitutional bishop, brushed aside their objections. "Kings are in the moral world what monsters are in the physical world," he proclaimed. The motion to abolish an institution central to French life for fourteen centuries was thus passed by acclamation.[9]

It was left to journalists to explain to the public the significance of the sudden transformation of their country into a republic like those imagined by Rousseau and Mably before 1789. A republic, the editor of the *Révolutions de Paris* wrote, "is a government where everyone is free, where no one is the master, where every citizen cares for his country as much as the head of a household does for his family." An honest republican, he added, "is a citizen who sees his fellows as equals. . . . A good republican . . . cares above all for the common good, which he prefers to everything else; he is not a cold egoist." Becoming republicans would not be easy, the writer admitted. "Citizens!," he exhorted them, "You must resign yourselves in advance to privations, and resolve to make sacrifices." The republic would have little room for dissent. Replying to the Girondin minister Roland, who had urged acceptance of political differences, the journalist wrote, "To preach tolerance at this moment is to invite slacking and disorganization."[10] His vision of the republic proved prophetic: the new regime would promote lofty ideals, but it would demand much from its citizens, and it would treat those who resisted harshly.

At the moment when the deputies to the Convention voted to declare France a republic, they had no assurance that their assembly would survive long enough to carry out any of its measures. As they were holding their first session, the future of the Revolution was being decided on a muddy battlefield in northeastern France, not far from where Louis XVI's escape attempt had been stopped a year earlier. News of the Battle of Valmy reached Paris on September 22. It had been fought two days earlier against the same Prussian forces that had captured Verdun on August 29, helping to trigger the September massacres. Dumouriez, who had left his position as war minister to command the French forces in the field, succeeded in instilling a new spirit into the troops, who had been demoralized both by their defeats earlier in the year and by the defection of his predecessor, Lafayette. The war effort drew energy from a wave of patriotic volunteers. Gabriel Noël, an educated young man who had joined the army a year earlier, and who now considered himself an experienced veteran, was not impressed by his new comrades. "They think everything will yield to them," he wrote in a letter. "But it's one thing to cut off heads, to hang people, to be killers and another to fight the Prussians." He added: "I saw one detachment of these Parisians led by a woman at their head, with a saber in her hand. What folly!"[11] Rough and inexperienced as they were, the new soldiers nonetheless gave the army an advantage in numbers and in fighting spirit.

As the Prussians advanced toward Paris, Dumouriez saw an opportunity to cut them off from their supply lines. His colleague General François Christophe de Kellermann massed his guns in front of a windmill near the village of Valmy, a position the enemy would have to break through to foil the French maneuver. The cannon of Valmy were the product of one of the military reform efforts undertaken in the last decades of the old regime: the lightweight and easily maneuverable field artillery had been designed by General Jean-Baptiste Gribeauval to respond to the deficiencies revealed by the defeats of the Seven Years' War. The new cannon would later prove essential to the victories of Napoleon Bonaparte, though he was not present at Valmy to witness their first success.

As Kellermann reported to the Convention, he had held the Prussians off for fourteen hours with continuous gunfire. Then, sticking his hat with its tricolor cockade aloft on the point of his sword and crying "Vive la nation!" he had urged his men forward as the army band blared out the revolutionary song "Ça ira," whose lyrics assured the soldiers that "despotism will die, liberty will triumph." The celebrated German author Johann Wolfgang von Goethe, who was with the Prussian forces, witnessed the demoralization of his own side as they realized that they would not easily be able to "skewer the whole French army and roast and eat it." Goethe later recalled that as the Prussian soldiers sat around a campfire, someone asked him what he thought the unexpected defeat meant, and he replied, "from here and now a new epoch of world history begins." Privately, as he contemplated "a great nation torn out of its frame," he anticipated that "after our unfortunate campaign, the world would also obviously be torn out of its frame."[12]

Once his effort to regain contact with his supply train had failed, the duke of Brunswick, the Prussian commander whose threatening manifesto had galvanized French resistance, requested an armistice so that he could withdraw from French soil. The negotiations gave the victorious French officers a chance to tell the Prussian commander what they thought of his "insane presumption" that he could "try to dictate laws to a people whom the whole of Europe could not conquer even if all the despots united against them." Villagers who talked to a Prussian army officer, Frédéric-Christian Lankhard, during the invasion of 1792 explained their loyalty to the Revolution by telling him "that the crushing taxes that used to weigh on them had been abolished, that they could now think, work, aid each other freely, enjoy life and the fruits of their labor in peace and build up some savings. . . . [I]n short, they were now conscious that they were men and no longer slaves at the mercy of the nobles and the priests."[13] Buoyed by their success at Valmy, the French decided to carry the war to their enemies. By the end of September, one French army had invaded the Italian kingdom of Savoy in the southeast, while another crossed the Rhine River, the prelude to an advance that soon reached Mainz. In October, Dumouriez led the main French force north into Belgium, and on November 6, he overwhelmed the Austrian forces at Jemappes, clearing the way for the occupation of the region's principal city, Brussels.

The victory at Valmy and the conquests that followed it dispelled the sense of looming disaster that had hung over France since the start of the war. It also provided precious time for the new republic to consolidate itself. Nevertheless, the atmosphere of heightened distrust and fear of treason that had grown so intense in the previous months quickly seized the Convention. The same weekly issue of the *Révolutions de Paris* that gave readers their first explanation of what the proclamation of the republic would mean also reported that on September 25, just three days after the deputies had seemed so united, the depth of their divisions had become obvious.

Spokesmen for the Girondin faction launched an all-out assault on Robespierre, Danton, and Marat. They were accused of plotting to set up a three-man dictatorship modeled after the triumvirate that had sealed the doom of republican government in ancient Rome. Robespierre and Danton denied the accusation, but Marat proudly acknowledged that he indeed favored a temporary dictatorship to defend the Revolution. "If you aren't yet up to my level, too bad for you," he announced. He then pulled a pistol out of his pocket, held it up to his head, and shouted, "If you had voted to condemn me, I would have blown out my brains in front of you."[14] He and other Montagnards denounced prominent Girondins who had made last-minute contacts with the king just prior to the August 10 uprising, accusing them of having betrayed the Revolution. It was the opening salvo in a conflict that would overshadow everything else the Convention did for the next eight months.

The chasm of distrust between Girondins and Montagnards widened steadily as the deputies grappled with the most explosive question on their agenda: what to do with the deposed Louis XVI. The king was now referred to simply as "Louis Capet," the dynastic name he had never used. The justification for the uprising of August 10 had been the claim that the king had betrayed the country, and there was strong pressure from the Commune and the sans-culotte activists to avenge those who had died in the fighting. Although there were no openly declared royalists in the Convention, the deputies knew that sympathy for the king remained strong in many parts of the country. Trying him threatened to test the population's loyalty to the new republican regime. Left alive, however, Louis XVI would remain a rallying point for opponents of the Revolution, and if he was in fact guilty of treason, letting him go unpunished would make it seem as though there were no price for betraying the nation.

At the beginning of October, barely a week after their session had begun, the Convention appointed a committee to examine the question of the king's fate. Dominated by Girondin sympathizers, the committee professed to be overwhelmed by the number of documents it had to examine; furthermore, to the king's enemies, it seemed suspiciously incapable of finding incriminating evidence in them. A second committee was charged to examine the question of whether the king could constitutionally be put on trial, and if so, who would judge him. Meanwhile, at the end of October, the Girondin spokesman Jean-Baptiste Louvet shook the Convention by accusing Robespierre of encouraging violence and plotting to make himself a dictator. The young British poet William Wordsworth, drawn to Paris by the spectacle of the Revolution, was in the gallery that day: years later, in his autobiographical work *The Prelude*, he recalled the dramatic moment when Louvet "took his station in the Tribune, saying, 'I, Robespierre, accuse thee!'" A week later, Robespierre replied, justifying the insurrection of August 10. Yes, there had been violence, he said, but there had been no other way to overthrow the monarchy and save the country. "Do you want a Revolution without a revolution?" he demanded. Even his Girondin colleagues recognized that Louvet had lost the argument.[15]

Robespierre's victory cleared the way for the debate about whether and how the king might be tried. From the legal point of view, there was a serious obstacle: the Constitution of 1791 had declared that the only punishment that could be inflicted on the king for violation of the laws was removal from the throne; otherwise, he was "inviolable," immune to judicial punishment for any of his actions. The youngest member of the Convention, the twenty-five-year-old Louis-Antoine de Saint-Just, provided the strongest argument for overriding the constitution. Addressing his colleagues for the first time, Saint-Just made an indelible impression as he argued that Louis XVI's crime was not what he had done, but what he was. "Judge a king like a citizen! The idea will astound posterity. . . . One cannot reign innocently. . . . Every king is a rebel and a usurper," Saint-Just insisted.[16] No trial was necessary to justify his execution: the mere fact that he had claimed to rule over men who deserved to be free was sufficient.

Saint-Just's implacable logic made it impossible for the Convention to let Louis XVI escape judgment, but the majority of the deputies were not prepared to endorse an execution without a trial. Sending him before an ordinary criminal court would underline the fact that Louis was a citizen like any other, but it created a thorny legal issue, since the authority of the existing courts came from the Constitution of 1791, which had declared that the king could not be held liable for his actions. To create a special court would take time and raise new complications. The alternative was for the Convention itself to act as both the king's prosecutor and the court to judge him. The deputies understood that this approach violated the principle of separation of powers embodied in Article 16 of the Declaration of Rights, but there seemed to be no practical alternative.

As the debate about procedures dragged on, the Girondin minister Roland committed a blunder that seriously compromised both him and his political allies. On November 20, 1792, he accompanied the locksmith Gamain, who had taught Louis XVI his craft so many years earlier, to the Tuileries Palace, where Gamain showed him a secret safe, the so-called *armoire de fer*, full of papers hidden by the king. Although he should have been aware of how controversial his action would be,

Roland went through the papers by himself before reporting the discovery to the Convention. Roland's failure to have witnesses present as he examined the papers—which included Mirabeau's letters to the king—allowed the Montagnards to charge that he might have suppressed evidence of his own allies' possible contacts with the court. As the Girondins made it increasingly clear that they opposed executing the king, the suspicions generated by Roland's handling of the *armoire de fer* weighed ever more heavily on them. "By itself, the crime of removing documents from the monster Capet deserves death," the Lyon Montagnard Joseph Chalier wrote.[17]

As Girondins and Montagnards battled over the king's fate, they both kept a wary eye on the reactions outside their meeting hall. The Girondins' demands for the prosecution of those responsible for the September massacres, and their suggestion that the Convention needed an armed guard made up of men from the provinces, created hostility between them and the sans-culotte militants in the capital. In Paris, agitation about high food prices was escalating again, and popular spokesmen demanded that the deputies take action against the king. Jacques Roux, a former priest who put himself forward as a spokesman for the poor, tied the two issues together in a fiery speech on December 1, 1792, "about the judgment of Louis the Last, the pursuit of speculators, of hoarders and traitors," delivered to the assembly of the Observatoire section. Roux warned the deputies that "if they do not strike a tyrant in the midst of his misdeeds, the sovereign nation will call them before its supreme tribunal." From Versailles, where buyers representing Paris cleaned out the local markets, Jean-Marie Goujon wrote to the Convention to decry "this class of capitalists and property-owners whom the unfettered freedom [of commerce] makes the masters of the price of grain." He demanded that the government impose price controls.[18] In the provinces, opinions about the king were divided. The Girondins tried to win support by denouncing the behavior of the population in the capital, a tactic that further alienated the sans-culottes. Brissot and his allies also warned that trying and executing the king risked widening the war. Other European monarchies had cut off diplomatic relations with France after the insurrection of August 10 and made it clear that they were concerned about Louis's fate.

Finally, on December 6, the Convention decided that the legislators themselves would try the king. Louis would have legal counsel and would be permitted to respond to the charges against him. Even though most of the Girondins supported the idea of a trial, they lacked a coherent strategy, so the decision benefited their Montagnard rivals, who had a clear goal in mind. The indictment, drawn up by a special committee, alleged that all of the king's actions, from the time he tried to impose his program at the royal session of June 23, 1789, to the day he issued orders to his troops in the Tuileries Palace on August 10, 1792, had been part of a consistent effort to cripple or overthrow the Revolution. On December 11, Louis was brought from his prison and interrogated before the deputies by Bertrand Barère, who told him, "The French people accuse you of having committed a multitude of crimes in order to establish your tyranny by destroying its liberty." Since the deputies did not know about the secret letters Marie-Antoinette had sent to the Austrian court and to Fersen, which would have provided convincing evidence of the royal couple's collusion with foreign powers, Louis was able to respond that his acts had always been legitimate exercises of his powers. In spite of the humiliating circumstances of his appearance at the Convention, he impressed onlookers with his dignified demeanor. "This conduct has made a considerable revolution in the minds of people here," an English spy wrote, "and those that were perhaps indifferent to what had passed before begin now to regret the approaching and most probably loss of a sovereign, whose life they considered as sacred."[19]

For his defense, the king enlisted François-Denis Tronchet, a distinguished barrister. Several others volunteered to assist him, including the women's rights activist Olympe de Gouges, a self-proclaimed monarchist. The king accepted an offer of help from his former minister Malesherbes, the onetime protector of Diderot and d'Alembert's *Encyclopédie* who would later pay with his life for his devotion to his sovereign. Eventually he added Raymond de Sèze, a specialist in courtroom orat[...] his team. On December 26, the king was again transported ac[...] to the Convention's meeting hall. Before an overflow crowd, [...] forward what the legal team had decided were the only a[...]

to sway the deputies: the constitution's promise that the king would be immune to prosecution, and the unfairness of the Convention acting as both the king's accuser and his judge. At the end of the session, Louis XVI delivered a short statement. "In speaking to you, perhaps for the last time," he said, "I declare to you that my conscience reproaches me for nothing. . . . My heart is torn to find in the accusation the charge of having wanted to shed the blood of the people."[20]

The Girondins now proposed that the question of the king's guilt and punishment should be put to a vote of the people. The Montagnards, despite their theoretical commitment to democracy, denounced this "appeal to the people" as a delaying tactic and an invitation to civil war. The deputy Barère convinced a majority of the deputies that turning over the determination of the king's guilt to the people would be an abandonment of the basic principle of representative government: "It would be to impose on the sovereign the job the sovereign has ordered you to do." Barère's speech turned the tide in the debate: the majority voted against the Girondins. Meanwhile, the tension in the streets was growing, making it clear that the legislators needed to reach a decision on the king's guilt and punishment themselves. Hébert's *Père Duchêne* demanded that they stop stalling and "shorten the pig in the Temple" by sending him to the guillotine. Disturbances broke out after performances of a political play, *L'ami des lois* (The friend of the laws), in which the leading Montagnards were stingingly caricatured. Royalist sympathizers were still able to publish pamphlets on the king's behalf, and on January 11, 1793, rioters in Rouen cried "Long live the king!" In Paris, the Spanish ambassador, acting on behalf of his own Bourbon sovereign, tried to bribe Convention deputies to save the king's life. Thomas Paine, who had allied himself with the Girondins, made a last effort to head off a possible execution, suggesting that Louis XVI be exiled to the United States. There, "far removed from the miseries and crimes of royalty," he said, "he may learn, from the constant aspect of public prosperity, that the true system of government consists not in kings, but in fair, equal and honorable representation." His suggestion was ignored.[21]

The process of voting on the king's fate took the deputies four agonizing days, starting on January 14, when they settled on the three questions to be decided: Was the king guilty of treason? Should there be an appeal to the people? And what penalty should be inflicted on him? On the first question, 691 legislators voted to find the king guilty of treason, with 27 others declining to cast a vote; none asserted his innocence. The Girondins made their stand on the second question, but they could muster only 287 votes against 424 to refer the king's sentence to a popular vote. At 8:00 p.m. on January 16, after a day of parliamentary delays, the deputies began filing to the tribune to cast the most emotionally difficult of their votes: for or against the king's execution. By this time, every deputy knew how much was at stake in his decision. To condemn the king to death was to do away with the living symbol of the country, a figure to whom much of the population still felt a strong attachment. It meant risking an internal conflict with those who might not accept the decision, and expanding the foreign war from a limited conflict with two major powers into a struggle against all the other European monarchies. Dozens of legislators felt compelled to justify their votes, lengthening the session long into the night.

The very first voter, Jean-Baptiste Mailhe, injected a new element of confusion into the proceedings by voting for the death penalty, but with the provision that if the majority supported that decision, the Convention would then take an additional vote on whether to suspend the execution. A number of other voters seized on Mailhe's formulation, which allowed them to vote to condemn the king to death while making it clear that they hoped the sentence would not actually be carried out. All but one of the twenty-four deputies from Paris opted for death, including the king's own cousin, the former duc d'Orléans, whose vote sent a tremor of shock through the room. The principal alternative to voting for death was to hold the king in prison until the end of the war and then to banish him, a proposition that received 319 of the 721 votes cast. Immediate execution was the choice of 361 deputies, the narrowest possible majority, but an additional 26 voted for Mailhe's suggestion that the sentence be suspended or for some other formulation that left doubts about their actual intentions. A handful of deputies were not in Paris at this time, and the deputies did not want such a momentous question to be decided by a margin so narrow that their votes might change the outcome; they therefore resigned themselves to one more ballot, on the question of whether the death sentence should be carried out immediately. The final count on the question of immediate execution was 380 in favor, 310 against. The king's head would fall.

Louis XVI, who had spent some of his time in prison rereading David Hume's history of the English Revolution, expected this outcome. He had already prepared his last will and testament. When the devoted Malesherbes burst into tears after telling him, "Sir, they have voted for death!" the king comforted him with a prolonged hug. The execution was set for January 21, 1793. On the evening of the 20th, the king said a last farewell to his family. In the morning, he heard Mass and took the wedding ring off his finger, asking his loyal valet, Jean-Baptiste Cléry, to deliver it to Marie-Antoinette. The streets were lined with troops as the king's carriage took him across the city to the large public square at the western end of the Tuileries Gardens—today's Place de la Concorde—where the guillotine had been erected. On the previous day, a Montagnard deputy, Michel Le Peletier de Saint-Fargeau, had been stabbed to death in the Palais-Royal by a royalist. The Commune was on guard to prevent any last-minute effort to rescue the king. In spite of a cold rain, a large and mostly silent crowd lined the streets. Their feelings were hard to read: as the chronicler Nicolas Ruault wrote, "one could not let one's thoughts show, for fear of angering the militants who ran around with a triumphant air."[22]

The king's carriage took over an hour to go from the Temple to the execution site. A journalist with royalist sympathies claimed that once the king had exited the carriage and started up the stairs to the scaffold, the priest who accompanied him blessed him with the words, "Son of Saint Louis, rise to heaven." As Louis reached the top of the scaffold, "he wanted to step forward to speak," according to the account in the *Révolutions de Paris*. "Voices cried to the executioners . . . to do their duty; nevertheless, while they were strapping him down, he distinctly pronounced these words: 'I die innocent, I forgive my enemies, and I wish that my blood will be of use to the French and that it will appease the anger of God.' At ten minutes after ten, his head was separated from his body, and then shown to the people. Cries of 'Long live the Republic!' were heard from all directions."[23] Below the scaffold, a few people dipped handkerchiefs in the king's blood to create relics.

"We have done it," the Montagnard deputy Philippe Le Bas wrote. "The road back is cut off, we have to go forward, whether we want to or not, and now one can really say, 'live free or die.'" For royalists, the king's death was as traumatic as the loss of a family member. "We will cherish our private grief, but we will not share it with anyone else," one journalist wrote. For revolutionary militants like Hébert, the "Père Duchêne," however, the event was an occasion to celebrate. His only concern was that Louis's "wife and his bugger of a family are still alive: you won't have any rest until they are destroyed." Their joint responsibility for Louis XVI's death now fused the *régicides*, the deputies who had voted for the action, together: they knew there would be no pardon for them if the Revolution was defeated. The Girondins and other deputies who had voted against the decision were in disarray. The radical Jacobin Club in Marseille started a campaign against the deputies who had voted to spare the king, calling them "traitors and disturbers" and demanding that they be expelled from the Convention.[24] Political activists now realized that the stakes in their quarrels were literally life or death: if the monarch could be sent to the guillotine, all citizens were just as vulnerable.

As they absorbed the shock of the king's execution, the revolutionary leaders also had to brace themselves for a wider war. Victories won by the revolutionary armies in Belgium, Germany, and the Italian Alps during the long-drawn-out debate in the Convention about the king's trial lifted the fear of foreign invasion, but they raised pressing questions about what should be done with the territories the French occupied. In a few regions, the French occupation went relatively smoothly. In Savoy, a part of the northern Italian kingdom of Piedmont, General Anne-Pierre Montesquiou summoned delegates to a national convention of the Allobroges, the name the Romans had given to the inhabitants of the region. Within four days, the deputies had enacted laws duplicating all the major reforms the French had taken three tumultuous years to agree on. The population was French speaking and had no strong attachment to the Italian part of the kingdom, from which it was separated by the Alps. By the end of November, the Convention had agreed to turn Savoy into a new department named for its highest mountain, Mont Blanc, and absorb it into the French nation.

Greater difficulties arose in other conquered regions. The situation in Belgium was particularly complicated and it exacerbated the tensions in the Convention between the Girondins, who were closely identified with General Dumouriez, and the Montagnards. Dumouriez had long had contacts with the Belgian revolutionaries who had unsuccessfully risen up against their Austrian rulers in 1789–1790, and one of his close allies, the French foreign minister Pierre Lebrun, was a revolutionary exile from the region. Concerned with keeping the population peaceful after he occupied the area, and above all with obtaining food and other supplies for his troops, Dumouriez allowed the reestablishment of traditional institutions, even if they violated the precepts of the French Revolution. "The Revolution is far from being accomplished in Brabant," he warned Paris. "The cabal of priests and the old Estates rules three-quarters of the country." The deputies in the Convention had different aims: French conquests should spread the ideals of liberty and equality. Their first "propaganda decree," passed on November 19, 1792, to provide guidelines for the republic's armies, declared that the French nation would "grant fraternity and aid to all peoples who wish to recover their liberty." It was an open-ended promise of assistance to revolutionary movements in other countries, and a threat to more conservative elements of their populations. Olympe de Gouges, perhaps inspired by the fact that Dumouriez had appointed the Fernig sisters, women volunteers in his army, as aides-de-camp, dashed off a five-act play celebrating his conquest of Brussels. In the play, she had him announce, "Your sex now equals ours; that's the result of this powerful revolution."[25]

Events in Belgium quickly led to a sharp change in French policy. Dumouriez complained that the promise of aid to movements for liberty was alienating the more conservative elements of the population. He also came into violent conflict with the war ministry in Paris, whose Montagnard minister, Jean-Nicolas Pache, had given jobs to allies more distinguished for their political radicalism than for their competence in organizing supplies for the army. Meanwhile, hardheaded radicals in the Convention demanded to know why France should pay the cost of bringing liberty to its neighbors. On December 15, 1792, a second propaganda decree specified that the property of the ousted rulers of occupied territories and the property of the Catholic Church in those territories would be expropriated. In addition, the new governments set up with French backing would be expected to pay the costs of French assistance. All "feudal" privileges in occupied countries were to be immediately abolished, and anyone "refusing liberty and equality, or renouncing them," was to be declared "an enemy of the people."[26]

This combination of demands spurred resistance to the French "liberators," not only in Belgium but in other occupied territories. The idea that the populations of liberated territories should pay for the maintenance of the French army, and that they should immediately adopt the full revolutionary program as well, created resentment. Even local activists who sincerely embraced the ideals of republicanism found themselves in a difficult situation: they needed French support, but this meant accepting the occupiers' heavy financial demands. Moreover, they would have to overlook the widespread pilfering that developed as church and noble property was expropriated. As the extent of opposition to French-imposed republicanism in Belgium became clear, members of the Brussels Jacobin Club were reduced to threatening their compatriots that "if you do not want to be free, very well, you will have to do so in spite of yourselves."[27] Across the Rhine in Mainz, in an area occupied by the troops of General Adam Philippe Custine, an enthusiastic group of "German Jacobins" formed a club to advocate for a republican constitution. Initially, they won support from some of the city's artisans, shopkeepers, and clerks, but frictions between the French troops and the civilian population undermined enthusiasm for the new regime. Under French supervision, the Mainz Jacobins staged the first elections ever held in Germany on February 24, 1793, but few citizens were willing to swear the oath to liberty and equality required in order to vote. A week after declaring themselves an independent republic, the deputies to the new National Convention of Free Germans voted to ask to be annexed to France. By the time the French Convention accepted their petition on March 30, however, Mainz was under siege by Prussian troops. For the German Jacobin activists, the experience was a bitter lesson: French demands had made it impossible for them to win support from their countrymen, and then the French army proved unable to protect them.

While the French tried to promote republicanism in the territories they had occupied in the fall of 1792, they also found themselves facing a greatly expanded war. As Brissot and other Girondins had warned, Louis XVI's execution turned opinion abroad against the Revolution and drew several major new opponents into the conflict. The addition of the Dutch Republic to the list of France's enemies showed that it was not only monarchies that saw revolutionary France as a mortal danger. More significant, however, was the start of war with Britain. On January 1, 1793, the Girondin deputy Armand Kersaint optimistically imagined how a global conflict with the British would change the world. The Irish and the Scots were ripe for revolt, French corsairs would chase British merchantmen from the seas, and revolutionary movements in the empires of Britain's allies would create free republics in Mexico and Brazil. France would send troops to India to assist Tippoo Sultan, the ruler of Mysore, in his struggle against the British East India Company. Finally, patriotic French fishermen would ferry an army across the Channel. There was no doubt in Kersaint's mind that "it is on the ruins of the Tower of London that we will sign . . . the treaty which will determine the destiny of nations and which will establish the freedom of the world."[28]

Kersaint's forecasts were unrealistic, but he was prophetic in anticipating that the two decades of nearly uninterrupted conflict between France and Britain that began in 1793 would have repercussions all over the globe. More pragmatically, Danton focused on the war's consequences in Europe. France, he told the deputies at the end of January, could no longer hope to reach any peaceful compromise with the other rulers of Europe. "You have thrown down a challenge to them. This challenge is the head of a king," he said. Regardless of the consequences, France should simply annex the territories it had occupied, particularly in Belgium, and make them full-fledged parts of the revolutionary republic. "Nature has marked out France's limits," he insisted.

"We will reach them in all four directions: the ocean, the banks of the Rhine, the Alps, the Pyrenees." Such an expansion would overturn the traditional balance of power on the continent, giving France resources that no other state could hope to match. Danton's claim that France deserved to reach its "natural frontiers" also challenged the principle of national sovereignty: he assumed that the Dutch, Belgians, Germans, and Italians would happily accept new identities as French citizens. Other deputies amended his proposition to make it clear that these populations would have little real choice: French generals would oversee elections in the territories they occupied, and commissioners sent by the Convention would determine their validity. Those who refused to participate in these elections would be considered to have shown that they "do not want to be friends of the French people" and would be treated appropriately.[29]

For a few weeks at the beginning of 1793, events seemed to justify Danton's optimism. From Belgium, Dumouriez sent his troops north to invade the Dutch Republic, which had just entered the war. The French had the support of the Dutch Patriots, who were eager to avenge their defeat in 1787. If they had been able to add the Netherlands to their conquests in Belgium, they would have gained a strategic advantage against the British, for whom a hostile power in control of the Low Countries always represented a mortal threat. From across the Atlantic came encouraging news: the commissioners dispatched to Saint-Domingue the previous June had successfully implemented the law of April 4, 1792, granting rights to free men of color. Even the unruly white colonists had welcomed the news of the August 10 uprising in Paris, and they had cooperated in purging the colonial army of its royalist officers. In response, French colonists who had sought safety in London signed a secret treaty promising to support British occupation of France's Caribbean islands.

Hoping to turn the Western Hemisphere into an active front in the looming war with Britain and Spain, the Convention sent Edmond-Charles Genêt to be its representative in the United States. They instructed him to organize an expedition from Kentucky to challenge Spanish rule in the Mississippi valley, and to equip privateering vessels in American ports to harass British shipping. The newly minted French republicans assumed that the United States, bound to France by the treaty of alliance signed in 1778, would be eager to join their international crusade against monarchy. On March 7, 1793, France declared war on Spain, whose Bourbon king had been consistently hostile to the Revolution since 1789. France now faced armed enemies on all its European borders as well as in the Caribbean, where the Spanish colony of Santo Domingo, today's Dominican Republic, occupied the eastern end of the island of Hispaniola whose western half belonged to France. The Spanish promptly made an alliance with the black insurgents who had risen up against slavery in the French colony and appointed their leaders, including Toussaint Louverture, as generals in the Spanish army.

Even as the war expanded, the National Convention tried to fulfill its obligation to give France a new constitution. The elimination of the hereditary monarchy gave the deputy Condorcet, the most important surviving philosophe in revolutionary politics, the chance to apply the rational principles of reason and mathematics to the problem of creating a genuinely democratic polity. Nearly twice as long as its predecessor, Condorcet's declaration of rights tried to avoid the ambiguities of the 1789 document. It provided, for example, explicit definitions of the kinds of oppression that citizens were entitled to resist. It firmly rejected any wealth-based restriction on the right to vote or hold office, essential features of the Constitution of 1791. "Since the entire code of our civil laws consecrates civil equality, isn't it better that political equality be fully applied as well?" Condorcet asked. Education and welfare were added to the list of individual natural rights, and Condorcet, a longtime abolitionist, included a provision that "no one can sell himself; his person is not an alienable property." This formulation avoided confronting the situation of the blacks in the French colonies, who had been sold into bondage by others.[30] In general, however, Condorcet strongly defended property-owners' rights, repeating the dogma formulated decades earlier by the Physiocrats about their absolute authority to buy, sell, and transport anything they owned.

The most original aspect of Condorcet's proposal was his attempt to create an election system that would truly reflect the will of the people. Almost alone among the politicians of the revolutionary era, Condorcet had thought deeply about the mathematical problems concealed in the seemingly simple idea of elections as expressions of the popular will. Even before 1789, he had identified what is still known as the "Condorcet paradox," the fact that, in a contest with more than two choices, it may be impossible to determine if there is a result that truly satisfies a majority of voters. His constitutional plan provided for a complicated procedure "so elaborate that it is impossible to summarize it," according to one journalist.[31] Citizens would participate directly in local "primary assemblies," which would meet every year to choose deputies to the national legislature and ministers to run the executive branch of government. The same assemblies could also propose laws and demand referenda on measures passed by the national legislature.

Critics disliked the idea of giving local primary assemblies such an easy means of demanding potentially controversial referenda. The same arguments that had been used to defeat the Girondins' proposal to hold a national referendum on the king's fate applied. The procedures would also be too time consuming, the critics said. "Who could accept that in order to propose a new law, or repeal one already voted, one would keep five million men occupied for six weeks?" Marat demanded. Annual month-long elections for deputies and ministers would have made political campaigning almost continuous. The idea of leaving the choice of ministers to the people had democratic appeal, but there would be no assurances that the men elected would work together to pursue common goals. More than a month earlier, with little fanfare, the deputies of the Convention had already begun to shape a very different kind of government, one that came into being with little input from the population but that they believed would be able to provide strong national leadership. On January 1, 1793, they had appointed a Committee of General Defense, chosen from members of the other major committees of the legislature and charged to "occupy itself uninterruptedly with the measures which the next campaign and the present state of affairs require."[32] It was the first step toward the creation of a new kind of executive authority, one that could act more decisively than the 749-member Convention itself and that would not be restricted by constitutional limits. By the time the Convention returned to the question of the constitution two months later, dramatic new crises had made the need for a strong and decisive government even more pressing, and Condorcet's democratic utopia was quickly shelved.

Despite the resolution of the question of the king's fate and the optimism generated by the military victories at the end of 1792, the survival of the Revolution was still very much in doubt in the first months of 1793. As the winter wore on after yet another disappointing harvest, food prices climbed again, setting off a new wave of disorder. Throughout the country, the grain marketing system was breaking down. When merchants tried to make purchases in the countryside to bring to the cities, they often faced opposition from local populations, who blocked shipments out of their districts. In the cities, local authorities faced pressure to set limits on the price of grain and bread and to borrow money in order to assure supplies. Meanwhile, agents from the army and buyers for the government in Paris scoured the countryside to keep the soldiers fed, outbidding other would-be purchasers. The Convention deputies and Roland, the Girondin interior minister, continued to defend the principle of free trade; laws passed in early December 1792 threatened the death penalty for anyone interfering with the free circulation of grain. Local authorities in the Seine-Inférieure department complained that "the principles [of free trade], however true, are in no way applicable to our situation": without an adequate supply of bread at an affordable price, they could not maintain order.[33]

In Paris, hungry women demanded that the Jacobin Club let them use its premises to demand measures to deal with the crisis, arguing that the issue should have priority over discussions about a new constitution. Frustrated by the male revolutionaries' reluctance to intervene in the workings of the marketplace by setting a limit on the price of necessities, women took the lead in a wave of assaults on merchants' warehouses. They seized the goods they wanted, such as the soap that laundresses needed, and sold them at what they regarded as a fair price. The Montagnard leader Robespierre, with his attention focused on what he and other politicians regarded as more important matters, tried to maintain his reputation as a friend of the common people while condemning such interference with the marketplace. "When the people rises up, should it not have a goal worthy of itself?" he asked. "Should it be preoccupied with insignificant merchandise?" Such appeals had little chance of silencing the demands voiced in pamphlets denouncing the high prices of goods. The author of one such pamphlet, titled "The Last Outcry of the Sans-Culottes," also denounced speculation on the revolutionaries' paper currency, which had fallen to barely half of its nominal value. He complained that "not one death sentence has been imposed on these bloodsuckers, who rob you more brazenly than the bandits who haunt lonely roads."[34]

Even as legislators tried to talk the common people out of causing disruptions over economic matters, they were also asking them to make a greater commitment to the war effort. The expansion of the war required more soldiers, especially since many of the volunteers who had put on uniforms in 1791 insisted that their engagement had only been for one year: some of them headed home after the victories at Valmy and Jemappes. On February 24, 1793, the Convention called for a levy of 300,000 new troops. Unmarried men between the ages of eighteen and forty were liable for service; the exemption of married men resulted in a wave of quickly arranged weddings. The country's thousands of local governments were assigned quotas of recruits and told to decide for themselves how to fill them if they could not find enough volunteers. This obligation put officials in conflict with their reluctant constituents. Despite the Convention's insistence that the country was now fully committed to equality, the decree allowed wealthier men to pay for substitutes. Local authorities in one small town protested this, saying it was wrong that "the indifferent rich man should slyly watch the patriot exhaust his strength and fortune while he himself contributes nothing from his effort or his fortune to the defense of la Patrie."[35] Resistance to the draft was widespread, and only about 150,000 men were actually recruited.

The unpopular troop levy sparked the most serious revolt yet against the Revolution, the uprising in the western department of the Vendée. Beginning in the first week of March, peasants in the region began assembling to resist the draft call; in some cases, they physically attacked the local officials and National Guards who tried to enforce it. Heavily outnumbered by hostile peasants, republicans fled to larger cities, allowing the movement to spread. Peasants quickly found leaders. Some of these leaders—such as Jacques Cathelineau, a middleman for some of the region's textile merchants and a devoted Catholic, and Jean-Nicolas Stofflet, an ex-soldier and game warden—emerged spontaneously from the ranks of commoners. Others, including the abbé Barbotin, were refractory priests. Barbotin was "electrified by the idea that religion was going to be avenged" for the attacks the revolutionaries had made on it.[36]

After their first victories, the peasants also appealed to local nobles. Disgruntled though they were with the Revolution, most nobles were initially reluctant to join a revolt against the new regime: they knew the terrible risks that would be involved. But when peasant insurgents insisted that they were ready to die for religion and the monarchy, a number of nobles decided to cast their lot with the movement. A former naval captain, François Charette, and the twenty-one-year-old nobleman Henri de la Rochejaquelin were among them. With his white-plumed hat, the dashing young La Rochejaquelin became an icon of the movement. His elegance contrasted with the rough clothes and broad peasant caps of the men he led, who were initially armed only with sharp farm implements. As the Vendeans marched, "the sound of conversations was mixed with the clatter of wooden shoes," an observer wrote. "The clashing of their scythes and pikes deafened our ears."[37] Calling themselves the "Catholic and Royal Army," the Vendeans pinned images of the Sacred Heart, a sign of religious devotion, to their coats. The wooded terrain of the *bocage*, the center of the Vendée region, favored the rebellion: republican troops using the sunken roads common in the region were exposed to ambushes by enemies who knew the area.

Within days, local officials were desperately appealing for help as the uprising threatened to overturn the republican regime throughout the western part of the country. "Everywhere they sound the tocsin, everywhere they pillage, they murder, they burn, everywhere the patriots fall victim to the fury and the fanaticism of the rebels," the administration of the Lower Loire department wrote on March 11, 1793.[38] With the army having sent almost all its men to the frontiers, there were few troops available to deal with the crisis. Reports of especially gruesome massacres in the small town of Machecoul, where republican prisoners were tied together with ropes to form "rosaries" and then killed, inflamed patriotic opinion throughout the country, just as the stories of the September massacres had galvanized opponents of the Revolution.

Although the call for army recruits was the spark that set off the Vendée revolt, the peasants' hostility to the republic had deeper roots. In 1789, peasants in the Vendée, like those in most of the rest of the country, welcomed the proclamation of the "abolition of feudalism." As time passed, however, the revolutionary reforms disappointed them. Feudal dues had not been very onerous in the area, and attitudes toward the local nobles were less hostile than in many other places. The confiscated church lands put up for sale in the region had gone mostly to bourgeois inhabitants of local towns, and peasants had seen little improvement in their situation. The Church had been a vital part of rural community life in the Vendée, and peasants had opposed the Civil Constitution of the Clergy. General Jean-Baptiste Canclaux, the republican commander in the large Breton city of Nantes, recommended that the government consider a conciliatory policy of quietly allowing the local clergy to resume their functions. He also thought the government should abandon its effort to force the region to supply more troops. Instead, the Convention responded on March 19, 1793, with a decree saying that any participants in the uprising caught bearing arms, or even just wearing a white royalist cockade, would be subject to immediate execution and the confiscation of their property. Although the peasant insurgents were promised amnesty if they gave up their arms, their representatives refused. They responded by insisting on "the free exercise of a religion that was that of our fathers": "We cannot live under a republican government that we can only see as a source of divisions, troubles, and war," they added. To the accusation that they were acting as supporters of France's foreign enemies, they replied, "We call out to them with all our strength . . . certain that they are our friends."[39]

News of the Vendée rebellion reached Paris just as the capital was reeling from the sudden collapse of the military effort in Belgium. On March 8, 1793, the Austrians launched a counteroffensive that threatened to cut the republican army off from its communications with France. The Convention sent deputies to the assemblies of the sections throughout the capital to find new volunteers for the army. One of them, André Jeanbon Saint-André, reported that the members of the section of the Louvre had been ready to "fly to the defense of the country," but first they wanted the Convention to "punish the traitors and annihilate the intriguers at home."[40] The deputies responded by reviving the Revolutionary Tribunal, the special court set up after August 10 to try those accused of political crimes. As before, there would be no appeal from the tribunal's sentences, and any death penalties imposed were to be carried out within twenty-four hours. Because the Girondins had supported Dumouriez, they were the main targets of militant anger. In the Convention, the Montagnard deputy Pierre Joseph Duhem unloosed a violent diatribe against the journalists who supported them, "these libelous insects who are the only, the real obstacles to the progress of the Revolution." On the night of March 9, sans-culotte militants rampaged through the narrow streets of the Latin Quarter where the printing shops of the leading Girondin newspapers were housed, smashing presses and scattering type.

While Paris seethed, Dumouriez saw his hopes of keeping control over Belgium disintegrating. From his headquarters in Louvain, he dispatched a letter to the Convention so strongly worded that the military committee refused to read it publicly. Dumouriez blamed the Convention and the agents it had sent to Belgium for not providing the supplies needed to keep up the struggle against the enemy. He asserted that the policies dictated by the propaganda decree of December 15, 1792, had "exasperated the spirits of the Belgians." On March 11, 1793, Dumouriez prohibited the clubs set up in Belgium from involving themselves in politics, making it clear that he would not support any effort to import French revolutionary institutions to the territories he occupied. A week later, on March 18, the Austrians won a crushing victory over the French forces at Neerwinden. Demoralized, the army retreated toward the border. At Neerwinden, one key part of the French army had been commanded by Francisco Miranda, a general born in the Spanish American colony of New Granada, who was closely linked to the Girondins. Another unit had been under the orders of the duc de Chartres, the son of the duc d'Orléans. In Paris, this led to demands for emergency measures against foreigners and the Orléans family.

Like Lafayette after August 10, 1792, Dumouriez now decided to use his army to overthrow the revolutionary government he considered responsible for the disaster he had suffered. "Paris is overwhelmed by tyranny, assaults, crimes; anarchy is devouring us," he wrote to the Convention at the end of March. "It is time for the army to speak up, to purge France of assassins and agitators, and give our unhappy country the peace that it has lost through the crimes of its representatives." The Convention hastily dispatched several deputies to meet with him, but Dumouriez had them arrested and turned them over to the Austrians. To Dumouriez's surprise, however, his troops and his subordinate officers resisted his orders, just as they had refused to follow Lafayette. Deeply disillusioned by their commander's behavior—"Who can one trust now? This Dumouriez whom the French Republic regarded as its savior, has thrown off the mask," the volunteer Gabriel Favier wrote to his mother—the soldiers nevertheless retained their loyalty to the country. "He saw himself abandoned by the whole army and obliged to flee . . . to save his life," Favier concluded.[41]

Dumouriez's treason threatened disaster for the Girondins, who had applauded his denunciations of their radical Montagnard opponents and insisted that the victor of Valmy was indispensable to the war effort. Marat, who had asserted repeatedly that "Dumouriez is a creature of the Brissotin faction," crowed in triumph: he had predicted that Dumouriez would desert to the enemy two weeks before it happened. But the crisis also undermined Danton, who had made several visits to Dumouriez's headquarters during the winter and returned each time to assure his colleagues that the general could be trusted. Rumors swirled that Danton had profited from his visits by sharing in the looting of Belgian property. He reacted by going on the offensive against the Girondins. As the Montagnard deputies cheered, Danton announced that "there cannot be any further truce between the Mountain, between the patriots who wanted the death of the tyrant, and the cowards who, wanting to save him, spread lies about us all over France." In the enthusiasm that followed Danton's speech, the Convention hastily passed a decree that would come back to haunt him a year later: it voted that the parliamentary immunity that protected deputies could be ignored if there were "strong presumptions" that they sympathized with "the enemies of liberty, of equality, and of republican government." The decree turned the disputes between rival factions into a blood sport, in which the losers could find themselves sent before the Revolutionary Tribunal.[42]

Even as the divisions within the Convention deepened, the deputies began to work out solutions to the overwhelming problems facing them. Within a few months, they would create a revolutionary government very different from the government by assembly that had prevailed since the summer of 1789. Unforeseen by any of the political thinkers of the Enlightenment or the earlier stages of the Revolution, the new government proved capable of moving swiftly and taking decisive actions, but it also imposed drastic punishments on dissenters and created new and lethal divisions among the most radical revolutionaries. The Revolutionary Tribunal set up in March was the first of what became the main pillars of the regime. Its establishment was followed by a decree on March 21, 1793, ordering the creation of "surveillance committees" in every commune in the country. The initial function of the committees was to make lists of all foreigners living in their jurisdictions, but they were also ordered to register all citizens over the age of eighteen and make them show that they had legitimate sources of income and had performed their "civic duties." The requirement that all adults follow this procedure to obtain a "certificate of *civisme*" gave the surveillance committees great power. A decree on March 28 consolidated previous laws against émigrés. They were "banished in perpetuity from French territory" and declared "civilly dead." Their property was confiscated by the state, and they were threatened with execution if found on French soil.[43] The law also punished anyone who assisted an émigré, such as relatives who sent money or tried to protect their property through fictitious sales or other means; the decree thus affected not only those who had left the country but many who remained in it.

As revolutionary legislation began to impinge more and more directly on ordinary people's lives, institutions capable of enforcing those laws were also taking shape. On April 6, 1793, the Convention set up a Committee of Public Safety to replace the less effectual Committee of General Defense established in January. Smaller than its predecessor—it originally had only nine members—the Committee of Public Safety was charged with overseeing the ministers and could overrule their decrees. The committee's meetings were secret, allowing it to thrash out decisions without falling victim to the divisions in the Convention. To make sure it did not become independent of the Convention, its powers had to be renewed every month. The creation of the new committee had broad support in the Convention. The Girondin Maximin Isnard had been among the first to demand "a firm, bold and pure hand" to take charge of the government, and Barère, regarded as independent of both the Girondins and the Montagnards, told his colleagues, "In every country, when flagrant conspiracies have occurred, it has been recognized as necessary to resort to temporary dictatorial authority."[44] In addition to Danton, who dominated the committee for the first three months of its existence, the Convention chose primarily deputies from the Plain, the group of legislators who had avoided taking clear positions in its internal disputes.

Two days after creating the Committee of Public Safety, the Convention formalized the practice of dispatching deputies "on mission," a measure begun in March 1793 to supervise the drafting of men for the army. Now deputies were also assigned to the armies at the front; before long, they would also be sent to oversee local governments and to make sure they followed the Convention's orders. These "proconsuls," invested with "unlimited power" by the Convention, could give orders to generals and local officials, appoint subordinates to carry out their instructions, and spend whatever money they thought was necessary to ensure the defense of the country, provided they immediately notified the Convention of their actions. Armed only with tricolor sashes, hats with tricolored plumes, and medallions to establish their authority, the deputies on mission frequently encountered strong opposition. Those who accepted missions were primarily the more determined and energetic *conventionnels*: a large majority of them voted with the Montagnards in the Convention, whereas the Girondin supporters showed a marked reluctance to take on such missions. The Girondins may have hoped to reduce the number of their opponents present in Paris, but the result was to strengthen the Montagnard influence with the army and the provinces.

Even as the Convention approved measures to make its authority more effective, control of the Convention and of France's major cities continued to seesaw back and forth, bringing the country to the brink of a civil war between republicans. In Paris, the Girondins, who had been the intended targets of the decree abolishing parliamentary immunity, succeeded in turning it against their archenemy: on April 14, 1793, they had the controversial journalist-deputy Marat indicted for having called for an uprising to purge the Convention. An old hand at hiding from the police, Marat went underground for several days. Meanwhile, his supporters in the streets threatened to "cut off thousands of heads" if he were convicted.[45] Marat finally surrendered himself, confident that the trial would end in his favor. The prosecutor Antoine-Quentin Fouquier-Tinville, a Montagnard sympathizer, let him dominate the proceedings, and the courtroom erupted with applause when he was acquitted. When an enthusiastic crowd carried Marat to the Convention's meeting hall on their shoulders, the Girondins realized that their ill-conceived assault had only reinforced his popularity.

In the section assemblies, in the municipal assembly of the Commune, and in the Jacobin Club, hostility toward the Girondins, and even toward the Convention as a whole, was rising rapidly. On April 8, a delegation from the Bonconseil section had denounced Brissot, Vergniaud, and other leading members of the group to the Convention. "What are you waiting for before you indict them?" the militants demanded. Two days later, Robespierre took up the charge, accusing his enemies of conspiring with foreign governments to "give us a king with an aristocratic constitution. . . . They hope to force us into this shameful situation through the force of foreign armies and domestic disorders."[46] On April 15, Jean-Nicolas Pache, the radical mayor of Paris, and Jacques-René Hébert, who had finally managed to eliminate competing versions of his Père Duchêne character, appeared at the Convention to present a petition. It had been drawn up by a committee meeting secretly in the Evêché, the former seat of the archbishop of Paris, and thirty-five of the forty-eight Paris sections had backed it. The petition demanded the expulsion of twenty-two Girondin deputies. The Evêché committee, made up of activists who had become frustrated by the Convention's reluctance to act against the Girondins, now became the center of activity for an effort planning an insurrection. The planners aimed to use the tactics of August 10 to put the radicals in power.

Paris was not the only part of France torn apart by popular unrest and conflicts between rival revolutionary factions. In Marseille, the radicals who controlled the local Jacobin Club reacted violently to the news of the military collapse in Belgium in early March, calling for the immediate dismissal of the Girondin deputies and rallying militants in other cities to support their position. The club's actions set off a backlash in Marseille itself, where more moderate republicans set out to conquer the city's section assemblies and turn them against their rivals. At the end of April, they drove out the pro-Montagnard deputies on mission sent from Paris and arrested the local radical leaders. Events took a similar course in Lyon, where a faction headed by a local Montagnard, Joseph Chalier, took control of the government in early March and created its own local Committee of Public Safety. The radicals imposed a maximum price on basic foods and set up a local militia to enforce it. As in Marseille, opponents mobilized their supporters to turn the sections against the city government. From Paris, the embattled Girondins encouraged the sections in the two cities, while the Montagnards feared that if they did not act quickly, they might be overwhelmed by a backlash from the provinces.

Despite the turbulent atmosphere in Paris and in the Convention, the deputies did not forget that they were supposed to be drafting a new constitution. Robespierre used the resumption of the debate on the subject on April 24 to give a powerful statement of his political ideas. In a bow in the direction of populism, he proposed to include in the new constitution's declaration of rights an article stating that "any institution that does not postulate that the people is good and that magistrates are corruptible is vicious." In response to Condorcet, who had made an emphatic defense of absolute property rights and free enterprise in his draft declaration, Robespierre proposed a very different definition of the right of property. Even as he assured his audience that he only wanted to "make poverty honorable" and promised that he would not advocate a redistribution of property, he dismissed the rich as "mudstained souls who only value gold," insisting that "the extreme disproportion of fortunes is the cause of many evils and many crimes." The revolutionaries of 1789 had considered the wealthier strata of the population to be the more enlightened and virtuous citizens. Robespierre clearly thought the opposite.[47]

Robespierre proposed to consider property legitimate only if it did not "prejudice the security, or the freedom, or the existence, or the property of our fellow men." Among other things, this notion justified measures to force grain merchants to sell their stocks at prices fixed by the authorities. From his principles, Robespierre also drew the conclusion that citizens whose income was at or below the subsistence level should be entirely exempt from taxes, a suggestion Condorcet had already made in his proposal. Robespierre added that tax rates on those with more wealth should be progressive. The wealthy should fund welfare programs, which Robespierre considered "an obligation of those who have a surplus." Whereas the militant agitators in the streets emphasized the issue of bread prices, Robespierre wanted to assure that they would be able to earn enough to support themselves. He hoped to accomplish this by incorporating into the Declaration of Rights an article stating that "society is obliged to provide for the subsistence of all its members, either in providing work for them, or in assuring the means of existence to those who are not able to work." This basic principle of modern welfare states had been foreshadowed early in the Revolution by the proposals of the National Assembly's welfare committee, but Robespierre now recommended giving it constitutional status.[48]

Claiming to be outlining eternal principles, Robespierre was in fact keeping a close eye on the political situation that surrounded him. His proposed declaration of rights was a weapon against his Girondin foes and an invitation to the popular militants to help the Montagnard deputies defeat them. One of the Girondins' arguments against the petition of the Paris sections demanding their expulsion from the Convention was that no one section of the country had the right to speak for the citizenry as a whole. Robespierre's draft declaration conceded that only the entire people was sovereign, but it insisted that "every assembled section of the sovereign should have the complete liberty to express its will." Going beyond the original Declaration of Rights' reference to a right of resistance to oppression, Robespierre defined what constituted a pretext for such resistance and added language stating that when rights were violated, "insurrection is . . . the most sacred of rights and the most indispensable of duties." This made it clear that he, and by extension the rest of the Montagnards, would accept a popular uprising to eliminate the Girondins from the Convention.[49]

Outside the Convention, protests of all kinds multiplied. On May 1, 1793, women from Versailles angrily complained to the deputies that "every day, mothers, weighed down with families, are forced to stand at the door of a bakery from 4 in the morning until ten"; they reminded them that "our husbands are fighting for the salvation of the republic." On the same day, representatives of the always restive Faubourg Saint-Antoine demanded that a maximum price be set for grain; they also wanted all unmarried men, including priests, to be drafted into the army, plus an emergency tax on the rich. "The burden of the revolution has so far been borne only by the class of the poor," they complained. "It is time that the rich and the egoists also become republicans." They threatened to stage an insurrection if their demands were not met.[50]

Pressed by the demands from the women and the Faubourg Saint-Antoine militants, on May 3 the Convention reluctantly approved an emergency measure to establish a maximum price for grain. It also instituted procedures intended to compel farmers and grain merchants to put whatever supplies they had on the market. The decision meant abandoning the liberal economic principles that most of the deputies—Girondins and Montagnards alike—held as articles of faith. A little-known deputy, Jean Desvars, protested the decision in a way that amounted to a textbook summary of free-market principles. "I want to avoid government intervention in matters concerned with subsistence, and searches of private property, equally dangerous for liberty," he insisted. "Respect property, because it is the first law of societies." The problem was that the market was visibly not functioning, and even Desvars conceded that a system of price controls was needed. A Girondin, François Buzot, agreed, although he also criticized "the weakness we have shown in not sticking to the principles of free transportation and commerce." For the more radical deputies, those principles were precisely the problem. "The unconstrained freedom of the grain trade allows free rein to the insatiable greed of the merchants," one of them contended. Recognizing that it was politically impossible to wait for "the natural course of things to reduce the price of goods," as another Girondin deputy advised, the Convention endorsed the maximum, as well as the state intervention in the economy that it implied.[51]

The violent quarrels that shook the Convention had their miniature equivalents in the neighborhood assemblies of the sections in Paris, often with drastic consequences for their participants. Jacques Ménétra took part in a political struggle for control of the Bonconseil section, a radical stronghold, when a group of *jeunes gens*, young men from the middle class in the section, tried to take over in the first week of May, in order to oppose an attempt by the Commune to force them to report for army duty. On May 4, these young men packed the meeting of the section's assembly and managed to replace its officials with their own choices. To celebrate their victory, they drafted an address to the Convention affirming their support for the Girondins and their abhorrence of the anarchy imposed by their opponents, who had succeeded in "obtaining a tyrannical authority." Ménétra had a particular dislike for the man who read their message to the Convention, one Isidore Langlois, whom he criticized "for not doing guard duty though he knew well how to denounce people in the section." That evening, Ménétra and the other radical militants, aided by comrades from other Paris neighborhoods, physically assaulted their rivals, hauling several of them off to jail. Langlois, after the heady experience of being publicly praised by the Girondin spokesman Vergniaud at the Convention in the morning, had to go into hiding that same night.[52]

By mid-May, the military situation along France's frontiers had stabilized. The Austrians recovered their Belgian territories and took a few French cities near the frontier, but they were not threatening to march on Paris. In the west, the Vendée rebellion continued, but the rebels were no longer expanding their territory. The violent political struggle in the cities was now the major threat to the country's survival. For the militant women activists in Paris, the situation presented an opportunity. On May 10, 1793, they announced the formation of the Society of Revolutionary Republican Women. Its leaders, Pauline Léon and Claire Lacombe, supported the economic program of the radical agitators known as the Enragés; Léon would marry one of the main Enragé spokesmen, Théophile Leclerc, in November. On May 19, the *citoyennes* of the society accompanied a delegation from the Cordeliers Club to the Convention to demand the creation of a revolutionary army made up of sans-culottes to enforce measures like the maximum. Women's direct participation in political protests remained controversial even among the male militants, however. The president of the Montblanc section assembly, who opposed the presence of women at its meetings, filed a complaint with the police after he was "insulted in the most outrageous fashion" by women protesters.[53]

In the last two weeks of May, the factional conflict in the Convention and in the country at large reached a peak. On May 18, Barère, still regarded as a centrist, won enough support from other deputies to create a "Commission of Twelve" to investigate the rumors of a plot to stage a popular insurrection in Paris. Evidence was plentiful: police agents concurred that "the uprising is inevitable and very close, if we do not adopt measures of relief for the people." Even Robespierre was coming in for criticism because, as one militant put it, "he begins to talk to us of prudence!" Brissot, the main target of the popular movement, told a friend that "they are preparing a Saint Bartholomew's Day massacre for us." On May 24, the Commission of Twelve provoked a confrontation by issuing arrest warrants for Hébert, the "Père Duchêne," and for a leading Enragé spokesman, Jean Varlet. When a delegation from the Paris Commune denounced the arrests, the Girondin Isnard, presiding over the Convention, intemperately replied that if the militant movement did not cease its threats, it would provoke such a reaction that "one will search on the banks of the Seine to see if Paris ever existed."[54]

Not necessarily friendly to Hébert and Varlet, Robespierre and his supporters in the Convention nevertheless refused to let the Girondins defeat the popular movement. Rallying their forces in the Convention on May 27, they won a vote to abolish the Commission of Twelve and have Hébert and Varlet released from prison. The next day, however, momentum swung back to the Girondins, who won a roll-call vote to reinstate the commission. Robespierre had consistently warned against an excess of violence that would leave the country without a recognized government, but on the evening of May 29, he told the Jacobin Club, "I am unable to tell the people how to save itself."[55] It was an invitation to the militant activists to set their plans in motion. Once again, as on July 14, 1789, and August 10, 1792, the fate of the Revolution would be decided in the streets of Paris.

# 14

# THE REVOLUTION
# ON THE BRINK

*June–December 1793*

E VEN FOR A POPULATION INURED TO CHAOS AFTER FOUR YEARS OF REVOLU-
tion, the summer and fall of 1793 were times of extraordinary upheaval. Enemy armies threatened the country from all directions, and
within its borders, new provincial uprisings against the radical Montagnards joined the royalist rebellion in the west. In the capital, male and
female activists demanded drastic measures to help the common people
survive economically, challenging the authority of both the National
Convention and the Commune. Across the Atlantic, many of the country's prized colonies threatened to slip out of its control, and in France's
most valuable overseas possession, Saint-Domingue, revolutionary officials took the extraordinary step of offering freedom to the black slaves,
overturning the institution of slavery so central to all the European
colonial empires. Both in France and abroad, many doubted that the
movement that had begun with such high hopes in 1789 could possibly
survive. In the midst of this hurricane of conflicts, an improvised set of

institutions took shape that would enable revolutionary leaders to carry out an unprecedented mobilization of the country's resources and fight off the threats facing it. The Revolution that emerged from the cauldron of mid-1793, however, was a very different kind of movement than the one that had begun in 1789.

The explosion that had been building up ever since the execution of Louis XVI finally erupted in Paris on the night of May 31, 1793. With neither the Girondin nor the Montagnard faction in the Convention able to achieve solid control of the national legislature, "both sides began to look for victory by mobilizing support from outside," wrote the deputy René Levasseur. The Girondins counted on their backers in the provinces; in early May, Vergniaud, their leading orator, told his constituents in Bordeaux, "There is not a moment to lose. If you show real energy, you will compel the men who are provoking a civil war to back down."[1] In response, the Montagnards put their fate in the hands of the popular movement in the capital. The journée of May 31 to June 2, 1793, began by following the script of the uprising of August 10, 1792. In the middle of the night of May 30, members of the insurrectionary committee that had been meeting since mid-March to plot against the Girondins declared themselves the representatives of the sovereign people. They installed a dependable military commander, François Hanriot, as head of the military units of the Paris sections, announced that the assemblies of the sections would now meet in continuous, permanent sessions, ordered the sounding of the tocsin to assemble the troops, and informed the Commune that they were calling for an insurrection.

On August 10, the main target of the uprising had been the king, who was blamed for betraying the country and the war effort. The insurrection of May 31 was aimed at the Convention, whose members had been elected by the people. This assault on the deputies risked leaving France with no recognized government at all. For this reason, and because they feared another massacre like the one that had taken place the previous September, even radicals who had supported the August journée initially hesitated to endorse the insurrection. These men included Pierre Gaspard "Anaxagoras" Chaumette, the principal official of the Paris municipal government, and Hébert, the sans-culottes' favorite journalist. "I witnessed Chaumette . . . shout, cry, tear his hair, and make the most violent efforts to convince [us] that the Comité central was effecting the counter-revolution," one of the Evêché committee members later testified.[2]

Once the Commune decided that it had no choice but to back the movement, the problem was to put enough pressure on the Convention to force the ouster of the Girondin leaders without completely destroying the national legislature's authority. Added to the original insurrectionary committee, representatives of the Commune tempered the movement's list of demands, which had originally called for drastic economic measures meant to benefit the poor, the creation of a revolutionary army to force rural farmers to deliver grain at an affordable price, and a complete purge of government personnel.

Early on May 31, armed sans-culottes surrounded the Tuileries Palace, now the Convention's meeting place. Some of them pushed their way into the assembly hall, where they mingled with the deputies in a scene of complete confusion. The Convention still hesitated to expel any of its own members, and as the first day of the insurrection came to an end, the militants who had launched it were badly frustrated. During the night, the insurrectionary committee had acted on its own to arrest Madame Roland, whom they viewed as the symbol of the Girondins, and made sure that Hanriot's armed men would return to surround the Convention again. The day of June 1 brought no resolution: the Convention still refused to bow to the demonstrators' demands. On June 2, a Sunday, crowds even larger than those of the previous two days gathered in the center of Paris. "All the deputies were surrounded to the point where they could not leave," a Jacobin member reported; the deputy Grégoire had to allow four armed men to escort him to the latrines.[3] The sense of urgency was heightened by the arrival of reports from Lyon, where anti-Montagnard forces had taken control of the city's sections on May 29; in a reversal of the situation in Paris, they had used them to overthrow the radical city government.

In the name of the Committee of Public Safety, the centrist deputy Barère appealed to the Girondin leaders to voluntarily step down as a patriotic gesture to end the crisis. A few of the Girondins gave up their seats, but others indignantly refused to yield to the pressure of the crowd. The Convention passed a decree ordering the withdrawal of the armed forces surrounding it; Hanriot responded by threatening an artillery bombardment. This was too much even for many of the Montagnard deputies. Danton protested that "the majesty of the Convention had been outraged." Led by the Convention's president, Marie-Jean Hérault de Séchelles, the majority of the deputies marched out the door to confront the sans-culottes. At each entry to the Tuileries grounds, the result was the same: Hérault ordered the armed crowd to let the deputies pass, but the militants refused. When he confronted Hanriot directly, according to a newspaper account, the general "backed his horse up a few paces, raised his saber . . . and uttered the order, 'To arms, cannoneers, to your guns.'" Then "the artillerymen lit their fuses, the cavalrymen raised their sabers, the infantry pointed their guns at the Convention."[4]

Recognizing that they were at the mercy of the armed crowd surrounding them, the deputies reassembled in their hall, where the Montagnard leaders insisted that they yield to the will of the people. Marat, who had been denouncing the Girondins for years, now had the chance to personally edit the list of those to be expelled from the Convention and arrested. In the end, it included twenty-nine deputies and the ministers Pierre Lebrun and Étienne Clavière. There was great confusion about who was responsible for carrying out the measures against the Girondins; most of them were able to go into hiding or escape from Paris.

The Girondins' defeat on June 2 ended the violent conflict within the Convention that had threatened to paralyze the revolutionary government, but there was no certainty that the rest of the country would follow the capital's lead. The Montagnard deputies in the Convention, the majority of the Jacobin Club, and the authorities of the Paris Commune, who were all eager to see Brissot, Roland, and their supporters finally ousted, had been willing to go along with the insurrection movement, but none of these groups intended to cede their own power to the militants who had launched it.

Among those who were most confused by the situation were the group of antiracist activists who had been pushing the Convention to take a more radical position against slavery and to send a military unit of free men of color to fight against the British and Spanish in the colonies. In March 1793, the former Saint-Domingue plantation owner Claude Milscent had become the first to call for the immediate and unconditional abolition of slavery. In the newspaper of the Cercle social, he wrote that it was no longer possible to "defend two such contradictory constitutions, and fight ceaselessly on the one hand against slavery and on the other to keep it."[5] Julien Raimond pushed for the creation of an "American Legion," to be commanded by the black composer Joseph Boulogne, chevalier de Saint-Georges. On June 3, immediately after the defeat of the Girondins, the Commune leader Chaumette, an ardent abolitionist, and Jeannette Odo, an elderly woman of color, led a delegation from the group and appeared at the Jacobin Club. Odo was supposedly 114 years old, and her appearance set off a round of applause. However, because their cause had long been supported by Brissot, Robespierre denounced them, and when they asked to address the Convention the next day, their request was rejected.

Of greater concern to the Montagnards who now controlled the Convention was the reaction to the journée in the provinces. Moderates sympathetic to the Girondins and hostile to the pretensions of the Paris sans-culottes dominated the administrations of many of the departments. Forty-seven of the departments sent letters to the Convention denouncing the journée of May 31–June 2; only thirty-four others either applauded the events in Paris or said nothing at all. In most cases, the anti-Montagnard departments did little else to respond to the events. Local movements against Parisian radicalism had already taken control of two key cities, Lyon and Marseille, however, and even before the uprising, Caen, the capital of the Calvados department in Normandy, had issued a call to create an armed force to protect the moderate deputies in Paris.

On June 9, a general assembly of delegates from the sections of Caen declared the city in insurrection against the Convention; they then sent messengers to incite other parts of Normandy and Brittany to join the movement. In Bordeaux, the capital of the department of Gironde that had given the Girondin faction its name, news of the measures against the deputies led to the formation of a Popular Commission that took over governmental powers and announced its determination to resist the Montagnards. In the Mediterranean island of Corsica, the young Napoleon Bonaparte was among those who had to decide whether to back the Jacobin central government or to join a revolt against it. The revolt was led by Pasquale Paoli, who was determined to declare the island's autonomy. Bonaparte and his family sided with the Convention's representative in the island. They were forced to flee to the mainland as Paoli not only rejected that body's authority but put Corsica under the protection of the king of England.

The outbreak of resistance in the provinces hardened the Montagnards' attitude toward the Girondins. The Montagnards now denounced their opponents as *fédéralistes* (federalists) bent on breaking up the "one and indivisible" republic proclaimed after the overthrow of the monarchy. Federalism—the idea that a country could be made up of relatively autonomous local units loosely bound together—was the political system adopted by the United States: there, the constitution of 1787 had created a central federal government that left important powers to the states. In France, however, the idea suggested a retreat to the old regime, where the provinces had had different laws, and this, the revolutionaries believed, would undermine the common national identity they wanted to promote. In the midst of a foreign war and the other crises facing the country, weakening the powers of the central government also seemed like a recipe for disaster.

Above all, the participants in the provincial revolts denounced the excessive influence of the Paris population, the sections and clubs of the capital, on the Convention. They called for the abolition of the Revolutionary Tribunal and the Committee of Public Safety, the improvised institutions that had strengthened central authority, and for the recall of the deputies sent "on mission" from Paris. They insisted that they were not in rebellion against the Convention, but could only recognize its authority when it had "recovered its liberty, its integrity," by readmitting the expelled deputies and renouncing "the laws that it did not pass freely." If the Convention deputies were too divided to accomplish their

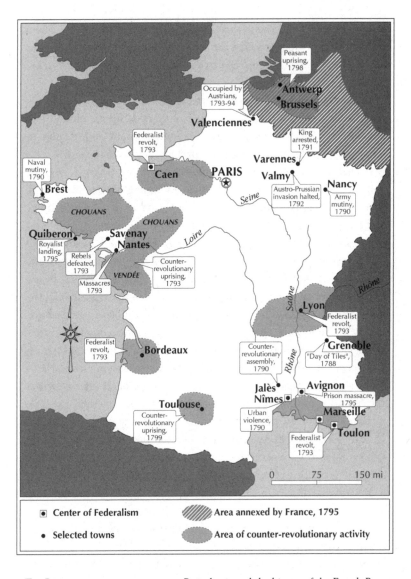

THE REVOLUTION IN THE PROVINCES: Paris dominated the history of the French Revolution, but many important events, from the Great Fear of 1789 to counterrevolutionary uprisings, occurred far away from the capital, and even in France's overseas colonies, as this map shows. The ability of the revolutionary government to establish control over the provinces was decisive in determining the Revolution's outcome. *Credit: Richard Gilbreath.*

tasks, the rebels told them, they should call for new elections.[6] There was nothing obviously "federalist" about this program; but there was also no hint of how it could be carried out in the circumstances facing France in June 1793.

Initially at least, the so-called federalist movements were led by middle-class political figures who had supported the Revolution and endorsed the creation of the republic. Things would soon change in some areas as the military situation became increasingly desperate for the rebel leaders, who found themselves forced to ally with royalists, and even, in the Mediterranean port city of Toulon, with foreign forces. From the outset, the federalists often had the backing of urban artisans and shopkeepers, the same milieus from which the radical sans-culottes of Paris were drawn. In Lyon, for example, where the Revolution had disrupted demand for the silk cloth that was the city's main product, weavers often sided with the merchants in longing for an end to up-heaval, rather than sympathizing with attacks on the rich. Unlike the revolt in the Vendée, the federalist movements had little peasant back-ing: while their participants included some members of the constitu-tional clergy, as well as some Protestants, such as Rabaut Saint-Étienne, they were not willing to make common cause with the refractory clergy and their supporters. The Vendée rebellion was still spreading even as the federalist protests unfolded, but the two movements had too little in common to allow them to join in fighting the national government. In early June, even as residents of the Breton port city of Nantes were expressing their opposition to the recent journée in Paris, they were also desperately fighting off a Vendean assault.

While the provincial centers of opposition to the Convention tried to organize themselves, leaders in other cities debated their own course. In Perpignan, the local newspaper denounced the "fatal day of May 31"; but how, the editor exclaimed, was it possible to "send forces marching on Paris! Recall our battalions from the frontiers! When these frontiers are menaced or ravaged by the numerous phalanges of foreign tyrants."[7] Meanwhile, in Paris, Montagnard deputies moved swiftly to exploit their control of the national legislature. That control was not yet complete:

many Girondin supporters remained in the assembly, where they repeatedly protested that important decisions could not be taken when so many departments were not fully represented, because their deputies had been arrested. By June 19, seventy-five deputies had signed a petition protesting the arrest of their colleagues. To assure support, the Montagnard majority quickly passed a series of laws meant to show their concern for the poor. These included measures to put land confiscated from émigrés up for sale in small lots so that peasants could bid on it; a law proposing the parceling out of village common lands so that all peasants would own at least a small plot; an expansion of welfare for the indigent; and an emergency tax on the rich.

As Danton's friend Pierre Philippeaux put it, "the surest means of calming the agitated departments" was to complete work on the constitution, whose provisions had been debated at intervals since the introduction of Condorcet's draft in February. A new constitutional committee produced a draft in just a week. Hérault de Séchelles, spokesman for the committee, hailed the proposal as "one of the most popular [constitutions] that has ever existed." Nevertheless, the document ignored most of the genuinely radical and utopian ideas that deputies had put forward during the preceding months. Jean-François Barailon proposed allowing single women to vote; moreover, he thought that since all citizens were "equal in fact and in rights, we ought to all be dressed the same," in a "truly national costume." Jacques-Nicolas Billaud-Varenne, a radical Montagnard who would wind up on the Committee of Public Safety, denounced the evils of economic inequality and proposed to reduce it by limiting the amount of land that any one individual could own; he also wanted to impose a heavy tax on inheritances and redistribute wealth to poorer citizens.[8]

The 1793 constitution largely incorporated the declaration of rights that Robespierre had proposed in April, with its promise of a right to work. Equality, mentioned but not defined in the 1789 declaration, now got an article of its own and took precedence over liberty. In contrast to the elaborate electoral procedures that Condorcet had proposed in his effort to overcome the mathematical difficulties inherent in voting systems, the new system would be simple: instead of sending delegates to electoral assemblies as they had in the elections of 1791 and 1792, voters would choose representatives through direct elections in single-member districts. Originally, the constitutional draft proposed that every law be submitted to a popular vote; this was amended to provide that laws would be presumed to be approved unless primary assemblies in more than half the departments objected to them. Disagreement surfaced briefly about a provision saying the nation would never make peace with an enemy whose forces were occupying French territory. Fearing that this stipulation might commit the country to dragging on hopeless conflicts, the deputy Louis-Sébastien Mercier asked whether France had made a "pact with victory." A Montagnard, Claude Basire, shot back, "We have made a pact with death," an example of the exaggerated patriotic rhetoric that was becoming a hallmark of this new phase of the Revolution.[9]

To the Montagnards, the new constitution embodied the ideals of democracy, republicanism, and national unity. All vestiges of the monarchy were completely effaced, and the once-mighty ministers whose "despotism" the revolutionaries had denounced were demoted to mere "chief agents of the administration" who were not to have "any personal authority." Many moderate deputies voted for the Constitution of 1793, as one of them later wrote, hoping that it would end "the anarchy and the disregard for the laws" in France by "at least establishing and fixing a form of government."[10] As the Convention had promised in its opening session, the constitution was put to a vote in local assemblies all over the country, even in areas where the federalist movements were resisting the national government. Given the chaotic conditions in much of the country, electoral participation was surprisingly high, above the levels in the legislative elections of 1791 and 1792, and discussions about the document were often animated. With 1,801,918 votes cast in favor and only 11,610 opposed, the new constitution could claim a stronger popular endorsement than any of the other government charters drawn up during the revolutionary decade.

The Paris radicals who had played such a central role in the insurrection of May 31–June 2, 1793, remained dissatisfied, however. The Montagnards had ignored many of their key demands, including the immediate trial and punishment of the Girondins, the imposition of price controls to force down the price of bread, and the establishment of a revolutionary army of sans-culottes to pressure farmers into bringing out the grain reserves that the militants were sure they were hoarding. Jacques Roux delivered a furious diatribe that fully justified his reputation as one of the agitators known as the "Enragés." "You have just finished writing a constitution that you are going to submit to a vote of the people. But did you include a ban against speculation in it? No! Did you announce punishments for hoarders and monopolists? No! All right: we tell you that you haven't finished the job," he roared.[11] Worried that the Enragés were cutting into his popular support, Hébert, the firebreathing "Père Duchêne," prevented the Commune assembly from criticizing the constitution. Preoccupied with the multiple crises facing the country, however, the National Convention did nothing to put the document into effect.

The completion of the constitution coincided with intensified conflict within the country. On June 24, after more than half of the targeted Girondin deputies had escaped from Paris, the Convention jailed the remaining members of the group. On June 28, delegates from ten departments in Normandy and Brittany gathered in Caen to discuss organizing a march on Paris. By this time, however, it was already clear that few men were ready to volunteer for such an expedition. In Bordeaux, efforts to create an insurrectionary army also fell flat. Meanwhile, the Convention was rallying its forces to crush the uprisings. On July 8, the Montagnard Saint-Just delivered a vehement indictment of the Girondins, accusing them of "a conspiracy to reestablish tyranny and the old constitution" by putting Louis XVI's son on the throne. Five days later, on July 13, the small military force the federalists had assembled in Normandy was easily dispersed, effectively ending the one rebellion that directly threatened Paris. "They had calculated according to the initial movement of excitement, and they didn't seize it," Pétion, one of the deputies expelled from the Convention who had taken refuge in Normandy, wrote dejectedly.[12] Even as the federalist rebellion in the northwest was crumbling, however, resistance elsewhere was becoming more serious. On July 12, Lyon officially declared itself at war with the Convention. Fortunately for the Montagnards, deputies on mission in the area and local military commanders prevented the Lyonnais from linking up with the rebels in Marseille, who had sent troops to occupy a number of other cities in their region.

On the same day that the Norman federalist army was defeated, Paris was jolted by an assassination that struck fear into the hearts of all supporters of the Revolution. Charlotte Corday, a young noblewoman from Normandy who was sympathetic to the federalist cause, talked her way into the apartment of the journalist and deputy Marat, the "Friend of the People," by passing him a note claiming that she could give him important information about the federalist conspiracy in her home region. She found the ailing Marat sitting in his bathtub, trying to ease the pain from a skin disease, and quickly stabbed him to death. Corday made no effort to escape. She admitted her sympathy for the Girondins but insisted that she had acted solely on her own initiative. She told her interrogators, "I knew he was ruining France. I killed one man to save a hundred thousand." The calm courage she showed at her trial impressed onlookers. Condemned to death, "she wrote to her family and asked for a painter, saying that she would certainly be celebrated in history," one journalist wrote.[13]

The assassination of Marat set off a theatrical outpouring of grief in Paris, even among politicians who had criticized his extremism. The artist Jacques-Louis David, now a Montagnard deputy, quickly worked out the design of the classic painting in which he managed to imbue the figure of Marat slumped in his bathtub with a timeless dignity. David also oversaw an elaborate Roman-style funeral meant to apotheosize his friend, but the solemnity of the event was undermined by the terrible stench emanating from the journalist's body, which putrefied quickly in the searing summer heat. That a woman "had shown the example to men," as the Girondin Pétion, who had met Corday in Caen, put it, stoked accusations that women could not be trusted; the Society of Revolutionary Republican Women tried to counter such attacks by insisting on playing a major role at Marat's funeral. The Cordeliers Club, where Marat had spoken so often, had his heart, "the precious remains of a god," conserved in an urn that was hung from the rafters of its meeting room.

Whatever their true feelings about Marat, supporters of the Revolution saw Corday's crime as evidence that hidden enemies surrounded them. Robespierre insisted that "the honor of a dagger is also reserved for me." That the assassin had been a young and beautiful woman struck one journalist as particularly threatening: "No one looked less like a creature thirsty for blood," he wrote.[14] News that the Lyon federalists had executed their local Montagnard radical Chalier on July 16, 1793, added to the sense that no patriot's life was safe. Together with the deputy Michel Lepeletier, who had been assassinated at the time of Louis XVI's trial, Marat and Chalier were elevated to the status of martyrs whose blood demanded to be avenged.

Marat's assassination coincided with a shift of power in the Convention. Since April, the assembly had relied on the Committee of Public Safety to give overall direction to the government. At first, Danton, the popular tribune, was the most visible member of the committee, but by July it was evident that he and his supporters lacked a clear policy to deal with the crises facing the country. On July 10, the Convention ousted Danton from the committee, leaving it without a dominating personality. That situation changed on July 27, when the assembly added Robespierre to the group. Although he already had a national reputation dating back to his defiant defense of democratic principles in the National Assembly, Robespierre had never had any direct governmental responsibility. For the next year, he would be the central figure in the revolutionary government, and history would remember him as the most visible leader in the Revolution's most radical phase, responsible both for the successful defense of the movement and the extreme methods it used to defeat its opponents. Although he had a personal authority that none of the other committee members could match, Robespierre was never a revolutionary dictator in the mold of V. I. Lenin or Mao Tse-tung. Throughout Robespierre's short time as the most prominent participant in the revolutionary government, he shared power with the other members of the Committee of Public Safety. His colleagues never hesitated to argue with him, and on some crucial issues, he was in the minority within the group.

In the struggle for power in the summer of 1793, Robespierre's guiding principle was that the authority of the Convention needed to be maintained, even as he warned that there were still disloyal members among the deputies. He denounced agitators who stirred up the anger of the populace about food prices, accusing them of trying to provoke another round of attacks on shops "by the people, or really by criminals disguised in the clothing of people." He also singled out the Enragé Jacques Roux, asking whether "this priest, who in concert with the Austrians denounces the best patriots, can have pure views or legitimate intentions." In his view, leadership needed to be in the hands of "men who love the people without saying so, who work tirelessly for its good without boasting." Yet he shared with the sans-culotte militants a conviction that the Revolution was threatened by conspiracies of all sorts. At times, he called for the dismissal of all the army's generals as well as the government's officials. The man who in 1791 had delivered one of the Revolution's most eloquent defenses of press freedom now exhorted the Jacobins to "fall on all the odious journalists . . . whose existence becomes more pernicious to society every day."[15]

As the summer of 1793 wore on, pressure to find ways to defeat the Revolution's enemies grew. The Convention tried to shore up rural support for the Revolution by decreeing, on July 17, that peasants would not have to pay any more compensation for abolished feudal privileges, but they had long since stopped making those payments anyway. On July 26, the Convention passed a sweeping decree declaring that "monopoly is a capital crime."[16] The law denounced speculators who hoarded supplies of any of a long list of foodstuffs and raw materials and ordered all those dealing in such goods to register their stocks with local authorities. The measure made almost every economic transaction suspect and empowered government officials and surveillance committees to invade homes, businesses, and peasant barns looking for violations. Even so, the Enragés and much of the population of Paris remained unsatisfied: bread prices did not come down, and the privileges of the rich remained. Suspicions that nobles and relatives of émigrés were contributing to the crippling shortage of hard currency by smuggling gold and silver out of the country added to the sense that enemies of the Revolution were deliberately exacerbating the economic difficulties that weighed on the poor.

The last days of July brought a wave of bad news from the frontiers. Besieged by Prussian forces for four months, the French forces occupying

Mainz finally surrendered, ending the effort to spread republican principles to Germany. In northern France, civilians panicked by the Austrian bombardment of the city of Valenciennes forced its garrison to evacuate, allowing the enemy to take a key position on French soil. Suspicion fastened on General Adam Philippe Custine, who had led the French occupation of Mainz before being transferred to command of the army in the north: Robespierre compared him to Dumouriez and accused him of being in the pay of the British. As the chronicler Ruault put it, "in the eyes of the sans-culottes incompetence and treason are more or less the same." Custine's trial by the Revolutionary Tribunal dragged on for much of the month of August, intensifying fears about the loyalty of military officers who, like him, came from noble families. Meanwhile, the campaign against the rebels in the Vendée and Brittany was also going poorly. In the Convention, Barère complained that none of the bickering republican commanders there understood how to fight the kind of elusive enemy they were facing: "Your army is like that of a Persian king," he said. "It has one hundred and sixty baggage wagons, whereas the brigands march with their weapons and a scrap of black bread in their sack."[17]

In the face of these setbacks, the Convention tried to recapture the spirit of enthusiasm and unity that were now remembered as the hallmarks of the early stages of the Revolution by taking aim at remaining vestiges of elitism. In addition, they staged a great public festival to celebrate the popular vote in favor of the new constitution. On August 8, 1793, after listening to the artist David denounce the academies that had overseen artistic and scientific endeavors as "monstrous corporations, survivals of the royal and ministerial regime that have been tolerated for too long" (the Jacobin priest Grégoire chimed in by claiming that they had "tried to monopolize glory and guard for themselves the exclusive privilege of talent"), the Convention voted to do away with them. A pamphleteer called for "a sans-culotticized science" and accused the "savants" of the academies, like priests, of "employing a mystical language, to avoid enlightening those they called profane."[18] Even the descendants of the philosophes now found themselves stigmatized as enemies of equality.

The Festival of Republican Unity, on August 10, was David's most elaborate production. Participants followed an itinerary that took them across the city to perform a series of symbolic rituals. At the Bastille, the Revolution's birthplace, they drank water that poured from the breasts of a giant statue of a woman representing Nature, the source of liberty and equality. Deputies and public officials were deliberately mixed in the procession with ordinary citizens in their working clothes; the official account of the festival emphasized that "the African, whose face is blackened by the fire of the sun, marched hand in hand with the white man. . . . [A]ll were equal as men, as citizens, as members of the Sovereign." In an unprecedented public recognition of the role women had played in the Revolution, an arch of triumph celebrated the heroines of the October Days of 1789. The Convention's president, Hérault de Séchelles, saluted their achievement, but then reminded them that they now had a more traditional role to play: "Liberty, attacked by all the tyrants," he said, "needs a people of heroes to defend it; it is up to you to give birth to them!"[19]

Having honored the conquerors of the Bastille and the heroines of the October Days, the procession moved on to the Place de la Révolution, where a statue of Liberty had been erected on the spot where Louis XVI had been guillotined. Here, Hérault de Séchelles set fire to an assemblage of objects symbolizing the old regime: thrones, crowns, scepters, coats of arms. As the flames roared, three thousand birds were released into the air. The birds bore tricolor ribbons with the message, "We are free! Imitate us!" At the festival's final site, on the Champ de Mars, participants had to pass under a carpenter's level suspended from a tricolor ribbon, a Masonic symbol meant as "a visible representation of the social equality that keeps all men on an equal plane." David had erected a colossal statue of Hercules; the demigod held a bundle of sticks in one hand while preparing to crush a monster under his feet with a club. In case the crowd did not initially grasp the statue's symbolism, Hérault's speech explained it to them: "This giant whose powerful hand brings together in a single bundle the departments that make its grandeur and its force is you! This monster whose criminal hand wants to break the bundle and separate what nature has united is federalism!"[20]

No one could mistake the role that the people were called on to play two weeks later, on August 23, when, to overcome the military crisis, the deputies decreed a *levée en masse*, that is, a "total mobilization" of the nation's population and resources. Whereas previous draft calls had affected only men of military age, the *levée en masse* demanded a universal effort. "The young men shall go to battle; the married men shall forge arms and transport provisions; the women shall make tents and clothes, and shall serve in the hospitals; the children shall turn old linen into lint; the old men shall repair to the public places, to stimulate the courage of the warriors and preach the unity of the Republic and hatred of kings," the decree said. The measure looked backward to the revolutionaries' idealized image of the patriotism of the ancient Greeks and Romans, but it also looked forward to the age of total war in the twentieth century. Theoretically meant to raise seven hundred thousand new troops, the levy only produced about two-thirds that number. The many calls for volunteers in the previous two years meant that there were few enthusiastic recruits left to send. In his village, the schoolteacher Delahaye wrote, "there was general desolation at the departure of these poor young men."[21] Nevertheless, the decree effectively conveyed the message that all individual interests were now overridden by the need to defend the country.

The day before the *levée en masse* was decreed, the Convention's forces opened their assault on the rebel city of Lyon, the most significant of the remaining federalist strongholds. The city's population had actually voted to accept the Constitution of 1793, hoping that their action might open the way to a negotiated end of the conflict with the Convention, but the government in Paris was in no mood to make concessions. With no choice but to hope that a foreign invasion might divert the Convention's forces before the city had to surrender, the leaders of the revolt accepted the support of royalists like Louis François Perrin de Précy, who was named Lyon's military commander. The presence of royalists among the defenders served the Montagnards' propaganda interests. As the Convention's forces tightened the noose around Lyon, the federalist movements south of the city faced drastic choices. Marseille, one of the major centers of resistance in the spring of 1793, surrendered. In Toulon, however, the home base of France's Mediterranean fleet, moderates and royalists accepted an offer from the British to land troops and help defend the city in exchange for the disarmament of the French warships in the harbor.

Like General Dumouriez's treason, the surrender of Toulon caused a furious reaction in Paris. The news arrived on September 4, 1793, just after confirmation of another sensational disaster, the destruction of the city of Cap Français, the main port of the Caribbean colony of Saint-Domingue. The burning of the city, which caused somewhere between three thousand and ten thousand deaths, resulted in a huge economic loss, as warehouses full of sugar and coffee went up in flames. It was the most extensive incident of urban violence in the entire course of the Revolution. The first reports of the event, which had taken place on June 20, were highly confused. They gave the impression that the two republican civil commissioners sent to the island a year earlier, with the support of the now disgraced Brissot, had staged a colonial version of a federalist revolt. "The national commissioners [Étienne] Polverel and [Léger-Félicité] Sonthonax have usurped a dictatorial authority in the island, and their criminal ambition is the cause of these latest misfortunes," noted the Montagnard Committee of Public Safety spokesman André Jeanbon Saint-André, speaking to the Convention on September 3.[22] He said nothing about the truly revolutionary step the commissioners had taken. On the night of June 20, after the commissioners and their free colored defenders had nearly been overwhelmed by their opponents in Cap Français, Polverel and Sonthonax had offered immediate freedom to any black slaves who would take up arms to support them.

Up until this moment, the French authorities in Saint-Domingue had been doing their best to defeat the black insurgents who had risen up in August 1791; many of the same men had enrolled themselves in the Spanish army when that country joined the war against France in early 1793. When they arrived in the colony in September 1792, Polverel and Sonthonax had publicly sworn that they would resign their posts rather than obey any decree from France ordering the abolition of slavery. Nevertheless, both men were personally critical of slavery; in September 1790, Sonthonax, the younger and more outspoken of the two, had written an anonymous article in the *Révolutions de Paris* predicting that "the day will come—and the day is not too far off—when you will see a curly-haired African, relying only on his virtue and good sense, coming to participate in the legislative process in the midst of our national assemblies."[23] The emergency they found themselves facing on June 20 gave the commissioners a justification for acting in accordance with their personal convictions, although they had no assurance that the Convention in Paris would approve of their decision.

The commissioners' initial offer was limited to men capable of joining the army. But they soon realized that recruiting loyal black soldiers required extending the scope of emancipation, first to the wives and children of those men who volunteered, and then, by the end of August 1793, to all blacks in the colony. Furthermore, the commissioners' concept of emancipation was constrained by their determination to maintain the plantation system that made the colony so valuable to France. Ignoring one idealistic white colonist who thought that, as long as plantation owners' property rights over their slaves were going to be ended, the moment had come to create a society based on "the community of goods among all the individuals," they drew up plans under which blacks would be legally free but still obligated to work in the sugar fields.[24]

There were thus good reasons for many blacks to remain suspicious of the French officials' intentions. Toussaint Louverture, who by this time was serving as a general in the Spanish army, condemned the French republicans for executing the king and persecuting the Church and indignantly rejected their emancipation offer. "You try to make us believe that Liberty is a benefit that we will enjoy if we submit ourselves to order," he wrote to Sonthonax and Polverel, "but as long as God gives us the force and the means, we will acquire another Liberty, different from that which you tyrants pretend to impose on us."[25] Persuaded by his Spanish allies that revolutionary France was about to be overrun by its foes, Louverture and the other black leaders saw no point in accepting promises that might never be fulfilled. Nevertheless, the crisis of June 20, 1793, which culminated in the burning of Cap Français and the flight of the majority of the colony's white population, opened the largest breach in the system of slavery in the history of the Americas. Within a few months, not only would Louverture change sides, becoming one of the strongest defenders of the measures

Sonthonax and Polverel had taken, but the Convention would extend the abolition of slavery to the rest of the French Empire.

The destruction of Cap Français had an immediate impact in the United States. Refugees fleeing the island flooded into the port cities of Norfolk, Baltimore, and Philadelphia in early July. The young American republic was revolutionary France's only ally, but the efforts of the French emissary Edmond-Charles Genêt, one of Brissot's diplomatic nominations, to pull the United States into conflict with Britain and Spain were putting great strain on the relationship. When Genêt first arrived in the spring of 1793, "Democratic Republican" supporters of Thomas Jefferson welcomed him ecstatically, seeing the French Revolution as a logical extension of the American movement. The Federalists, who followed President George Washington, however, warned against allowing republican enthusiasm to drag the country into wars for a "foreign interest." The angry clashes over Genêt's mission marked the creation of America's first political parties. The arrival of the Saint-Domingue refugees, some of whom brought black slaves or free colored mistresses with them, raised fears that "French Negroes" would incite slave rebellions. By the end of July, Washington's cabinet had agreed to demand that the French recall Genêt. Ironically, in Paris, the Committee of Public Safety had already decided to dismiss him, not because he had alienated the American government but because he was a Brissotin. The Genêt affair marked the beginning of a separation between the world's only two democratic republics and left the French feeling that they were truly isolated in a hostile world.

Combined with the catastrophic news from Toulon, the reports of the upheaval in Saint-Domingue provoked yet another popular insurrection against the Convention on September 5, 1793. The organizers of this journée were not the obscure section militants who had started the movement of May 31, but rather the leaders of the Commune, Chaumette and Hébert, and radical members of the Jacobin Club, such as the deputies Billaud-Varenne and Collot d'Herbois, who were determined to force the Committee of Public Safety to adopt more extreme measures to save the country. The demonstrators bore placards calling for "war on tyrants, hoarders and aristocrats," and their slogan was to "make terror the order of the day." Their most concrete demand was one that had been on the populist agenda since the spring: the formation of a revolutionary army of sans-culottes to comb the countryside, rooting out opposition and hunting for grain supplies. Billaud-Varenne, for his part, suggested a new committee to replace the Committee of Public Safety and achieve what it had not, the extermination of the Revolution's enemies.[26]

The members of the Committee of Public Safety had grave reservations about creating a revolutionary army. Coordinating the fourteen separate armies already in the field and keeping them from competing with each other for desperately needed supplies was already stretching the government's resources to the limit. The revolutionary army would be under the control of populist allies of Hébert, who had little respect for the Committee or the Convention. Unleashing armed bands of militants in the countryside threatened to spread further chaos and to alienate the rural population. Nevertheless, the popular pressure was impossible to resist. In the Convention, Danton once again showed his talent for improvisation. He moved to create a revolutionary army, but to put the Committee of Public Safety in charge of organizing it. At the same time, however, the ability of the Paris sections to mobilize against the Convention would be reined in by ending their right to remain in permanent session, which allowed them to constantly stir up public opinion, and limiting them to just two short meetings per week. In an apparent gesture to the sans-culottes, Danton proposed that workers and artisans who attended the sections be paid for coming. It was a clever maneuver because the participants would have an interest in getting their money, which would be at risk if they disrupted the regular workings of the government. To ward off criticism of the Committee of Public Safety, the deputies added the two firebrands Billaud-Varenne and Collot d'Herbois to its membership.

As the crowd dispersed, few recognized that, thanks to Danton, the Convention had eluded the militants' demand to officially declare "terror the order of the day," a step that would have committed the government to satisfying the radicals' call for a wave of repression unrestrained by the law. Nevertheless, the journée of September 5 set the stage for a sharp intensification of measures aimed at real and imagined enemies of the Revolution and a dramatic expansion in the power of the central government. Terror—the swift punishment of opponents and the demand for unquestioning obedience to official decrees—was an openly acknowledged means of carrying out these decrees. The idea that the law should inspire terror in the souls of those tempted to violate it had a long history in the old regime. Montesquieu, however, had given the word a negative connotation, identifying it as the principle of despotic regimes. In the first years of the Revolution, Marat had been almost alone in praising popular violence as a way of creating "this mood of terror that is healthy and so indispensable to achieve the great work of the constitution."[27] By mid-1792, many revolutionaries had come to share the idea that the Revolution's enemies needed to be intimidated through terror; both the Girondin Vergniaud and the Montagnard Danton spoke of making the royal court experience the fear it had long inspired in the people.

What was new in the late summer of 1793 was the concept of terror as a systematic method not just to defend the Revolution, but to achieve its positive aims. "Yes, terror is on the order of the day, and should be for the egoists, for the federalists, for the rich who have no pity, for the ambitious who are dishonest, for the shameless intriguer, for the coward disloyal to the country, for all those who do not feel the dignity attached to the title of a free man, the pure republican. . . . No compromise, France must be either entirely free or perish completely, and all methods are justified to uphold such an admirable cause," wrote the *Révolutions de Paris*.[28] The revolutionaries did not use the phrase *le règne de la terreur* (reign of terror), which, along with the word *terroriste* (terrorist), was invented by opponents of Robespierre after his overthrow in 1794, to discredit the system it described. Nevertheless, these terms are undeniably accurate as descriptions of the policies followed in late 1793 and the first half of 1794 by the men who held power in France for the ten months that followed the September journée. Convinced that the survival of liberty and equality in the world depended on the survival of the French Republic, and fearful that they themselves would not survive if the Revolution was defeated, they fully intended to instill fear—not just in their enemies, but in the citizenry at large.

In February 1794, when the scope of this policy had become clear, Robespierre unhesitatingly defended it, telling his listeners that without terror, "virtue is impotent." What justified the terror of the Revolution in his eyes—and what made it different from the uncontrolled violence of the common people—was that it was an instrument of justice carried out through the law, not simply a weapon of the strong deployed to over-awe the weak. To its victims, this insistence that revolutionary terror was a form of law and justice was what made it particularly objectionable. From her prison cell, Madame Roland, long one of the Revolution's most devoted supporters, denounced "the rule of these hypocrites who, always dressed in the mask of justice, always speaking the language of the law, have set up a tribunal to carry out their vengeance."[29] Given her situation, she could hardly have appreciated how sincerely men like Robespierre believed that what they were doing was necessary and justified. But it was the intensity of that conviction that allowed Robespierre and many other participants in the Revolution to tolerate the all-too-real abuses of power that Madame Roland identified so astutely.

After the journée of September 5, 1793, it was clear that, in spite of the elaborate celebration of the new constitution a month earlier, there was not going to be any move to actually put it into effect by holding elections for a new legislature. Robespierre denounced the "insidious proposition" of replacing the Convention's "purified members" with "envoys of Pitt and Cobourg," referring to the foreign enemies of the Revolution.[30] Until the war was won and the security of the country assured, the Convention elected in 1792 would continue to govern the country. Moreover, until the Convention decided otherwise, the Committee of Public Safety, now clearly dominated by the most radical Montagnards, would be the center of policy making. The committee ruled from September 1793 to July 1794. The only body that shared authority with it was the Committee of General Security, which oversaw the police and the Revolutionary Tribunal.

The Convention moved swiftly to give these two "committees of government" broadened powers. On September 17, 1793, the "law of suspects" authorized the arrest of "those who, by their conduct, associations, talk, or writings have shown themselves partisans of tyranny or federalism and enemies of liberty." In addition to this wide and vague definition of suspects, the law targeted a number of specific groups: anyone who could not show that they earned their living honestly, any former public officials who had been suspended or dismissed from their posts, all relatives of émigrés who had not "steadily manifested their devotion to the Revolution," and anyone who had emigrated from France in the early years of the Revolution, even if they had returned before the deadline set by the law passed in 1792. The surveillance committees created in March 1793 were charged with carrying out the law. In Paris, the Commune issued a list of "characteristics that render people suspect," including "those who speak cryptically of the misfortunes of the Republic, show pity for the people and are always ready to spread bad news with apparent sorrow, . . . those who affect, in order to appear republican, an excessive austerity and severity," and "those who not having done anything against liberty, also haven't done anything for it," criteria elastic enough to take in anyone. Those who feared arrest tried to look like good patriots by dressing like sans-culottes and subscribing to the *Père Duchêne*. "The image of the orator smoking his pipe . . . served as an icon of safety on the dressing tables of the prettiest women, in the studies of the learned, in the salons of the rich and in business offices," one Parisian later recalled.[31]

Local authorities were told to establish prisons to hold suspects "until the peace"; those arrested did not necessarily have to be charged or brought to trial. As was customary at the time, prisoners had to pay for their own food and expenses. A former military officer caught up in the dragnet remembered his captors looking him over and deciding, "He's tall, he looks self-confident, he's a suspect." Recounting the incident further, he added: "I object, I invoke the law, justice, no one listens; outbreaks of laughter echo through the vaults." The guards strip-searched him, took his clothes and valuables, and threw him into a cell with eighty other prisoners. It was "without beds, without chairs, just old mattresses covered with vermin." Even individuals who were not imprisoned were placed under onerous surveillance. In the small town of Langres, a devout Catholic nun wrote that "around 300 women are obliged, since they are called suspects, to check in at the town hall every day. Age, illness, nothing matters to them."[32] The country of the rights of man had now created a prison system on a scale without precedent in the Western world; by the summer of 1794, half a million men and women had experienced it.

Two weeks later, the Convention embarked on an equally sweeping effort to regulate the country's economy. Expanding the system of price controls imposed on grain and bread the previous April to a long list of other essential commodities now became a priority. Even as they praised the virtues of the common people, the deputies had come to be deeply suspicious of what one of them called "the greed and the bad faith of the cultivators"; they believed that farmers were not selling their produce at a fair price and that they were too reluctant to accept the Revolution's depreciated assignats in payment. The law of the general maximum, enacted on September 29, 1793, aimed to stabilize the prices of foodstuffs, textiles, and basic materials for industrial production and to ensure adequate supplies for the armies. Prices of regulated items were set at 1790 levels augmented by a third to account for inflation. The law also set limits on wages, which were to be one and a half times what they had been in 1790. In theory, this amounted to an increase for workers, but only if they could actually find goods in the market at the government-imposed prices. Meanwhile, the law authorized local officials to punish workers and company owners "who refuse[d], without legitimate grounds, to do their usual work."[33] Jean-Marie Goujon had been one of the first to use the word *maximum* in this way; it had appeared in his letter to the Convention the previous November. He now suddenly found himself elevated to a position of national importance: the Committee of Public Safety appointed him as one of three members of the commission charged with administering price controls throughout the country. Just two years earlier, he had been giving highflown speeches about the Revolution's love for the common people; now he was entrusted with satisfying their most pressing practical needs.

Together with the law against hoarding and speculation, the law of the maximum drastically limited the freedom of economic enterprise that had been a central aspect of the 1789 revolutionaries' original concept of rights. Patriotic businessmen at first promised to respect the law. "It has cost me more than 50,000 livres," one wrote. "I made the sacrifice without effort and without regret, because a crisis in commerce was necessary to stop the ongoing and limitless increase in the most necessary goods." Cumbersome to administer, the maximum soon spawned a flourishing black market as customers with money tempted suppliers by offering to pay more than the legal price for scarce commodities. Workers pressured employers to pay them more than the official rate. Only the threat that violators would find themselves jailed as suspects or even sent before the Revolutionary Tribunal forced a grudging acceptance of regulations that were often unworkable. In its original form, for example, the law did not take into account the cost of transporting commodities from their place of origin, an omission that discouraged the shipment of goods to distant markets. Much of the work of the revolutionary armies created after the journée of September 5, 1793, consisted of pressuring peasants to sell their crops at the official price and intimidating workers to do their jobs for what they considered inadequate wages, activities that increased the population's resentment of the Revolution. "The revolutionary army has been badmouthed throughout the countryside," a police observer wrote. "The peasants, already upset about the price limit, are not at all disposed to let them peacefully enter their homes and seize . . . the produce they have stored."[34]

For all of its defects, however, the law of the maximum did make it possible to keep the urban population fed and the armies supplied through the winter and spring of 1794. The revolutionary government's threat to punish those who refused to accept assignats stopped the precipitous decline in the paper currency's value. After falling to less than 30 percent of its nominal value in September 1793, the assignat rose to over 50 percent of that value in December, even as the mass of money in circulation kept rising. With all the other demands they faced, local officials had little time or energy to collect taxes; the vast majority of government revenue came from the ongoing sale of church and émigré properties, which continued at a steady pace throughout the Terror. Since payments were accepted in assignats, the government got much less than full value from these sales, but they provided what the Convention's fiscal expert Pierre Cambon called "incalculable resources for the conquest of liberty."[35]

To give their policies a legal basis, on October 10, 1793, the Convention deputies endorsed a decree presented by the Montagnard Saint-Just, a member of the Committee of Public Safety, declaring that "the provisional government of France is revolutionary until the peace." "In the circumstances in which the Republic finds itself," Saint-Just proclaimed, "the constitution cannot be put into effect; it would be turned against itself. It would protect attacks against liberty, because it would not allow the violence necessary to stop them." The decree consecrated the power of the Committee of Public Safety, giving it the authority to direct ministers and generals. A more detailed decree issued two months later, on December 4, or 14 frimaire Year II, according to the new revolutionary calendar that the Convention had by then adopted, reversed the decentralization of power that had been one of the central features of the revolutionary process. The decree declared that "the National Convention is the sole motive center of the government" and converted elected local officials into "national agents"; they would be responsible for carrying out the laws passed by the Convention as well as orders issued by the Committee of Public Safety.[36] What the absolute monarchy had dreamed of possessing through its system of intendants was now available to its revolutionary successor: a national bureaucracy that would, at least in theory, immediately implement the policies of the central government throughout the country. Napoleon would later call the Terror the only serious government France had during the revolutionary decade.

The necessity of winning the war provided the main justification for the rapid expansion of the revolutionary government's powers. Although the most heated rhetoric of 1793 was directed against the domestic enemies—the federalists and the Vendée rebels—the bulk of the army was still deployed against foreign foes. Fortunately for the French, the invaders showed much less urgency about pursuing their campaigns than the revolutionaries did in fighting them off. After driving the French out of Mainz, the Prussians shifted their attention to their eastern frontier, joining the Russians in a partition of Poland that was meant to end the reform movement there. In the southeast, the Piedmontese fought to regain the province of Savoy that France had annexed a year earlier, and in the south, Spanish forces took a few border fortresses. These fronts were far from Paris, however: the real threat to the republic was in Belgium. Still following the playbook of eighteenth-century warfare, Austrian and British forces moved slowly and cautiously, laying siege to fortified positions rather than seeking to destroy the French armies in the field. In addition, the allies divided their forces, with the British attacking the coastal port of Dunkirk, while the Austrians sent the bulk of their troops to Maubeuge, hundreds of miles away.

In the fall of 1793, the French inflicted significant defeats on both their opponents in the north. On September 6, General Jean-Nicolas Houchard's victory at Hondschoote broke the siege of Dunkirk. As in their more famous retreat from the same port in 1940, the British had to abandon much of their materiel and leave the conflict on the continent to their allies. Rather than being praised for his victory, Houchard was promptly arrested for not following it up with enough vigor. On November 15, he was guillotined, his fate a warning to other republican generals. Meanwhile, on October 6, General Jean-Baptiste Jourdan defeated the Austrians at Wattignies, forcing them to give up their effort to capture Maubeuge. While the Austrians managed to retreat in good order, their offensive was ended for the year, giving the French precious time to prepare the fresh troops that the *levée en masse* was producing for future combat.

As military operations wound down for the year, the revolutionaries undertook new campaigns aimed not just at defending the accomplishments of the Revolution but at changing the world. Already at the beginning of August, in the midst of civil war and military calamities, the assembly had applauded a lengthy report presenting a new system of weights and measures, what we now know as the metric system. The new system was derived from nature itself: the meter was defined as one ten-millionth of the meridian, or the distance from the earth's pole to the equator; the liter was the volume of a cube defined in terms of the meter; and the gram the weight of a specified fraction of a liter of water. The creators of the metric system saw it as universal, a "symbol of the equality and a gauge of the fraternity that should unite all men." The fact that they had been able to approve the reform in the midst of so many other preoccupations was important to the revolutionaries. "Philosophy will someday be pleased to contemplate . . . the genius of the sciences and of humanity transcending the storms of revolutions and wars," the deputies assured themselves.[37]

Another campaign altered everyday speech by eliminating the distinction between the polite form of address, *vous*, customarily used to address one's social superiors, and *tu*, reserved for addressing intimates, children, and those of inferior rank. A petition to the Convention promised that if *tutoiement*, the use of the familiar second-person singular form, was made mandatory, "these principles will be a basic demonstration of our equality, since no man, no matter who he is, will be able to think of distinguishing himself by saying 'tu' to a sans-culotte." There were some objections: one journalist worried that men would take advantage of the new usage to claim a familiarity with women that would "tear down the last barrier between the two sexes."[38] Nevertheless, like the replacement of *monsieur*, a term of respect, with the egalitarian *citoyen*, the use of *tu* became commonplace. The drive for equality also underlay the law passed on 12 brumaire Year II, granting illegitimate children equal shares of their parents' inheritance. This provision was made retroactive to 1789 a few months later, even though it required reopening estates that had been settled for some years. The law of 12 brumaire prohibited paternity suits, on the optimistic assumption that fathers would no longer need to be pressured to recognize their children.

The transition to the revolutionary calendar was more of a challenge than many of the other changes the revolutionaries introduced, because the rhythm of time was so closely tied to religious observance. The plan to introduce a new calendar presented to the Convention by the deputy Gilbert Romme on September 20, 1793, was explicitly meant to show that the world had entered a new era. Romme's report denounced the Gregorian calendar as the product of "an ignorant and credulous people." He added, "For eighteen centuries it served to anchor in time the progress of fanaticism, the abasement of nations."[39] The new calendar started the year on September 22, which, by happy coincidence, as Romme pointed out, was a date significant both in nature, marking the fall equinox, and in history, where it commemorated the proclamation of the French Republic in 1792, which was retrospectively declared to be Year I. The year would now be divided into twelve thirty-day months, each with three ten-day weeks, or *décades*, and days would be divided into ten hours of one hundred minutes each, an idea that never caught on. Among the many advantages of the new calendar, according to its proponents, was that workers would now be idle only one day out of ten instead of one day out of seven, which would supposedly allow them to earn more income. The shift was also meant to wean the population away from regular church attendance, since Sunday would no longer be a day of rest.

Initially, the months, *décades*, and days were simply numbered. Philippe Fabre d'Eglantine, a deputy who had been a poet and playwright, came up with an elegant scheme that linked the new months to the cycle of the seasons. A common suffix linked the three months of each part of the year, and their names evoked the prevailing weather. Thus the three months of the fall were vendémiaire, the month of the grape harvest, or *vendange*; brumaire, the month of *brumes*, or fall fogs; and frimaire, the month of frost. After a winter of nivôse, pluviôse, and ventôse (snow, rain, and wind), French citizens would greet the spring and its months of germinal, when plants sprouted; floréal, when they flowered; and prairial, when they began to ripen. Messidor (named for the harvest) and thermidor (for heat) hailed the maturing crops in the fields that would be ready in fructidor, the month of fruits. The seasons in Fabre's scheme were those of European France: the newly emancipated black citizens of tropical Saint-Domingue had to adopt months named for cold and snow that did not correspond to their climate. Since the revolutionaries could not alter the fact that nature had made the solar year 365 days long, each year ended with five "sans-culottide days," plus an additional day in leap years, each of which would be a festival dedicated to a moral virtue that strengthened the republic.

Persuading the population to adopt the revolutionary calendar became one of the revolutionaries' main preoccupations, an effort that would only end in the Year XIV, when Napoleon decreed a return to the Gregorian calendar. Use of the new dates was mandatory on all legal documents. Enthusiasts for the new calendar saw it not just as a simpler, more rational, and, thanks to Fabre d'Eglantine, more poetic way of keeping track of time, but as a way for citizens to reaffirm their commitment to the republic in acts of everyday life. For the same reason, opponents of the Revolution stuck to the old calendar and especially to the ritual of Sunday observance as a way of demonstrating their hostility to the new regime. The war over the calendar thus became one of the most contested battlegrounds in the revolutionary struggle.

The introduction of the revolutionary calendar coincided with a sudden and intense campaign to dismantle the Catholic Church altogether. For many revolutionary militants, this de-Christianization campaign was the logical culmination of the Enlightenment critique of revealed religion and the revolutionary program of insisting on exclusive loyalty to the nation. Although the Constitution of 1793 had promised freedom of worship, pressure on the Church had been building up throughout the year. Revolutionaries demanded that priests demonstrate their trustworthiness by renouncing their "unnatural" vows of chastity: they should now marry. A law passed in July 1793 forbade bishops from punishing clergy who did so. Local officials closed churches or converted them to "temples of reason" for the staging of civic ceremonies.

Deputies on mission, such as Joseph Fouché, a onetime Oratorian priest sent to the Nièvre who later became Napoleon's much-feared minister of police, promoted the antireligious policy vigorously. With support from local militants, he closed churches and had signs posted in cemeteries telling mourners "Death is an eternal sleep," a direct rebuke to the Christian dogma of the eternity of the soul. At the cathedral of Reims, where the kings of France had traditionally been crowned, the deputy Philippe Ruhl destroyed the phial holding the sacred oil, supposedly dating back to the time of Clovis, with which each of them had been anointed. Priests and nuns as well as church buildings became targets. "I ordered all the curés to marry," one revolutionary commissioner reported. "Some twenty promised to marry within two months, and I have authority to find wives for them." Over all, some eighteen thousand parish priests, about a third of the total, officially gave up their status during the de-Christianization campaign, and some six thousand married.[40]

In Paris, the Commune's *procureur*, Chaumette, was an equally enthusiastic supporter of de-Christianization. Along with his allies—particularly Hébert, the author of the *Père Duchêne*, whose influence was at its height—Chaumette organized a series of events to mark what the de-Christianizers saw as their epochal victory over superstition. Escorted by Chaumette, Jean-Baptiste Gobel, the constitutional bishop of Paris, told the Convention that he was abandoning his religious functions. Only Grégoire, who was a longtime Jacobin but also a firmly committed Catholic, had the courage to take a public stand against the tide. "They harass me now to submit an abdication, which they will not get from me," he announced; in an act of defiance, he continued to wear his ecclesiastical robes to the Convention even after that body had banned them from public places.[41]

To consolidate what he considered a victory over superstition, Chaumette presided over a hastily organized Festival of Reason staged in the symbolic heart of Paris Catholicism, the expropriated cathedral of Notre Dame. The *Père Duchêne* gleefully described the scene for its readers: "The pious, male and female, [were] saddened to see their saints ousted from their niches. . . . In place of that altar or really of that stage for charlatans, a throne had been constructed for liberty. In place of a dead statue, there was a living image of that divinity, a masterpiece of nature . . . a charming woman, beautiful like the goddess she represented." After the ceremony, the crowd took their "goddess," armed with a pike and coiffed with a red liberty bonnet, to the Convention, where she was seated next to the assembly's president. Meanwhile, in the streets, "the most ludicrous masquerades presented themselves in every quarter," the Englishwoman Helen Maria Williams wrote. "The revolutionary ladies and the priestesses of Reason had sanctified themselves with the clothing belonging to the Virgin."[42]

The de-Christianizers' violent assault on the Church was not simply an extension of the philosophes' campaign against organized religion. It also drew energy from the long-standing popular anticlericalism of ordinary men like Jacques Ménétra, who resented the clergy's privileges and their interference with ordinary people's lives. Customary forms of mockery that had been used to ridicule cuckolded husbands and other violators of community norms, such as being promenaded through town on the back of an ass, were now turned on the Church. In the department of Loir-and-Cher, a cart filled with "the remnants of royalism and superstition" was "pulled along by a donkey dressed in a surplice and neckband, and bearing the inscription, 'I am more useful than a king.'" After attending a Festival of Reason in a small town, a police observer who personally endorsed the policy nevertheless made an astute observation about the limits of popular support for it. In public, "the people takes giant steps toward the abolition of prejudices and religious superstitions," he commented, but in their private lives, "not having anything to substitute for the cult they have just overturned, if some accident, some misfortune befalls them, they think it is a punishment from heaven." In one parish, five newborns had died in two *décades*. "That was enough to trouble minds, terrify mothers, and make them blame this coincidence on the absence of baptisms." Another official noted that the closing of the churches angered both older women, who often "took advantage of the long journey [to services] to exchange old stories with other old gossips," and younger women, who had looked forward to Sunday dances. These comments help explain why women often remained more committed than men to their faith.[43]

The de-Christianization movement had critics even among supporters of the Revolution. In the south, where the Spanish invaders were posing as defenders of the Church, local authorities warned the Convention that "if the people . . . hear the apostles of the Revolution trying to persuade them that all religion is based on fable, or on inept absurdities . . . they will be led to rebel against a new system which seems to be forcing them to renounce their religion and their religious beliefs." In the Convention, Robespierre opposed the movement, saying that "we must be careful not to give hypocritical counter-revolutionists, who seek to light the flame of civil war, any pretext that seems to justify their calumnies." He urged the deputies on mission not to give the impression that "war is made on religion itself."[44] The disagreement between the radical de-Christianizers and the majority of the Committee of Public Safety hinted at a growing tension between populists like Hébert and Chaumette, on the one hand, and the Montagnard leaders in the Convention, who were determined to keep extremism under control, on the other.

Despite the tensions over the de-Christianization campaign, the revolutionaries remained united about the necessity of crushing domestic revolts that threatened the Revolution. On October 9, Lyon surrendered, ending the most serious of the federalist uprisings. On October 17, the republican armies, after suffering a string of humiliating defeats in the Vendée throughout the summer, finally won a major victory at Cholet. Rather than retreating south toward the areas where most of their fighters came from, the main rebel force, accompanied by thousands of women and children, unexpectedly crossed the Loire River and began a desperate march to the north; they hoped to reach a point on the coast where they could receive support from the British. The sixty thousand participants in this march heavily outnumbered the scattered republican units in the region; they were not stopped until their attempt to capture the Norman port of Granville, close to the famous abbey of Mont-Saint-Michel, was beaten back on November 14. With the threat of foreign intervention in western France ended, the republicans could turn their efforts to punishing the participants in the uprising.

Punishment of the enemies of the Revolution was one of the most strident demands of the radicals in Paris. They had wanted the revolutionary army units to incorporate revolutionary tribunals and to be equipped with mobile guillotines, so that convicted suspects could be executed immediately. The Convention's committees feared letting the process of repression get out of hand and resisted these demands; they did, however, approve a series of high-profile political trials in Paris that captured public attention throughout the fall of 1793. The first prominent victim was Marie-Antoinette, whom many revolutionaries now called simply "the widow Capet." After Louis XVI's execution in January, she remained in the Temple prison. In the indictment presented by the Revolutionary Tribunal's prosecutor, Antoine-Quentin Fouquier-Tinville, on October 14, 1793, the misogynist hatred that had followed the queen from the time of her marriage was given full rein. She was accused of having been, "throughout her stay in France, the curse and the parasite of the French," of having held "conspiratorial meetings . . . under cover of night" at which all the calamities of the Revolution had been plotted, and of having taught Louis the "dangerous art of dissimulation." From her exile in London, Madame de Staël insisted that the queen's fate concerned all French women: "Your empire is doomed if ferocity prevails, your fate is sealed if your tears flow in vain." Hébert's assertion that Marie-Antoinette had taught her son to masturbate and had often shared her bed with him justified de Staël's fear that attacks on the queen would strengthen prejudices against her sex. Marie-Antoinette won a moment of sympathy when she appealed to the women in the audience, saying that "nature refuses to reply to such a charge made against a mother."[45]

Most of the details cited by witnesses to prove the queen's involvement in opposing the Revolution were either irrelevant or misleading; in the absence of the letters she had actually written to the Austrian court and to her lover Fersen, truly damning evidence of her efforts to enlist foreign support was not available. No more than the king at his trial did she dare admit that she had seen it as her duty to do everything possible to preserve the monarchy, even if it meant deceiving the revolutionary politicians she dealt with and secretly appealing to other monarchs to invade France. The verdict was never in doubt, and on October 17, 1793, the queen, dressed in a simple white dress that she had deliberately chosen as a sign of her innocence, was taken to the guillotine. In its usual vindictive style, Hébert's *Père Duchêne* called on the sans-culottes to silence anyone who showed the slightest sympathy for "the abominable fury who wanted to load you down with irons."[46]

Marie-Antoinette's trial had barely ended when the Revolutionary Tribunal took up the case of the Girondins who had been expelled from the Convention on June 2. Several of them, including the philosopher Condorcet and the former minister Roland, were still in hiding, but twenty-two others, including Brissot and Vergniaud, were brought to court. Their trial posed problems that the case of the violently unpopular queen had not. Sending elected representatives of the people to the guillotine was a dangerous precedent, even if the Girondins themselves had been the first to make such an attempt when they had Marat tried the previous April. Using tactics that would be copied by dictatorial regimes in modern times, André Amar, the spokesman for the Committee of General Security, made all the members of the group collectively responsible for anything any one of them had done; took actions out of context to create an appearance of guilt; and painted everything the defendants had done in the previous three years as part of a long-planned conspiracy to serve the interests of the king and France's foreign foes. But the worst crime of the Girondins, Amar insisted, was their hypocrisy: "They have taught all the enemies of the Revolution the execrable art of assassinating liberty by adopting its slogans."

As a political lesson for the population, the trial was not a great success. At the Jacobin Club, Hébert complained that the publication of the proceedings was spreading the impression that "there is no proof against the accused." Alarmed that the courtroom-wrangling threatened to drag on indefinitely, the prosecutor, Fouquier-Tinville, appealed to the Convention to change the rules and permit the jury to declare that it had heard enough evidence to reach a verdict. The deputies followed his advice, but the jurors at first resisted. In the end, however, all twenty-two defendants were sentenced to death. "A great movement broke out among the condemned men," the official account reported. "Many cried 'Long live the Republic!' Others swore at their judges."[47] Vergniaud supposedly said, "The Revolution, like Saturn, devours its own children." In classic Roman fashion, the deputy Charles Valazé managed to stab himself to death; the court ordered that his body be taken to the place of execution and buried along with those of the other defendants.

Knowing that they had little chance of escaping their fate, several of the Girondins spent their time in prison or in hiding writing their memoirs. Brissot retraced the youthful education that had imbued him with "a love of independence, a hatred of despotism," and that had led him to ask why Louis XVI, born the same year as him, "was on the throne, while I was born the son of a cook." Madame Roland found solace in the thought that someday her story "might occupy the time of some unfortunate captive, who will forget his own situation in taking pity on mine." Perhaps the most moving testimonial left behind by any member of the group was that of Condorcet, who managed to stay in hiding through the winter of 1793–1794. In his last months, before he was arrested and committed suicide, he devoted himself not to a personal memoir, but to a *Sketch of the Progress of the Human Mind*, in which he retraced the rise of civilization and reaffirmed his belief that "the day will come when the sun will shine, all over the earth, on free men, who will know no master except their reason."[48] Like Anne

Frank's assertion 150 years later in her diary that "in spite of everything, I still believe that people are basically good at heart," Condorcet's optimism won him the sympathy of posterity.

Certainly the Girondins were not the traitors the Montagnards made them out to be at their trial. They had consistently supported revolutionary democracy. Brissot and Condorcet deserve recognition for their dedication to the abolition of slavery and racial prejudice, and Condorcet was an eloquent supporter of women's equality. Nevertheless, they bore some responsibility for their own fate. Their advocacy of war in April 1792, their loyalty to Dumouriez, and, above all, their inconsistent attitude toward the king cast grave doubt on their judgment and honesty. Their attempt to negotiate with Louis just prior to the uprising of August 10, 1792, and their subsequent attempt to avoid his execution, after voting to condemn him for treason in January 1793, caused others to suspect them of wavering in their loyalty to the Revolution. Their inflammatory verbal attacks on the Montagnards and the Paris sans-culottes in the weeks prior to their defeat on May 31, 1793, added to their unpopularity, and the actions of their supporters in the provinces left them vulnerable to the accusation that they were dividing the country at a moment when it faced foreign invasion and civil war. In his impassioned calls for war, Brissot himself had welcomed the fact that it would encourage a hunt for traitors; he had helped to create an atmosphere in which he and his friends found themselves put into that category.

The sentences on Brissot and his colleagues were carried out on October 31, 1793. The prisoners embraced each other and defiantly sang "La Marseillaise"; meanwhile, the hostile crowd shouted "Down with the traitors." It was the largest mass execution yet carried out with the guillotine, but the executioners were by now well practiced at their craft: the twenty-one Girondins and eleven other men were dispatched in just thirty-eight minutes. Rosalie Jullien, whose husband was a Montagnard deputy, wrote to her son that the Girondins "were justly snuffed out by the blade of the law." She worried, however, that the revolutionaries might lose "our humanity and the sense of pity that distinguishes man from the rest of the animals." The bloodbath could have been much worse: Robespierre had personally intervened to prevent seventy-three other deputies from being tried along with them. They had all been imprisoned after the journée of September 5 for signing a petition the previous June in favor of their arrested colleagues. "Let's not seek to multiply the number of the guilty," he told the Jacobins. "Let the heads of the tyrant's widow and the chiefs of the conspiracy fall, but after these necessary examples, let's be sparing of blood."[49]

Despite Robespierre's promise, the trial of the Girondins was quickly followed by a series of prosecutions of other prominent political figures. Madame Roland, accused of being the mastermind behind the Girondin conspiracy, made plans with a close friend so that there would be a witness to the words she planned to say on her way to the guillotine: "Oh! Liberty! What crimes are committed in your name!" Olympe de Gouges was tried because she had composed pamphlets and posters demanding that the voters be allowed to decide whether they wanted a republic or a monarchy, which constituted, in the prosecution's eyes, proof that she questioned the sovereign people's endorsement of the constitution. When she asked for a lawyer, prosecutors mocked the woman who had demanded that members of her sex had the same rights as men, telling her that she had "enough spirit to defend herself."[50]

Bailly, the former mayor, who had led the deputies in swearing the Oath of the Tennis Court on June 20, 1789, had to stand shivering for hours in the November rain while the guillotine was erected at the Champ de Mars, the site of the massacre in July 1791 that he was condemned for ordering. When one of his guards accused him of trembling with fear, he replied, "I'm cold, my friend." Barnave, who had argued so strongly for the king's reinstatement in 1791, was accused, among other things, of having destroyed the colonies, a charge that also figured in the indictment against Brissot. Barnave objected that they could not both be guilty of that crime, since they had advocated opposing policies, but the court ignored him. The king's cousin the duc d'Orléans, elected to the Convention as a Montagnard deputy in September 1792, had voted for Louis XVI's execution, but he now fell victim to accusations that he had plotted to get the throne for himself. Madame du Barry, the notorious mistress of Louis XV, was dragged out of retirement and tried as a symbol of the corruption of the old regime; unlike most victims, who strove to show courage in their last moments, she shrieked in terror as she was dragged onto the scaffold.

The high-profile trials and executions in Paris were paralleled by merciless measures against the thousands of more ordinary individuals who had participated in revolts against the Montagnard government. On October 12, 1793, three days after the rebel city of Lyon surrendered, the Convention issued a bloodcurdling decree announcing that a monument was to be erected on its site with an inscription reading, "Lyon made war against liberty; Lyon no longer exists"; what remained of the settlement would be called Ville-Affranchie (Liberated City).[51] Determined to make the punishment of the defeated rebels an object lesson for the enemies of the Revolution, two deputies on mission, Collot d'Herbois and Fouché, planned a spectacular mass execution in Lyon at the beginning of December, when they had several hundred victims chained together and mowed down by cannon. The idea was to strike the enemies of the republic with the force of a thunderbolt, but the result was too gruesome even for the executioners. Soldiers had to wade into a mass of bleeding bodies to finish off dozens of wounded victims with sabers and bayonets. The Montagnards reverted to less theatrical methods of execution, the guillotine and the firing squad, but some 1,900 Lyonnais were put to death for their role in the uprising. In accordance with the Convention's decree, the facades of the houses of the city's wealthier inhabitants were demolished, creating a visible reminder of its punishment.

Even harsher measures were adopted against the insurgents of the Vendée. A decree of November 5, 1793, ordered the complete destruction of towns that sheltered their fighters, and an agent of the Committee of Public Safety proposed expelling the entire local population and resettling the region with good patriots from other parts of France. Overwhelmed by the number of rebels they had captured, republican authorities carried out mass executions and let hundreds of others die from diseases in the overcrowded prisons. In Nantes, the largest city in the region, the Convention deputy Jean-Baptiste Carrier oversaw a series of atrocities in which prisoners, including women and children, were tied together and forced into overcrowded boats, which were then towed into the Loire River and deliberately sunk, drowning the victims. Although the worst actions seem to have been carried out by members of the revolutionary army without specific orders from Carrier, he defended what he called these *déportations verticales* (vertical deportations).[52]

Like the September massacres in Paris, the *noyades* (drownings) in Nantes became an inextricable part of the black legend of the Revolution. So did the operations of the *colonnes infernales* (infernal columns) commanded by General Louis-Marie Turreau, who was put in command of the forces that were ordered to devastate the core region of the Vendée at the beginning of 1794. "We are going to bring fire and flames, the rifle in one hand and the torch in the other. Men and women, everything will be put to death," the republican soldier François-Xavier Joliclerc wrote to his family.[53] As Turreau's columns pushed through the countryside, they often massacred the entire population of villages, including even revolutionary supporters, and also burned farms and houses and slaughtered livestock. The devastation they caused was counterproductive: peasants who might have reluctantly reconciled themselves to living under the republic were driven instead to desperate resistance. Although the Vendée rebels could no longer assemble large armies, as they had in the spring and summer of 1793, they and the *chouans*, bands of peasant rebels in Brittany, continued to tie up considerable republican forces throughout 1794.

As it brought the full weight of its forces to bear on rebellious regions of the country, the revolutionary government also strove to extend its control over the capital. The decree Danton had put forward on September 5 ended the Paris sectional assemblies' permanent sessions and greatly reduced their potential for mobilizing protests. Jacques Roux and other Enragé spokesmen were now in jail—Roux would commit suicide in January 1794—and the government seized on a clash between the militants of the Society of Revolutionary Republican Women and the marketwomen of Les Halles, a food market in Paris, to launch a campaign against female activists. After the passage of the law of the maximum in September, the members of the society had confronted marketwomen who evaded the regulations of the maximum and who ostentatiously refused to wear patriotic tricolor cockades. A police report claimed that the militants' pressure for the women to put on the cockades was only a beginning. "When they have the cockade, they say, they will demand civic cards, want to vote in our assemblies, share administrative positions with us."[54]

In response to these complaints, the Convention took up the issue of women's involvement in politics. Amar, the spokesman for the Committee of General Security, hinted that the Revolutionary Republican Women were stirring up trouble to disrupt the trial of the Girondins; he thought they did not possess "the moral and physical strength" to exercise the same rights as men. One deputy objected, asking, "Unless you are going to question whether women are part of the human species, can you take away from them this right which is common to every thinking being?" Nevertheless, the Convention voted to ban women's political clubs. When the leaders of the Republican Women turned to the Commune, whose radical initiatives they had supported so often during previous months, its leader, Chaumette, denounced women's activism as contrary to nature. "Since when is it permitted to give up one's sex? . . . Is it to men that nature confided domestic cares? Has she given us breasts to feed our children?"[55] In case his audience missed the seriousness of his warning, he reminded them of the recent executions of Madame Roland and Olympe de Gouges. In the face of this opposition, the women who had tried to use the revolutionaries' own principles to claim equal rights were forced into silence.

# 15

# THE ARC OF TERROR

*January–July 1794*

THE FIFTH DAY OF THE REVOLUTIONARY MONTH OF NIVÔSE YEAR II WAS December 25, 1793, Christmas Day, according to the old calendar. For the deputies of the National Convention it was an ordinary working day, notable only because Maximilien Robespierre delivered a speech laying out "the principles of revolutionary government." Few considered Robespierre a spellbinding orator. Usually, when the members of the Committee of Public Safety had something to communicate to the Convention, Barère spoke for them: his highflown eloquence won him the nickname "the Anacreon of the guillotine," a reference to a famous Greek poet. Robespierre did not have the powerful physical presence of Mirabeau or Danton. His voice was high-pitched and thin and he needed glasses to see his texts, which he read slowly and carefully, making sure the journalists in the hall had time to catch his words. He did not even look like a proper revolutionary. By the fall of 1793, most of the politicians affected the appearance and speech of the sans-culottes, letting their hair grow, wearing the clothes of the common people, and adopting the crude language of Hébert's *Père Duchêne*. Robespierre continued to appear in a powdered wig and wore "a suit that came from an earlier time," in the words of Jean-Victor Colchen, from the Ministry of Foreign Affairs. "He called me *Monsieur* and not citizen, and refrained from using the familiar 'you' [*tu*]," Colchen reported.[1]

Nevertheless, when Robespierre delivered one of his carefully thought-out speeches to the Convention or the Jacobin Club, his colleagues knew they needed to listen closely. In the four and a half years since he had arrived at the Estates General as a deputy for the provincial town of Arras, Robespierre had achieved a moral authority unmatched by any other revolutionary leader. Once he was appointed to the Committee of Public Safety, he emerged as a leader—not as a dictator, but as the figure best able to find the delicate balance that would preserve the authority of the government while satisfying public pressure for strong measures to protect the Revolution.

The moment Robespierre had chosen for his speech was a favorable one. Six days earlier, on December 19, the Convention's forces had retaken Toulon, the naval port on the Mediterranean that had surrendered to the British at the end of August. The victory owed much to the energy of the twenty-four-year-old artillery officer Napoleon Bonaparte, a bumptious young man who had not hesitated to write directly to the Committee of Public Safety to promote his plan for the campaign: he would drive the enemy fleet away by seizing a key promontory from which French cannon could dominate the harbor. Among those impressed with Bonaparte's abilities was Robespierre's younger brother Augustin, a deputy on mission, who told his older sibling that the young officer was a man of "transcendental merit."[2]

Robespierre did not single out Napoleon Bonaparte or any other individual for praise in his speech, however. Instead, he used the "miracle of Toulon" to make an argument for the importance of the revolutionary government proclaimed by his fellow committee member Louis-Antoine de Saint-Just in October. He also laid out the path the committee intended to follow in using the powers it had been given by the decree of 14 frimaire Year II three weeks earlier. "The theory of revolutionary government is as new as the Revolution that created it," Robespierre announced. The men of 1789 had had no inkling of the magnitude of the task on which they were embarking; they had thought that proclaiming the principles of liberty and equality would suffice to assure their triumph. By 1793, however, it had become clear that replacing one political and social order with another one based on different principles required a passage through the fires of revolution. "Revolution is the war waged by liberty against its enemies," Robespierre proclaimed, and that war could not be limited by routine laws. The goal of revolutionary government was to render itself unnecessary by giving the nation a firm constitution, "that which crowns the edifice of freedom once victory has been won and the nation is at peace." Robespierre's vision of what a good society endowed with "civic liberty" would look like had not changed since 1789. "Under a constitutional government little more is required than to protect the individual against abuses by the state," he insisted. But to get to that point, "revolutionary government is obliged to defend the state itself against the factions that assail it from every quarter. To good citizens revolutionary government owes the full protection of the state; to the enemies of the people it owes only death."[3]

With the recent victories of the revolutionary armies at Hondschoote, Wattignies, and Toulon, had the moment to revert to constitutional government arrived? "The ship of the constitution was certainly not built to remain on the ways forever," Robespierre admitted, "but should we launch it when the storm is at its height?" Only enemies of the Revolution, he claimed, wanted the constitution to be put into effect immediately. No one who understood the political situation in Paris could mistake the message of the rest of Robespierre's speech, in which he outlined the policy that he and the Committee of Public Safety intended to follow. The revolutionary government, he promised, would permit neither "anarchy or disorder" nor "arbitrary rule." Its challenge was to "sail between the twin reefs of weakness and temerity, moderatism and exaggeration: moderatism which is to moderation what impotence is to chastity, and exaggeration whose resemblance to energy is like that of dropsy to good health." Sitting in the audience were men for whom Robespierre's words sounded a warning: for more than a month, some deputies had been calling for an end to the harshest forms of the

Terror, while others had been insisting that it needed to be made even more ferocious.

As he positioned himself and the Committee of Public Safety between the two extremes he condemned, Robespierre was haunted by another fear: two months earlier, in mid-October, Philippe Fabre d'Eglantine, the man who had given the revolutionary calendar its poetic sheen, had sought out Robespierre and Saint-Just. Swearing them to secrecy, Fabre, a friend of Danton's, had accused a number of prominent figures in revolutionary politics of being part of a "foreign plot." It was funded by the British and the Austrians, he said, and was designed to destroy the Revolution from within by putting forward ever more extreme measures and pitting good patriots against each other. Such accusations sometimes have real foundations, of course, as nations can find ingenious ways of meddling in each other's politics. But Fabre's allegations, for which he had no serious evidence, were calculated to take advantage of Robespierre's weakness for conspiracy theories, sowing maximal confusion. He named the Prussian baron and Convention deputy Anacharsis Cloots and several other foreigners who had been active in the radical Cordeliers Club; they were considered supporters of Hébert, the "Père Duchêne." He also threw suspicion on a member of the Committee of Public Safety itself, Hérault de Séchelles, the committee's only *ci-devant* member from a noble family, who shared a house with an Austrian, Pierre-Jean Berthold Proli, who was on Fabre's list.

Denouncing enemies of the Revolution was the duty of a good patriot, but Fabre's motives were far from pure. He himself was at the center of a scheme to profit from the changes taking place in the nation during the Revolution: it involved selling off the assets of the chartered monopoly companies that had been set up under the monarchy. Fabre had personally forged a decree liquidating the India Company that Calonne had established in the mid-1780s, and it had enabled him to pocket thousands of livres. By inciting Robespierre and Saint-Just to start a hunt for conspirators in the ranks of revolutionary militants, he hoped to divert suspicion from himself.

Robespierre kept the details of Fabre's allegations secret, but rumors about them made many politicians nervous. Among those who were worried was the deputy François Chabot, an ex-monk and former Cordeliers member who had attracted attention to himself by marrying a sister of the Frey brothers, wealthy Austrian Jewish bankers. In doing so, he had acquired an impressive dowry that many suspected was actually money gained through corruption. In an effort to protect himself, Chabot, like Fabre, also went to Robespierre with a tale of conspiracy: he exposed the plot to embezzle money from the India Company and blamed it on royalists working to discredit the Convention. Although there was more evidence to support Chabot's denunciation than Fabre's—he even showed Robespierre a bundle of assignats that he claimed had been given to him as a bribe—Chabot's all-too-visible connection with wealthy foreigners worked against him. He was arrested, and the snowballing tangle of accusations poisoned the political atmosphere further. It was increasingly difficult for anyone to know whom they could trust.

Many of the men coming under suspicion were associates of the most prominent of the former Cordeliers in the Convention, Danton, whose own reputation was hardly spotless. Returning from a month-long visit to his rural hometown, Danton rallied a loose coalition of political figures who came to be known as the Indulgents, and they began to call for an end to the excesses committed in the aftermath of the journée of September 5. Robespierre shared some of the concerns of the Indulgents, and he was more closely linked through friendship with one of them, the former journalist and deputy Camille Desmoulins, than with any other leading political figure. Above all, Robespierre opposed the violent de-Christianization campaign, which reached its peak in early November. When he denounced the "extraordinary and sudden intensity, the exaggerated and overdone zeal" of the war on religion in a speech on November 21, Robespierre surely had in mind Fabre's story about the foreign plot to destroy the Revolution by promoting extremism.[4]

For Camille Desmoulins, the Indulgents' campaign was a chance to reclaim the spotlight he had occupied early in the Revolution. Although everyone remembered the young lawyer's role in stirring up the crowd in July 1789, as well as the success of his *Révolutions de France et de Brabant*, Desmoulins had found himself treated as an immature lightweight in the Convention. Taking up his pen to launch a new periodical, the *Vieux Cordelier* (Old Cordelier), he thrust himself back into the center of attention by denouncing revolutionary extremists. Drawing parallels with Roman history, he argued that patriotic leaders trying to govern for the good of the people could easily be undermined by enemies who would answer each proposal with "one even more populistic, in order to thus kill principles and patriotism by pushing them to the point of extravagance."[5]

Robespierre, Desmoulins's friend since their schooldays, reviewed the content of the first two numbers of the *Vieux Cordelier* before they appeared and found nothing objectionable in them. But Desmoulins was not content to simply echo Robespierre's attacks on the "Hébertistes" and the de-Christianization campaign. In his third issue, under the guise of describing how the Roman emperors had tyrannized their citizens by "changing simple glances, sadness, compassion, sighs, even silence, into crimes," he strongly condemned the law of suspects; in his fourth, addressed explicitly to Robespierre, he called for a "clemency committee" to consider the release of "these two hundred thousand citizens whom you call suspects, since there is no detention for suspicion in the Declaration of Rights." In its obsession with uncovering its enemies, he charged, the Revolution had forgotten its true purpose, the establishment of "liberty, which is happiness, which is reason, which is equality, which is justice."[6] This was too much for more orthodox members of the Jacobin Club: one of them warned Desmoulins that he had "been edging toward the guillotine for a long time."[7]

Desmoulins's calls for clemency coincided with the peak of the repression directed against the counterrevolutionary rebels of the Vendée and the Lyon federalists. Reports about the drowning of prisoners in Nantes and the mass execution of suspects in Lyon led to protests in Paris against the conduct of the deputy Jean-Baptiste Carrier and the commander of the revolutionary army, Charles-Philippe Ronsin. Sent to Lyon to ensure punishment for the rebels there, Ronsin issued a chilling proclamation: "We must make the bloody Rhône, on its way down to the sea, cast up on its banks the corpses of the cowards who have killed our brothers."[8] Swayed by pleas that too many innocent victims were being swept up in the mass killings, the Convention, on December 17, ordered the arrest of Ronsin and several of his associates. Ronsin and his vociferous defender, Hébert, still had strong support among the Paris sans-culottes, however, as police reports on street-corner conversations indicated. They also had influential allies in the Convention. The deputy Jean-Marie Collot d'Herbois, who had collaborated with Ronsin in organizing the executions in Lyon, rushed back to Paris to demand the general's release. Collot protested to the Jacobins, "They want to moderate the revolutionary movement. Ah! Does one direct a tempest?" The Père Duchêne rejoiced: "The giant has appeared, and all the dwarfs who plagued the best patriots have returned a hundred feet underground."[9]

Robespierre's speech of December 25, delivered just two days after Collot d'Herbois's intervention and on the same day as the release of Desmoulins's fifth Vieux Cordelier, was thus an effort to ward off the contradictory pressures that the Indulgents and the Hébertistes were putting on the Committee of Public Safety. Behind the scenes, the members of that committee and their colleagues on the Committee of General Security continued frantically trying to make sense of the welter of accusations Fabre and Chabot had made. Ronsin and his colleagues from the revolutionary army were kept in jail while the committees pressed their police agents to let them know whether the Cordeliers Club might be plotting yet another sans-culotte uprising to support them.

When Desmoulins was called on the carpet by the Jacobins, Robespierre made an effort to protect his old friend, calling him "a thoughtless child . . . who has been led astray by bad company." It would be sufficient punishment if the offending issues of the Vieux Cordelier were solemnly burned in the presence of the club members. Although he knew what he was risking, Desmoulins refused to accept such a humiliation. "Robespierre said my issues must be burned; I reply to him, in the words of Rousseau: Burning is not an answer!"[10] He and Danton were in a perilous position: a few days later, on January 17, 1794, Fabre d'Eglantine's forgeries caught up with him, and he, Chabot, and several others with links to the Indulgents were arrested. The Committee of Public Safety member Hérault de Séchelles shared their fate, a demonstration that no member of the Convention was immune to the forces that could precipitate a downfall. As the danger to the Indulgents mounted, the tide seemed to shift in favor of the Hébertistes, and on February 2, the Convention ordered Ronsin's release.

In the midst of these tense maneuvers between the political factions, the colonial question and the issue of slavery, the greatest contradiction of the revolutionaries' claim to be defending liberty, suddenly resurfaced. As we have seen, the news of the destruction of Cap Français had helped inspire the journée of September 5, 1793. The Convention had initially accepted the proslavery colonists' version of that event, blaming Sonthonax and Polverel and their Girondin patrons. Robespierre himself had endorsed the white colonists' accusations against Sonthonax and Polverel in a major speech laying out the Committee of Public Safety's foreign policy on November 17, 1793. The Paris revolutionaries' alliance with the slaveowners was threatened in late December, however, when word arrived that the remaining white colonists in Saint-Domingue had allowed British forces to occupy towns on the colony's western coast. The colonists' representatives in the capital persuaded the Montagnards to accept their argument that the whites were "forced to choose between death or subjection to the king of England."[11] On January 23, 1794, the colonists were jolted by the news that three men from Saint-Domingue—a white ally of Sonthonax and Polverel, a black man, and a man of mixed race—had appeared in Paris with documents showing that they had been elected as the colony's deputies to the Convention: their mission to get the assembly to endorse the emancipation of the slaves that Sonthonax and Polverel had carried out.

The white colonists managed to get their allies on the Committee of General Security to issue arrest warrants for the members of this "tricolor" delegation from Saint-Domingue, but before they could be imprisoned, the men met with several members of the Committee of Public Safety, which ordered their release. Barère, always a good judge of the way the wind was blowing in that committee, stunned the proslavery lobbyists by telling them that he now realized that "the whites are aristocrats in that colony and that the men of color and the Negroes are patriots."

Having never previously shown much interest in the question of slavery, the embattled Dantonists suddenly embraced the cause and persuaded the Convention to accept the Saint-Domingue deputies' credentials. The African-born Jean-Baptiste Belley, a former slave, and James Mills, a mixed-race planter, became the first black men to sit in the legislature of a European country, preceding by more than seventy years the black senators and representatives in the United States elected during Reconstruction. On February 4, one day after they had been admitted, Louis Dufay, the white member of the group, delivered a three-hour speech to the Convention. He justified the actions that Sonthonax and Polverel had taken after the sailors' mutiny in Cap Français the previous June and promised that "your colony of Saint-Domingue, cultivated by free hands, will be more flourishing. . . . [I]t will soon dominate the entire archipelago of the Gulf of Mexico."[12]

Dufay was careful to justify the measures Sonthonax and Polverel had taken as expedients to deal with a crisis, rather than casting them as the fulfillment of the Revolution's principles of liberty and equality. He did not have the support of the Committee of Public Safety: although it had freed him and his colleagues from prison, none of the committee members were even present to hear his speech. Instead, they were holding an emergency meeting with the representatives of the white colonists, who pleaded with them to head off any attack on the slave system. As the lobbyists exited the meeting, they learned that it was too late. Fired with enthusiasm by Dufay's words, the deputy René Levasseur immediately moved to "decree as of this moment that slavery is abolished throughout the territory of the Republic," insisting that "I want all men to be free, without distinction of color." The Dantonist Jean-François Delacroix told the assembly not to "dishonor itself with a longer discussion," and in a matter of minutes, the institution that had been fundamental to the creation of France's overseas empire was struck down.[13]

Not only were the blacks declared free, but they were immediately granted full rights as French citizens. A wave of emotion reminiscent of the night of August 4, 1789, when the National Assembly had declared the feudal system abolished, ran through the room: the deputies had finally faced up to the greatest contradiction of the principles of liberty and equality in the French Empire. The Convention's president embraced the two black deputies as other members cheered.

Even longtime supporters of abolition were shocked by the suddenness of this shift. Grégoire, a consistent advocate of racial equality in the Revolution's early years, feared that Levasseur's motion would be "disastrous . . . the political equivalent of a volcano." Perhaps aware of the unease many deputies felt about the radicalism of their action, Danton let his allies push the motion through before demonstrating, for one final time, his uncanny ability to combine daring and caution. He predicted that, thanks to the Convention's actions, "as of today, England is dead": the enslaved blacks in its colonies would surely rise in revolt and disrupt its economy. But he urged the deputies, some of whom wanted to send the news to the colonies immediately, to leave the decree's implementation to the Committee of Public Safety.[14] It was his last significant intervention in revolutionary politics before his arrest.

Perhaps Danton hoped the Committee would be grateful to him for upholding its authority. The committee did in fact decide against sending the decree to the French colonies in the Indian Ocean, fearing that the plantation owners there would simply turn the islands over to the British. And one prominent committee member remained unreconciled to the decision. A few weeks later, while debating what charges to bring against Danton at his trial, Robespierre tried unsuccessfully to have him specifically blamed for the passage of a decree "whose likely result was the loss of our colonies."[15] It was a measure of how thoroughly obsessed he was with the idea of a foreign conspiracy against French interests. Far different was the reaction of Toussaint Louverture, the black general who had rejected the offer of freedom from local revolutionary officials in Saint-Domingue in August 1793. When news of the Convention's proclamation reached Saint-Domingue, he broke with the other leaders of the black movement and their Spanish backers and announced his conversion to the republican cause. His soldiers became the core of the French army that kept the colony from falling into the hands of the country's enemies.

On the other side of the political spectrum from Danton, the Commune's *procureur*, Chaumette, also seized on the abolition decree to stage his last significant political action. "This decree is not the work of men," he told the Commune assembly on February 6. "It is more the work of the Eternal . . . who wants all men henceforth to be nothing more than a family of brothers." On February 18, Chaumette presided over a great ceremony in Notre Dame to hail what he regarded as nothing less than a return to humanity's original state of nature and the beginning of a new era in human history. Several other French cities staged their own celebrations. In the small Norman town of Bernay, "members of the popular society surrounded their new brothers, took them in their arms and put liberty caps on their heads; hymns and scenes of joy completed this touching tableau."[16]

As they applauded the idealistic decree abolishing slavery, the revolutionaries were also mobilizing for a military effort on a scale never before seen in European history. By January 1794, some 670,000 men were in uniform, far surpassing the 400,000 that Louis XIV had commanded at the height of his wars a century earlier. The *levée en masse* decreed in August 1793 had swelled the army's ranks, but it took time before the raw conscripts could be used on the battlefield. "Brave in combat, the volunteers did not yet understand the soldier's trade," the deputy Levasseur wrote. The new men had to be convinced that following orders was compatible with their status as free citizens. "When a soldier obeys his superior, it is certainly only the law and not the individual that he obeys," one battalion commander explained. The relative lull in fighting after the victories in the fall provided valuable time to drill the new men and indoctrinate them with revolutionary values. "It is not by numbers and discipline alone that you should expect victory," Saint-Just proclaimed in February 1794. "You will achieve it only as the republican spirit makes progress in the army."[17] Copies of the *Père Duchêne* and patriotic festivals in which soldiers and ordinary citizens proclaimed their shared values helped instill patriotic attitudes.

For some time, the Convention had been pressing the army to combine the remaining veterans from the prerevolutionary professional units with the patriotic volunteers from the National Guard who had been recruited in 1791 and 1792 as well as the newer recruits drafted in 1793. A Convention decree of January 10, 1794, made this *amalgame* (amalgamation) official policy: all existing units would be formed into *demi-brigades*, with one-third of their men coming from the old army and the remainder from the newer recruits. All would now wear the same uniforms and be paid at the same rate.

From the beginning of March, officers and men elected councils to decide on day-to-day matters affecting their units, a practice reflecting the democratic values of the volunteers. Most of the rank-and-file soldiers in the new combined army had joined after 1789, but the officer corps still consisted mainly of men whose careers had started before the Revolution. The massive emigration among nobles who opposed the Revolution opened opportunities for men such as Napoleon Bonaparte and for talented noncommissioned officers from the Third Estate. Aware that the soldiers lacked the discipline to execute the close-order maneuvers characteristic of traditional eighteenth-century warfare, Lazare Carnot, the Committee of Public Safety's military expert, and the generals planned to rely on superiority in numbers and violent attacks with the bayonet. Lazare Hoche, one of the army's young rising stars, tersely summarized the revolutionary army's doctrine as "no maneuvers, no skill, steel, firepower and patriotism."[18] In the midst of the crises of 1793, there had been no time to think of an overall military plan. For 1794, Carnot was determined to concentrate as many forces as possible on the Belgian frontier, both to protect Paris and to defeat the Austrian army, the country's most dangerous opponent.

As the soldiers prepared for the coming campaign, the entire country strained to provide them with the tools they would need. To supply muskets, rifles, and cannon, the government created a huge weapons workshop, the Manufacture d'armes de Paris (Arms Manufacture of Paris). Skilled workers were exempted from military service and promised pay above the rates of the maximum. To obtain adequate supplies of saltpeter, a crucial ingredient in gunpowder, municipal officials and even schoolchildren fanned out to find deposits in damp cellars, where it can form on walls when the potassium nitrate in brickwork reacts with moisture; they had the right to invade private property in their search. The Convention hosted a festival at which the Paris sections presented their saltpeter harvests, decorated with revolutionary symbols.[19] The revolutionaries mobilized the country's scientists to find new methods for refining the precious material into gunpowder. They also instructed the scientists to develop improved procedures for extracting bronze from church bells and royal statues to be used to forge cannon. The thousands of popular societies and clubs that now spanned the country gathered supplies for the soldiers; in an effort to build up the army's mounted troops, the government encouraged each club to raise money to recruit and equip a cavalryman.

To promote the unity required to undergird the war effort, the Montagnard leaders announced a campaign against the regional languages spoken in some parts of the country. All citizens, Barère told the Convention, should be taught to speak "the most beautiful language of Europe, the first one that clearly consecrated the rights of man and citizen, the one that has the mission to transmit to the world the most sublime ideas of liberty." The regions where non-French languages were common—Brittany, Alsace, Corsica, and the Basque country—were all, as he noted, peripheral parts of the country exposed to foreign invasion, and ensuring their loyalty was therefore especially important. "Federalism and superstition speak Breton," he warned. "Emigration and hatred of the Republic speak German; the counterrevolution speaks Italian, and fanaticism speaks Basque."[20] In addition to supplying the army with soldiers, the popular societies spread across the country were exhorted to find schoolteachers who could spread the national language. It was an ambitious program that would only be realized under France's Third Republic a century later.

To justify the demands it was making, the revolutionary government needed to convince the general population and soldiers alike that they would benefit from military victory. Although it struggled to provide welfare benefits for needy civilians, the Convention made heroic efforts to ensure subventions for the families of soldiers and pensions for those who were wounded or for their widows. In the early days of the revolutionary month of ventôse, as the Committee of Public Safety prepared its move against the Hébertistes in Paris, who had tried to identify themselves with the cause of the common people, Saint-Just proposed a set of decrees to demonstrate the revolutionary government's concern for the lower classes. Although the Convention had always hesitated to suggest a redistribution of property to benefit the poor, Saint-Just proposed a new principle: "Whoever has shown himself the enemy of his country cannot own property there." It would be only just, he insisted, for the wealth of the people's enemies to be given to poor citizens: "The properties of patriots are sacred, but the goods of conspirators are there for all those in need." He promised that this measure would end begging, "which dishonors a free country," and that it would transform society. "Happiness is a new idea in Europe," he concluded.[21]

In the twentieth century, after the Russian revolutionaries attempted to create a communist society, Saint-Just's ventôse decrees were often hailed as pioneering attempts to challenge the oppressive reign of private property. In reality, neither he nor any other member of the Convention imagined a socialist society with collective ownership of property. The idea of confiscating the property of opponents of the Revolution followed logically from the measures already taken against the Church and the émigrés. The promise to award confiscated property to poor deserving patriots, rather than putting it up for sale, was more radical, but the purpose was to create new small-scale property-owners who would be loyal to the republic rather than to undermine the principle of property itself.

In private jottings that were not published at the time, Saint-Just concluded that, to create a just society, "one must give everyone some land." He added that "there should be neither rich nor poor," but his main concern was to create what he called "institutions" or social practices that would promote virtue and loyalty to the republic. To that end, he wanted boys to be taken away from their families at age five and taught to be farmers and soldiers. Adults would be required to make an annual declaration of their friends, which meant not just posting their names publicly but accepting responsibility for their behavior: if a man committed a crime, his friends would be banished.[22] In Saint-Just's mind, the ventôse decrees were at best a first step toward the creation of such a moral republic. Even so, they would not have had much appeal to the urban sans-culottes, whose spokesmen the Committee of Public Safety was about to strike down: few Paris workers and artisans had any desire to become peasants.

Unaware of the danger he faced, Hébert took Saint-Just's speeches as a signal to intensify his own campaign against the Indulgents. On the day after passage of the second ventôse decree, he led the Cordeliers Club in demanding the immediate trial of the seventy-three Convention deputies still being held in prison for signing a petition in favor of the Girondins in June 1793; he and the other Cordeliers also demanded the arrest of Desmoulins and his supporters. Carrier, the deputy who had overseen the mass drowning of prisoners in Nantes, roused the club members by exclaiming, "A holy insurrection, that's how you should resist the scoundrels." Hébert directly criticized Robespierre, and the group voted to drape a veil over the framed copy of the Declaration of Rights on their wall "until the people shall have recovered their sacred rights."[23] The hotheaded speeches at the meeting gave the Convention's committees the pretext they needed to start preparing for the arrest of the leading Cordeliers, but the Hébertistes, even though many of them were veterans of previous Paris journées, did nothing to actually plan an uprising. Collot d'Herbois, the Committee of Public Safety member who had defended terroristic policies in December, disappointed the Cordeliers by telling them to temper their demands. Hébert was personally embarrassed when an informer revealed that, in the midst of his denunciations of food hoarders, he had received a substantial package of salt pork at his home, which he claimed he planned to distribute to the poor.

On March 14, 1794, 24 ventôse Year II, the committees pounced, ordering the arrests of Hébert and Ronsin along with Ronsin's second-in-command, François-Nicolas Vincent, and the president of the Cordeliers, Antoine-François Momoro, as participants in a foreign plot to overthrow the government. The Hébertistes, charged with plotting to starve the capital and massacre the deputies of the Convention, found themselves thrown together with several foreigners, notably the Prussian Anacharsis Cloots, the Austrian Proli, and other defendants who had nothing to do with the group. Meanwhile, the leading suspects in the India Company scandal were also arrested, a signal that the committees intended to pursue Danton's associates from the other side of the political spectrum. On March 17, Chaumette, the dominant figure in the

Paris Commune, was jailed to make sure the municipal government did not become a source of support for the Hébertistes. When they were brought to the Luxembourg prison, the Hébertistes were jeered by the other inmates, a group that included many men who had been arrested because of denunciations by sans-culotte militants. An elderly prisoner gave Chaumette a lesson in revolutionary grammar: "I am a suspect, you are a suspect, he is a suspect, we are suspects, you are suspects, they are all suspects."[24]

The remaining Cordeliers Club members rushed to separate them-selves from their arrested comrades, putting an end to the organization's status as a populist alternative to the Jacobins. Knowing what their employers wanted to hear, the police agents working for the Committee of General Security assured them that public opinion was overwhelmingly supportive of the arrests. Inadvertently, their reports revealed that the measures taken to bar women from politics had not been fully effective. "Women said that the more they had loved the Père Duchêne, the more they now despised him," one policeman wrote, although he added that "a very few said that perhaps they weren't guilty." However, other women, "wives of good sans-culottes," were disillusioned by the affair. "What is going to become of us, since we are so badly betrayed by so many men in whom we had the greatest confidence?" they asked.[25]

The Hébertist defendants were initially confident that they would be released, and the Committee of Public Safety was correspondingly nervous about the potential public reaction to their arrests. Hébert was charged with trying to "destroy commerce in declaiming without distinction against all citizens engaged in it," thereby exacerbating food shortages. Ronsin, who had been commander of the revolutionary army, was painted as a potential Cromwell who could have used his soldiers to break up the Convention. Hébert's success in presenting himself as the voice of the sans-culottes had perhaps made him imagine that he was too popular to be treated the way so many of his past targets had been. A police observer commented that he hardly spoke in response to questions at the trial: "The contrast between the public indignation that overwhelms him now and the almost universal love of which he was the object . . . is well designed to reduce him to a kind of stupor."[26] Unlike the other members of the group, he was unable to keep up a brave front as he was taken to the guillotine: whereas Ronsin faced his fate with courage, Hébert appeared completely shattered.

With the death of Hébert, "the Père Duchêne," the overtly populist current of the Revolution lost the man who had known, better than anyone else, how to turn the blunt speech of the common people into a genuine political force. For the first time since 1789, a conflict between the leaders in power and a movement from below that wanted to push the Revolution in a more extreme direction ended with the decisive defeat of the radicals. The middle-class Jacobins who sent him to the guillotine were conscious of the danger that Hébert's claim to speak to the common people in their own idiom created. The *Journal de la Montagne*, a semi-official paper, condemned him for making "a separate category of a more vulgar class of people, who spoke a more vulgar language," insisting that "today, when equality has brought all men together, language should be the same for all."[27] Forced to accept the language of the educated Jacobins, however, the readers who had recognized themselves in Hébert's pages were bound to feel alienated from the Revolution.

No one had done more than the *Père Duchêne* to fan fears of counterrevolutionary conspiracies and betrayals by bourgeois politicians, or to encourage the punitive impulses that so often came to the surface during the Terror. What Hébert and the other populist agitators lacked was a coherent program. Demands for stricter price controls did not address the causes of the shortages plaguing the urban population; reiterated calls for insurrections and executions were not a convincing alternative to the policy being followed by the governing committees. The charges on which the Hébertistes were convicted were trumped up, but the overworked members of the Committee of Public Safety, straining to mobilize the country's resources for war and to keep the economy from collapsing, had little tolerance for agitators who seemed to have no comprehension of the real problems facing the country. The dissolution of the revolutionary army, announced during the Hébertistes' trial, was popular outside of Paris, and a wave of arrests of militants accused of sympathies with the "conspirators" extended the impact of the repression throughout the country.

Even before the Hébertistes had been dispatched to the guillotine, Robespierre warned that the governing committees had a second faction in their sights. The moderates gathered around Danton would not be allowed to profit from the defeat of their enemies. The committees were in agreement about putting Fabre and the other deputies involved in the India Company scandal on trial, as well as Hérault de Séchelles, who was embroiled in a separate affair of corruption, but they were deeply divided about whether to include Danton and Desmoulins as well. Saint-Just, an expert in such matters, drew up the indictment, but the question of whom to include was too sensitive for one person to decide. The more hotheaded committee members—Collot d'Herbois and Billaud-Varenne from the Committee of Public Safety and Amar and Jean-Henri Voulland of the Committee of General Security—insisted on the danger the Indulgents represented: their calls for clemency might persuade the deputies of the Plain, the silent backbenchers of the Convention, to turn against the Terror and the men who had conducted it. The more practical committee members, such as Lazare Carnot and Robert Lindet, thought arresting a revolutionary hero like Danton was too risky. "Think carefully, a head like Danton's will cost many others," Carnot warned.[28]

The crucial vote was Robespierre's. Despite their differences, he knew what Danton had done for the Revolution at many critical moments, and his personal friendship with Camille Desmoulins went back to their schooldays. Just days before the committees made their fateful decision to have Danton arrested, Robespierre agreed to attend a dinner with him organized by mutual friends who hoped to reconcile them. Accounts of the words exchanged between them are unverifiable, but Danton reportedly suggested that some of the politicians who had been sent to the Revolutionary Tribunal had been innocent, and Robespierre replied that by Danton's standards, no conspirator would ever be found guilty.[29] The encounter convinced Robespierre that Danton would not abandon his criticism of the governing committees; he was also aware that Desmoulins had prepared a seventh issue of his *Vieux Cordelier* that contained such a stinging attack on the Committee of Public Safety that his printer had refused to publish it.

At the decisive meeting with the other members of the governing committees, Robespierre proposed letting Danton justify himself in front of the Convention before taking action. "You can run the risk of getting guillotined, if such is your will," Marc-Guillaume Vadier of the Committee of General Security replied. "For myself, I prefer to avoid this risk, by getting them arrested at once." Once he agreed to the decision, however, Robespierre combed through his memories of interactions with Danton from the start of the Revolution for evidence that could be twisted to justify an indictment. Danton had once urged him, when Barnave and Lameth were leading the Jacobins, to ease up on his criticism of them: proof of conspiratorial intentions. In another private conversation, Danton had mocked Robespierre's obsession with virtue by remarking that he knew of no virtue greater than that "which he practiced every night with his wife": evidence of the love of pleasure that would make a man susceptible to corruption.[30]

In Robespierre's view, the survival of the Revolution depended on maintaining the unity and authority of the committees. If Danton and Desmoulins could not be persuaded to end their agitation, they would have to be eliminated, regardless of his personal feelings for them. Desmoulins learned about the Incorruptible's decision the hard way. "I am lost," he told a friend. "I went to visit Robespierre, and he had me turned away from his door." The arrest warrants for Danton, Desmoulins, and their allies were executed on the night of March 30, 1794 (10 germinal Year II). The news caused a sensation. "People are stunned and don't know what to think," a police agent reported. At the Convention, the deputy Louis Legendre, one of Danton's closest associates, caused a commotion by reporting the news. Resolute after his initial hesitation, Robespierre denied the Dantonists any chance of defending themselves. "Pale with anger and seemingly impelled by the sense of a great danger," according to one witness, he silenced opposition by announcing, "We shall see on this day if the Convention knows how to break a false idol."[31]

Camille Desmoulins knew better than to expect a good outcome at his trial: when the prosecutor made him state his age, he replied that he was thirty-three, "the age of the sans-culotte Jesus" when he stood before Pilate. Danton, who claimed credit for establishing the Revolutionary Tribunal in March 1793, had ignored warnings of his impending arrest. "I was tipped off, and I couldn't believe it," he said when he found himself in prison. Told to give his name and address, he said, "I will soon be living nowhere; as for my name, you will find it in the pantheon of history." He was nevertheless determined to put up a brave front. "Provided they let us speak at length," he assured his colleagues, "I am sure of routing my accusers and if the French people is what it ought to be I shall have to ask it to pardon them!" Furnished with nothing but the vaguest accusations of conspiracy and corruption against the defendants, the prosecutor, Antoine-Quentin Fouquier-Tinville, found himself on the defensive: Danton took control of the courtroom, bellowing so loudly that his voice could be heard in the street outside. The officially published transcript of the proceedings made the reason for Fouquier's difficulties clear: readers could imagine Danton roaring, "Is it from a revolutionary like me, so strongly committed, that you expect a cold defense? Men like me cannot be bought; on their brows are imprinted, in ineffaceable characters, the seal of liberty, the genius of republicanism; and I am accused of having crawled at the feet of vile despots!"[32]

By the third day of the trial, Fouquier-Tinville had warned the Committee of Public Safety that he could not guarantee the outcome unless the defendants were silenced. Saint-Just rushed to the Convention to denounce the "revolt of the guilty" who were disrupting the courtroom: "They admit their crimes by resisting the laws," he said. The deputies obediently voted a decree giving the prosecutor the right to remove such defendants from the courtroom, for anyone behaving in such a manner "resists or insults the justice of the nation." Protesting that "we are going to be judged without being heard," Danton and the others defiantly shouted "take us to the scaffold" as they were hustled away. As he awaited execution, Danton had a few choice words for the former colleagues responsible for his fate. Another prisoner heard him say, "If I left my balls to Robespierre and my legs to Couthon the Committee of Public Safety could last a bit longer." Still in full possession of his sense for the theatrical as he mounted the scaffold the next day, Danton told the executioner, "Don't forget to show my head to the people; it's worth seeing."[33]

Following so quickly on the heels of the execution of the Héber-tistes, the deaths of Danton and his colleagues showed that the govern-ing committees would not tolerate any public criticism of their policies. No one, no matter how great their contributions to the Revolution, was safe. This warning struck home not only with the public at large but with the members of the Convention. Inside the Paris prisons, which had ironically become one of the few places where people could speak freely, inmates did not hesitate to predict the fate of the Committee of Public Safety itself. A prisoner in Saint-Lazare imagined Danton tell-ing Charon, the boatman who collected coins from the dead to ferry them across the river Styx in Greek mythology, to keep the change: "I'll pay for Couthon, Saint-Just and Robespierre."[34] More than any other episode of the Revolution, the drama of Danton's sudden fall from rev-olutionary hero to victim has had an irresistible attraction for creative artists. His conflict with Robespierre is the theme of *Danton's Death*, a classic drama by the nineteenth-century German playwright Georg Buchner; of the Polish filmmaker Andrzej Wajda's film *Danton*, made in 1983; and of the British historical novelist Hilary Mantel's first major work, *A Place of Greater Safety*, published in 1992.

Casting Danton's death as the outcome of a duel with Robespierre is an effective dramatic device, but it distorts the historical significance of the crushing of the Indulgent faction. Robespierre was not the only member of the governing committees who saw Danton as a threat; in-deed, Robespierre put himself at risk by his repeated efforts to defend Danton and Desmoulins while also trying to guide them back into the fold of orthodoxy. He and the other revolutionary leaders faced a real di-lemma: to permit a reexamination of the premises of the Terror threat-ened to discredit the revolutionary movement as a whole. The fact that some of Danton's supporters, particularly Fabre d'Eglantine, were truly guilty of crimes cast legitimate suspicion on Danton himself. At the moment when the Indulgents were sent to trial, the Vendée rebellion still smoldered, in spite of the ferocious measures taken to stamp it out, and the military campaign of 1794 that would drive foreign invaders off French soil had not yet begun. Having barely survived the rebellions, betrayals, and violent factional disputes of the previous twelve months, the members of the governing committees were more concerned about a resurgence of such conflicts than about the possible excesses to which their policies might lead.

The execution of the Dantonists sent a clear message: so long as the revolutionary government remained in power, no public challenge to its leadership would be allowed. To strengthen its authority, on 14 germinal Year II (April 3, 1794) the Convention abolished the ministries that had theoretically continued to direct government policies and put their officials directly under the control of the Committee of Public Safety. Among those affected by this change was Jean-Marie Goujon, rewarded for his consistent devotion to the revolutionary cause by being named as a minister just before the office was eliminated. Instead, he replaced the recently executed Hérault de Séchelles in the Convention, a remarkable achievement for a young man who, only four years earlier, had been just an anonymous participant in the Festival of the Federation. Goujon had always clung to the hope that the purity of the revolutionary cause would bring all its acolytes together, but the elimination of the Hébertistes and Dantonists only intensified the conflicts at the top of the movement. By late spring, Carnot later remembered, the Committee of Public Safety had to move its meetings to an isolated room, "so that the people would not be able to observe the storms that agitated us."[35] Distrust between the members of that committee and their colleagues on the Committee of General Security was so strong that Robespierre and Saint-Just set up a parallel police network of their own. Many Convention deputies had been close to members of one or the other of the factions that were now eliminated, and they feared that they might find themselves following their former friends to the guillotine. For the moment, however, they did not dare to take any action against the seemingly all-powerful committees.

The newspapers, whose power to affect public opinion had been demonstrated so effectively by Hébert and Desmoulins, now offered readers only edifying stories about revolutionary soldiers' heroism in battle, and about public ceremonies in which citizens and officials joined in proclaiming their support for the Convention and its policies. For writers and artists willing to support the government, Year II nevertheless offered opportunities. The output of revolutionary songs, poems, and plays reached a peak as publishers and theater managers tried to demonstrate their patriotism. Patriotic spectacles such as Sylvain Maréchal's *The Last Judgment of Kings*, which portrayed monarchs from all over Europe being overthrown by their subjects, then shipped to a remote island and swallowed up by a volcano, and staged reenactments of glorious events, such as the recapture of Toulon, played to packed houses. Although the Jacobins had excluded women from politics and army service, playwrights often allowed them to demonstrate their national loyalty on stage. In one play about Toulon, a woman merchant sacrifices her wealth to serve as a spy against the British; in another, a republican mother disguises herself so she can avoid being recognized as she observes her son, who is a soldier, to make sure he is a good patriot. More than forty different versions of revolutionary playing cards were published in which the kings, queens, and jacks of traditional decks were replaced with allegorical figures representing different aspects of liberty and equality, or with pictures of revolutionary soldiers and sans-culottes. Even in their leisure-time activities, good patriots were supposed to constantly reaffirm their support for the Revolution.

From the daily police reports they received, the governing committees knew that this enthusiasm had its limits. Ordinary Parisians continued to complain about shortages of food and other necessities. A system of bread rationing assured the population of a minimum of calories, but many wanted to see meat and other commodities subjected to the same regime. When the rates of the *maximum* were revised in March 1794, "everyone said that [they were] very favorable to the people of the countryside and the merchants," according to police reports. The authorities used the law's restrictions on wages to deter workers from pushing for higher pay; strikers were punished for undermining the war effort. The requirement that everyone have a *carte de civisme* from their local surveillance committee in order to claim their bread ration or to travel made people dependent on overworked officials, who were accused of taking bribes to protect suspects, and of using their powers to harass their personal enemies. "Every day one hears it said that [the surveillance committees] are composed of intriguers who exploit the nation and oppress the citizens," a police observer wrote.[36]

Paradoxically, although in the middle months of Year II the revolutionary government's control over the population reached its peak, this was also the moment when ordinary people played their greatest role in public life. The former nobles and prosperous lawyers who had dominated city governments at the outset of the Revolution were now replaced by men from more modest backgrounds. In Lorraine's capital of Nancy, artisans and shopkeepers, 12 percent of the city council in 1790–1791, now made up 36 percent of its membership; in Bordeaux, merchants, 55 percent of the council in 1790–1791, saw their representation drop to 33 percent, barely ahead of the 32 percent of their colleagues who were artisans or shopkeepers.[37]

Jacques Ménétra, who never could have dreamed of holding any politically significant office in the old regime, held so many different posts in his Paris section during the Terror that later he could not remember them all. He was a member of the surveillance committee, an assistant to the local justice of the peace, chair of the saltpeter commission, and a candidate for a seat in the Commune's assembly.[38] In theory, every town and village was supposed to have both a council and a surveillance committee, and all but the smallest communities also had a popular society or political club, meaning that a substantial fraction of the male population had some kind of political responsibility. Despite the Convention's ban on women's participation in politics, they frequently attended meetings as spectators, keeping the men under observation and making sure they carried out their responsibilities. Charles Dickens's character Madame Defarge in A Tale of Two Cities, a vengeful shopkeeper's wife who takes her knitting and goes every day to jeer the defendants at the Revolutionary Tribunal, had her real-life equivalents, female militants who saw it as their patriotic duty to make sure the juries knew that the people wanted their enemies punished.

The thousands of citizens who found themselves occupying political positions in Year II had little chance to contest revolutionary orthodoxy, but they were often nearly overwhelmed with the tasks imposed on them. In addition to the traditional responsibilities of maintaining public order and collecting taxes, they were now expected to recruit soldiers for the army and to come up with the funds for their uniforms and weapons. Under the law of suspects, they not only had to identify potential enemies of the Revolution but also had to set up and administer prisons for those who were arrested. Saint-Just's ventôse decrees obliged local governments to identify émigrés and others whose property might be confiscated, as well as deserving patriots who might receive a share of it. Few communes did much to implement that law. They were more active in carrying out a subsequent decree, one presented by Barère on 22 floréal (May 11). The measure provided funds to set up a comprehensive welfare system in rural areas. Village councils quickly prepared lists of peasants and artisans over the age of sixty who could no longer support themselves, as well as poor mothers with children; they were also obligated to recruit *officiers de santé* (health officers) to provide free medical care for the indigent. In addition, with churches across the country closed, local officials and popular societies were supposed to organize civic rituals to mark the *décadi*, or tenth day of the republican calendar, and to observe the national festivals decreed from Paris. From Paris, too, came an unprecedented flood of paperwork, putting a great strain on newly minted officials who often had only rudimentary writing abilities.

One challenge local officials were happy to accept was the Convention's order that they prepare a special celebration for the 20th day of prairial Year II (June 8, 1794). For the first time, the entire population was mobilized to take part in a festival staged simultaneously throughout the country. The idea was a personal initiative of Robespierre's; indeed, no other action taken during the year he served as a member of the Committee of Public Safety was so directly identified with him. Barely a month after the execution of the Dantonists, in what proved to be the last of his major speeches, the Incorruptible called for the inauguration of a "cult of the Supreme Being." Three months earlier, in his speech on the principles of political morality, Robespierre had proclaimed the necessity of virtue as the basis for the republic and denounced the factions that he alleged were conspiring to undermine it. Now, with those factions defeated, he could make the triumph of virtue a lasting one. In messianic terms, Robespierre announced that "all has changed in the physical order; all must change in the moral and political order. One half of the world revolution is already achieved, the other half has yet to be accomplished."[39]

As he called for the recognition of what he labeled "the universal religion of nature," Robespierre was careful to distinguish his proposed cult both from the *fanatisme* (fanaticism) of the radical atheists, who had shut down the churches during the de-Christianization campaign, and the "priest-made religions" that they had attacked. Robespierre had clearly been inspired by his cherished Rousseau's concept of a civil religion that could bind society together. He hoped that a formal declaration that "the French people recognizes the existence of the Supreme Being, and the immortality of the soul," and a list of moral duties—"to detest bad faith and despotism, to punish tyrants and traitors, to assist the unfortunate, to respect the weak, to defend the oppressed, to do all the good one can to one's neighbor, and to behave with justice towards all men"—would unite all citizens and make it possible to end the conflicts that had racked the Revolution.[40]

The artist and Convention deputy Jacques-Louis David, the republic's designated "pageant master," set to work to plan the 20 prairial "Festival of the Supreme Being" in the capital, and municipal governments throughout the country were told to imitate it as best they could. In Paris, it took four hours for the procession to make its way from the center of the Tuileries Gardens to the Champ de Mars on the other side of the Seine. Marchers watched as a papier-mâché figure of "Hideous Atheism" was set on fire, revealing a plaster statue of "Wisdom" concealed inside. On the Champ de Mars, David erected an artificial mountain, the symbol of the Jacobin Montagnards, with platforms on its sides to hold groups ranging from mothers with newborn babies to white-haired patriarchs. A choir sang hymns specially composed for the occasion, and an oxcart laden with freshly harvested crops stood nearby, representing the bounty of nature. As in the earlier festival marking the acceptance of the constitution, an oversized statue of Hercules, mounted on a column, symbolized the might of the people.

His colleagues elected Robespierre as president of the Convention for the occasion, giving him the right to march at the head of their group. As he led them in the procession, he held a sheaf of wheat to honor the products of agriculture. Behind him, deputies who resented

VUE DE LA MONTAGNE ELEVÉE AU CHAMP DE LA REUNION
*pour la fête qui y a été célébrée en l'honneur de l'Être Suprême le Decadi 20 Prairial de l'an 2ᵉ de la Republique Française.*
*A Paris chez Chéreau Rue Jacques, aux deux Colonnes, près la Fontaine Severin. N.° 257.*

FESTIVAL OF THE SUPREME BEING: At the height of the Reign of Terror, the Festival of the Supreme Being offered the population a glimpse of the peaceful and prosperous future the Montagnards wanted to believe lay just over the horizon. This engraving shows David's artificial mountain, the statue of Hercules, and the oxcart bearing nature's bounty. *Source: Library of Congress.*

his preeminence muttered words like "dictator" and "tyrant"; at least one of them later claimed he had intended to assassinate him if the opportunity had presented itself. Whatever the thoughts of the deputies, most of the participants entered into the spirit of the occasion. According to one witness, "the Festival of the Supreme Being was a total success. It was believed to be the prelude to a general amnesty. . . . The weather was beautiful. The crowds were so large that it seemed that Paris had risen from the dead, rejuvenated, busy and sparkling; the ladies dared once more to appear with their old finery and every face shone with friendliness." Joachim Vilate, a member of the Revolutionary Tribunal, claimed to have encountered Robespierre, "his face . . . transformed with joy," as he watched the "glorious spectacle" he had called into be-ing.[41] The widespread expectation that the festival was a signal that the Terror was about to end encouraged even prisoners to demonstrate their patriotic loyalty: they staged their own versions of the event, building miniature mountains in the courtyards of their jails and chanting ap-propriate hymns. In some cases, their families were allowed to join them for the day, adding to their hope that they might soon be freed.

Robespierre's mood of exaltation did not last. Just two days later, on 22 prairial Year II (June 10, 1794), his close ally Couthon presented the Convention not with a proposal for an amnesty, but with a decree intensifying the Terror. The law of 22 prairial drastically curtailed the rights of defendants tried by the Revolutionary Tribunal: they no longer had any right to counsel, death became the only penalty for all offenses, and the "conscience of the jurors, enlightened by the love of the *Patrie* [homeland]," was sufficient to determine a verdict. Up to this point, the Revolutionary Tribunal had often acquitted as many as half of the sus-pects brought before it; in the two months of its operation after the passage of the law of 22 prairial, the conviction rate rose to 80 percent.[42] In the weeks that came to be known as *la Grande Terreur* (the Great Terror), the Paris tribunal sent over 1,300 people to the guillotine.

The reasons for this sudden escalation, so out of tune with the expectations raised by the Festival of the Supreme Being, are unclear. The difficulties the Revolutionary Tribunal had encountered during the Danton trial no doubt created pressure to simplify its procedures and re-duce the ability of defendants to justify themselves. Pressures also came from some of the deputies on mission. The deputy Étienne Maignet, ea-ger to speed up the punishment of counterrevolutionaries in the south-ern Rhône valley, received permission to set up a *commission populaire* (popular commission) in the town of Orange with authority to carry out executions. Having approved such measures for the Orange com-mission, which would order 332 executions during its own version of the Great Terror, the Committee of Public Safety may have thought that Paris should step up its executions as well. Two bungled assassination attempts against Robespierre and Collot d'Herbois at the beginning of the month of prairial reminded the Montagnard leaders of the fate of Marat. Robespierre seemed almost to look forward to sacrificing his life, writing privately that "surrounded by their assassins, I have already placed myself in the new order of things where they wish to send me." Other revolutionaries wanted sterner actions to deter such attacks.[43]

As dangerous as open resistance to the Committee of Public Safety had become, some Convention deputies understood the threat represented by the law of 22 prairial and tried to at least delay its approval, or to require that the Convention be given the right to approve the arrest of any of its members. Their efforts were the first sign of the opposition that would lead to Robespierre's overthrow less than two months later. Robespierre reinforced their fears by openly painting his critics as men "who spoke continually, fearfully, and publicly of the guillotine, regarding it as something which had its eye on them for debasing and troubling the national convention."[44]

The officials of the Revolutionary Tribunal, overwhelmed by the number of inmates in the Paris prisons, immediately put the law's expedited trial procedures to use. Martial Herman, a colleague of Fouquier-Tinville's, demanded the committee's authorization to "purge the prisons in a single blow and rid the soil of Liberty of this garbage, these dregs of humanity." Prison informers, dubbed *moutons* (sheep) by the other inmates, furnished the prosecutors with lists of names that were used to make up ever-larger *fournées* (oven-loads) of men and women who were sentenced for imaginary conspiracies. Among the victims were distinguished public figures such as Malesherbes, who had volunteered to defend Louis XVI at his trial; intellectuals, including the chemist Antoine Lavoisier and the era's leading poet, André Chénier, whose brother, the playwright Marie-Joseph Chénier, sat in the Convention; clergy who had embraced the Revolution, such as the Paris archbishop Jean-Baptiste Gobel and the former deputy Adrien Lamourette; and ordinary men and women who had muttered too loudly about the price of bread. The guillotine was transferred to a location on the eastern edge of the city so that the spectacle of several dozen executions a day would not provoke a negative reaction. In private, the chronicler Ruault lamented that the revolutionary leaders, who had done great things to save the country, were making themselves "execrable now by the horror and the multiplication of unnecessary punishments. . . . No citizen is sure of being alive in two more days."[45]

The impression that the Terror had turned into an irrational and un-controlled bloodbath was accompanied by an improvement in the military situation. The tide was clearly turning in the republic's favor. In May, French forces won a decisive victory over the Spanish, securing the country's southern border. On June 1, 1794, the French Atlantic fleet, its discipline restored by Committee of Public Safety member André Jeanbon Saint-André, confronted the British off Brittany in order to protect a convoy carrying a massive grain shipment from the United States. The British captured or sank a number of French warships, but the French crews performed bravely; they prevented the enemy from intercepting the merchant ships and their much-needed cargo. On land, the crucial encounter was the Battle of Fleurus, fought in Belgium on June 26. For the first time in the history of warfare, aviation was used for military purposes: the French put up a tethered hot-air balloon as an observation post, which "contributed a lot to the success of the day," a French soldier later remembered.[46] As Carnot had hoped when he decided to deploy the bulk of French forces on the northern frontier, the Austrian army was forced to retreat, clearing the way for a renewed French occupation of Belgian territories that would last until Napoleon's defeat in 1814.

The Austrian commanders were deeply discouraged by their situation. "How is it possible that a well-equipped, balanced, disciplined army had been defeated by an enemy with raw troops, lacking cavalry, and with inexperienced generals?" one asked. A young German officer who would, years later, help defeat Napoleon, offered an answer: "The terrible position the French found themselves in, surrounded by several armies which sought (or so they believed) to enslave them and condemn them to eternal misery, inspired the soldier with courage, induced the citizen to make voluntary sacrifices, gathered supplies for the army and attracted the civilian population to the colors."[47] The Prussians withdrew from the fighting in order to concentrate their forces in Poland, where a revolutionary movement led by Tadeusz Kościuszko, who had been an officer in the American revolutionary army, broke out in March 1794. In an effort to free their country from foreign domination, the Polish revolutionaries went beyond the limited reform program proclaimed in 1791 and announced the abolition of personal serfdom and other reforms in favor of the peasants. The Polish "Jacobins" posed a more immediate threat to the country's neighbors, all of them dependent on serfdom, than the events in France. A coalition of Russian, Prussian, and Austrian troops crushed Kościuszko's movement, but the campaign in Poland diverted crucial resources from the war against France and led Prussia to begin secret negotiations with Paris.

For true believers in the Revolution, the daily executions in Paris and the good news from the armies proved that the movement's conclusive success could not be disputed. Rosalie Jullien and her husband joined other Parisians in a "fraternal banquet" to celebrate the anniversary of July 14. Rich and poor came together to share a common meal at tables set up in the streets. "We drank to the health of the Republic, of the Convention, of the Mountain. It is such a simple joy, so decent in spite of the crowd and the mixture, that nothing equals these pleasures for propagating equality," she wrote to her son. The increasingly suspicious Robespierre saw the banquets in a different light. He worried that they provided the wealthy with an opportunity to curry favor with the poor by plying them with food and drink. At his behest, Barère denounced them in the Convention: "Fraternity does not consist of meals in the streets; there can be nothing in common between the opulent egoist, who sighs for inequality and kings, and the sans-culotte, full of candor, who loves only the Republic and equality."[48]

The religious coloration of the Festival of the Supreme Being offered Robespierre's enemies an opening to attack him. On 27 prairial Year II (June 15, 1794), Marc-Guillaume Vadier, a member of the Committee of General Security, delivered a long report on a supposed conspiracy centered around an elderly woman, Catherine Théot, who had proclaimed herself to be a religious prophetess, the "Mother of God." Robespierre intervened to prevent the case from being sent to the Revolutionary Tribunal. His attitude allowed his colleagues to insinuate that he was protecting a cabal of religious fanatics and even that he saw himself as a messianic figure. After a furious quarrel with his committee colleagues, during which Robert Lindet shouted at him, "The nation is not only one man!" Robespierre stopped attending the group's meetings; for nearly a month, he appeared in public only to attend a few sessions of the Jacobin Club.[49]

Despite having spent his revolutionary career denouncing conspiracies, Robespierre failed to take any effective steps to counter the one forming against him. Several of his colleagues on the Committee of Public Safety, including both the radicals Billaud-Varenne and Collot d'Herbois and more moderate figures, such as Carnot and Barère, were ready to turn against him, and he had alienated most members of the Committee of General Security as well. Robespierre's most dangerous enemies were men who had played a leading role in the Terror, notably Joseph Fouché, who had launched the de-Christianization campaign in the fall of 1793; Jean-Lambert Tallien, who had overseen the repression following the federalist uprising in Bordeaux; and Paul Barras, who had been on mission in Marseille. That Robespierre might turn against the more violent terrorists, and then fulfill his 1793 promise to reinstate constitutional protections, did not appear impossible, and indeed, many of his biographers have suggested as much.

If Robespierre had such an idea, he was singularly inept in pursuing it. When he denounced Fouché, whose commitment to de-Christianization had deeply offended him, and succeeded in having him expelled from the Jacobin Club, this merely drove Fouché to step up his plotting. Exploiting rumors that Robespierre had settled on the names of the opponents he planned to have arrested, Fouché warned other deputies, "You are on the list, you are on the list as well as myself, I am certain of it!"[50] While the plotters were reaching out to the members of the Plain, the men who had kept their heads down during the dangerous factional struggles of the previous two years, and to disaffected members of the government committees, the Incorruptible remained in isolation, meeting only with a few loyalists at his home. His opponents feared that he might find support from the Paris Commune, whose head official, Claude-François Payan, named to replace Chaumette after the latter's arrest, was an unswerving follower of Robespierre. The sectional military battalions, whose intervention had forced the Convention to expel the Girondins on June 2, 1793, were still commanded by François Hanriot, another Robespierrist. Since the fall of the Hébertistes and Chaumette, however, the Commune had carried out policies imposed by the Committee of Public Safety that had alienated the working population whose support had made the journées of 1792 and 1793 successful.

City officials rigorously suppressed workers' protests about wages and working conditions, insisting that they disrupted the war effort, and on May 5, 1794, Payan banned the meetings of the sectional assemblies in which ordinary Parisians had been able to make their voices heard. The sans-culottes had little reason to listen to calls for support from men who had effectively silenced their movement.

During the critical weeks before the final crisis, Robespierre may have been ill or even suffering a kind of nervous breakdown; in any event, the keen political instincts that had propelled him to the center of the revolutionary stage had clearly deserted him. In the first days of that month, Barère, a moderate at heart but a man who had long been a faithful ally of Robespierre's, made a final effort to avoid a confrontation. On 4 thermidor (July 22), the members of the two committees met without Robespierre. In exchange for promises that his ventôse decrees calling for the distribution of land to the poor would be implemented, Saint-Just promised to persuade Robespierre to put aside his differences with his colleagues. On the following day, Robespierre joined the group and reluctantly endorsed the agreement, but only after making personal attacks on several of his colleagues that raised doubts about his sincerity. He then disappeared again for two days, drafting a speech about whose content the others could only speculate.

On the morning of 8 thermidor (July 26), Robespierre made his long-awaited reappearance at the Convention. He had written out a lengthy speech, but it lacked his usual organization and clarity. He painted a grim picture of a revolution in greater danger than ever before from factions and unnamed conspirators in the pay of foreign interests. Anyone who hoped that Robespierre might advocate a tempering of the Terror must have shuddered when he called the revolutionary government's policies "the thunderbolt of retribution launched by the hand of liberty against crime." Above all, listeners were struck by the personal tone of the speech. Over and over again, he complained that he was being unjustly persecuted. "What . . . am I that they should accuse me? A slave of liberty—a living martyr of the Republic!" he protested. Even as Robespierre indignantly refuted the charge that he sought dictatorial power, it was clear that he had reached the point of considering every trace of opposition as evidence of conspiracy. That same evening, he appeared at the Jacobin Club. The divisions among the members of the Committee of Public Safety were on full display. When Billaud-Varenne and Collot d'Herbois tried to prevent Robespierre from speaking, he replied, "It is easy to see that factious persons among us fear to be unveiled in the presence of the people." After he succeeded in delivering his oration, his opponents were shouted down with cries of "Conspirators to the guillotine!"[51] The organizers of the movement against him realized that they had to act immediately, before Robespierre could strike.

According to the agreement made by the members of the two governing committees several days earlier, the Convention session on 9 thermidor (July 27) was supposed to open with a speech by Saint-Just. Before he had time to read more than a few lines, Tallien interrupted and began an all-out assault on Robespierre and his two main allies on the Committee of Public Safety, Saint-Just and Couthon. Robespierre tried to seize the podium but was silenced by roars of "Down with the tyrant!" and "It is Danton's blood that is choking him!" The Convention voted to arrest Hanriot, the commander of the section battalions. Vadier brought up Robespierre's defense of Catherine Théot; Tallien accused him of cowardice on August 10, 1792, when he had not appeared in public; and finally, several deputies took the decisive step of moving for his arrest. "Is one man to be the master of the Convention?" one of them demanded. Robespierre's younger brother Augustin and his friend Philippe Le Bas showed their devotion by demanding to be arrested with him, and the Convention added the names of Saint-Just and Couthon to the decree. "They meant to form a triumvirate which recalls the bloody proscriptions of Sulla," asserted the deputy Stanislas Fréron, who had once been a proponent of the most extreme terrorist measures.[52]

The five arrested deputies initially submitted to the authority of the Convention, but the jailers at the prisons to which they were sent, all appointees of the pro-Robespierre city government regime, refused to take responsibility for incarcerating them. The National Guard commander, Hanriot, initially evaded arrest and dashed around the city, ordering the sections to send their battalions to the Hôtel de Ville, the seat of the city government that had so often served as a counterweight to the national government during previous revolutionary journées. Instead of immediately launching an attack on the nearby Convention, however, the Commune's loyalists remained at the Hôtel de Ville, losing their best opportunity to overwhelm their opponents. While news of the day's confusing events circulated around the city, many citizens went about their ordinary routines; at the Place du Trône, the relatively isolated location to which the guillotine had been relocated, the executioner dispatched forty victims who might have survived a few days later.

As the sun set at 7:30 p.m., guardsmen from several of the sections gathered in the square in front of the Hôtel de Ville, although many of them were still unsure of the nature of the crisis and undecided about whom to support. Listening to the alarm bells sounding across the city, prisoners in the Luxembourg were terrified: cut off from news, they feared a repetition of the 1792 September massacres. The Convention appointed the deputy Paul Barras to command the forces on its side. Informed of the arrested deputies' escapes and of Hanriot's activities, the assembly decreed that they were now "outside the law" and subject to immediate execution without a trial when they were captured. Most of the sections rallied to the Convention's side, and some of them sent messages to their guard units, ordering them to return from the Hôtel de Ville. Inside the building, an insurrectionary committee was cobbled together, but no orders were given to the increasingly confused soldiers in the square outside. It was after 9:00 p.m. when the first of the outlawed deputies, Augustin Robespierre and Le Bas, reached the Hôtel de Ville. Maximilien Robespierre showed little enthusiasm for joining them; he had never actually taken a personal role in any of the Revolution's insurrections. When he finally arrived, after 10:00 p.m., he avoided appearing in the Commune's large meeting hall, which was filled with militants eager for leadership; instead he met only with the members of the insurrectionary committee, who "treated him as a brother, and told him they would protect him."[53]

Aware of the mortal danger facing them, Robespierre and his supporters debated how to phrase their call for support. Couthon wanted to denounce the Convention as a nest of conspirators, but Robespierre still insisted on respecting the assembly's legitimacy. Meanwhile, the guards-men who had assembled at the Place de Grève in front of the Hôtel de Ville began to drift away. Some returned to their sections; others joined the army that Barras was assembling. The blustering Hanriot, appar-ently unaware that his forces were dissolving, continued to issue orders. He told them, "If you see [Convention] deputies leading patrols to make proclamations, seize them. . . . Lots of energy, firmness, and the people's cause will triumph!"[54] By the time the Convention's forces arrived at the Hôtel de Ville prepared for a confrontation, around 1:00 a.m., they found the Place de Grève deserted. Entering the building, they discov-ered that the Robespierrists, recognizing that the population had not rallied to their cause, had already given up the fight. Le Bas shot him-self; Augustin Robespierre and Hanriot were badly injured jumping out of windows. The paralyzed Couthon, who had only joined the group at the Hôtel de Ville a few minutes before the end, was dragged out of his wheelchair and beaten up. Maximilien Robespierre was bleeding badly from a pistol ball that had smashed his jaw and could not speak; he had apparently tried unsuccessfully to kill himself.

The prisoners were taken back to the offices of the Committee of Public Safety, where their wounds were treated, and then transferred to the Conciergerie prison while the guillotine was set up in the Place de la Concorde. Finally, at 7:30 p.m. on 10 thermidor (July 28), the behead-ings commenced. As carts took the victims to their fate, "it was a holi-day, all the elegant people were at their windows to see them pass; they applauded and clapped their hands all along the rue Saint-Honoré," Nicolas Ruault wrote. Robespierre suffered a final indignity when the executioner ripped the bandage from his jaw, leaving him screaming in pain as the blade came down.

Over the next two days, more than a hundred of those who had ral-lied to his side on 9 thermidor (July 27) were also put to death. Hardly anyone dared to express any sympathy for the victims. Rosalie Jullien, whose son Marc-Antoine had been a favorite of the Incorruptible, was typical in the speed with which she accommodated herself to the new state of affairs. "The quickness of events is as miraculous as their im-portance," she wrote to her son, "and six hours was perhaps the whole space that destiny used to carry out such extraordinary changes." She regretted only that "the infamous Robespierre" had "dragged excellent patriots in his fall."[55]

The temptation to put all the blame for the violence and excesses of the Terror on Robespierre's shoulders was understandable. But thousands had played a part in those events, including the remaining members of the Committee of Public Safety, who all kept their positions. Certainly Robespierre was no innocent. He never indulged in the open advocacy of bloodshed that had characterized Marat and Hébert, and he never personally participated in the streetfighting of the Paris journées, or the campaigns of repression that many of his Convention colleagues oversaw in the provinces. But he justified such violence as inevitable and necessary if the goals of the Revolution were to be achieved. Robespierre's idealization of the people gained him a popular following that lasted well into the period of the Terror, even though he lacked the ability to deal with the common people that accounted for Danton's success. But Robespierre was also, at least until the last months of his remarkably short public career—he was just thirty-six when he died—a gifted politician, capable of sizing up the forces at work in the complicated situations he confronted and taking effective steps to achieve his goals.

Robespierre's greatest weakness was the counterpart of his total commitment to his principles: he could only think of those who did not share his convictions as people motivated by selfish interests, and therefore easily corruptible and liable to engage in conspiracies. Some of those he opposed were indeed either corrupt, or willing to use unconstitutional means to oppose the basic principles of the Revolution, or both, including Louis XVI and Marie-Antoinette, General Dumouriez, Fabre d'Eglantine, and the other participants in the India Company affair. After the war that he had opposed was under way, Robespierre was certainly justified in regarding foreign governments as dangerous foes. Increasingly, however, he came to lump all those who differed with him together with the Revolution's genuine enemies and to support ever more violent measures against them.

Once Robespierre became convinced that all those who disagreed with him were tied to a foreign-backed plot that brought together federalists, de-Christianizers, Indulgents, and royalists, all of them capable of disguising themselves as good patriots, it became increasingly difficult for him to trust anyone. Despite his professed devotion to the people, he came to see even grumbling about food shortages and low wages as signs of conspiracy. The reluctance of many other revolutionaries to pay more than lip service to the moral principles incorporated in the cult of the Supreme Being added to his isolation. By the time of thermidor, the Incorruptible had become a potential threat to almost all of his colleagues: too strongly identified with the revolutionary government to be ignored, but too unpredictable to be trusted. By the same rules he had applied to the leaders of the other revolutionary factions he had helped to eliminate, he had to be destroyed. His death, however inevitable according to the logic of the political system he had done so much to create, nevertheless left a yawning void. Robespierre was the last figure who could truly claim to have embodied the vision of liberty and equality that had inspired so many participants in the Revolution. His execution meant the abandonment of the utopian hopes that had been expressed in the Declaration of the Rights of Man and Citizen, leaving his successors to struggle with the question of what values the revolutionary movement and the republic now stood for.

The events of 9 thermidor ended Robespierre's career, but the way in which the day's victors rushed the Robespierrists to the guillotine indicated that they were not yet ready to abandon the methods of the Terror. Many of those who soon came to be known as the "thermidorians" had been as responsible as Robespierre, Saint-Just, and Couthon for its policies. The human cost of the period of revolutionary government was high, but it had successfully warded off the combined forces of the other European powers, as well as the royalist uprising in the west and the federalist revolts. With great difficulty, it had kept the urban population from facing actual starvation and had provided its armies with enough supplies to enable them to prevail. While its more extreme measures had alienated a good part of the population, the revolutionary government had also inspired real support from thousands of ordinary people, who served as local officials, engaged themselves as militants, participated in public festivals, and put up with the sacrifices demanded of them. No one could claim that the Terror had respected the ideals of liberty proclaimed in 1789, but it was not easy to completely dismiss the argument that Robespierre had made when he had insisted that ordinary rules could not be followed in an emergency situation as drastic as that facing the country in the Year II. Although the Terror restricted liberty, it continued to promote the other great revolutionary ideal of equality, embedding it deeply in the minds and daily habits of the population. Even in hindsight it is difficult to say that the basic achievements of the Revolution could have been preserved in 1793 and 1794 without something resembling a revolutionary dictatorship.

# 16

# THE REPUBLIC'S NEW START

*July 1794–October 1795*

AT THE END OF HIS LETTER DESCRIBING THE EVENTS OF 9 THERMIDOR Year II (July 27, 1794), the Convention deputy Jean Dyzez wrote, "We shall now have to wait several days to know what course events will take." His uncertainty reflected the fact that the thermidorians had no defined goals beyond ridding themselves of Robespierre and his closest allies. Even as they denounced the supposed dictator on 9 thermidor, the thermidorians promised to maintain the republic and continue all-out war against its enemies. When some deputies demanded the abolition of the Revolutionary Tribunal and the surveillance committees, essential instruments of the Terror, the thermidorian leaders Tallien and Billaud-Varenne rushed to preserve them, provided that Robespierrist loyalists, such as the dreaded prosecutor Fouquier-Tinville, were purged. "Beware above all of that fatal moderatism which by speaking of peace and mercy is able to turn everything to its account," Barère demanded. "Let the revolutionary movement not hesitate on its purifying course; and let the Convention still terrify traitors and kings, conspirators within and despotic governments without."[1]

Yet the victors of thermidor quickly realized that, after striking down the man who had symbolized the Terror, they could not simply continue it. Their challenge, as one historian has put it, was to "exit from the Terror" without undoing the revolutionary republican regime it had been created to protect.[2] In this endeavor, the thermidorians have generally been regarded as failures. Just as the revolutionaries discredited the monarchy by calling it "the old regime," Napoleon and his supporters justified their overthrow of the post-thermidorian Republic in 1799 by describing it as hopelessly weak and corrupt; the fact that Napoleon himself and most of his political associates had played major roles in that period was conveniently overlooked. With the exception of Napoleon, the second half of France's revolutionary decade also failed to bring strong personalities to the fore. Whereas Mirabeau, Danton, and Robespierre had boldly thrust themselves into the limelight, the men who took control of the republic's destinies after thermidor were hesitant to do so and refrained from taking public positions from which they could not retreat. Typical of this style was Sieyès, the most important of the men of 1789 to reemerge as a major figure after thermidor. His laconic vote in January 1793 for "death, without discussion," after Louis XVI's trial had protected him from accusations of moderation during the Terror, but when asked what he had done during that period, he replied simply, "I survived." The caution and political flexibility that characterized politicians after thermidor created a new atmosphere of distrust among them: no one knew who would stand by his publicly proclaimed principles and who was secretly prepared to welcome the return of the monarchy or the abandonment of other major revolutionary changes.

Until Napoleon's coup d'état of 18 brumaire Year VIII (November 9, 1799), however, France's leaders and its citizens did not know that the republic would prove so ephemeral. To many of them, thermidor appeared to have given the movement a fresh start, an opportunity to correct the mistakes that had led to the Reign of Terror and to create institutions that would truly protect liberty and equality. The years from 1794 to 1799 also saw a dramatic expansion of the Revolution's impact outside of France. Military conquests swelled French national pride and shook centuries-old institutions such as the papacy and the Holy Roman Empire. The spectacle of formerly enslaved blacks exercising the rights of French citizens, and of a black man, Toussaint Louverture, becoming the governor of a major colony, shocked defenders of slavery and racial hierarchy throughout the Western Hemisphere. The French invasion of Egypt in 1798 signaled the beginning of modern European incursions into the Muslim world, initiating conflicts that continue to the present day. The second half of the revolutionary decade of the 1790s is thus an essential part of the revolutionary saga.

In death, Robespierre was transformed into the dictator he had never been during his lifetime. By caricaturing him as a pathological monster, the thermidorians were able to blame him for all the excesses of the Reign of Terror and cast themselves as innocent victims. An anonymous pamphlet claimed that only their courage had disrupted a plan to "assassinate the National Convention and marry Capet's daughter [the child of Louis XVI and Marie-Antoinette] to Robespierre to reign together and have 80,000 citizens killed." Reproached along with other members of the Committee of Public Safety for having gone along with Robespierre's policies, Billaud-Varenne replied, "Have we forgotten that, in the National Convention, Robespierre soon became the man who, fixing all regard upon his own person, gained so much confidence that it rendered him preponderant?"[3] As soon as news of his fall reached them, local officials and popular societies hastened to join in denouncing "the audacious dominator of the people and of its representatives . . . this tiger thirsty for blood," and applauding those who had overthrown him.[4]

The thermidorians quickly learned, however, that by overthrowing Robespierre, they had unleashed forces they could not control. In a small town in northern France, the writer Charles Lacretelle saw how people crowded around to hear the details. "All these passers-by, who the day before avoided each other out of a reciprocal distrust, now greeted and talked to each other like old friends. It was clear that the terror, once it had been lifted from their spirits, could not be reinstilled." Just five days after 9 thermidor, popular pressure led the Convention to repeal the law of 22 prairial and replace it with rules allowing juries to acquit defendants if they concluded that they had not acted with criminal intent. Four days later, the Convention ordered the release

ROBESPIERRE GUILLOTIN-
ING THE EXECUTIONER:
Thermidorian propaganda
blamed Robespierre for all
the excesses of the Terror.
In this caricature, the guillotine has multiplied, with
each machine representing
a different group of victims.
*Credit: © Musée Carnavalet /
Roger-Viollet.*

of suspects who had been unjustly arrested. When Tallien personally
went to the Luxembourg prison to open the gates for some of them, "a
crowd of people gathered, covered him with blessings, embraced him,
embraced those who were restored to freedom. . . . Tears of joy and of
emotion flowed from all eyes," a journalist reported. But the opening of
the prisons set in motion a chain reaction of reproaches and accusations
as former suspects began seeking the dismissal or punishment of those
who had accused them. They raised an embarrassing question: "Is it
possible that Robespierre alone did all this evil?"[5]

Sensing the strength of this movement, the thermidorian leaders began to separate themselves not only from Robespierre but also from the policies of the Terror. On 2 fructidor Year II (August 19, 1794), when one deputy revived the call to "maintain terror everywhere as the order of the day," Tallien replied, "Terror is the weapon of tyranny." Tallien then called for an end to denunciations of former nobles and others merely on the basis of their status in the old regime. On 11 fructidor (August 28), Tallien delivered a long speech laying out an analysis of the Terror as a "system" and evoking the psychological mechanisms that made it work. It was not at all in his usual style—many suspected that someone else had written it. He said that a government based on terror "implies also an absolute power . . . which owes neither obedience nor accountability to anyone." Fear, "when it has become a habitual state of mind, makes men think only of themselves and of the least worthy part of themselves, I mean their physical survival. It breaks all ties, extinguishes all affection, it turns people away from fraternity, from society, from morality," he continued, anticipating the most probing twentieth-century analyses of totalitarianism. Tallien, during his mission to Bordeaux, had fallen in love with a strikingly beautiful and wealthy female "suspect," Thérèse de Cabarrus. He may have had his relationship with her in mind when he added that the Terror had altered the interactions between men and women: "The experience of a year has shown that the art of making men tremble is an infallible means of corrupting and degrading women."[6]

Tallien's actual proposals were more cautious than his analysis of the Terror's psychology. He wanted the Convention to reaffirm that France's government would continue to be revolutionary as long as the war continued, and he squelched any talk of holding new elections. Nor did he suggest putting the new constitution of August 1793, which had been approved with such ceremony, into effect. When he called for justice, not terror, to be the "the order of the day," however, he nevertheless stirred up heated debates about the responsibility for the Terror. The deputy Laurent Lecointre demanded the indictments of Billaud-Varenne, Collot d'Herbois, Barère, and four members of the Committee of General Security for having "covered France with prisons, with a thousand Bastilles." In his first major intervention in a Convention debate, Jean-Marie Goujon rose to object to the danger of calling the entire Revolution into question: "It is the Convention that is accused, it is the French people who are put on trial." The Dantonist Louis Legendre warned that reexamining past events might discredit not only politicians but also "those who burned the chateaux at the beginning of the Revolution," the peasants whose uprising against feudalism in 1789 had made the movement possible.[7]

A public disaster, the explosion of a gunpowder magazine on the rue de Grenelle in Paris, which killed and injured hundreds of victims and did more physical damage to the city's buildings than any of the revolutionary journées, momentarily revived fears of counterrevolutionary plots and diverted attention from politics. But opinion was turning against the Jacobins, and other deputies insisted on denouncing aspects of the Terror that continued to affect the country. On 14 fructidor Year II (August 31, 1794), Grégoire, who even at the time of the de-Christianization campaign had opposed the destruction of artistic monuments linked to the church and the monarchy as "vandalism," presented a lengthy report on that subject. The scientist-deputy Antoine-François Fourcroy joined him, reminding the Convention that "they wanted to burn the libraries; they paralyzed education. . . . [H]ow could you expect citizens to be educated, when all educated men were persecuted, when it was sufficient to have knowledge, to be a man of letters, to be arrested as an aristocrat?" A few weeks later, Edmond Dubois-Crancé denounced accusations against the wealthy, "all those whose fortune sets the talents and the industry of the people in motion, who were pillaged, who were murdered under the accusation of being aristocrats."[8] His speech signaled a campaign against the economic controls associated with the Terror.

The movement that would soon become known as the "thermidorian reaction" was not limited to Paris. Within days of the overthrow of Robespierre, ousters, and, in some cases, arrests, of local officials and activists who had carried out the policies of the Terror began to spread. One of those swept up in the hunt for provincial Robespierrists was Napoleon Bonaparte, the young artillery officer whose career had been advanced by Maximilien's brother Augustin during his mission to Provence. For twelve days, Bonaparte was put under house arrest in Nice. Even after he was freed, his career was derailed for some time. At the local level, the targets were often the most active members of revolutionary committees, who were accused of having carried out arbitrary arrests and abusing their powers; local Jacobins were frequently clapped in jail as the suspects they had earlier imprisoned were released.

As open criticism of the policies inherited from the revolutionary government mounted, the improvised coalition between those who still identified themselves with the revolutionary government and those who were prepared to abandon it fell apart. On 17 fructidor (September 3), the Jacobin Club, the rallying point of those who still identified themselves with the Montagnard regime, expelled Tallien and his close ally Stanislas Fréron, two of the main architects of 9 thermidor. But the Terror's defenders were thrown on the defensive by the start of the trial of ninety-four men from the Breton city of Nantes who had been arrested during the Terror by the deputy Jean-Baptiste Carrier when he was on mission there in the fall of 1793. Testimony at the trials brought out the atrocities Carrier had committed and ordered; as a result, the diehard Jacobins suffered a "terrible blow in public opinion," according to a police report. The defendants were acquitted, and their accusers, the militant terrorists operating under Carrier who had persecuted them and carried out the mass killings in Nantes in late 1793 and early 1794, were themselves put on trial. The former terrorists insisted that Carrier had told them to "empty the prisons" and eliminate not only the Vendean captives but also "the hoarders, the merchants, the federalists, the rich, the moderates": in other words, the bourgeoisie.[9] The trial of the Nantes terrorists precipitated a decisive shift in the political atmosphere. There were cries in the streets and even in the courtroom demanding that Carrier, who was still a sitting member of the Convention and an active participant in the meetings of the Jacobin Club, be put on trial along with the other defendants.

The campaign against Carrier was not entirely spontaneous: after being expelled from the Jacobin Club, some of the thermidorian plotters, particularly Tallien and Fréron, embarked on an all-out war against the remaining defenders of the revolutionary government. Although they were former extremist revolutionaries themselves, they were now willing to ally themselves with people who opposed the movement. Tallien's young wife, Thérèse de Cabarrus—"humanity incarnated in the most ravishing form," as one of her admirers put it—took an active role in her husband's campaign.[10] Her salon became a recruiting ground for former members of moderate and counterrevolutionary political factions whose loyalty to the republic was often suspect. A cohort of young men took over newspapers whose previous editors had fallen victim to the Terror and joined Fréron, whose *Orateur du peuple*, with its circulation of fifteen thousand, had become the most popular political journal in the country, in denouncing the Jacobins.

In addition to waging a war of words, journalists set out to take over Paris's streets and public places. One of these was Isidore Langlois, who had competed with Jacques Ménétra for control of the Bonconseil section in the spring of 1793. Langlois had spent much of the Terror in prison. Aware of the symbolic power of clothing, he and his friends deliberately adopted a costume that announced their distance from the sans-culottes, with their crudely made coats and floppy red liberty caps. Langlois and his allies wore a tailored jacket, a high silk collar, and a top hat. Armed with heavy canes, these *muscadins*, as the members of the thermidorian *jeunesse dorée* (gilded youth) were called, made it their mission to break up gatherings of their opponents in the streets and other places, to the delight of the *merveilleuses*, their female equivalents, whose revealing dresses and extravagant jewelry signaled a rejection of republican austerity. By the beginning of 1795, the jeunesse dorée had acquired an anthem, "Le reveil du peuple" (The awakening of the people), composed by one of their members. Its opening verse was, "French people, people of brothers, / Can you see without a shudder of horror, / Crime unfurling its banners of carnage and terror?" It was sufficient to send a message to any supporters of the Revolution within listening range: if they responded by singing "La Marseillaise," a fight was sure to break out.

The defenders of the Terror were steadily losing ground. The Convention barred the Jacobin clubs from corresponding with each other, thus isolating the Paris club from its network of provincial support.

Members of the jeunesse dorée attacked the dwindling number of Paris Jacobins, and by mid-November, the once mighty club was closed and the deputy Carrier was bound over for trial. Seizing on lurid details from the Nantes trial, which included unsubstantiated claims that the killers had sworn oaths sealed with swigs of their victims' blood, the newspapers made the label *buveurs du sang* (blood-drinkers) a synonym for "Jacobins," fatally damaging their opponents' public image. As other Montagnard deputies had feared, Carrier's attempt to justify himself created problems for all those who had seen the Terror as a harsh but necessary policy. "Today, when things are calm," Carrier argued, "these horrors make us shudder, but remember the times and the circumstances. . . . At the time, we were persuaded that one could not be a patriot without going to extremes. . . . The decrees said to burn and to exterminate. I declare that I told the Convention what I had done. . . . I came back to the Convention, I was well received there, and a year later I am attacked!"[11] Nevertheless, for most of the deputies, the need to demonstrate that the republic itself could punish those who had committed excesses in its name justified Carrier's conviction and execution. The prosecution of Carrier coincided with demands for the rehabilitation of victims of the Terror. Politically, the most burning issue was the fate of "the 73," the Convention deputies imprisoned in the fall of 1793 for having signed a petition in favor of the Girondins. The surviving members of the group and several other deputies, such as Thomas Paine, were released from prison in late October and allowed to resume their seats in the Convention on December 8, 1794. Their readmission tilted the balance of power in the assembly even further toward repudiation of the Terror.

As the deputies debated the policies of the Terror period, members of the population also made their views heard. Widows began a vigorous campaign to recover the property of husbands who had been executed as suspects and to have their names cleared of the accusations of treason. Legislators were inundated with petitions critical of the revolutionary laws on divorce and inheritance. "The social order is entirely overturned," complained the author of one letter objecting to the new rules about the division of family property. Critics maintained that the egalitarian divorce law approved in 1792 had made it dangerously easy for women to "escape the severe observation of a husband"; moreover, the equal division of inheritance, they said, gave women too much independence. "No doubt man is endowed by nature to be the master of woman," one man wrote. "Today, by the law, he becomes her slave." Women did not suffer these challenges in silence. An *Address of the Women Citizens of the Former Normandy* called the inheritance law a necessary correction to practices that had left daughters impoverished while "their brothers lived in idleness and opulence."[12] Although many thermidorian legislators expressed sympathy with charges that revolutionary laws had undermined the basis of authority within the family, for the moment, the major provisions of the laws governing marriage and inheritance were left unchanged.

As the Convention grappled with explosive issues raised by the re-examination of what had been done during the Terror, it still tried to move forward with the remaking of French society. Even during the most troubled moments of 1794, the Convention's Committee on Public Instruction had kept working on plans to replace the patchwork school system of the old regime, for example, which had been crippled by the campaign against the Church. In the heated atmosphere of 1793, the Convention had enacted and then suspended or ignored two proposals: the first, and the most radical, was to have all male children educated in boarding schools; the other was to give parents subsidies to help pay for their children's education at whatever schools they chose. Nothing had actually been done to create a new school system, however. On 7 brumaire Year III (October 28, 1794), the deputy Joseph Lakanal finally introduced a comprehensive proposal on elementary education. His recommendation was founded on the conviction that a common education, shared equally by all citizens and financed by the state, was essential to guarantee the perpetuation of the Revolution's accomplishments. "An enlightened people should be able to keep itself free," his report promised. "How could it be so weak as to suffer chains, if it has a proper idea of man? If it views tyranny with all the horror that it inspires?" The task was a daunting one: Lakanal calculated that a national elementary school system would require 24,000 schools with nearly 40,000 teachers to accommodate some 3.6 million children, 15 percent of the national population. "The goal of our legislators seems to be to make the French not only the freest people, but the most educated in the universe," an approving journalist wrote.[13]

Although the Lakanal law, extensively debated and finally passed on 27 brumaire (November 17), foreshadowed the national educational system that France would finally establish at the end of the nineteenth century, it was too costly and ambitious to be successfully implemented in 1794. Lakanal had more success with his proposal to establish teacher training colleges in Paris and the departments to prepare instructors to provide secondary education. The institution now known as the École normale supérieure (ENS) opened its doors in January 1795 and has attracted many of the country's most outstanding students ever since. The ENS was just one of a number of educational and research institutions founded during the thermidorian period. The École polytechnique, intended to train engineers, had been established a month earlier; like the ENS, it is still a prestigious part of France's higher education system. In December 1794, the Convention passed legislation to establish modern medical schools as well. Their curriculum would be based on reforms proposed in the early years of the Revolution, ending the traditional separation of theoretical medicine from clinical practice and surgery.

The thermidorians, who had abolished the prerevolutionary royal academies in 1793, completed their system of academic institutions just before the final dissolution of the National Convention in October 1795 by creating the Institut national (National Institute), now known as the Institut de France. Unlike the old academies, the Institut was intended as a completely meritocratic institution, with no seats reserved for members chosen on the basis of social status. With separate sections devoted to the natural sciences, the social sciences, and arts and literature, the institute was designed to promote research and invention in all areas of culture. Together with the Musée national d'histoire naturelle (National Museum of Natural History), a center for biological research created in 1793, the new schools and the Institut national gave France a set of scientific and cultural institutions unmatched anywhere else in the world.

The thermidorian Convention's legislation on schooling and the creation of new institutions to replace the abolished royal academies closed the breach between the Revolution and the country's scientists and intellectuals that had opened up during the Terror. Robespierre had denounced them as atheists, and major figures, such as the chemist Antoine Lavoisier and the philosopher-deputy Condorcet, had been executed or driven to suicide. Among the crimes the thermidorians now heaped on Robespierre's head was his alleged effort to "persuade the people that enlightenment is dangerous and only serves to mislead them." In April 1795, the Convention sponsored the first publication of Condorcet's *Sketch of the Progress of the Human Mind*, which had affirmed the inevitable triumph of reason; the work provided an ideological legitimation of the republic. Even during the Terror, however, writers and savants imbued with the secular spirit of the eighteenth century had refused to believe that the revolutionary movement would entirely reject them. At the end of April 1794, a group of them had put out the first issue of a new journal, the *Décade philosophique*, welcoming the democratization of intellectual and artistic life: "No more obstacles or humiliations for developing genius; no more injustices to fear, no need to court the powerful, no need to accept humiliations," it proclaimed.[14] Careful to toe the official revolutionary line in the months before thermidor, the *Décade philosophique* subsequently became the central organ for those who saw the post-Robespierrist republic as a chance to create a society governed by the dictates of science and reason.

At the same time as they were taking actions that encouraged the disciples of the Enlightenment to embrace the republic, the thermidorians also had to grapple with the religious issues that had fueled so much of the violence of the Terror period. Even though the Convention, at Robespierre's urging, had condemned the violent de-Christianization campaign in December 1793 and promised that freedom of worship would be respected, public religious observances of any kind had virtually ceased. Refractory priests, or *non-jureurs*—those who had refused to take the government-imposed oaths—were in hiding, in prison, or in exile, and many of the constitutional Catholic clergy and Protestant ministers who had taken the oath—the *jureurs*—had renounced their religious functions altogether. The Enlightenment-inspired intellectuals who dominated France's new academic institutions remained critical of religion and opposed any governmental backsliding that might allow the Church to recover its influence. In their circles, the most-discussed new book of 1795 was Charles-François Dupuis's *Origine de tous les cultes, ou religion universelle* (The origin of all cults, or universal religion), a milestone in the comparative study of religion. Dupuis argued that religious beliefs were human creations inspired by efforts to placate the forces of nature. In his view, the light-bringer "designated by Christians under the name of Christ, is nothing but the sun, or the divinity adored by all peoples, under so many different forms and names."[15]

A thermidorian law passed on a revolutionary calendar "leap day," 2 jour complémentaire Year II (September 18, 1794), cut off the salaries that had continued to be paid to priests of the constitutional church: legally speaking, the church and the state were now completely separated. In practice, private gatherings for religious purposes were tolerated, but public worship remained restricted. Grégoire, the leader of the remaining constitutional clergy and the country's most dedicated defender of religious liberty, complained that "freedom of worship exists in Turkey; it does not exist in France." Many of the thermidorians had been leading proponents of de-Christianization, and they were not sympathetic. The Dantonist Legendre retorted, "I thought that we were sufficiently advanced in revolution to not occupy ourselves any further with religion."[16]

Grégoire finally persuaded his colleagues to pass a law protecting religious observances as long as they were organized as private initiatives. The law of 3 ventôse Year III (February 21, 1795) treated all religions equally and implied a policy of state neutrality, committing France to accepting religious diversity. Catholics were quick to resume regular worship. "Our churches are not big enough to hold all those who want to go hear mass," a Paris newspaper wrote.[17] The law did not satisfy either the remaining supporters of the constitutional church, who continued to call the government's attention to what they regarded as the subversive activities of their more numerous refractory opponents, or those Catholics who continued to reject the revolutionary church reforms. From their refuges in neighboring countries, exiled refractory bishops sent "apostolic vicars" to try to restart regular worship in parishes that had lost their priests during the Terror. The bishops were concerned not only to defy the hostility of the republican government, but also to limit the spread of new forms of Catholic worship that had been organized by laymen and laywomen during the Terror: the people had become accustomed to holding "white masses" in the absence of priests, an initiative that threatened to undermine the Church's traditional hierarchy.

The returning refractory priests found many allies among women. "These women who should be caring for their households, seeing to the happiness of their husbands and the raising of their children, go from family to family and bore or disturb them with their ridiculous theological gabbling," the journal of the constitutional clergy complained. As for the refractory priests themselves, it said, "they redo confessions, remarry people, rebaptize. . . . [T]hey commit a bunch of extravagances that go against the simple and healthy notions of religion." Among other things, the "constitutionals" accused their rivals of warning that the purchasers of expropriated church properties would have to return them, a threat bound to unsettle the new owners. The adherents of the refractory church were relieved to be able to receive the sacraments again, and in some communities they did recover the use of the church buildings. "Public worship, June 29, BY THE GRACE OF GOD," the nun Gabrielle Gauchat noted in her journal.[18] But they still longed for the restoration of such manifestations of the Catholic Church's privileged position in public life as the ringing of church bells and the right of priests and other religious to wear their distinctive clothing in public.

The easing of restrictions on religious worship was accompanied by measures to temper some of the most rigorous edicts against the émigrés who had fled the country during the Terror. A law of 20 nivôse Year III (January 10, 1795) permitted the return of peasants or artisans who had left after the journée of May 31, 1793, when the Girondins had been ousted from the Convention. This edict benefited thousands of Alsatian peasants who had crossed the Rhine with the retreating Austrian army, as well as silkworkers from Lyon who had fled to escape repression after the federalist revolt. Grégoire's law on religious freedom permitted émigré priests to return if they were willing to swear an oath to defend liberty and equality; they no longer had to approve the Civil Constitution that the pope had condemned.

As the thermidorians eased the campaign against the Church and offered amnesty for some of the émigrés, they also tried to bring the conflicts in the rebellious regions of the west under control. Even before Robespierre's fall, the Committee of Public Safety had recalled General Louis-Marie Turreau and ended the indiscriminate killing of civilians in the Vendée. On February 17, 1795, François Charette, the main Vendean leader, signed a treaty at the chateau of La Jaunaye. Its provisions included permission for the refractory church to hold services in the region and a promise that its inhabitants would not be conscripted for the army or required to pay taxes for a period of ten years. By the late spring of 1795, the government in Paris thought it had finally ended the civil war that had cost thousands of lives and threatened the very survival of the Revolution.

The end of active fighting in western France coincided with military advances beyond France's frontiers. Throughout the fall, French soldiers consolidated the advantages they had gained in Belgium after their victory at Fleurus. The soldiers at the front paid a high price for these successes, but many of them continued to voice patriotic sentiments in their letters home. "It's been two months that we've been sleeping on the same straw in our gopher holes," a captain in the Army of the Rhine wrote to his mother in late 1794. "However, the hope of seeing our country triumph over all its enemies makes us bear our sufferings with patience." The thermidorians seized on these military achievements to fan an increasingly aggressive form of nationalism. When the war had begun in 1792, it had been heralded as an idealistic crusade to bring freedom to other people. During the desperate struggles to beat off invaders, patriotism meant defending French territory. Now victories were celebrated as proof of French superiority over other countries. Good news from the Caribbean added to the sense that France was reaffirming its position as a world power. The republican commissioner Victor Hugues ousted the British from Guadeloupe, and a letter from Saint-Domingue announced that "Toussaint Bréda has taken Saint-Michel and Saint-Raphaël," two towns in Spanish Santo Domingo. It was the first mention in the French press of the black general Toussaint Louverture.[19]

At the beginning of 1795, the French invaded the Netherlands. The approach of the French revived the Dutch republican movement, which had challenged the authority of its ruler, the stadholder Willem V, before being crushed by Prussian intervention in 1787. A number of Dutch Patriots had taken refuge in France. In 1793, they had hoped that Dumouriez's invasion would reach their country and formed a military legion to participate in his campaign. The collapse of the first French invasion of the Low Countries had disappointed them, but they continued to agitate for the "liberation" of their homeland. Inside the country, Patriots formed a network of clubs disguised as "reading societies" to prepare for a revolutionary uprising once French aid was close enough to support them.

While Dutch republicans prepared to enact their own version of 1789, the French republicans were no longer in the mood to encourage radical upheavals; the thermidorian Committee of Public Safety was more concerned with obtaining military advantages against the British and economic resources for its own war effort. Thanks to a bitterly cold winter whose effects were causing the French government increasing concern at home, military developments unfolded quickly. By mid-January, the multiple branches of the Rhine River that traditionally obstructed invading armies were frozen over, allowing the French to break through the enemy defenses and reach Amsterdam. As the French advanced, the leaders of the Dutch club movement ousted the stadholder's supporters from local governments and proclaimed a "Batavian Republic." As far as the Dutch republicans were concerned, they had carried out their own revolution, albeit with French support, and their hope was to be recognized as an independent ally rather than being treated like their neighbors in Belgium.

The victorious French generals saw things differently. One of them advised the Committee of Public Safety that "it was the ice, the indefatigable courage of our troops and the talents of our generals which delivered [Holland] and not any revolution. It follows from this that there can be no reason to treat her any differently from a conquered country."[20] The French were convinced that the Netherlands, whose wealth they greatly overestimated, could be tapped for almost unlimited amounts of money. They initially planned to annex several key pieces of Dutch territory to strengthen their military position. Dutch opposition led to some softening of the terms, as did belated French recognition of the danger of alienating the population, but the price of becoming a *république soeur* (sister republic) was still substantial for the Dutch: an indemnity of 100 million Dutch florins, the obligation to pay for the French army of occupation, and entry into the war on the French side. These provisions resulted in the disruption of the country's overseas trade and the loss of most Dutch overseas colonies to the British. The arrangements created a model that the French would follow as they expanded their conquests in the years that followed.

In January 1795, the Prussian government agreed to enter negotiations with France, signaling its intention to withdraw from the coalition of major powers opposing the republic. For the French, whose diplomacy was now under the direction of the veteran revolutionary Sieyès, the negotiations offered an opportunity to obtain a natural frontier on the Rhine through annexation of various occupied German territories. The Treaty of Basel, signed on April 5, 1795, included clauses promising that Berlin would not object to these annexations if the French eventually negotiated a general peace with the Holy Roman Empire. In return, the French would make sure Prussia was compensated with land elsewhere in Germany. If republican France succeeded in ending the war on favorable terms, a reshaping of the entire map of Germany that would transform the balance of power in Europe would now be a necessary consequence.

At the same time that French diplomacy was detaching Prussia from the enemy coalition, negotiations were under way with the Bourbons of Spain. In addition to gains along their southern frontier, the French pressed for concessions in the Americas, indicating that the republic had no intention of abandoning its overseas empire. Initially, Sieyès and the Committee of Public Safety hoped to regain the whole of the Louisiana Territory, which France had ceded to Spain after the Seven Years' War. "It is more important than one can say in a letter to have a continental [American] colony at the end of a revolution," the instructions sent to the French negotiator read.[21] In the end, the French had to settle for the eastern half of the island of Hispaniola, which had been divided between their colony of Saint-Domingue and Spanish Santo Domingo, today's Dominican Republic. The peace with Spain put the French in a favorable position. Only one significant continental power—Austria—remained at war with them, and it was now clear that the other states of Europe were prepared to live with a republic that had executed its king.

The success of the republic depended not only on victories abroad but also on the government's ability to retain the loyalty of its population at home. That loyalty was tested to the limit in the first half of 1795. The icy temperatures that froze the Dutch rivers and facilitated the French victory there in January were part of a cold wave such as Western Europe had not seen in nearly a century. For the population, the timing could not have been worse. Since the fall of 1794, the deputies of the Convention had abandoned their attempt to regulate the economy through the maximum. Initially, the idea of not enforcing the law of the maximum had some popular support. Workers of all kinds had rebelled against its limits on their wages, and merchants at Paris's central market, the Halle, insisted that "free trade in edible goods, no more maximum, complete liberty," was "the only way to bring down the cost of food."[22] Most of the deputies were at heart believers in the virtues of economic freedom, and the practical problems of enforcing the maximum were painfully evident. The moderate deputy Antoine Thibaudeau called the law "the sole source of all the misfortunes we have suffered." In his view, it had "covered France with a swarm of black marketeers and ruined the men of good faith who respected your laws."[23] On 4 nivôse Year III (December 24, 1794), the Convention abolished all price limits on goods, although it left local authorities with the power to requisition food supplies if necessary.

However necessary the abolition of the maximum may have been, in the short run it proved catastrophic for much of the population. The harvest of the fall of 1794 was below normal, and the end of the Terror sent the Revolution's paper currency into a disastrous free fall. For the poor, the combination of short supplies and diminishing purchasing power led to destitution. Their problems were compounded by the government's decision to lay off workers who had been employed in the workshops set up to supply the army. The cold weather that set in toward the end of 1794 made the situation apocalyptic. Supplies of firewood and coal, needed for heating and cooking, ran short as the Seine froze, cutting off the normal transportation route for those bulky commodities.

The reports from the Paris police for the last months of 1794 and the first part of 1795 could easily have been titled "Les misérables." Week after week, police observers chronicled the difficulties the population faced in obtaining bread. Grain reserves shrank and bakers could not obtain fuel to heat their furnaces. Daily rations were cut, finally dwindling to a mere half a pound, but even at that level, supplies often ran out before all customers had been served. Fearing that they would be left out, women began lining up outside the bakeries in the early morning hours; eventually, some began standing in the cold before midnight, prepared to stay all night to get food for their families. At the quays on the Seine, the distribution of firewood and coal provoked daily scuffles. An unusually outspoken police report laid out the situation in stark terms:

> It is of the greatest importance and of the greatest justice to come to the aid of the most indigent class, which cannot manage to procure what it most urgently needs because of the enormity of the rapid rise in prices. It is above all of the greatest importance to reassure this hardworking and useful class about the supply of bread, which is, so to speak, its only food. . . . It is to be feared that, if worries about this essential matter continue, the ill-intentioned will take advantage of the general discontent to cause some violent commotions.[24]

Another constant theme in the police reports from late 1794 and early 1795 were the activities of the jeunesse dorée. The deputy Stanislas Fréron had turned the members of the group into an anti-Jacobin strike force. Well enough off to ignore the mounting hunger in the streets, the young men gathered daily in cafés in the Palais-Egalité to talk politics and coordinate editorial campaigns in the numerous newspapers they controlled. In the afternoons and evenings, they set out to harass their foes. During the fall, they frequently clashed, not always successfully, with militant women who had turned the public galleries of the Convention into one of the few remaining Jacobin strongholds. In one incident, a woman punched a jeunesse dorée member and told him, "It would be better for you to go to the front like our husbands." In January 1795, the jeunesse dorée began to rid the Paris theaters and other public places of the busts of Marat that had been put up after his assassination in 1793. "A hundred young men gathered in the foyer, overturned the bust and threw it in the fire," two police agents at the Théâtre des Arts reported on 14 pluviôse Year II (February 2, 1794).[25] A few weeks later, Marat's ashes were expelled from the Pantheon; jeunesse dorée members seized the urn containing them and dumped the contents into a sewer. Plaster busts and urns were not their only targets: when actors and actresses who had supported the Jacobin movement appeared on stage, the young men greeted them with catcalls, demanding that they apologize for their actions and sing the anthem of the jeunesse dorée, the "Réveil du peuple" (Awakening of the people) with its violent lyrics.

The political meaning of the language and behavior of the jeunesse dorée was ambiguous. In public, members of the group affirmed their loyalty to the Convention and to the republic, but they had a broad definition of "blood-drinkers." Their newspapers hailed the reopening of the churches and religious schools, whose teachers would now be able to teach their students "the principles of religion, without which a man can only be a brigand and an entire nation a horde of criminals." Another paper questioned the need for continuing the war: "If we really want peace, let us give up the Rhine frontier." The police were aware that royalist sentiments were circulating among the population: a report in early March mentioned mysterious individuals who would ask people they passed in the streets, "How much is fifteen plus two?" After the respondent gave the answer, "Seventeen," the reply was, "That's what we need." It was an easily decoded reference to the imprisoned Dauphin, who was regarded as "King Louis XVII" by those who remained loyal to the monarchy.[26]

In their newspapers, the young men of the jeunesse dorée aggressively criticized not just Jacobins but the poor in general. For the first time since 1789, sentimental rhetoric about the common people was replaced with contempt. The *Gazette française* had no sympathy for the working women who expressed fears about the impact of the abolition of the maximum: "Most of them can't remember the past and can't think ahead to the future," the paper's editor wrote. The right-wing writers' sympathies went instead to members of the wealthier classes who had suffered during the Revolution. "Their fate is only more appalling, because in them humiliation is joined to misfortune," Charles Lacretelle wrote. As agitation about bread shortages mounted, the jeunesse dorée broke up groups complaining about food prices. In response, workers from the city's faubourgs began to strike back at "the golden million, the muscadins, the shopkeepers and Fréron's young men."[27] There were fights in the Palais-Egalité in which the young men were thrown into its fountain.

The men who fought the young dandies around the Palais-Egalité and the women who egged them on had their own political ideas. At times, the police overheard mutterings that bread had never been so scarce under the monarchy, and they worried about a possible movement of popular royalism. More often, however, the poor seemed to be reviving the ideas of the Enragés of 1793 and the Montagnards of 1794. "They talked about the regime prior to 9 thermidor," one police agent reported, "when goods were not so costly and silver was on a par with the assignats." Toward the end of the month of ventôse, a printed poster calling for "bread and the Constitution of 93" appeared on walls in the faubourgs of Saint-Antoine and Saint-Michel, the traditional breeding grounds for insurrections. Aware of the rising anger in the streets, the deputies of the National Convention responded on 1 germinal Year III (March 21, 1795) by passing a harsh "law of high police" proposed by Sieyès. The measure authorized the repression of any opposition to the government, increasing the perception that the Convention had turned against the poor.

If anyone thought the 9th of thermidor had brought the sequence of tumultuous revolutionary journées to an end, events on 12 germinal (April 1) showed otherwise. On that morning, some Paris sections cut the bread ration to its lowest level yet: a quarter of a pound per person. It was too much for the long-suffering population. "A very numerous crowd forced their way into the Convention's hall, loudly demanding bread, the Constitution of 1793 and the release from prison of the patriots," the Moniteur reported. With support from the spectators in the galleries, several deputies from the Convention's extreme left called on their colleagues to accept the people's demands, which were voiced by one of the marchers: "It is time that the indigent class not be the victim of the egoism of the rich and the selfishness of the merchants. . . . Render justice against Fréron's army, these *messieurs* with their big sticks."[28]

As the session dragged on—the deputies would not finally adjourn until 6:00 a.m. the following morning—the demonstrators gradually departed. But the thermidorians turned what had started like a reenactment of the popular uprisings of 1792 and 1793 into a remake of the day Robespierre was overthrown. Their anger mounting as they proceeded, the deputies decreed the immediate deportation of three former members of the pre-thermidor Committee of Public Safety: Billaud-Varenne, Collot d'Herbois, and Barère. They also wanted the arrest of six of their colleagues who had endorsed the demands of the crowd earlier in the day as well as of several former Robespierrists who had escaped earlier purges. The deputies to be deported would be sent to Cayenne, a remote French colony on the coast of South America that was nicknamed "the dry guillotine" because of its unhealthy climate.

With the situation still explosive in Paris, the country was also rocked by a series of violent outbreaks in the Rhône valley in the southeast, where the political passions aroused by the federalist revolts in 1793 and their violent repression in 1794 combined with the desperation generated by the rigorous winter and the food shortages that went along with it. In Lyon, young men similar to the Parisian jeunesse dorée joined with survivors of the executions ordered by Fouché and Collot d'Herbois a year earlier; they formed an organized network that publicly identified former "terrorists" and demanded their punishment. On 15 floréal Year III (May 4, 1795), a crowd of over thirty thousand people stormed the city prisons, where many former Jacobins had been incarcerated; they killed over one hundred of the prisoners, dumping their bodies in the Saône River. When the deputy on mission in the city called on the killers to obey the law, they answered, "At the moment, your voice is stifled by the cries of our massacred relatives who cry out for vengeance."[29] In the months that followed, similar massacres took place in Marseille and other nearby cities. All over the region, former revolutionary activists in other towns fled their homes to escape the wave of *Terreur blanche* (White Terror) that the authorities seemed unable or unwilling to control. Just as denunciations of "blood-drinkers" could be counted on to incite hatred of former Jacobins, references to the *égorgeurs* (cutthroats) *du Midi*, the anti-terrorist murder gangs of the region known as the Midi in the southeast of France, became a reliable tool for republicans, who used it to rally their followers against suspected opponents of the Revolution.

Spring brought an end to the bitter cold in Paris, but months remained before the arrival of the new harvest. In the meantime, supplies dwindled to the point where the poor, who depended on the daily bread ration for their sustenance, faced literal starvation. "All one sees in the streets are pale and pinched faces, showing the effects of sadness, exhaustion, hunger and misery," a journalist wrote.[30] People fainted from hunger in the streets, and the police reported an alarming increase in suicides. Determined not to go back to the policies of Year II, the government continued to allow pastry shops to sell fancy cakes to clients with money, even as bakers had so little flour that they were unable to furnish their customers with the minuscule daily bread ration, which at times was cut to a mere two ounces. Riots outside the bakeries were a daily occurrence, and illegal assemblies in the sections showed that the defeat of the germinal uprising had done nothing to silence popular discontent. Convinced that the Convention's deputies had lost all interest in their fate, the population increasingly wanted to see them replaced by new legislators chosen by the democratic procedures promised in the Constitution of 1793.

Acutely aware of the danger of a renewed insurrection, the Convention's military committee summoned troops to Paris. As in July 1789, however, the soldiers showed an alarming tendency to sympathize with the people. Members of one unit swore that "they were not going to kill people half-dead from hunger." On 30 floréal Year III (May 19, 1795), a printed call for an "Insurrection of the people, to obtain bread and reconquer its rights," circulated in the streets. It urged the citizens to march on the Convention. The germinal uprising had been a demonstration; the journée that took place a few days later, on 1 prairial Year III (May 20, 1795), was a genuine attempt to replace the government. The anonymous authors of the "Insurrection of the people" summoned the men and women of Paris to act on behalf of the entire nation. Justifying their revolt on the grounds that the Convention was "making the people die inhumanely from hunger," they demanded the immediate arrest of all the members of the Convention's governing committees, implementation of the Constitution of 1793, immediate national elections, and a new assembly. In the meantime, Paris would be put under a state of emergency: the city's barriers were to be closed except for those bringing in provisions and all public officials suspended from office. "The people will not stand down until it has ensured the subsistence, the happiness, the tranquility and the freedom of all the French," the document promised.[31]

More than any other journée of the Revolution except for the October Days of 1789, the uprising of 1 prairial Year III was the work of women. All over the city, groups of them ran through the streets exhorting their neighbors to join the march on the Convention. They invaded the offices of the sections to demand that their battalions be mobilized "for the good cause," sometimes threatening the recalcitrant with knives or appropriating the guard units' drums to sound the call to arms.[32] By the time the Convention began its session at 11:00 a.m., women had filled the galleries, shouting and gesticulating at the deputies. The men were slower to arrive, but by the middle of the afternoon, armed battalions from the Faubourg Saint-Antoine, the traditional stronghold of popular militantism, assembled outside the deputies' meeting hall. As on 12 germinal, the Convention counted on National Guard battalions from the more bourgeois sections of the city to come to its aid, but the prairial insurrection was so widespread—the crowd, estimated at thirty-five thousand, was the largest of any of the revolutionary journées—that even those units proved unreliable.

At exactly 3:33 p.m., according to the Moniteur's account, the attackers battered down the door to the assembly hall and surged into the room, driving the legislators from their benches. In the confusion, the deputy Jean-Bertrand Féraud was killed and his head sawed off: for all the violence the Revolution had seen, this was the first and only time a legislator was actually murdered in the assembly's own meeting place. For several hours, the conservative thermidorian François Boissy d'Anglas sat immobile in the president's chair, even when members of the crowd thrust the pike holding Féraud's severed head in his face: he was determined to prevent the crowd from intimidating the legislators into approving any of the decrees they repeatedly demanded. By evening, the crowd was becoming impatient: their insurrectionary plan depended on getting the Convention to endorse their demands. When Boissy d'Anglas finally yielded the chair to another deputy, several of the Convention's remaining Montagnards, including the idealistic Jean-Marie Goujon, put forward motions that won the support of the popular militants: the release of political prisoners jailed after 9 thermidor and 12 germinal; a requirement that bakers make only one kind of bread, to be shared equally with all customers; broader rights for the section assemblies; and the arrest of journalists who "poisoned public spirit." The deputies who proposed these measures later defended themselves by claiming they had hoped to calm the crowd and get them to disperse. The alternative, the Montagnard Gilbert Romme claimed, would have been to allow the exasperated demonstrators to "seize the right to speak, to deliberate, to exercise authority, and to complete the dissolution of the national representation."[33]

Romme and the other Montagnard deputies then moved to replace the Committee of General Security, which was at that moment coordinating efforts to defeat the insurrection, with a provisional commission. Even though Goujon's mother had come to urge him not to keep the oath to "live free or die" that he had made at the time of the Festival of the Federation in 1790, he accepted a place on the commission. Knowing that he might have to keep his promise; he told a colleague, "The people are suffering, someone must sacrifice himself for them."[34] This effort to replace the governing committees allowed their opponents to charge that the Montagnards had tried to overthrow the lawful government. By now it was almost midnight, and most of the demonstrators had dispersed. Suddenly, troops loyal to the thermidorians entered the meeting hall; it was the first time in the Revolution that soldiers were deployed among the deputies. Boissy d'Anglas retook control of the proceedings, and the deputies quickly annulled all the decrees passed earlier in the evening. They also decreed the arrest of fourteen of their Montagnard colleagues, who were accused of collaborating with the insurgents.

Parliamentary decrees were not enough to end the uprising, however. Agitation in the sections resumed the next morning, and unauthorized assemblies sent representatives to a general meeting to create a city-wide communal assembly. This threat to resurrect the Paris Commune, which had been abolished after thermidor, caused alarm in the Convention: many deputies remembered only too well how the insurgents of August 10, 1792, had used a similar assembly to overthrow the monarchy. Many of the section battalions again converged on the Convention with their artillery. "Today we have the force and the section of Montreuil is determined to sweep away all the beggars of the Convention," one gunner announced.[35] Some of the deputies addressed the tense crowd in a last-ditch effort to convince the insurgents that it would take urgent action to deal with the hunger crisis and prepare the implementation of the constitution. They were just persuasive enough to defuse the situation, and by 11:00 p.m., most of the armed men who had threatened them had gone home.

After two days of inconclusive confrontations, the insurgents were tired and uncertain of what to do next. Meanwhile, the Convention assembled reliable military forces. Their immediate objective was to recapture the apprentice lockmaker Jean Tinel, who had been arrested and condemned to death for carrying the head of the massacred deputy Féraud on a pike. As he was being taken to the Place de Grève to be executed on the evening of 3 prairial (May 22), Tinel was freed by a crowd and taken back to the Faubourg Saint-Antoine in triumph. The Convention's forces also had a broader aim, however: they meant to break the power of the populace of Paris once and for all. Only "good citizens who had wealth to protect" were summoned to take up arms. All told, the Convention's forces amounted to more than twenty thousand men. The faubourg residents lacked leadership and yielded without a serious fight once the military operation against them began. Tinel was captured and executed, and a wave of arrests swept up not only active participants in the just-concluded journées, but all the revolutionary militants active during the Terror. Shaken by the role that women, "either misled or incited by the enemies of liberty," had played in the uprising, the Convention passed decrees ordering them to "retire . . . to their homes" and forbidding them to form groups in the street. Taken over by the *honnêtes hommes* (literally, "honest men"), the advocates of stern measures to enforce order, the Paris sections wreaked vengeance on the defeated "terrorists, assassins, blood-drinkers, thieves and agents," as the assembly of the Brutus section called them.[36]

A military commission was set up to try the leading insurgents as speedily as possible. Of the thirty-six death sentences it pronounced, the most important were those imposed on six Montagnard Convention deputies, including Goujon, Romme, and Ernest Duquesnoy, who had taken sides with the demonstrators on the evening of 1 prairial. Friends had managed to smuggle a knife and a pair of scissors into the prison; rather than submitting to execution, the condemned men each stabbed themselves and then passed the blades on. "I want my blood to be the last that flows," Duquesnoy said as he lay dying. "May it consolidate the Republic."[37] Their gesture, which evoked the stoic courage of ancient Roman republicans, immortalized them as the "martyrs of prairial." Their dedication to their principles stood in sharp contrast to the opportunism of thermidorian leaders like Tallien and Barras, who had identified themselves with radicalism during Year II but were now leading the campaign against the former terrorists. For the moment, the thermidorians were in firm control of the Convention, but a network of former Montagnards, including Goujon's comrade Pierre-François Tissot, remained loyal to the ideals that had motivated the martyrs of prairial and hoped for an opportunity to reinvigorate the republican movement.

Although democratic republicanism still had significant support in the country, the defeat of the prairial uprising marked the end of the Parisian popular movement that had exercised such a powerful influence on the course of the Revolution. There would not be another revolt of the lower classes in the city's streets until the July Revolution of 1830 a generation later. Even had the prairial insurgents succeeded in disrupting the Convention, it is doubtful that they would have found enough support outside the capital to revive the militant republicanism of the Terror. The triumphant thermidorian leaders of the Convention could now ignore popular demands for bread: the demoralized sansculottes were left to fend for themselves until the new harvest brought some relief.

Shaken by the germinal and prairial uprisings, the deputies decided to make it clear that the democratic constitution of 1793 would never be put into effect. From the time of Robespierre's overthrow, there had been some sentiment for returning to the Constitution of 1791. Since Louis XVI's son, the Dauphin, was only ten years old, there were those who thought the Convention could appoint a regency council to run the government; they assumed the boy could be indoctrinated to accept the role of a constitutional monarch when he came of age. The child's health had been broken by his long imprisonment in the Temple, however, and on June 8, 1795, he died. The throne now fell to Louis XVI's brother, the comte de Provence, who had escaped from France at the time of the flight to Varennes in 1791. He was now living in the Italian city of Verona. Had he been willing to come back under the terms of the Constitution of 1791, he might well have been welcomed, but such an arrangement would have required him to forge a compromise with some of the men who had overthrown the monarchy and voted for the execution of his brother. In a declaration issued on June 24, 1795, the comte de Provence proclaimed himself the rightful ruler of France under the name Louis XVIII. Comparing himself to Henri IV, who had battled his way to the throne and ended the wars of religion in France two hundred years earlier, Louis XVIII refused to accept any of the changes the revolutionaries had made. The thermidorians, as far as he was concerned, were "treacherous and cruel usurpers" who deserved punishment. If he returned to France, he would restore the "ancient and wise constitution" of the monarchy, the authority of the Catholic Church, and the distinctions between the three orders that had been abolished in 1789.[38]

Louis XVIII's intransigent stance forced even those politicians who might have secretly been inclined to hope for a restoration to work toward a more stable republican constitution. Just as the news of Louis XVIII's proclamation arrived in France, the royalist cause suffered a further setback: the defeat of a British-backed attempt to land an army of French émigrés in Brittany. The plan's architect, Joseph de Puisaye, had won the support of the British, who put some 4,500 troops ashore on the Quiberon Peninsula on the south coast of Brittany at the end of June 1795. This force was a mixture of émigré nobles devoted to the royalist cause and captured French soldiers whom the British pressured into joining the expedition.

The émigrés succeeded in linking up with chouan rebels in the area, but the republican general, Lazare Hoche, prevented them from expanding outside their Quiberon beachhead. Expected British reinforcements never arrived, and on July 21, 1795, Hoche's men captured the fort that commanded the entry to the peninsula. "It was a total debacle," wrote Gaston de Lévis, the onetime noble deputy to the National Assembly who had fled France in 1792 and joined the counterrevolutionary forces, in a letter to his wife.[39] The thermidorian deputy Tallien, rumored to be among the deputies who would have accepted a constitutional monarch, showed no mercy to the émigré nobles. In accordance with the decree sentencing any émigré captured "with arms in hand" to death, he had 748 of them executed, although the rank-and-file soldiers and chouan rebels were pardoned; Lévis was one of the few nobles who managed to escape back to England. The disaster at Quiberon caused lasting damage to the royalist cause. Supporters of constitutional and absolutist monarchy blamed each other for the catastrophe, and conspiracy theories that the British might have deliberately set the expedition up to fail as a way of weakening their traditional enemy sowed distrust between the émigrés and their hosts.

Meanwhile, the deputies of the Convention were turning their attention once again to the original goal of the Revolution: making a constitution that would finally bring order and stability to the country while protecting the principles of liberty and equality proclaimed in 1789. Because of his crucial role in 1789, Sieyès expected to dominate the committee appointed to draft the new constitution, but he quickly realized that his colleagues disagreed with him about many crucial points. He promptly resigned, nursing a grudge that would resurface four years later. The remaining members of the committee, moderate thermidorians and former Girondins, were in general agreement on two points: that the political influence of the common people needed to be sharply reduced, and that there needed to be a real division of powers to prevent a recurrence of the kind of dictatorial authority that the Convention had exercised during the Terror.

The argument that only owners of property could be trusted to make rational decisions had justified the distinction between active and passive citizens adopted in 1789, but in the wake of the germinal and prairial uprisings, it was voiced far more crudely. "Poets, novelists, dishonest philosophers have praised the simplicity, the incorruptibility, the honesty of villagers, of artisans. . . . This portrayal is far from the truth," a Paris newspaper announced as the deputies debated whether to restrict the right to vote to owners of property. "Selfishness and jealousy are passions that tear the human heart beneath thatched roofs as beneath gilded ceilings." Some writers, reasoning from the proposition that owners of property had a right to order anyone else off their land, concluded that non-property-owners were in no sense citizens, since those who did own property could unite and expel everyone else from the country. "The non-property-owner . . . cannot have any role in the government, and he is limited to obeying the laws *that are imposed on him*, violating them when he can and being hanged when he is caught," one pamphleteer wrote. Charles Duval, whose *Journal des hommes libres* (Journal of free men) would be the most dogged defender of democracy until Napoleon's seizure of power, expressed his indignation at conservatives who "tell you openly that even the word 'democracy' should be forgotten." He observed sourly that "in 1793 it was common to treat great landed property as a violation of the rights of men," whereas "now it is fashionable to place [the exercise of] national sovereignty in landed property."[40]

Duval was fighting a losing battle: in his speech outlining the principles that the Committee of Eleven had decided to follow in drafting the new constitution, Boissy d'Anglas, the hero of the prairial days, left no doubt about their determination to exclude the poor from meaningful political participation. "We must be governed by the best," he proclaimed. "The best are those who are best educated and most interested in the maintenance of the laws: now, with very few exceptions, you find such men only among those who, owning a piece of property, are devoted to the country that contains it, to the laws that protect it, to the tranquility that maintains it."[41] The assembly settled on a system of indirect elections, with electoral colleges that would actually choose the deputies. They set a high property qualification for members of the electoral colleges, rather than for the deputies themselves, claiming that in this way, poorer citizens could still be elected.

Unlike the first two revolutionary constitutions, the Constitution of 1795, or Year III, established a bicameral legislature. "I will pause only briefly to remind you of the unavoidable dangers of a single assembly," Boissy told his colleagues. "To help me, I have your own history, of which you are all aware."[42] The example of the Convention had shown that "an unexpected circumstance, an enthusiasm, a popular misconception," could easily lead a single assembly to enact unwise laws. The example of the United States' constitution, with its provision for a popularly elected House of Representatives and a more restricted Senate, showed that a republic with a two-house legislature could exist. Since revolutionary France had definitively rejected any kind of federal system, however, there was no obvious basis for two different assemblies, and the Convention was certainly not willing to create a hereditary upper chamber like the British House of Lords. Instead, both chambers of the new assembly would be elected by the same voters, but the larger of the two, the Conseil des cinq-cents (Council of Five Hundred), open to deputies as young as twenty-five, would propose laws, while the Conseil des anciens (Council of Elders), whose 250 members had to be over the age of forty and married or widowed, would give them a second consideration and propose amendments. One-third of the deputies in both councils would be elected every year. The design of the new government's executive branch was even touchier than the creation of two legislative chambers. Proposals to create an American-style presidency chosen by the voters were rejected: the former Girondin Louvet warned that such a system might allow the electors to install a Bourbon prince in power. Instead, the constitution created a five-man executive council, to be known as the Directory. Its members were to be chosen by the legislature rather than being elected by the people, which the constitution makers feared would give the directors too much authority. According to the constitution's provisions, one member of the Directory would be replaced each year.

As in 1789 and 1793, the question of whether to include a declaration of rights in the constitution generated fierce debates. Some wanted to do away with a declaration altogether, arguing that, as conservatives had predicted in 1789, the original one had provided grounds for attacks on laws that supposedly violated individual natural rights. The declaration they finally adopted retained the basic format of the earlier versions but was unmistakably more conservative. The 1795 declaration's first article specified that it listed only the "rights of man in society," ruling out the appeals to natural rights that conservatives feared. In a reversal of the order in the 1793 declaration, liberty was defined before equality, and there was no mention of the right of insurrection that had been acknowledged in the two previous declarations. A proposal to include welfare rights in the declaration was scuttled because it might justify demands that the government provide "work or bread," as the insurgents had demanded in germinal and prairial.[43] Religious freedom was not mentioned in the declaration, although a clause of the constitution, which ran in the end to 377 articles, protected it, while also forbidding state support for any religious organization. Freedom of the press was included in Article 355, which also reiterated the 1791 ban on guilds and the promise of unrestricted economic freedom. During the Terror, these freedoms had been limited without any constitutional basis; Article 355 foresaw the possibility of their suspension in a crisis, but promised that any such action would only be in effect for at most a year.

Despite its conservative coloration, the 1795 declaration of rights retained some of the language of its more radical predecessors. It reaffirmed that "the law is the general will" and that "sovereignty resides essentially in the universal body of citizens," and it acknowledged that all citizens had a right to participate in debates about the laws and the election of deputies, even if the constitution's other provisions severely limited the influence of poorer voters. It also enshrined basic protections for legal defendants, repeated the 1793 declaration's provision that men could not sell themselves into slavery, and restated the 1789 declaration's insistence on the need for a division of powers in the government to prevent the rise of what Sieyès, anticipating the twentieth-century term "totalitarianism," called a *ré-totale*, a regime that claimed total power over its citizens, as opposed to a *ré-publique*, in which laws only concerned public affairs. The new constitution's most obvious deviation from its predecessors was the inclusion, alongside the list of rights, of a "declaration of duties," an idea that had been rejected in 1789. The declaration of duties was striking, above all, for its banality: citizens were admonished to "do nothing to others that you would not want them to do to you," and urged to obey the laws, respect property, and be prepared to defend their country. The deputies, some of whom were notorious for their dissolute behavior, declared self-righteously that "no one is a good citizen if he is not a good son, a good father, a good brother, a good friend, a good husband."[44]

Although the Constitution of 1795 reflected a rejection of many of the initiatives taken during the Revolution's radical phase, one of the Convention's most radical measures was reaffirmed: the abolition of slavery and the granting of citizenship to the blacks in the colonies. White colonists attempted to turn the republican commissioners Sonthonax and Polverel's emancipation of the slaves in Saint-Domingue into one of the "crimes" of the Terror, but a parliamentary commission dominated by former Girondin allies of Brissot upheld their actions. Not only did the white colonists' offensive against the commissioners fail, but the thermidorian Convention explicitly made abolition and black citizenship part of the new constitutional order. The deputy Jacques Defermon successfully urged his colleagues to "remove all anxiety, all uncertainty about their situation," from the minds of the emancipated blacks. His arguments were not entirely idealistic: he emphasized the contributions of Toussaint Louverture, "an intrepid soldier who accepts orders, and an enterprising leader," and his five thousand black soldiers in the war against the British, and he claimed, with some exaggeration, that the production of sugar and coffee was rapidly recovering thanks to the efforts of blacks who were now free laborers. Boissy d'Anglas, the spokesman for the constitutional committee, told the assembly, "The abolition of slavery was solemnly decreed, and you would not want to change it. . . . It is the one act of justice that tyranny had you pass; you would surely not want to seem less attached than it was to these eternal principles."[45] Twelve years before the British Parliament finally banned the slave trade—but not the practice of slavery—and a full seventy years before the United States ended slavery, republican France reaffirmed the promise of universal freedom and racial equality made in February 1794.

After making the Caribbean colonies and their mostly black population integral parts of France, the Convention acted to extend the country's boundaries in Europe. Having been torn apart by their own revolution and then fought over by the French and Austrian armies, the population of Belgium had resigned itself to the idea that annexation was the only solution that could bring peace. Even longtime opponents of this outcome, the deputy Joseph-Étienne Richard reported, now said, "You have made us so unhappy, the state of uncertainty, anxiety and suffering in which you keep us is so insupportable, that we would rather be part of France than stay as we are."[46] Divided into French-style departments, Belgium formed a part of the country until the defeat of Napoleon in 1814. The situation of the German territories the French had conquered on the west side of the Rhine was more complicated. The leaders of the Convention made no secret of their determination to keep them, but gaining international recognition of their absorption depended on reaching a peace agreement with the Austrians, the protectors of the Holy Roman Empire, and on winning at least the acquiescence of the inhabitants. Some of the latter wanted to create an independent republic of their own rather than being forcibly turned into French citizens. In September 1795, French armies crossed the Rhine, threatening to drive deep into German territories, but they could not force the Austrians to sue for peace, making it clear that the war would continue into the following year.

After three exhausting years, the surviving deputies of the Convention finally prepared to end their work. The primary assemblies were summoned to vote on whether to approve the new constitution and to choose electors, who would in turn choose new deputies. On 5 fructidor Year III (August 22, 1795), however, the Convention created an uproar when it required that two-thirds of the deputies to the new legislative councils be chosen from its own ranks. Their argument was that the complete turnover of personnel following the National Assembly's decision in 1791 to bar its members from sitting in the second legislature had put the destiny of the Revolution in the hands of inexperienced men who had been unprepared for the problems facing them. The deputies' real fear was that if the voters were given complete freedom, they would almost certainly reject nearly all the *conventionnels* in favor of men who had no commitment to the republic.

The "Two-thirds Decree" was an easy target for critics of every stripe, and the young journalists who had been active in the jeunesse dorée saw an opportunity to whip up opposition to politicians who seemed determined to keep themselves in power indefinitely. "How dare you tell the people to perpetuate you once again and to see before its eyes forever the spectacle of its torturers and of its eternal shame?" one of them demanded. With the sans-culotte activists marginalized after the defeats of the germinal and prairial uprisings, the young men and their middle-class supporters had taken control of many of the Paris section assemblies. Using the rhetoric of popular sovereignty, they prepared to stage an insurrection of the well-to-do rather than of the common people. What they would do if they succeeded was unclear even to them: as Charles Lacretelle, one of their leaders, wrote later, "we avoided explaining what form of government ought to be adopted." Although their republican opponents denounced them as royalists, the official agents of Louis XVIII had no direct contact with the Parisian agitators. "Are they really for us?" one royalist conspirator wondered.[47]

On 1 vendémiaire (September 23), the first day of the republican Year IV, the results of the referendum on the constitution and the Two-thirds Decree were announced. Overall participation in the election was only half of what it had been in the vote on the democratic constitution of 1793. According to the official figures, 914,853 votes had been cast in favor of the new document, with 41,892 opposed. Only 167,758 voters favored the Two-thirds Decree, however, while 95,373 were against it. To achieve a positive result, the vote-counters ignored the results in Paris sections that reported a unanimous no-vote on the decrees rather than providing a numerical figure, and the yes-vote total included large numbers of ballots from army units whose soldiers had little sense of the atmosphere among civilians. One army lieutenant who arrived in Paris just after the vote was struck by the contrast he encountered. "The soldiers are misled; most of them don't know how badly the government is doing," he wrote. "Here people are suffering and they see clearly."[48]

The dubious nature of the election results gave the right-wing militants in the conservative Paris sections the pretext they needed to call for an insurrection. The Convention added fuel to the fire by moving troops close to Paris and issuing weapons to some of the sans-culottes who had been disarmed after the popular uprisings in the spring. "Are we going to see the reappearance of those days of horror and bloodshed that we have experienced?" the Lepeletier section, the center of the movement, asked as it tried to galvanize the rest of the city to support its call to arms. The Convention was not well prepared to defend itself. The Paris military commander, General Jacques-François Menou, suspected of sympathizing with the royalists, was abruptly dismissed, and the deputy Barras, who had organized the defense during the prairial uprising, was again appointed to command its forces. A number of officers who were in Paris without assignments volunteered to assist him; one of them was the young Napoleon Bonaparte, whom Barras knew from his mission to Toulon in 1793. Released from prison shortly after thermidor but offered only an unappealing assignment fighting the Vendée rebels, Bonaparte had been so discouraged about his prospects that he had asked for permission to accept a position with the Ottoman army. On the night of 12 vendémiaire (October 4), he took charge of placing artillery pieces to cover the streets and bridges leading to the Convention's meeting place in the Tuileries.

The insurgents who attacked the Convention on 13 vendémiaire (October 5) outnumbered the Convention's defenders, but they were mostly inexperienced civilians; they were facing trained soldiers and they lacked artillery. In later years, Bonaparte would claim credit for having driven the assailants away from their strongpoint, the church of Saint-Roch on the rue Saint-Honoré, with "a whiff of grapeshot" from his cannon. In fact, the battle for the church raged for over an hour and both sides suffered casualties. "We killed a lot of their people; they killed thirty men and wounded sixty," Napoleon Bonaparte wrote to his brother Joseph. In contrast to its treatment of the prairial insurrection, the Convention made little effort to punish the movement's instigators. The Paris city gates were deliberately left open so that the most compromised activists could escape, and only two participants were executed. Nevertheless, their supporters were demoralized. "One doesn't see foolish and mutinous young men, former aristocrats always sighing for their illusions, priests ready to serve the altar of discord," the police reported. "Even the prostitutes no longer provoke sedition."[49]

Although the Convention treated the rebels with leniency, the failed vendémiaire uprising had significant political results. The Paris section assemblies, in which so many political movements had been launched, were permanently abolished; there would not be another mass mobilization in the streets of the capital until the July Revolution of 1830. For the first time since 1789, troops from the regular army had been deployed against the citizens of Paris. They had obeyed orders to fire on them, a sign that the soldiers no longer identified with the civilian population. Above all, the vendémiaire movement rescued the career of the twenty-six-year-old general from Corsica. "It is to him and to his wise and timely dispositions that we owe the defense of this enclosure," Barras told the deputies. In the aftermath of the insurrection, Bonaparte was named to command the "army of the interior," the forces charged with maintaining order inside the country. Barras introduced the socially awkward young officer into his fashionable circle. There he met Josephine Beauharnais, a Creole woman from Martinique whose first husband had been executed during the Terror. Seven years older than Bonaparte and the mother of two children, Josephine was "not at all what one could call beautiful," his younger brother Lucien recalled, but her spirit and sophistication bowled him over.[50] In early March, Bonaparte was given command of the French army in Italy; it was his first chance to command troops in the field. Just after his appointment to the post, he and Josephine were married, with the thermidorian deputies Tallien and Barras as witnesses.

The defeat of the vendémiaire insurrection allowed the Convention to proceed with its plan to implement the Constitution of 1795. In the three years since they had first assembled in 1792, with foreign armies deep inside French territory and the shock of the September massacres still reverberating, the surviving Convention deputies had lived through a seemingly unending series of crises. They had declared a republic and executed a king. They had seen dozens of their colleagues guillotined, and they recognized only too well how easily they themselves might have suffered the same fate. They had shuddered at the news of military defeats and commanders' betrayals, and they had cheered reports of unprecedented victories. They had struggled to satisfy the demands of the popular movement and to defeat dangerous counterrevolutionary revolts. They had improvised a revolutionary dictatorship and had then strived to dismantle it without yielding power to their enemies. They knew they had written an extraordinary chapter in history, even if they still had no way of knowing what its sequel would be.

The last days of the National Convention were hectic and disputatious, leaving little time or energy for reflection. Knowing that they were not going to be represented in the new councils, committed radicals poured out their anxieties and fears in final speeches; some even wanted to annul the results of the elections of candidates whose loyalty to the republic was dubious. Others denounced "unrestrained infernal speculation that doubles, triples, quadruples, decuples the price of goods," and lamented that "the wisest and most virtuous republicans are chased from all public positions; the émigrés return everywhere along with the deported priests." Conservative deputies angrily replied that "the Terror still hovers over this meeting hall." Trying to steer a middle course, Marie-Joseph Chénier opined that "a great people, after numerous revolutionary crises, should raise a temple to forgetting." Even as he called for setting aside "the labels of moderates, Girondins, terrorists, which serve only to tear us apart," however, he also called for the permanent banishment of all royalists.[51]

As it had all through its session, the Convention alternated outbursts of partisan passion with constructive initiatives. On the body's next-to-last day, Pierre Daunou pushed through the final version of the law establishing a national system of public education and setting up the Institut national, "the representative body of the republic of letters." Pierre-Charles-Louis Baudin des Ardennes, charged with presenting an amnesty law that would prevent any further prosecutions for political acts committed during the Convention's session, insisted that it should also include the abolition of the death penalty, "this punishment that nature abhors." He argued that it was fitting that the assembly, which had begun its work three years earlier by abolishing the monarchy, should end it by banning another "plague . . . that oppresses humanity." The Convention responded by voting that executions should end once the war had been won. It also endorsed Baudin's call to rename the Place de la Révolution, where Louis XVI had been guillotined, the Place de la Concorde, the "square of harmony." Finally, reminded that the hour when the Convention had promised to officially dissolve itself had already passed, the presiding officer declared its work ended. "Union, friendship, harmony among all the French, that's the way to save the Republic," he intoned. More than one deputy must have reflected that an assembly that had displayed so few of those qualities could hardly ensure that its successors would enjoy them.[52]

# 17

# THE REPUBLIC IN QUESTION

*October 1795–September 1797*

R ETURNING TO FRANCE IN MID-1795 AFTER SEVERAL YEARS IN EXILE, MA-dame de Staël recognized that hardly anyone loved the new Directorial constitution. Determined to regain the influence she had wielded through her salon in the first years of the Revolution, she set out to persuade her friends that "the founders of the constitution of 1791 should be the defenders of the constitution of 1795." Most of her friends would have preferred a constitutional monarchy. But although France, Madame de Staël wrote, could "stay as a republic, . . . to become a constitutional monarchy she would have to pass through military dictatorship."[1] The common people might resent the elitist nature of the new government, but the experience of the Terror had left them too disillusioned to rise up against it. Madame de Staël's ambivalent endorsement of the Directorial republic reflected the challenge facing the new regime: it had few true supporters, and the strongest argument in its favor was that the alternatives—the return of the intransigent Louis XVIII or a resurgence of militant Jacobinism—were too frightening to contemplate. Madame de Staël hoped that the same reasoning that had converted her to republicanism would convince the country's leaders to put aside partisan and personal differences. That was a lot to ask of them, however. Many of the politicians charged with making the government function now had to work with colleagues who had sent them to prison during the Terror or who had threatened them with execution.

The unpopular Two-thirds Decree that gave a majority of seats in the councils to former Convention deputies ensured that most of the new legislators had at least some reason to want the new constitution to succeed. In spite of the law of 3 brumaire Year IV (October 25, 1795) excluding relatives of émigrés, refractory priests, and other presumed counterrevolutionaries from the carefully crafted electoral assemblies, however, the voters consistently chose the most moderate members of the Convention, along with new men who were often suspected of royalist sympathies. François Boissy d'Anglas, the man who had stood up to the prairial demonstrators, was elected in thirty-six different departments, and Jean Denis Lanjuinais, a conservative former Girondin, in over thirty. Largely excluded from national government and often fearful of the local officials installed during the thermidorian period, the former supporters of the Jacobin movement and the revolutionary government of Year II saw the new constitution as an abandonment of the democratic ideals embodied in the Constitution of 1793. Republican militancy was still widespread in the armies, as soldiers remembered comrades who had died to defend the Revolution; the generals, however, could easily imagine themselves replacing the squabbling politicians in Paris.

The first obligation of the two new councils was to elect the five members of the Directory who were to form the government's executive branch. Emmanuel Sieyès, resentful about the Convention's rejection of his constitutional proposals, refused a seat on the Directory, a sign that the new political system did not even have the support of key members of the republican elite. The men chosen were a representative sample of the deputies who had survived the Terror without abandoning their republican convictions. All had voted for the execution of the king, giving them a strong reason to oppose the return of the Bourbons. Only one director, Jean-François Rewbell, had been a member of the National Assembly. Lazare Carnot, a former member of the Committee of Public Safety of the Year II, had survived the thermidorian purges that his fellow director Paul Barras had helped engineer, but questions about his political past still lingered, whereas Étienne-François Letourneur was regarded as a political nonentity. Louis-Marie Larevellière-Lépeaux had been forced to go into hiding during the Terror because of his ties to the Girondins, and he retained a strong suspicion of former Montagnards, including Carnot, Rewbell, and Barras. The director with the highest public profile was Barras, a former aristocrat whose unsavory reputation for corruption was offset by his record of overseeing campaigns against the federalist revolts in the Midi and organizing the defense of the Convention during the prairial and vendémiaire uprisings. Fairly or not, Barras's controversial personality and his longevity—he was the only director to keep his place throughout all four years of the regime's existence—made him a symbol of a government whose other members were mostly men earnestly struggling to avoid political catastrophe.

To underline the fact that the new constitution made the executive branch of the government independent of the legislature, the directors and their families were housed in the Luxembourg Palace, more than a mile from the Tuileries, where the councils held their sessions. On official occasions, the directors wore elaborate costumes: their embroidered cloaks and elaborately feathered hats were a windfall for satirical cartoonists and marked a sharp break with the affected simplicity that had prevailed during the Terror. Larevellière-Lépeaux worried that the palace's luxury—and the company of Barras, "a real spreader of corruption"—would be bad for his teenage daughter. Hoping to avoid constant squabbles, the directors divided up their responsibilities. Carnot, as he had during the Terror, oversaw military affairs, while Letourneur managed the navy. Larevellière-Lépeaux claimed domestic issues as his domain; he had a special interest in religious affairs, where he actively promoted a deist cult, Theophilanthropy, and opposed concessions to the Catholic Church. The irascible Rewbell was the Directory's main voice on foreign policy. Barras supervised the police and kept a close eye on the various factions competing for influence in the capital.

The architects of the 1795 constitution had given the new government precious time to consolidate its hold on power. The first legislative elections were not due to be held until April 1797, but the time was needed, for the Convention had also left its successors a host of unresolved problems. The harvest that year was insufficient to reassure the population about the food supply; the Paris police continued to warn their superiors about the frustrations of the women who gathered in the streets of the Faubourg Saint-Antoine, where "the most outrageous epithets are hurled at the government."[2] Despite the defeats of the uprisings of 1795, the agents were convinced that neither the former revolutionary militants nor the counterrevolutionary agitators of the jeunesse dorée had given up their hopes of overturning the new regime. The provinces were no calmer: although peasant protests were on the wane, local governments remained as desperate as the authorities in Paris to find grain for their populations, even at the price of confrontation with farmers. Years of upheaval had created an atmosphere of lawlessness in many regions, where robber bands, some of them with a distinct royalist coloration, spread fear and insecurity.

The collapse of the Revolution's paper currency was a major source of unrest; the assignat had lost so much value that the smaller denominations were literally not worth the paper they were printed on. Peasants with scarce grain to sell demanded payment in coin, while urban workers who paid in assignats faced ever-higher prices for bread and other necessities. Among the victims of the currency's depreciation was Jacques Ménétra, who sold his workshop in exchange for a payment due six months later, "when it was no longer worth the trouble to collect." In March 1796, the Directory abandoned the assignat and replaced it with a new form of paper money, the *mandat*, backed by the real estate the government still possessed and planned to put on the market. Within a month, the new currency lost 80 percent of its value. Writing more like a financial analyst than a policeman, the author of one police report accurately predicted that the confiscated lands, "which are the only resources of the government to meet the indispensable expenses of the war, will not produce the sums that one would have expected; they are going to fall into the hands of speculators who, flush with *mandats* they have acquired at bargain prices, will give them to the government at their face value and resell [the purchased national lands] for metallic money under the very eyes of the authorities whom they blame for the situation." The fact that public officials often bought such properties and even justified their gains added to the Directory's image problem. "From the start of the Revolution," one deputy wrote, "I thought that one should do things honestly . . . but not take stoicism to the point of neglecting one's own interests."[3]

By the end of the year, the government decided that it had no choice but to abandon paper currency altogether. To prevent the complete ruin of individuals who had made contracts during the period of inflation, debts were calculated according to the approximate value of paper currency at various dates during the Revolution, making the settlement of financial affairs immensely complicated. To convince public opinion of the necessity of the severely deflationary return to metallic currency, the private Dijon Company was given the right to collect whatever mandats remained in public treasuries around the country in exchange for an advance of solid currency to the government. The company amassed a much larger sum in mandats than the government expected and swiftly sold them to other speculators, who used them to buy up national lands at fire-sale prices before the government's deadline for their retirement. A lengthy and ultimately unsuccessful lawsuit against the Dijon Company kept the scandal in the news for more than a year, severely damaging the Directory's public standing.

More aggressively than previous revolutionary regimes, the Directory tried to use newspapers to build support for itself by subsidizing papers representing different currents of post-thermidorian republicanism. The favoritism shown to these loyal journalists irked their competitors, even when they shared the political views of the subsidized papers, and it did nothing to diminish the popularity of newspapers critical of the Directory. Left-wing journalists, who now looked back nostalgically on the days of Robespierre, were as active as the royalists. The *Journal des hommes libres* kept the Jacobin tradition alive, and René Lebois's *Ami du peuple* laid claim to the heritage of Jean-Paul Marat. A political amnesty was proclaimed as the new constitution went into effect, allowing the counterrevolutionary journalists who had incited the vendémiaire uprising to resume their attacks on the government.

Alarmed by the popularity of newspapers advocating either the restoration of the monarchy or a return to democratic radicalism, in April 1796 the Directory encouraged the councils to pass a heavy-handed law imposing the death penalty on anyone who advocated changes to the Constitution of 1795. The Directory also encouraged writers to make the case for its version of socially conservative republicanism as the only alternative to the extremes of royalism or *anarchie* (anarchy), the government's label for Jacobin democracy. Madame de Staël's new lover, the Swiss-born Benjamin Constant, became the most articulate proponent of this argument. In a widely read pamphlet titled *The Strength of the Present Government of France*, he contended that whereas it had been legitimate for the philosophes of an earlier generation to criticize the abuses of the long-established French monarchy, the very fragility of the new republican order made it a moral duty for responsible citizens to avoid driving men in power to extremes. If conservatives would recognize that the major accomplishments of the Revolution could not be undone, Constant promised, they could have a constructive influence, but he feared that they were bent on doing just the opposite. "They see that the Revolution was a terrible and disastrous thing, and they conclude from this that what they call a counter-revolution will be a happy event. They are not aware that this counter-revolution will itself only be a new revolution."[4] Reversing Constant's argument in another pamphlet, *On the Weakness of a Newly Founded Government*, Adrien Lezay replied that in a constitutional system, it was the government that needed to follow the dictates of public opinion, not the other way around. "The authorities can vex, oppress, insult the class of citizens called the *honnêtes gens* [wealthy property-owners]" whom Constant was urging to give up their conservative sentiments, Lezay wrote, but they would "always be the key to a national majority."[5]

As much as they differed with one another, Constant and Lezay were united by their opposition to any kind of social radicalism, such as the campaign Gracchus Babeuf launched in the winter of 1795–1796 in his *Tribun du peuple*. Babeuf's prerevolutionary occupation as a *feudiste*, an expert in the drafting of documents concerning seigneurial rights, had given him an intimate acquaintance with the ways in which wealthy landowners exploited the poor. Attracted to radical ideas even before 1789, he had led a troubled career on the fringes of revolutionary politics and journalism and spent the Terror period in prison. Released after thermidor, he founded a *Journal de la liberté de la presse* (Journal of the freedom of the press) that denounced Robespierre for having silenced the popular movement. He quickly decided that the plotters who had overthrown the Incorruptible and ended the Terror were an even greater danger to the common people than the Montagnards, however, and renamed his paper the *Tribun du peuple*, claiming to speak for the interests of the poor.

Until the fall of 1795, little had distinguished Babeuf from other militants calling for the implementation of the democratic constitution of 1793. Now he went beyond his predecessors by calling for a world in which all people would truly be equal. This would be accomplished through the abolition of private property and the creation of a society in which all goods would be held in common and shared equally among the population. According to the laws of nature, Babeuf proclaimed, "land doesn't belong to anyone, it belongs to all. . . . Whatever anyone has taken beyond what is needed to feed him is a theft from society." Babeuf had no sympathy for the idea that hard workers or talented individuals should receive extra rewards from society. "It is absurd and unjust to claim greater compensation for someone whose job requires more intelligence and more effort and thought; none of that increases the needs of his stomach."[6]

Babeuf envisioned a communistic society that would end all the ills besetting humanity. "This government will do away with . . . envy, jealousy, greed, pride, deception, duplicity, all the vices. What is more (and this is no doubt the essential point), with the universal, special, perpetual worry that eats away at each of us about how we will live tomorrow, next month, next year, in our old age, and what will become of our children and their children." The regime of private property rights created by the Constitution of 1795, Babeuf claimed, was worse than the slave code that "the harsh colonists imposed on the blacks in our islands." For those who know how the attempt to create communist societies in the twentieth century led to the development of oppressive bureaucracies, Babeuf's optimism about a "common administration" that would "suppress private property, assign everyone with skills to the task he knows and oblige him to deposit what he makes in the common warehouse" is hard to credit. His assurance, in a response to his critics, that "the people responsible for preserving this system" would "never be tempted to preserve their authority in defiance of the will of the people" now seems as unconvincing as his cavalier unconcern about the limits on individual freedom that would be necessary to ensure that everyone would contribute fairly to the common welfare.[7]

Described in glowing terms in the early nineteenth century by his Italian disciple Filippo Buonarroti, Babeuf's communist ideas inspired generations of revolutionaries, from Karl Marx to the Bolsheviks. They were determined to realize the promise that Babeuf's followers had made when they predicted that the French Revolution would prove to be only "the forerunner of a greater and more imposing revolution, which would be the last one."[8] In 1796, however, even Babeuf's small circle of followers recognized that his ideas were too extreme to attract a mass following. The sans-culottes who had poured into the streets during the revolutionary journées and the peasants who had forced the abandonment of seigneurial rights dreamed of making themselves economically independent, not of doing away with private property. Nevertheless, the all-too-obvious suffering of the poor under the Directory convinced Babeuf that if the masses were properly led, they could be inspired to rise up and topple the regime, creating an opportunity for a determined group of leaders to implement his ideas. Along with being the forerunners of modern communism, Babeuf and his followers were thus the first to imagine revolution as a calculated process directed by a vanguard of conspirators whose goals might be unknown to the mass of their followers.

In the fall of 1795, as Babeuf was setting down his ideas in his newspaper, other radicals tried to revive the club movement in Paris. The Jacobin Club remained banned, but a new "Club du Panthéon," so called because it met near the shrine to the heroes of the Revolution, provided a forum for agitation against the socially conservative Directory and in favor of the implementation of the more radical constitution of 1793. Whether or not they fully grasped the fact that Babeuf's ideas went far beyond a return to the principles of that document, many former Jacobins—including thirty-two former Montagnard Convention deputies and the widows of the revolutionary martyrs Michel Lepeletier and Marat—subscribed to his newspaper. Ex-revolutionaries in the provinces also embraced it. When he announced that a new installment of the journal had been published, the leader of a group in the Burgundian town of Autun wrote to Babeuf, "the greatest silence descends, joy is depicted on every face, our spirits are enlivened, courage is reborn, and we are ready to fall on the enemy."[9] Concerned about this resurgence of militant Jacobinism, the Directory ordered General Bonaparte, the commander of its interior forces, to shut the Pantheon Club; his execution of the order showed how completely the onetime protégé of Augustin Robespierre had now separated himself from any association with the revolutionary left.

Driven underground, Babeuf and his closest supporters resorted to conspiratorial methods. By the end of March 1796, he and three close associates, Félix Lepeletier, Pierre-Antoine Antonelle, and the atheist playwright Sylvain Maréchal, had constituted themselves as an "Insurrectional Directory of Public Safety." Unable to operate openly, they relied on the subscription list of Babeuf's *Tribun* and their familiarity with former revolutionary activists to identify potential supporters. In the "Declaration of Insurrection" that they planned to issue when they launched their movement, the Babouvists denounced the Directorial government as "oppressors" who had "outraged, degraded, and done away with the qualities and the institutions of liberty and democracy" and "murdered the best friends of the republic." In his memoirs, Buonarroti admitted that the uprising would have begun with "a day of justified and healthy terror," but once the directors and their allies in the legislature had been eliminated, "indulgence and forgetting would have followed."[10]

The Babouvists found support among former sans-culotte militants as well as among the soldiers of the Legion of Police, a force recruited to guard the Directory and other government institutions. The plotters also hoped to win the support of some former Montagnard deputies. They did manage to enlist one celebrated figure, Drouet, the provincial postmaster who had recognized Louis XVI in Varennes in June 1791, and some of their agents had contacts with the director Barras, a political chameleon who at least wanted to know what was brewing in militant circles. Unlike Barras, the other directors were alarmed by the growing agitation and reports of the Police Legion's untrustworthiness. Carnot, in spite of his past as a member of the Committee of Public Safety during the Terror, took the lead in demanding measures to quash any radical agitation. Thanks to a double agent, on May 10, 1796, the police were able to round up the leading Babouvists and finally the *Tribun du peuple* himself, who had been living in hiding for several months.

Although many observers found it hard to take a plot seriously when it had been put together by a committee whose members were unknown even to their own supporters, the Directory seized the opportunity to portray itself as the defender of property and social order. The *Nouvelles politiques*, a conservative newspaper, put forward the official view: "However inconceivable the conspiracy that has just been discovered may appear, in view of the audacity of the enterprise, the atrocity of its goal, and the difficulties of its execution, it is nevertheless certain that it existed."[11] The Directory launched a nationwide wave of arrests of revolutionary militants, over a hundred of whom were accused of involvement. The government's decision to indict Drouet, a sitting member of the legislature, complicated plans for trying the Babouvists: under the constitution, charges involving deputies had to be heard by a special "High Court," and the trial did not begin until February 1797. The delay gave the republican opposition time to reorganize itself in order to counter accusations that its members adhered to Babeuf's communist ideas.

The members of the Directory hoped that the arrest of Babeuf and his supporters would win them support from moderates and property-owners. Although the authors of the Constitution of 1795 had tried to turn property-owners into the pillars of a conservative republic, the property-owners were reluctant to give the regime real support. But they also frustrated the advocates of a return to monarchy. From his observation post in the Swiss capital of Bern, the well-informed journalist Jacques Mallet du Pan described the majority of them as "royalists of opinion": they "admitted the necessity of a king," he said, "but they want one who will be a child of the Revolution, chosen by the nation. . . . They hope thus to guarantee their security, dispel the fear of vengeance, and reassure the purchasers of national properties."[12] In the absence of a plausible alternative to Louis XVIII, these "royalists of opinion" saw themselves as obliged to compromise with the Directory and accept a government headed by men who had voted for the execution of the king.

Mallet du Pan recognized that there were also "royalists of conspiracies," men who remained convinced that the population would welcome a Bourbon restoration if they could strike a sudden blow against the republic. He also realized, however, that the disastrous landing at Quiberon in 1795 and the subsequent defeat of the vendémiaire uprising had left them demoralized. Royalist agents hoped that Jean-Charles Pichegru, the commander of the Army of the Rhine, might turn against the republic. Pichegru accepted money from the royalists and encouraged them to circulate propaganda among his troops. In March 1796, however, he was recalled to Paris. His replacement, Jean-Victor Moreau, shared his lack of enthusiasm for the republican cause but was not prepared to try to stage a military coup. The royalist cause faced further setbacks in the early months of 1796, as the firmly republican General Lazare Hoche suppressed a revival of *chouannerie* in Brittany. Two of the main chouan leaders, Jean-Nicolas Stofflet and François Charette, were captured and executed.

Although the practical chances of a return to the old regime remained slim, the early years of the Directory were a time of creative ferment among counterrevolutionary thinkers, particularly those who found themselves stranded in the scattered refuges of the emigration outside France. The revolutionary regime's continued survival, even after the excesses of the Reign of Terror, challenged conservatives to explain how such a disaster could have occurred and to put forward new arguments as to how it might be defeated. One influential answer was offered by a French émigré priest, the abbé Augustin Barruel. As early as 1793, Barruel had argued that the Revolution was the result of a deliberate conspiracy "meditated for a long time in France by men who, under the name of philosophes, seemed to have divided up the tasks. Some wanted to overthrow the throne, others the altar."[13] In publications during the Directory period, Barruel elaborated on his theory, claiming that the Enlightenment authors, the Freemasons, and the German Illuminati, a secret society founded in the 1780s, had worked together to subvert monarchies and the Christian faith, and that the

French Revolution had been the culmination of their destructive plans. Barruel's conspiracy theory has continued to attract disciples down to the present day, despite the implausibility of his claim that the entire European Enlightenment was a conspiracy to overthrow the French monarchy. In fact, the radical revolutionaries of 1793 had closed the Masonic lodges that Barruel blamed for the upheaval.

Other émigré writers posed more thought-provoking challenges to the postulates underlying the revolutionary movement. Joseph de Maistre, a French-speaking nobleman who had been driven from his home in the kingdom of Savoy by the French invasion, and Louis de Bonald, a provincial nobleman from Auvergne in southern France, both published major works in 1796 that went beyond both Barruel and Edmund Burke in questioning the very possibility of a society based on rational deductions from the axiom that individuals possess natural rights. De Maistre saw the events of the Revolution as God's way of demonstrating to humanity the profound sinfulness of faith in human reason. "The Divinity has never showed itself more clearly in any human event," he wrote. "If it makes use of the vilest instruments, it is to punish in order to regenerate." The revolutionaries had erred in thinking that a political constitution could emerge from the deliberations of an assembly and be reduced to writing, or that there were general principles common to all societies. "They cite America," de Maistre commented. "Nothing makes one more impatient than the praise heaped on this baby in diapers: let's see it grow up." In any event, the idea that human beings were meant to live peaceful and happy lives contradicted de Maistre's Christian convictions about God's inscrutable purposes. In a chapter titled "On the Violent Destruction of the Human Species," he argued that war was an inevitable and necessary aspect of the world and that the suffering of the innocent was part of the divine plan: "There is no punishment that does not purify."[14]

De Maistre's violent assault on the political correctness of his day made him a precursor of the militant Catholicism that would later be a major feature of nineteenth-century French life. Bonald shared de Maistre's intense Catholicism and his rejection of the individualism and rationalism of the Enlightenment and the Revolution, but the alternative he proposed was different. His fundamental postulate was that individuals had no existence outside of the social units to which they belonged, the family, the state and the religious community, and that, to prevent conflicts, each of these units needed a single ruler—the father in the family, the king in the state, and the pope in the church. "Man only exists for the sake of society, and society forms him only for its purposes," he wrote, an assertion that turned the revolutionaries' assumption that society was a creation to serve the needs of its individual members on its head.[15] Bonald's argument would have an important influence on the development of modern sociology.

Threatened by radical conspirators, faced with the barely concealed hostility of much of the country's propertied class, and still mired in a desperate financial crisis, the directors hoped that military successes would shore up the regime's position and provide a source of desperately needed revenue. Whether the republican armies could respond to these hopes was by no means sure. The number of soldiers had fallen by at least a third since its peak in early 1794. Short of funds, the government had been unable to pay the troops regularly or ensure adequate supplies. "The poor armies are reduced to a fragment of bread, sleeping on straw, badly clothed, without shoes, marching in snow-covered mountains," one soldier wrote.[16] Although regulations introduced in 1795 strengthened the authority officers had over their men and did away with elected soldiers' councils, discipline was hard to maintain; this was especially true on foreign territory, where the hungry men could not be stopped from seizing provisions from the population. Years later, Jean-François Noël remembered with pride how he had stood up for his comrades when General Jean-Baptiste Jourdan, commander of the Army of Sambre-et-Meuse, threatened to punish them for looting: "A lively indignation seized me; I advance to the middle of the long circle formed by the generals and superior officers; in a few words characterized by military frankness . . . I demand, in the name of my brothers in arms, that the soldier be given the food and equipment the law promises him."[17]

All the French armies were in a similar condition in early 1796, but at the beginning of May, news reached Paris of the first of a stunning series of victories won by the Army of Italy under its new commander, the twenty-six-year-old Napoleon Bonaparte. Ever since he had helped defeat the federalist uprising in Toulon in December 1793, Bonaparte had dreamed of leading a French invasion of northern Italy. During his time in Paris, he had drawn up campaign plans, and at the beginning of March, his patron Barras made sure he would have the opportunity to implement them. The older and more experienced officers already serving in the Army of Italy quickly recognized Bonaparte's intelligence and force of will. "He questioned us on the position of our divisions, on their equipment, on the spirit and effective force of each corps, traced the course we were to follow, announced that the next day he would hold an inspection, and on the following day attack the enemy," General André Masséna recalled.[18] Bonaparte made an equally strong impression on the men, although the eloquent words with which he later claimed to have won their loyalty—"You are hungry and naked. The government owes you much; it can give you nothing"—and his promise to lead them "into the most fertile plains on earth," where they would "find honor, glory, and riches," were only composed when he dictated his memoirs after his defeat at Waterloo.[19]

Bonaparte managed to split the enemy armies facing him and quickly overwhelmed the war-weary Piedmontese. Going beyond the bounds of his authority, he acted as a diplomat as well as a general, sure that his promise to extort badly needed cash from the defeated Savoyard monarchy would assuage any concerns the Directory had about his conduct. Losing no time, he then headed for Milan, the capital of the Austrian province of Lombardy. The crucial battle took place at Lodi, where the French troops had to storm a bridge under heavy Austrian fire. After the victory, Bonaparte, acutely aware of the value of publicity, commissioned engravings showing him leading the perilous charge; it was one of the many exaggerations that would mark his career as a propagandist. Even though he had not been so reckless as to risk his own life, he had been able to inspire his men to heroic efforts, and they now dubbed him "the little corporal," a token of their special loyalty to their commander. Lodi fired Bonaparte's ambitions. "I no longer regarded myself as a simple general," he said in his memoirs, "but as a man called upon to decide the fate of peoples. It came to me then that I really could become a decisive actor on our national stage."[20] While the Austrians retreated to the fortress of Mantua, blocking the road through the Alps to Vienna, the French general turned his attention to the small states of central Italy and the possessions of the papacy. Throughout the peninsula, the arrival of the French unleashed feverish political excitement; in Italian history, the *triennio*, the three years from 1796 to 1799, are remembered as the moment when the movement to unify the country began. In Italian cities, Enlightenment ideas had found an audience long before 1789, and Italian "Jacobins" now saw an opportunity to put them into practice. In contrast to the Netherlands, however, where the organized Patriot movement had been poised to take power as soon as the French arrived, in Italy revolutionary politics were a novelty, and there was no clear consensus on how the new ideas might be implemented.

While the bourgeois lawyers and journalists and the reform-minded nobles who made up the Italian Jacobin movement debated whether to support the creation of a unified nation-state or a federation that would respect the historical and cultural diversity of the peninsula, the French were primarily interested in appropriating the region's resources. To satisfy Bonaparte's demand for a "contribution" of twenty million francs, the Milanese had to turn over the contents of the province's public treasury, the funds held by its charitable institutions, and even the objects held by the municipal pawnshop. As they had in the Low Countries, the French took part of their tribute in the form of paintings and other art objects, which were then sent to Paris as symbols of the republic's claim to be the center of European culture. "By virtue of its power and the superiority of its culture and its artists," the *Moniteur* said, "the French Republic is the only country in the world which can provide a secure refuge for these masterpieces."[21] Bonaparte sent some of the money extorted from the territories he occupied back to France, providing the Directory with badly needed funds; he was also able to pay his soldiers part of their wages in cash, solidifying their loyalty to him.

Bonaparte's successes in Italy set him apart from the other French generals. In Paris, Carnot regarded Germany, where the largest French forces were engaged, as the principal theater of war. However, the campaign there in 1796, which began with the armies of Generals Jourdan and Moreau crossing the Rhine and advancing into enemy territory, ended in defeat in late August. Both French armies had to fight their way back to their starting points, leaving behind them a population thoroughly antagonized by the invaders' seizure of food supplies and anything else they could get their hands on. Meanwhile, in northern Italy, Bonaparte successfully repelled repeated Austrian attempts to break the siege of Mantua. The fortress finally surrendered on February 2, 1797, after celebrated Napoleonic victories at Arcole and Rivoli. The loss of Mantua not only ended any further Austrian hopes of recovering their possessions in northern Italy, but left their own capital of Vienna vulnerable to a French attack from the south.

Well aware ever since Dumouriez's invasion of Belgium in 1792 of the ways in which ambitious generals tended to develop their own policies, the Directory's agents tried to keep Bonaparte from defying the government's instructions. By this point, French politicians had abandoned any interest in spreading the ideals of liberty and equality. "There can be no question of republicanizing Italy. The people are not at all inclined to accept liberty, neither are they worthy of this boon," the Directory's representative in Genoa wrote. Nor did the Directory have any interest in promoting the unification of the small states into which the peninsula was divided into a larger entity, "a giant whose great size would be a cause of embarrassment to us one day," as Barras put it.[22] As far as the directors were concerned, Bonaparte's conquests were worthwhile only for the resources that could be wrung out of them and because they might be used as bargaining chips to bring Austria to the peace table, where they might obtain its consent to the French annexation of German territory on the west bank of the Rhine.

Bonaparte, however, had his own ideas. In the fall of 1796 he allowed the formation of a "Cispadane Republic" to unify the small principalities and the portions of the Papal States he had occupied south of the Po River. He assured the Directory that he would see that the new republic's constitution would reflect the views of Italian moderates and not those of supporters of "pure democracy." The moderates, he wrote, were "the rich property-owners and priests who, in the last analysis, always sway the mass of the people," and they were the ones who had to be won over if the French cause was to triumph.[23] Although

Bonaparte ruthlessly repressed any opposition that might threaten the French grip on the areas he had conquered, he was eager to conciliate the Catholic Church and prevent the development of anything resembling the Vendée revolt in France. "As long as ministers of religion hold true principles . . . I will respect them, their property and their customs, as they contribute to public order and the common weal," he promised. He made no objection to the Cispadane Republic declaring Catholicism as the state religion, even though the idea ran strongly counter to the Directory's policy in France.[24]

The end of 1796 brought the usual halt to military operations in northern Europe, and bad weather disrupted the most ambitious French military project, an attempt to land troops in Ireland to spark an uprising of the population against British rule. There was no slowdown in Bonaparte's operations in Italy, however. After capturing Mantua, he turned his attention south. When he took Ancona, a port in the pope's territories along the Adriatic Sea, his mind was captivated by the prospect of establishing French dominance over the eastern Mediterranean: "From here one can . . . be in Constantinople in ten days."[25] His immediate goal was to compel the papal diplomats to accept a draconian treaty as the price of keeping him from marching on Rome. In the Peace of Tolentino, the Vatican ceded much of its Italian realm to the Cispadane Republic. Bonaparte demanded a payment of thirty million livres and the usual tribute of art treasures to be sent to Paris.

Bonaparte's soldiers soon found themselves marching north again as their commander set out to impose his will on the Austrian enemy that France had been fighting for five years. By April 7, 1797, the French army was at Leoben, barely twenty miles from Vienna. Rather than conquering Vienna in the name of the Revolution, Bonaparte wanted to make a deal: he hoped to secure Austrian consent to France's annexation of Belgium and the German territories west of the Rhine, as well as recognition of the republic he had created in northern Italy. In exchange, he was prepared to promise the Austrians that France would invade the centuries-old Republic of Venice, a neutral state that had tried to stay out of the conflicts in the peninsula, and then turn its territory over to them. It was a proposal as cynical as the partition of Poland that Austria, Prussia, and Russia had recently concluded, and for the time being it had to be kept secret, not only from the Venetians, but also from the Directory in France, which had not given its ambitious general authority to do any such thing. The public accord Bonaparte reached with the Austrians at Leoben was much more limited: it gave France Belgium but not the Rhineland or northern Italy. Knowing that the Directory, whose own priority was to plant France's frontier on the Rhine, would not be pleased, Bonaparte threatened to resign and return to Paris: he was sure that the shaky government would not take the risk of disavowing its most glorious general.

Meanwhile, on the other side of the Atlantic, Toussaint Louverture, the black leader whose switch from the Spanish to the French side in 1794 had saved the Caribbean colony for the republic, was, like Bonaparte, converting military success into political power. After joining the French ranks, Louverture assiduously courted the French military governor, Étienne Laveaux, who was left in command when the civil commissioners Sonthonax and Polverel were recalled in June 1794. Louverture professed affection for Laveaux, addressing him as "Papa," and urged the black population to show gratitude for the French republic that had freed them from slavery. But he also called on them to remember that "it was I who first raised the standard of insurrection against tyranny,"[26] and therefore, it was his orders that must be obeyed. Like Bonaparte, he won the loyalty of his soldiers by making sure they had food, ammunition, and uniforms and by leading them to success in battle. Most of Laveaux's white troops had succumbed to tropical diseases, and he was grateful for Louverture's support. He recommended him for appointment as a general in the French army, and the thermidorian Convention accepted this advice in the summer of 1795.

Just as Bonaparte skillfully navigated the many crosscurrents of Italian politics, Louverture managed the complexities of Caribbean colonial society. He balanced expressions of concern for the black population with gestures to win the trust of the remaining whites, as well as of the mixed-race population, which had been legally free before the abolition of slavery. Most of the former slaves longed to divide up the plantations and claim plots of land for themselves, but Louverture upheld the rights of landowners and insisted that the blacks needed to prove themselves worthy of freedom "by their submission to the laws, by their work and by their obedience." He expected the whites to recognize his essential role in keeping the black population in check. In December 1795, when he stage-managed the election of deputies to represent the West Province of Saint-Domingue in the French legislature, he instructed them to report "the great and memorable services he had rendered to the country and to all the citizens who lived under his kind and humane command." Like Bonaparte, Louverture rejected the Directory's hostility to the Church; at one point, he urged the republican Laveaux to "imitate Jesus Christ who died and suffered so much for us."[27]

Reassured that the threat of a British takeover of Saint-Domingue had receded, in January 1796 the Directory dispatched a new civil commission to the colony. Its most prominent member was Sonthonax, who had granted freedom to the black population there in 1793; one of his colleagues was Julien Raimond, the longtime representative of the free colored population, who thus became the first man of part-African descent appointed to such a position. Sonthonax was now married to a woman of color whom he had met in Saint-Domingue on a previous mission, giving him additional credibility with the population.

The civil commissioners arrived in June 1796, just after a political crisis had significantly altered the balance of power in the colony. On March 20, one of Louverture's rivals, the mixed-race general Jean-Louis Villatte, had staged a coup, arresting Laveaux and proclaiming himself governor. Assembling his black troops, Louverture had restored Laveaux to office, but it was now clear that Louverture himself was the one who held the real power in Saint-Domingue. Although both Sonthonax and Louverture were strongly committed to the abolition of slavery, the two men were soon locked in a struggle for control of the colony. Many blacks revered Sonthonax for giving them freedom, and Louverture resented the white man's popularity. He strengthened his own position by arranging to have Laveaux elected to the French legislature, where he became a strong defender of the black general; after Laveaux's departure for France in late 1796, Louverture replaced him as the colony's governor. The French general Donatien Rochambeau, who had accompanied Sonthonax, met with Louverture and recognized his ambition; he predicted that "he will someday oblige the agents of the Directory to give way to all his wishes."[28]

Saint-Domingue was not the only colony the Directory had to worry about. The French commissioner Victor Hugues had retaken Guadeloupe from the British in mid-1794. He then executed many of the white plantation-owners who had earlier welcomed the invaders and ruled the island as a virtual dictator until 1798. Ignoring orders from the metropole to implement the Constitution of 1795, Hugues refused to grant full freedom to the former black slaves. Blacks nevertheless made up most of the army. They also made up most of the crews of the numerous privateering vessels that Hugues armed to disrupt British commerce in the region. Hugues's privateers seized American merchant vessels engaged in trade with the British colonies as well. Hugues thus dragged France into a "quasi-war" with the United States that widened the gulf between the republics on the two sides of the Atlantic. Slavery was ordered abolished in Cayenne, the thinly populated French colony on the South American mainland, but the Directory introduced a new form of servitude there by designating it as a penal colony for political prisoners deported from France. In February 1796, the Directory dispatched commissioners to France's two remote island colonies in the Indian Ocean, the only French territories where the 1794 abolition decree had not yet been implemented. When the commissioners finally reached the Île de France after their four-month voyage, the white colonists hustled them back onboard before they could proclaim the law. The Directory took no action against the rebellious white colonists, fearing that if it antagonized them, they would turn the island over to the British. The government's passivity raised doubts about its determination to maintain the abolition of slavery.

Meanwhile, politics in France itself devolved into a tense stalemate. The arrest of the Babouvists alienated the Directory from the remaining Jacobins, but it did not win the government any genuine support from royalists, who were already looking forward optimistically to the legislative elections scheduled for April 1797. A republican friend of Carnot's, alarmed that the former member of the Committee of Public Safety had led the repression of the Babeuf plot, warned him that the royalists were just waiting for the opportunity to try to seize power, telling him,

"You deprive yourself every day of the support of those whose survival is attached to yours."[29] An attack on the army camp of Grenelle in early September 1796, blamed on left-wing agitators, only widened the gap between the government and the republicans. In the streets, according to the police, people called the arrested suspects "workers who were led astray"; they refused to believe that "unfortunates without resources, without weapons, without money could have come up with the idea of attacking a well-defended camp."[30]

Determined to show that it was on guard against any revival of militant republicanism, the Directory took a more ambivalent attitude toward the right-wing movement. Carnot was convinced that the Directory needed to reach an understanding with the more moderate members of this group, as they represented the opinions of the restricted electorate created by the Constitution of 1795. Other members of the Directory, however, feared that concessions to the right would lead to an eventual restoration of the monarchy. The deputies, journalists, and royalist agents who made up the political right were themselves divided, both about their ultimate goals and about the best strategy for pursuing them. Since late 1794, conservative politicians had been meeting at a member's home on the rue de Clichy. At this "Clichy Club," the differences between the rival currents were aired. At one extreme were the true royalists, who were determined to restore the Bourbon dynasty and willing to resort to force to overthrow the Directory. At the other were cautious republicans who thought that Louis XVIII's stubbornness made a return of the monarchy impossible; they wanted to concentrate on consolidating social order and giving the Constitution of 1795 a conservative interpretation. In the middle were constitutional monarchists who considered any republican government fundamentally unworkable; they were equally unhappy, however, with the prospect of a return to the old monarchy. The British agent William Wickham, charged by his government with making sense of "that strange mass of persons and parties that forms the present feeble opposition to the Government at Paris," concluded that little was to be hoped for from them.[31]

In public, the conservative deputies and the journalists who were allied with them limited themselves to pushing for revisions to the social legislation passed during the Revolution's radical phase. A proposal for a comprehensive civil law code, put forward in June 1796, would have restored the exclusive right of husbands to manage family property. It would also have reduced the inheritance rights of adopted children and children born out of wedlock. Only a narrower law excluding illegitimate children from any share of their father's estate was actually passed. Denunciations of the divorce law—one speaker said it "allow[ed] a man to change wives like his clothes, and women to change husbands like their hats"—drew applause, but failed to win legislative approval.[32] The conservatives also cast themselves as the "peace party." They were willing to abandon goals such as the annexation of the German territories on the west bank of the Rhine and spoke critically of Bonaparte's aggressive policy in Italy. "In propagating the Revolution beyond our borders, we make war perpetual," the journalist Charles Lacretelle wrote.[33] Such criticisms alienated the increasingly influential generals and allowed the Directory's supporters to question their opponents' loyalty to the nation. Since the Directory had committed itself to maintaining the abolition of slavery in Saint-Domingue, the conservatives made common cause with the displaced white plantation-owners, claiming that the government was doing nothing to protect their rights to their land in the colony. "What white man would be brave enough to live without protection or any guarantee in the midst of these same individuals whose hands are stained by the blood of his fellows?" one colonist demanded.[34]

At the beginning of 1797, the government arrested a group of royalist plotters led by the abbé Brottier, hoping to show that it was targeting extremists on both the right and the left. Its propaganda campaign enjoyed only limited success, however. Right-wing journalists were exasperated at having their cause tarred by association with a plot that "could not have any real hope of success and that had only one purpose, that of troubling, dividing, and rupturing the constitutional order." The response reflected their irritation at seeing their plan of taking over the government by legal means disrupted.[35] According to the constitution, elections to replace one-third of the deputies in the two councils were to take place in April. The conservatives and the royalists could hardly conceal their impatience: they were sure that the electoral assemblies, made up of wealthy property-owners with bad memories of the Terror, would favor them. "Tremble, you who were the plague of your country!" a widely circulated pamphlet warned the ex-*conventionnels* who had to stand for reelection.[36] Divided among themselves, the members of the Directory did nothing to ward off the looming republican debacle; the start of the trial of Babeuf and his fellow conspirators, which overlapped with the election campaign, riveted the attention of the remaining republican radicals but served to remind conservatives of the dangers of anarchy.

The right's only problem was a lack of overall coordination. Supported by the British, the former National Assembly deputy Antoine d'André formed a royalist network, the Philanthropic Institute, which tried to select candidates who could be counted on to follow a common program. But he could not control the more than thirty right-wing newspapers publishing in Paris, many of them edited by men who thought they would make excellent deputies, or the dozens of local notables who were determined to put themselves forward with or without his organization's endorsement. Reviewing the outcome six months later, another conspirator who had worked with d'André wrote that when he had begun his work, two months before the voting, "I had reason to believe that a party had been formed for the reestablishment of the monarchy [and] that this party had connections in the departments. How surprised I was to discover that all this only existed on paper. . . . Nothing had been done! Even in Paris there was no party, no organization!"[37] The electoral assemblies did indeed reject almost all the former members of the Convention, and the deputies they chose were overwhelmingly conservatives. But the new deputies were not in agreement on how to promote their ideas.

As the more experienced right-wing politicians tried to gather their colleagues in the Clichy Club, the directors argued among themselves about how to react to the election outcome. Rewbell wanted to declare the results invalid and prevent the new deputies from taking their seats, a policy that would have provoked an immediate constitutional crisis. Carnot argued that they should instead try to compromise with the more moderate conservatives. The outcome of the Babeuf trial, which had dragged on for three months in the provincial city of Vendôme, added to the difficulty of the government's situation. The defendants and their skillful lawyer, Pierre Réal, successfully discredited much of the evidence designed to prove the existence of a conspiracy, even though Babeuf undermined this strategy by boasting of his intentions and arguing for his communist vision. In the end, most of the sixty defendants were acquitted; Babeuf and his associate Augustin Darthé were condemned to death, not for conspiracy but for violating the press law passed in 1796 that prohibited advocating a return to the policies of the Terror. Like the Montagnard "martyrs of prairial," Babeuf and Darthé stabbed themselves, but they lived long enough to be dragged to the guillotine. The republican press denounced their "barbarous executions," which seemed particularly excessive in view of the relatively light sentences imposed on the royalists who had been arrested in the Brottier conspiracy.[38]

Allowed to take their seats in the legislative councils, the conservative deputies of the "new third" showed their strengths and weaknesses immediately. They were able to dictate the choice of a new director to replace Letourneur, François Barthélemy. Barthélemy, a former aristocrat and diplomat, lacked energy and experience in domestic politics and soon proved unable to stand up to his more determined colleagues. Their choice to lead the Council of Five Hundred, General Pichegru, was a stronger personality, but his treasonous contacts with the royalists left him badly compromised. The republican directors learned of them in July 1797 thanks to correspondence seized by Bonaparte in Italy. The conservatives' first legislative initiative, an attack on the Directory's policy in Saint-Domingue, backfired. After denouncing the emancipation of the blacks in the colony as a measure adopted "more out of hatred for the whites than out of attachment to the Negroes," the conservatives could not stop themselves from condemning the entire republican phase of the Revolution and the legislators who had supported it. "You know what evils the atrocious decrees slipped through for the past five years by these same men have caused in France," a proslavery legislator declared. The comment provoked a furious response from the former Convention deputy Merlin de Thionville, a thermidorian who had been willing to compromise with the conservatives; he now objected that the speaker wanted "to start a trial of those who, in spite of him, founded the Republic."[39]

The uproar caused by this debate damaged the chances of an alliance between the more aggressive members of the Clichy Club and the moderate republicans who might have been prepared to form a coalition with them. The Clichyens regained some momentum when Camille Jordan, a member of the new third, proposed loosening the restrictions on public religious observances and ending the ban on the ringing of church bells to announce Catholic services. Unlike the defenders of slavery, Jordan was able to appeal to the principle of religious freedom incorporated in the republic's own constitution and even to revive the Jacobins' sentimental language about the "simple and good men who cover our countrysides and make them productive through their useful work." He demanded that these villagers be given the freedom to "follow in peace the religion of their heart." He artfully compared the "philosophical superstition that makes us fear bells" to the "popular superstition that attaches the women of our villages to them."[40]

By this time, the constant repetition of political clichés had deprived parliamentary speeches of the galvanizing effect they had often had earlier in the Revolution. Jordan's defense of religious freedom was one of the last orations that truly made a public impact. He was undoubtedly correct in arguing that much of the population would have welcomed the return of church bells and religious burial ceremonies. The commentaries on his proposals showed how far apart the republicans and their opponents were. The *Sentinelle*, edited by Jean-Baptiste Louvet, one of the Girondin deputies the Montagnards had expelled from the Convention in 1792, opposed Jordan's claim that religion had a positive impact on morality. Priests, he insisted, could not edify the people: "To enlighten men, one has to be enlightened oneself, and not have an interest in abasing the reason of one's fellows."[41] The persuasiveness of Jordan's promise that greater freedom for Catholics would end their hostility to the republic was also undercut by the right-wing newspapers. One of them complained that his "project seems to propose the toleration of a superstitious cult rather than the protection due to a true religion, a religion that one can call that of France."[42]

To counter the royalists and the Clichy Club, the Directory looked for support from the army. Although Bonaparte's policy in Italy was socially conservative, he was enraged by the French right-wingers' denunciations of his invasion of the historic republic of Venice. When journalists demanded that he explain how he could "still talk about the inalienable sovereignty of peoples while trafficking in their blood and their rights," he realized that he had no choice but to support the republican government in Paris.[43] Although the French constitution forbade the army from taking political sides, Bonaparte encouraged his men to pass resolutions that echoed the radical rhetoric of the Year II. Bonaparte told his men, "I know that you are profoundly affected by the misfortunes that threaten the country. . . . Mountains separate us from France; you would cross them with the speed of an eagle, if necessary, to uphold the constitution, defend liberty, protect the government and the republicans."[44] Responding to secret orders from Barras, Hoche, another strongly republican commander, marched units from his army toward the capital. From the other side of the Atlantic, Toussaint Louverture, alarmed by news of the Clichy Club's hostility toward black emancipation, sent a proclamation reminding the French that "it was the blacks who, when France was threatened with losing the colony, used their arms and their weapons to conserve it." He warned that the black population, "with the Constitution in one hand . . . will defend the liberty it guarantees."[45]

Hoping to ward off a violent outcome, the centrist deputy Antoine Thibaudeau scurried from meeting to meeting. He exploited his contacts at the salon of Madame de Staël to obtain information that he could use to persuade the directors to make concessions that would win over the more moderate right-wingers. Then he encountered deputies from the Clichy Club to argue against the royalists who were determined to provoke a violent confrontation with the government. Barras kept his intentions so well concealed that Carnot was deceived into thinking that he could count on him to support the kind of compromise Thibaudeau and others were promoting. On 27 messidor Year V (July 15, 1797), Carnot proposed that the Directory signal its willingness to accommodate the councils by dismissing the more markedly republican government ministers. To his consternation, Barras voted instead with his more militant colleagues, Rewbell and Larevellière-Lépeaux, to remove the ministers who were most open to compromise with the conservative legislators. At the same moment, reports reached Paris that Hoche's troops had crossed the limit prescribed in the constitution, which stated that military units were not to come closer than twenty miles to the capital. Right-wing journalists called the Directory's actions "a declaration of civil war."[46]

Despite having soldiers at hand, the "triumvirs," as the press now took to calling Barras, Rewbell, and Larevellière-Lépeaux, did not act. Barras had ordered Hoche to bring his soldiers to Paris without informing his two colleagues beforehand, and the general was not willing to back a military coup without their support. In the summer, throughout the month of thermidor and the first half of fructidor, the two rival camps watched each other warily. The Directory encouraged its supporters in the councils to form a reunion of their own, the Club de Salm, also known as the Constitutional Circle, to rival the gathering at Clichy, and its establishment inspired former Jacobins in some provincial cities to form their own Constitutional Circles. To replace the hesitant Hoche, Bonaparte dispatched one of his generals, Pierre Augereau, to be ready to command republican forces. Barras reached out to networks of former activists in the Paris faubourgs, making sure they would support the Directory if necessary. Sensing that they were in mounting danger, the right-wing deputies in the councils organized a military force of their own, officially designated as a guard for the independence of the legislature, and recruited civilian supporters from the former jeunesse dorée.

The tension building up in the capital reminded some observers of the weeks preceding the journée of August 10, 1792, but the confrontation, when it came, was almost bloodless. On the night of 17 fructidor Year V (September 3, 1797), printed proclamations announcing a coup were posted on the walls. These included copies of documents that Bonaparte had forwarded from Italy providing evidence of the treason of General Pichegru, one of the leaders of the Clichy Club. Uniformed soldiers surrounded the councils' meeting halls. The recently elected director Barthélemy was arrested, while Carnot managed to escape.

On the morning of 18 fructidor (September 4), the deputies from the two councils whom the coup organizers considered trustworthy were told that the three triumvirs were acting to forestall an elaborate royalist plot. They were asked to endorse the arrest and deportation to Cayenne of sixty-five supposed counterrevolutionary conspirators, including the two other directors and fifty-three deputies. Election results in more than half of the country were invalidated, unseating over a hundred deputies, who were replaced with dependable republicans. Invoking the constitutional article that authorized restrictions on press freedom in case of an emergency, the Directory banned more than thirty right-wing newspapers and ordered the arrest of their editors and publishers. Most of the politicians and journalists on the list managed to evade the police. Madame de Staël, who had dined with Barras on the night before the coup, tipped off the thermidorian leader Boissy d'Anglas and other acquaintances, and the Directory showed little zeal in hunting down the escapees. Augereau's troops made sure there was no overt resistance to the coup, and a few groups of excited republican militants who had responded to Barras's appeals were told to disperse.

The coup d'état of 18 fructidor demonstrated that the post-thermidorian republican elite would not allow themselves to be ousted from power through the mechanisms of the constitution they themselves had created. To justify their actions, the police minister, Jean-Marie Sotin, presented a report on "the vast project for the restoration of royalty that, prior to the 18 fructidor, was carried out all over the Republic." He had no trouble showing that numerous émigrés had been finding ways to return to France, often with the connivance of local officials, and that there was widespread support for the restoration of Catholic worship, or, as he put it, the "resurrection" of "fanaticism." The enthusiasm for the deputies of the new third voiced in numerous letters intercepted by the police, he claimed, proved that "a large number of the members of the two Councils" were "supporters, protectors, correspondents, [and] accomplices" of the royalists.[47] From the defeated right-wing movement's point of view, the ease with which the unpopular republicans crushed them showed that they had never had the support they had counted on. Years later, the journalist Charles Lacretelle concluded that his readers may have shared his views, but what they really wanted were leaders who, "without excessively alarming the republicans, without costing us any effort, without asking us to take up arms, would one day pass this simple decree: Louis XVIII is proclaimed king of France.'[48]

Superficially, the coup seemed to demonstrate not only the weakness of the right-wing opposition but also the strength of the Directorial republic. Barras, Rewbell, and Larevellière-Lépeaux provided a textbook lesson on how an unpopular regime could outmaneuver its opponents. At the same time, unlike the victors of the revolutionary journées of 1792 and 1793, they managed to stay just within the letter of the law and to keep control of the situation after their victory. There was no upsurge of popular radicalism after fructidor, and the institutions of the regime—the Directory and the legislative councils—remained intact, even if the principle that the government should reflect the will of the electorate was clearly violated. The unceremoniously ousted Carnot and Barthélemy were replaced with dependable republicans, the vacancies in the councils were promptly filled, and the routine of parliamentary debate resumed. Even freedom of the press was not stamped out: many of the banned right-wing newspapers quickly reappeared under new names, and the republican newspapers continued to disagree among themselves vigorously enough to make it clear that public debate was still alive.

Despite these reassuring appearances, however, the fructidor coup did mark a major change in the nature of the republican regime. Even though the victors managed to give their actions a veneer of constitutionality, they had clearly violated the fundamental postulate of representative government, the principle that the will of the voters should be respected. To be sure, the narrowly restricted electorate created by the mechanisms of the Constitution of 1795 was hardly the whole of the French people, but the fructidor coup was not carried out in order to make the system more democratic. Instead, the self-proclaimed defenders of republicanism turned to the generals and their armies to provide the support they needed to defeat the royalists. Despite the constant references to the ways in which Julius Caesar and Oliver Cromwell had used military force to overthrow the republican institutions of ancient Rome and Puritan Britain that punctuated French revolutionary debates, the leaders of the Directory took the risk of inviting the military into politics. For the moment, their gamble succeeded: the generals, even the ambitious Napoleon Bonaparte, accepted the authority of the "Second Directory" that emerged from fructidor. But the coup d'état that Barras and his colleagues had carried out set a precedent that would come back to haunt them.

# 18

# FROM FRUCTIDOR
# TO BRUMAIRE

*September 1797–November 1799*

Like the defeat of the Girondins on May 31, 1793, and the crushing of the royalist insurrection on 13 vendémiaire Year IV (October 5, 1795), the blow struck against moderates and counterrevolutionaries on 18 fructidor Year V (September 4, 1797) was followed by a surge of republican militancy. Fortified with two new reliably republican members, Philippe-Antoine Merlin de Douai and Nicolas-Louis François de Neufchâteau, the Second Directory took strong measures to ensure that the regime would not be threatened by hostile political forces. Abroad, French armies made the year following the coup the peak of republican expansion. Under the tricolor flag, the republic's troops drove British invaders out of the positions they had occupied in Saint-Domingue, reached the summits of the Swiss Alps, overthrew the governments of the southern half of the Italian Peninsula, and crossed the Mediterranean to win battles on the banks of the Nile. The Second Directory's successes intensified the conviction that France was a "great nation, accustomed to victory," as the poet and legislative deputy Marie-Joseph Chénier wrote.[1] Even as the regime demonstrated its ability to defeat its enemies at home and abroad, however, its leaders remained aware that they still had not won the hearts of their own population, many of whom refused to accept the republican institutions that were supposed to transform them into loyal citizens. Indeed, even among the republic's governing elites there was much dissatisfaction with the system created in 1795. When the tide of war turned against the French in 1799, the republic's survival was quickly put into question.

The victors of fructidor lost no time in following up their triumph. The republican press formed a thunderous chorus to justify the coup. "In great political crises, it is simply impossible to stick to the ordinary legal procedures that conspirators never appeal to except when they are trying to overturn them," the *Décade philosophique*, the organ of the country's secular intellectuals, intoned.[2] Benjamin Constant, eager to be recognized as the regime's designated political philosopher, insisted that "in the entire republic, there should not be a single officeholder, from the administrator of the smallest commune to the holders of supreme executive authority . . . who is not committed to republican liberty."[3] In addition to ousting supporters of the Clichy Club from the Directory and the councils and banning their newspapers, the Directory systematically purged local administrations throughout the country, making sure they would follow orders from Paris. The councils joined in by reinstating harsh laws against émigré nobles and priests. Emboldened by their strengthened position, the directors declared a partial bankruptcy, disguising it as a consolidation of the state's obligations, thus finally freeing themselves from the unsustainable burden of debt that had brought down the monarchy. Bondholders were told that they would receive only one-third of what they were owed. They had to take what comfort they could in the promise that at least a part of their investment would now be secure.

Debates in the post-fructidorian legislature sometimes veered toward actions reminiscent of the Terror. In a fit of ideological zeal, the legislators approved a law depriving all former nobles remaining in France of their civic rights, in spite of objections that the measure punished thousands of individuals who had never violated any laws. The government needed "all possible means to defeat the enemies of the social contract," one journalist proclaimed.[4] In practice, exemptions were made for nobles who had been elected to any of the previous revolutionary assemblies and for those who were currently holding office or serving in the army; otherwise, figures as prominent as the director Paul Barras would have had to give up their positions. Émigré priests whose return had been tolerated before the coup were not as fortunate as former nobles: between 10,000 and 11,000 of them were arrested in the two years after fructidor, and some 1,500 were interned on islands off France's west coast. The republican rhetoric against the clergy reached levels not seen since the de-Christianization campaign of 1793. "A man who becomes a priest has abandoned his reason; he is an imbecile or a hypocrite," one polemicist declared.[5]

The fructidorians' assertion that the republic had only narrowly escaped being overthrown by royalists had a consequence the coup leaders had not anticipated: it encouraged the revival of a genuine popular republicanism. Constitutional Circles quickly spread throughout Paris and popped up in cities and towns all over the country. Once again, as they had during the time of the National Convention, artisans, shopkeepers, and clerks, "men without much education who have no assets other than their moral and political virtue," as a police commissioner in Bordeaux put it, insisted on their right to participate actively in civic affairs.[6] The success of the movement showed that neither the memory of the excesses committed during the Terror nor the repression of activism in the years since thermidor had stamped out the desire for a more democratic society. Even more threatening to conservatives were new stirrings of activism among some of the working-class women of the capital. When a group of them staged a demonstration, one journalist asked how the government could tolerate these "shameless women, who could become at any moment, as they were more than once, the nucleus of a formidable riot."[7]

In the face of this recrudesence of popular politics, the government's propagandists reverted to the claim that it was protecting the country from both royalism and "anarchy," their code word for the Jacobin spirit. The supporters of the Constitutional Circles responded vigorously. "When an architect rebuilds a house, he does not call the inevitable disorder of the shapeless materials assembled with great difficulty 'anarchy,'" the *Courrier de la Gironde* editorialized.[8] To counter the spread of the Constitutional Circles, the government imposed a stamp tax on newsprint, forcing editors to raise the price of subscriptions. As the *Journal des hommes libres* complained, the law was openly aimed at papers intended for a popular audience, whose readers "are not rich, but nevertheless have need of an antidote to evil opinions."[9] Directorial officials cracked down on the Constitutional Circles' practice of *ambulation*, in which members of one club would get around the ban on club networks by walking to a neighboring town or village to meet with fellow activists. The Directory's version of republicanism consisted above all in an intensified effort to impose law and order in the countryside. The *gendarmerie*, a police force authorized before fructidor, was turned into a larger and more professional organization. A law passed in mid-January 1798 allowed members of robber bands to be tried by military commissions, which worked faster than the regular courts and meted out harsher punishments.

The government's hardline policies within the country were mirrored by a more aggressive foreign policy. In the months prior to fructidor, France had been engaged in peace talks with the British government. Blaming the British for the supposed royalist conspiracy that had provoked the coup, the Directory broke off these negotiations. Recognizing that they could not hope for any further concessions from France, where the Directory was now exhorting Bonaparte to make even greater demands, the Austrians hurried to conclude an official treaty that would consolidate the informal agreement made at Leoben six months earlier. By the terms of the Treaty of Campo-Formio, signed on October 17, Bonaparte turned over Venice and its territories on the Italian mainland to the Austrians. In exchange, they recognized the independence of the Cisalpine Republic and abandoned their claims to their former province of Lombardy. The Austrians recognized France's acquisition of Belgium and promised to support the French demand for the German territories on the west bank of the Rhine River; in return, the French would see that Austria was eventually compensated at the expense of smaller German states in the Holy Roman Empire.

The Directory was not happy with the Campo-Formio treaty, and two of its five members even refused to sign it. They had wanted a firmer Austrian agreement to recognize French gains along the Rhine, and they were upset that Bonaparte, by turning over Venice and its surrounding territories to Austria, had left the enemy with a strategic foothold in Italy. Nevertheless, when the general returned to Paris at the end of November 1797, the government had no choice but to honor him with an elaborate public ceremony in the courtyard of the Luxembourg Palace. The foreign minister Talleyrand, who had returned from exile the previous year, praised Bonaparte's achievements and his modesty and insisted that as they honored his accomplishments, "all French republicans should feel greater." Bonaparte's own speech was short and devoid of exaggerated rhetoric, but his concluding words—"When the happiness of the French people will be secured by better organic laws, all of Europe will become free"—conveyed the message that he did not regard the Constitution of 1795 as satisfactory. Bonaparte gave a picture of what he meant by "better organic laws" in a letter addressed to the leaders of the "Ligurian Republic" he had established in Genoa. In the letter, he blamed revolutionary policies for having alienated the Church and the nobility in France, thereby creating endless domestic conflicts, and called for "coolness, moderation, wisdom, reason in the conception of decrees." At a moment when the Directory was intensifying its rhetoric against priests and former aristocrats, its leading general was clearly thinking in very different terms.[10]

Having defeated kings, instituted republics, and negotiated treaties in Italy, Bonaparte was ready to claim a major role in France for himself. In public, he cultivated an air of humility; when a theater audience, learning that he was in attendance, called for him to take a bow, he refused to show himself. Elected as a member of the Institut national's section on science and technology, he flattered the intellectuals who had honored him by saying that "before I become their equal, I will for a long time be their pupil."[11] Privately, he sounded out politicians about the possibility of changing the age requirement for election to the Directory so that he could claim a seat, or about altering the constitution; he also talked to other generals to test their willingness to support a military coup.

Some journalists were already hailing him as a providential figure. "Bonaparte the demigod has appeared to achieve victory, to fulfill the idea I have conceived of man, and to show us the value of wisdom conjoined with valor," one wrote. Madame de Staël found him different from any of the other political figures she had met. "I had seen men very worthy of respect; I had also seen dangerous-seeming men: nothing in the impression that Bonaparte made on me recalled any of them." Bonaparte, for his part, found the ambitious de Staël irritating; when she asked him whom he considered "the first among women," he snapped, "the one who bears the most children." Crowds gathered whenever he appeared in public and the press reported his every move, but Bonaparte did not let this popularity go to his head. When his companion and aide Louis-Antoine Fauvelet de Bourrienne remarked that "it must be nice to see his fellow citizens so eager to see him," Bonaparte replied, "They would be just as eager to see me if I were being taken to be executed."[12] Concluding that the time was not right for an attempt to overthrow the Directory, he accepted a mission to inspect troops being assembled for a possible invasion of England and left the capital.

As the Directory pondered what to do with one ambitious general, another military man was also causing concerns. By mid-1797, Toussaint Louverture had won his battle of wills with the French civil commissioner Sonthonax, peremptorily ordering him to return to France as a legislative deputy for Saint-Domingue. Sonthonax's commitment to defending the freedom of the black population remained unswerving: he strongly supported a new law on the colonies, passed on January 1, 1798, that outlined procedures for dividing the overseas territories into departments with the same civil institutions as in metropolitan France; it also guaranteed that "black or colored individuals . . . [would] enjoy the same rights as an individual born in French territory." But Sonthonax also warned the government against Louverture's growing ambitions and claimed that the black general's "superstitious and unenlightened mind has made him dependent on counter-revolutionary priests who, in Saint-Domingue as in France, use all possible means to overthrow liberty." The Directory replaced Sonthonax with Joseph Hédouville, a general known for having sternly repressed rebels in the Vendée, but Hédouville quickly realized that he was helpless in the face of Louverture's firm control of the black troops in the colony. "With him, you can do anything; without him, you are powerless," a veteran white officer in Louverture's army told Hédouville.[13]

Like Bonaparte, Louverture conducted his own foreign policy. In August 1798, he negotiated a treaty with the commander of the British forces, Thomas Maitland, providing for the redcoats' withdrawal from the territories they had occupied since 1793; in exchange, he tipped the British off about a Directory-backed plot to provoke a slave insurrection in Jamaica. Louverture also established his own connections with the United States, undermining the French position in the ongoing "quasi-war" between the two republics. Franco-American relations had already deteriorated because of French seizures of American merchant ships; they became even worse when Talleyrand demanded a hefty bribe from American representatives who had come to Paris to try to resolve the conflict between the two countries. Known as the "XYZ Affair," because the American government referred to Talleyrand's intermediaries as X, Y, and Z, rather than publishing their names, this demand scandalized the Americans. President John Adams's supporters in the United States proceeded to push for a declaration of war against France. Toussaint Louverture courted American sympathy by forbidding French privateering raiders from using Saint-Domingue as a base. Although Americans from the southern states had qualms about forging ties with an island of blacks who had successfully revolted against slavery, a law imposing a trade embargo on France, passed in February 1799, contained an exemption, known as "Toussaint's clause," permitting American commerce with Saint-Domingue.

While the French colony of Saint-Domingue was threatening to escape from the Directory's control, the French government was tightening its control over the sister republics it had sponsored in the Netherlands and Italy and extending French influence to new parts of Europe. Ever since the French invasion in 1795, Dutch republicans had been deadlocked between a radical "unitary" faction that wanted a strong centralized government and a "federalist" party that hoped to preserve a significant role for the country's historic provinces. On January 22, 1798, the advocates of centralism, supported by Dutch and French troops, arrested their leading opponents and imposed a constitution reflecting their ideas. The coup in the Netherlands served as a model for a similar reshaping of the government in the Cisalpine Republic, where the newly created legislative councils tried to assert some independence from France by objecting to the terms of a proposed treaty of alliance. The treaty required the Italians to pay eighteen million francs a year to support a French army and stipulated that the French would be allowed to name the commander of the Cisalpine's own troops. The more militant Italian Jacobins exploited the Directory's annoyance with this resistance to eliminate their moderate rivals.

Meanwhile, Switzerland had been added to the list of French-dominated sister republics. Like the Netherlands and Venice, Switzerland had been one of Europe's traditional republics; the legendary hero William Tell, leader of a revolt against Austrian rule in the fourteenth century, was part of the pantheon of revolutionaries the French themselves honored as predecessors. As in other old-regime republics, however, wealthy urban elites dominated the rest of the population, and even some peasants were prepared to welcome the French and their promise to promote social equality. The director Jean-François Rewbell dismissed the country as a "crazy formless assemblage of governments . . . all despotic and all enemies of the French Republic."[14] Opponents of the oligarchical government in Bern, the center of the loose confederation of the Swiss cantons, secretly encouraged a French invasion, which took place in January 1798. By this time, the script for creating new republics was familiar: the new Helvetic Republic was proclaimed on March 22, 1798, and its constitution, edited beforehand by the French directors Rewbell and Merlin de Douai, was put into effect on April 12. Rather than destroying monarchy throughout Europe as they had promised in 1792, the French had now overthrown all of the continent's historical republican regimes.

The crucial question of what kind of republicanism would prevail in France itself still remained unsettled. The purge of the councils in fructidor meant that more than half the deputies would be replaced in the elections of April 1798. During the winter, the directors sent agents, disguised as road inspectors, to report on the political atmosphere in the provinces. Many wrote back that the roads were indeed in bad shape—that is, that either unrepentant conservatives or resurgent neo-Jacobins threatened to dominate the upcoming vote. The energized supporters of the Constitutional Circles worked to bring about the success of the democratic values that had been eclipsed since the overthrow of Robespierre, and they had been figuring out the tactics necessary for success in an electoral system. A republican journalist in Marseille wrote that, "for the first time since the constitution was inaugurated, republicans are cheerful at the prospect of coming freely to the primary assemblies, without having to fear the arbitrary blows of magistrates who have sold out to the royalist faction."[15]

As the first reports of the radicals' strong showing in the electoral assemblies poured in, the Directory and its supporters struck back, claiming that royalists and neo-Jacobins were colluding to "assassinate the Republic," as the government's commissioner in Bordeaux proclaimed. "Both want to overthrow the republican government; both are aiming at the same goal, by different means, and that goal is nothing else but the reestablishment of monarchy, by frightening terror or atrocious reaction."[16] In fact, centrist deputies willing to support the Directory prevailed in most departments, but the government was determined to keep the candidates of the Constitutional Circles from scoring even a partial victory. Where it faced defeat, the Directory told its supporters to claim that legal procedures were being violated; they were then to create a schism by walking out of the electoral assemblies and forming their own rival group. Even when the breakaway assembly had many fewer participants than the original one, the government's loyalists in the councils would pronounce its candidates legally elected. On 22 floréal Year VI (May 11, 1798), the directors staged a new coup d'état, overturning all or part of the results in nearly half the departments and ousting 127 newly elected legislators, including the prairial martyr Goujon's loyal friend Tissot. The Décade philosophique justified what it admitted was a violation of legal principles in view of the necessity of teaching the voters "to be sensible in their choices."[17] The French Directory ordered coups modeled after the floréal purge carried out in the sister republics, where the radicals installed after fructidor were replaced by more moderate figures. This succession of upheavals directed from Paris undermined the pretense that the governments of the Batavian, Cisalpine, and Helvetic republics had any autonomy and discredited them in the eyes of their own populations.

With the opposition movements in France on both the right and the left temporarily sidelined, the "Directorials" were free to steer "the vessel of the Republic" on what they advertised as a middle course between "the two abysses that these factions keep open on both sides of it." By this time, the utopian hopes that had energized the revolutionaries in the first years after 1789 had largely been forgotten, but François Poultier d'Elmotte, an otherwise obscure legislative deputy and editor of the most popular pro-Directory newspaper of the period, the *Ami des lois*, still had a vision of the goal that he wanted to believe France would eventually achieve. In a series of articles on "the hundredth year of the Republic" published in the summer of 1798, he imagined a society in which "general abundance, a more or less equal distribution of wealth, not as a result of a violent redistribution of land, but by the gradual influence of the laws on inheritance and taxation, will have made the excessive inequality of fortunes disappear, as well as all crimes, the result of extreme wealth and extreme need." The revolutionary wars would have ended long ago, and Europe would peacefully accept the moral superiority of France, which would intervene whenever necessary to protect the oppressed against tyrants. The five-member Directory would still be lodged in the Luxembourg Palace, where they would receive the public every *décadi* and resolve all their complaints. Although he was a deputy himself, Poultier did not even mention the legislature, the constitutional mechanism by which the people's will was supposed to be represented. Poultier's dream failed to anticipate the dramatic changes in technology and society to come: changes that would transform France from a country of oxcarts and villages to one of railroads and cities by the time one hundred years had passed. In 1798, with the memory of the upheavals of the previous few years still fresh in everyone's mind, the notion of liberty and equality having been achieved without further conflict was an attractive one.[18]

François de Neufchâteau, who was appointed as interior minister in 1798 after a short term as a member of the Directory, bombarded the government's commissioners in the departments with circulars aimed at making Poultier's vision a reality. A lengthy set of instructions sent out in September 1798 told them to make sure to visit every corner of their assigned territories on a regular basis. They were to take the pulse of the local "public spirit" and try to improve it by promoting the opening of schools and public libraries. The government wanted its agents to promote new farming methods that promised to increase production. They were to be equally active in encouraging commerce and manufacturing. A precocious environmentalist, the minister lamented the widespread destruction of woodlands by peasants seeking firewood; he went into raptures about "the attraction that we cannot avoid having" to newly planted trees. To pay for all this, the commissioners were to make sure that taxes were being collected. At the national level, one of François de Neufchâteau's more successful innovations was the staging of annual expositions of agricultural products and manufactures. The first industrial exposition, held in the summer of Year VI, served as an opportunity to celebrate new technologies: a prize was awarded, for example, to a factory from the Vendée for its textiles. The offerings in the exhibits showed that the country was recovering from "the disasters of a war that ravaged everything there," according to the official report on the exposition, which boasted that France was overcoming Britain's lead in technology.[19]

The Directorial republic's positive ambitions were always paired with concern that nefarious enemies might sabotage its initiatives. François de Neufchâteau's circulars, even as they instructed local officials to be sure that hospitals and other institutions serving the poor in their area were properly managed, veered off into attacks on the religious charities of the past, which "were too indulgent of laziness." The poor were to be put to work, and the money spent to feed them was to be kept to a minimum. A long and detailed circular about schools, which were seen as crucial institutions for promoting social equality, mixed progressive notions, such as the abolition of physical punishments and the creation of student councils to administer discipline, with warnings against any reversion to religious traditions.[20]

All of François de Neufchâteau's ideas about improving the lives of French citizens depended on the government having enough revenue to pay its expenses and enough soldiers to maintain its armies. The

National Assembly had enacted a basic tax on land and a business license tax. The Second Directory added two new taxes, one on luxuries that fell primarily on the rich and one based on counting the doors and windows in buildings, a rough measure of property value. The basic taxes put in place under the Directory became the basis of the national revenue system and successfully kept French governments out of the kind of financial crises that had brought down the old regime, at least until the immensely expensive wars of the twentieth century forced the imposition of new levies, including an income tax.

After the *levée en masse*, which had provided the men for the mass armies that saved the country in 1793 and 1794, republican France had no regular system for conscripting new soldiers. With no end to the war in sight, in September 1798 the councils established a permanent system of military conscription. The plan, proposed by General Jourdan, made all men between the ages of twenty and twenty-five liable to be called for service for up to five years, with the actual number to be drafted each year determined by the army's needs. The law fell equally on the rich and the poor: there was no provision to allow wealthier families to pay a substitute to take their son's place, as had been permitted under the first revolutionary draft calls. Republican journalists applauded the idea of universal military service. Young men would be cured of "all the false ideas contrary to the interests of their country . . . all the germs of royalism or anarchism," one wrote, adding that it would result in an army "with which no ambitious chief can become dangerous for the Republic." The Jourdan law was passed during a momentary lull in major military operations, and it was initially assumed that only a minority of the men eligible each year would actually have to serve. But when the war flared up again at the end of 1798, draft quotas were immediately raised. As in 1793, protests erupted in regions where opposition to the republican regime was strong. In the Belgian departments annexed in 1795, protesters called on "all young men affected by the requisition" to join an uprising "to fight for our fatherland and our religion against the French barbarians."[21] Despite this resistance, the Jourdan law created the basic mechanism by which Napoleon would later fill the ranks of his armies.

While ministers and deputies grappled with the practical difficulties of establishing a functioning regime, intellectuals like Madame de Staël outlined a theoretical justification for the Second Directory's top-down republicanism. In a long manuscript titled *On the Current Circumstances That Could End the Revolution and the Principles That Should Found the Republic in France*, de Staël argued that what citizens really needed was freedom to pursue their own private interests rather than the right to participate actively in politics. The Revolution had brought about some crucial changes that needed to be protected, she claimed, including the abolition of hereditary social privileges and the substitution of a republic for the monarchy, but the people were not yet educated enough to fully appreciate them. "It is necessary, in France, until the moment when public instruction will have trained a new generation in liberty, to extend several portions of the conserving power among the hands of republicans," she wrote, indicating her approval of the coups of fructidor and floréal. Not only did Staël want to restrict the freedom of voters; she also demanded limits on the freedom of the press, since newspapers were "capable of leading citizens into error about what they should do." Indeed, they constituted "a means of governing or revolutionizing so powerful that one cannot remove it from the authorities' surveillance."[22]

De Staël differed from the directors and from the intellectuals who formed a good part of her circle of friends because of her conviction that, rather than trying to impose an unhistorical civic religion on the population, the French Republic ought to adopt the Protestantism she shared with her friend and lover, Benjamin Constant. The rationalist scientists and philosophers who had filled the places in the Institut national opposed the thought of making any concession to Christian beliefs. Pleased to be freed from the restrictions of the old regime that had so irritated the philosophes of the Enlightenment, and supported by the government against the attacks on elitism that had threatened them during the Revolution's radical phase, the country's academics were among the most enthusiastic supporters of the socially conservative republic established in 1795. Several of them, such as the prominent doctor Pierre Cabanis, were deputies or held other political positions, and their prestigious magazine, the *Décade philosophique*, gave the regime its unqualified endorsement.

In 1798, one of the group's leading figures, Antoine Destutt de Tracy, published several essays outlining a "science of ideas," which he called *idéologie*—he and his colleagues came to be called "the Idéologues." Building on the ideas of Condorcet, whose posthumously published *Sketch of the Progress of the Human Mind* served as an inspiration, and of the French Enlightenment philosopher Étienne Bonnot de Condillac, the Idéologues were convinced that their rationalist methods could unify all human knowledge, from psychology and medicine to physics and astronomy.

The Idéologues' efforts to promote empirical scientific methods laid the basis for the development of modern social science and for genuine advances in medicine and in the natural sciences. They promoted clinical studies, for example, in medical research. The Idéologues were among the leading supporters of the Second Directory's vigorous campaign to impose the republican calendar on the population. Between April and September 1798, four new decrees and laws sought to ban references to the old months and days of the week and impose the ten-day rhythm of the *décade* on every aspect of public life. To promote the civic ceremonies held on the *décadi*, the laws required public officials and schoolchildren to attend and made it the only day on which marriage ceremonies could be performed. As local officials in the Lot-et-Garonne department explained, citizens' "civil conduct, their pursuit of their affairs, even the choice of their pleasures should be regulated from now on by a calendar that does not belong to any one religion."

The director Larevellière-Lépeaux made himself the patron of the cult of Theophilanthropy, an effort, like Robespierre's Cult of the Supreme Being, to create a new form of worship that could take the place of the Church. The promoters of the new religion invented ceremonies to accompany the registration of births, marriages, and deaths and wanted to institute catechism classes to teach their principles to children. Peasants dragooned into attending ceremonies on the *décadi* made a point of coming in their work clothes, and women, still the backbone of resistance to religious innovation, sometimes staged riots to prevent government-imposed ceremonies from being held in the churches. However much the notion of changing the nation's religious practices might appeal to intellectuals and republican militants, the effort was one of the most resented aspects of the Directory's policies.

The union of politicians and intellectuals that promoted the unsuccessful effort to remake France's religious practices had more success in promoting a new colonial policy. The abolition of slavery triggered a rethinking of the purpose of extending French rule to overseas territories. In 1796, advocates of a different kind of overseas expansion, under the leadership of Henri Grégoire, revived the Society of the Friends of the Blacks and added "and the Colonies" to its name. They argued that if France did nothing, Britain would dominate the non-European world. The French republic, they proposed, should try to gain influence in Africa by bringing civilization to benighted populations. "In their native land, the Africans are unaware of all the advantage they can draw from their soil and their climate for their own use and that of others. . . . Do they not have an urgent need for moral and physical instruction?"[23] The prospect of acquiring new colonies in sub-Saharan Africa was remote as long as the British controlled the Atlantic, but there were opportunities elsewhere. In an *Essay on the Advantages to Be Gained from New Colonies*, the Directory's foreign minister, Talleyrand, pointed to Egypt, whose climate, he claimed, was suitable for growing the sugar and cotton France could no longer obtain from its Caribbean islands.

Recently returned from three years of exile in the United States, Talleyrand had concluded that territorial expansion was one way of diverting the restless energy generated by the Revolution away from internal political disputes. Napoleon Bonaparte, the very incarnation of restless energy, was already dreaming of Egypt himself. In the summer of 1797, he had written to the Directory that "the time is not far off when we will realize that, in order to truly destroy England, we need to take Egypt." By taking Egypt, France would be able to threaten Britain's connection to India, its most valuable overseas holding. In addition to what the capture of Egypt could do for France's strategic position, Bonaparte, inspired by the example of Alexander the Great, dreamed of what such a conquest could do for him. "I do not have enough glory," he told his loyal aide, Bourrienne. "This little Europe doesn't offer enough. It is necessary to go to the Orient, all the great reputations come from there."[24]

The Egyptian expedition sealed the alliance between the general and the republican intellectual elite who had already welcomed

Bonaparte as a member of the Institut national. A long two-part article in the Idéologues' journal, the *Décade philosophique*, made the case
for what would come, in the nineteenth century, to be called France's
*mission civilisatrice* (civilizing mission) in the non-European world. The
Middle East, the article's author announced, was the region of the world
where "the fate of people is the most deplorable, and where it would be
the most useful to change it." The *Décade's* editorialist admitted that it
would be hard to deal with the native population's "religious fanaticism,"
but he was confident that "the invincible ignorance of the Muslims, or
the contempt that they profess for those they call unbelievers," could be
overcome. Anticipating one of the great dividing lines between Europeans and Muslims down to our own day, he concluded that the only real
obstacle to a successful transformation of the Middle East would be "the
system of morality, especially with regard to women."[25]

Recognizing that the Arab populations of Egypt and Syria would
resist any effort to transform their countries in line with enlightened
principles, the author of the *Décade* article put forward another revolutionary proposal: the creation of a Jewish state in Palestine. Europe's
Jews would provide the resources and the energy to bring the region
into the modern world. "We know how much they long for their ancient
homeland and the city of Jerusalem! . . . They will come running from
the four corners of the world, if one gives them the signal." Another
pro-Directory journalist expanded these ideas into a proposal for the
convocation of a Jewish national assembly that would make a formal
treaty with France and finance the establishment of a sister republic
in the ancient Holy Land. The Directory's ambitions thus led both to
the idea of a European mandate to spread its civilization to the rest of
the world and to the first manifesto of modern Jewish nationalism or
Zionism, even though this proposal for a Jewish homeland was probably
drawn up by a non-Jew.[26]

Bonaparte's expeditionary force set sail for Egypt on May 19, 1798. In
total, there were 56 warships and 309 merchant vessels carrying 36,800
men and their supplies. Among the voyagers were some 170 scientists,
artists, and experts on antiquities, tokens of the French ambition to

bring European civilization to Egypt and to uncover the country's legendary past. The French evaded the British admiral Horatio Nelson, who had been sent to intercept them, and came ashore at the historic city of Alexandria. Bonaparte issued a proclamation designed to win over the local population. He claimed that the French had come to free Egypt from the tyranny of the Mamelukes, the military caste employed by the Ottomans to control the country. "Egyptians, you will hear that I have come to destroy your religion; it is a lie, do not believe it! . . . I respect, more than the Mamelukes, God, his prophet Mohammed and glorious Koran." The Ottoman envoys in Paris, who had been honored by the directors and who had even invited Bonaparte and his wife to dinner, were shocked that the French, "exhibiting dishonesty, deception and perfidy . . . allowed their hypocritical actions to become public in attacking without warning, like thieves, the sacred land of Egypt."[27]

Advancing as quickly as possible across the desert terrain, the French neared Cairo, where Egyptian forces confronted them on the banks of the Nile, within sight of the pyramids. "Soldiers, forty centuries look down on you!" Bonaparte told his troops. The French won a decisive victory, and four days later, Bonaparte entered the city and set up his headquarters. He ordered the creation of an assembly of local inhabitants to govern the city and promised its members that he would "bring justice, respect for properties, enlightenment, and thereby reopen, for a people worthy of improvement, the sources of happiness." Given that "the army's treasury faced many difficulties in meeting the needs of the soldiers," as Bonaparte delicately put it in his memoirs, the local population, like those in other countries the French had occupied, found themselves forced to pay a heavy indemnity. As Bonaparte was settling into his role as ruler of Cairo, news reached him of a disaster on the coast: on August 2, 1798, Nelson's fleet caught the French at anchor off the port of Aboukir. "The whole beach was covered with the debris of our vessels," a French officer wrote.[28] Napoleon's army was now trapped in the country it had conquered, with no way to get home.

The scientists and intellectuals Bonaparte had brought along wasted no time in creating an "Egyptian Institute" modeled after the institute in France. The French savants undertook research on practical problems, such as water purification, and explored the antiquities they encountered

*Cairo Raso ai Republicani in Agosto 798.*

**NAPOLEON IN EGYPT:** The French invasion of Egypt in 1798 marked the beginning of European colonial expansion in the Middle East. Napoleon's expedition enjoyed enthusiastic support from republican France's intellectual elite. This engraving, published in Italy at the time, shows Napoleon Bonaparte being greeted by local dignitaries. *Source: Bibliothèque nationale de France.*

that had previously been unknown to Europeans. The inscriptions on one of their discoveries, which became known as the Rosetta stone, eventually provided the key to reading ancient hieroglyphics, thus opening the way to understanding the civilization that had created the pyramids. A few members of Egypt's religious minorities were admitted to the Egyptian Institute, but Muslims kept their distance. Despite their professions of respect for Islam, one wrote, the French "are a sect of philosophers who reject the Law and claim that they obey nature." Efforts to compel local Muslim officials to wear the tricolor cockade antagonized them, as did the demolition of gates within the city and sacred tombs, which the French removed in an effort to make it easier for their troops to move around.

Hostility toward the French exploded on October 21, 1798, when the population rose in revolt. The Egyptian chronicler Abd al-Rahman al-Jabarti wrote that "the people went beyond all limits, committed every excess, assaulting and mistreating individuals, pillaging and stealing."[29] Some 250 French were killed, and at least ten times as many Egyptians. Despite Bonaparte's promise to respect religion, the French soldiers who put down the revolt showed little regard for Muslim holy places. When they entered the famous Al-Azhar Mosque, one of the strongholds of the rebellion, "they treated the books and Qu'ranic volumes as trash, throwing them on the ground," al-Jabarti wrote. "They guzzled wine and smashed the bottles in the central court." Any illusion that the ideas of the French Revolution could easily be transposed to the Middle East was shattered. Bonaparte now dismissed the Cairo population as "the most brutish and savage rogues who exist in the world."[30]

Bonaparte now found himself stranded in the Middle East, with no way of extricating his army. Fearing that Turkish forces might attack Egypt from the north, he decided to take the initiative and invade Palestine, resulting in atrocities that badly stained his reputation. When the city of Jaffa refused to surrender, French troops "slaughtered men, women, the elderly, children, Christians, Turks," the mathematician Étienne-Louis Malus wrote. One of Bonaparte's subordinates had persuaded the Turkish garrison to surrender in exchange for a promise that their lives would be spared, but Bonaparte decided that he could neither leave several thousand enemy soldiers behind as he continued his advance nor spare the food and resources to care for them. French troops, ordered to execute the unarmed prisoners, ran out of ammunition and had to wade into piles of fallen bodies to finish off the wounded with their bayonets. "I could not stand the horrible sight," one officer wrote. "I fled, ashen and ready to faint."[31] The massacres at Jaffa widened the gulf between the French claims that they were bringing civilization to the Middle East and the reality of military occupation. They also demonstrated the lengths to which Bonaparte would go to achieve his aims. From Jaffa, he continued his advance north, but found himself stopped at the port of Acre, where he had to undertake a lengthy siege while an epidemic of plague decimated his troops.

Meanwhile, events in Europe were threatening to end any chance of Bonaparte seizing power. The Treaty of Campo-Formio that he had negotiated had ended the war against Austria, but it was a fragile agreement. When the French aided local revolutionaries in February 1798 in creating a republican government in Rome that drove Pope Pius VI into exile, the Austrians complained that France was expanding its sphere of influence without offering them any offsetting compensation. Austria responded by making an alliance with the last remaining independent Italian state, the kingdom of Naples, which occupied the southern part of the peninsula. The ruling dynasty of Naples, a branch of the Bourbons, was irrevocably hostile to the French Republic, and the Neapolitans' enthusiasm for a war with France only increased when Admiral Nelson arrived with his fleet after his victory at Aboukir. Through the influence of his lover Emma Hamilton, the wife of the British ambassador and a close confidante of the queen of Naples, Nelson saw that Naples was brought into an anti-French coalition that included not only Britain and Austria but also Russia. The Russian ruler, Tsar Paul I, the honorary head of the Knights of Malta, was eager to take revenge for Bonaparte's occupation of that island on his way to Egypt. The British determination to find continental allies was intensified after the Directory sent French troops to assist the uprising of the United Irishmen, a revolt against British rule that broke out in the spring of 1798. Irish exiles had worked for years to cultivate French support for their cause, and the news of the revolt inspired orators at the Paris festival for July 14 to promise that "all France will arm if necessary to help you."[32] Although the French expedition was quickly defeated, rebellion in Ireland was the London government's greatest fear. The British were convinced that the threat could only be eliminated by destroying the French Republic.

The French found themselves facing a formidable "Second Coalition" whose combined forces outnumbered the republic's armies, which were now worn down by many years of almost continuous combat. The Neapolitan invasion of the Roman Republic on November 23, 1798, started a new round of fighting as furious as anything seen during the first years of the revolutionary wars. Enemy armies never crossed France's frontiers during the conflict, but they threatened the nation's predominance and the system of sister republics it had fostered to extend its influence. The French quickly beat back the Neapolitan invasion of Rome and drove south, forcing the Bourbon king, Ferdinand IV, to flee Naples and take refuge in the island of Sicily. Against the wishes of the Directory, which had no desire to become responsible for defending yet another distant client state, the French general Jean-Étienne Championnet oversaw the proclamation of a "Parthenopean Republic."

Unlike Rome, whose life was dominated by the Catholic Church, Naples had a cultured elite imbued with the ideas of the Enlightenment, and even educated members of the local nobility embraced the Jacobin cause. Eleanora Pimentel Fonseca, whose literary talents had earned her admission to the city's learned academy before the Revolution, took a leading role in the movement and edited its newspaper, the *Monitore Napoletano*. The lower classes of the crowded city, the *lazzaroni*, and the impoverished peasants in the kingdom's rural areas, in contrast, rallied to the banners of religion and monarchy. Pimentel was sure that "the people distrust the patriots because they do not understand them," and that propaganda written in the local dialect would win them over, but her efforts had little effect.[33] The new republic found itself plunged into a civil war similar to the bloody conflict of the Vendée in France. Acting with the support of King Ferdinand, an aristocratic churchman, Cardinal Fabrizio Ruffo, recruited peasants and the region's endemic rural bandits to form an "Army of the Holy Faith." It would go on to terrorize supporters of the republic and townspeople in general.

Faced with a widespread popular uprising, the Neapolitan republicans were dependent on French troops to defend them. Beginning in April 1799, however, the forces of the anti-French coalition, led by an energetic seventy-year-old Russian general, Alexander Suvorov, won victories in northern Italy that forced the French to hastily evacuate the peninsula, lest the troops there be cut off. Abandoned to their fate, the leaders of the Neapolitan movement surrendered to Ruffo's forces in exchange for a promise that their lives would be spared. Returning from his Sicilian exile, King Ferdinand was in no mood to spare his enemies. Admiral Nelson encouraged his vindictive instincts, and 119 of the leading figures in the Parthenopean Republic, including Eleanora Pimentel, were hanged from the yardarms of his ships, a warning to republicans everywhere of the fate threatening them if France was defeated. Meanwhile, the French were engaged in a desperate struggle against Suvorov's army in Switzerland. The cascade of bad news from the armies, exaggerated by royalists who circulated reports from foreign newspapers, did nothing to encourage young men to respond to their draft notices. The Directory tried to revive patriotism by exploiting an outrage committed by the Austrians, whose troops had waylaid three French deputies returning home from the German city of Rastadt in May, after negotiations about the implementation of the Treaty of Campo-Formio were broken off. Two deputies were killed, and their diplomatic papers were stolen. "There are crimes that only need to be told to the people in order to exhort it to vengeance," one pro-government paper wrote. But the population, according to the police, reacted with indifference.[34]

The bad news from the armies coincided with the annual election season in France. The interior minister, François de Neufchâteau, supervised an all-out campaign to influence the voters' choices, and especially to warn them against "the successors of Robespierre and Marat." His heavy-handed purge of local officials in the run-up to the elections proved counterproductive: in many communities, men ousted from office took the lead in opposing the candidates the government endorsed. The electoral assemblies were tumultuous. Crowds often surrounded the meeting rooms and even interfered in the proceedings: in one canton in the southwestern department of the Landes, a woman grabbed the urn used to hold the ballots and broke it over an opponent's head. In Marseille, the governmental commissioner complained that the local National Guard had backed the anarchists. "Instead of the majestic and respectable spectacle of a united people summoned to exercise its rights," he wrote, the city's primary assemblies "presented only a scandalous assemblage of smokers, drinkers and babblers crazed by revolutionary maxims."[35] As in 1798, many assemblies split into two or even three rival groups, each claiming that the members of the other had violated legal procedures.

The results were a clear repudiation of the Directory: only 56 of its 141 officially endorsed candidates were chosen. What the voters actually wanted was less clear. Candidates backed by the Constitutional Circles did well. They found allies among more moderate republicans who were alarmed by the military defeats that the Directory seemed unable to halt and disheartened by the atmosphere of corruption that hung over the regime. In contrast to what had happened in 1798, however, the deputies who had not been up for reelection, charged with deciding between rival claimants when the electoral assemblies had split, followed a consistent policy of seating the candidate backed by the largest number of voters. This approach allowed a number of neo-Jacobins to take their seats. The annual drawing of lots among the directors forced Rewbell, one of the group's strongest personalities, to give up his position. The councils showed their attitude toward the directors by replacing him with Sieyès, who had never ceased to criticize the Constitution of 1795 and call for its revision or replacement.

Sieyès "brought nothing to the government except a difficult character, a spirit of discontent, an extreme fear of revolutionaries, and projects for overturning the constitution that he hoped to modify to suit his own ideas," Goujon's friend Pierre-François Tissot later wrote.[36] In the councils, the new deputies wasted no time in attacking the remaining members of the Second Directory. They demanded that the Directory explain how it had happened that "two months have barely gone by since Italy was republican and victorious under our banners," and that it was now "invaded by a ferocious victor." They also wanted to know what the executive branch of the government planned to do to revive the economy and to reassure "the friends of liberty, so long proscribed and pursued by royalists," in the provinces.[37]

When the directors made no response, on 28 prairial Year VII (June 16, 1799) the two councils declared themselves in permanent session and forced the director Jean-Baptiste Treilhard from office, charging that he had not met the strict constitutional requirements when he was elected a year earlier. He was replaced by Louis-Jérôme Gohier, who was considered to be close to the neo-Jacobins. Behind the scenes, Barras, always determined to end up on the winning side, and Sieyès pressured Larevellière-Lépeaux and Merlin, the two remaining holdover members of the Directory, to resign. In the Council of Five Hundred, the deputy

Bertrand du Calvados thundered, "You have no power to do any good, you will never have the confidence of your colleagues or that of the people or that of its representatives."[38] The two recalcitrant directors finally gave in two days later. Their immediate replacements were Roger Ducos, an ally of Sieyès, and Jean-François-Auguste Moulin, one of the many generals who had complained about the Second Directory's failure to provide the army with adequate resources.

As he reluctantly wrote out his resignation, Larevellière-Lépeaux grumbled, "I tell you, the republic is doomed."[39] The "coup" of 30 prairial (June 18) was the third time in less than two years that political pressures had resulted in the overturning of constitutional procedures. Whereas the coups of fructidor and floréal had clear winners and losers, however, the coup of 30 prairial was more ambiguous. Some of the political figures who carried it out were neo-Jacobins eager to revive the democratic energy of the Revolution's radical period; others shared Sieyès's view that the republic needed a new constitution that would make the government more independent of the electorate. In the wake of the coup, the councils quickly moved to dismantle several of the Second Directory's policies. The restrictions imposed on the press after the fructidor coup were struck down, and a new electoral law prohibited the tactic of initiating deliberate schisms in the electoral assemblies. Journalists of all political colors immediately took advantage of their restored freedom. Once again, the *Père Duchêne* appealed to the common people, thanks to the efforts of René Lebois, a veteran of the far left. Royalist writers who had been in hiding since fructidor also resurfaced, denouncing the republican government and the continuing persecution of the Catholic Church.

A new Jacobin club began to hold public sessions in the Manège, the former meeting hall of the Convention in the Tuileries Palace. "Ask liberty to tell you what she calls her children," the new *Père Duchêne* wrote. "She will respond, 'Jacobins.'" The *Journal des hommes libres*, as ever the voice of the neo-Jacobin movement, ran articles arguing that the revolutionary dictatorship of Year II had been necessary to save the republic; it hinted that similar measures were needed again. Tissot insisted that "if, within a month, the legislature hasn't taken great measures, the slaughter of the patriots is assured." Alarmed by this sign of revived republican militancy, opponents gathered outside the meeting hall, shouting, "Down with the Jacobins! Down with the blood-drinkers!" and even "Long live the king!" A royalist journalist told readers that it was unnecessary to report on club meetings "where they did nothing but give out inarticulate cries," but they could be assured that they would be told "what is most important, that is, most horrible."[40]

During the first month after the 30 prairial coup, the councils passed several decrees that reflected the influence of the Jacobin movement. A revised version of Jourdan's conscription law summoned five years' worth of draftees at once to rebuild the beleaguered armies. To suppress counterrevolutionary agitation in the provinces, the legislators voted for a "law of hostages" on 24 messidor (July 12) to deter "attacks and acts of brigandage committed out of hatred for the republic." Under the law, relatives of émigrés and former nobles could be arrested and their property seized, regardless of whether there was any evidence that they had been involved in criminal acts. The former philosophe André Morellet objected, asking, "Is this the freedom that this same Republic that has given to the blacks of our colonies the rights of man . . . gives to the French?"[41] There was also vigorous debate about a law requiring wealthier taxpayers to contribute to a forced loan, which was finally approved in early fructidor (mid-August).

The neo-Jacobins' successes in the first month after the prairial coup were made possible because a number of more moderate deputies joined them in dismantling the policies of the Second Directory. Soon, however, this tactical alliance began to fall apart. On 29 thermidor (August 16), the neo-Jacobins tried to persuade the Council of Five Hundred to indict the three former directors who had been ousted in prairial. The prospect of a return to the high-profile public trials of the past scared the moderates, even though a neo-Jacobin spokesman promised that the only punishment they wanted to inflict on the former directors was to make them sweep the streets of Paris while dressed in their official costumes. Sieyès immediately went to work to undermine the neo-Jacobin allies with whom he had cooperated just two months earlier. Among those who joined him was Bonaparte's younger brother Lucien, who had succeeded in claiming a seat in the Council of Five Hundred as a representative for Corsica, the family's place of origin. In a widely noted speech, he swore that France would see "no more scaffolds, no more terror, no more of the execrable regime of 1793."[42] A few days later, Sieyès persuaded his colleagues to name Joseph Fouché, the former terrorist and leader of the thermidor conspiracy against Robespierre, as minister of police. Having long since renounced any sympathy with the radicalism of 1793–1794, Fouché put his formidable organizational skills to use to repress the neo-Jacobins, whose club was closed in mid-August.

As it contended with the neo-Jacobins in Paris and the provinces, where nearly 250 clubs had sprung up, the Directory also had to face a new royalist uprising, timed to coincide with offensives by the republic's foreign enemies. The rebels began an insurrection in the countryside around the southwestern city of Toulouse on August 5, 1799, counting on support from royalist groups in Brittany and the Vendée. They hoped that a planned landing of British and Russian troops in the Netherlands, as well as the advance of Austrian and Russian troops in Italy and Switzerland, would keep the Directory from sending troops to oppose them. News of the royalist uprisings inspired the neo-Jacobins in Paris to make one more attempt to swing the majority of the legislative councils in their favor. General Jourdan's motion to declare "the country in danger," however, seen as a prelude to revolutionary measures like those taken in 1792 and 1793, failed by a vote of 171 to 245.

The new Directory's position should have been consolidated by a turn in the tide of the foreign war. On September 19, 1799, General Guillaume Brune inflicted a crushing defeat on the Anglo-Russian invasion force in the Netherlands. A week later, General André Masséna won a decisive victory over the Russians at Zurich, ending the threat to the Helvetic Republic. The improvement in the republic's political and military situation did nothing to dissuade Sieyès from pursuing the goal he had had in mind since his election to the Directory three months earlier. Convinced that the Constitution of 1795 was fatally flawed, he was determined to replace it. He had decided early on that he would need a prominent general as a partner, preferably one without marked political ambitions of his own. During the summer he had settled on Barthélemy Joubert, a young commander who had served under Bonaparte in Italy. Hoping to build up Joubert's reputation, Sieyès had him sent to Italy; in mid-August, his troops won a hard-fought victory at the Battle of Novi, but the general had the misfortune of being killed in the fighting. Sieyès turned to other options, but by the beginning of October he had still not found an officer willing to play the role of his "sword" in a coup. And then, on October 9, 1799, the commander of the Army of Egypt unexpectedly landed at the southern French port of Fréjus.

After his invasion of Palestine failed to produce a decisive victory over the Turks, Bonaparte had begun making preparations to return to France well before he finally took ship on August 22. Four months earlier, he had received a letter from his brother Joseph urging him to come home, both for political reasons and to deal with the infidelities of his wife, Josephine. After organizing the retreat of his forces back to Cairo and winning a battle at Aboukir against a Turkish army, which had been transported there by the British, Bonaparte decided that his soldiers would be able to hold out for some length of time without him. When he had negotiated an exchange of prisoners with the British following the affair at Aboukir, they had given him newspapers from Europe informing him that almost all of his conquests in Italy had been lost. Bonaparte realized that France was facing the possibility of military disaster. He did not have the courage to inform his soldiers, or even General Jean-Baptiste Kléber, who would be left in command of the stranded expeditionary force, of his departure. "That bugger has deserted us with his breeches full of shit," Kléber exclaimed when he learned what Bonaparte had done.[43]

Technically, Bonaparte had abandoned his post, and the director Barras later claimed that when he and his colleagues learned of his arrival in France, they discussed having him arrested and shot. By this time, however, the general had already been given ecstatic welcomes in all the towns he passed through as he headed to Paris. In Lyon, "all the houses were lighted up and covered with flags. . . . [T]here was dancing in the public squares, and the air was filled with cries of 'Long live Bonaparte who comes to save the country.'"[44] Once he reached the capital, Bonaparte's first order of business was to resolve a family drama. His brothers and sisters pressed him to break with Josephine, but he reconciled with her instead. He wanted to avoid being distracted by divorce proceedings while he pursued his main goal of finding a route to power. Reinstalled in his house on a street renamed rue de la Victoire in his honor, Bonaparte plunged into a round of encounters with political insiders to see what opportunities were open to him.

As he sized up the situation, Bonaparte had the assistance of several key figures who saw an alliance with him as a way of furthering their own ends. Talleyrand, who had been dismissed as foreign minister after the coup of 30 prairial, played a key role thanks to his broad range of contacts. Pierre-Louis Roederer, like Talleyrand, had connections across the political spectrum, as well as with the intellectuals of the Idéologue movement. The latter remained sympathetic to the general because he had brought them into his Egyptian venture. Bonaparte's brother Lucien, a member of the Council of Five Hundred, was also deeply involved in these political intrigues. Many of Bonaparte's fellow generals shared his contempt for the civilian politicians running the country and were prepared to accept his leadership. Some neo-Jacobins might have been prepared to cooperate with Bonaparte as well—one of their complaints against the Directory was that it had deliberately sent the general into "exile" in Egypt. He had a lengthy but acrimonious meeting with General Jean Bernadotte, the military leader closest to the neo-Jacobin party. The neo-Jacobins' democratic program had no appeal for him, however. "After having triumphed with them," he later said, "I would have had to triumph over them."[45] He met with the two least political members of the Directory, Gohier and Moulin, to explore the possibility of getting himself appointed to that body, but they were not willing to help him.

Realizing that the opposition of these two directors left him with no way of gaining power through legal means, Bonaparte turned to potential allies who were open to the idea of a coup. Sieyès was the leading candidate. As soon as the news of Bonaparte's return reached Paris, General Jean-Victor Moreau, with whom Sieyès had been negotiating, pointed out the obvious: "There is your man! He will make your coup much better than me."[46] Sieyès would have preferred a general with a more pliant personality, but he had no real alternative. He had already worked out a plan in which the Council of Elders, where he had a firm group of supporters, would activate a constitutional provision allowing for the declaration of a state of emergency. That would trigger the transfer of both legislative assemblies to a location outside of Paris, where the Council of Five Hundred could be pressured into voting for a new regime.

From Bonaparte's point of view, the main disadvantage of joining Sieyès's plot was that the veteran revolutionary politician assumed that Sieyès would make the key decisions about the new constitutional arrangements to replace the Directory. The general would be expected to simply lend his popularity to the operation and accept a secondary role afterward. The alternative to Sieyès was Barras, who had helped launch Bonaparte's career by calling on him to put down the counterrevolutionary vendémiaire uprising in 1795. A meeting between the two men on the night of October 30, 1799, did not go well: Barras told his former protégé that he was too inexperienced to assume a political role. By the following morning, when several of Barras's former allies who had gone over to Bonaparte convinced him that he had made a terrible mistake, the general had already committed himself to Sieyès.

In just over a week, the plotters finalized their plans. Early on the morning of 18 brumaire Year VIII (November 9, 1799), letters were delivered to 150 members of the Council of Elders summoning them to an emergency meeting—another 100 who were considered unlikely to go along with the coup were not informed. One of the plotters told them that the country was menaced by a terrible conspiracy and that if they did not act at once, "there will be no more representative body, no more liberty, no more Republic." The sleepy-eyed deputies were befuddled by the lack of any evidence of an imminent uprising, but they voted to appoint Bonaparte the commander of the troops in Paris and to order the transfer of the councils to the small town of Saint-Cloud west of the city. The plotters had chosen this location because it would keep crowds from forming who might oppose their plans; it would also allow them to surround the deputies with loyal troops.

As the Council of Elders was meeting, Bonaparte assembled other military leaders at his own home. Once he received the decree appointing him as military commander of Paris, he set off for the Tuileries, the seat of the legislature. Addressing the troops assembled around the building, he justified his action as a matter of national security. "In what shape did I leave France, and in what shape do I find it now! I left you in peace, and I find war! I left you with conquests, and the enemy threatens our frontiers! . . . [T]his state of things cannot last; in three months it would have led us to despotism. But we want the Republic . . . based on equality, morals, civil liberty and political tolerance. With a good administration all will forget the factions of which they were members in order to become French."[47]

While Bonaparte was busy at the Tuileries, Talleyrand took charge of ousting the three potentially hostile directors from the Luxembourg. Barras was given a generous bribe and exiled to his country estate, his political career at an end; his colleagues Gohier and Moulin realized that resistance was futile. Meanwhile, printed posters and pamphlets prepared in advance were being distributed throughout the city celebrating Bonaparte and justifying the coup. "It cannot be that a man so eminent by his services remains excluded from leadership," one propaganda piece insisted.[48] None of the publications announcing the coup made any mention of Sieyès, the man who had really set it in motion.

The day of 18 brumaire had gone off without a hitch, but the plotters still had to deal with the councils, which were due to reassemble at the former royal palace in Saint-Cloud on the following morning. At a meeting on the evening of 18 brumaire, Sieyès, Bonaparte, and the other principal conspirators argued for hours about how to persuade the legislators to agree to abandon the Constitution of 1795. Sieyès, the civilian, favored forceful action: he wanted to arrest the neo-Jacobin deputies in the Council of Five Hundred before they could voice any opposition. Bonaparte, the military man, demurred: he wanted to maintain a facade of legality, so that the new regime would not bear the stigma of having been imposed by force. Both Bonaparte and Sieyès realized that their scheme could still fall apart if the deputies really stood up to defend the existing constitution, as they had six months earlier when they forced the members of the Directory to resign. On the morning of 19 brumaire (November 10), as a carriage transporting him to Saint-Cloud crossed the Place de la Révolution, where Louis XVI and Robespierre had both been executed, Bonaparte's aide, Bourrienne, said to his companion, "Tomorrow we will sleep at the Luxembourg or we will end up here."[49]

If the 18th of brumaire had been a model of a well-executed coup d'état, the 19th was a lesson on the dangers of improvisation. Whereas the plotters had succeeded in keeping potential opponents from attending the previous day's early-morning session of the Council of Elders, this time the full membership of both assemblies arrived, including the neo-Jacobin deputies. They were accompanied by several thousand soldiers, including the councils' official guards, who could not be counted on to support the coup, and by a large crowd of civilian spectators. It was well past noon before the two councils officially began their sessions in their improvised chambers. The conspirators' plan was to have the Council of Elders immediately approve a decree appointing three provisional consuls to replace the Directory and small committees drawn from the two councils to draft a new constitution. Lucien Bonaparte, the president of the Council of Five Hundred, would then ram the measure through that body, and the two councils' meetings would be suspended.

Instead of bowing to the conspirators' pressures, the Council of Elders held an angry debate. The deputies who had been kept away from the previous day's session demanded evidence of the conspiracy that justified their transfer to Saint-Cloud. "We are no longer in the times when the Committee of Public Safety said, 'Take my word,' and dictated decrees to the representatives of the nation," one deputy exclaimed.[50] Meanwhile, the neo-Jacobin opponents of the coup in the Council of Five Hundred ignored Lucien Bonaparte's efforts to silence them and demanded instead that all the council members individually swear a new oath of loyalty to the Constitution of 1795. By 4:00 p.m., Napoleon Bonaparte, his nerves on edge, had decided to address the Council of Elders in person. Challenged to declare whether he supported the constitution, he turned on the deputies, telling them, "The Constitution! Every faction invokes it, and every faction violates it; all of them despise it; it cannot save us, since no one respects it anymore." Called on to provide evidence that the republic was in such jeopardy that emergency measures were needed to save it, he repeated his claim that only he represented "the great party of the French people." Finally, discarding any effort at persuasion, he addressed himself to "the brave soldiers whose bayonets I see," openly threatening the legislators. "Remember that I

march accompanied by the god of victory and the god of good fortune!"
he told the recalcitrant deputies.[51]

Even the loyal Bourrienne admitted that "there was not the slightest sense in everything he managed to get out. . . . Bonaparte was no
orator." As soon as he left the meeting room, new opposition to his allies' demands for action broke out. "All measures should be approved
by the whole legislative body, and in accordance with the constitution," one deputy insisted.[52] Meanwhile, Bonaparte, accompanied by
two grenadiers, had forced his way into the palace's Orangerie, where
his brother Lucien was surrounded by angry Jacobin deputies shouting,
"Death to the tyrant! Down with the dictator! Long live the Republic
and the Constitution of the Year III!" As they saw Napoleon Bonaparte
advancing toward the speaker's podium, the Jacobins turned on him,
screaming, "Outlaw him! Outlaw him!" Dragged out of the room by the
grenadiers and several officers who had rushed to his defense, Bonaparte
seemed stunned and unable to speak coherently. Inside, Lucien struggled to keep the deputies from immediately voting to declare his brother
"outside the law."

Once Bonaparte recovered his wits, he, Sieyès, and the other plot
leaders appealed to the soldiers gathered outside the palace. Lucien
Bonaparte emerged to galvanize them with the false claim that "the immense majority of the Council is at this moment terrorized by a few deputies with stilettos." Napoleon Bonaparte himself seconded him, saying,
"I wanted to speak to them; they have responded to me with daggers."
Led by General Joachim Murat, soldiers entered the Orangerie. The pretense that a transfer of power was being carried out through legal means
was completely abandoned. "All honest men leave or I will no longer
be answerable for my actions!" an officer announced. The Council of
Elders, informed that its sister body had been forcibly dispersed, made
a last effort to assert itself, passing a resolution that announced the appointment of a provisional government but that also called for the re-
convening of the two assemblies a month later, a move that exasperated
the plotters. To make sure of their success, they were obliged to round up
enough of the now dispersed members of the Council of Five Hundred
to hold a semblance of a parliamentary session. There, the members of
the council were intimidated into voting for a resolution naming Sieyès,

Ducos, and Bonaparte to run the government as provisional consuls and replacing the councils with two committees that would draw up a new constitution. The remaining members of the Council of Elders were then pressured to approve the measure. It was not until 3:00 a.m. on 20 brumaire (November 11) that the newly named consuls could take their oath of office. Lucien Bonaparte proclaimed that "from today, all the convulsions of liberty are at an end."[53]

As the exhausted participants in the drama of Saint-Cloud straggled back to Paris, they had little real idea what the events of the past two days portended for the republic and the legacy of the Revolution. Napoleon Bonaparte's stumbling performance had created doubts about his ability to play the leading role he had cast for himself; perhaps he would soon find himself outmaneuvered by Sieyès and the other veteran politicians who had organized the overthrow of the Directory. At the same time, however, the use of troops to chase the elected representatives of the nation out of their meeting hall raised the specter of a genuine military dictatorship. In his angry harangue to the Council of Elders, Bonaparte had accused the republic's own leaders of discrediting the Revolution's principles, citing the coups they had carried out on 18 fructidor Year V (September 4, 1797); 22 floréal Year VI (May 11, 1798); and 30 prairial Year VII (June 18, 1799). The absence of popular reaction to the overthrow of the Directory showed how little support there was for the regime created in 1795. The lack of enthusiasm for the Constitution of 1795 was not a mandate for its replacement by one-man rule, however. Much would still have to happen before, in December 1804, the French would again find themselves living under a hereditary ruler.

# 19

# THE SLOW DEATH OF
# THE REPUBLIC

## *1799–1804*

D ESPITE BONAPARTE'S AWKWARD PERFORMANCE AT SAINT-CLOUD ON THE
19th of brumaire, the coup proceeded as its plotters had planned:
the browbeaten remnants of the two councils authorized them to draw
up a new constitution. Like the thermidorians, who, after overthrowing
Robespierre, had immediately blamed him for the extremism of the Terror, the brumairians put all the blame on those who had been in power
before them. They inundated the country with propaganda insisting
that, under the Directory, the country had been on the verge of catastrophe, and that only their intervention had saved it from "tyrannical disorganizers."[1] The undeniable successes of the new regime during
its early years make it easy to conclude that revolutionary republicanism
was indeed bankrupt by 1799 and that an authoritarian regime suited
the country much better. At the time of the brumaire coup, however,
neither Bonaparte himself nor anyone else knew what kind of government was going to take the place of the Directory and what aspects of

the French Revolution's legacy it would preserve or undo. Like all the other episodes of the Revolution, the unraveling of the republic after 1799 was a story whose outcome was not determined in advance.

The victors of brumaire claimed they had acted to save the republic, not to destroy it. They referred to their coup by its date in the revolutionary calendar, and even as they denounced the Directory, they filled 90 percent of the new government's national offices with men who had served it.[2] Bonaparte himself—he would not start to be referred to by his first name, Napoleon, until his power was firmly established several years later—was a "child of the Revolution," one of the thousands of ambitious men who had reached positions they could never have dreamed of occupying before the transformations of 1789 and the political intrigues of the Directory years. He had fought under the tricolor flag and identified himself with the enlightened secularism of the Institut national, whose scientists and philosophers had eagerly welcomed him as a member. His driving ambition was clear, but what policies it would lead him to embrace—and, equally importantly, whether he could persuade political elites and the population at large to follow him—remained unknown.

The brumairians' propaganda emphasized Bonaparte's role in a way that had no precedent in the revolutionary era. An illustrated broadsheet included verses calling him "the immortal friend of the French," and "the god of light." But even his closest collaborators were not sure the young general really had the skills to become an effective political leader. Just thirty years old when he assumed power, Bonaparte had little experience in the labyrinth of French revolutionary politics; men like Sieyès, who had spent a decade mastering the art of politics, expected to outmaneuver him. Pierre-Louis Roederer, the political chameleon who had ushered Louis XVI out of power on the morning of August 10, 1792, and survived to help usher Bonaparte in seven years later, noted the general's poor public speaking ability: "He had trouble finding resounding words, graceful expressions and the rhythm that he sought for."[3] Even Bonaparte's influence over the military was by no means completely assured: there were other ambitious generals prepared to step forward if he should stumble.

The new men in power were able to tap into genuine dissatisfaction with the Directory. In addition to the political conflicts and rural criminality that plagued many regions, ten years of revolutionary disorder had taken their toll on the country's physical and social infrastructures. Officials dispatched to survey conditions shortly after the brumaire coup reported bridges, canals, harbors, and public buildings everywhere in urgent need of repair. Sent to inspect Normandy's hospitals, the scientist Antoine-François Fourcroy lamented that "the sick are without body linen or in torn rags, the beds lack blankets"; another inspector noted a large number of abandoned infants in the Provence region and estimated that 95 percent of them died.[4] Local governments lacked the revenue to cope with these problems, and the central government's resources were taken up by seemingly endless war. In spite of these problems, however, the Directory had been improving the efficiency of its administrative machinery, and conditions in most of the country were better than in 1795. Having survived the military crisis of 1799 and shown that it could keep the more extreme neo-Jacobins at bay, the regime would not necessarily have collapsed if it had not been deliberately undermined by its own leaders.

A Paris police report noted that "the satisfaction inspired by the revolution of 18 brumaire has nothing of the exaltation or the enthusiasm that arise and vanish almost at once," suggesting that much of the population, including the observers themselves, were waiting to see what the new men in power would do and whether they would be any more effective than their predecessors before fully embracing them. To some, brumaire looked like a takeover by the army. "This revolution has a military character, one cannot deny it," wrote Christine Reinhard, the wife of the ousted Directory's last foreign minister. Others expected that the coup would open the door to a return of the Bourbon monarchy. Even Bonaparte understood that the ease with which he and his associates had overthrown the Directory did not make their own position secure. In a discussion with some of his advisers in early 1800 about modifying the law against the émigrés who had fled the country during the Revolution, he remarked, "We govern today; tomorrow, others may inscribe us on the list of émigrés."[5]

The brumairians' first moves reflected their own uncertainty about what course to follow. The plotters' propaganda posters covered the walls of Paris with their version of the coup. Joseph Fouché's police cracked down on theaters that rushed to stage unauthorized plays about the coup, but at the same time, newspapers, still operating with considerable freedom, published reports that contradicted the official account that Bonaparte's life had been threatened. The consuls revoked the law of hostages that the councils had passed before the coup, under which relatives of émigrés and former nobles could be arrested and their property seized. They also revoked the law forcing the rich to contribute to a loan to the government that had been passed around the same time as the hostage law. These decisions indicated that the consuls wanted to dissociate themselves from the militant republicanism that had flared up during the crisis of the spring and summer of 1799. When a wallposter announced the pending publication of "the *Père Duchêne*'s farewell to the French," the police moved quickly to prevent any reappearance of the mythical sans-culotte spokesman.[6] Throughout the country, the provisional consuls carried out a drastic purge of local officials, dismissing some 70 percent of them; in general, their replacements were drawn from the wealthier and more conservative members of the local population.

All this suggested a conservative turn, but when the consuls announced that they were going to send nearly sixty Jacobins into exile in French Guyana, there was a strong backlash. "People thought it marked the return of arbitrary measures and the reestablishment of a system execrated by the public," wrote Jean-Jacques Cambacérès, who would soon be appointed as second consul, and the idea was quickly shelved. The brumairians also took steps to counter rumors that "the deported priests are going to return, the dominant Catholic cult is going to be reestablished, and they will be able to hold solemn mass on Christmas eve." The Idéologue Pierre Cabanis, one of the legislators involved in drafting the new constitution, promised his former colleagues that the basic achievements of the Revolution would be protected. "No, there will not be any reaction," he insisted. "No, the properties acquired by purchasers of national lands will remain as sacred in your eyes as those of other citizens."[7]

The public's confusion about the brumairians' intentions reflected the fact that Sieyès, Bonaparte, and their supporters had toppled the Directory without having agreed on what should replace it. When Antoine Boulay de la Meurthe, one of Sieyès's collaborators, remarked to him on 19 brumaire that everyone assumed "that you have a constitution all prepared," he was surprised to discover that the man who had just demolished the Constitution of 1795 did not have a replacement ready. Sieyès insisted that he wanted to "return to the ideas of 1789," but the original revolutionaries would hardly have recognized his ideas as a fulfillment of their program. Deeply distrustful of "brute democracy," Sieyès adopted the principle that "no one should be named to a function by those over whom he exercises authority," which meant abandoning the fundamental principle that citizens should choose those who made the laws under which they lived.[8] In place of elections, he proposed that the property-owning citizens of each commune should draw up a list of "notables" eligible for office. Local notables would then meet and designate 10 percent of their number as potential officeholders at the departmental level. The departmental notables would in turn nominate 10 percent of their group as potential national officeholders, and the central government would then choose among them for the new legislative assemblies and other national offices. In Sieyès's mind, this system, in which "confidence comes from below, authority from above," still qualified as a form of representative government, since all those in the pool of notables would have been designated by their fellow citizens as potential officials. It would not, however, allow voters to decide who would actually hold office.

Sieyès was determined to replace the turbulent elected legislatures of the revolutionary decade with institutions insulated from popular opinion. His plan provided for a *Corps législatif* (Legislative Body) of three hundred members, who would vote on proposed laws but have no power to initiate or even debate them. Their votes would be cast after listening to members of a second house, the Tribunat (Tribunate), with a smaller number of members. The tribunes would be allowed to discuss draft laws submitted to them by the government but not to introduce proposals on their own. Sieyès's constitutional plan also included a third body, ultimately named the Sénat (Senate). The senators would be responsible for deciding whether laws approved by the other two houses violated the constitution. Sieyès had proposed such a constitutional jury in 1795 and had been humiliated when the thermidorian Convention unanimously rejected the idea; this time, he only had to convince one person—Bonaparte—to accept it. In theory, the Senate, whose members would be chosen for life and given substantial endowments meant to ensure their independence, would have served a purpose similar to the US Supreme Court.

Bonaparte was for the most part ready to accept Sieyès's ideas for the elimination of meaningful elections and his tripartite legislature. What concerned him about Sieyès's plan, however, was the design for the executive branch of the new government. Sieyès proposed a government headed by a *grand électeur* (grand elector) who would have a lavish salary; his powers, however, would be limited to choosing two consuls, one to conduct foreign policy and the other responsible for domestic matters. If the grand elector exceeded his largely ceremonial authority, the Senate could "absorb" him, making him an ordinary member of their body. Bonaparte recognized that Sieyès intended to designate him as grand elector, leaving him with a fancy title but no real power. "He thought or pretended to think that this whole theory had been imagined just to make him ridiculous and dispose of him in a couple of months," Boulay de la Meurthe recalled. An angry meeting nearly resulted in a complete break between the two men, with Bonaparte threatening to claim power on his own, even if it made him look like a dictator.[9]

Sieyès soon realized that he could not stand in Bonaparte's way, and Bonaparte realized that it would be foolhardy to shred the veil of legality justifying the coup. "It was obvious, in reality, that it was Bonaparte whom the nation wanted to see in charge of affairs," Boulay wrote. "It was necessary to give him enough power so that he could . . . employ his popularity, his energy and his genius for the good of the country."[10] Roederer, always a master at finding compromises, proposed transforming Sieyès's grand elector into a *premier consul* (first consul) with power to direct the government. He was to be flanked by two other consuls to avoid making it seem as though France were reverting to one-man rule. The other two consuls, however, would have no real power.

Once the new executive structure was set, Bonaparte told Sieyès to select the consuls, knowing that his fellow-conspirator-turned-adversary would have no choice but to nominate him as first consul. He also left it to Sieyès, who knew the personalities in the Paris political scene better than he did, to choose most of the members of the new legislative bodies. Rather than accept a purely subordinate position as second consul, Sieyès agreed to become president of the Senate. Bonaparte quickly arranged to have Sieyès granted a valuable property outside of Paris; his acceptance of the gift destroyed Sieyès's reputation as a statesman uninterested in acquiring wealth. Christine Reinhard understood Sieyès's situation: "His hands are now tied and he cannot aspire to anything else," she wrote. Even though she realized that the new administration would cost her husband his job, she was pleased with the outcome. "I trust in the genius of Bonaparte; he will not let us down! He would not have escaped from a thousand dangers, he would not have miraculously crossed the sea, if his destiny was not to be fulfilled."[11] Her attitude was shared by much of the population.

The second and third consuls, Jean-Jacques Cambacérès and Charles-François Lebrun, were carefully selected. The appointment of Cambacérès, a former Convention deputy who had voted for the execution of Louis XVI in 1793, reassured former Jacobins, while Lebrun, a constitutional monarchist who had been a deputy in the National Assembly, did the same for moderate royalists. Bonaparte allowed one of the Paris newspapers to underline the message of their appointments in an article that quoted him as saying, "Positions will be open to Frenchmen of all opinions, provided that they are intelligent, capable, and virtuous."[12] The new Senate, Legislative Body, and Tribunate were composed overwhelmingly of former Directorial deputies. Men who did not find a seat in the assemblies were often appointed to administrative positions or to the newly created Conseil d'état (Council of State), a body of legal experts set up to draft legislation. The Council of State remains one of the lasting contributions of the Napoleonic regime to French political life. Despite the presence of a few former Montagnards, such as the police minister Fouché, however, the new government of the Consulate firmly closed the door to the neo-Jacobins, whose movement had enjoyed a brief revival in 1799.

On 24 frimaire Year VIII (December 15, 1799), barely a month after the brumaire coup, the new Constitution of 1800 (or the Year VIII) was published. The consuls announced that "the Revolution is settled according to the principles which started it; it is finished." The new document differed from its predecessors of 1791 and 1795 in a number of ways. As the veteran legislator Antoine Thibaudeau pointed out, the new document "said nothing about the freedom of worship, of the press, the public nature of judicial proceedings": in fact, it included no declaration of rights at all. The Constitution of 1795 had foreseen the possibility that specific rights might be suspended in a crisis; the new document authorized the suspension of the entire constitution in case of "troubles that threaten the security of the state." Another significant change was the document's announcement that "the regime of the French colonies is determined by special laws," a clause that raised the possibility that slavery, abolished in 1794, might again be legalized. The *Journal des hommes libres*, still identified as a Jacobin organ but now controlled by Fouché, admitted that republicans "have the right to regret that a number of principles that were so dear to them have been passed over in silence in the new social pact." The journal reminded its readers of "the futility of the efforts they made, in other times, to put into practice and carry out, even with their most beloved lawmakers, the most just and most accepted things." Less committed to the new regime, the royalist *Gazette de France* saw no chance that the head of the government would be restrained by the constitution. "One should not delude oneself in politics," its editorialist wrote. "The French have no safeguard against the preponderance of the executive power, and if it is just and wise, it will be so because that is in its interest."[13]

In one respect, Bonaparte did pay homage to the dogma of popular sovereignty. Over Sieyès's objections, he insisted that the new constitution be submitted for a vote, even demanding that almost all adult men be allowed to participate, regardless of their wealth or income. This populist gesture was not really meaningful: citizens were required to write down their vote along with their name and address, and the new institutions were put into effect even before the plebiscite was held, with members of the new legislative bodies simply named by the consuls. The government announced that over 3 million citizens had voted yes, and only 1,562 had said no. In reality, however, Lucien Bonaparte, the interior minister, intervened again, as he had at Saint-Cloud on 19 brumaire, to save his brother from embarrassment: only 1.6 million votes had actually been cast, fewer than the 1.8 million who had endorsed the Jacobin constitution of 1793. Lucien systematically padded the figures so that the new regime could claim a stronger endorsement than its democratic predecessor.[14] The plebiscite allowed Bonaparte to present himself as the chosen representative of the French people, in contrast to the members of the three legislative bodies, none of whom had been elected.

From the start, Bonaparte made no effort to conceal his annoyance with any public criticism. When Benjamin Constant made a motion critical of the government in the Tribunate, "the First Consul's anger went beyond all limits," Christine Reinhard wrote. "He wanted to take draconian measures, annul the latest elections to eliminate the supporters of Sieyès from all the chambers." As the new ruler's authoritarian tendencies became apparent, even many of the men who had participated in the brumaire conspiracy began to have second thoughts about having helped him seize power. By late spring, the police were reporting that Sieyès was holding mysterious meetings with former Jacobins. "He stubbornly saw Bonaparte as an auxiliary that the moderate party could rein in whenever it wanted," Madame Reinhard told her mother.[15]

On 27 nivôse Year VIII (January 17, 1800), shortly after the start of the legislative session, the consuls announced a return to the old-regime system of licensing periodicals and banned all but thirteen of the newspapers appearing in Paris. Journalists and publishers, who had survived many attempts at repression during the Revolution, tried their usual tactics, creating new papers under different titles, but this time they faced a regime determined to enforce its edicts. Within a few months, all vestiges of the republican press were suppressed. The Consulate tolerated the creation of an outspokenly counterrevolutionary daily paper, the *Journal des débats*, whose editors had earlier put out journals that supported the vendémiaire uprising in 1795 and the Clichy Club in 1797; it quickly became by far the most widely read publication in the country and a genuine influence on public opinion. While the *Journal des débats* avoided overt political commentary, its literary critic Julien-Louis Geoffroy waged a relentless campaign against the ideas of the Enlightenment. Determined to combat the influence of the Idéologues' *Décade philosophique*, the *Journal* emphasized the value of social order and encouraged a return to religion.

Imposing order on society was also the main motivation behind the policies Bonaparte put in place in the first months of the Consulate. Now housed in the former royal palace of the Tuileries, where he began to revive public rituals reminiscent of the royal court, he moved quickly to replace the elected departmental and local administrative bodies created during the Revolution with appointed officials called *préfets* and *sous-préfets* (prefects and subprefects). The prefects took the place of the government commissioners the Directory had appointed, but whereas the Directory's system had still been something of an improvisation, the new top-down administrative structure quickly took on an air of permanence. Under this system "the movement of power will be rapid," a pro-government journalist wrote. "It will find its orders carried out everywhere, with no opposition, it will always have the instruments it needs and no obstacles against it."[16] The prefects reminded many of the old regime's intendants, against whom so much of the revolutionaries' anger had been directed in 1789. But the intendants had always faced resistance from the parlementary courts, provincial assemblies, and other local institutions. Now that the Revolution had abolished these obstacles to centralized rule, the prefects had a much easier time enforcing the government's orders. The prefectorial system proved so effective that every subsequent French government has maintained it, although today the appointed prefects share power with elected departmental and regional councils.

Even as the new government silenced former republicans and allowed a revival of conservative ideas in the press, it could not ignore the threat of royalist agitation. This was so especially in the western regions, where opposition to the Revolution flared up again. Bonaparte wasted no time in dealing with the problem. He dispatched troops, but also opened negotiations with rebel leaders, trying to persuade them that his regime would be an acceptable substitute for the monarchy. In other regions, where rural banditry had become endemic during the Directory, the new government extended the repressive measures already deployed by its predecessor, placing large areas under a state of siege and establishing military tribunals that did not hesitate to impose death sentences.

As the government sought to end the long-running armed conflict in western France, it also sought to find a solution that would permit many of those who had emigrated during the Revolution to return to the country. Although the Constitution of the Year VIII maintained the existing laws against émigrés, the consuls announced that no further names would be added to the list of those penalized for having fled before the brumaire coup. Sensing that the atmosphere had changed, a number of émigrés took the chance of returning, even if they were unable to get themselves officially removed from the dreaded list. Bonaparte's own attitude on the issue was inconsistent: he wanted to promote reconciliation, but he was aware of the strong feelings in the army about aristocrats who had fought against France. The émigrés, for their part, brought their own resentments with them. Many of them discovered, as one put it, that "except in a few special or unusual cases one does not get one's property back. The young men have to go into the army, the young women have to continue to work as they did in emigration; the old die of hunger." François-René de Chateaubriand, a young nobleman who had fled in 1792 and spent years in Britain and America, was relieved to be able to come back to his native country, but he could not shake the memory of his family members being guillotined during the Terror. Walking in Paris, he had the feeling of "putting my foot in blood." Bonaparte was conciliatory toward émigrés and domestic royalists, but only those who were willing to accept the new regime. When Louis XVI's older brother Louis XVIII wrote to Bonaparte, promising a handsome reward if he used his position to reinstate the monarchy, Bonaparte's reply was unequivocal: "You must not hope to return to France; you would have to march over 100,000 dead bodies. Sacrifice your own interest to the peace and the happiness of France. History will be grateful to you."[17]

As energetic as the new government was in dealing with domestic matters, Bonaparte and his supporters knew that the key to cementing their power was to bring the war they had inherited from the Directory to a victorious conclusion. Despite the successes of the French armies in September 1799, the conquests in Italy that Bonaparte had made were now in enemy hands. Moreover, the promise of Austrian acceptance of French gains in northern Europe that he had extracted in the Treaty of Campo-Formio had been broken. As the campaigning season neared, he assembled a reserve army near Dijon, a strategic location that kept the enemy guessing whether he would march north to invade Germany or south to try to reclaim Italy. In mid-May, Bonaparte made his decision: he would lead his forces over the Alps to take the Austrian army besieging Genoa, the last French foothold in Italy, in the rear. This daring maneuver surprised the Austrians and Bonaparte quickly reoccupied Milan, the capital city of Lombardy, but the critical battle at Marengo, fought on June 14, 1800, came within a hair's-breadth of ending in disaster. Not expecting an Austrian attack, Bonaparte had dispersed his forces and found himself badly outnumbered; he was rescued at the last minute by the arrival of General Louis Desaix, who was killed even as his troops launched a successful charge. Desaix's misfortune meant that he was not around to contest Bonaparte's account of Marengo as a battle won by his own strategic brilliance. The dramatic victory consolidated Bonaparte's power at home, although it took another six months of fighting before General Jean-Victor Moreau's victory at the Battle of Hohenlinden drove the Austrians to sue for peace.

The Treaty of Lunéville, signed in February 1801, restored all the gains that France had obtained four years earlier at Campo-Formio and even added to them. The Austrians officially recognized France's annexation of the German territories west of its self-proclaimed "natural frontier" on the Rhine. The government in Vienna then had to convene a congress of the rulers of the Holy Roman Empire to work out compensations for the various princes whose possessions had been taken by the French. The process overturned the complicated arrangements that had governed central Europe for several centuries. Initially, it led to expanded French influence in Germany, as local rulers competed to win Bonaparte's backing for their claims. In the long run, it opened the way for the rise of a German nationalist movement seventy years later, when Otto von Bismarck created a unified German Empire after defeating France in the war of 1870–1871, definitively ending the era of French dominance in Europe.

Together with the increasingly successful campaign to restore law and order in the countryside, the peace with Austria increased Bonaparte's popularity and allowed him to embark on further initiatives that might otherwise have been too controversial to pursue. As the Consulate became more solidly entrenched in power, its domestic opponents were left with no method of opposing it other than conspiracy. Both royalists and militant republicans circulated clandestine pamphlets justifying assassination as a legitimate response to Bonaparte's dictatorial behavior. The police broke up several plots, but on 3 nivôse An IX, Christmas Eve 1800, as Bonaparte's carriage was taking him to the opera, an "infernal machine," a horse-cart loaded with gunpowder—the revolutionary era's version of a car bomb—exploded nearby. It narrowly missed its target but killed several passersby.

Even before the police investigation had begun, Bonaparte was convinced that the plot was the work of republican militants. He demanded immediate vengeance: "Blood must flow; we need to shoot as many guilty ones as there were victims, fifteen or twenty, deport two hundred of them, and take advantage of this opportunity to purge the Republic of them."[18] The Senate was bullied into approving arbitrary measures, including the creation of special courts to hold expedited trials of defendants accused of threatening public security. Over one hundred former Jacobins and sans-culotte activists were shipped off to Guyana or the Seychelles in the Indian Ocean, where most of them died. Meanwhile, Fouché's agents carried out one of the first modern forensic investigations, showing the remains of the horse that had been attached to the cart to Paris blacksmiths. One of them recognized it and identified the horse's owner; he turned out to be a royalist conspirator. Several of the perpetrators were promptly arrested and executed, although the mastermind behind the plot escaped, ending his life as a Catholic priest in Charleston, South Carolina. Despite the revelation of the royalist nature of the plot, Bonaparte refused to reconsider the measure he had ordered against the Jacobins. Although the Consulate still maintained

PROPAGANDA FOR THE BRUMAIRE COUP: The plotters who overthrew the Directory made skillful use of the media to consolidate their power. This broadsheet showed the youthful Napoleon Bonaparte flanked by the older men who had agreed to serve as second and third consuls. They hold scrolls inscribed with promises to pay state debts, achieve peace, and inspire "love of the laws." *Source: Bibliothèque nationale de France.*

a facade of republicanism, the first consul was determined to destroy the last traces of revolutionary radicalism.

The increasingly arbitrary and authoritarian nature of Bonaparte's regime widened the gap between the republican intellectuals who had helped carry out the brumaire coup and the man they had incautiously helped put into power. Objecting to the special tribunals, the tribune

Pierre Daunou warned that the arguments of the government's advocates could be used to justify "suspension of individual rights, of all the social guarantees; military taxes; arbitrary arrests; indefinite detentions; arbitrary inquisitions." In his private meditations, Benjamin Constant now regretted that he and his friends had been so ready to sabotage the noisy public politics of the Directory in the name of order. Bonaparte, Constant lamented, was extending the principles of the army into all areas of national life. "The military spirit slips into all civil relations. One imagines that for liberty, as for victory, nothing is more appropriate than passive obedience."[19] In the face of the new realities, Constant and his friends developed the intellectual bases for a principled defense of individual liberties that would bear fruit under the less repressive regimes that followed Napoleon in the nineteenth century. For the moment, however, their protests went unheeded.

The affair of the "infernal machine" convinced Bonaparte of two things: the fragility of his regime as long as he appeared to be the only person holding it together, and the necessity of making peace with Britain in order to end that country's support for the royalists. He was not yet in a position to deal with the first problem by making his rule hereditary, but the victory over Austria gave him the leverage to bring the British to the peace table. A preliminary agreement was signed on October 1, 1801, in which the British agreed to return almost all the overseas territories they had seized from France and its allies in exchange for French withdrawal from Egypt and the southern half of the Italian Peninsula. Great celebrations were held in Paris in early November, timed to coincide with the anniversary of the brumaire coup. A final treaty was signed in the northern French city of Amiens on March 25, 1802. For the first time since April 1792, France was no longer at war. In his memoirs, Talleyrand, Napoleon's foreign minister, wrote, "One can say, without the least exaggeration, that, at the time of the peace of Amiens, France enjoyed in the world a power, a glory, and influence as great as the most ambitious spirit could want for his country."[20]

In Bonaparte's mind, one of the most important consequences of the peace of Amiens was Britain's agreement to let France immediately launch a naval expedition to regain full control of its Caribbean colonies. When Bonaparte took power in late 1799, Saint-Domingue was embroiled in a violent civil war between Toussaint Louverture and André Rigaud, the leader of the island's free people of color. The Directory's last commissioner, General Joseph Hédouville, had encouraged Rigaud to challenge the black strongman. In the smaller island of Guadeloupe, a revolt of the free population of color forced the French general Edme Desfourneaux to flee in early October 1799.

Bonaparte was determined to reimpose metropolitan control over the colonies and restore France's status as a world power; indeed, he bargained with Spain to reclaim Louisiana—the vast territory in the Mississippi valley that Louis XV had ceded after the Seven Years' War in 1763—in order to create an American empire. As long as the British navy prevented the dispatch of a large number of troops to the Caribbean, however, he did not specify what the "special laws" would be that the new constitution foresaw for the colonies. In December 1799, Bonaparte issued a proclamation promising the population of Saint-Domingue that "the sacred principles of the liberty and equality of the blacks will never be attacked or modified." Louverture was not reassured. He was aware that the new French ruler had already promised that slavery would not be disturbed in colonies where the 1794 law had not been applied. He also knew that Bonaparte had appointed a number of former advocates of slavery to important government positions. Thus, Louverture told the Consulate's representative, "We are free today because we are the strongest. [Bonaparte] maintains slavery in Martinique and the Île Bourbon; we will also be enslaved when he becomes the strongest."[21]

As he waited for the moment when he could take action overseas, Bonaparte consulted former colonists about what policy he should adopt. Some of the responses were unexpected: the former Saint-Domingue Convention deputies Louis Dufay and Jean-Baptiste Belley, whose presence on 16 pluviôse Year II (February 4, 1794) had persuaded the Convention to pass its historic decree abolishing slavery, had turned against Toussaint Louverture and urged intervention to remove him. The former lobbyist for the white slaveowners, Pierre-François Page, however, concluded that it was now too late to overturn the policy of emancipation. Bonaparte's personal views were not favorable to the egalitarian policies the Convention and the Directory had adopted. In 1801, when the pending return of Martinique brought the question of slavery to the fore, Thibaudeau heard him deliver a veritable racist tirade: "I am for the whites, because I am white; I have no other reason, and that one is good. How could one grant freedom to Africans, to men who have no civilization, who don't even know what a colony is, what France is?"[22] Bonaparte may have been influenced by his wife, Josephine, whose family owned land in Martinique, although he rarely let her offer him advice. In 1802, she permitted the author of *The Errors of Negrophilism*, a violent tract against the abolition of slavery, to dedicate his work to her.

Yet Bonaparte did not let his personal beliefs about race and slavery keep him from thinking of ways to profit from Toussaint Louverture's successes. In early 1801, he drafted a letter appointing the black leader as captain-general of the colony. Rather than sending the letter, however, Bonaparte then changed direction, deciding to dismiss Louverture and expel him from the French army altogether. After defeating Rigaud's forces in early 1800, the black general had defied instructions from the French government and occupied the Spanish colony of Santo Domingo (today's Dominican Republic), which formed the eastern half of the island of Hispaniola. In February 1801, Louverture put Philippe Roume, the last remaining French official in the colony, under house arrest, and in April he convened an assembly to draft his own constitution for Saint-Domingue. On the other side of the Atlantic, Bonaparte had already given orders for an expeditionary force to be assembled and deployed to the Caribbean before he received a copy of Louverture's constitution, but the contents of the document confirmed his worst fears. He increased the number of troops being sent to the colony.

In his constitution, Louverture carefully avoided declaring independence, instead appropriating the language of the French constitution of 1800 to assert that he was merely establishing the "special laws" that it promised for the colonies. Whereas the consular constitution had omitted any declaration of rights, Louverture's document used the language of liberty and equality. It declared slavery "forever abolished," stated that "all men are born, live, and die free and French," that men of all colors could hold "all types of employment," and that "the law is the same for everyone, with regard to both protection and punishment." Even as it appealed to the doctrine of natural rights, however, the Louverturian constitution also went beyond Bonaparte's own charter in establishing an authoritarian government, to be headed by Louverture himself "for the rest of his glorious life." The only theoretical check on his power was an assembly whose members he himself would choose. Catholicism was declared the state religion and divorce outlawed. Despite the abolition of slavery, Louverture instituted a system of forced labor; he even foresaw the possibility of the Saint-Domingue government purchasing captives brought from Africa in order to promote "the revival and expansion of agriculture." The social conservatism underlying Louverture's constitution was not far from Bonaparte's own views, but the first consul was infuriated by the black governor's disregard for his authority. Louverture's initiative helped inspire a movement against the white governor of Guadeloupe, where a mixed-race military officer, Magloire Pélage, took power with the support of black soldiers in the army who "thought that they were going to be re-enslaved," according to one report.[23]

The expedition that sailed from France in the fall of November 1801 was one of the largest overseas military efforts mounted by a European government up to that time. It took well over a hundred ships to transport the more than twenty thousand troops destined for the two islands. As commander of the army bound for Saint-Domingue, Bonaparte appointed his own brother-in-law Victoire Leclerc, who was married to his sister Pauline. Leclerc's instructions laid out a three-part plan: Initially he would reassure the population about its rights and negotiate with Toussaint Louverture, "in order to take possession of the strongholds and get ourselves into the country." Once he had secured the colony's strategic points, Leclerc was to become "more demanding" and remove Louverture from his position; meanwhile, he would incorporate the black soldiers and officers into his own army. Finally, he would arrest the black officers, have them "shot like rebels" if they resisted, and disarm the black population, leaving them no way of opposing French authority. The plan echoed an anonymous proposal published in France several years earlier by a proslavery pamphleteer. That writer had explicitly recommended pretending that slavery would not be reintroduced until the colony had been secured militarily, when the blacks could be "defeated and kept in complete subjection to forestall misfortunes."[24]

Informed of Bonaparte's hostile reaction to his constitution and the impending arrival of the military expedition, Louverture prepared to fight back. When the French fleet reached the northern port of Cap Français, which had been rebuilt in the years since the devastating fire of 1793, he set his own plan in motion. Henri Christophe, one of Louverture's commanders, burned the city once again and withdrew into the countryside. Leclerc was able to bring his forces ashore, but he encountered ferocious opposition from Louverture's army and from guerrilla bands in the island's mountains. The black forces inflicted heavy casualties on the French and massacred whites who they feared would side with the invaders. Nevertheless, by the end of April, the French had gained the upper hand. In accordance with his instructions, Leclerc allowed Christophe, Jean-Jacques Dessalines, and other black officers to keep their ranks and incorporated their men into his own army. Abandoned by his own supporters, Toussaint Louverture agreed to give up his position as governor of the colony and retire to his rural plantation.

News of these military successes in the Caribbean paved the way for one of Bonaparte's most emphatic repudiations of the revolutionary principles of liberty and equality: on May 20, 1802, the Convention's law of 16 pluviôse Year II was repealed, legalizing the decision to maintain slavery in the colonies where it had not been abolished in 1794. The decision aroused a certain amount of opposition: a third of the tribunes and sixty-three members of the Legislative Body voted against it. The repeal law said nothing about Saint-Domingue and Guadeloupe, but the threat to black freedom was unmistakable. The re-legalization of slavery was followed by another law prohibiting "blacks, mulattoes or other people of color, of either sex," from entering France's European territory. Convinced that the prerevolutionary days were rapidly returning, slave-ship captains set sail for the African coast. Whites who had fled Cap Français after the 1791 slave uprising hastened to return to the colony to resume their trades. One of these, a tailor named Norbert Thoret, reopened his shop in Cap Français and was soon employing forty workers to make uniforms for French officers. "If things had remained tranquil," he later wrote, "it is certain that I would quickly have made a great fortune."[25]

The sense of security among the white population in Saint-Domingue was reinforced in June 1802, when Leclerc accused Toussaint Louverture of secretly encouraging black resistance to the French. Caught off-guard on his own plantation, Louverture was arrested and hustled onboard a warship bound for France; there, he was separated from his family and imprisoned in the Fort de Joux, near the Swiss border. Bonaparte refused to read the lengthy memorandum Louverture wrote to justify his conduct. Unaccustomed to the cold, dank European climate, Louverture fell ill and died in April 1803. By that time, General Leclerc was also in his grave, along with much of his army, decimated by a deadly yellow fever epidemic. As the ranks of white soldiers dwindled, Louverture's officers changed sides again, galvanized by reports concerning Guadeloupe: they had heard that an armed revolt there, led by the mixed-race Louis Delgrès, had been defeated by the French commander Antoine Richepance, but that the rebels, refusing to surrender, had blown up their last stronghold—committing suicide in the process—to cries of "No slavery! Long live death!"[26] The blacks in Guadeloupe, Martinique, and France's Indian Ocean colonies would not gain their freedom until 1848, when another revolution finally toppled slavery in the French Empire.

In Saint-Domingue, the French effort to quash black resistance failed. In October 1802, the mixed-race general Alexandre Pétion and the black generals Jean-Jacques Dessalines and Henri Christophe launched a revolt that openly aimed at gaining independence from France. In the winter of 1802–1803, Bonaparte poured thousands more troops into the struggle. Most of them, like their predecessors, ended up dying on the island; total French losses ultimately came to around fifty thousand soldiers and sailors. The expedition's fate was sealed after May 1803, when the fragile peace of Amiens collapsed and the British navy once again cut off French communications with the Caribbean. Leclerc's successor, General Donatien Rochambeau, resorted to brutal tactics, importing tracking dogs from Cuba to hunt down black rebels in the mountains and asphyxiating prisoners in the holds of warships. Nevertheless, by the end of 1803, he was compelled to surrender, and what had been France's most valuable overseas possession became the independent nation of Haiti. As the looming defeat in Saint-Domingue destroyed his dream of creating an empire in the New World, Bonaparte hastily offered the Louisiana Territory to the Americans, launching the new country on the career of expansion that would make it a world power.

The abandonment of the abolition of slavery and the experiment that had made France, from 1794 to 1802, a multiracial polity was the Consulate's most devastating retreat from the promises of the Revolution. Of more immediate concern to the population in metropolitan France, however, was Bonaparte's policy toward the Catholic Church. From the start of the Consulate, he had taken steps foreshadowing an end to the revolutionary campaign against the Church. Shortly after the coup, deportations of refractory priests to Guyana were stopped, and Catholics were allowed to resume Sunday worship services. Priests were still required to take an oath of loyalty to the constitution, however, which most of them refused to do, and many officials, particularly the police minister, Fouché, remained strongly hostile to the Church. "We don't know what to say about this government," the Savoyard priest François Molin wrote in his diary in March 1800. "They free some and imprison others." But pressure for a broader agreement between the government and the Church was growing. After his survey of the western provinces, the scientist and official Antoine-François Fourcroy concluded that "it is an error of some modern philosophers, which I myself shared, to believe in the possibility of spreading instruction sufficiently to destroy religious prejudices."[27]

Bonaparte was nevertheless moving toward an agreement with the Church that would end the religious conflict that the National Assembly had started with the Civil Constitution of the Clergy. When he occupied Milan in June 1800, Bonaparte had called on the local clergy to mount a public ceremony to celebrate his victory and spoke of "removing every obstacle that might hinder complete reconciliation between France and the head of the Church."[28] The new pope chosen in 1800, Pius VII, had indicated, during the French invasion of Italy in 1797, that coexistence between the Church and republican ideas was possible. Informed of Bonaparte's "glorious and fortunate decision" to open negotiations about a restoration of the Church, he responded positively. Bonaparte originally conceived of a one-sided bargain in which he would use the pope to force recalcitrant émigré clergy into line, as he explained to one member of the Council of State. "The people need a religion. That religion must be under the control of the government. At the moment, fifty émigré bishops paid by England direct the French clergy. Their influence must be destroyed; the Pope's authority is necessary for that." In exchange for giving the Church legal protection in France, he would have the pope order all the bishops of the French Church to resign their posts. This would include both those who had gone into exile to oppose the Revolution and those, like the constitutional church leader Henri Grégoire, who had embraced the Civil Constitution. Those who were willing to go along with the new order of things would then be reappointed. "The pope will confirm the sale of the church's property; he will bless the Republic," Bonaparte said to one Council of State member. He assured his listener that his determination had nothing to do with any personal attachment to Catholicism. "They will say that I am a Papist; I am nothing; I was a Muslim in Egypt, I'll be Catholic here for the good of the people."[29]

The Concordat required many concessions from the Church. First, the Church would have to accept the permanent loss of the property that had been expropriated in 1789. In exchange, the government agreed to resume the payments to the clergy that had been abolished in 1795. But the government would now nominate bishops, who would still receive their religious consecration from the pope. This arrangement was basically a return to the practices of the prerevolutionary Gallican Church, but after an experience that had shown how hostile a French government could be to religion. The Concordat recognized Catholicism as "the religion of the majority of the French," rather than granting it special status, and it guaranteed freedom of worship to the country's Protestants and Jews. The rights of citizens who did not subscribe to any religion were also secured. After Pius VII agreed to Bonaparte's terms and signed the agreement, the French government unilaterally added a number of so-called "organic articles" to its provisions. Among other things, these additions prohibited the Vatican from communicating directly with the French clergy and required that church services include prayers for the salvation of the republic and the consuls. In later years, priests were ordered to tell their congregants that military service was a religious obligation.

In order to prevent the Catholic population from drifting away from the Church altogether, Pius VII accepted what was, from his point of view, a highly unfavorable agreement. As the negotiations leading to the Concordat began in 1800, the refractory priest Molin worried in his diary that "the torch of faith may finally go out in our unfortunate country." No new priests were being trained, and after so many years of disruption, the laity were in a state of "astonishing stupidity" about their faith. One government official remarked that peasants had fallen out of the habit of going to confession, taking communion, and avoiding meat on Fridays. "Where there are no priests, the schoolteacher officiates and they are happy," he wrote.[30] The Concordat gave the Church a chance to reestablish itself in national life and to restore priests' authority over the laity. Bonaparte's willingness to acknowledge the pope's control over the French Catholic hierarchy in order to silence the quarreling refractory and constitutional bishops marked a major shift of power within the Church. French rulers and clergy had long resisted "Ultramontanism," the recognition of the authority of the Vatican "beyond the mountains." By invoking the pope's authority to silence dissent in the French Church, Bonaparte helped set changes in motion that culminated in the First Vatican Council of 1870, which consecrated the doctrine of papal infallibility and created the modern, highly centralized Catholic Church.

The Concordat was officially put into effect on Easter Sunday, April 18, 1802, with a great ceremony at Paris's Notre Dame cathedral. The grand medieval structure, which had been the setting for the revolutionary Festival of Reason and the celebration of the abolition of slavery, now resumed its religious function. The returned émigré writer Chateaubriand timed the release of his *Genius of Christianity*, an eloquent response to the critiques of religion propagated by the philosophes and the Revolution, to coincide with the ceremony; lavishly praised by the conservative press, it marked a turning point in public opinion. The promulgation of the Concordat and the ceremony at Notre Dame did not succeed in returning the whole of France to the Catholic faith, however. In his memoirs, written during the Consulate, Jacques Ménétra still lambasted the "ancient Gothic prejudices of the clergy." When Bonaparte tried to persuade the writer Constantin Volney that the country wanted him to reestablish the Church, he was so irritated by Volney's response—"If France asked you to bring back the Bourbons, would you do it?"—that he kicked him in the stomach, knocking him to the floor. A British visitor, Henry Redhead Yorke, did not think the sight of Bonaparte and other dignitaries at the Easter ceremony, "assembled together in one place to adore a God in whom they had no faith, and to profess a religion which they despised," would do much to restore the people's faith. He noted ironically how the first consul, who "had worshipped the altar of Atheism some years before in Paris, . . . afterwards knelt down before the Pope at Rome, and embraced the religion of Mahomet in Africa."[31]

Many army officers were especially disgruntled about the restoration of Catholicism. One group of generals, forced to attend the Mass at Notre Dame, ousted some of the priests from their seats, "insulting them, making them flee, and taking their places." After the ceremony, when Bonaparte asked one of the officers what he thought of it, he responded, "It is a shame that the million or so men who got themselves killed destroying what you have reestablished were not there." A small band of writers, some of them linked to the Idéologues, kept up a dogged campaign to discredit religious belief. Marie-Joseph Chénier ridiculed Chateaubriand and his circle in his Les nouveaux saints (The new saints), and the popular author Pigault-Lebrun rushed out a work meant to show that "the edifice of religion is the costume of Harlequin, an assembly of pieces whose clashing nuances shock the eye, as the whole shocks reason." Bonaparte knew, however, that he could ignore these critics: unlike the supporters of the Church, they were incapable of causing widespread disturbances. At the beginning of 1803, he targeted the last stronghold of the anticlerical Idéologues, the Institute's Class of Moral and Political Sciences. The group was broken up and replaced with a conservatively oriented Class of History and Ancient Literature, whose members were told to avoid "any historical, religious, or political discussions."[32]

The reinstatement of slavery and the Concordat were two unmistakable signs that the era of the Revolution was truly drawing to a close: a government based on very different principles from those of 1789 was now in place. In March 1802, Bonaparte used the compliant Senate to carry out a purge of the Tribunate and the Legislative Body. Benjamin Constant and other Idéologues who had initially supported the brumaire coup but had then become vocal critics of the first consul's authoritarian tendencies were ousted. "The nation's will is that the government should not be stopped from doing good," Bonaparte told Cambacérès. Shortly after the celebration of the Concordat, Bonaparte abandoned another of the Revolution's hallmark policies by pushing through a law giving amnesty to the vast majority of the émigrés who had fled France during the Revolution. The Paris police reported animated debates about the measure in the streets and cafés, but Bonaparte was sure that the public would approve "as long as the sale of national lands is respected."[33]

The peace of Amiens and the Concordat increased Bonaparte's popularity, and he was eager to use the opportunity to strengthen his already extensive powers. According to the Constitution of 1800, his appointment as first consul was only for ten years, but many of his supporters wanted to declare him consul for life. Bonaparte, concerned about appearances, avoiding making the request himself, but when the legislators hesitated to take the initiative, he outmaneuvered them by calling for another plebiscite: the population could decide whether he should be named first consul for life. His loyal supporter Pierre-Louis Roederer argued that Bonaparte deserved "a gift worthy of his devotion: that of the time necessary to assure the happiness of France."[34] The results of the election were announced at the beginning of August 1802, giving Bonaparte a resounding victory: 3,568,885 voters said yes and 8,374 said no. In contrast to the 1800 referendum, the vote count in 1802 was relatively honest and reflected a genuine endorsement of the regime.

Bonaparte further underlined his determination to break with the ideas of the Revolution by creating the Legion of Honor, an award recognizing those who had rendered outstanding service to the country and to ensure their loyalty to the regime. Defenders argued that the Legion did not contradict the dogma of equality because all male citizens could earn membership, which carried no legal privileges and was not hereditary. To many former revolutionaries, however, the Legion looked like a revival of the monarchy's practice of giving out titles and decorations rather than relying on citizens' selfless love of their country. In the Council of State, a former Convention deputy objected to this handing out of "baubles." Bonaparte shot back, "It is with baubles that men are led."[35] Despite the purge carried out earlier in the year, there was vociferous opposition to the Legion of Honor in the Tribunate and 110 no-votes in the Legislative Body, the highest number cast against any of Bonaparte's measures. Like many of the Consulate's innovations, however, the Legion of Honor became a permanent feature of French life, surviving even under democratic regimes.

Just as the revolutionaries had tried to remodel civil society according to their ideas about liberty and equality, Bonaparte and his supporters sought to instill certain values; however, now it was to make sure the principles of order and respect for authority pervaded all aspects of French life. Their most powerful tool for achieving their goals was the unified civil law code, which the Council of State hammered out in hundreds of sessions starting in 1800, often with Bonaparte in attendance. It was finally completed in 1804. The new Code civil des Français (Civil Code of the French) showed how key concepts of the Revolution could be interpreted in ways that served very different purposes than those the revolutionaries of 1789 had had in mind. The new set of laws did reflect the revolutionaries' determination to make the independent male individual the basic unit of society: all adult men now had the same legal rights. The code's definition of property consolidated the abolition of the old regime's panoply of feudal, seigneurial, and communal rights and erected safeguards against the limitations on economic individualism proposed by revolutionary radicals. The drafters accepted the view of Jean-Baptiste Say, whose *Treatise on Political Economy*, destined to shape economic thinking for decades afterward, appeared in 1803. Say insisted on "the freedom that men should have to dispose of their persons and their goods; freedom without which social happiness and property are meaningless words."[36] The code's provisions were framed to favor property-owning patriarchs, who were to rule over their families and their employees as Bonaparte now ruled over France.

Whereas the Revolution's civil legislation, especially the laws concerning the family, had tended to equalize the rights of men and women, the Civil Code gave husbands authority over wives and fathers authority over children. Husbands now had full control of the family's property, and married women could only work or conduct businesses with their permission. The authority of fathers over children was enhanced by a revision of the Revolution's egalitarian law on inheritance giving them the right to award a part of the family estate as they wished, meaning that they could privilege favored heirs. "Natural" children and unwed mothers were deprived of the rights that had been granted to them under revolutionary legislation; in the interest of protecting family property, paternity suits were prohibited, and such children could not claim any inheritance, even if their fathers acknowledged them.

Marriage remained a civil contract, but it was no longer an agreement between equal partners. The Civil Code stated that "the husband owes protection to his wife, the wife owes obedience to her husband," a provision that Jean-Étienne Portalis, the spokesman for the code, justified on the grounds that "conjugal society . . . can only exist if one spouse is subordinate to the other."[37] Bonaparte, already thinking about ending his childless marriage with Josephine in the interest of founding a dynasty, made sure that divorce remained legal, although a majority of the Council of State favored abolishing it. Under the Civil Code, the husband could bring divorce proceedings much more easily than the wife, who could only initiate a suit in cases of extreme cruelty, or if her spouse brought another woman into the family home. The egalitarian "family councils" established by the revolutionary law of 1792 were abolished, and the number of divorce cases dropped sharply. Women who married foreigners lost their French citizenship.

Women were shut out of the Council of State's discussions about their status under the new Civil Code. Madame de Staël, whose circle of friends had included many participants in the brumaire coup, initially hoped that her salon would become the intellectual center of the new regime, but she quickly realized that the first consul had no tolerance for her. "Advise her not to block my path, no matter what it is, no matter where I choose to go, otherwise I will break her," Bonaparte warned one intermediary. The prominent women militants from the Revolution's radical years were mostly dead by this time, but a few new voices still spoke out on behalf of their sex. In 1801, in the midst of the Civil Code debates, Fanny Raoul wrote, "For the same reason that I don't want women to dominate, I also don't want them to be dominated. . . . Civil liberty and equality; that is what I ask for them. Isn't there some middle point between sovereign authority and absolute nullity?" Although Raoul stopped short of demanding political rights for women, as the radicals of 1793 had, she wanted women to be allowed to pursue the full range of professional careers and not to be confined to poorly paid manual occupations and domestic service.[38] Her protest showed that some women still remembered the issues that had been raised about women's rights during the revolutionary decade, but her pamphlet had no immediate impact.

In addition to coming down strongly on the side of patriarchal authority, the Civil Code and other laws gave employers advantages over their workers: in case of disputes, for example, the testimony of the employer was automatically accepted. In addition, a prerevolutionary law requiring workers to have a *livret*, or work passport, was reinstated. Workers could not leave a job unless they had permission from their previous employer. Employers were thus given a powerful weapon over their workforce; they were expected to assist the government in keeping the urban lower classes under control. Peasants, still the overwhelming majority of the population, retained more independence under the new law code. Its provisions on property safeguarded the landholdings that many of them had acquired or expanded as church lands and émigré properties were sold off, and they were no longer beholden to seigneurs. Thomas Holcroft, one of the many British visitors who hastened to visit after the peace of Amiens ended the rupture between the two countries, wrote that "although there are still many wretched cottages, the peasants are in general better dressed and they seem to be, if not in good humor, at least calmer and better disposed."[39]

The Consulate eliminated the election of village mayors, but in exchange it provided a consistent and relatively efficient system of local administration that peasants largely accepted. Bonaparte hoped that rural society would be dominated by wealthy landowners, the "masses of granite" on whom he counted to hold together a society that he feared was otherwise nothing more than "grains of sand." Unlike the seigneurs of the old regime, however, wealthy landowners no longer had any legal authority over the rest of the population.[40] Despite its masculinist and authoritarian coloration, the Civil Code was perhaps the most successful achievement of Bonaparte's Consulate. Compared to the tortuous complexities of old-regime civil law, the new law code, renamed the Code Napoléon (Napoleonic Code) in 1807, was clear and consistent. With its biases against women and workers considerably modified, it remains the basis of French society today. Introduced in territories under French control during the Napoleonic period, it also remains the basic legal framework in neighboring countries such as Belgium, the Netherlands, western Germany, and Italy, as well as in the American state of Louisiana.

By the time the Civil Code was completed in 1804, the regime's evolution from an authoritarian republic to a new form of monarchy was nearly complete. Bonaparte's decision to take the final steps in that direction was hastened by the resumption of the war with Britain in May 1803. The ostensible pretext for the renewal of the conflict was the British refusal to remove their forces from the Mediterranean island of Malta, as promised in the Treaty of Amiens; in reality, neither side had been truly committed to the terms of the agreement. British manufacturers were disappointed when they discovered that Bonaparte had no intention of opening the French market to their products; his advisers remembered how unpopular Calonne's free trade treaty of 1786 had been, and they intended to make Europe a protected sphere for France's own industries. On his side, Bonaparte complained that the British refused to extend official recognition to the sister republics France had reestablished in Italy and Switzerland after the Treaty of Lunéville with Austria. He also objected to the protection the British continued to extend to émigré bishops who refused to accept the Concordat, as well as to the comte d'Artois, Louis XVIII's younger brother, and other royalist exiles. He was incensed by the vitriolic attacks on him in the British press and refused to accept that the British tradition of press freedom made it impossible for the government to prevent them. The British ambassador told his government, "I am persuaded that the First Consul, if he makes war on us, will be motivated more by the irritation our journals cause him than by the dispute itself."[41]

The resumption of hostilities led the British government to give the green light for a new royalist plot against Bonaparte's life. The chouan conspirator Georges Cadoudal, who had helped organize earlier attempts, joined with General Jean-Charles Pichegru, who had been exiled after fructidor, to recruit a network of agents; their plan was to seize the first consul on the route to his wife Josephine's country estate at Malmaison. With Bonaparte out of the way, the comte d'Artois would land in France and announce the restoration of the monarchy. The plotters made contact with General Jean-Victor Moreau, who was still popular in the army. Moreau's resentment of Bonaparte's predominance was well known. The French police caught wind of the conspiracy but had difficulty tracking down the main participants, especially Cadoudal. Moreau was arrested, but the potential assassins were still at large. By February 1804, Bonaparte's nerves were on edge as rumors about an impending attack swirled. "Some master, who for five months has not been able to sleep for more than two hours at a time!" a royalist spy wrote.[42] On February 28, 1804, Paris was declared in a state of siege.

Finally, in early March, Pichegru and Cadoudal were caught in Paris. Bonaparte decided that it was not enough to punish the conspirators who had planned to kill him: he wanted to strike back at the Bourbon family. He suspected that the duc d'Enghien, the son of the prince of Condé, who had been living in exile in the German state of Baden, had been involved in the plot. On March 15, 1804, French soldiers, violating Baden's neutrality, staged a raid and captured him. He was brought to Paris, where a military tribunal, convened in the middle of the night, sentenced him to death, even though there was no evidence that he had known anything about the assassination plot. The police minister Fouché later claimed to have said, "It's worse than a crime, it's a blunder." Many royalists who had accepted Bonaparte's rule nevertheless condemned this direct blow against the Bourbon family. From Bonaparte's point of view, the execution was an exercise of *raison d'état*. "It was necessary to show the Bourbons, the cabinet of London, all the courts of Europe, that this is not a children's game," he told a senator.[43]

In Bonaparte's mind, the execution of the duc d'Enghien was also a necessary step to justify his decision to convert the Consulate into a hereditary empire. In her history of the Revolution, written after Bonaparte's fall, Madame de Staël deciphered the logic of his actions. "He thought it was necessary, on the one hand, to reassure the revolutionaries that the Bourbons would not return, and to prove to the royalists, on the other, that by supporting him, they were definitively breaking with the old dynasty."[44] With Bonaparte's encouragement, a campaign began to urge him to found a new dynasty, a step that would assure the survival of the regime even if something happened to him. The Senate passed a resolution asking him to consider "what would happen to the ship of the Republic if it had the misfortune to lose its pilot. . . . You have saved us from the chaos of the past, you have allowed us to enjoy benefits in the present, guarantee us for the future."[45] Only a few legislators—including Carnot, the former "organizer of victory," now in the Tribunate, and, in the Senate, the former constitutional bishop Grégoire—withheld their approval. On May 18, 1804, the Senate voted that Bonaparte, who promptly followed the precedent of other royal families by calling himself "Napoleon" rather than using his family name, would be declared "Emperor of the French." Condemned to death along with nineteen of his accomplices, the conspirator Cadoudal remarked, "We wanted to establish a king, we established an emperor." As in 1800 and 1802, a plebiscite was held to legitimate the change in the constitution. The approval rate was substantial—with 3,572,329 voting in favor and only 2,569 against—but more than half the eligible voters did not participate.

On December 2, 1804, a grand coronation ceremony at Notre Dame marked the end of the republic that had been born out of the revolutionary movement twelve years earlier. A reluctant Pius VII was pressured into coming from Rome to bless the ceremony. Nevertheless, to underline the subordinate role of the Church, Napoleon crowned himself, rather than following precedent by letting the pope do so. The gesture was somewhat awkward: the artist Jacques-Louis David, commissioned to create a huge painting of the ceremony, chose instead to highlight the moment when Napoleon crowned Josephine as empress. Crowds lined the Paris streets, but one observer later wrote that "little enthusiasm was shown." Others agreed. One onlooker remarked that those who were present did not express the "élan that a sovereign jealous of receiving the testimony of love for these subjects might have desired."[46]

One of the emperor's first official acts was to abandon the republican calendar and its implicit message that the French Revolution had marked a new era in the history of the world. Napoleon swore an oath "to maintain the integrity of the territory of the Republic; to respect and cause to be respected the laws of the Concordat and of freedom of worship, of political and civil liberty, and the sale of nationalized lands; to raise no taxes except by virtue of the law; to maintain the institution of the Legion of Honor; to govern only in view of the interests, the well-being and the glory of the French people."[47] Aside from the vague reference to political and civil liberty, the only outcomes of the Revolution that he explicitly promised to uphold were religious freedom and security for purchasers of church and émigré properties. Louis XVI could have subscribed to most of the oath: he, too, had considered himself obligated to defend French territory, to impose only legal taxes, and to look after the welfare and glory of his subjects. Five years after the coup d'état of 18 brumaire, France did indeed seem to have returned to its point of departure; Napoleonic propagandists had already begun to cast him as the founder of a fourth dynasty, following in the footsteps of the Merovingians, the Carolingians, and Capetians.

Although the inauguration of the Napoleonic Empire did mark a turning away from many of the fundamental ideas of the Revolution, it was not simply a return to the past. Napoleon abolished the celebration of the anniversary of the storming of the Bastille, but the memory of the events of the Revolution remained in people's minds. However manipulative it may have been, the plebiscite held to endorse the change was a concession to the principle of national sovereignty: unlike Louis XVI, Napoleon claimed to rule by the will of the French people, not "by the grace of God." He would, within a few years, begin to establish a new nobility, peopled primarily by his leading generals and civil officials, but its members did not enjoy the legal privileges that had set the old aristocracy apart from the rest of the population. Members of the clergy were acutely aware that they no longer held the special position they had occupied before 1789. Within a few years, relations between the emperor and the pope deteriorated to the point that Napoleon had Pius VII seized and held as a prisoner. The army of the old regime had gone into battle under the white flag of the Bourbon dynasty; that of the Napoleonic Empire fought and died for the tricolor flag created by the revolutionaries.

Even though the Napoleonic Empire differed in important ways from the absolute monarchy overthrown in 1789, its principles were equally far removed from those articulated by the revolutionaries of the 1790s. Liberty was now reduced to the right of adult men to conduct their private affairs as they chose; the radical idea that women might also deserve such freedom was firmly rejected, and the blacks in France's colonies were deprived of the freedom they had gained in 1794. Equality was also defined in narrow terms that reinforced hierarchical authority structures in the family and the workplace. The idea that citizenship implied a right to a voice in government and lawmaking was abandoned, as was any notion that a free constitution required a balance of powers. Freedom of expression was sharply curtailed, and critics like Madame de Staël were forced into exile. Napoleon's exaltation of military success continued a tradition rooted in the aggressive nationalism of the revolutionary wars, and the population tolerated the high human toll of his wars, although the impact of that toll was diluted in France as his army recruited more troops from its non-French-speaking territories.

Above all, Napoleon broke with the Revolution by imposing a system of one-man rule on France. His power was not restrained by the traditional institutions that had limited the authority of the old regime's absolute monarchs, and he paid only the merest of lip service to the revolutionary notion that power should ultimately be based on the consent of the people. As dictatorships go, the Napoleonic regime was fairly benign: the number of those held as political prisoners was never very large, and ordinary people were able to go about their lives without constantly fearing arrest. Compared to the Reign of Terror or the twentieth-century dictatorships of Stalin and Hitler, Napoleon's actions were much more predictable. Capable of harshness when he thought it was necessary, as the executions of the Turkish prisoners at Jaffa and of the duc d'Enghien showed, the emperor was not a sadist.

For much of his reign, Napoleon was genuinely popular: there is little reason to doubt that the majority of the population preferred his rule to the tumult of the Revolution. Onetime Jacobins as prominent as the former Committee of Public Safety members Carnot and Barère accommodated themselves to his rule, as did royalists who had opposed the Revolution. Jacques Ménétra, retired from his trade, was free to write his memoir, recalling, in his unpunctuated style, "the good and the evil that the Revolution has done all the assaults the days the nights the punishments and the fate of our unfortunate friends who perished in the time of Terror when good men feared for their lives."[48] In 1810, determined to provide himself with a male heir to perpetuate his dynasty, Napoleon divorced Josephine. Like Louis XVI, he married a Habsburg princess, and the match showed that Europe's monarchs were prepared, however reluctantly, to accept his legitimacy. The fatal flaw of Napoleon's regime was its dependence on military success. His inability to restrain his ambition, already evident in the catastrophic expedition to Saint-Domingue under the Consulate, led him into other disastrous adventures, first in Spain and then in Russia. Without those defeats, it is not inconceivable that his regime would have consolidated itself successfully.

When Napoleon returned from the exile he had accepted after his defeat in 1814 and launched his dramatic "Hundred Days," he tried to rally the population by reviving the spirit of 1789: he roused volunteer units, made up of men called *fédérés* like the soldiers of 1792, and had the liberal political philosopher Benjamin Constant draft an "Additional Act" to the imperial constitution, telling him, "Bring me your ideas: public debate, free elections, ministers with real responsibility, freedom of the press."[49] Napoleon's appeal to the principles of the Revolution was not enough to overcome the foreign coalition aligned against him, but it was a sign that those principles were now deeply ingrained in the minds of much of the French population. Even Napoleon realized that the ideals of the Revolution lived on.

# Epilogue

N APOLEON WAS THE FIRST OF MANY LEADERS WHO THOUGHT THEY COULD turn the page on the French Revolution. After his defeat, the other European powers restored the Bourbon monarchy, with Louis XVI's brother, who had been calling himself Louis XVIII since the death of his brother's son in 1795, as king. No matter how much Louis XVIII might have liked to return to the old regime, he sensed that he could only govern the country if he granted a written constitution, shared power with an elected parliament, and allowed freedom of religion and expression. The abolition of the provinces and the parlements, the unification of the country's laws, and the ending of aristocratic privileges had all become so ingrained that they could not be reversed. A heavy-handed attempt to re-Catholicize the country provoked a revival of Enlightenment ideas that contributed to the Revolution of 1830, when ordinary Parisians turned out in the streets, as their ancestors had in the 1790s, to overthrow the Bourbons. Survivors of the Revolution, such as Lafayette and Talleyrand, helped install the son of the revolutionary era's duc d'Orléans as a "citizen king" who brought back the Revolution's tricolor flag. In 1848, another revolution ended monarchy in France for good and created a Second Republic based on universal male suffrage. Napoleon's nephew imitated his uncle, overthrowing the republic in 1851 and proclaiming himself Emperor Napoleon III, but he could not stop the progress of democracy. When Bismarck's newly unified Germany defeated this Second Empire in 1870, France turned again to republicanism, which has remained the country's form of government ever since, except for the period of German occupation during World

War II. July 14—Bastille Day—became the country's national holiday, and "La Marseillaise" was firmly established as its national anthem.

In 1886, France presented a colossal statue of Liberty to the American people as a symbol of the two countries' shared commitment to the ideals that had inspired their two revolutions a hundred years earlier. By then, those ideals had spread to many other parts of the world, such as the republics of Latin America. After World War I, the empires that had fought against revolutionary France—Austria, Germany, Russia, Turkey—disintegrated, replaced by nation-states with democratic constitutions. This apparent triumph of the ideas of 1789 was short-lived and incomplete: communist and fascist regimes destroyed freedom in many countries, and even democracies like Britain and France refused to extend it to their overseas colonies. A yet more destructive world war, however, spurred a reaffirmation of the democratic and republican traditions rooted in the French Revolution. The Universal Declaration of Human Rights, proclaimed in 1948, three years after the defeat of Germany and Japan in World War II, was modeled on the Declaration of the Rights of Man and Citizen of 1789. By explicitly affirming racial equality and women's rights and incorporating social, economic, and cultural rights, such as the right to education, social security, and health care, the drafters of the Universal Declaration acknowledged the importance of the radical ideas first voiced during the French movement.

The year 1989 was marked by two important events: the two hundredth anniversary of the French Revolution, and the collapse of the communist dictatorships of Eastern Europe. An American political scientist, Francis Fukuyama, wrote a best-selling book, *The End of History*, asserting that the principles of democratic freedom and capitalist free enterprise—two powerful aspirations of the French revolutionaries—had finally achieved global hegemony. Like Thomas Paine's optimistic assessment of the French Revolution in 1792, Fukuyama's conclusion was premature. In the three decades since the lavish bicentennial celebration in Paris in 1989 and the fall of the Berlin Wall, the world has seen a resurgence of authoritarian regimes even in countries that seemed to have embraced democracy. Religious movements of many sorts have fought back against the secularization of public life associated with the French Revolution. In many non-Western countries, the liberal world order whose roots go back to the ideas of 1789 is still criticized as a facade for the maintenance of European and American hegemony, and Toussaint Louverture's appeal for "another liberty" in place of that outlined in the Declaration of the Rights of Man still echoes.

At the time of the French Revolution's bicentennial in July 1989, no one knew that the communist bloc would not survive the year. Criticism of the French Revolution at that time came primarily from those who emphasized the ways in which the movement, especially in its radical phase during the Terror, foreshadowed the Bolshevik Revolution of 1917 in Russia. In the aftermath of the collapse of Soviet-style communism, it is easier to see how the two revolutions differed. The French revolutionaries never abandoned their faith in individual freedom and a market economy, even when crises drove them to suspend those principles. After the fall of Robespierre, the French republicans "exited from the Terror." They did so clumsily and at the cost of considerable popular suffering, but it is remarkable, considering the passions the Revolution had unleashed, that they were able to do so at all. In Russia after 1917, on the other hand, dictatorship became a permanent principle of government.

If the French Revolution does not deserve to be tarred with the same brush as the Russian Revolution, its legacy nevertheless remains troubling in a number of ways. The ease with which Sieyès and Napoleon undermined the institutions created by the revolutionaries is a reminder that ideals such as liberty and equality are not inevitably bound to prevail. The history of the Revolution shows how difficult it can be to achieve a consensus on what liberty and equality mean, and how efforts to promote those values can arouse the resistance of groups ranging from religious believers to the owners of property. The great drama of the French Revolution enables us to appreciate the power of the beliefs that were expressed in the Oath of the Tennis Court in 1789, the Festival of the Federation in 1790, and the cheers that greeted the abolition of slavery in 1794. However, the same intense emotions also produced the drive for war in the spring of 1792, the backlash against women's rights in 1793, the excesses of the Terror and the hollowing out of democracy after thermidor in 1794. The French Revolution was the laboratory in which all the possibilities of modern politics, both positive and negative, were tested for the first time.

As I have striven, in the course of writing this book, to bring the actors and the ideas of the French Revolution alive for today's readers, I have learned about many aspects of this endlessly complicated event that were new to me, even after more than forty years spent studying and teaching about the subject. One story that has particularly intrigued me is that of Jean-Marie Goujon, the "prairial martyr" whose name has appeared often in these pages, and his friend Pierre-François Tissot, who survived him by more than half a century. Their letters and writings helped me understand the enthusiasm that powered the Revolution. As an apostle of liberty and equality, Goujon tried to reach out to the common people and inspire them. In the critical years of the Revolution, he went beyond preaching and devoted himself to the urgent matter of making sure the population had food to eat. He was fortunate in that he did not join the National Convention until after the bloody purges of the Girondins, the Hébertistes, and the Indulgents, and he was absent from Paris on 9 thermidor Year II (July 27, 1794), which spared him from having to take sides for or against Robespierre. There is every reason to believe that, as he and his fellow defendants argued at their trial after the prairial uprising, he supported some of the crowd's demands in a sincere effort to prevent bloodshed and preserve some of the Convention's authority.

A casualty of the passions of the Revolution, Goujon was just twenty-nine when he died. Contrasting his life with that of his friend Tissot, who did so much to preserve Goujon's memory, is a thought-provoking exercise. The two were both seized by emotion at the Festival of Federation in 1790. At the same time that Goujon married in 1793 in a republican ceremony, Tissot married his friend's sister. Tissot lacked Goujon's charisma and speaking ability, but as Goujon's political career took off, Goujon was able to employ Tissot in various administrative posts. On the fateful day of 1 prairial Year III (May 20, 1795), while Goujon was at his post at the Convention, Tissot was in the gallery with the demonstrators, where he successfully avoided arrest. For some years after Goujon's execution, Tissot remained involved with the radical left. He participated in the Babeuf conspiracy and, under the Consulate, was on the list of former Montagnards scheduled for deportation after the December 1800 assassination attempt against Napoleon. Some of his friends, however, convinced the first consul to spare him.

After 1800, Tissot abandoned his radicalism. To support not only his own family but also Goujon's widow and his younger brothers, he went into business, opening a factory to make lanterns in Paris's Faubourg Saint-Antoine. As a manufacturer, he made his small contribution to the movement of technological progress—a movement that would eventually allow the world to escape from the poverty that had made the ideals of the French Revolution so hard to realize in the 1790s. Tissot also embarked on a literary career, obtaining a reputation for his translations of Latin poetry. Gradually, he embraced Napoleon's regime. He was rewarded with a teaching post at the Collège de France in 1813, shortly before the empire fell. Under the Bourbon Restoration, he was active in the moderate liberal opposition, and when that regime was overthrown in 1830, he reached the pinnacle of glory by being elected to the Académie française (French Academy). Author of one of the first histories of the French Revolution, Tissot lived long enough to become one of the few participants in the movement of 1789 who was still alive to witness the proclamation of France's Second Republic in 1848.

Two young men seized with the spirit of liberty in 1789, two young men who followed the revolutionary movement's shift toward ever more radical positions until 1794, two men who kept the republican faith even after Robespierre's overthrow, and whose destinies diverged only because one spoke up at the Convention during the prairial uprising and the other escaped unnoticed. Which of the two best epitomizes the true meaning of the Revolution: Goujon, who sacrificed his life rather than abandon the ideals he had embraced, or Tissot, who eventually accommodated himself to the sober realities of life after 1800? Without idealists like Goujon, the Revolution would never have imprinted itself on the minds of its contemporaries and of posterity; without pragmatists like Tissot, its principles might have been completely repudiated. Through the stories of Goujon and Tissot, we can perhaps come to some understanding of the complexities of the Revolution's impact on the lives of those who experienced it, and the ways in which its legacy was perpetuated.

# Acknowledgments

A *New World Begins* is the product of fifty years spent studying and teaching about the French Revolution, and it would be impossible to name all those who have helped shape my understanding of the subject. The Marxist philosopher Herbert Marcuse, with whom I took an undergraduate course on social and political philosophy in the revolutionary year of 1968, first showed me that the Revolution was more than a simple demonstration of the rightness of liberty and equality, introducing me to the conservative critiques of Edmund Burke, Joseph de Maistre, and Louis de Bonald. A succession of distinguished French historians, from Jacques Godechot, François Furet, and Daniel Roche during my years of graduate study to scholars of my own generation, such as Jean-Clément Martin, Marcel Dorigny, and Pierre Serna, welcomed me to their seminars and introduced me to the many conflicting ways in which the most controversial event in their country's history can be interpreted. My good friend the late Pierre Rétat and I shared a common passion for the study of the era's press, and I am saddened that his recent passing means that he will not be able to see this book.

It has been my good fortune to be part of an extraordinarily talented cohort of English-speaking historians of the subject, as well as specialists from Germany, Italy, Israel, and other countries, many of whom have also become friends. It would truly not be possible to mention all of those from whose varied insights I have profited, but a few deserve special mention. In the 1970s, I learned vital lessons about research from fellow graduate students such as Michael Sibalis, who took me on daring expeditions into the back rooms of the French Archives nationales (National Archives) in quest of card indexes that were officially off limits to readers. Patrice Higonnet's unique perspectives on the subject have challenged me to refine my own views since my student days at Harvard. Lynn Hunt, who was beginning her long career at Berkeley when I was finishing my dissertation there, has been an inspiration throughout my career, and her support was crucial in getting this project off the ground. Keith Baker was an invaluable source of support in the early phase of my career. Timothy Tackett's exemplary scholarship and intellectual integrity are, I hope, reflected in these pages. I owe special gratitude to Jack Censer, with whom I have debated the French Revolution for almost half a century. He read the manuscript carefully and offered many valuable suggestions. My agent Lisa Adams provided invaluable guidance on courting publishers, and Basic Books editors Dan Gerstle, Brandon Proia, and Lara Heimert have been excellent partners in moving the project toward completion. As much as I owe to my fellow scholars, the interpretation of the Revolution offered in this book is, for better or for worse, my own. Unless otherwise indicated in the notes, so are the translations from French sources.

I began the project that resulted in this book during a year at the National Humanities Center in Durham, North Carolina, in 2012–2013, and its timely completion was greatly assisted by a National Endowment for the Humanities Public Scholar Program fellowship in 2017. Other institutions that have supported my research on the French Revolution over the years include the Newberry Library, the John Simon Guggenheim Foundation, the Fulbright Foundation, the Institute for Advanced Studies, the John Carter Brown Library at Brown University, the American Council of Learned Societies, the American Philosophical Society, the Social Science Research Council, the Council for European Studies, and the University of Kentucky. Like all historians of the French Revolution, I owe a debt of gratitude to innumerable librarians and archivists, particularly the staffs of the Bibliothèque nationale de France (National Library of France), the Archives nationales (National Archives), the Bibliothèque historique de la Ville de Paris (Historical Library of the City of Paris), the Newberry Library, the John Carter Brown Library, the Widener Library at Harvard University, the University of California Libraries, and the W. T. Young Library of the University of Kentucky. Completing this project left me in awe of the wealth of digitized resources now accessible on this subject, so it seems appropriate to also thank the invisible staffs of the Bibliothèque nationale's Gallica project, the Internet Archive, Google Books, and the Hathi Trust, among others.

In 2005, when my father, the historian of philosophy Richard H. Popkin, died, I inherited the letters he wrote to my grandmother during my childhood. In one of them, written during my first stay in France in 1953, when I was four years old, he describes trying to satisfy my curiosity about what happens to people after they die by taking me to see Napoleon's tomb in Paris's Invalides church. Whether or not that experience subconsciously sparked my interest in the era of the French Revolution, I certainly owe much of my passion for history and scholarship to his example. My mother, Juliet Popkin, was not a published author, but she loved books and constantly urged me to perfect my writing. For two decades, she ran a small independent literary agency, and nothing would have given her greater pleasure than to help promote this project. Both of my parents' commitment to books owed much to the example of my father's mother, Zelda Popkin, author of thirteen novels and an autobiography. Her book-lined apartment in Manhattan was a veritable shrine to literature. I have not imitated her writing routine, which consisted of sitting down at her typewriter at 9:00 a.m., working steadily until 1:00 p.m., and then pouring herself a double glass of scotch, lighting another of her innumerable cigarettes, and relaxing for the rest of the day, but she, like my parents, has been in my mind as I have worked on *A New World Begins*, which is dedicated to my three book-loving ancestors.

# Notes

## Preface

1. *The Kentucky Almanac, for the Year of the Lord 1794* (Lexington, 1793).
2. Letter, March 31, 1776, in Adams Family Papers (electronic version), Massachusetts Historical Society.
3. *Annales patriotiques et littéraires de la France*, June 8, 1792 (*Annales patriotiques* hereafter).
4. Paul Butel, *Histoire des Antilles françaises* (Paris: Perrin, 2007), 150–151; Pierre Bardin, "La population noire dans le Paris du XVIIIe siècle," http://www.ghccaraibe.org/articles/2015-art20.pdf.
5. Saint-Just, speech of 8 vent. II, in Charles Vellay, ed., *Oeuvres complètes de Saint-Just*, 2 vols. (Paris: Charpentier and Fasquelle, 1908), 2:238. Several websites offer tools for converting dates in the French revolutionary calendar to the standard Gregorian calendar. See, for example, Napoléon & Empire, www.napoleon-empire.com, and French Revolutionary Calendar, www.windhorst.com/calendar.

## Chapter 1: Two French Lives in the Old Regime

1. Jacques-Louis Ménétra, *Journal of My Life*, ed. Daniel Roche, trans. Arthur Goldhammer (New York: Columbia University Press, 1986), 124–125.
2. Louis XIV, *Mémoires de Louis XIV pour l'instruction du Dauphin* (Paris, 1860), 250.
3. Ménétra, *Journal*, 18.
4. Ibid., 24.
5. Ibid., 22.
6. Ibid., 21–22.
7. Jean-Louis Soulavie, *Mémoires historiques et politiques du règne de Louis XVI*, 6 vols. (Paris: Treuttel and Wurtz, 1801), 2:46–47.
8. Madame Campan, *Mémoires secrets sur la vie privée de Marie-Antoinette*, 3 vols. (Paris: Baudouin frères, 1823), 1:53; Ménétra, *Journal*, 176.
9. Citations in Derek Beales, *Joseph II*, 2 vols. (Cambridge: Cambridge University Press, 1987), 1:374; Alfred d'Arneth, ed., *Correspondance secrète entre Marie Thérèse et le Cte de Mercy d'Argenteau, avec les lettres de Marie-Thérèse et Marie-Antoinette*, 3 vols. (Paris: Firmin Didot, 1874–1875), 2:88, 2:10, 1:189.

10. Pierrette Girault de Coursac, *L'éducation d'un roi: Louis XVI* (Paris: Gallimard, 1972), 172; *Mémoires secrets pour servir à l'histoire de la république des lettres en France, depuis MDCCLXII jusqu'à nos jours* (London: John Adamson, 1777–1789), 28:166 (Mar. 8, 1785).

11. Ménétra, *Journal*, 26, 276.

12. Madame Roland [Manon Philipon], *Mémoires de Madame Roland*, ed. Paul de Roux (Paris: Mercure de France, 1966), 218.

13. Citations in John Lough, *France on the Eve of Revolution: British Travellers' Observations, 1763–1788* (Chicago: Dorsey Press, 1987), 62; Ménétra, *Journal*, 45.

14. Ménétra, *Journal*, 92–93, 73.

15. Philippe Girard, *Toussaint Louverture: A Revolutionary Life* (New York: Basic Books, 2016), 53–54.

16. Citations in Steven Laurence Kaplan, *Provisioning Paris: Merchants and Millers in the Grain and Flour Trade During the Eighteenth Century* (Ithaca, NY: Cornell University Press, 1984), 2.

17. Louis-Sébastien Mercier, *Panorama of Paris*, ed. Jeremy D. Popkin (University Park: Penn State University Press, 1999), 31.

18. Ménétra, *Journal*, 167, 173.

19. Ibid., 177, 174.

20. Ibid., 182, 180.

21. Campan, *Mémoires*, 1:201–202.

22. Based on previously unknown documents, Evelyn Farr, *I Love You Madly: Marie Antoinette and Count Fersen* (London: Peter Owen, 2016), makes a persuasive case for the reality of a love affair that previous scholars often doubted.

## Chapter 2: The Monarchy, the Philosophes, and the Public

1. Louis XVI, *Réflexions sur mes entretiens avec M. le comte de Vauguyon* (Paris: J.-P. Aillaud, 1851), 86, 88; Louis XV, declaration to Paris Parlement, Mar. 3, 1766 (Popkin translation).

2. Louis XVI, *Réflexions*, 89.

3. Ibid., 212.

4. Arthur Young, cited in John Lough, *France on the Eve of Revolution* (Chicago: Dorsey Press, 1987), 10.

5. Denis Diderot, Sept. 26, 1762, in Peter France, ed., *Diderot's Letters to Sophie Volland* (London: Oxford University Press, 1972), 125.

6. Voltaire, *Candide*, trans. Lowell Bair (New York: Bantam Books, 1959), 118, 120.

7. Jean-Jacques Rousseau, "Letter to Voltaire Regarding the Poem on the Lisbon Earthquake," Aug. 18, 1756, in T. Besterman, ed., *Voltaire's Correspondence* (Geneva: Institut et musée Voltaire, 1958), 30:115.

8. Denis Diderot, "Prospectus," in Stephen J. Gendzier, ed., *The Encyclopedia: Selections* (New York: Harper Torchbooks, 1960), 38–39.

9. Denis Diderot, "Political Authority," in Gendzier, *Encyclopedia*, 185; Paul Thiry d'Holbach, "Representatives," in Gendzier, *Encyclopedia*, 219.

10. François Quesnay, "Grains," in Gendzier, *Encyclopedia*, 126, 132; Louis de Jaucourt, "Peuple," in *The ARTFL Encyclopédie*, encyclopédie.uchicago.edu.

11. Jaucourt, "Egalité," in *ARTFL Encyclopédie*; Louis de Jaucourt, "Woman," trans. Naomi J. Andrews, in "The Encyclopedia of Diderot and D'Alembert:

Collaborative Translation Project," University of Michigan Library Digital Collections, https://www.lib.umich.edu/database/link/8785.

12. Articles on "Woman" by Antoine-Gaspard Boucher d'Argis and Joseph-François-Louis Desmahis, trans. Naomi J. Andrews, in "Encyclopedia of Diderot and D'Alembert"; Diderot, "Enjoyment," in Gendzier, *Encyclopedia*, 96.

13. Articles "Nègre," by Samuel Formey, and "Nègres, commerce," anonymous, in ARTFL *Encyclopédie*.

14. Rousseau, "Political Economy," in Gendzier, *Encyclopedia*, 190, 191, 193, 197.

15. Article "Belloi, Pierre-Laurent Burette de," in *Encyclopédie méthodique: Histoire* (1784), 1:587; Denis Diderot, *Entretiens sur le fils naturel*, in Diderot, *Oeuvres*, ed. M. Tourneux (Paris: Garnier, 1875), 7:150–151.

16. Mably citation in Johnson Kent Wright, *A Classical Republican in Eighteenth-Century France: The Political Thought of Mably* (Stanford, CA: Stanford University Press, 1997), 88.

17. Citations in Antoine de Baecque, *Les eclats du rire: La culture des rieurs au XVIII siècle* (Paris: Calmann-Lévy, 2000), 66.

18. Citations in Matthew Levinger, "La rhétorique protestaire du Parlement de Rouen (1753–1763)," *Annales E.S.C.* 47, no. 3 (1990): 602.

19. Memorandum cited in Julian Swann, *Politics and the Parlement of Paris Under Louis XV, 1754–1774* (Cambridge: Cambridge University Press, 1995), 268; Louis XVI, *Réflexions*, 103, 104.

20. Citations in Swann, *Parlement of Paris*, 328.

21. *Journal historique de la Révolution opérée dans la Constitution de la Monarchie française, par M. de Maupeou, Chancelier de France* [new ed., revised, corrected, and augmented], 7 vols. (London, 1776), 1:1–2, 2:339–340, 1:69.

## Chapter 3: The Monarchy Adrift

1. *Journal historique de la Révolution opérée dans la constitution de la monarchie française* [new ed., revised, corrected, and augmented], 7 vols. (London, 1776), 6:17 (May 22, 1774).

2. Citations in Durand Echeverria, *The Maupeou Revolution: A Study in the History of Libertarianism* (Baton Rouge: Louisiana State University Press, 1985), 32.

3. *Journal historique*, 7:330–331.

4. Cynthia A. Bouton, *The Flour War: Gender, Class, and Community in Late Ancien Régime French Society* (University Park: Penn State University Press, 1993), 90.

5. "Remonstrance of the *Cour des Aides*," trans. in James Harvey Robinson, ed., *Translations and Reprints from the Original Sources of European History* (Philadelphia: University of Pennsylvania Press, 1912), reprinted in The College History Staff, *History of Western Civilization* (Chicago: University of Chicago Press, 1977), 76, 64.

6. *Espion anglois* [new ed.] (London: John Adamson, 1779), 1:314 (June 6, 1775).

7. Citations in Jean-Pierre Poirier, *Turgot: Laissez-faire et progrès social* (Paris: Perrin, 1999), 183.

8. Remonstrances of the Parlement of Paris, trans. Keith Baker and Ellen Ross, in The College History Staff, *History of Western Civilization*, 87, 90.

9. *Gazette de Leyde*, Sept. 16, 1774; citations in Joël Félix, *Louis XVI et Marie Antoinette: Un couple en politique* (Paris: Payot, 2006), 184.

10. Citations in Félix, *Louis XVI*, 266.

11. Louis-Sébastien Mercier, *Panorama of Paris*, ed. Jeremy D. Popkin (University Park: Penn State University Press, 1999), 196.

12. Letter of Pierre Céleron de Blainville, May 8, 1785, cited in Gabriel Debien, *Les esclaves aux Antilles françaises (XVIIe–XVIIe siècles)* (Basse-Terre and Fort-de-France: Sociétés d'histoire de la Guadeloupe et de la Martinique, 1974), 486.

13. Citations in Charles Walton, "The Fall from Eden: The Free-Trade Origins of the French Revolution," in Suzanne Desan, Lynn Hunt, and William Max Nelson, eds., *The French Revolution in Global Perspective* (Ithaca, NY: Cornell University Press, 2013), 51.

## Chapter 4: "Everything Must Change"

1. Jean Egret, *The French Pre-Revolution, 1787–1788*, trans. Wesley D. Camp (Chicago: University of Chicago Press, 1977), 2; Morellet, letter of Mar. 13, 1787, in *Lettres de l'abbé Morellet à Lord Shelburne* (Paris: Plon, 1898), 222.

2. Charles-Alexandre Calonne, "Objections et réponses," in Hans Glagau, *Reformversuche und Sturz des Absolutismus in Frankreich* (Munich, 1908), 352, 365.

3. *Mémoires secrets pour servir à l'histoire de la république des lettres en France, depuis MDCCLXII jusqu'à nos jours* (London: John Adamson, 1777–1789), 34:63.

4. Minutes of the Société Gallo-Américaine, John Carter Brown Library, Brown University, Codex Fr. 15.

5. Pierre-François Tissot, "Vie de Goujon," in Françoise Brunel and Sylvain Goujon, eds., *Les martyrs de prairial: Textes et documents inédits* (Geneva: Georg, 1992), 101–102.

6. Honoré Gabriel de Riquetti, comte de Mirabeau, *Des lettres de cachet et des prisons d'état* (Hamburg, 1782), 96.

7. Citations in Guy Chaussinand-Nogaret, *Mirabeau* (Paris: Seuil, 1982), 103.

8. Vivian R. Gruder, *The Notables and the Nation: The Political Schooling of the French, 1787–1788* (Cambridge, MA: Harvard University Press, 2007), 21.

9. Alfred d'Arneth, ed., *Correspondance secrète entre Marie Thérèse et le Cte de Mercy d'Argenteau, avec les lettres de Marie-Thérèse et Marie-Antoinette*, 3 vols. (Paris: Firmin Didot, 1874–1875), 2:108, cited in John Hardman, *Overture to Revolution: The 1787 Assembly of Notables and the Crisis of France's Old Regime* (New York: Oxford University Press, 2010), 92.

10. Le Blanc de Castillon, cited in Egret, *Pre-Revolution*, 13.

11. Citations in Hardman, *Assembly of Notables*, 136.

12. Honoré Gabriel Riquetti de Mirabeau, *Dénonciation de l'agiotage* (Paris, 1787), 8, 65.

13. Vivian Gruder, "Les notables à la fin de l'ancien régime," *Dix-huitième siècle*, no. 14 (1982): 45, 48; Pierre Casselle, *L'anti-Robespierre: Jérôme Pétion ou la Révolution pacifique* (Paris: Vendémiaire, 2016), 70.

14. Citations in Gruder, *The Notables and the Nation*, 46; *Correspondance secrète*, May 20, 1787, cited in Egret, *Pre-Revolution*, 34.

15. Florimond Claude, comte de Mercy-Argenteau, *Correspondance secrète avec l'Empereur Joseph II et le Prince de Kaunitz*, ed. A. Ritter von Arneth and Jules Flammermont, 2 vols. (Paris: Imprimerie nationale, 1889), 112; Alexis de Tocqueville, *The Old Regime and the Revolution* (Garden City, NY: Doubleday Anchor, 1956), 214.

16. Citations in Egret, *Pre-Revolution*, 92.

17. Jules Flammermont, *Les remonstrances du Parlement de Paris au XVIIIe Siècle*, 3 vols. (Paris, 1898), 3:674.

18. Citations in Louis Gottschalk, *Lafayette Between the American and the French Revolution* (Chicago: University of Chicago Press, 1950), 375.

19. Amis des noirs, session of Mar. 18, 1788, in Marcel Dorigny and Bernard Gainot, eds., *La Société des amis des noirs, 1788–1799: Contribution à l'histoire de l'abolition de l'esclavage* (Paris: Editions UNESCO, 1998), 109.

20. Letter of Jan. 6, 1788, in Oscar Browning, ed., *Despatches from Paris, 1784–1790*, 2 vols. (London: Camden Society, 1909–1910), 2:4.

21. Flammermont, *Remontrances*, 3:745–746.

22. Guy-Marie Sallier-Chaumont, *Annales françaises* (Paris: Leriche, 1813), 153; Brunel and Goujon, *Les martyrs de prairial* (Geneva: Georg, 1992), 227; citations in Egret, *Pre-Revolution*, 149.

## Chapter 5: A Nation Aroused

1. Jean Sgard, *Les trente recits de la Journée des Tuiles* (Grenoble: Presses Universitaires de Grenoble, 1988), 36.

2. Ibid., 34.

3. *Délibération de la ville de Grenoble, du samedi 14 juin 1788* (Grenoble, 1788), 2, 3.

4. *Assemblée des trois-ordres de la province de Dauphiné* (Dauphiné, 1788), 16, 9.

5. *Lettre écrite par plusieurs citoyens du clergé, de la noblesse & des communes de Dauphiné, à Mm. les syndics-généraux des Etats de Béarn* (Grenoble, 1788), 6.

6. Jean Egret, *The French Pre-Revolution, 1787–1788*, trans. Wesley D. Camp (Chicago: University of Chicago Press, 1977), 171; C. A. Dauban, ed., *Lettres en partie inédites de Madame Roland*, 2 vols. (Paris: Plon, 1867), 2:557, letter of June 2, 1788.

7. Citations in Egret, *Pre-Revolution*, 179, 162.

8. Citations in Joël Félix, *Louis XVI et Marie Antoinette: Un couple en politique* (Paris: Payot, 2006), 396.

9. Egret, *Pre-Revolution*, 180, 181.

10. A. Sayous, ed., *Mémoires et correspondance de Mallet du Pan*, 2 vols. (Paris: Amyot, 1851), 1:152–153.

11. Joseph Charon, *Lettre ou mémoire historique sur les troubles populaires de Paris en août et septembre 1788* (London, 1788), 19.

12. *Journal de Paris*, July 31, 1788.

13. Citations in Lynn Avery Hunt, *Revolution and Urban Politics in Provincial France: Troyes and Reims, 1786–1790* (Stanford, CA: Stanford University Press, 1978), 41.

14. Sayous, *Mémoires et correspondance de Mallet du Pan*, 163; Dauban, *Lettres de Madame Roland*, 2:572.

15. Vivian R. Gruder, *The Notables and the Nation: The Political Schooling of the French, 1787–1788* (Cambridge, MA: Harvard University Press, 2007), 337–338.

16. Citations in Robert D. Harris, *Necker and the Revolution of 1789* (Lanham, MD: University Press of America, 1986), 328.

17. Citations from "What Is the Third Estate?" in John Hall Stewart, ed., *A Documentary Survey of the French Revolution* (New York: Macmillan, 1951), 42–56.

18. Citations in Lucas de Montigny, *Mémoires biographiques, littéraires et politiques de Mirabeau*, 8 vols. (Brussels, 1834), 7:205; Marc Bombelles, *Journal*, ed. Jean Grassion and Frans Durif, 2 vols. (Geneva: Droz, 1982), 2:260.

19. *Détail de ce qui s'est passé à Rennes le 26 janvier 1789* (Rennes, 1789); *Mémoire des députés de l'ordre des avocats au Parlement de Bretagne, concernant la malheureuse affaire, arrivée en cette ville les 26 et 27 janvier 1789* (Rennes, 1789), 23.

20. Henri Fréville, *L'intendance de Bretagne*, 3 vols. (Rennes: Plihon, 1953), 3:265.

21. Gilbert Shapiro and John Markoff, *Revolutionary Demands: A Content Analysis of the Cahiers de Doléances of 1789* (Stanford, CA: Stanford University Press, 1998); John Markoff, *The Abolition of Feudalism: Peasants, Lords, and Legislators in the French Revolution* (University Park: Penn State University Press, 1995); citations in J. M. Roberts, ed., *French Revolution Documents*, 2 vols. (Oxford: Blackwell, 1966), 1:75; Jacques Bernet, ed., *Journal d'un maître d'école* (Villeneuve-d'Ascq: Presses Universitaires du Septentrion, 2000), 183.

22. Markoff, *Abolition of Feudalism*, 31.

23. Citations in Roberts, *French Revolution Documents*, 1:55–57; Jérôme Mavidal and Emile Laurent, eds., *Archives parlementaires: Première série* (Paris, 1867–1913) (AP hereafter), 3:736.

24. Timothy Tackett, *Becoming a Revolutionary: The Deputies of the French National Assembly and the Emergence of a Revolutionary Culture (1789–1790)* (Princeton, NJ: Princeton University Press, 1996), 19–47.

25. Citations in ibid., 46.

26. "Journal historique du Comité Colonial de St. Domingue," Library of Congress ms. MMC 2671, Sept. 26, 1788; citations in Guy Chaussinand-Nogaret, *Mirabeau* (Paris: Seuil, 1982), 133.

27. Hervé Leuwers, *Robespierre* (Paris: Pluriel, 2016), 111–119; citations in Charles-Élie, Marquis de Ferrières, *Correspondance inédite (1789, 1790, 1791)*, ed. Henri Carré (Paris: Armand Colin, 1932), 13; Elisabeth Badinter, ed., *Correspondance inédite de Condorcet et Mme. Suard, M. Suard et Garat (1771–1791)* (Paris: Fayard, 1988), 249–250.

28. Ferrières, *Correspondance*, 37–38.

29. *Gazette de Leyde*, Apr. 19, 1789 (Paris, Apr. 9); citations in Michèle Grenot, *Le souci des plus pauvres: Dufourny, la Révolution française et la démocratie* (Rennes: Presses Universitaires de Rennes, 2014), 116; [Antoine-François Lemaire], *Les vitres cassés par le véritable Père Duchesne, député aux Etats-Généraux* (Paris, 1789).

30. *Remontrances, plaintes et doléances des dames françois* (Paris, March 1789), in Albert Soboul, ed., *Les femmes dans la Révolution française*, 2 vols. (Paris: EDHIS, 1982), vol. 1, no. 5.

## Chapter 6: Revolution in a Tennis Court

1. François Mège, ed., *Gaultier de Biauzat: Sa vie et sa correspondance*, 2 vols. (Paris: Lechevalier, 1890), 2:26.

2. Citations in Georges Lefebvre, ed., *Recueil des documents relatifs aux séances des Etats généraux*, 2 vols. (Paris: CNRS, 1953), 1:66–67, 76, 69.

3. Citations in Antoine de Baecque, *1789: L'Assemblée Nationale* (Paris: Assemblée Nationale, 1989), 56; Guy Chaussinand-Nogaret, *Mirabeau* (Paris: Seuil, 1982), 151.

4. Charles-Élie, Marquis de Ferrières, *Correspondance inédite (1789, 1790, 1791)*, ed. Henri Carré (Paris: Armand Colin, 1932), 45–46; *Supplément au Journal de Paris*, May 14, 1789.

5. Adrien Duquesnoy, *Journal d'Adrien Duquesnoy*, ed. Robert de Crèvecoeur (Paris: Picard, 1894), 29, 19, 9; Ferrières, *Correspondance*, 56.

6. Jacques-Pierre Brissot, *Sur la nécessité de rendre dès ce moment la presse libre, et surtout pour les journaux politiques* (Paris, 1789), 10; Duquesnoy, *Journal*, 28.

7. *Journal des Etats-généraux*, no. 1 (May 28, 1789), no. 2 (June 6, 1789); Arthur Young, *Travels in France During the Years 1787, 1788 and 1789*, ed. Constantia Maxwell (Cambridge: Cambridge University Press, 1950), 134.

8. Young, *Travels in France*, 134, 142–144.

9. AP, 8:85, Third Estate session of June 10, 1789.

10. Ferrières, *Correspondance*, 68; J. J. Brethe, ed., *Journal inédit de Jallet* (Fontenay-le-Comte: Robuchon, 1871), 87; *Journal des Etats Généraux*, June 13, 1789.

11. Citations in Timothy Tackett, *Becoming a Revolutionary: The Deputies of the French National Assembly and the Emergence of a Revolutionary Culture (1789–1790)* (Princeton, NJ: Princeton University Press, 1996), 146, and AP, 8:110.

12. AP, 8:128–129.

13. Citations in Munro Price, "The 'Ministry of the Hundred Hours': A Reappraisal," *French History* 4 (1990): 325; Montmorin, letter of June 22, 1789, in Lefebvre, *Recueil*, 2:200.

14. Citations in John Hall Stewart, ed., *A Documentary Survey of the French Revolution* (New York: Macmillan, 1951), 90–98.

15. Citations in Chaussinand-Nogaret, *Mirabeau*, 176.

16. Young, *Travels in France*, 154; Ferrières, *Correspondance*, 76.

17. *Point du jour*, June 28, 1789; Young, *Travels in France*, 159.

18. Citations in Tackett, *Becoming a Revolutionary*, 158; Stewart, *Documentary Survey*, 44; Jeremy D. Popkin, "Saint-Domingue, Slavery, and the Origins of the French Revolution," in Thomas E. Kaiser and Dale Van Kley, eds., *From Deficit to Deluge: The Origins of the French Revolution* (Stanford, CA: Stanford University Press, 2011), 242–245.

19. AP, 8:217.

20. AP, 8:212; *Lettre des dames de Paris, à Messieurs les officiers du camp* (Paris, 1789), in Albert Soboul, ed., *Les femmes et la Révolution dans la Révolution française*, 2 vols. (Paris: EDHIS, 1982), vol. 1, no. 9.

21. Duquesnoy, *Journal*, 144.

22. Marc Bombelles, *Journal*, ed. Jean Grassion and Frans Durif, 2 vols. (Geneva: Droz, 1978, 1982), 2:341.

23. Citations in Price, "Ministry," 335; Claudine Pailhès, ed., *Ecrire la Révolution, 1784–1795: "Lettres à Pauline"* (Cahors: La Louve, 2011), 150–151.

## Chapter 7: A People's Revolution

1. AP, 8:110.

2. *Point du jour*, June 21, 1789, speech of June 19.

3. Camille Desmoulins, letter to his father, July 16, 1789, in Jules Clarétie, *Oeuvres de Camille Desmoulins* (Paris, 1874), 2:330.

4. Letter from a Paris merchant, July 15, 1789, published in *Affiches américaines*, Sept. 19, 1789.

5. "Procès-verbal de l'assemblée générale des électeurs de Paris," in L. G. Wickham Legg, *Select Documents Illustrative of the History of the French Revolution* (Oxford: Clarendon Press, 1905), 1:55.

6. AP, 8:228.

7. Louis-Abel Beffroy de Reigny, *Supplément nécessaire au Précis exact de la prise de la Bastille, avec des anecdotes curieuses sur le même sujet* (Paris: Baudouin, 1789), 6.

8. Citations in Jacques Godechot, *La Prise de la Bastille* (Paris: Gallimard, 1965), 371.

9. Jean-Sylvain Bailly, *Mémoires de Bailly*, 3 vols.(Paris: Baudouin, 1821–1822) 1:364; Godechot, *Prise de la Bastille*, 290.

10. Letter of Paris merchant, July 15, 1789.

11. Godechot, *Prise de la Bastille*, 298.

12. Hans-Jürgen Lüsebrink and Rolf Reichardt, *The Bastille: A History of a Symbol of Despotism and Freedom*, trans. Norbert Schürer (Durham, NC: Duke University Press, 1997), 120.

13. Bailly, *Mémoires*, 1:390.

14. AP, 8:227–229.

15. AP, 8:233.

16. Citations in Godechot, *Prise de la Bastille*, 309; AP, 8:236.

17. Adrien Duquesnoy, *Journal d'Adrien Duquesnoy*, ed. Robert de Crèvecoeur (Paris: Picard, 1894), 210; Charles-Élie, Marquis de Ferrières, *Correspondance inédite (1789, 1790, 1791)*, ed. Henri Carré (Paris: Armand Colin, 1932), 90; citations in Godechot, *Prise de la Bastille*, 17–18.

18. Citations in Godechot, *Prise de la Bastille*, 319, 318; Jefferson citations in Julian Boyd et al., eds., *Papers of Thomas Jefferson*, 43 vols. (Princeton, NJ: Princeton University Press, 1950–2017), 15:291.

19. Letter of Jean Antoine Huguet, July 18, 1789, cited in François Mège, ed., *Gaultier de Biauzat: Sa vie et sa correspondance*, 2 vols. (Paris: Lechevalier, 1890), 2:185.

20. *Gazette de Leyde*, July 24, 1789 (Paris, July 17).

## Chapter 8: From the "Great Fear" to the Declaration of Rights

1. John Markoff, *The Abolition of Feudalism: Peasants, Lords, and Legislators in the French Revolution* (University Park: Penn State University Press, 1995), 271, 300–301.

2. *Nouvelles de Bretagne, de ce qui s'est passé le 17 & 18 juillet 1789* (Paris, 1789), 4, 8–9; *Suite des Nouvelles de Bretagne* (Paris, 1789), 1, 7.

3. Lynn Avery Hunt, *Revolution and Urban Politics in Provincial France: Troyes and Reims, 1786–1790* (Stanford, CA: Stanford University Press, 1978), 73–91; Arthur Young, *Travels in France During the Years 1787, 1788 and 1789*, ed. Constantia Maxwell (Cambridge: Cambridge University Press, 1950), 183.

4. Young, *Travels in France*, 186, 188.

5. Citations in J. M. Roberts, ed., *French Revolution Documents*, 2 vols. (Oxford: Blackwell, 1966), 1:135; Maurice Wahl, *Les premières années de la Révolution à Lyon, 1788–1792*, (Paris: A. Colin, 1894), 106; Jacques Bernet, ed., *Journal d'un maître d'école* (Villeneuve-d'Ascq: Presses Universitaires du Septentrion, 2000), 196.

6. Citations in Roberts, *French Revolution Documents*, 1:143–144.

7. Victor Advielle, ed., *Histoire de Gracchus Babeuf et du Babouvisme*, 2 vols. (Paris: Editions du CTHS, 1990 [1884]), 55; Claude Perroud, ed., *Lettres de Madame Roland*, 2 vols. (Paris: Imprimerie nationale, 1902), 2:53.

8. Citations in Michel Biard, *La Révolution hantée* (Paris: Vendémiaire, 2017), 78.

9. AP, 8:344.

10. Adrien Duquesnoy, *Journal d'Adrien Duquesnoy*, ed. Robert de Crèvecoeur (Paris: Picard, 1894), 267.

11. Aug. 4 decrees in John Hall Stewart, ed., *A Documentary Survey of the French Revolution* (New York: Macmillan, 1951), 107–110.

12. *Courier de Provence*, no. 23 (Aug. 3–5, 1789).

13. Young, *Travels in France*, 207, 226.

14. Stewart, *Documentary Survey*, 110, 112.

15. Adrien-Joseph Colson, *Lettres d'un bourgeois de Paris à un ami de province, 1788–1793* (Saint-Cyr-sur-Loire: Christian Pirot, 1993), 64.

16. Advielle, *Histoire de Gracchus Babeuf*, 1:57.

17. Honoré Gabriel Riquetti de Mirabeau, *Aux Bataves*, in Stéphane Rials, *La Déclaration des droits de l'homme et du citoyen* (Paris: Hachette, 1988), 519; Sieyès, *Délibérations*, in Rials, *Déclaration*, 538; Condorcet, in Rials, *Déclaration*, 546–550.

18. [Dupont de Nemours], cahier of Third Estate of Nemours, in Rials, *Déclaration*, 552, 554; Rials, *Déclaration*, 567–568 (Jefferson Papers, 15:230ff).

19. Citations in Timothy Tackett, *Becoming a Revolutionary: The Deputies of the French National Assembly and the Emergence of a Revolutionary Culture (1789–1790)* (Princeton, NJ: Princeton University Press, 1996), 182; *Journal de Paris*, Apr. 22, 1789.

20. Antoine de Baecque, *L'An 1* (Paris: CNRS Éditions, 1988), 60, 62.

21. Rials, *Déclaration*, 591, 600.

22. Ibid., 606–608.

23. De Baecque, *L'An 1*, 104, 106, 123.

24. Ibid., 124.

25. François Mège, ed., *Gaultier de Biauzat: Sa vie et sa correspondance*, 2 vols. (Paris: Lechevalier, 1890), 2:247.

26. De Baecque, *L'An 1*, 150.

27. Ibid., 158.

28. Ibid., 164, 165, 166; Duquesnoy, *Journal*, 309–310.

29. De Baecque, *L'An 1*, 173, 175, 176–177; Duquesnoy, *Journal*, 310–311.

30. De Baecque, *L'An 1*, 185, 186.

31. Ibid., 187.

32. Ibid., 195–196.

33. AP, 29:264, 266–267.

34. Antoine-François Delandine, *Mémorial historique des Etats généraux* (Paris, 1789), 190; "Déclaration des droits des citoyennes du Palais-Royal," in Rials, *Déclaration*, 691; "Dom Bougre aux Etats Généraux," cited in Jeffrey Merrick and Bryant T. Ragan, eds., *Homosexuality in Early Modern France* (New York: Oxford University Press, 2001), 177.

## Chapter 9: Constitution-Making and Conflict

1. Adrien Duquesnoy, *Journal d'Adrien Duquesnoy*, ed. Robert de Crèvecoeur (Paris: Picard, 1894), 311–312.

2. Vernier, letter of Aug. 30, 1789, cited in Timothy Tackett, *Becoming a Revolutionary: The Deputies of the French National Assembly and the Emergence of a Revolutionary Culture (1789–1790)* (Princeton, NJ: Princeton University Press, 1996), 189; AP, 8:513.

3. Citations in Keith Michael Baker, *Inventing the French Revolution* (Cambridge: Cambridge University Press, 1990), 281, 296.

4. AP, 8:604–605.

5. Guy Chaussinand-Nogaret, *Mirabeau* (Paris: Seuil, 1982), 213.

6. Annie Duprat, ed., *"Les affaires d'état sont mes affaires de coeur"* (Paris: Belin, 2016), 51; Maillard, cited in Darline Gay Levy, Harriet Branson Applewhite, and Mary Durham Johnson, eds., *Women in Revolutionary Paris, 1789–1795* (Urbana: University of Illinois Press, 1979), 37.

7. Maillard testimony, in Levy et al., *Women in Revolutionary Paris*, 38–39; citations in Louis Gottschalk and Margaret Maddox, *Lafayette in the French Revolution: Through the October Days* (Chicago: University of Chicago Press, 1969), 330, 340.

8. Duquesnoy, *Journal*, 402; citations in Levy et al., *Women in Revolutionary Paris*, 48, 50.

9. Marie-Antoinette, letter to Mercy d'Argenteau, Oct. 10, 1789, in Évelyne Lever, *Correspondance de Marie-Antoinette (1770–1793)* (Paris: Taillandier, 2005), 497.

10. *Etrennes nationales des dames*, in Albert Soboul, ed., *Les femmes dans la Révolution*, 2 vols. (Paris: EDHIS, 1982), vol. 1, no. 18; *Requête des dames, à l'Assemblée nationale*, in ibid., vol. 1, no. 19; *Patriote françois*, Oct. 10, 1789.

11. Citations in Bronislaw Baczko, *Politiques de la Révolution française* (Paris: Gallimard, 2008), 364; Archives historiques nationales, Madrid, Papeles de Estado, 3942, liasse 2, cited in Albert Mousset, *Histoire d'Espagne* (Madrid: Société d'éditions françaises et internationales, 1947), 322.

12. Ad. de Bacourt, ed., *Correspondance entre le Comte de Mirabeau et le Comte de la Marck, pendant les années 1789, 1790 et 1791*, 2 vols. (Brussels: Pagny, 1841), 1:250.

13. *Révolutions de Paris*, no. 1 (July 12–19, 1789).

14. *Ami du peuple*, Sept., 18, 1789; Keralio letter, n.d. [fall 1789], in AP, 12:446.

15. Johann Heinrich Campe, *Briefe aus Paris zur Zeit der Revolution geschrieben* (Hildesheim: Grstenberg, 1977 [1790]), 51.

16. Marie-Joseph Chénier, "Discours prononcé devant MM. les représentans de la Commune," in Chénier, *Charles IX, ou l'École des rois* (Paris: Bossange, 1790), 165.

17. Patrick Kessel, *La nuit du 4 août 1789* (Paris: Arthaud, 1969), 272; Duquesnoy, *Journal*, 462.

18. Citations in Kessel, *Nuit du 4 août*, 275; George Rudé, *Robespierre* (Englewood Cliffs, NJ: Prentice Hall, 1967), 14.

19. *Ami du peuple*, Nov. 19, 1789.

20. Adrien-Joseph Colson, *Lettres d'un bourgeois de Paris à un ami de province, 1788–1793* (Saint-Cyr-sur-Loire: Christian Pirot, 1993), 93.

21. Lucas de Montigny, *Mémoires biographiques, littéraires et politiques de Mirabeau* (Brussels, 1841), 8 vs., 6:390; Caroline Chopelin-Blanc, *De l'apologétique à l'Église constitutionnel: Adrien Lamourette (1742–1794)* (Paris: Honoré Champion, 2009), 330.

22. Citations in Nigel Aston, *Religion and Revolution in France, 1780–1804* (Washington, DC: Catholic University Press, 2000), 133; AP, 9:424.

23. Abbé d'Eymar, Oct. 13, 1789, in AP, 9:420.

24. Citations in Ted W. Margadant, *Urban Rivalries in the French Revolution* (Princeton, NJ: Princeton University Press, 1992), 94.

25. *Journal de Lyon*, Dec. 31, 1789; citations in Kessel, *Nuit du 4 août*, 281.

26. Citations in Lynn Hunt, *The French Revolution and Human Rights*, 2nd ed. (Boston: Bedford / St. Martin's Press, 2016), 83–84.

27. Ibid., 84–86; Frances Malino, *A Jew in the French Revolution: The Life of Zalkind Hourwitz* (Cambridge, MA: Blackwell, 1996), 81.

28. Alexandre Lameth, *Histoire de l'Assemblée constituante*, 2 vols. (Paris, 1828–1829), 1:399.

## Chapter 10: A New World Divided

1. Alexandre Lameth, *Histoire de l'Assemblée constituante*, 2 vols. (Paris, 1828–1829), 2:452.

2. Charles-Élie, Marquis de Ferrières, *Correspondance inédite* (1798, 1790, 1791), ed. Henri Carré (Paris: Armand Colin, 1932), 241.

3. Letter of July 15, 1790, in Françoise Brunel and Sylvain Goujon, eds., *Les martyrs de prairial* (Geneva: Georg, 1992), 256–257.

4. *Bulletin de la Société départementale d'archéologie et de statistique de la Drôme* 42 (1908): 391; *Confédération de Lyon, le 30 mai 1790* (Lyon: Aimé de la Roche, 1790), 26.

5. AP, 16:95; *Annales de l'éducation du sexe, ou Journal des demoiselles*, no. 8, 7; *Ami du peuple*, July 7, 1789.

6. Citations in J. M. Roberts, ed., *French Revolution Documents*, 2 vols. (Oxford: Blackwell, 1966), 1:196.

7. Citations in ibid., 1:209.

8. Citations in Nigel Aston, *Religion and Revolution in France, 1780–1804* (Washington, DC: Catholic University Press, 2000), 135; Gwénaël Murphy, *Les réligieuses dans la Révolution française* (Paris: Bayard, 2005), 50; Jean-François de Vauvilliers, *Le témoignage de la raison et de la foi contre la Constitution civile du clergé* [new ed.] (Paris: Desaint, 1791), iii.

9. AP, 15:742; C. Bloch and A. Tuetey, *Procès-verbaux et rapport du Comité de mendicité de la Constituante, 1790–1791* (Paris: Imprimerie nationale, 1911), 41.

10. AP, 12:715, 717–718.

11. Baron de Menou, in AP, 12:715.

12. Citations in Timothy Tackett, *Religion, Revolution, and Regional Culture in Eighteenth-Century France: The Ecclesiastical Oath of 1791* (Princeton, NJ: Princeton University Press, 1986), 218; *Moniteur universel*, Feb. 21, 1791.

13. Citations in Aston, *Religion and Revolution*, 141, and Dale Van Kley, *The Religious Origins of the French Revolution* (New Haven, CT: Yale University Press, 1996), 357.

14. Citations in Aston, *Religion and Revolution*, 149.

15. Citations in Laurent Dubois and John Garrigus, *Slave Revolution in the Caribbean, 1789–1804* (Boston: Bedford / St. Martin's Press, 2006), 64–65; letter from Governor Peinier, Oct. 10, 1789, in Archives nationales (AN hereafter), C 9 A 162.

16. Citations in Marcel Dorigny, ed., *Les bières flottantes des négriers: Un discours non prononcé sur l'abolition de la traite des Noirs (novembre 1789–mars 1790)* (Saint-Étienne: Publications de l'Université de Saint-Etienne, 1999), 16–17.

17. *Annales patriotiques*, Feb. 26, 1790.

18. Pierre Bernadeu, "Tablettes manuscrites," Bibliothèque municipale de Bordeaux, Microfilm 1698/5, p. 60.

19. AP, 15:643, 644.

20. Claudine Pailhès, ed., *Ecrire la Révolution, 1784–1795: "Lettres à Pauline"* (Cahors: La Louve, 2011), 262; AP, 15:651.

21. AP, 16:373.

22. AP, 16:375; Charles-Élie, Marquis de Ferrières, *Correspondance inédite* (1789, 1790, 1791), ed. Henri Carré (Paris: Armand Colin, 1932), 211–212.

23. Alexandre Lameth, in AP, 17:506.

24. *Révolutions de Paris*, no. 56 (1790), cited in Aline Cordani, "Metz et l'affaire de Nancy," *Les cahiers lorrains*, no. 2-3-4 (1989): 141–171.

25. F. C. de la Coudraye, *Opinion sur le nouveau projet d'organisation (de la marine militaire)* (Paris: Imprimerie nationale, 1791), 11.

26. Arthur Chuquet, ed., *Paris en 1790: Voyage de Halem* (Paris: Chailley, 1890), 222, 215.

27. Ibid., 226, 229.

28. Charles Popham Miles, ed., *The Correspondence of William Augustus Miles on the French Revolution*, 2 vols. (London: Longmans, Green, 1890), 1:203, 205.

29. Chuquet, *Voyage de Halem*, 213; *Révolutions de Paris*, no. 69 (1790): 175, cited in *Voyage*, 214.

30. Etta Palm d'Aelders, in Darline Gay Levy, Harriet Branson Applewhite, and Mary Durham Johnson, eds., *Women in Revolutionary Paris, 1789–1795* (Urbana: University of Illinois Press, 1979), 69.

31. Alfred Bougeart, *Les Cordeliers: Documents pour servir à l'histoire de la Révolution française* (Paris, 1891), 157, 133; citation from R. B. Rose, *The Making of the Sans-Culottes* (Manchester: Manchester University Press, 1983), 97.

32. *Courrier politique et littéraire du Cap Français*, June 24, 1790.

33. *Gazette de Paris*, Apr. 4, 1791.

34. Edmund Burke, *Reflections on the Revolution in France* (New York: Anchor Books, 1973), 48, 100, 74.

35. Ibid., 73, 89, 90.

36. William Godwin, *Memoirs of the Author of A Vindication of the Rights of Women*, eds. Pamela Clemit and Gina Luria Walker (Peterborough, Ontario: Broadview, 2001), 73; *Patriote français*, Jan. 2, 1791.

37. Citations in Aston, *Religion and Revolution*, 154.

38. AP, 21:7–8; Tackett, *Religion, Revolution, and Regional Culture*, 20, 25.

39. Marillet diary, cited in Richard Ballard, *The Unseen Terror: The French Revolution in the Provinces* (London: I. B. Tauris, 2010), 48.

40. Adrien-Joseph Colson, *Lettres d'un bourgeois de Paris à un ami de province, 1788–1793* (Saint-Cyr-sur-Loire: Christian Pirot, 1993), 189; Pailhès, *Ecrire la Révolution*, 315–316, 279; *Discours d'un curé de campagne à ses paroissiens, relativement au serment* (1791), 1.

41. *Révolutions de Paris*, Apr. 17–24, 1791; Marie-Antoinette citation in Munro Price, *The Road from Versailles: Louis XVI, Marie-Antoinette and the Fall of the French Monarchy* (New York: St. Martin's Press, 2003), 153.

42. *Révolutions de Paris*, Apr. 17–24, 1791; AP, 25:646, 651.

43. Citations in Carmela Ferrandes, "Le *Journal de la maladie et de la mort de Mirabeau* de Pierre-Jean-Georges Cabanis," *Dix-huitième siècle*, no. 39 (2007): 201–209; Jean-François Thénard and Raimond Guyot, *La conventionnel Goujon (1766–1795)* (Paris: Félix Alcan, 1908), 22; P. Fromageot, *Pierre-François Tissot (1768–1854)* (Versailles: L. Bernad, 1902).

44. *Journal des décrets de l'Assemblée nationale*, Feb. 16, 1791, cited in Michael P. Fitzsimmons, *From Artisan to Worker: Guilds, the French State, and the Organization of Labor, 1776–1821* (Cambridge: Cambridge University Press, 2010), 46.

45. AP, 27:210.

46. AP, 27:212; Pierre Nicolas Berryer, cited in Michael P. Fitzsimmons, *The Parisian Order of Barristers and the French Revolution* (Cambridge, MA: Harvard University Press, 1987), 65.

47. AP, 25:680, 685, 683.

48. *Patriote français*, Dec. 1, 1790.

49. *Patriote français*, Jan. 5, 1791.
50. *Patriote français*, Apr. 30, 1791.
51. *Gazette universelle*, May 12 and 13, 1791.
52. Citations in Hervé Leuwers, *Robespierre* (Paris: Pluriel, 2016), 179–180.
53. Guillaume Raynal, "Adresse à l'assemblée nationale," May 31, 1791.

## Chapter 11: A Runaway King and a Constitutional Crisis

1. Citations in Timothy Tackett, *When the King Took Flight* (Cambridge, MA: Harvard University Press, 2003), 49.
2. Evelyn Farr, *I Love You Madly: Marie Antoinette and Count Fersen* (London: Peter Owen, 2016), 135, 138; *Mémoires de madame la duchesse de Tourzel* (Paris: Plon, 1883), 312.
3. Citations in Munro Price, *The Road from Versailles: Louis XVI, Marie-Antoinette and the Fall of the French Monarchy* (New York: St. Martin's Press, 2003), 181.
4. Citations in Tackett, *When the King Took Flight*, 8, 22, 23; Victor Fournel, *L'Evénement de Varennes* (Paris, 1890), 311.
5. Citations in Tackett, *When the King Took Flight*, 79.
6. *Mémoires de madame la duchesse de Tourzel*, 339.
7. *Moniteur universel*, June 22, 1791; *Geschichte der gegenwärtigen Zeit* (Strasbourg), June 26, 1791; J. M. Roberts, ed., *French Revolution Documents*, 2 vols. (Oxford: Blackwell, 1966), 1:298.
8. *Patriote françois*, June 22, 1791; letter from William Miles's daughter, Paris, June 27, 1791, in Charles Popham Miles, ed., *The Correspondence of William Augustus Miles on the French Revolution*, 2 vols. (London: Longmans, Green, 1890), 1:304; citations in Sian Reynolds, *Marriage and Revolution: Monsieur and Madame Roland* (Oxford: Oxford University Press, 2012), 146.
9. Thomas Paine, citation in Moncure Daniel Conway, *The Life of Thomas Paine* (New York: B. Blom, 1970 [1908]), 307; Sigismond Lacroix, ed., *Actes de la Commune de Paris pendant la Révolution*, ser. 2, 5:112; *Annales patriotiques*, June 22, 1791; *Journal de la cour et de la ville*, June 27, 1791; *Gazette de Paris*, June 23, 1791.
10. Lacroix, *Actes de la Commune*, ser. 2, 5:113; police report in David Andress, *Massacre of the Champ de Mars: Popular Dissent and Political Culture in the French Revolution* (Woodbridge, Suffolk: Boydell Press, 2000), 150.
11. Citations in Serge Bianchi and Roger Dupuy, eds., *La Garde nationale entre nation et peuple en armes: Mythes et réalités, 1789–1871* (Rennes: Presses Universitaires de Rennes, 2006), 395; Thomas Lindet, cited in Georges Michon, *Essai sur l'histoire du parti feuillant: Adrien Duport* (Paris: Payot, 1924), 240.
12. *Argus patriote*, June 26, 1791, cited in Michon, *Essai*, 235.
13. *Gazette universelle*, July 10, 1791; citations in Farr, *I Love You*, 216, and Michon, *Essai*, 246.
14. Citations in Michon, *Essai*, 254, 256–257.
15. Citations in Albert Mathiez, *Le Club des Cordeliers* (Paris: H. Champion, 1910), 122.
16. Citations in Andress, *Massacre*, 198.
17. Nicolas Ruault, *Gazette d'un Parisien sous la Révolution, 1783–1796* (Paris: Perrin, 1976), 257.
18. Barnave to Marie-Antoinette, July 25, 1791, in Évelyne Lever, *Correspondance de Marie-Antoinette (1770–1793)* (Paris: Taillandier, 2005), 562; Marie-Antoinette to

Barnave, Aug. 7, 1791, in ibid., 575; Marie-Antoinette to Mercy d'Argenteau, Aug. 26, 1791, in ibid., 585.

19. *Gazette de Leyde*, May 20, 1791.

20. Citations in Farr, *I Love You*, 192; Pillnitz Declaration, in John Hall Stewart, ed., *A Documentary Survey of the French Revolution* (New York: Macmillan, 1951), 223–224; declaration of the comtes de Provence et d'Artois, in L. G. Wickham Legg, *Select Documents Illustrative of the History of the French Revolution* (Oxford: Clarendon Press, 1905), 2:134; Jean Philippe Guy le Gentil Paroy, *Mémoires du comte de Paroy*, ed. Etienne Charavay (Paris: Plon, 1895), 292–293.

21. Citations in Michon, *Essai*, 309, 327; Adrien-Joseph Colson, *Lettres d'un bourgeois de Paris à un ami de province, 1788–1793* (Saint-Cyr-sur-Loire: Christian Pirot, 1993), 202.

22. Pierre-François Tissot, "Vie de Goujon," in Françoise Burnel and Sylvain Goujon, *Les martyrs de Prairial* (Geneva: Georg, 1992), 119, 128–129.

23. *Gazette universelle*, Sept. 12 and Sept. 25, 1791.

24. Citations in Michael D. Sibalis, "The Regulation of Male Homosexuality in Revolutionary and Napoleonic France," in Jeffrey Merrick and Bryant T. Ragan, eds., *Homosexuality in Modern France* (New York: Oxford University Press, 1996), 82.

25. AP, 31:674.

26. *Révolutions de Paris*, Sept. 24–30, 1791; Sylvain Maréchal, *Dame Nature à la barre de l'Assemblée nationale* (Paris, 1791), 3.

27. Olympe de Gouges, "Declaration of the Rights of Woman," in Darline Gay Levy, Harriet Branson Applewhite, and Mary Durham Johnson, eds., *Women in Revolutionary Paris, 1789–1795* (Urbana: University of Illinois Press, 1979), 87–96.

28. Charles-Élie, Marquis de Ferrières, *Correspondance inédite (1789, 1790, 1791)*, ed. Henri Carré (Paris: Armand Colin, 1932), 430.

## Chapter 12: A Second Revolution

1. Claude Perroud, ed., *Lettres de Madame Roland*, 2 vols. (Paris: Picard, 1911), 386; cited in F.-A. Aulard, ed., *La Société des Jacobin: Recueil des documents pour l'histoire du club des Jacobins à Paris*, 6 vols. (Paris: Jouaust, 1889–1897), 3:203.

2. Evelyn Farr, *I Love You Madly: Marie Antoinette and Count Fersen* (London: Peter Owen, 2016), 160, letter of Sept. 26, 1791; Évelyne Lever, *Correspondance de Marie-Antoinette (1770–1793)* (Paris: Taillandier, 2005), 658, letter of Oct. 31, 1791.

3. Walter Markov and Albert Soboul, *Die Sansculotten von Paris: Dokumente zur Geschichte des Volksbewegung, 1793–1794* (Berlin: Akademie-Verlag, 1957), 2.

4. *Feuille villageoise*, Sept. 29, 1791.

5. Citations in Peter McPhee, *Revolution and Environment in Southern France, 1780–1830* (New York: Oxford University Press, 1998), 60.

6. Serge Bianchi and Roger Dupuy, eds., *La Garde nationale entre nation et peuple en armes: Mythes et réalités, 1789–1871* (Rennes: Presses Universitaires de Rennes, 2002), 172.

7. *Feuille villageoise*, Sept. 29, 1791; citations in Peter McPhee, *Living the French Revolution* (Basingstoke: Palgrave Macmillan, 2006), 96–97.

8. Claudine Pailhès, ed., *Ecrire la Révolution, 1784–1795: "Lettres à Pauline"* (Cahors: La Louve, 2011), 279.

9. Olympe de Gouges, *L'Esclavage des noirs, ou l'heureux naufrage* (Paris: Veuve Duchesne, 1792), 4; Jacques-Pierre Brissot, *Discours de J. P. Brissot, député, sur les causes*

*des troubles de Saint-Domingue, prononcé à la séance du premier décembre 1791* (Paris: Imprimerie nationale, 1791).

10. Letter of Nov. 23, 1791, in Lever, *Correspondance*, 682; Jacques Godechot, "Fragments des Mémoires de Charles-Alexis Alexandre sur les Journées Révolutionnaires de 1791 et 1792," *Annales historiqes de la Révolution française*, no. 126 (Apr. 1952): 153.

11. Citations in C. J. Mitchell, *The French Legislative Assembly of 1791* (Leiden: Brill, 1988), 44.

12. Brissot [first discourse, Dec. 16, 1791], 3, 5, 6, 15.

13. Brissot, *Deuxième discours*, Dec. 30, 1791, 15, 27, 26.

14. Letter of Dec. 16, 1791, in Lever, *Correspondance*, 735.

15. Robespierre, speech of Jan. 2, 1792, at Jacobins, in *Discours de Maximilien Robespierre sur la guerre* (Paris, 1972), 18; Perroud, *Lettres de Madame Roland*, 2:419; Gabriel Noël, ed., *Au temps des volontaires 1792: Lettres d'un volontaire de 1792*, 2nd ed. (Paris: Plon, 1912), 27.

16. Lever, *Correspondance*, 771.

17. Citations in Patricia C. Howe, "Charles-François Dumouriez and the Revolutionizing of French Foreign Affairs in 1792," *French Historical Studies* 14 (1986): 386; Becquey, cited in Mitchell, *Legislative Assembly*, 79.

18. *Créole patriote*, July 28, 1792.

19. Citations in Mona Ozouf, *Festivals and the French Revolution*, trans. Alan Sheridan (Cambridge, MA: Harvard University Press, 1988), 69.

20. Citations in Étienne Joliclerc, ed., *Joliclerc Volontaire aux armées de la Révolution* (Paris: Perrin, 1905), 56–57.

21. Annie Duprat, ed., *"Les affaires d'état sont mes affaires de coeur"* (Paris: Belin, 2016), 82; Jean-Marie Roland de la Platière, *Lettre de M. Roland, ministre de l'intérieur, au roi* (Paris, 1792), 3, 6, 8.

22. Godechot, "Fragments des Mémoires," 180.

23. *Créole patriote*, July 3, 1792; Godechot, "Fragments des Mémoires," 183–184.

24. Brissot, speech of July 9, 1792, in AP, 46:264, 272.

25. F.-A. Aulard, ed., *Mémoires secrets de Fournier l'Américain* (Paris: Société de l'histoire de la Révolution française, 1890), 71; *Trompette du père Duchêne*, July 8, 1792.

26. Nicolas Ruault, *Gazette d'un Parisien sous la Révolution, 1783–1796* (Paris: Perrin, 1976), 450.

27. Aulard, *Mémoires secrets de Fournier l'Américain*, 71.

28. Citations in Mitchell, *Legislative Assembly*, 245n.

29. Ruault, *Gazette*, 452, 454.

30. Rosalie Jullien, cited in Lindsay Porter, *Popular Rumour in Revolutionary Paris, 1792–1794* (Cham, Switzerland: Palgrave Macmillan, 2017), 86; *Révolutions de Paris*, no. 162 (Aug. 11–18, 1792).

31. Ruault, *Gazette*, 458.

32. Citations in Philip Dwyer, *Napoleon: The Path to Power* (New Haven, CT: Yale University Press, 2008), 99.

33. André Fribourg, *Discours de Danton* (Paris: Société de l'histoire de la Révolution française, 1910), 155.

34. Citations in Henri Wallon, *Le Tribunal Révolutionnaire de Paris* (Paris: Hachette, 1880–1882), 17; Adrien-Joseph Colson, *Lettres d'un bourgeois de Paris à un ami de province, 1788–1793* (Saint-Cyr-sur-Loire: Christian Pirot, 1993), 221.

35. Fribourg, *Discours de Danton*, 156, 165.

36. Noël, *Au temps des volontaires*, 238–239.

37. *Créole patriote*, Aug. 24, 1792 (evening edition); *Mémoires, corrrespondance et manuscrits du général Lafayette*, 4 vols. (Brussels: Société Belge de Librairie, 1837–1838), 4:215, letter of Sept. 3, 1792.

38. Fribourg, *Discours de Danton*, 173.

39. *Révolutions de Paris*, no. 165, Sept. 1–8, 1792.

40. François Jourgniac Saint-Méard, *Mon agonie de trente-huit heures* (Paris: Desenne, 1792), 24, 25.

41. *Révolutions de Paris*, no. 165, Sept. 1–8, 1792; citations in P. J. B. Buchez and P. C. Roux, *Histoire parlementaire de la Révolution française*, 40 vols. (Paris: Paulin, 1834–1838), 17:433.

42. Citations in Buchez and Roux, *Histoire parlementaire*, 17:385.

43. Citations in John Hardman, *French Revolution Documents* (Oxford: Blackwell, 1973), 2:9.

44. *Feuille du Matin*, Nov. 27, 1792; *Révolutions de Paris*, no. 165, Sept. 1–8, 1792.

45. *Créole patriote*, Sept. 2, 1792 (evening edition).

46. Danton, speech of March 10, 1793, in AP, 60:63.

## Chapter 13: A Republic Born in Crisis

1. Citations in Gérard Noiriel, "L'identification des citoyens: Naissance de l'état civil républicain," *Genèses* 13 (1993): 4.

2. Citations in ibid., 13.

3. AP, 49:611.

4. Jean-François Thénard and Raimond Guyot, *La conventionnel Goujon (1766–1795)* (Paris: Félix Alcan, 1908), 56; Françoise Brunel and Sylvain Goujon, eds., *Martyrs de prairial: Textes et documents inédits* (Geneva: Georg, 1992), 311, 313.

5. Citations in Hervé Leuwers, *Robespierre* (Paris: Pluriel, 2016), 235.

6. René Levasseur, *Mémoires de R. Levasseur, de la Sarthe, ex-Conventionnel*, 4 vols. (Paris: Rapilly, 1829–1831), 1:48.

7. Citations in Norman Hampson, *Danton* (London: Duckworth, 1978), 88.

8. André Fribourg, ed., *Discours de Danton* (Paris: Société de l'histoire de la Révolution française, 1910), 177.

9. Grégoire, speech of Sept. 21, 1792, in *Réimpression de l'ancien Moniteur*, Sept. 22, 1792.

10. *Revolutions de Paris*, no. 168, Sept. 22–29, 1792.

11. Gabriel Noël, ed., *Au temps des volontaires: Lettres d'un volontaire de 1792*, 2nd ed. (Paris: Plon, 1912), 267, letter of Sept. 17, 1792.

12. Jean-Paul Bertaud, *Valmy: La démocratie en armes* (Paris: Juilliard, 1970), 30; Goethe, *Campagne de 1792*, citation in *Die Französische Revolution im Spiegel der deutschen Literatur* (Leipzig: Reclam, 1975), 249–250.

13. General Galbaud, in AN, D XXV 49, d. 473; Jean Vidalenc, *Les Emigrés français, 1789–1825* (Caen: Ozanne, 1963), 156; Frédéric-C. Lankhard, *Au temps des volontaires* (Paris, 1915), 72.

14. Daunou, cited in John Hardman, *French Revolutionary Documents* (Oxford: Blackwell, 1973), 2:23.

15. Citations in David P. Jordan, *The King's Trial: Louis XVI vs. the French Revolution* (Berkeley: University of California Press, 1979), 54.

16. Citations in Albert Soboul, *Le procès de Louis XVI* (Paris: Julliard, 1966), 74.

17. Chalier, letter of Feb. 3, 1793, in Walter Markov, *Revolution im Zeugenstand: Frankreich, 1789–1799*, 2 vols. (Frankfurt: Fischer, 1987), 2:352.

18. Citations in Soboul, *Procès de Louis XVI*, 89, and Brunel and Goujon, *Martyrs de prairial*, 30, 32.

19. Citations in Jordan, *King's Trial*, 108–109, 112.

20. Citations in ibid., 136.

21. Citations in Soboul, *Procès de Louis XVI*, 166, 179, 186; Michael Walzer, *Regicide and Revolution* (New York: Columbia University Press, 1992), 212.

22. Nicolas Ruault, *Gazette d'un Parisien sous la Révolution, 1783–1796* (Paris: Perrin, 1976), 320.

23. Charles Lacretelle, *Dix années d'épreuves pendant la Révolution* (Paris: Allouard, 1842), 133–134; citations in Soboul, *Procès de Louis XVI*, 233.

24. Citations in Soboul, *Procès de Louis XVI*, 250; *Révolution de 92*, Jan. 23, 1793; *Père Duchêne*, no. 212 (January 1793); Michael L. Kennedy, *The Jacobin Clubs in the French Revolution: The Middle Years* (Princeton, NJ: Princeton University Press, 1988), 332.

25. Citations in Janet L. Polasky, *Revolution in Brussels, 1787–1793* (Hanover, NH: University Press of New England, 1987), 229; propaganda decree in John Hall Stewart, ed., *A Documentary Survey of the French Revolution* (New York: Macmillan, 1951), 381–382; Olympe de Gouges, *L'entrée de Dumouriez à Bruxelles* (Paris: Regnaud, 1793), 74.

26. Propaganda decrees in Stewart, *Documentary Survey*, 381–383.

27. Citations in Polasky, *Revolution in Brussels*, 257.

28. AP, 56:116.

29. Citations in Albert Sorel, *L'Europe et la Révolution française*, 8 vols. (Paris: Plon, 1908), 4:278–279, 280.

30. Condorcet, speech of Feb. 15, 1793, in AP, 58:595.

31. *Journal de Perlet*, Feb. 19, 1793.

32. Marat, *Journal de la République française*, Feb. 26, 1793; citations in Stewart, *Documentary Survey*, 398.

33. Citations in Judith A. Miller, *Mastering the Market: The State and the Grain Trade in Northern France, 1700–1860* (Cambridge: Cambridge University Press, 1999), 147.

34. *Robespierre*, speech of Feb. 25, 1793, in Marc Bouloiseau et al., eds., *Oeuvres de Maximilien Robespierre*, 11 vs. (Paris: Société des Etudes Robespierristes, 1910–2007), 9:275; citations in Markov, *Revolution im Zeugenstand*, 359.

35. Citations in Jean-Paul Bertaud, *The Armies of the French Revolution: From Citizen-Soldiers to Instrument of Power*, trans. R. R. Palmer (Princeton, NJ: Princeton University Press, 1988), 93.

36. Citations in Félix Deniau, *Histoire de la Vendée*, 6 vols. (Angers, 1876), 1:277n.

37. Citations in ibid., 299.

38. Citations in ibid., 1:365.

39. Citations in ibid., 1:367, 370, 372.

40. *Réimpression de l'ancien Moniteur*, March 11, 1793 (Convention session, March 9).

41. Citations in Levasseur, *Mémoires*, 134; Lucien Duchet, ed., *Deux volontaires de 1791: Les frères Favier de Montluçon* (Montluçon: A. Herbin, 1909), 93, 97.

42. *Journal de la République française*, Mar. 20, 1793; Levasseur, *Mémoires*, 1:139; *Réimpression de l'ancien Moniteur*, Apr. 3, 1793 (Convention, Apr. 1).

43. Stewart, *Documentary Survey*, 415.

44. Isnard, Apr. 3, 1793, in AP, 61:278; Barère, *Réimpression de l'ancien Moniteur*, Apr. 8, 1793.

45. Citations in Olivier Coquard, *Marat* (Paris: Fayard, 1993), 394.

46. *Réimpression de l'ancien Moniteur*, Apr. 9, 1793; AP, 61:532.

47. *Robespierre*, speech of Apr. 24, 1793, in Bouloiseau et al., eds., *Oeuvres de Maximilien Robespierre*, 9:459–463.

48. Ibid.

49. Ibid.

50. *Réimpression de l'ancien Moniteur*, May 4, 1793 (Convention, May 1).

51. *Réimpression de l'ancien Moniteur*, May 4, 1793 (Convention, May 3).

52. Jacques-Louis Ménétra, *Journal of My Life*, ed. Daniel Roche, trans. Arthur Goldhammer (New York: Columbia University Press, 1986), 226; *Bulletin de la Convention*, May 5, 1793; P. J. B. Buchez and P. C. Roux, *Histoire parlementaire de la Révolution française*, 40 vols. (Paris: Paulin, 1834–1838), 26:357–358; Isidore Langois, petition to Committee of General Security, AN, F 7 4764.

53. Citations in Darline Gay Levy, Harriet Branson Applewhite, and Mary Durham Johnson, eds., *Women in Revolutionary Paris, 1789–1795* (Urbana: University of Illinois Press, 1979), 152–153.

54. Citations in Morris Slavin, *The Making of an Insurrection: Parisian Sections and the Gironde* (Cambridge, MA: Harvard University Press, 1986), 18; Hardman, *French Revolution Documents*, 2:62, 64, 67.

55. Aulard, *Société des Jacobins*, 5:213.

## Chapter 14: The Revolution on the Brink

1. René Levasseur, *Mémoires de R. Levasseur, de la Sarthe, ex-Conventionnel*, 4 vols. (Paris: Rapilly, 1829–1831), 1:247; citations in Alan Forrest, *Society and Politics in Revolutionary Bordeaux* (Oxford: Oxford University Press, 1975), 99.

2. Citations in Morris Slavin, *The Making of an Insurrection: Parisian Sections and the Gironde* (Cambridge, MA: Harvard University Press, 1986), 96.

3. Citations in ibid., 113.

4. Citations in ibid., 114; *Journal de Lyon*, June 27, 1793, cited in Pierre Rétat, *1793: L'esprit des journaux* (Saint-Etienne: Publications de l'Université de Saint-Etienne, 1993), 162.

5. *Bulletin des amis de la vérité*, Mar. 2, 1793.

6. Citations in Paul R. Hanson, *The Jacobin Republic Under Fire: The Federalist Revolt in the French Revolution* (University Park: Penn State University Press, 2003), 246–247.

7. *Echo des Pyrénées*, June 22, 1793.

8. AP, 66:252, 254, 257; Jean-François Barailon, *Projet de Constitution*, in AP, 67:188–189; Billaud-Varennes, *Les elements du républicanisme*, in AP, 67:240, 244.

9. Citations in P. J. B. Buchez and P. C. Roux, *Histoire parlementaire de la Révolution française*, 40 vols. (Paris: Paulin, 1834–1838), 28:209, Convention, June 28, 1793.

10. Pierre Toussaint Durand-Maillane, cited in John Hardman, ed., *French Revolutionary Documents* (Oxford: Blackwell, 1973), 135 (*Mémoires*, 141–145).

11. *Réimpression de l'ancien Moniteur*, June 28, 1793 (Convention, June 25), cited in Jeremy D. Popkin, *A Short History of the French Revolution*, 6th ed. (Boston: Pearson, 2014), 68–69.

12. Citations in Buchez and Roux, *Histoire parlementaire*, 28:212; Hardman, *French Revolutionary Documents*, 103.

13. Citations in Olivier Coquard, *Marat* (Paris: Fayard, 1993), 410; Rétat, *Esprit des journaux*, July 29, 1793, 195; and *Quotidienne*, July 18, 1793, 192.

14. Citations in Pierre Casselle, *L'anti-Robespierre: Jérôme Pétion ou la Révolution pacifiqique* (Paris: Vendémiaire, 2016), 535; Buchez and Roux, *Histoire parlementaire*, 28:395, 341; Rétat, *Esprit des journaux*, 189.

15. Citations in R. R. Palmer, *Twelve Who Ruled: The Year of the Terror in the French Revolution* (Princeton, NJ: Princeton University Press, 1969 [1943]), 36–37; F.-A. Aulard, ed., *La Société des Jacobins: Recueil des documents pour l'histoire du club des Jacobins à Paris*, 6 vols. (Paris: Jouaust, 1889–1897), 5:350 (speech of Aug. 14, 1793).

16. John Hall Stewart, ed., *A Documentary Survey of the French Revolution* (New York: Macmillan, 1951), 469.

17. Nicolas Ruault, *Gazette d'un Parisien sous la Révolution, 1783–1796* (Paris: Perrin, 1976), 342; Buchez and Roux, *Histoire parlementaire*, 28:361 (speech of July 26, 1793).

18. Citations in Françoise Waquet, "La Bastille académique," in *La Carmagnole des muses* (Paris: Armand Colin, 1988), 24; Jean-Luc Chappey, "'Repenser la Terreur' par les sciences?" in Michel Biard, ed., *Les politiques de la Terreur, 1793–1794* (Rennes: Presses Universitaires de Rennes, 2008), 401.

19. Buchez and Roux, *Histoire parlementaire*, 28:440, 443.

20. Ibid., 28:445, 446.

21. Stewart, *Documentary Survey*, 469, 473; Léonor Dupille, *Un maître d'école à silly-en-Multien, 1771 à 1803* (Dammartin en Goële, n.d.), 41.

22. *Nouvelles politiques*, Sept. 4, 1793.

23. *Révolutions de Paris*, Sept. 18–25, 1790, cited in Robert Louis Stein, *Léger-Félicité Sonthonax: The Lost Sentinel of the Republic* (Rutherford, NJ: Fairleigh Dickinson University Press, 1985), 21.

24. Richebourg to Sonthonax, Aug. 26, 1793, in Jeremy D. Popkin, *You Are All Free: The Haitian Revolution and the Abolition of Slavery* (New York: Cambridge University Press, 2010), 270, 275–276.

25. Citations in Popkin, *You Are All Free*, 276.

26. Palmer, *Twelve Who Ruled*, 46–48.

27. *Ami du peuple*, June 13, 1790, cited in Gerd van den Heuvel, "Terreur, Terroriste, Terrorisme," in Rolf Reichardt and Eberhard Schmitt eds., *Handbuch politisch-sozialer Grundbegriffe in Frankreich, 1680–1820* (Munich: R. Oldenbourg, 1985), 3:99.

28. *Révolutions de Paris*, no. 212 (Aug. 3–Oct. 28, 1793), cited in van den Heuvel, "Terreur," 3:110.

29. Robespierre, "On Political Morality," cited in Richard Bienvenu, ed., *The Ninth of Thermidor: The Fall of Robespierre* (New York: Oxford University Press, 1968), 32–49; Madame Roland, *Mémoires de Madame Roland* (Paris: Mercure de France, 1966), 236.

30. Buchez and Roux, *Histoire parlementaire*, 28:459.

31. Stewart, *Documentary Survey*, 478; Walter Markov and Albert Soboul, *Die Sansculotten von Paris: Dokumente zur Geschichte des Volksbewegung, 1793–1794* (Berlin: Akademie-Verlag, 1957), 214; Pierre Paganel, *Essai historique et critique sur la Révolution française*, 2 vols. (Paris: Panckoucke, 1815), 2:259.

32. "Mémoire d'un prisonnier, première partie: Mon séjour à la Mairie et à la Force," *Paris pendant l'année 1795*, June 27, 1795; Gabrielle Gauchat, *Journal d'une Visitandine pendant la Terreur* (Paris: Poussielgue-Rusand, 1855), 107.

33. Thuriot, cited in Levasseur, *Mémoires*, 2:121; Stewart, *Documentary Survey*, 499–500.

34. Citations in Gérard Gayot and Jean-Pierre Jessenne, "Institutions et politiques économiques, politiques sociales," in Biard, *Politiques de la Terreur*, 220; Pierre Caron, *Paris pendant la Terreur*, 6 vols. (Paris: Picard, 1910–1978), 1:249.

35. Citations in Jean-François Belhoste, "Le financement de la guerre de 1792 à l'an IV," in *Etat, finances et économie pendant la Révolution française* (Paris: Imprimerie nationale, 1991), 342.

36. Citations in Hardman, *French Revolutionary Documents*, 2:157; Stewart, *Documentary Survey*, 482.

37. *Réimpression de l'ancien Moniteur*, Aug. 2, 1793 (Convention, Aug. 1).

38. Petition to Convention, in Markov and Soboul, *Sansculotten*, 188; citations in Rétat, *Esprit des journaux*, 272.

39. AP, 74:550–551.

40. Dupille, *Un maître d'école*, 42–43; Richard Cobb, *The People's Armies: The Armées révolutionnaires, instrument of the Terror in the Departments, April 1793 to floréal Year II* (New Haven, CT: Yale University Press, 1987), 468; Michel Vovelle, *The Revolution Against the Church: From Reason to the Supreme Being*, trans. Alan José (Columbus: Ohio State University Press, 1991), 63–65, 84.

41. Citations in Joseph F. Byrnes, *Priests of the French Revolution: Saints and Renegades in a New Political Era* (University Park: Penn State University Press, 2014), 102.

42. *Père Duchesne*, no. 309 (Nov. 1793); Helen Maria Williams, *Letters Containing a Sketch of the Politics of France* (London: G. G. and J. Robinson, 1795), 2:185.

43. Citations in Vovelle, *Revolution Against the Church*, 106, 158, and Caron, *Paris pendant la Terreur*, 1:256.

44. Citations in Cobb, *People's Armies*, 472, and Palmer, *Twelve Who Ruled*, 118.

45. *Réimpression de l'ancien Moniteur*, Oct. 16, 18, 19, 1793; Madame de Staël, *Réflexions sur le procès de la Reine*, in *Oeuvres complètes de Mme la baronne de Staël*, 2 vols. (Paris: Treuttel and Würtz, 1820), 2:32.

46. Citations in Rétat, *Esprit des journaux*, 251.

47. *Créole patriote*, 7 bru. II (Oct. 27, 1793); *Réimpression de l'ancien Moniteur*, vol. 18, trial session of 9 bru. II (Oct. 30, 1793).

48. Claude Perroud, ed., Jacques-Pierre Brissot, *Mémoires de Brissot*, 2 vols. (Paris: Picard, 1912), 1:1–2; Madame Roland [Manon Philpon], *Mémoires de Madame Roland*, ed. Paul de Roux (Paris: Mercure de France, 1966), 201, 238; Condorcet, *Esquisse d'un tableau des progrès de l'esprit humain*, ed. Alain Pons (Paris: Flammarion, 1988), 271.

49. Citations in Lindsay A. H. Parker, *Writing the Revolution: A French Woman's History in Letters* (New York: Oxford University Press, 2013), 116; Hervé Leuwers, *Robespierre* (Paris: Pluriel, 2016), 293.

50. Citations in Olivier Blanc, *La dernière lettre* (Paris: Pluriel, 1984), 168.

51. Citations in W. D. Edmonds, *Jacobinism and the Revolt of Lyon, 1789–1793* (Oxford: Clarendon Press, 1990), 280.

52. Citations in Jean-Clément Martin, *La guerre de Vendée, 1793–1800* [new ed.] (Paris: Editions Seuil, 2014), 219–220.

53. Étienne Jolicler, ed., *Joliclerc Volontaire aux armées de la Révolution* (Paris: Perrin, 1905), 155.

54. Darline Gay Levy, Harriet Branson Applewhite, and Mary Durham Johnson, eds., *Women in Revolutionary Paris, 1789–1795* (Urbana: University of Illinois Press, 1979), 200.

55. Citations in ibid., 215, 217, 219.

## Chapter 15: The Arc of Terror

1. Citations in David P. Jordan, *The Revolutionary Career of Maximilien Robespierre* (Chicago: University of Chicago Press, 1985), 186.

2. Citations in Philip Dwyer, *Napoleon: The Path to Power* (New Haven, CT: Yale University Press, 2008), 147.

3. Citations from George Rudé, ed., *Robespierre* (Upper Saddle River, NJ: Prentice Hall, 1967), 59.

4. F.-A. Aulard, ed., *La Société des Jacobins: Recueil des documents pour l'histoire du club des Jacobins à Paris*, 6 vols. (Paris: Jouaust, 1889–1897), 5:528 (1 fri. II [Nov. 21, 1793]).

5. Camille Desmoulins, *Le Vieux Cordelier*, ed. Matton aîné (Paris: Ebrard, 1834), no. 2, 13 (20 fri. II).

6. Desmoulins, *Vieux Cordelier*, no. 3, 36; no. 4, 62, 61.

7. Aulard, *Société des Jacobins*, 5:569 (1 niv. II [Dec. 21, 1793]).

8. Citations in Morris Slavin, *The Hébertistes to the Guillotine: Anatomy of a 'Conspiracy' in the French Revolution* (Baton Rouge: Louisiana State University Press, 1994), 72.

9. Aulard, *Société des Jacobins*, 5:574 (Dec. 23, 1793); citations in Slavin, *Hébertistes*, 79.

10. Citations in Marisa Linton, *Choosing Terror: Virtue, Friendship, and Authenticity in the French Revolution* (Oxford: Oxford University Press, 2013), 212.

11. Citations in Jeremy D. Popkin, *You Are All Free: The Haitian Revolution and the Abolition of Slavery* (New York: Cambridge University Press, 2010), 352.

12. Citations in ibid., 354, 360.

13. Ibid., 362.

14. Henri Grégoire, *Mémoires*, ed. Hippolyte Carnot (Paris: Editions de Santé, 1989), 81; Popkin, *You Are All Free*, 362.

15. Albert Mathiez, *Etudes sur Robespierre (1758–1794)*, ed. Georges Lefebvre (Paris: Editions sociales, 1958), 146.

16. Chaumette, cited in Popkin, *You Are All Free*, 369; Jean-Claude Halpern, "Les fêtes révolutionnaires et l'abolition de l'esclavage en l'An II," in Marcel Dorigny, ed., *Les abolitions de l'esclavage de L. F. Sonthonax à V. Schoelcher, 1793–1794–1848* (Paris: Editions UNESCO, 1995), 194.

17. René Levasseur, *Mémoires de R. Levasseur, de la Sarthe, ex-Conventionnel*, 4 vols. (Paris: Rapilly, 1829–1831), 2:42; citations in Jean-Paul Bertaud, *The Armies of the French Revolution: From Citizen-Soldiers to Instrument of Power*, trans. R. R. Palmer (Princeton, NJ: Princeton University Press, 1988).

18. Marcel Reinhard, *Le Grand Carnot*, 2 vols. (Paris: Hachette, 1952), 2:106.

19. *Réimpression de l'ancien Moniteur*, 4 ger. II (March 24, 1794).

20. Bertrand Barère, *Rapport du Comité de salut public sur les idiomes*, 8 plu. II (Jan. 27, 1794) (Paris: Imprimerie nationale, 1794).

21. Louis-Antoine de Saint-Just, *Oeuvres choisies* (Paris: Gallimard, 1968), 201, 206.

22. Ibid., 337, 341–342, 344.

23. Citations in Slavin, *Hébertistes*, 97.

24. *Almanach des prisons* (Paris, Year III), 85.

25. Adolphe Schmidt, *Tableaux de la Révolution française*, 3 vols. (Paris, 1869), 2:157.

26. Citations in Slavin, *Hébertistes*, 225; Schmidt, *Tableaux de la Révolution*, 2:182.

27. *Journal de la Montagne*, 18 plu. II.

28. Reinhard, *Grand Carnot*, 2:137–138.

29. Ernest Hamel, *Histoire de Robespierre*, 3 vols. (Paris, 1865–1867), 3:468–469.

30. Citations in Linton, *Choosing Terror*, 221, 222–223.

31. Citations in Hamel, *Histoire de Robespierre*, 3:474; Pierre Caron, *Paris pendant la Terreur*, 6 vols. (Paris: Picard, 1910–1978), 6:226; P. Fromageot, *Pierre-François Tissot (1768–1854)* (Versailles: Bernard, 1902), 11; Linton, *Choosing Terror*, 225.

32. *Almanach des prisons*, 93; *Réimpression de l'ancien Moniteur*, 15 ger. II (Apr. 4, 1794); citations in Norman Hampson, *Danton* (London: Duckworth, 1978), 167; *Bulletin du Tribunal criminel révolutionnaire*, no. 4:21 (Year II).

33. *Réimpression de l'ancien Moniteur*, 16 ger. II (Apr. 5, 1794); *Bulletin du Tribunal criminel révolutionnaire*, no. 4:26; citations in Hampson, *Danton*, 174.

34. *Almanach des prisons*, 176.

35. Citations in Reinhard, *Grand Carnot*, 2:151.

36. Caron, *Paris pendant la Terreur*, 6:95, 224.

37. Lynn Hunt, *Politics, Culture and Class in the French Revolution* (Berkeley: University of California Press, 1984), 163–164.

38. Jacques-Louis Ménétra, *Journal of My Life*, ed. Daniel Roche, trans. Arthur Goldhammer (New York: Columbia University Press, 1986), 223–228.

39. Robespierre, "On the Cult of the Supreme Being," in Rudé, ed., *Robespierre*, 69.

40. Rudé, *Robespierre*, 71.

41. Citations in Jonathan Smyth, *Robespierre and the Festival of the Supreme Being* (Manchester: Manchester University Press, 2016), 138, 137.

42. John Hall Stewart, ed., *A Documentary Survey of the French Revolution* (New York: Macmillan, 1951), 529; Anne Simonin, "Les acquittés de la Grande Terreur: Réflexions sur l'amitié dans la République," in Michel Biard, ed., *Les politiques de la Terreur, 1793–1794* (Rennes: Presses Universitaires de Rennes, 2008), 183–184.

43. Citations in Linton, *Choosing Terror*, 250.

44. Citations in Richard Bienvenu, ed., *The Ninth of Thermidor: The Fall of Robespierre* (New York: Oxford University Press, 1968), 104.

45. Citations in Olivier Blanc, *La dernière lettre* (Paris: Pluriel, 1984), 62; Nicolas Ruault, *Gazette d'un Parisien sous la Révolution, 1783–1796* (Paris: Perrin, 1976), 352, 357.

46. Jean-François Noël, *L'ombre et la lumière*, ed. Denis Jeanson (Tours: Denis Jeanson, 1988), 111.

47. Citations in T. C. W. Blanning, *The French Revolutionary Wars, 1787–1802* (London: Arnold, 1996), 116–117.

48. Annie Duprat, ed., *"Les affaires d'état sont mes affaires du coeur"* (Paris: Belin, 2016), 306; citations in Bienvenu, *Thermidor*, 126.

49. Citation in Gérard Walter, *Robespierre* (Paris: Gallimard, 1946), 418.

50. Citations in Bienvenu, *Thermidor*, 112 (from Fouché's memoirs, 1:17–22).

51. Citations in Bienvenu, *Thermidor*, 143, 155, 154, 182–183.

52. Bienvenu, *Thermidor*, 189–191; Peter McPhee, *Robespierre: A Revolutionary Life* (New Haven, CT: Yale University Press, 2013), 218; Bienvenu, *Thermidor*, 199–200.

53. Bienvenu, *Thermidor*, 211.

54. Paul Sainte-Claire Deville, *La Commune de l'An II* (Paris: Plon, 1946), 287.

55. Ruault, *Gazette*, 361; Jullien, *"Les affaires d'état"*, 318–319.

## Chapter 16: The Republic's New Start

1. Citations in Richard Bienvenu, ed., *The Ninth of Thermidor: The Fall of Robespierre* (New York: Oxford University Press, 1968), 235, 247.

2. Bronislaw Baczko, *Comment sortir de la Terreur* (Paris: Gallimard, 1989).

3. Citations in ibid., 28, and Bienvenu, *Thermidor*, 317.

4. Citations in Baczko, *Comment sortir*, 62, 63.

5. Charles Lacretelle, *Dix années d'épreuves pendant la Révolution* (Paris: Allouard, 1842), 181; citations in Baczko, *Comment sortir*, 101, 119.

6. Citations in Bienvenu, *Thermidor*, 304–305; *Réimpression de l'ancien Moniteur*, 13 fruc. II (Convention, 11 fruc.).

7. Citations in Bienvenu, *Thermidor*, 312; *Réimpression de l'ancien Moniteur*, 13 and 14 fruc. II.

8. *Réimpression de l'ancien Moniteur*, 16 fruc. II, 1 vend. III.

9. F.-A. Aulard, ed., *Paris pendant la réaction thermidorienne et le Directoire*, 5 vols. (Paris, 1898), 1:104; *Procès-criminel des members du comité révolutionnaire de Nantes, et du ci-devant représentant du peuple Carrier* (Paris: Toubon, Year III), 1:35, 244.

10. Lacretelle, *Dix années d'épreuves*, 196.

11. *Réimpression de l'ancien Moniteur*, 8 niv. III (trial proceedings, 21 fri. II).

12. Citations in Suzanne Desan, *The Family on Trial in Revolutionary France* (Berkeley: University of California Press, 2004), 255, 259; *Adresse des citoyennes de la ci-devant Normandie, département du Calvados, sur la loi du 17 nivôse* (Year III), 4.

13. Joseph Lakanal, *Rapport et projet de loi sur l'organisation des écoles primaires* (Paris: Imprimerie nationale, 1794), 2, 3; *Décade philosophique*, 2:393, 464.

14. *Réimpression de l'ancien Moniteur*, 8 vend. III; *Décade philosophique*, Apr. 29, 1794.

15. Charles-François Dupuis, *Origine de tous les cultes, ou religion universelle*, 6 vols. (Paris: H. Agasse, 1795), 1:xiv.

16. *Réimpression de l'ancien Moniteur*, 4 niv. III (Convention, 1 niv.).

17. *Abréviateur universel*, 24 vent. III, cited in Aulard, *Réaction thermidorienne*, 1:559.

18. *Annales de la religion*, May 2, 9, 1795; Gabrielle Gauchat, *Journal d'une Visitandine pendant la Terreur* (Paris: Poussielgue-Rusand, 1855), 240.

19. Ernest Picard, *Au service de la nation: Lettres de volontaires, 1792–1798* (Paris: Félix Alcan, 1914), 63; *Réimpression de l'ancien Moniteur*, 22 plu. III.

20. Citations in Simon Schama, *Patriots and Liberators* (New York: Knopf, 1977), 201.

21. Citations in Albert Sorel, *L'Europe et la Révolution française*, 8 vols. (Paris: Plon, 1908), 4:312.

22. Citations in Aulard, *Réaction thermidorienne*, 1:147.

23. *Réimpression de l'ancien Moniteur*, 20 fri. III (Convention, 17 fri.).

24. Citations in Aulard, *Réaction thermidorienne*, 1:556.

25. Citations in Dominique Godineau, *The Women of Paris and Their French Revolution*, trans. Katherine Streip (Berkeley: University of California Press, 1998), 296; Aulard, *Réaction thermidorienne*, 1:446.

26. *Gazette française*, 3 vent. III, in Aulard, *Réaction thermidorienne*, 1:502; *Courrier universel de Husson*, 2 ger. III; Aulard, *Réaction thermidorienne*, 1:513.

27. *Gazette française*, 5 niv. III, in Aulard, *Réaction thermidorienne*, 1:327; citations in Jeremy D. Popkin, *The Right-Wing Press in France, 1792–1800* (Chapel Hill: University of North Carolina Press, 1980), 109; *Messager du soir*, 2 ger. III, in Aulard, *Réaction thermidorienne*, 1:587.

28. *Réimpression de l'ancien Moniteur*, 13 ger. III.

29. Citations in Renée Fuoc, *La réaction thermidorienne à Lyon (1795)* (Lyon: Editions de Lyon, 1957), 127n.

30. Citations in Kåre Tønnesson, *La défaite des sans-culottes* (Oslo: Presses Universitaires d'Oslo, 1959), 235.

31. Citations in ibid., 248; *Réimpression de l'ancien Moniteur*, 4 prair. III.

32. Godineau, *Women of Paris*, 335–336.

33. Romme, in Françoise Brunel and Sylvain Goujon, *Les martyrs de prairial: Textes et documents inédits* (Geneva: Georg, 1992), 395.

34. Brunel and Goujon, *Martyrs de prairial*, 188.

35. Citations in Tønnesson, *Défaite des sans-culottes*, 301.

36. Dominque Godineau, *Citoyens tricoteuses: Les femmes du people à Paris pendant la Révolution française* (Paris: Perrin, 2004 [1988]), 330–331; Walter Markov and Albert Soboul, *Die Sansculotten von Paris: Dokumente zur Geschichte des Volksbewegung, 1793–1794* (Berlin: Akademie-Verlag, 1957), 494.

37. *Annales patriotiques*, 30 prair. III; and *Courrier français*, 30 prair. III, in Aulard, *Réaction thermidorienne*, 2:21.

38. Louis XVIII, "Declaration of Verona," in Paul H. Beik, ed., *The French Revolution* (New York: Harper and Row, 1970), 325–329.

39. Claudine Pailhès, ed., *Ecrire la Révolution, 1784–1795: "Lettres à Pauline"* (Cahors: La Louve, 2011), 524.

40. *Postillon des armées*, 1 mess. III; Adrien Lezay-Marnésia, *Les ruines, ou voyage en France, pour servir de suite à celui de la Grèce* (Paris: Migneret, Year III), 32–33; *Journal des hommes libres*, 4 and 5 mess. III.

41. Boissy d'Anglas, speech of 5 mess. III, in Beik, *French Revolution*, 318, 319.

42. Ibid., 320, 321.

43. *Journal des hommes libres*, 17 mess. III (Convention, 15 mess. III).

44. Citations in John Hardman, ed., *French Revolutionary Documents* (Oxford: Blackwell, 1973), 2:341–342.

45. Defermon, speech of 5 ther. III, in *Réimpression de l'ancien Moniteur*, vol. 25 (10 ther. III); Boissy d'Anglas, speech of 22 thermidor III, in *Réimpression de l'ancien Moniteur*, vol. 25 (23 ther. III).

46. Citations in Sorel, *Europe et la Révolution française*, 4:399.

47. Citations in Henri Zivy, *Le treize vendémiaire An IV* (Paris: Alcan, 1898), 18, 28, 17.

48. Election figures in ibid., 35; letter of lieutenant Enée in ibid., 124.

49. Citations in Philip Dwyer, *Napoleon: The Path to Power* (New Haven, CT: Yale University Press, 2008), 176; police report, cited in Zivy, *Vendémiaire*, 98n.

50. *Réimpression de l'ancien Moniteur*, 23 vend. IV (Convention, 18 vend.); citations in Dwyer, *Path to Power*, 188.

51. *Réimpression de l'ancien Moniteur*, 1 bru. IV (Convention, 26 vend.), 9 bru. IV (Convention, 2 bru.), 4 bru. IV (Convention, 29 vend.), 7 bru. IV (Convention, 1 bru.).

52. *Réimpression de l'ancien Moniteur*, 3 bru. IV (Convention, 27 vend.), 9 bru. IV (Convention, 2 bru.), 12 bru. IV (Convention, 3 bru.), 14 bru. IV (Convention, 4 bru.).

## Chapter 17: The Republic in Question

1. Anne-Louis Germaine de Staël, *Réflexions sur la paix intérieure*, in de Staël, *Oeuvres complètes de Mme la baronne de Staël*, 2 vols. (Paris: Treuttel and Würtz, 1820), 2:110, 104.

2. F.-A. Aulard, ed., *Paris pendant la réaction thermidorienne et le Directoire*, 5 vols. (Paris, 1898), 3:2.

3. Jacques-Louis Ménétra, *Journal of My Life*, ed. Daniel Roche, trans. Arthur Goldhammer (New York: Columbia University Press, 1986), 236; Aulard, *Réaction thermidorienne*, 3:175 (18 flor. IV); Victorin Laval, ed., *Lettres inédites de J.-S. Rovère à son frère Simon-Stylite* (Paris: H. Champion, 1908), 152–153.

4. Benjamin Constant, *De la force d'un gouvernement actuel de la France et de la nécessité de s'y rallier* (Paris, 1796); final citation from K. Steven Vincent, *Benjamin Constant and the Birth of French Liberalism* (New York: Palgrave Macmillan, 2011), 55.

5. Adrien Lezay-Marnésia, *De la faiblesse d'un gouvernement qui commence, et de la nécessité où il est de se rallier à la majorité nationale* (Paris: Mathey, 1796), 32.

6. *Tribun du peuple*, no. 35 (9 fri. IV).

7. *Tribun du peuple*, no. 36 (20 fri. IV), no. 35, 105–106; "Réponse à une lettre signée M. V.," in Filippo Buonarroti, *Conspiration pour l'égalité dite de Babeuf* (Paris: Editions sociales, 1957), 2:151.

8. "Manifeste des égaux," in Buonarroti, *Conspiration pour l'égalité*, 2:95.

9. Citations in R. B. Rose, *Gracchus Babeuf: The First Revolutionary Communist* (Stanford, CA: Stanford University Press, 1978), 219.

10. "Acte d'insurrection," in Buonarroti, *Conspiration pour l'égalité*, 2:166; Buonarroti, *Conspiration pour l'égalité*, 1:123.

11. *Nouvelles politiques*, 23 flor. IV.

12. Letter of Nov. 28, 1795, in André Michel, ed., *Correspondance inédite de Mallet du Pan avec la Cour de Vienne (1794–1798)*, 2 vols. (Paris: Plon, 1884), 372–373.

13. Augustin Barruel, *Histoire du clergé pendant la Révolution française* [new ed.] (Brussels, 1801), 2.

14. Joseph de Maistre, *Considérations sur la Révolution française* (Lyon: J. B. Pelagaud, 1880), 8, 56, 46–47.

15. Louis de Bonald, *Théorie du pouvoir politique et religieuse* (electronic edition), Les classiques des sciences sociales, University of Quebec and Chicoutimi, classiques. uqac.ca, 9.

16. Citations in Jean-Paul Bertaud, *The Armies of the French Revolution: From Citizen-Soldiers to Instrument of Power*, trans. R. R. Palmer (Princeton, NJ: Princeton University Press, 1988).

17. Jean-François Noël, *L'ombre et la lumière*, ed. Denis Jeanson (Tours: Denis Jeanson, 1988), 125.

18. Citations in Philip Dwyer, *Napoleon: The Path to Power* (New Haven, CT: Yale University Press, 2008), 198.

19. Dwyer, *The Path to Power*, 200.

20. Citations in Andrew Roberts, *Napoleon: A Life* (New York: Penguin, 2015), 91.

21. Citations in T. C. W. Blanning, *The French Revolutionary Wars, 1787–1802* (London: Arnold, 1996), 162.

22. Citations in Blanning, *French Revolutionary Wars*, 173.

23. Citations in Giorgio Candeloro, *Storia dell'Italia moderna*, 11 vols. (Milan: Feltrinelli, 1977 [1957]), 1:219.

24. Citations in Owen Chadwick, *The Popes and European Revolution* (Oxford: Clarendon Press, 1981), 453.

25. Citations in Albert Sorel, *L'Europe et la Révolution française*, 8 vols. (Paris: Plon, 1908), 5:148.

26. Citation in Jeremy D. Popkin, *A Concise History of the Haitian Revolution* (Malden, MA: Wiley-Blackwell, 2012), 73.

27. Citation in Popkin, *Haitian Revolution*, 72–73.

28. Rochambeau, "Mémorial," in Newberry Library, Ms. Ruggles 410.

29. Citations in Marcel Reinhard, *Le Grand Carnot*, 2 vols. (Paris: Hachette, 1952), 2:187.

30. Aulard, *Réaction thermidorienne*, 3:448.

31. William Wickham, *The Correspondence of the Right Honourable William Wickham*, 2 vols. (London: Bentley, 1870), 1:357.

32. Citations in Jean-Louis Halperin, *L'impossible Code Civil* (Paris: Presses Universitaires de France, 1992), 245–246.

33. *Nouvelles politiques*, 19 mess. IV.

34. [Jean-Baptiste Laplace], *Réflexions sur la colonie de Saint-Domingue*, 2 vols. (Paris: Garnéry, Year IV), 1:190.

35. *Nouvelles politiques*, 18 plu. V.

36. [André Dumont], *Manuel des assemblées primaires et électorales de France* (Hamburg, 1797), v, vi.

37. Letter to Wickham, Oct. 1797, in Charles Ballot, *Le coup d'état du 18 fructidor An V* (Paris: Société de l'histoire de la Révolution française, 1906), 166–167.

38. Citations in Isser Woloch, *Jacobin Legacy: The Democratic Movement Under the Directory* (Princeton, NJ: Princeton University Press, 1970), 66.

39. Vincent-Marie Viénot de Vaublanc, *Discours sur l'état de Saint-Domingue*, (Paris: Imprimerie nationale, Year V), 15; *Réimpression de l'ancien Moniteur*, 21 prair. V (Council of 500, 15 prair.).

40. Camille Jordan, *Rapport sur la police des cultes* (Paris: Imprimerie nationale, 29 prair. V), 5, 24.

41. *Sentinelle*, 26 prair. V.

42. *Invariable*, 12 mess. V.

43. *Europe politique*, 4 prair. V.

44. *Correspondance de Napoléon Ier*, 60 vols. (Paris: Imprimerie impériale, 1858–1869), 3:180–181.

45. Toussaint Louverture, cited in Laurent Dubois and John Garrigus, *Slave Revolution in the Caribbean, 1789–1804* (Boston: Bedford / St. Martin's Press, 2006), 148–153.

46. *Tableau de la France*, 1 ther. V.

47. Ballot, *Coup d'état de 18 fructidor*, 158–167.

48. Charles Lacretelle, *Précis historique de la Révolution française*, 5 vols. (Paris: Treuttel and Würtz, 1820), 5:27.

## Chapter 18: From Fructidor to Brumaire

1. Marie-Joseph Chénier, "Le Vieillard d'Ancenis: Elégie sur la mort du général Hoche," in *Victoires, conquêtes des Français de 1792 à 1815: Couronne poétique* (Paris: Panckoucke, 1821), 27:133.

2. *Décade philosophique*, 30 fruc. V.

3. Citations in Pierre Serna, *La République des girouettes* (Paris: Champ Vallon, 2005), 444.

4. *Conservateur*, 15 vend. VI.

5. *Sentinelle*, 26 vend. VI.

6. Citations in Isser Woloch, *Jacobin Legacy: The Democratic Movement Under the Directory* (Princeton, NJ: Princeton University Press, 1970), 88.

7. *Bulletin de Paris*, 21 bru. VI.

8. *Courrier de la Gironde*, cited in Anne de Mathan and Gilles Feyel, "Le Courrier de la Gironde, 1797–1799," in Gilles Feyel, ed., *Dictionnaire de la presse française pendant la Révolution*, 5 vols. (Ferney-Voltaire: Centre International d'Étude du XVIII Siècle, 2005–2012), 4:203.

9. *Journal des hommes libres*, 13 bru. VI.

10. Louis-Antoine Fauvelet de Bourrienne, *Mémoires de M. de Bourrienne, ministre d'état, sur Napoléon* (Paris: Garnier, 1899), 2:24, 27; Patrice Gueniffey, *Le dix-huit brumaire: L'épilogue de la Révolution française* (Paris: Gallimard, 2008), 133–134.

11. Bourrienne, *Mémoires*, 2:33.

12. *Journal de Paris*, 1 plu. VI, cited in Serna, *Girouettes*, 452; citations in Patrice Gueniffey, *Le dix-huit brumaire*, 149–150; Bourrienne, *Mémoires*, 2:32.

13. Citations in Laurent Dubois and John Garrigus, *Slave Revolution in the Caribbean, 1789–1804* (Boston: Bedford / St. Martin's Press, 2006), 154–155; Léger-Félicité Sonthonax, *Discours prononcé par Sonthonax, sur la situation actuelle de Saint-Domingue* (Paris: Imprimerie nationale, Year VI), 18; Beaubrun Ardouin, *Etudes sur l'histoire de Haïti*, 11 vols. (Port-au-Prince: Dalencour, 1958), 3:86.

14. Citations in Marc H. Lerner, "The Helvetic Republic: An Ambivalent Reception of French Revolutionary Liberty," *French History* 18, no. 1 (2004): 60.

15. Citations in Woloch, *Jacobin Legacy*, 280.

16. Citations in Mathan and Feyel, "Courrier de la Gironde," 4:203.

17. *Décade philosophique*, May 19, 1798, cited in Serna, *Girouettes*, 448.

18. Ibid.; "L'An centième de la République," in *Ami des lois*, 13 prair. VI, 26 prair. VI, 16 mess. VI.

19. François de Neufchâteau, *Recueil des lettres circulaires, instructions, programmes, discours*, 2 vols. (Paris: Imprimerie de la République, Year VII), 1:160–173, 1:240; *Première exposition des produits de l'industrie française* (Paris: Imprimerie de la République, Year VII), 24.

20. François de Neufchâteau, *Recueil*, 1:168.

21. *Clef du Cabinet*, 23 ther. VI; citations in T. C. W. Blanning, *The French Revolutionary Wars, 1787–1802* (London: Arnold, 1996), 239.

22. Citations in Andrew Jainchill, *Reimagining Politics After the Terror: The Republican Origins of French Liberalism* (Ithaca, NY: Cornell University Press, 2008), 134–135; Madame de Staël, *Des circonstances actuelles qui peuvent terminer la Révolution, et des principes qui doivent fonder la République en France*, ed. J. Vienot (Paris: Fischbacher, 1906), 35.

23. Citations in Alyssa Sepinwall, *The Abbé Grégoire and the French Revolution* (Berkeley: University of California Press, 2005), 152.

24. Citations in Robert Solé, *Bonaparte à la conquête de l'Egypte* (Paris: Seuil, 2006), 12.

25. L. B., "Considérations sur l'Egypte et le Syrie," *Décade philosophique*, 20 ger. VI (Apr. 9, 1798).

26. L. B., "Suite des considérations sur l'Egypte et la Syrie," *Décade philosophique*, 30 ger. VI (Apr. 19, 1798); *Ami des lois*, 20 prair. VI (June 7, 1798).

27. Citations in Solé, *Bonaparte*, 46; Stéphane Yerasimos, ed., *Deux Ottomans à Paris sous le Directoire et l'Empire* (Paris: Actes Sud, 1998), 115.

28. Napoleon I, *Campagnes d'Egypte et de Syrie*, 450, 453; François Pairault, *Gaspard Monge, le fondateur de Polytechnique* (Paris: Taillandier, 2000), 373; Solé, *Bonaparte*, 90.

29. Citations in Solé, *Bonaparte*, 113.

30. Shmuel Moreh, ed. and trans., *Napoleon in Egypt: Al-Jabarti's Chronicle of the French Occupation, 1798* (Princeton, NJ: Markus Weiner, 1975), 93; citations in Juan Cole, *Napoleon's Egypt: Invading the Middle East* (New York: St. Martin's Press, 2007), 204.

31. Citations in Patrice Gueniffey, *Bonaparte, 1769–1802* (Paris: Gallimard, 2003), 313, 315.

32. Citations in Marianne Elliott, *Partners in Revolution: The United Irishmen and France* (New Haven, CT: Yale University Press), 216.

33. Citations in R. R. Palmer, *The Age of the Democratic Revolution*, 2 vols. (Princeton, NJ: Princeton University Press, 1959–1964), 2:385n, 386.

34. *Clef du cabinet*, 15 flor. VII; F.-A. Aulard, ed., *Paris pendant la réaction thermidorienne et le Directoire*, 5 vols. (Paris, 1898), 5:522.

35. Citations in Bernard Gainot, *1799: Un nouveau Jacobinisme?* (Paris: Editions du Comité des travaux historiques et scientifiques, 2001), 34, 56.

36. Pierre-François Tissot, *Histoire complète de la Révolution française*, 6 vols. (Paris: Baudouin, 1837), 6:362.

37. P. J. B. Buchez and P. C. Roux, *Histoire parlementaire de la Révolution française*, 40 vols. (Paris: Paulin, 1834–1838), 38:49, 51.

38. Tissot, *Histoire complète*, 6:368.

39. Ibid., 6:371.

40. Citations in Gainot, *1799*, 478; P. Fromageot, *Pierre-François Tissot (1768–1854)* (Versailles: L. Bernard, 1902), 15; *Feuille du jour*, 6 ther. VII.

41. André Morellet, *Observations sur la loi des otages* (Paris, Year VII), 11.

42. Buchez and Roux, *Histoire parlementaire*, 38:89.

43. Citations in Andrew Roberts, *Napoleon: A Life* (New York: Penguin, 2015), 201.

44. Citations in Gueniffey, *Dix-huit brumaire*, 224.

45. Citations in ibid., 251.

46. Citations in Luca Scuccimarra, *La Sciabola di Sieyès: Le giornati di brumaio e la genesi del regime bonapartista* (Bologna: Il Mulino, 2002), 130.

47. Buchez and Roux, *Histoire parlementaire*, 38:175–176.

48. Citations in Gueniffey, *Dix-huit brumaire*, 275.

49. Bourrienne, *Mémoires*, 3:82.

50. Buchez and Roux, *Histoire parlementaire*, 38:185.

51. Ibid., 38:187–193; Gueniffey, *Dix-huit brumaire*, 287.

52. Bourrienne, *Mémoires*, 3:85; *Mémoires historiques sur le dix-huit brumaire* (Paris: Gauthier, 1799), 60.

53. Citations in Philip Dwyer, *Napoleon: The Path to Power* (New Haven, CT: Yale University Press, 2008), 502, and Gueniffey, *Dix-huit brumaire*, 306.

## Chapter 19: The Slow Death of the Republic

1. *Tableau historique des causes qui ont amené la Révolution du dix-huit brumaire*, 1.

2. Werner Giesselmann, *Die brumairianische Elite* (Stuttgart: Klett, 1977), 408.

3. *Tableau historique*, 4; cited in Pierre-Louis Roederer, *Oeuvres du comte P. L. Roederer*, 8 vols. (Paris: Firmin-Didot, 1866), 3:302.

4. Félix Rocquain, *L'état de la France au 18 brumaire* (Paris, 1874), 135, 186, 33.

5. F.-A. Aulard, ed., *Paris sous le Consulat: Recueil des documents pour l'histoire de l'esprit public à Paris*, 4 vols. (Paris: Cerf, 1903–1909), 1:3; Christine Reinhard. *Une femme de diplomate: Lettres de Madame Reinhard à sa mère, 1798–1815*, (Paris, 1900), 95; citations in Roederer, *Oeuvres*, 3:310.

6. Aulard, *Paris sous le Consulat*, 1:30.

7. Jean Jacques Régis Cambacérès, *Mémoires inédits*, 2 vols. (Paris: Perrin, 1999), 1:443–444; François Aulard, ed., *L'état de la France en l'an VIII et L'an IX* (Paris: Cerf, 1897), 74; Pierre-Jean-Georges Cabanis, *Quelques considérations sur l'organisation sociale en général et particulièrement sur la nouvelle constitution* (Paris: Imprimerie nationale, 1799), 36.

8. Antoine Boulay de la Meurthe, *Théorie constitutionnelle de Sieyès* (Paris: Paul Renouard, 1836), 3, 10.

9. Cambacérès, *Mémoires inédits*, 1:464n; Boulay de la Meurthe, *Théorie constitutionnelle*, 48.

10. Boulay de la Meurthe, *Théorie constitutionnelle*, 71.

11. Reinhard, *Femme de diplomate*, 102–103.

12. *Diplomate*, 23 fri. VIII, in Aulard, *Paris sous le Consulat*, 1:50.

13. P. J. B. Buchez and P. C. Roux, *Histoire parlementaire de la Révolution française*, 40 vols. (Paris: Paulin, 1834–1838), 38:301; A.-C. Thibaudeau, *Mémoires sur le Consulat* (Paris: Ponthieu, 1827), 109; Jacques Godechot, ed., *Les constitutions de la France depuis 1789* (Paris: Garnier-Flammarion, 1970), 161; *Journal des hommes libres*, 27 fri. VIII, in Aulard, *Paris sous le Consulat*, 1:58; *Gazette de France*, Dec. 30, 1799.

14. Isser Woloch, *The New Regime* (New York: W. W. Norton, 1994), 109.

15. Citations in Philip Dwyer, *Citizen Emperor: Napoleon in Power* (New Haven, CT: Yale University Press, 2013), 15; Reinhard, *Femme de diplomate*, 114.

16. *Publiciste*, 20 plu. VIII, in Aulard, *Paris sous le Consulat*, 1:143.

17. Citations in Jean Vidalenc, *Les Emigrés français, 1789–1825* (Caen: Ozanne, 1963), 133; Dwyer, *Citizen Emperor*, 79; Thierry Lentz, *Le Grand Consulat, 1799–1804* (Paris: Fayard, 1999), 220, 247.

18. Thibaudeau, *Mémoires sur le Consulat*, 2:29.

19. Citations in Andrew Jainchill, *Reimagining Politics After the Terror: The Republican Origins of French Liberalism* (Ithaca, NY: Cornell University Press, 2008), 256, 281; K. Steven Vincent, *Benjamin Constant and the Birth of French Liberalism* (New York: Palgrave Macmillan, 2011), 117.

20. Citations in Lentz, *Grand Consulat*, 295.

21. Citations in Jeremy D. Popkin, *A Concise History of the Haitian Revolution* (Malden MA: Wiley-Blackwell, 2012), 105.

22. Thibaudeau, *Mémoires sur la Consulat*, 119.

23. Citations in David Geggus, ed., *The Haitian Revolution: A Documentary History* (Indianapolis: Hackett, 2014), 160–162, and Frédéric Régent, *Esclavage, métissage, liberté: La Révolution française en Guadeloupe, 1789–1802* (Paris: Grasset, 2004), 394.

24. Citations in *Lettres du Général Leclerc*, ed. Paul Roussier (Paris: Société de l'histoire des colonies françaises, 1937), 263–274; *De l'affranchissement des noirs, ou Observations sur la loi du 16 pluviôse* (Paris, n.d.).

25. Claude Wanquet, *La France et la première abolition de l'esclavage, 1794–1802* (Paris: Karthala, 1998), 646; Yves Bénot and Marcel Dorigny, eds., *Rétablissement de l'esclavage dans les colonies françaises* (Paris: Maisonneuve et Rose, 2004), 564; Norbert Thoret, *La Vie aventeureuse de Norbert Thoret, dit "L'Américain"* (Paris: Editions du Port-au-Prince, 2007), 26.

26. Laurent Dubois, *A Colony of Citizens: Revolution and Slave Emancipation in the French Caribbean, 1787–1804* (Chapel Hill: University of North Carolina Press, 2004), 400.

27. Christian Sorrel, ed., *Les carnets 'retrouvés du Curé Molin: Un prêtre dans la tourmente* (Montmélian: La Fontaine de Siloë, 2008), 285–286; Rocquain, *État de la France*, 148, 150.

28. Citations in Nigel Aston, *Religion and Revolution in France, 1780–1804* (Washington, DC: Catholic University Press, 2000), 320.

29. Citations in Rafe Blaufard, *Napoleon: Symbol for an Age* (New York: Bedford / St. Martin's Press, 2008), 62; Thibaudeau, *Mémoires sur le Consulat*, 2:152–153.

30. Sorrel, ed., *Carnets*, 320; Report of Lacuée, in Rocquain, *État de la France*, 253–254.

31. François-Yves Besnard, *Souvenirs d'un nonagénaire: Mémoires de François-Yves Besnard*, 2 vols. (Paris: H. Champion, 1880), 1:197–198; Jacques-Louis Ménétra, *Journal of My Life*, ed. Daniel Roche, trans. Arthur Goldhammer (New York: Columbia University Press, 1986), 217; Henry Redhead Yorke, *Letters from France, in 1802* (London: H. D. Symonds, 1804), 269.

32. Rodney Dean, *L'église constitutionnelle, Napoléon et le concordat de 1801* (Paris: A. and J. Picard, 2004), 496; citations in Dwyer, *Citizen Emperor*, 83; Pigault-Lebrun, *Le citateur* (Paris: Bibliothèque nationale, 1888 [1803]), 1; citations in Martin S. Staum, *Minerva's Message: Stabilizing the French Revolution* (Montreal: McGill-Queen's University Press, 1996), 226.

33. Citations in Lentz, *Grand Consulat*, 321; Cambacérès, *Mémoires*, 1:619.

34. Citations in Lentz, *Grand Consulat*, 338–339.

35. Citations in ibid., 396.

36. Jean-Baptiste Say, *Traité d'économie politique*, 2 vols. (Paris: Crapelet, 1803), 1:xviii.

37. Citations in Suzanne Desan, *The Family on Trial in Revolutionary France* (Berkeley: University of California Press, 2004), 299.

38. Citations in Maria Fairweather, *Madame de Staël* (London: Constable, 2005), 275; Fanny Raoul, "Opinion d'une femme sur les femmes," in Geneviève Fraisse, ed., *Opinions des femmes, de la veille au lendemain de la Révolution française* (Paris: Côté-femmes, 1989), 155.

39. Citations in Henri Fauville, *La France de Bonaparte vue par les visiteurs anglais* (Aix-en-Provence: Édisud, 1989), 166.

40. Citations in Lentz, *Grand Consulat*, 427.

41. Citations in Fauville, *La France de Bonaparte*, 192, 196.

42. Citations in Lentz, *Grand Consulat*, 534.

43. Lentz, *Grand Consulat*, 537, 550.

44. Staël, *Considérations sur la Révolution française*, 396; cited in Lentz, *Grand Consulat*, 551.

45. *Moniteur*, 16 flor. XIII (May 6, 1804), cited in Lentz, *Grand Consulat*, 562.

46. Citations in Lentz, *Grand Consulat*, 581; Dwyer, *Citizen Emperor*, 163.

47. Citations in Dwyer, *Citizen Emperor*, 166.

48. Ménétra, *Journal*, 237.

49. Citations in Godechot, *Constitutions de la France*, 227.

# Index

Index

Credit: University of Kentucky

**Jeremy D. Popkin** holds the William T. Bryan Chair of History at the University of Kentucky. He is the author of many books, including *You Are All Free: The Haitian Revolution and the Abolition of Slavery* and *Revolutionary News: The Press in France, 1789–1799*. He lives in Lexington, Kentucky.